2 –

2|12

CHILE

GUIDE

BE A TRAVELER - NOT A TOURIST!

OPEN ROAD TRAVEL GUIDES SHOW YOU
HOW TO BE A TRAVELER – NOT A TOURIST!

Whether you're going abroad or planning a trip in the United States, take Open Road along on your journey. Our books have been praised by **Travel & Leisure, The Los Angeles Times, Newsday, Booklist, US News & World Report, Endless Vacation, American Bookseller, Coast to Coast,** *and many other magazines and newspapers!*

Don't just see the world – experience it with Open Road!

ABOUT THE AUTHORS

Becky Youman and Bryan Estep lived, worked, and traveled in Chile for three years before writing Open Road's *Chile Guide*. They have contributed to the *Santiago News Review*, *Big World*, and *Transitions Abroad* among other periodicals. In addition to their stint in Chile, they have called Brazil, Argentina, and Mexico home; they now live in Arroyo Grande, California.

BE A TRAVELER, NOT A TOURIST - WITH OPEN ROAD TRAVEL GUIDES!

Open Road Publishing has guide books to exciting, fun destinations on four continents. As veteran travelers, our goal is to bring you the best travel guides available anywhere!

No small task, but here's what we offer:

• All Open Road travel guides are written by authors with a distinct, opinionated point of view – not some sterile committee or team of writers. Our authors are experts in the areas covered and are polished writers.

• Our guides are geared to people who want to make their own travel choices. We'll show you how to discover the real destination – not just see some place from a tour bus window.

• We're strong on the basics, but we also provide terrific choices for those looking to get off the beaten path and experience the country or city – not just see it or pass through it.

• We give you the best, but we also tell you about the worst and what to avoid. Nobody should waste their time and money on their hard-earned vacation because of bad or inadequate travel advice.

• Our guides assume nothing. We tell you everything you need to know to have the trip of a lifetime – presented in a fun, literate, no-nonsense style.

• And, above all, we welcome your input, ideas, and suggestions to help us put out the best travel guides possible.

CHILE

GUIDE

BE A TRAVELER - NOT A TOURIST!

Becky Youman & Bryan Estep

OPE ROAD PUBLISHI G

1st Edition

Copyright ©1999 by Becky Youman & Bryan Estep
- All Rights Reserved -
Library of Congress Catalog Card No. 98-68683
ISBN 1-892975-05-X

ACKNOWLEDGMENTS

We'd like to acknowledge and thank the following people whose help and input added to the quality of this book: Julie Gardner, Marcelo Cienfuentes, Rolf Wagner, Maria Soledad Rojas, Gabriela Neria, Fidel Pinilla, Felix Elias, Juan, Roberto Movillo, Juan Carlos Ruiz, Andy, Mr. and Mrs. Morgano, German Claro, Enrique Cuesta, Sergio Cano, Viviana de la Riva, Viviana Flores, Jorge Cristie Aguirre, Ivo Depetris, Manuel Daire, Charles Jacobsthal, Rony Pollak, Guillermo Pollak, Heinz Dieter Hermann, Carlos Ojeda, Patricia Paredes, Sunny Castillo, Rick Geyer, Jason Gursky, David and Susana Santos, Jeff Winge, Victor, Phil Hayes, and Rebecca Cannel.

Jonathan Stein, our publisher, deserves particular recognition for his guidance.

We'd also like to thank the people who facilitated our vagrancy by giving us working space: Dudley and Sandy Youman, Bill and Susie McCaleb, Daniel and Vivian Charney, John, Laurie, and Cooper Chahbandour, Jeff Estep, Ace and Alice Forsythe, and Steve and Ellen Miura.

A special thanks to Continental Airlines and Sernatur.

Cover photos courtesy of Becky Youman & Bryan Estep. Maps by James Ramage.

All information, including prices, is subject to change. The authors have made every effort to be as accurate as possible, but neither they nor the publisher assume responsibility for the services provided by any business listed in this guide; for any errors or omissions; or any loss, damage, or disruptions in your travel for any reason.

TABLE OF CONTENTS

MAPS

SIDEBARS

SIDEBARS

SIDEBARS

1. INTRODUCTION

Chile's lanky physique stretches over half the length of South America to offer travelers a staggering array of nature-blessed destinations. The country's diverse terrain features craggy shorelines, high plains ruptured by conical volcanoes, vast chromatic deserts, fertile orchard-patched valleys, mossy rain forests, and rugged, glacier-crammed mountains. This guide is designed not only to reveal Chile's splendors, but also to help you choose among the alluring options to create an itinerary that best fits your time-frame and interests.

In addition to offering detailed coverage of the country's most popular attractions, restaurants, and hotels, we share information about lesser-known jewels that we have discovered during our years living in the country. Let our experience guide your travels in Chile – whether you go for exhilarating outdoor adventures, intriguing museums, or body-pampering resorts.

Chile's single greatest gift is her nature. The country's national parks, renowned for their biological diversity and superior maintenance, occupies nearly one-fifth of Chilean territory! This guide equips you, regardless of budget or athletic bent, to experience the wonders of these preserves. You can visit flocks of pink flamingos electrifying vast salt flats; Andean mountaintops revered by the ancients; wild rolling rivers conquerable in professionally guided rafts; and colonies of dandified penguins. We give detailed information on popular parks such as the extraordinary, spire-sculpted Torres del Paine in Patagonia as well as less visited reserves, such as those in the great, untamed wilderness of the Austral Region.

For many people, culinary exploration is an important part of the travel experience, so we guide you to our favorite Chilean foods and restaurants. From simple to sumptuous, the dining choices and dishes we highlight will leave you satisfied, whether you order Parmesan-dusted razor clams at the most discerning restaurant in town or a hot chicken pie in the local fire station's dining room.

Our strongest recommendations focus on unique Chilean locales. When recommending hotels we prioritize quality, regional culture, and personality. While both upscale travelers and backpackers will find reviews on establishments to fit their budgets, the often overlooked mid-range traveler will benefit from our eclectic list of reasonably priced, distinctive lodging alternatives. It is our hope that your travels in Chile will leave you with the same sense of awe and admiration that the country has inspired in us.

2. OVERVIEW

Chile is a land endowed with an abundance of natural wonders. Each section of the country, from the stark, mesmerizing north to larger-than-life Chilean Patagonia, is brimming with extraordinary attractions.

One unexpected plus is that the destinations are much less crowded than you might imagine. Even a short distance from densely populated Santiago, you can find yourself practically alone in a vast national park. This is especially true if you travel outside the peak austral summer months of January and February. Meanwhile there is ample infrastructure in several strategically located towns, such as San Pedro de Atacama and Pucón, to make you comfortable and facilitate your exploration of the natural wonders that surround them.

You will encounter an enchanting variety of animal life in Chile. The birds you will see in your travels include stands of gloriously pink flamingos, chatty flocks of brilliant green parrots, solitary condors, and throngs of formally attired penguins. Many of the country's mammals seemed to have stepped right out of a Dr. Doolittle film, including *vizcacha*, a rabbit with a long, squirrel-like tail, and the *pudú*, a deer roughly the size of a large house cat.

Chile's cities are culturally distinct and quite manageable. Even Santiago offers a solution to its rush hour traffic with an efficient subway system. Other than the capital, there are no cities in Chile with a population over 400,000 people. In addition to their appealing size, the towns consistently offer a good variety of hotels, restaurants, and diversions.

THE PEOPLE

Chile is an accommodating country for independent travelers. The people are friendly, the economy strong, and the police trustworthy. Chileans can be shy at first, especially the country folk, but if you make an effort to communicate they'll flood you with a wave of smiles and rapid, slang-filled Spanish. Chileans are refreshingly honest, so you can generally relax those self-protective barriers.

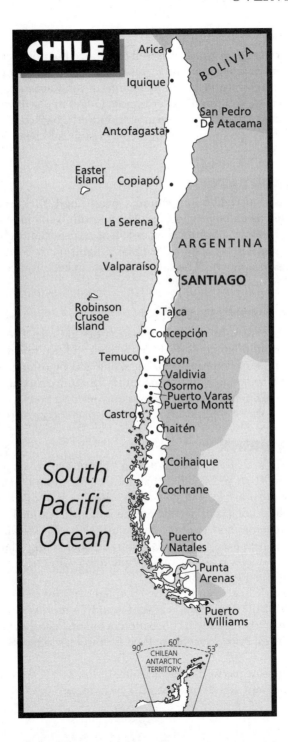

CHILE

Arica

Iquique

BOLIVIA

San Pedro
De Atacama

Antofagasta

Easter
Island

Copiapó

La Serena

ARGENTINA

Valparaíso

SANTIAGO

Robinson
Crusoe
Island

Talca

Concepción

Temuco • • Pucon

Valdivia

Osormo

Puerto Varas

Puerto Montt

Castro

Chaitén

Coihaique

Cochrane

*South
Pacific
Ocean*

Puerto
Natales

Punta
Arenas

Puerto
Williams

90°   60°   53°

53°

CHILEAN
ANTARCTIC
TERRITORY

LODGING

The structure for travelers is well developed but not overly so. There are excellent lodging options in most cities and towns ranging from sprawling old-time resorts to intimate inns. If you want to get completely away from it all, you can discover remote lodges in places you'll be hard pressed to find on the map. Even more removed is backcountry camping, which will take you to some of the most pristine and beautiful environs you'll ever see.

TRANSPORTATION

Chile is an incredibly long country, measuring 4,270 km (2,669 miles) from the northern border to Cape Horn – with 6,435 km (about 4,022 miles) of coastline – but there is excellent transportation between the distinct regions. Reasonably priced plane flights out of Santiago can get you places in a hurry. The cities are also linked by fleets of clean, comfortable buses.

SPORTS & RECREATION

There are plentiful sporting opportunities in Chile. The Andes are a paradise for mountain and river sports like kayaking, rafting, mountain climbing, trekking, mountain biking skiing and fly fishing. The central valleys and beaches provide opportunities for tennis, surfing, swimming, and scuba diving. After you've exhausted your own body, you can cheer on others at one of the spectator sports such as soccer or rodeo.

FOOD & DRINK

Chile is a seafood lover's dream. There are so many delicious possibilities of fish and shellfish that it will be hard to try them all during the course of your trip. Two of our favorites are *machas a la parmesana*, scrumptious razor clams served on the half shell, capped with melted Parmesan cheese; and *centolla*, an exquisitely rich Chilean king crab. Some of the best food in Chile is the traditional country fare. *Pastel de choclo*, for example, is a delicious hot pie filled with crispy corn niblets, chicken, beef, and vegetables.

A trip to Chile would not be complete without tasting pisco, the national drink of Chile. Pisco, a type of brandy, is most commonly served in the form of a pisco sour, a concoction of lemon juice, powdered sugar, and egg whites. Pisco sours are at their best when served cold with fresh seafood.

Chilean wine has won world acclaim. Its low cost and consistent high quality will tempt you to order it with every meal.

CHILE'S REGIONS

Santiago

Santiago, the unchallenged nucleus of the country's industrial, commercial, and political activity, is a city of contrasts. The tidy, arboreal uptown appears to be one of the most modern, bustling, well-planned cities in Latin America, while the downtown historical center was inspired by the architectural grandeur of old Europe. In the summer, with up to one-fifth of the city migrated to the beaches, genial breezes dry-clean the sky to reveal the Andes Range as a spectacular rocky curtain behind the city. Conversely, in the winter the city feels like a dungeon due to the damp cold and smog that grimly envelop the capital.

The original **Historical Center** *(centro)* is composed of grand post-independence public buildings and tall office buildings. You could easily entertain yourself for several days in this part of town with visits to the museums, historical buildings, and seafood market.

Sparkling modern uptown, **Providencia** and **El Bosque**, tapers off into a suburbia of shopping malls and family residences in **Las Condes** at the foothills of the Andes. It's here you'll find pleasant hotels, many excellent restaurants, and the beautiful artisan market **Los Dominicos**.

Bohemian **Bellavista** whirls with activity from its theaters and bars into the early hours of the morning. Good shopping and the must-visit **Pablo Neruda Museum** draw you here during the day. The best views in town are from **San Cristóbal Hill** which you can summit by tram around the corner from Neruda's home.

Nature lovers and sports enthusiasts have a field day here. Three excellent ski resorts, numerous hiking trails and mountain biking are all accessible from town as day trips.

The Central Region

The 650 km stretch of land around Santiago is a worthy vacation destination in its own right. With two mountain chains, fertile valleys, sparkling beaches, roaring rivers, ski resorts, vineyards and interesting cities, it holds its own against the other areas of the country. The best part is that almost every destination in the region is within three hours of Santiago. Just head out of the city in any direction and you'll be delighted with what you find.

The most visited area, the **Central Coast**, offers a variety of beach experiences. In **Zapallar** you'll find a gorgeous little town with excellent restaurants, profuse gardens, and a delightful horseshoe bay. Traveling south you'll discover two laid-back fishing villages, **Maitencillo** and **Horcón**, where you can watch the waves crash along open stretches of coastline. If you prefer to be pampered, you can always check in at

Marbella, the five star spa and golf resort. Or, if you prefer a more high-energy scene, you should head straight to **Viña del Mar** with its throngs of people and bustling casino.

Any visit to the Central Region would be incomplete without an excursion to the fascinating port city of **Valparaíso**. An engaging jumble of streets and houses stacked on hills and spilling over the edges of cliffs, a trip to "Valpo" is a step back in time. **Pablo Neruda's house** in Isla Negra is another priority on the coast. Discover more about the life of this intriguing Chilean personality at his whimsical seaside paradise. If you like to hang ten, you can't miss mellow **Pichilemu**, "The Surf Capital of Chile."

To the northeast of Santiago you pass through the Aconcagua river valley to the **Portillo**, one of the finest ski areas in the country. You can test your mettle on the area resorts' steep slopes against the US and European teams that train there in the austral winter. Down in the valley around **Los Andes**, small, colonial towns, with adobe buildings and thatched roofs, seem to be from another age. Old churches and monasteries abound in the region, as does the influence of Teresa de Los Andes, the first Chilean saint.

Head northwest from Santiago and you'll find the Quillota Valley where greenhouses, fruit orchards, and vineyards abound. Visit the sleepy weekend retreat of **Olmué** to access **La Campana National Park**. The summit of La Campana offers a glimpse of the entire width of the country with the fat peak of Argentina's **Aconcagua** towering to the east and the hazy Pacific Ocean in sight to the west.

Cajón del Maipo, to the southeast, is filled with adventures. Rafting, hiking and mountain climbing are all available just a few hours from Santiago. At the base of the lovely purple peak of **El Morado** you can study the sensual blue crevasses of a slowly moving glacier. The more sedentary can enjoy the view from a summer cabin after a session at the hot springs.

If you've had enough sightseeing and just want to relax, head south of Santiago to **Lago Rapel**. Water-skiing, fishing, swimming and lounging fill your to-do list here. National Reserves such as **Los Cipreses** and **Siete Tazas** give you the chance to see wild parrots flying in iridescent flocks against canyon walls turned golden by the setting sun. Continuing south, you plough through the fertile farmland that brings a cornucopia of goods to the Chilean table. Fresh produce stands dot the highways and will undoubtedly entice you to stop and sample the merchandise. **Chillán**, surrounded by smoking volcanoes, is the last city in the Central Region. Its famous ski resort has a spa with thermal baths heated by volcanic activity.

The North

The geography of the north changes so dramatically from east to west that you have the chance to see beaches, desert, Amerindian farmers, llamas and alpacas, volcanoes and flamingo-filled lakes in a single day. From the five main traveler's hubs in the region, you can venture out for a stunning display of diversity.

The northernmost hub, **Arica**, lies just a few kilometers from the border with Peru. From this pleasant ocean-side city you cross fertile valleys and stop by lovely pre-colonial villages as you climb to **Lauca National Park**. Vast, isolated high plains, broken by green lakes and purple volcanoes, teem with fascinating bird and wildlife. Semi-nomadic Amerindians herd their alpaca as their ancestors have done for hundreds of years.

Iquique, with its ornate turn-of-the-century architecture, enjoys its reputation as a hopping beach metropolis. From Iquique you can follow geoglyphs through the **Atacama Desert**, the world's driest, to reach the *sierra* on the western edge of the Andes. Oasis villages, such as **Pica**, offer welcome shade and fresh swimming holes.

From the hub of **Calama**, a small mining city, you cross the desert to marvel at strange rock formations and vast salt flats. The area around funky **San Pedro de Atacama** is a spot where natural wonders are literally overwhelming. Foreign lunar landscapes and spouting geysers are continually backed by a brilliant blue sky. Hiking, mountain biking, and horseback riding are popular ways to experience this land.

From the mining city **Copiapó** you can head towards the sea to explore the strange coastal landscape at **Pan de Azúcar National Park** or relax in **Bahía Inglesa**, a quiet bayside town. Chile's highest mountain, **Ojos de Salado**, and remote high mountain lakes await discovery to the west.

The last hub, **La Serena**, is another famous beach getaway. To the east you'll find lush green valleys, such as **Elqui**, backed by purple desert hills, internationally famous observatories, and, if it's been a rainy winter, a profusion of wildflowers blanketing the desert.

The Lake District

The Lake District could have just as easily been named the Volcano District, as it is home to a majority of Chile's majestic, snow-capped volcanoes. It is not unusual to turn your head on a sunny day and see four or five distinctly shaped volcanoes posing behind the quilted pastureland. Lying at the base of many of these volcanoes are the magnificent lakes for which the region is named.

Pucón, on **Lake Villarica**, and **Puerto Varas**, on **Lake Llanquihue**, are the two most popular bases in the area. Adventure seekers flock to the region eager to hike, climb, horseback ride, ski, raft, kayak and fish to their hearts' desires.

You can pick one of the less frequented, intimately beautiful lakes and spend the day making your own discoveries of unexpected waterfalls and crystal clear streams. These amazing undeveloped lakes include some of the **Siete Lagos** as well as **Lago Rupanco** and **Lago Ranco**.

In addition to lakes and volcanoes, the Lake District is home to numerous magnificent national parks. Scenes from the extraordinary **Conguillío** and **Huerquehue National Parks** will stay with you long after you leave the country. **Puyehue National Park**, with its stunning lookout point, is famous for its thermal baths and comfortable lodging. **Vicente Pérez Rosales**, near Puerto Varas, contains the cool, emerald-green waters of Lago Todos Los Santos that visitors ferry across to the Argentine border.

Attractive river cities near the coast round out your trip to the region. Two of these, **Concepción** and **Valdivia**, are noted for their fine universities, old forts, and palpable German influence.

Chiloé

One of the most intriguing destinations in Chile, Chiloé offers a rich, distinctive culture developed during centuries of isolation. On the island you can enjoy unique architecture; friendly, hardworking people; colorful legends; and some of the best food in Chile.

Chiloé is a seafaring culture, with the family vehicle as likely to be a motorboat as a car. You will find the diminutive vessels transporting the most unwieldy of cargo, from furniture to farm animals.

The main city, **Castro**, has excellent options for hotels and restaurants, the country's best modern art museum, an unforgettable church, and is a centralized location for day trips. The small town of **Dalcahue** is a shopper's dream with thick, colorful, handmade wool sweaters and other items. To truly experience what it is like to live on the island, you can lodge with *Chilote* families that participate in the agricultural-tourism program.

The Austral Region

The Austral Region, also called **Aisén**, is often compared to Alaska. While this is an appropriate comparison due to the area's rugged mountains, giant glaciers, and unforgiving remoteness, it falls short. The Austral region is this and so much more. It is also painted deserts, fertile valleys, raw jungle, and golden *pampa*.

Once you leave **Coyhaique**, the hub, you are immediately struck by the isolation of the region. To the west you can visit remote **Laguna San Rafael**, where the San Valentín glacier drops dramatically into the sea. If you travel the **Austral Highway** (really a single lane gravel road) to the north, you'll pass through the overwhelming primordial rain forests of **Quelat National Park**. Continuing north, the rushing emerald waters of **Futulefú** beckon world-class kayakers from around the globe. The road almost peters out by the time it reaches **Pumalin**, the largest private park in the world, home to glaciers, rivers, volcanoes, and huge stands of *alerce*, the South American sequoia.

South of Coyhaique you'll find lakes and rivers whose colors are similar to the bright blues and greens of food coloring. The deep azure of **Lago General Carrera** dominates the landscape of this part of the Austral Region before it drains into the Río Baker near **Bertrand**. Sporting opportunities abound in all the region, but Bertrand is justifiably famous for fly fishing, horseback riding and rafting. If you really want to get remote, try **Villa O'Higgins**, tucked between the northern and southern ice fields and accessible only by plane.

Chile Chico, on the eastern part of Lago General Carrera, basks in over 300 sunny days a year. Cross through desert canyons with incredible rocky spires and wind shaped formations to reach **Jeinimeni National Park**.

Magallanes-Chilean Patagonia

Chilean Patagonia is a skinny continental tail dangling precariously near the frozen jaws of Antarctica. **Punta Arenas**, the main hub of the region and southernmost city in the world, was forged by immigrant pioneers whose elegant, turn-of-the-century mansions have been preserved by an economic Rip Van Winkle effect. Rooftops painted in bold primary colors stand in stark contract to the intense windswept skies. **Tierra del Fuego** lies in sight across the narrow **Straight of Magellan**. Don't miss the **Ottaway Penguinera** where thousands of penguins waddle around in formal attire.

To the northeast, **Puerto Natales** is the gateway city for the world showpiece **Torres del Paine National Park**. This vast nature-lover's playground, centered on the **Paine Massif**, focuses on the massif's granite spires, **Torres**, and two-tone horns, **Cuernos**, sculpted by the wind and weather. **Glacier Grey**, more than six km wide and 60 meters tall, fills in one entire side of the massif before calving into the lake of the same name. Fascinating wildlife adds an extra element to the spectacular scenery. There is a full range of lodging options in the park, making overnight stay possible for more than just backpackers. All types of travelers can follow the hiking trails that unfold the wonders of this amazing place.

Off the Continent

Chile's non-continental holdings cover the range from a Polynesian island to a slice of Antarctica. Throw in the islands upon which the story of Robin Crusoe is based and you've got the ingredients for some great adventure tales.

Easter Island, in the middle of the Pacific, beckons travelers with its tropical climes, warm waters, and unique archaeological heritage. Its large *moai* sculptures are an image of the island known around the world.

People are drawn to **Antarctica** by the wildlife and spectacular scenery. The dramatic frozen landscape, clear air, and abundance of penguins and whales make for an unforgettable experience.

Robinson Crusoe Island, the largest of the Juan Fernandez archipelago, is the site where Alejandro Selkirk was rescued after almost four and a half years, becoming the inspiration for Daniel Defoe's *The Incredible and Amazing Adventures of Robinson Crusoe*. You'll worry less about being left ashore than having to leave. With outstanding hikes, isolated beaches, and inexpensive and abundant lobster, getting shipwrecked here is more a dream than a nightmare.

3. SUGGESTED ITINERARIES

Chile is so geographically diverse that your experience in the country will depend greatly on the regions you choose to visit. If you had time to travel the country completely, from one end to the other, you would find constant, yet varied allure. More than likely you will not be so lucky, so you are faced with narrowing down the destinations to those that will be most worthwhile for you.

What's the best way to go about doing that? Our strategy is to focus on the areas that are most strikingly unique, those that look the least like home.

It is the two extremes of Chile, the **North** and **Magallanes-Chilean Patagonia** that have the most to offer travelers in this regard. In addition to these two areas, your itinerary will be perfectly complemented if you have time to experience the distinct culture and savory food of **Chiloé**.

Magallanes-Chilean Patagonia, with the justifiably famous **Torres del Paine National Park**, is a highlight of the country. Wildlife like cameloids, penguins, and rheas, and wild landscape such as rocky spires, wind-swept pampa, and intensely blue glaciers can all be seen at the end of the earth.

The north has two excellent yet distinct options. Surrounded by natural wonders, **San Pedro de Atacama** is a funky oasis town with good accommodations and restaurants. Multiple sporting options and comfortable temperatures draw people to the town year round. Another option in the north is **Arica** and **Lauca National Park**, an area of colonial villages, abundant wildlife, and the distinct Aymara culture of the high plains. Lauca, however, offers less infrastructure than San Pedro and adds the variable of high altitudes. We recommend and include itineraries for both places – you'll just have to make the decision between the two based on your personal preferences.

If you just don't have the travel time it takes to get to the two extremes of Chile, do not despair. There are many excellent options in the rest of the country. We offer six four-day itineraries that focus on different landscapes and activities. The idyllic **Lake District**, with scores of perfect volcanoes, and the dramatic **Central Coast** fall under this category.

If you have more time or want to concentrate on a certain part of the country, we highlight the best of the region at the beginning of each chapter. If you are really interested in getting off the beaten path, the **Austral Region** is waiting to be explored. However you ultimately decide to spend your time, you'll leave wanting to come back for more.

ITINERARIES

Most international flights arrive in Santiago in the early morning and depart late at night. This is great for squeezing the most out of your time here. Some people want to push it every minute on vacation, while others prefer to take a slower pace. These four-day itineraries offer a bit of both.

FOUR-DAY FLINGS
Beaches
Day 1
• Arrive Santiago
• Explore Santiago (see *One Very Busy Day in Santiago* sidebar in Santiago chapter)
• Dinner at one of the recommended Chilean restaurants

Day 2
• Drive to Zapallar
• Explore Zapallar

Day 3
• Drive along the coast from Zapallar to Valparaíso
• Explore Valparaíso

Day 4
• Drive to Isla Negra
• Return to Santiago
• Hike at El Arrayan or Yerba Loca or continue exploring Santiago
• Go to airport

Surf & Turf
Day 1
• Arrive Santiago
• Explore Santiago (see *One Very Busy Day in Santiago* sidebar in Santiago chapter
• Dinner at one of the recommended Chilean restaurants

Day 2
• El Morado National Park or La Campana National Park

Day 3
• Zapallar or Valparaíso/Isla Negra

Day 4
• Return to Santiago
• Hike at El Arrayan or Yerba Loca or continue exploring Santiago
• Go to airport

Multisport
Day 1
• Arrive Santiago
• Explore Santiago (see *One Very Busy Day in Santiago* sidebar in Santiago chapter)
• Dinner at one of the recommended Chilean restaurants

Day 2
• Fly to Temuco and drive to Pucón
• Horseback ride or mountain bike

Day 3
• Hike in Huerquehue National Park

Day 4
• Raft the Trancura
• Return to Santiago

Culture, Churches, & Food
Day 1
• Arrive Santiago
• Explore Santiago (see *One Very Busy Day in Santiago* sidebar in Santiago chapter)
• Dinner at one of the recommended Chilean restaurants

Day 2
• Fly to Puerto Montt and drive to Castro
• Explore Chiloé
• Dinner at El Sacho

Day 3
• Continue to explore Chiloé

• Dinner at Don Eladio

Day 4
• Drive to Ancud
• Lunch at Ostras de Caulín
• Return to Puerto Montt
• Return to Santiago

City Slicker
Day 1
• Arrive Santiago
• Explore Santiago Centro

Day 2
• Explore the rest of Santiago

Day 3
• Valparaíso or a Day Trip from Santiago

Day 4
• Return to Santiago

If you really want to push it you can continue traveling your first day to spend a sliver of time in the north or Magallanes-Chilean Patagonia. You'll be haggard and we don't recommend it, but here are the itineraries:

North – San Pedro de Atacama Option
Day 1
• Arrive Santiago
• Fly to Calama
• Drive to San Pedro

Day 2
• Visit Salar de Atacama
• Sunset at Valle de la Luna

Day 3
• Visit geysers
• Hike or mountain bike

Day 4
• Return to Calama
• Fly to Santiago

North – Arica/Lauca Option
Day 1
• Arrive Santiago
• Fly to Arica

Day 2
• Explore Arica and Azapa Valley

Day 3
• Travel to Lauca National Park and stay in Putre

Day 4
• Return to Arica
• Fly to Santiago

Torres del Paine
Day 1
• Arrive Santiago
• Fly to Punta Arenas
• Drive to Puerto Natales

Day 2
• Drive to Torres del Paine
• Explore park

Day 3
• Explore park
• Return to Puerto Natales

Day 4
• Return to Punta Arenas
• Fly to Santiago

SEVEN-DAY ITINERARIES
Torres del Paine/Chiloé
Day 1
• Arrive Santiago
• Explore Santiago (see *One Very Busy Day in Santiago* sidebar in Santiago
    chapter)
• Dinner at one of the recommended Chilean restaurants

Day 2
• Fly to Punta Arenas

• Drive to Puerto Natales and Torres del Paine

Day 3
• Explore park

Day 4
• Explore park

Day 5
• Explore park
• Return to Puerto Natales

Day 6
• Return to Punta Arenas
• Fly to Puerto Montt
• Drive to Castro

Day 7
• Explore Chiloé
• Return to Puerto Montt
• Fly to Santiago

The North
Day 1
• Arrive Santiago
• Explore Santiago (see *One Very Busy Day in Santiago* sidebar in Santiago chapter)
• Dinner at one of the recommended Chilean restaurants

Day 2
• Fly to Calama
• Drive to San Pedro
• Sunset at Valle del la Luna

Day 3
• Visit Salar de Atacama
• Mountain bike or hike

Day 4
• Visit geysers
• Return to Calama
• Fly to Arica

Day 5
• Explore Arica and Azapa Valley

Day 6
• Travel to Lauca National Park and stay in Putre

Day 7
• Return to Arica
• Fly to Santiago

The North & South
This one will wear you out and you spend most of your time traveling, but if you've just got to see both the North and Chilean Patagonia in a week, here it is.

Day 1
• Arrive Santiago
• Fly to Punta Arenas

Day 2
• Drive to Puerto Natales and on to Torres del Paine
• Explore park

Day 3
• Explore park
• Return to Puerto Natales

Day 4
• Return to Punta Arenas
• Change planes in Santiago
• Fly to Arica or Calama and follow rest of four-day itinerary

TEN-DAY ITINERARIES
The North & South
Day 1
• Arrive Santiago
• Explore Santiago (see *One Very Busy Day in Santiago* sidebar in Santiago chapter)
• Dinner at one of the recommended Chilean restaurants

Day 2
• Continue on to Punta Arenas, Puerto Natales and to Torres del Paine

Day 3
• Explore park

Day 4
• Explore park

Day 5
• Explore park
• Return to Puerto Natales

Day 6
• Return to Punta Arenas and on to Santiago
• Relax in Santiago or if you're a glutton for punishment fly to the north

Day 7 – San Pedro de Atacama Option
• Fly to Calama
• Drive to San Pedro
• Sunset at Valle del la Luna

Day 8 – San Pedro de Atacama Option
• Visit Salar de Atacama
• Mountain bike or hike

Day 9 – San Pedro de Atacama Option
• Visit geysers
• Mountain bike or hike

Day 10 – San Pedro de Atacama Option
• Return to Calama
• Fly to Santiago

Day 7 – Arica/Lauca Option
• Fly to Arica
• Explore Arica and Azapa Valley

Day 8 – Arica/Lauca Option
• Travel to Lauca National Park and stay in Putre

Day 9 – Arica/Lauca Option
• Return to Arica

Day 10 – Arica/Lauca Option
• Beach

• Fly to Santiago

14-DAY ITINERARIES
North, South, & Chiloé

If you have two weeks we recommend adding Chiloé or spending more time in each of the places on the ten-day itinerary. It's nice not to be on the move every day. If you're the type that has to keep moving, you can tack any of the four-day itineraries on to your trip.

Austral Region

If you really want to get remote however, you could try the following Austral Region trip.

Day 1
• Arrive Santiago
• Explore Santiago (see *One Very Busy Day in Santiago* sidebar in Santiago chapter)
• Dinner at one of the recommended Chilean restaurants

Day 2
• Fly to Balmaceda and drive on to Coyhaique
• Explore Coyhaique

Day 3
• Rent a 4WD vehicle and drive south to Puerto Ibañez
• Take the ferry to Chile Chico
• Spend the night in Chile Chico

Day 4
• Drive to Jeinimeni National Park
• Hike and fish
• Camp in Jeinimeni

Day 5
• Hike and fish
• Camp in Jeinimeni

Day 6
• Return to Chile Chico
• Spend the night in Chile Chico

Day 7
• Drive to Bertrand

• Spend the night in Bertrand

Day 8
• Backcountry horseback ride or hike

Day 9
• Backcountry horseback ride or hike

Day 10
• Raft the Rio Baker
• Spend the night in Bertrand

Day 11
• Drive to Coyhaique or camp in Cerro Castillo National Park and continue to Coyhaique in the morning

Day 12
• Drive to Quelat National Park
• Spend the night at Termas de Puyuhuapi

Day 13
• Get pampered at the Termas de Puyuhuapi
• Return to Puerto Cisnes (or Coyhaique if you are up for the drive)

Day 14
• Return to Coyhaique
• Fly to Santiago

4. LAND & PEOPLE

THE LAND

Extruded between the natural barriers of the Andes and the Pacific Ocean by the force of territorial ambition, Chile's slender frame stretches 4,300 kilometers.

The slender frame disguises Chile's expansiveness. Comparing it with the somewhat similarly shaped but stockier California, Chile possesses about twice the area, half the width, and three times the length. If laid diagonally across the United States, Chile would reach from Miami to Seattle.

Two parallel spines run most of the length of the country, the massive **Andes** to the east and the less prominent **Coastal Range** to the west. The Coastal Range ambles from the northernmost border to the island of Chiloé. The Andes, shared by Argentina and Chile at this latitude, consumes much of Chile's 110-mile average width. The chain curves to a continental finale in Tierra del Fuego. Both ranges are called *cordilleras*, but when a Chilean utters *la cordillera* with a tone of nostalgia or respect, you can be sure the speaker is referring to the Andes.

RAISE THE ROOF

*The Andes' formation began when South America collided with the oceanic **Nazca Plate**. The mountain range is a work in progress, which is emphasized by Chile's frequent earthquakes and volcanic activity. For perspective on the enormity of the remodeling job, consider that the Andes contain the highest peaks in the world outside of the Himalayas. Argentine Aconcagua measures 6,959 meters and Chilean Ojos de Salado stands 6,893 meters. The tectonic collision also created an inverse phenomenon, the **Peru-Chile Trench**. Chile is perched at the edge of a profound precipice that descends as far as 8,000 meters below sea level.*

Due to its longitudinal reach of over half the continent, Chile is endowed with considerable geographic diversity. Its regional divisions can be thought of as an inversion of the west coast of North America. The Arid north features the same clay-baked seaside deserts found in Baja California. The Metropolitan region is blessed with a pleasant fruit-bearing Mediterranean climate like that of California. Farther south, the Lakes District engenders mossy rain forests similar to those in Washington State. At the southern end of the string bean, Magallanes is set in a rugged, pristine wilderness frequently compared to Alaska.

The Arid North

The copper-rich desert region, which stretches from the northern border with Peru to La Serena, provides some of Chile's most fascinating landscape. Although known as one of the world's driest places, the hypnotic setting of chromatic, mineral-gorged hills under a sweeping blue sky is engagingly interrupted by unexpected greenery and wildlife.

The region is temperate despite the lack of rainfall, with the mean high temperature hovering around 81 degrees. The frigid **Humboldt Current**, which originates in Antarctica and follows the Chilean coast north, emits enough cool air to moderate the temperature. Condensation from the ocean creates a fog which moistens spiny vegetation on the coastal bluffs, then expires abruptly. From that point inland, precipitation ceases. Some areas of the Atacama desert have never recorded rainfall.

The more arid northernmost sector of the desert region is known as **Norte Grande**. Its terrain is composed of coastal desert, a transitional sierra strip, and the **Altiplano**, a high plain created by lava filling in the crevices of the Andes. There are several good national parks in the Altiplano that allow precariously close viewing of natural phenomena like bubbling sulfur springs and steam plumed geyser fields, as well as all four types of native cameloids that populate the reserves. Norte Grande's seemingly endless beaches are cherished for offering the least numbing of the country's frigid ocean bathing.

In the semi-arid southern portion, known as **Norte Chico**, the Coastal and Andes ranges begin to form their familiar double spine creating an intervening valley. Spring rains can miraculously transform the cracked, barren surface into a green carpet littered with wildflowers. Melting snow from the Andes produces rivers that carry water year round. Vegetation alongside the rivers creates green swaths through the desert, which nurture funky oasis towns. Some of the land is utilized for fruit production and cattle grazing, but it is vexed by frequent droughts. Vast, barren, salt flats that dominate large portions of the landscape are emblazoned by flocks of pink flamingos.

Central Chile

Central Chile's pleasant Mediterranean climate is characterized by long dry summers and mild winters with moderate rainfall. The coastal range and the Andes diverge to expose an orchard-patched valley made fertile by deposits of marine, glacial, and volcanic sediment over succeeding geological periods. The valley is intersected by rivers that bloat with spring and summer snow melt, such as the Aconcagua and Mapocho, the irrigation of which spurred dramatic agricultural progress.

Given the inviting climate and abundance of fine food and drink, it is no surprise that the region is home to 75% of Chile's population, including the capital city of Santiago. The natural environs also provide an extraordinary recreational arena. The Andes Range maintains its highest elevations in this region, towering like an monolithic wall on the east side of the valley. The combination of abundant snow and relatively mild temperatures creates excellent conditions for alpine skiing. Sun worshipers flock to the beautiful beaches along the coast in the summertime. The slopes and the beach are both about an hour from Santiago, so it would not be inconceivable to snow ski in the morning and dine on seafood at a beach side restaurant in the afternoon.

CENTRAL VALLEY FRUIT BASKET

The Central Valley is one of the world's fruit baskets. Peaches, apricots, plums, pears, apples, and avocados are among the leading crops. This is where Chilean vintners take advantage of the superlative grape growing conditions to produce Chile's internationally acclaimed wines.

The Lake District

Even the view of the map of Lake District is extraordinary. The cartographer's richly textured landscape includes myriad pinched and puckered volcanoes, lakes multiplying like giant amoebas, and an extensive river system that covers the entire surface in blue cobwebs.

Hundreds of rivers descend from the Andes to rush over volcanic rocks forming numerous white-water sections and waterfalls. Most drain into the ocean through larger rivers such as the Calle Calle. The lakes' formation began as glacier movement carved out deep cavities that subsequently clogged with volcanic debris and filled with glacier melt-off. The lakes are strikingly clear and utilized as popular retreats for summer recreation. A majority of Chile's volcanoes are located in this district with one sprouting up almost every thirty kilometers. During eruptions, flash flooding from snow and ice melt is a greater threat than lava flow.

Lush vegetation is supported by an extremely wet, temperate climate that is among the rainiest in the world. Some sections of the Andean foothills contain old growth forests including stands of the umbrella-shaped **Araucaria** or monkey puzzle tree. The northern portion of the Lake District is named for this magnificent conifer, the pine nuts of which were an important food source for the Mapuche Indians.

Much of the landscape is now pastureland set against a backdrop of lakes and conical volcanoes. These fields supply significant quantities of wheat, barley, berries, and dairy products. Salmon farming has developed rapidly in recent years, taking advantage of the abundant supply of clear running water. The timber and logging industries also play a vital role.

Three miles from the mainland is the damp fishing center of **Chiloé**, the second largest island in South America. The island and the archipelagos off the mainland's eastern coast are formed by the Coastal Range that descends into the Pacific Ocean beyond Puerto Montt.

Austral Region

The remote Austral Region consists of the area south of Puerto Montt, between Chaitén and Lago O'Higgins. Beyond the shores, thousands of rain-drenched islands are interwoven with fjords and channels. The verdant islands, most of which remain uninhabited, are formed by the highest peaks of the submerged Coastal Range poking out of the ocean. The extensive channel system provides the main routes of navigation, protecting ships from the turbulent open seas.

The Andes Range no longer demarks the border with Argentina, but rather forms the rugged, steeply ascending coastline. Cerro Macá, for example, rises abruptly out of the ocean to a height of nearly 3,000 meters. From the Austral Region to Punta Arenas, Chile's arable land and population centers lie on the eastern side of the Andes. Nearly constant rainfall supports extensive old growth forest in this area.

Whereas the Lake District's hydrography seems to be tamed so that it is integrated with its orderly settlements, the Austral Region's multi-hued rivers and lakes remain wild and unsullied. The frenetic, crystal

PABLO'S GEOGRAPHY

My slim nation has a body made up
Of night, snow, and sand
The silence of the world is in its long coast
– Pablo Neruda, *from his* **Discoverers of Chile**

green rapids of the **Futalefú** and the placid, turquoise waters of the **Baker River** draw rafters, kayakers, and fly fisherman from all over the world. Other principal rivers include the Palena, Cisnes, and Simpson. A 175,000 hectare lake, known as **Lago General Carrera** on the Chilean side, and **Lago Buenos Aires** on the Argentine side, is almost evenly split between the two countries. It is the second largest lake in South America, outsized only by Lake Titicaca.

The most unique topographical feature of the Austral region are two enormous ice fields which comprise the most expansive glacial area outside of the polar caps. The hundred meter thick ice sheets encase all but the highest peaks of the Andes Chain. The **Northern Ice Field**, *Campo de Hielo Norte,* stretches 100 km with an area of 4,500 square km. The **Southern Ice Field**, *Campo de Hielo Sur,* extends 320 km and comprises roughly 14,500 square km.

As opposed to normal glaciers that move in one direction, the Chilean ice fields expand outward in all directions. Plentiful snowfall provides building material for the glaciers which drop into oceanic channels to the west and feed into expansive lakes on the eastern side. You can view many of these colossal blue ice tongues from the luxury of your vehicle as you bump along the Austral Highway.

Magallanes-Chilean Patagonia

Severe weather is the dominant shaper of the landscape in the southernmost continental region. Pacific winds collide with the Andes to dump torrential rain on the western side of the mountains, then blow dry and cold across Patagonia. The endless rainy season on the western side creates resplendent forests. The eastern side becomes breezy Patagonian grasslands and scrub desert as the moisture dissipates completely.

The Andes consume the coastline, forming a west to east arch, until the end of the continental land mass is reached. The chain submerges below the **Magellan Strait** then, as a farewell, forms **Tierra del Fuego**, the largest South American island. Cape Horn, the southernmost point of the continent, lies to the south of Tierra del Fuego.

Magallanes' parks, the principal of which is the extraordinary **Torres del Paine**, are brimming with wildlife such as guanacos, rheas, and even flocks of giant green parrots squawking above the glaciers. Dense rookeries of Magellanic penguins inhabit the region's coastline and islands.

Both offshore and inland energy resources have recently been developed. Chile now meets 50% of its petroleum and 100% of natural gas needs with extraction from the region. Sheep farming, supported by the grassy pampas, also plays an important role.

Off the Continent

Chile's non-continental territories couldn't be more climatically distinct. They include the rainy Juan Fernández Islands, the subtropical Easter Islands, and a frosty slice of Antarctica.

Antarctica's ice-encrusted landmass lies a thousand kilometers from the tip of Tierra del Fuego. Tree and mammal fossils found beneath the layer of ice recount warmer times, before the continent floated its way to the North Pole. Currently it records the planet's coldest temperatures and is characterized by hurricane force polar winds. Daylight dominates the summer as sunlight continuously skims the horizon. Conversely, winter is mired in a trimester of darkness. The surrounding sea is a rich feeding area for penguins, seals, and whales due to an abundance of algae and krill, a tiny shrimp-like crustacean.

Chile asserts rights to a wedge of 1.3 million square km that overlaps claims by Argentina and England. This area includes the Antarctic Peninsula, the most hospitable area of continent because it is the only portion that extends beyond the Arctic circle. It is here that you are most likely to tread upon the 1% of land not covered by ice.

Easter Island, also known as **Rapa Nui**, is located 3,600 km west of the Chilean mainland. The 64 square mile Polynesian island was formed by the eruption of three volcanoes. The upper landscape is dominated by the volcanoes, while the lower unfolds into fields of pasture and volcanic rock. Pink coral beaches and high bluffs delineate the shoreline. There is some agriculture and fishing but tourism is the primary commercial activity.

The **Juan Fernández Islands** are 18 square miles of tempestuous solitude. Daniel Defoe's novel, *Robinson Crusoe,* was inspired by a Dutch sailor named Alexander Selkirk who was set ashore here in 1704 and remained stranded for four years until his rescue. The largest island in the archipelago, located about one thousand km from the Chilean coast, is named for the fictional character. Five hundred people reside on the rain- and wind-pounded Pacific island. Most engage in lobster fishing to make a living. The island's flora and fauna are noted for having developed in an isolated environment similar to that of the Galapagos.

THE PEOPLE

The most endearing Chileans will work their way into your subconscious to animate your memories long after your visit. Among the cast of characters playing out their roles in front of the Andean backdrop are amicable cowboys known as *huasos* and industrious miners forever demonstrating for requisite pay in return for their perilous labor. There are the earnest, somewhat intimidating, national police *carabineros*, the neatly outfitted mestizo *nanas* (nannies) pushing strollers with blonde *guaguas* (babies), and hair-netted factory women selecting nectarious fruit for export. There are the construction workers who scan the street for passing beauties to shower them with double-entendres, and the stylish Chilenas themselves, many of whom appreciate the compliment. There are resourceful street vendors, savvy, dedicated businessmen who push the economy's pedal to the metal, and introspective *mate*-sipping mountaineers who explore the half of Chile most of their compatriots never see.

THE ARTISTRY OF AN ASADO

When not at work, and they are there a lot because long hours are a point of pride, Chileans eagerly head to beaches and barbecues. If they can barbecue on the beach, all the better. The orchestration of an **asado** *by a skilled barbecuer is a fascinating exhibition. It is a dynamic performance, the objective of which is not to feed everyone at once, rather to feed everyone continuously for hours.*

The grill master is sure to first load the barbecue with spicy sausages that are launched sizzling onto crisp-crusted, soft-bodied **bolillo** *rolls, then garnished lavishly with* **pebre**, *a chunky concoction of diced tomatoes, onions, and cilantro. We often think of Jessica's hands, which were absolutely derelict at tying square knots, but whose dexterity mesmerized us as they juggled a salt shaker and carving knife over seared, crackling meat. She seasoned and sliced it piece by delicate piece while feeding our hungry trekking group the tantalizing morsels directly from her blade.*

In comparison to other Latin American countries, Chile is culturally muted. Some attribute the country's tightly held character to being a mountain culture. Others even consider it an island culture due to its isolated development until the advent of air travel and modern communications. The natural barriers of ocean, desert, and mountains have certainly created a distinct variant of the Spanish language. The society's reticence can also be ascribed to the years of dictatorship during which freedom of expression was brutally suppressed. This is changing though, especially with the under-30 generation who are as tuned in to the fashion and attitudes of MTV, as are young people in California.

Outwardly you will find Chileans to be modest about the country's formidable achievements. They frequently preface any discussion about the country with "Chile is a poor country" or "Although we are not as developed as your country..." However, Chileans also exhibit an intense national pride that is easily pricked by perceived slights, such being shut out of the North American Free Trade Agreement, or extolled, as demonstrated with the exuberant night-long celebrations set off by international athletics victories.

ON THE QUIET SIDE

"In Chile we are influenced by the eternal presence of the mountains that separate us from the rest of the continent, and a sense of precariousness inevitable in a region of geological and political catastrophes. Chileans are sober, circumspect, and formal, and suffer an acute fear of attracting attention, which is synonymous with looking ridiculous."
*– Isabel Allende, in her memoir **Paula***

Ethnic Composition

Chile is composed of a homogenous, mostly mestizo population of 14 million people. Although the majority of Chileans have brown hair and brown eyes, all color gradations can be found, ranging from the fair northern European to the darker Native American complexion. Cultural similarity throughout the country is due to the fact that most of the Chilean population was formed in a small section of the country, then spread to the north and south.

The roots of the Chilean mestizo can be traced back to colonial times. Spain was forced to protect its territory by sending a great number of soldiers. Since European women were few, miscegenation created a population with a mixture of Native American and Spanish blood, but one in which the Spanish element is greater than in other Latin American mestizo populations. Currently about two-thirds of the country defines itself as mestizo. Since Chile did not have a tropical plantation economy, few African slaves were brought to Chile.

WHAT'S IN A NICKNAME?

*Travelers of Asian and African heritage will surely receive unsolicited attention from curious Chileans due to the near non-existence of these races in the country's ethnic composition. Nicknames such as **Chino**, applied to all Asians, and **Negro**, for anyone with dark skin, are amicably intended as camaraderie builders. The same goes for **Gordo**, **Flaco**, **Gringo**, or any of a host of other nicknames describing physical characteristics that are commonly applied to strangers, friends, and family alike.*

Much of the indigenous population had been decimated by European diseases by the time of Chile's annexation of the Mapuche-controlled Araucania in 1880. In a recent census, about 1.3 million Chileans were listed as native American, most indicating their specific tribe as **Mapuche**. The indigenous way of life remains strongest for those who live on reservations in the Lake District, but it's difficult to distinguish between a Mapuche family and any other Chilean family living in the countryside. The most easily identifiable indigenous group is the population of 50,000 **Aymara** living in the Altiplano of Chile's northern Andes. They share similar dress and customs with their counterparts in Bolivia and Peru. There are also 28,000 native **Rapa Nui** on Easter Island.

During the 19th century, Chile sought to stimulate European immigration with land incentives. It had success in attracting German and Swiss migrants to the Lake District. That area of the country still shows strong Northern European influence in its architecture and cuisine. In fact, in many areas of the Chilean countryside you will see roadside stands advertising German pastries such as *kuchen* and strudel. Other prominent groups of immigrants during this time include English, Scottish, North American, and Croats. Another wave of immigrants arrived just before World War II composed primarily of Spanish, Italian, Arabs, and East European Jews. About a quarter of the population counts itself as being from European descent.

Urbanization

Chile is recognized as the most industrialized country in Latin America. The majority of Chileans live in urban areas. Chilean cities follow the usual Spanish colonial plan of a central plaza surrounded by a grid of streets forming square blocks. Relatively few architectural monuments remain from colonial times due to the devastation wrought by frequent earthquakes.

The most significant impact of urban development has been the disproportionate growth of Santiago. The Metropolitan Region of Santiago has more than 5 million inhabitants, over one-third of the country's population. It is the seat of the national government (except for Congress, which is now in Valparaíso), the nation's main financial, manufacturing, and commercial center, and the most important location for educational, cultural, and scientific institutions. Concepción and Valparaíso also receive a great influx of rural migrants.

In the countryside, the land reforms instituted from 1964-1973 were effective in breaking down the inefficient system of large estates. Pinochet's free market policies opened the way for unrestricted sale of rural land. The net result was an expansion of medium-size holdings. Agricultural workers now live mainly in towns or on small rural properties.

Income & Education

Chile's successful economic policies have earned a great deal of praise. Conflicting conclusions can be drawn, however, as to whether the wealth is being shared. Chile's class structure is composed of 10% upper class, 60% middle class, and 30% lower class. One comparative statistic indicates that Chile has the largest middle class in Latin America. Another figure shows income distribution remains among the most regressive in the world, with the highest decile of the population holding about 40% of the country's total income.

Oddly enough, it is at the beach where you might first notice Chile's rigid socio-economic stratification. As is true in most Latin American countries, Chileans socialize with the birds of the same economic feather. This unwritten rule is quite visible on the country's beaches. While the cities' inhabitants mix together like a stew, the highways sift vacationers into their income categories, to deposit them as purified strata onto each class's respective beach. A Central Coast drive from upper class Zapallar, to middle class Maitencillo, to lower class Quintero will make this particularly evident.

Chile's educational system is divided into eight years of free and compulsory primary education, four years of optional secondary education, and additional higher education. Private schools have relatively high enrollment. Chile's adult literacy rate of 96% is among the highest in Latin America.

Chilean universities are well respected. The most prominent of these are the state-run Universidad de Chile and private Universidad Católica in Santiago, as well as the private universities in Valparaíso, Concepción, and Valdivia.

Government

Chile is a democratic republic governed in accordance with a constitution written in 1981. Presidential elections are held every six years. There is a bicameral legislature consisting of the *Senado*, an upper chamber and a *Cámara de Diputados*, a lower chamber, both of which are elected by direct popular vote and convene in Valparaíso. The justices and prosecutors of the Supreme Court and the Courts of Appeals are appointed by the president from a list of nominees proposed by the Supreme Court.

The country is divided into 12 administrative regions with the capital of Santiago located in the separate Metropolitan Region. The regions are officially referred to by Roman numerals. The regions are divided into provinces, then into communes.

REGIONS BY NUMBER

Number	Name	Capital
Region I	Tarapacá	Iquique
Region II	Antofagasta	Antofagasta
Region III	Atacama	Copiapó
Region IV	Coquimbo	La Serena
Region V	Valparaíso	Valparaíso
Region VI	O'Higgins	Rancagua
Region VII	Maule	Talca
Region VIII	Biobío	Concepción
Region IX	Araucania	Temuco
Region X	Los Lagos	Puerto Montt
Region XI	Aisén	Coyhaique
Region XII	Magallanes	Punta Arenas

Religion

The great majority of Chileans consider themselves **Roman Catholic**. In the last census taken, about 78% listed themselves as Roman Catholic, 14% as Protestant, and 7% declared that they were either indifferent to religion or atheist. The Catholic Church was named in the original constitution as the established church of the Chilean government. All other religions were banned and the church maintained full authority over education, cemeteries, and civil registry.

Most of the authority and preferences were taken away from the church during the 19th century, but the official separation of church and state was not implemented until the 1925 constitution mandated it. The dominance of the Catholic Church, although no longer the official religion, still pervades scholastic, social, and political life.

Family Life

Indicative of Chilean society's conservatism is that fact that it is one of the last countries in the world without legalized divorce. The restriction is a toothless guise for the most part, since many couples simply separate, establishing new bonds outside of wedlock, and others have the marriages annulled by convincing the civil clerks that there was procedural error, such as an incorrect address on the wedding application. There is still considerable resistance to legalized abortion, although birth control is readily available and widely accepted.

Children generally continue to live in their parents' homes well into adulthood due to the strength of the family in Chilean social structure, as

DON'T EAT, DON'T DRINK, & BE MARY

Maríanismo, the belief that women should emulate the Virgin Mary in their daily lives, still holds strong in Chilean society. For example, young women rarely drink on an evening out, while their male companions are expected to indulge freely. When it comes to earthly pleasures, good girls don't.

well as the difficulty of supporting oneself on entry level salaries. Leisure time is frequently spent with extended families so people get to know their cousins well.

Statistical evidence, such as near equity in educational enrollment and prominent gains by women in fields such as law and journalism, points to an evolution of traditional gender roles. Despite such facts, you can observe a very different scenario in daily life. For example, there is strong belief that women can only reach full self-realization through motherhood, generating intense pressure on women to have children, a lot of them. The markings of this "baby culture" can be seen at the supermarket which has stork-adorned signs reserving parking spots and checkout lines specifically for expectant mothers. Chileans will routinely ask women, even strangers, about their child bearing record, expressing bewilderment or pity if the number is too low.

Language

Chilean Spanish has been recognized as one of the five main variants in Spanish America, and is one of the most challenging accents to understand. The language bounces through tones like a superball tossed in a small concrete room, ricocheting from baritone to soprano every other syllable, and losing word-endings in the tumult.

You should not feel that you have forgotten Spanish if you learned it in a classroom or in another Spanish speaking country, yet have difficulty understanding the Chileans. Even after spending years living and speaking Spanish in other countries, we were forced to ask Chileans to repeat themselves when we first arrived. We suggest watching some Chilean soap operas to acclimate your ear and pick up the daily vernacular.

Literature

Poetry is the literary vehicle most adeptly utilized by Chilean writers. It is through poetry that the artists have been best able to convey sentiments inspired by the extraordinary natural beauty that surrounds them, as well as sensations of love and solitude.

CHILE SPEAK

Here are a few of the most common slang expressions used in Chile:
- **Cachai?** - *"Understand?" or "Get it?" Usually used at the end of a explanation.*
- **Como 'ta allí?** - *"How's it going?" Usually spoken as one continuous word.*
- **Choro** - *"Cool." Commonly used as an exclamation, "Que chorro!"*
- **Huevón** - *This literally means "big testicles." Huevón has entered into such common usage, that it has lost most of its edge, but it still does not pass the do-you-say-it-to-your-grandmother? test. Some people tag it on to the end of every spoken sentence like "dude." Depending on the intonation, it can also mean "jerk."*
- **Luca** - *One thousand pesos.*
- **Paco** - *"Cop."*
- **Plata** - *Money.*
- **Pololo** - *"Boyfriend." A girlfriend is a polola.*
- **Po** - *A shortened version of pues, which means "well," "certainly," or "why." Frequently spoken at the beginning, middle, and/or end of a sentence as filler. It can also accentuate a response such as "Sí, po!"*

The earliest and most notable Chilean literary work is an epic poem by **Alonso de Ercilla y Zúñiga** (1533-1594), *La Araucana*. The poem describes the Spanish conquest of Chile and pays homage to the valiant battles waged by the Mapuche natives. **Vicente Huidobro** (1893-1948), was the pioneer of modern Chilean poetry. His works, such as *The Mirror of Water*, would serve as inspiration for future poets like Gabriela Mistral.

Chile's two most renowned poets, **Gabriela Mistral** (1889-1957) and **Pablo Neruda** (1904-1973) both brought literary glory to their country by winning the Nobel Prize. They are cultural icons in Chile of the same magnitude that Albert Einstein and Ernest Hemingway are in the United States. Other than both having spent much of their time out of the country in diplomatic posts, Mistral and Neruda differed dramatically in character and perspective.

Gabriela Mistral's stirring, personal poems deal with themes of love, death, and solitude. Her poetry is represented by five major works, the principal one being *Desolation*. The poem, understood to be autobiographical, narrates a story of love and tragedy. It describes a couple's first meeting, their romance, the lover's betrayal, and his unexpected suicide (the beau of Mistral's youth committed suicide). The healing and ultimate serenity are consistent with her later poems which speak of spiritual peace.

ROAD READING

We recommend the following books to enrich your travels in Chile:
Curfew, Jose Donoso. (Fiction).
History of Chile, 1808-1994, Simon Collier and William F. Sater.
   (History).
House of the Spirits, Isabel Allende. (Fiction).
How to Survive in the Chilean Jungle, John Brennan and Álvaro
   Toboada. (Dictionary of Chilean slang).
In Patagonia, Bruce Chatwin. (Travelogue).
Memoirs, Pablo Neruda. (Autobiography).
Paula, Isabel Allende. (Fiction).
Robinson Crusoe, Daniel Defoe. (Fiction).
Voyage of the Beagle, Charles Darwin. (Travel Journal).
Uttermost Part of the Earth, E. Lucas Bridges. (Biography/auto
   biography).
   Several anthologies of poems by Pablo Neruda and Gabriela Mistral
have been translated into English and are available in bookstores. The best
way to ease into Chilean poetry is to start with Neruda's playful odes.

Mistral began her career as a teacher and administrator, directing various secondary schools throughout Chile. In 1922, Mistral left Chile to assume diplomatic assignments that included posts in Europe, Central America, and the United States. She also represented Chile in the United Nations and took part in the creation of UNICEF. Due to her educational work and the spiritual themes of her poems, Mistral at times seems to be elevated to sainthood. In a biblically styled mural in Punta Arenas, it is easy to mistake Mistral for Moses. A shrine dedicated to Mistral in Santiago's San Francisco Colonial Museum is as devout and reverential as any built for a recognized Catholic saint.

In contrast, Pablo Neruda's poetry and deeds are highlighted by his love of women and nature, his interest in politics, his joy of simple things, and his devotion to life's diversions. Neruda's topics are as intangible as humanity's evolution and as simple as the watermelon, which he describes as "the great green whale of summer." His writings include the most popular book of poems ever published in Spanish, *Twenty Love Poems and a Song of Despair.*

Neruda was a convivial bigger-than-life force who most dominated the Chilean cultural panorama in the twentieth century. In addition to publishing fifty books in as many years, Neruda was active in politics, especially in promoting the Communism. Neruda's first diplomatic posting in Rangoon, Burma at the age of twenty-three was followed by foreign positions in Asia and Europe. While serving as a senator for the Communist Party in 1949, the party was outlawed. In a legendary act, Neruda fled across the Andes on horseback to escape persecution. He was allowed to return to Chile three years later. In 1971, his political ally and friend President Salvador Allende named him as ambassador to France. He returned to Chile in 1973 suffering from cancer, and died, twelve days after the military coup in which Allende died. Neruda's three houses, in Santiago, Valparaíso, and Isla Negra, have been converted into intriguing, enjoyable museums.

Only a handful of Chilean novelists have attained international distinction. The best known novelist in recent decades is **Isabel Allende**, a niece of President Salvador Allende. Her novels, such as *House of the Spirits* and *Eva Luna*, depict odd, enchanting characters in surreal settings.

Although some would dispute its merit as literature, the animated character **Condorito** is among the most-loved comic strips in Latin America. You can find his comic books available in all of the country's newsstands.

POETIC ENCOUNTERS

"Around this time, a tall lady who wore long dresses and flat shoes came to Temuco. She was the new principal of the girl's school. Her name was Gabriela Mistral.

I used to watch her passing through the streets of my home town, with her sweeping dresses, and I was scared of her. But when I was taken to visit her, I found her to be very gracious. In her dark face, as Indian as a lovely Araucanian pitcher, her very white teeth flashed in a full, generous smile that lit up the room.

I was too young to be her friend, and too shy and taken up with myself. I saw her only a few times, but always went away with some books she gave me."

– **Pablo Neruda**, *from his book* **Memoirs**

Music

The national folk dance of Chile is the *cueca*, which appeared during the first years of the republic. It has now become the traditional dance to celebrate Independence Day. Few Chileans know how to dance the cueca however. They prefer to gather around a pair of profesional entertainers who wave handkerchiefs and circle one another to perform the coquettish dance.

In the 1970's, the lyrics of the *Canción Nueva* music served as an outlet for political expression during the censorship imposed by the military regime. The Andean folk songs contained metaphorical significance understood by initiated listeners. The most highly publicized *Canción Nueva* figure was **Victor Jara** who was executed in 1973 while leading thousands of arrested political detainees in song in the National Stadium. As democracy and freedom of expression returned to the country in the 1980's, the movement's popularity waned.

Currently Chile contributes to the international music scene with tunes from groups such as **Los Tres** and **La Ley**. Chilean country music, such as that played by **Los Huasos Quincheros**, continues to be popular with Chileans of all ages. Tango bars are popular in the seaports of Valparaíso and Punta Arenas, while tropical music such as salsa and merengue is the preferred beat in northern Chile.

MÚSICA CHILENA

If you like to collect music as travel souvenirs, pick up CD's by these artists available in music stores like Feria de Discos. The counter people usually provide good recommendations if you tell them what type of music you like.

Congreso *(Canción Nueva/Rock/Pop)*
Chancho en Piedra *(Rock/Funk)*
Fulano *(Jazz/Rock Fusion)*
Inti Illimani *(Canción Nueva)*
Los Huasos Chincheros *(Chilean Country)*
La Ley *(Rock)*
Lucybell *(Pop/Funk)*
Los Tetas *(Pop/Rock)*
Los Tres *(Rock)*
Joe Vasconcello *(Rock/Jazz Fusion)*

5. A SHORT HISTORY

Chile has traditionally been one of South America's best educated and most politically stable nations. In modern times, this accomplishment has been overshadowed by General Agustín Pinochet's military regime, which ruled the country for seventeen years. From a broader historical perspective, however, Chile's record of civilian rule merits recognition as one rivaled by few others in the world. The country has enjoyed a constitutional and democratic government for most of its history as a republic, with military intervention occurring only at times of extraordinary social crisis.

While blessed with generally good fortune in its politics, Chile's persistent struggle has been the attempt to free itself of single country and single commodity economic dependence. Trade dependence began with colonial reliance on Spain, then later on England, and in modern times on the United States. In terms of export industries, mining has played an overwhelmingly dominant role in the country's economy, leaving it vulnerable to fluctuations in commodity prices and world economic downturns.

Although justifiably criticized for a brutal record of human rights abuses, the Pinochet regime proved to be the most productive catalyst for revolutionizing the economy. Its free market, diversified-export, economic strategy was so successful that it has been adopted as a model for progress by other developing nations. At the time of the transfer of power, in 1990, the civilian government inherited one of the strongest economies in Latin America, though one notably flawed by a high inequality of income distribution.

The two elected civilian administrations since the dictatorship have delicately attempted to distance themselves from the military, while trying to unify a polarized citizenry. An intrinsic part of this objective is establishing a more humane distribution of wealth without disrupting an unprecedented fourteen consecutive years of positive growth.

Conquest & Colonization

The first known European to set foot on Chilean territory was **Ferdinand Magellan**. He camped along the shores near Punta Arenas while passing through the strait during a 1532 voyage seeking a route to the Orient. **Diego de Almagro** led the first colonizing expedition into central Chile from Peru in 1535, but was disappointed by the lack of mineral wealth, so he disbanded the colony two years later.

The second Spanish colonial expedition from Peru to Chile was organized by **Pedro de Valdivia** in 1540. He founded the city of Santiago on February 12, 1541 and became the first governor of the Captaincy General of Chile. In that post, he reported to the viceroy of Peru rather than directly to Spain.

When Valdivia arrived, about one million Amerindians inhabited Chile, living in fragmented societies of hunters, gatherers, and farmers. There was no dominant central state such as those established by the Aztecs in Mexico and the Incas in Peru. The Inca empire, for its part, had penetrated far enough south to establish a few forts near present-day Santiago, but never colonized any current Chilean territory, nor did it establish a strong cultural presence.

A PLACE CALLED CHILE

There are a few of different theories about the origin of Chile's name. The most plausible one is that Chile derives its name from the indigenous word **tchilimapu**, *which designated the area of the Aconcagua Valley, north of present day Santiago. Tchili means "snow" or "cold" in Quechua, the language of the Incas, and mapu means land, so together it means "land of snow or cold."*

Though the conquistadors easily subdued the northern natives, forcing them to work in the fields and mines, they were not as successful with the **Mapuche** natives to the south. The **Araucanians**, as the Spanish called the Mapuche, were a mobile people who lived in scattered family clusters and small villages, feeding themselves through hunting, domesticating crops, and collecting pine nuts from araucaria trees.

Seeking slave labor, Valdivia established a fortress near the Biobío River, 600 km south of Santiago. In December 1553, an army of Araucanian warriors, organized by the legendary Mapuche chief **Lautaro** (Valdivia's former servant), assaulted the fort of Tucapel. Accompanied by only fifty soldiers, Valdivia rushed to the aid of the fort, but all of his men perished in the battle and the fort was destroyed. Valdivia was captured and killed by the warriors.

The Spanish soon reestablished the fort of Concepción on the Biobío River and seven new settlements farther south. A great Mapuche offensive in 1600 expelled the invaders from the seven cities. The Mapuche victory effectively fixed the frontier border at the Biobío River. The territory of Arauco was viewed, for two and a half centuries, as an independent nation. The Araucanian's fierce resistance and indefatigable military will was extolled by Alonso de Ercilla, the soldier-poet, in his renowned epic, *La Araucana*.

Warfare along the frontier border lessened in intensity during the following centuries. Cross-frontier trade developed as a common form of interaction. The Mapuches supplied cattle, horses, and ponchos in exchange for hardware, wine, and manufactured goods.

Society in colonial Chile was sharply divided along ethnic, racial, and class lines. Dominating the upper class were *peninsulares*, Spaniards born in the mother country, and the Creoles, Spaniards born in the colonies. Next were the mestizos, a mixed Spanish Amerindian race, forming the largest segment of society. On the bottom rung were the Amerindians and a few African slaves. Missionaries proved to be the valiant defenders of the indigenous population, but their attempts at conversion were futile.

Wage labor was rare in the colonial period. As in many parts of Latin America, the crown rewarded many conquerors according to the *ecomienda* system. This granted them natives to work large pieces of land in return for the obligation of civilizing and Christianizing them. The natives, in fact, were virtual slaves with little or no rights.

Later the mestizo and poor Spanish population became the main source of labor for the large haciendas known as *latifundos*. Initially these laborers were recruited to work the *latifundo* in exchange for the rent of a small plot of land for their personal cultivation. Gradually the agreements would evolve into permanent arrangements, although the workers were not legally bound to the land. Darwin described the living conditions on the *latifundos* as "feudal-like." Each *latifundo* was a self-contained community, growing its own food, weaving its own fabric, and organizing its own entertainment.

The fortunes of those outside of the *latifundo* system were even more precarious than those within it. With most of the arable land absorbed into the large estates, and no open frontier to settle, a permanent floating population of peons and vagabonds roamed the Central Valley in search of subsistence.

As the Hapsburg dynasty's rule ended in Spain in 1700, trade restrictions were loosened, allowing for direct Chilean trade with the Viceroyalty of the River Plate (modern day Argentina), England, and the United States. Foreign trade brought with it greater knowledge of the politics abroad, especially the spread of liberalism in Europe. This did not

FOLKLORIC HEROES

Two idealized characters whose existence can be traced back to colonial times are **huasos** *and* **rotos**.

You will observe a Chilean tenderness of heart toward the impoverished of their county. Any of the poor who are seen begging in the streets or who live in the shanty towns are sympathetically referred to as rotos, literally "the broken" or "the ragged." The label furnished the title of the book, El Roto, a 1920's novel by Joaquin Edwards describing the plight of the destitute. There is even a public square dedicated to them in Arica, the Roto Chileno Plaza.

Huasos, poncho-clad horsemen with broad-brimmed hats, are characterized by contentment, improvidence, and a strong gambling instinct. One thing is certain, the handsomely dressed cowboys are friendly. An hola invested will certainly get you hola with a smile and nod in return. Our favorite huaso was one we dubbed "The Whistling Huaso." He clopped along each morning on his horse among the handful of autos on Chile Chico's single paved strip, lips pursed, pushing forth a cheery, forthright tune which announced his arrival and faded in the distance as he moseyed from concrete to scrub land.

spur immediate change however, because most of the colony's elite remained staunchly loyal to the Spanish crown. Meanwhile, the new ideas of independence and democracy probably never reached the majority, most of which was illiterate.

Independence & Civil Wars

The timing of the independence was due entirely to the great upheaval caused by the Napoleonic wars in Europe. In 1808, having forced the Spanish king to abdicate, Napoleon placed his own brother on the Spanish throne. Chileans, like other Spanish Americans, were faced with the dilemma of deciding who was in charge in the absence of the divine monarch. The Creole leaders of Santiago decided on September 18, 1810 that they would self-govern as long as the imposter king ruled Spain. This date is celebrated as the country's independence day.

Chile's first experiment with self-government was led by **Jose Miguel Carrera**, an aristocrat in his mid-twenties just back from the war in Spain. His immediate task was to confront an army, headed by loyalists from Peru, sent to Chile to quell the creole subversion. The loyalists were successful in recruiting men for their regiment in southern Chile. The battles fought between the Creoles and the loyalists near the city of Concepción ground to a deadlock.

Carrera was a heavy-handed ruler who aroused widespread opposition. **Bernardo O'Higgins Riquelme** captained a rival creole faction. He and his allies believed that the battles against the loyalists should be fought for permanent independence rather than temporary self-rule. A power struggle developed into a civil war as the two men vied for leadership. In 1814, the loyalist troops took advantage of the internal strife to capture Santiago. O'Higgins, Carrera, and some 2,000 others retreated across the high Andean passes to the safety of Argentina.

The Spanish "reconquest" of Chile and the accompanying harsh rule by the loyalists erased any remaining loyalist sentiment among the Creoles. Even though the Spanish King Ferdinand had been returned to the throne, most Creoles became convinced of the necessity of full independence. It is important to recognize that the benefits of liberation were intended for the creole elite, not for the masses of Chileans. The Creoles wanted to assume the leadership roles previously occupied by the Iberian-born Spaniards without disturbing the existing social and economic order. The majority of troops on both sides, however, consisted of mestizos and native Americans who were coerced to do the actual fighting.

Long before the Chilean rebel's exodus to Mendoza, the Argentine general **José de San Martín** had been planning to use a liberated Chile as a launching point for a seaborne assault on the Viceroyalty of Peru. He considered victory in Peru as the key to the expulsion of the Spanish from all of South America. San Martín and O'Higgins' parallel objectives made them allies and close friends.

The combined armies of O'Higgins and San Martin crossed the treacherous Andean pass to initiate the offensive, then won Chile's formal independence when the army defeated the last large Spanish force in the Battle of Maipu in 1818. An assembly of Chilean leaders offered the government to San Martin, but he declined, preferring to focus on his objective of liberating Peru. O'Higgins was thus chosen as the Supreme Director of the State of Chile. He maintained this role as Chile's first president until 1823 and is revered as the father of the nation.

Unfortunately for O'Higgins, civil strife plagued his tenure in office. He is respected for having defeated the royalists and for his efforts to build schools. He alienated Liberals with his authoritarianism, however, and ruffled Conservative landowners with his proposed property reforms. Many also opposed Chile's costly involvement in the fight for the liberation of Peru. Amid mounting discontent, O'Higgins resigned and sought exile in Peru where he lived out his remaining years.

After O'Higgins' departure, civil conflict continued with Liberal presidents and constitutions rising and falling quickly throughout the 1820's. During this time commercial traffic accelerated. The trading community, much of which was composed of foreigners, clustered in the booming port of Valparaíso. The abolition of slavery in 1823 – long before most other countries in the Americas – was considered one of the Liberals few lasting achievements. In 1830 government troops lost a pivotal battle against rebelling Conservative forces, which dislodged the Liberal government from power for the first time since independence.

Rise of a Republic

The Conservative forces that came to power in 1830 established a foundation to make Chile the preeminent Latin American country in terms of stable civilian rule. Chile was viewed as a model republic, an example for her turbulent neighbors to emulate.

Chile's success in its constitutional government is partially credited to having fewer obstacles to overcome, as it was less disturbed by regional and ethnic conflicts. Its homogenous mestizo population was concentrated in the compact Central Valley making the country easier to manage than those with far-flung states. Conflicts with the Catholic Church that hindered other countries were minimal in Chile, since the Church had never been very wealthy or powerful here. To fully benefit from these advantages Chile relied on shrewd leaders, victories in wars against its neighbors, and continued economic growth.

The Chilean elite was cohesively united by familial and business networks. The Larraín clan, for example, consisted of multiple landed

THE PORTALES ERA

Although he never aspired to the presidency, Valparaíso merchant **Diego Portales Palazuelos** *dominated national politics from the cabinet and behind the scenes from 1830 until his death in 1837. He was a cousin of the head of the Larraín clan, but had no exalted opinion of the Basque-Castilian elite to which he belonged. Known for his sardonic wit and charm, he complained, "the families of rank would flail without the support of the white elephant of government, but regrettably, it is the only class available for the task of managing the republic."*

Portales' social character was that of a devotee of animated parties, guitar music, and female company while his public persona was markedly different, that of austere businessman and servant of the state. Though not alive for most of them, the years 1830-1871 became known as the "Portales Era." His vision of a framework of executive control that would eventually lead to a genuinely liberal government was implemented and evolved exactly as he had plotted.

and titled families known as "the eight-hundred." The Larraíns and their offspring, through marriage to other prominent families such as the Errázuriz and Vicuña, attained influential positions time and time again. The role of these family networks is a fundamental element of Chile's power structure.

General Joaquin Prieto Vial served as president from 1831-1841 in two successive terms of five years each. The main accomplishments during his administrations were implementation of the 1833 constitution, stabilization of the government, and victory over the Peru-Bolivia Confederation. Political and economic stability reinforced each other as his advisor Portales encouraged economic growth and free trade. Mining lured a large number of workers, traders, speculators, and prospectors to northern Chile. Most of the mines were small and shallow and relied on labor more than advanced extraction and processing technology.

Prieto and Portales feared that sword-rattling Bolivia, which had just formed a confederation with Peru, might attack Chile. Animosities rooted in the colonial period, as well as disputes over customs duties and loans exacerbated the conflict. Portales was taken captive by a Chilean rebel force who opposed the war. The captors killed Portales with thirty-five bayonet thrusts. Peruvian involvement was suspected in the assassination and war ensued. Quick Chilean land and naval victories made Chile lord of the West Coast. The triumph brought unity and patriotism to Chile, as well as convincing Europe and the United States to respect Chile's coastal sphere of influence.

Manuel Bulnes Prieto, a decorated general, was the ideal president (1841-1851) to establish executive control over the armed forces. Bulnes presided over continued prosperity as production from the farms and mines increased. New markets were created for wheat and flour by the population-swelling gold rushes in California and Australia. The hacienda structure was fortified by the increased demand. It simply employed more peasants in the exploitive tenant farmer workforce, rather than importing modern capital and technology. The haciendas increased their holdings and political clout to the detriment of future agricultural and economic development.

Manuel Montt Torres (president 1851-1861) strengthened the republican policies with openness to Liberal participation in the government. Montt was forced to put down two rebellions while in office, one at the beginning and the other at the end of his tenure. These brief civil wars, in which 4,000 Chileans died, were fueled by opposition to the landowners' inordinate power and influence. Montt's administrations were lauded for the establishment of railroad and telegraph lines as well as school construction that would make Chile one of the most literate nations in the hemisphere. He also continued to push back the southern Auracanian frontier, in part by encouraging German emigration.

In reaction to a Spanish seizure of Peruvian territory in 1864, Chile denied Spain coaling rights to its ports. The Chilean navy broke the ensuing Spanish blockade of Valparaíso, but as a final vengeful salvo, the retreating Spanish fleet severely shelled the city. Chile's role as the dominant coastal power was again enhanced by its success in the conflict.

Five Liberal presidents formed coalition cabinets from 1861-1891. Various parties arose and splintered into new groups during this time period. Secularization gradually gained ground, as the state assumed management of the civil registry formerly in the hands of the Church.

The **War of the Pacific** (1879-83) is Chile's most important historical event between its independence in 1810 and the military coup of 1973. The booty from this second war fought against Bolivia and Peru augmented Chilean territory with two northern provinces: Tarapacá from Peru and Antofagasta from Bolivia. It gave Chile control of the nitrate exports that dominated the national economy until 1920 as well as copper deposits that eclipsed nitrate revenues in the 1930's. Mining from the area contributes a major portion of the country's wealth today.

The discovery of silver, nitrates, and guano suddenly attracted attention to the previously neglected Atacama desert. The ill-defined Bolivia-Chile border took on new significance as the two nations began to vie vigorously for control of the desert area. When Bolivia increased taxes on Chilean mines in Bolivian territory, disregarding an existing treaty, Chile's jingoistic press and the public demanded that Aníbal Pinto's administration take military action.

Pinto, like most other politicians, knew of Peru and Bolivia's alliance. He feared Peru's formidable navy, but was swayed by patriotic mobs demonstrating in the capital. Chile faced an enemy whose combined forces outnumbered them two to one.

Chile overwhelmed the opposition on both land and sea with better-trained forces. It then took the war beyond the disputed border areas to occupy Lima, a humiliation the Peruvians never forgave. Chilean disenchantment with the lengthening conflict hastened the conclusion. Treaties were signed which returned some occupied territories to Peru, but which allowed Chile to retain Tarapacá and Antofagasta. Bolivia not only lost valuable mineral resources in the conflict, but also its vital link to the sea.

After the War of the Pacific, the military turned its energies to a definitive vanquishing of the Araucanians. The Chilean government had been whittling away at Mapuche-held territory in the 170 years since independence. Lack of centralized Araucanian rule and resistance made the final defeat in 1882 inevitable. Many Araucanians fled over the border

THE BATTLE OF IQUIQUE

*The emotional turning point in the War of the Pacific was the **Battle of Iquique** which took place on May 21, 1879. Two iron-clad warships from the Peruvian Navy cornered two antiquated Chilean ships in Iquique's harbor. Chilean Captain Arturo Prat's vessel, the Esmeralda was forced to engage in a direct exchange of fire with the mighty Huáscar. Prat promised his men that despite the odds, he was willing to fight to the death. He fulfilled this prophesy when, as his ship was sinking, he heroically boarded the Huáscar and was killed. Meanwhile, the other Chilean vessel, the Covadanga, lured its larger pursuer, the Peruvian Independencia, onto a sandbar, then circled back to destroy the grounded vessel with canon fire. The Battle of Iquique, and in particular, Prat's martyrdom served as inspiration for the Chilean military and is commemorated today in museums throughout the country.*

to settle in the Argentine pampas and the rest were herded into tribal reservations where they have lived mired in poverty for generations. Wealthy Chileans immediately carved out immense estates as no homestead act or legion of family farmers stood in their way. A few middle-class farmers from the central valley and Northern Europe moved in as well.

The downfall of **President Jose Manuel Balmaceda** (president 1886-1891) represented the only occasion in a hundred year period that the transfer of power was implemented by force. The rebellion was ignited by the growing strength of Congress and its demand for more leverage in the political process. The Conservatives and Navy sided with Congress while the Liberals and Army sided with the president. Brief bloody battles in Concón and Placilla, which cost about 6,000 lives, decided the civil war. The congressionalist force marched to the capital. Balmaceda was too proud a man to surrender. Having gained asylum in the Argentine embassy, he defended his cause with lyrical essays. On September 19, 1891 the day after the formal expiry of his presidential term, he shot himself in the head with his revolver. His demise is frequently compared to that of a later president, Salvador Allende.

Industrialization & Mass Democracy

The result of the congressionalist victory in the civil war was a Parliamentary Republic, which lasted from 1891-1925. During this period, Congress overshadowed the ceremonial office of the president. The congress was dominated by the landed elites who were accused of fixing elections by intimidating or bribing peasant voters. Lackluster presidents were handcuffed by congresses, which frequently used their power to replace presidential cabinet members. Quipped **President Ramón Barros Lucos** (namesake of the popular Barros Lucos sandwich) about the lack of executive power, "There are only two kinds of problems – those that solve themselves, and those that can't be solved."

With improved transportation and communication, Chile's cities grew rapidly. The government adopted policies to encourage growth of domestic industries. Exports of nitrate, which had fueled Chile's economy for decades, received a devastating hit when Germany developed a synthetic nitrate in 1913, leading to a collapse of international prices. Copper production picked up the slack, however, aided by massive investment in the three large American-owned mines. The copper companies became the government's favorite revenue source since they could be aggressively taxed without antagonizing local interest groups.

The middle class grew in size and its political power increased through the formation of new parties. Equally important was middle class presence among the top commanders in the armed forces. Life for the upper class was better than ever. So many headed for the Central Coast beaches in the summer, that there was not enough passenger space on the railway to keep up with demand.

Life wasn't so rosy for everyone. The ruling class was criticized for neglecting the dismal lot of the working class. Census data shocked the proud Chileans with revelations about the extent of poverty, illiteracy, and poor health among the vast majority of the population. The miners, for example, lived in shanties constructed out of chunks of desert and zinc roofs, affording little or no protection from the extreme swings in temperature for which the north is famous. Living conditions in the cities were every bit as bad. Frequently an entire family would be crammed into a single, unventilated room. The workers' homes were incubators of fatal diseases such as tuberculosis. At the end of World War I, the working class began to organize labor unions in the city, but any such attempts by miners or peasants were crushed.

The middle and working classes voted **Arturo Alessandri Palma** (1922-1925, 1932-1938) into power. His initiatives addressing social reforms, however, were blocked by a conservative congress. In a double coup, first military right wingers who opposed the president seized power in September 1924, then reformers in favor of the ousted president took charge in January 1925. The two colonels who led the second group, **Carlos Ibañez del Campo** and **Marmaduke Grove Vallejo**, returned Alessandri to the presidency.

A new constitution was written in 1925, the second major charter in Chilean history, and one which would remain in affect until 1973. The constitution increased presidential power, provided legal recognition of workers' right to organize, promised social welfare for all citizens, and recognized official separation of church and state. It also included a provision for the right of the state to infringe on private property for the public good.

Ibañez maneuvered himself to remain as the only minister in the cabinet so that all presidential decrees had to legally include his signature. President Alessandri resigned in protest and went into exile. Ibañez, (president 1927-31, 1952-58) rigged the election in his favor, then fortified his authoritarian reign with military support.

According to the League of Nations, no other nation's trade suffered more than Chile's from the economic collapse of the Great Depression. Unemployment reached almost 25%, government revenues plummeted, and Chile took its currency off of the gold standard. Unable to revive the economy, Ibañez resigned in 1931 rather than risk civil war. Alessandri returned to Chile to win the presidency again in the 1932 elections. Alessandri's rough but effective measures brought life to the shattered economy, aided by rising international prices for copper.

Chile attempted to continue its foreign policy tradition of neutrality during World War II, but finally severed relations with the Axis powers under pressure from Washington. Chile subsidized the Allied cause by accepting an artificially low price for it copper exports to the United States. After the war, the United States implemented support programs to facilitate new Chilean enterprises in industries such as steel, oil, and fishing. After displacing Britain as Chile's most important economic partner in the 1920's, the United States asserted an economic dominance that would last until the 1980's.

Chile quickly became enmeshed in the Cold War as Washington and Moscow meddled in its affairs. Communist activity was banned under the 1948 law entitled "Defense of Democracy." It is commonly understood that the government took such action under pressure from the United States. The crackdown was followed by an expanded scope of US loans, investments, and technical missions to Chile.

By 1952 Chileans suffered from a crisis of political faith. They were alienated by multi-party politics that produced reformist governments, slow growth, and spiraling inflation. The voters showed their displeasure by turning to two symbols of the past, the 1920's dictator Ibañez and Arturo Alessandri, the son of former president Jorge Alessandri. The politically unaffiliated Ibañez returned to the presidency in 1952, but his monetarist policies failed. Jorge Alessandri was then voted into the presidency in 1958, but his conservative administration also accomplished little of note.

LIKE FATHER LIKE SON

The Chilean electorate tends to favor chips off the ol' block when it comes to casting ballots for president. Sons of former presidents have been voted into their father's footsteps on five separate occasions:
- *Francisco Antonio Pinto (1827-1829) and son Aníbal Pinto (1876-1881)*
- *Manuel Montt (1851-1861) and son Pedro Montt (1906-1910)*
- *Federico Errázuriz (1871-1876) and son Federico Errázuriz (1896-1901)*
- *Arturo Alessandri (1920-1925, 1932-1938) and son Jorge Alessandri (1958-1964)*
- *Eduardo Frei (1964-1970) and son Eduardo Frei (1994-2000)*

Additionally, Chile's first president, General Bernardo O'Higgins (1817-1823), was the son of the colonial governor Ambrosio O'Higgins.

In the 1964 elections, a showdown was staged between **Eduardo Frei**, representing the Christian Democrats of the Center and **Salvador Allende** with the Popular Unity, a coalition of the Left. The two men were not that far apart in their political philosophies. Both recognized the need for and sought social change. Fueled by fear of godless communism spreading under Allende, the Right threw their support in favor of Frei, who earned 56% of the vote. For the first time in Chilean history, a new party, with a serious new agenda, broke the mold of traditional politics. The Christian Democrats possessed sincere aspirations of social reform combined with a fierce attachment to democracy. The party claimed that both capitalism and socialism could be transcended into a more equitable society.

One of the major achievements of the Frei administration was the "Chileanization" of the copper mines, that is, purchasing controlling interest from the American corporations, principally Anaconda and Kennecott. Critics complained that the companies received overly-generous terms. Nevertheless, copper production rose, and Chile received a higher return from the enterprises. The administration promoted the right of peasants to unionize and strike, and implemented land redistribution. Access to education was improved by the building of thousands of new schools. By 1970 primary education covered nearly all children.

The perennial Chilean problem of inflation and slow growth haunted Frei and the Christian Democrats in the last years of the presidency. Frei remained personally popular, but his party lost momentum by the time of the 1970 campaign.

The turbulent 1970 campaign featured a past president, Jorge Alessandri, as the candidate of the Right; a die-hard socialist, Salvador

Allende, who was running for the fourth time as the nominee of the Left's Popular Unity Party; and Rodomiro Tomic, who represented the Centrist Christian Democrats. To the surprise of pollsters, Allende, with 36% of the vote, squeaked by Alessandri with 35%. The democratic election of an avowed Marxist shocked the world.

The Allende experiment enjoyed a triumphant first year. A failed US-backed coup rallied support around Allende. The administration artificially fueled the economy by hiking wages and doubling the money supply. It also initiated its announced programs of accelerated agrarian reform, large-scale nationalization, and the confiscation and redistribution of property. The result of these radical policies, implemented in total disregard of a strong opposition, (two-thirds of the electorate voted for other candidates), would result in disastrous consequences.

The nationalization of the mines was a popular move initially, but one that did not play out as anticipated. Both production and profits plunged as squabbling political appointees failed miserably in their attempt to run the operations.

The agrarian reform was even more controversial. The administration fulfilled its promise of expropriating all large estates. Meanwhile, radical leftist elements organized peasants and Mapuches into groups that seized hundreds of properties without governmental approval. It was politically difficult for Allende to suppress these unauthorized expropriations without appearing to betray the socialist movement. Not only did former owners react angrily to the land seizures, violent struggles erupted among small farmers because the new policies conflicted with redistribution affected by the previous administration.

During the final two years of the administration the economy shrank, deficit spending snowballed, and inflation skyrocketed to over 500%. The government could not impose austerity measures because it lacked support in the opposition-controlled Congress. Allende's congressional adversaries were furious. They accused him of systematically violating the constitution by seizing property.

With politicians arguing the constitutional issues, the growing conflict between government and opposition factions regularly turned into violent confrontations. Allende twice decreed states of emergency to quell riotous demonstrations. Middle and upper-class business owners launched shutdowns. The copper miners, normally the staunchest allies of the left, walked off the job to protest falling real wages. Incensed by plans to create a state transportation enterprise, truckers went on strike. At the height of the stoppage more than 23,000 trucks were off the road. Given their vital role in the transportation of goods, the country suddenly found itself close to paralysis.

In response to Chile's closer alliance with the Soviet Union, the Nixon Administration engaged in overt ploys such as terminating financial assistance and blocking loans from multinational organizations. Covertly, Washington worked to destabilize the Allende administration by funding opposition political groups and by encouraging a military coup d'état. The $8 million allocated to the CIA for its operations against Allende has long been a matter of public record. Although no one can state definitively that the Nixon Administration caused the turmoil strangling Chile, especially when considering Allende's strife-inspiring initiatives, the destablization activities no doubt exacerbated the situation.

As chaos gripped the country, Allende sought to appease the military by including three generals in his most recently reshuffled cabinet. For the position of Army Chief of Staff, advisors to the president recommended the relatively unknown **General Augusto Pinochet**, who was reported to be strongly loyal to the presidency and constitution.

In 1973, after several days of intense plotting, the leaders of the armed forces, with support from the *Carabineros* (national police), made their pact to overthrow the government on September 11. The Army used the pretext of the annual September 19 military parade to mask the transfer of units into Santiago. The Navy, on its way to take part in annual joint maneuvers with the US Navy, returned to Valparaíso under the cover of darkness to seize the port, which it did without opposition.

President Allende, learning of the revolt in the morning, left his residence for the Moneda Palace. Shortly after he arrived, the *Carabineros* abandoned their positions, leaving the edifice to be protected by only a handful of loyal stalwarts. The president refused an offer of safe passage out of the country, opting instead to resist by returning fire with an assault rifle. As the insurgent army battled snipers positioned on rooftops around the square, the Air Force fired missiles at the Moneda. Allende broadcast a final moving speech over the one remaining radio station while the Moneda Palace burned. At about two o'clock that afternoon, Salvador Allende shot himself through the head with a machine gun.

Although the political objectives of Frei and Allende were similar, the inclusion of radical elements in Allende's coalition party and his inability to control them brought about devastatingly different results. The Left's opposition sought temporary support from the military to reign in the chaos, but they badly miscalculated. Pinochet's regime would maintain power for the next seventeen years.

The first phase of the dictatorship was dominated by unflinching repression. The Popular Unity parties were banned and other parties were placed in recess, until they too were banned in 1977. Pinochet purged the public administration, assigning all important national institutions to generals, colonels, and admirals. The military commanders closed Congress, censored the news media, sacked university faculty, burned books, and banned union activities. A strict night time curfew was enforced. This is referred to by the Chileans as the *toque de queda* for the horn that signaled its commencement each night and termination each morning (from the Spanish verb *tocar,* meaning "to play or sound").

During the first four years of the administration, thousands of civilians were murdered, jailed, tortured, brutalized, and exiled. The secret police, known as DINA (Dirección Nacional de Inteligencia) instigated terror that was not limited by Chile's borders. In Buenos Aires, agents murdered General Carlos Prats, the defense minister Pinochet had replaced in the Allende administration. In Washington D.C., a car bomb exploded, killing former Chilean ambassador to the US, Orlando Letelier.

Although aid and loans from the United States increased during the first three years of the regime under the Nixon and Ford administrations, relations became icy after the Letelier assassination and implementation of Jimmy Carter's human rights policies.

Under international pressure, prompted by the effective publicity efforts of the Catholic Church and the outlawed Chilean Communist Party, Pinochet called for the first "yes or no" plebiscite in 1977 to legitimize his regime. The government claimed that 75% of the voters endorsed Pinochet's rule. A ballot in 1980, at the height of an economic boom, would approve a constitution that included provisions for Pinochet's presidency to run eight more years when another "yes or no" plebiscite would be held in 1988.

Pinochet's economic strategy relied on a neoliberal, free market policy that reversed decades of protection for industrialists and unions. The new economic program was designed by civilian technocrats who were known as the "Chicago Boys" because many of them had studied at the University of Chicago. The strategy was effective in cutting inflation and deficits. Growth was encouraged by slashing tariffs. The result was five years of expansion, from 1976-1981, known as the "Chilean Miracle." One indisputable success was the increase of nontraditional exports, especially fruit, timber, and fish products, the revenues of which rose to equal those of copper sales.

Problems that the economic policies failed to resolve during these years, however, were double-digit unemployment and regressive income distribution. The economy collapsed in 1982 prompted by the world economic recession. Chile's woes were compounded by a foreign debt crisis.

Fine-tuning of the neoliberal policies, like reducing foreign debt, resulted in the highest sustained growth in Latin American history from the mid-eighties onward. Chile became the economic model for developing nations. One important change was transferring the national pension plans to private companies. Income distribution remained badly skewed, but the Pinochet regime pointed to its work of caring for the poorest of the poor. There were significant improvements in low-cost housing, sewerage, street-paving, domestic water supply, life-expectancy, and child nutrition. In 1970, Chile had one of Latin America's highest rates of infant mortality, and in 1990, one of the world's lowest.

The return to democracy began with a series of demonstrations in the years following the 1982 recession. Putting the economy back on track did not placate the Chileans, who yearned to re-embrace their democratic tradition. As the 1988 "yes or no" plebescite neared, the dormant political parties awoke. A united effort by the parties from the Center and the Left, known as *Concertación,* secured 54% for the "No" vote against Pinochet continuing for another eight year term, versus 43% for the "Yes" vote.

Pinochet agreed to observe the timetable for handing over the presidency which fixed elections for December 1989. A number of concessions were granted by Pinochet's regime before the elections, but Pinochet was adamant about retaining his position as commander-in-chief of the armed forces until 1998.

The vote in the presidential election reflected, almost exactly, that of the plebiscite. **Patricio Alywin** won 55% of the vote against two right-wing rivals who collected 43% between them. The challenges that confronted the septuagenarian Alywin required tact and skillful negotiating. His administration strove to effect a democratic transition without rankling the military; to tackle the delicate questions of human rights abuses arising from the previous regime; and to maintain economic growth while attending to the pronounced social inequities.

WHAT TO SAY ABOUT PINOCHET

Generous tact should be applied when engaging Chileans in discussions of politics. On our first visit to the country, we were surprised that our democratic virtuosity was rebuffed by hosts who were sympathetic to Pinochet. Many see the dictator as an old uncle who applied a firm hand for the good of the country. Conversely, there are an equal number of Chileans who seethe at the mention of Pinochet's name. Another significant sentiment is simple embarrassment that Chile was a political pariah for almost two decades.

Curious and cautious inquiry, with openness to unexpected opinions, seems to work well. Just be aware that you are likely to encounter polarized, highly-charged, emotional commentary when broaching the subject.

The elected government took several actions to redress the wrongs of the past decades. In September 1990, Salvador Allende was given a state funeral in Santiago that his widow described as a moment of "reparation and reconciliation." A Chilean human rights commission publicly revealed a grim panorama of repression. They documented over 3,000 deaths and strongly criticized the judiciary's support of the regime, although lack of prosecution of the culprits dismayed the families that suffered losses. Alywin engaged in numerous official visits to foreign countries to re-establish Chilean credentials with the simultaneous goal of export promotion. The government also tackled the social debt, increasing social spending by one-third.

The first four year presidential term was to be followed by six year terms beginning in 1994. The names in the next presidential duel were familiar ones. **Eduardo Frei**, son of the former president of the same name, ran for the Christian Democrat's coalition of the Left. **Arturo Alessandri**, a grandson of the former president of the same name, and a nephew of President Jorge Alessandri, represented the Right's United Democratic Party. Frei won with nearly 58% of the popular vote, vowing to pursue continued economic growth while seeking greater social justice.

Agustín Pinochet duly resigned his post of commander-in-chief in March 1998 according to schedule. After a military farewell parade, he traveled to the congressional building in Valparaíso where he was sworn in as Senator-for-life, a final perch he reserved for himself in the 1980 constitution. Protesters outside vocalized their opposition and a few congressional members were removed from the chamber while attempting to interrupt the swearing-in ceremony.

In November 1998, Pinochet was detained in London for extradition to Spain to face charges for the torture and murder of Spanish citizens that occurred while he was in power. The complicated international judicial process and resulting media coverage have opened old wounds and debate in Chile. The Chileans, for the most part, wish the polarizing issue would just go away, so they could move on. Others, especially friends and family of the regime's victims, celebrated the unexpected possibility of seeing justice done.

In a poignant, prophetic statement given to *The New Yorker* magazine the month before his detainment, Pinochet stated, "I was only an *aspirante* dictator. I've always been a very studious man, not an outstanding student, but I read a lot, especially history. And history teaches you that dictators never end up well."

6. PLANNING YOUR TRIP

BEFORE YOU GO

WHEN TO GO

Seasons in the Southern Hemisphere are inverse to those in the Northern Hemisphere. You can calculate what time of year it is by adding or subtracting six months. For example, the Southern Hemisphere's January would correspond to the Northern Hemisphere's July.

Many visitors like to visit Chile in the **austral summer**, which runs from December to February. Although technically summer begins on December 21, we include the beginning of December because that's when the summer vacations and high season pricing starts.

Planning your trip in the summer allows you to take advantage of the driest months, as well as the longest days. In the southern city of Punta Arenas, for example, you can expect about 15 hours of daylight and you will probably go to bed before it gets dark. The only geographical exception to summer weather being a plus is in the northern Altiplano because its distinct rainy season makes some of the park roads impassable. The downside of traveling during the summer is that Chilean and Argentine tourists pack the popular destinations and the hotels raise their prices. Some moderately priced hotels in the Lake District, for example, double their rates. The expensive and inexpensive hotels' seasonal adjustments are not so dramatic.

Spring, September through November, is a good time to travel in Chile. Flowers are blooming, even in the desert region, and the Central Valley really starts to warm up. The **fall** months of March to May start to get pretty nippy country-wide, and the winter rains may have already begun. You will definitely find lower prices and fewer crowds during these

WEATHER CHART

The weather chart demonstrates the climatic diversity within Chile's spindly stretch. Listed are the average high and low temperatures in each city in degrees Fahrenheit and precipitation in millimeters.

	January Low-High	Prcp	April Low-High	Prcp	July Low-High	Prcp	October Low-High	Prcp
Arica	66-80	0	61-76	0	58-67	0	60-70	0
Copiapó	58-92	0	49-85	0	41-86	5	50-88	0
Santiago	54-85	0	45-72	12	37-57	76	58-71	12
Temuco	50-73	40	44-63	73	40-52	180	44-61	83
Puerto Montt	50-65	59	44-60	107	39-50	264	42-55	122
Punta Arenas	44-59	22	38-50	28	32-39	31	39-50	27

seasons. The Central Coast beaches' ambience, for example, changes completely. Packed with raucous blanket to blanket crowds in the summer, they are vacant and serene in the off-season. Most tourist businesses scale down their staffs and some close, but there are always a few companies working the off-season market. Examples of this scaling back would be fewer departures per day on public transport and fewer camping areas open in each national park.

The **transitional months** of November and March are the best months to plan your trip. In these months you get an optimal combination of dry weather, small crowds, functioning services, and low season prices. If neither of these months work into your schedule, consider the first half of December as the next best alternative.

In **winter**, June to August, a damp, bone-chilling gray consumes Santiago. The Lake District is awash in rain. The Magallanes area and Torres del Paine are cold, but still alluring with few crowds and frequent blue skies. The northern desert temperatures drop to freezing at night, but warm up during the daytime.

Given the weather, alpine sports provide the greatest incentive for traveling to Chile in the winter months. There are four international-caliber resorts in the Santiago area and several smaller ones planted on volcanoes further south. It is important to note that snow levels differ radically from one year to the next. One winter will provide a huge base, intermittently topped off with luscious powder, allowing the resorts to operate through September. Another year will be nearly dry with so much uncovered earth on the slopes that only a few of the least rock-infested runs will be open. If skiing or snow boarding is your primary objective, consider checking conditions in June and July, then firming up your trip for August if there is a decent base.

WHAT TO PACK

Most items you could think of to buy for travel in the United States, such as personal care products, will be available in Chile. You will probably pay more for the items in Chile due to the 18% value-added sales tax. Niche products, like specialized camera or sports equipment, will be more expensive over and above the sales tax differential.

Medicine is widely available in Chile's pharmacies. For special medicine, you should try to bring sufficient quantities as well as a prescription with the drug's generic name. You will find that prescriptions are not required for many drugs that require them at home. We've entered pharmacies pointing toward the ailing body area and have been given prescription medication on the spot. The boxes normally do not indicate dosage or use so you should be sure to clarify this before leaving the pharmacy. Some of the smallest towns may not have pharmacies, but most will.

Health standards in Chilean are high. No vaccinations are mandatory, but the Centers for Disease Control suggest that you make sure you are up-to-date on typhoid, tetanus, polio, and hepatitis. Most of the tap water is potable so you will likely dodge stomach ailments, but consider packing bacterial fighting drugs just in case. You should also make sure your health insurance covers you in foreign countries.

TRAVELING WITH CHILDREN

Chileans love children and have lots of them. Because of Chile's strong Catholic ties, large families are a badge of honor. Much of the tourist infrastructure is set up to accommodate their large broods.

In the regions where Chileans generally vacation, the Central Coast and Lake District, there is no lack of hotels, cabins, and apart-hotels with facilities set up for children. Most have kitchens and bunk beds so that the whole family can stay together and save some money on meals. They also usually have playground areas. Many of the lodges and beach resorts count baby-sitting and children's programs as standard services. Family activities for youngsters and teens in these areas include hiking, horseback riding, fishing, swimming, and even rafting. Remember that many of the beaches have strong undertows so it is best to keep all bathers close to shore. The ski resorts are also excellent places for children. Almost all of them have children's lessons and programs so that Mom and Dad can spend as much or as little time skiing with the tykes as they like.

Chilean Patagonia and the Austral Region are generally not spots for family vacationers. The unpredictable weather, which can include strong winds and rain, tends to dampen younger hikers' enthusiasm.

The beaches of the north fill with Chilean and Argentine families in the summer and on holidays. Again, there are excellent, child-friendly lodging options. The national parks of the Altiplano might not be as attractive to children, as the travel distances are long and the altitude high.

You can probably find more baby-paraphernalia in Chile than you can at home, as the country produces its own as well as imports goods from both the United States and Europe. Diapers, formula, baby toiletries, and clothing can easily be found in major cities and resort areas.

When packing clothing, remember that Chile is chilly. The Humboldt Current flowing from Antarctica along the Pacific coast lowers the air temperature to levels that surprise unwitting visitors who imagined the South American tropics. While summer days in the Central Chile are consistently warm and California-like, temperatures cool down in the evenings, especially if you are in one of the national parks at higher elevations. The north of the country is particularly famous for wide swings in temperatures that make for toasty days and frosty nights. Shorts and short sleeves clothes are good for Central Chile's summer days. You should pack rain gear and warm clothing for trips south. If you are making the trip during the austral winter, pack ample winter wear.

Packing camping gear is worthwhile if you are planning to spend a lot of time in Chile's spectacular national parks. The best way to enjoy these parks is by camping under the stars of the Southern Hemisphere. If you only want to spend a few nights in the parks, you can make do without the gear by staying in one of the many parks that offer lodging. It is imperative that you make reservations in advance though, especially during the high season.

VISA, IMMIGRATION, & CUSTOMS

Most foreigners, including North Americans, are required to have a valid passport to enter Chile. Citizens of neighboring Andean countries may enter with a national ID card, but should contact the local Chilean consulate to confirm this.

North Americans are not required to process a tourist visa before going. Instead, you will fill out a tourist card, good for 90 days, on the plane. Blank cards are also available in the airport's immigration area. It is important to keep your copy of the tourist card safe because it will be requested upon leaving the country. You will also want to keep this tourist card handy because most hotels will discount the 18% sales tax known as **IVA** if you present it. Some nationalities outside of North America are required to process visas in advance through a Chilean consulate.

US citizens must pay a $25 visa fee in cash as they pass through customs. The authorities will staple a receipt into your passport, good for the life of your passport. This is a reciprocal fee charged only to citizens of countries that charge Chileans a fee to process visas for their countries.

For tourist visa extensions or for work visas, you have to go to **Departamento de Extranjería**, *Moneda 1342, Centro, open 9am-1pm* in Santiago. To contact the **Chilean Embassy in the US**: *1732 Massachusetts Ave., NW, Washington, DC 20036, Tel. 202/785-1746*. To contact the **Chilean Embassy in Canada**: *50 O'Conner Street, Suite 1413, Ottawa, Ontario K1P-6L2, Tel. 613/235-4402.*

Chilean Consulates in the US
• **Boston**: *79 Milk Street, Suite 600, Boston, MA. 02109. Tel. 617/426-1678*
• **Charleston**: *948 Equestrian Drive, Mount Pleasant, SC 29464. Tel. 803/ 792-2489*

- **Chicago**: *875 N. Michigan, Suite 3352, Chicago, IL 60611. Tel. 312/654-8780*
- **Honolulu**: *1860 Ala Moana Blvd., Apt. 1900, Honolulu, HI 96815. Tel. 808/9492850*
- **Los Angeles**: *1900 Ave. Of the Stars, Suite 2450. Los Angeles, CA. Tel. 310/785-0047*
- **Miami**: *800 Brickel Ave., Suite 1230, Miami, FL 33131. Tel. 305/379-8623*
- **New Orleans**: *P.O. Box 60046, New Orleans, LA 70160. Tel. 504/528-3364*
- **New York**: *866 United Nations Plaza, 3rd floor, New York, NY 10017. Tel. 212/888-5288*
- **Olympia**: *2946 Landgridge Loop NW, Olympia, WA 98503. Tel. 360/754-8747*
- **Philadelphia**: *Public Ledger Building Suite 1030, Philadelphia, PA 19106. Tel. 215/829-0594*
- **Salt Lake City**: *130 S. 500 East, Salt Lake City, UT 84102. Tel. 801/531-1292*
- **San Francisco**: *870 Market St., Suite 1058, San Francisco, CA 94102. Tel. 415/982-7662*
- **San Juan**: *1509 Lopez Landron Santurce, San Juan, PR 00911. Tel. 787/725-6365*
- **San Mateo**: *P.O. Box 9054 Menlo College, San Mateo, CA 94025. 415/688-3847*
- **Washington D.C.**, *1732 Massachusetts Ave. NW, Washington, DC 20036. Tel. 202/785-3159*

Chilean Consulates in Canada

- **Edmonton**: *4612 99th Street, Edmonton, Alberta T6E 5H5. Tel. 403/439-9839*
- **Montreal**: *1010 Sherbrooke Street West, Suite 710, Montreal PQ, H3A 2R7. Tel. 514/499-0405*
- **Ottawa**: *50 O'Conner Street, Suite 1413, Ottawa, Ontario K1P-6L2. Tel. 613/235-1176*
- **Toronto**: *170 Bloor Street West, Suite 800, Toronto, Ontario M5S 1T9. Tel. 416/924-0112*
- **Vancouver**: *1185 West Georgia, Suite 1250, Vancouver, BC V6E 4E6. Tel. 604/683-9181*
- **Winnipeg**: *810 Sherbrooke Street, Suite 410, Winnipeg, Manitoba R3A 1R8. 204/889-4410*

CUSTOMS ENTRANCE & REQUIREMENTS

All items which are considered traveler's personal belongings are allowed in duty free. In addition, you can bring in 20 packs of cigarettes, 500 grams of pipe tobacco, 50 cigars, 2.5 liters of alcoholic beverages, and up to $500 purchased in Duty Free. You can bring in a laptop computer, but they will tax you for a desktop model. Anything that appears to be commercial goods or falls outside of the category of traveler's personal belongings should be declared and is subject to duty.

BOOKING YOUR TRIP

Airline tickets to Chile do not come cheaply. Round-trip coach class tickets now range from $900-$1,400 depending on your starting point and the date you fly. Finding the cheapest time of the year on a seasonal basis isn't that cut and dry, because when its low season one direction, it is frequently high season in the other.

Ticket consolidators don't seem to be able to work the wonders that they do with tickets to Europe and Asia. You may get a hundred or maybe two hundred dollars knocked off the cost of your ticket, but you incur the non-monetary cost of almost complete inflexibility.

Airlines that fly non-stop to Santiago from the United States are **Continental** from Newark; **Lan Chile**, **United**, and **American** from Miami (American also flies to Chile from Dallas). Continental's new service from Newark is particularly attractive for East Coast residents because you can avoid the stopover in the dungeon-like environs of the Miami airport. Considering all of the mileage you earn by flying to South America, putting it in Continental's exceptional frequent flyer program seems like the way to go. For those travelling from the West Coast, the American flight from Dallas is the logical option.

The additional cost of adding a second South American destination, such as Buenos Aires, is usually minimal and worth investigating.

Santiago's modern and efficient **Arturo Merino Benítez Airport** is the entry point for most visitors. You will normally be processed through customs and immigration and retrieve your luggage faster than at other international airports. You can change money at the kiosk near the luggage carrousel or at the windows to the left of the customs exit. The most convenient way of obtaining Chilean currency with a good exchange rate is by utilizing the ATM machines located throughout the country. In the airport, the closest of the three ATM machines is in front of you as you leave customs. This is a free-standing ATM unit so they change its location occasionally, but you will find it somewhere near the customs exit.

FLYING HORIZONTAL

Most flights from the United States leave for Chile late in the evening. The eight to ten hour flight presents the challenge of sleeping in the sky, which if accomplished, eliminates jet lag on your first day. Often you can nab as many as three seats across in unoccupied economy class space to stretch yourself out horizontally. Those with elevated frequent flyer status can block one or both adjacent seats by calling the airline the day of the flight or by arranging it at the check-in counter. Those without this ability simply spread out in extra seats before boarding is finished. Eyes dart about the cabin as the squatters calculate whether the pivotal territory can be held until take-off or if someone will disrupt their plans of pleasant dreams with the dreaded phrase, "You're in my seat."

Eye shades, ear plugs, and half a sleeping pill also work wonders.

ECO-TRAVEL & ADVENTURE TRAVEL OPTIONS

Because Chile offers such a diverse array of outdoor activities, adventure travel and eco-travel have become the modus operandi rather than something you have to seek out. Every destination in Chile, even Santiago, is surrounded by spectacular arenas for outdoor play that will make thrill seekers giddy and nature lovers swoon.

Although **Pucón, Puerto Varas**, and **Torres del Paine** are probably the most well-known destinations for adventure travel, we describe lesser known locales in every destination chapter of this book. If you want the ultimate outdoor adventure in the most pristine wilderness, however, you should head to the **Austral Region**. Driving down the Austral Highway qualifies as adventure travel in itself. There are almost no people, enormous glaciers practically hang down to the road, and brilliant emerald streams appear all along the way, any of which you can call paradise. Imagine what it's like when you get a bit off of the highway.

Of course, the eco- and adventure name tags can become trite at times. We saw a place near Temuco advertising "eco-camping" ... as opposed to what?

For the most part you can just line things up when you get into the region. Both Puerto Varas and Pucón, for example, have travel adventure outfitters that organize excursions to climb, white water raft, horseback ride, and mountain bike. You can usually just show up and sign on to go that day or the next for any of the excursions they list. The outfitters supply all of the gear, even outdoor wear like goggles and gloves for volcano climbing.

There are a few cases, usually when the activity involves higher risk, such as rafting the **Futalefú**, or climbing one of the higher peaks, such as **Ojos de Salado**, that it is better to put things in motion before you go. In our destination chapters we cover enough basics, such as related travel adventure companies and climbing permit issuers, to at least get you started.

In addition to the travel adventure companies located in Chile which we list in the destination chapters, there are several packagers in the United States that will combine sets of activities, sometimes with a specific bent, such as photography or mountain climbing, and coordinate all aspects of your trip. Although you could do the same thing for yourself by using this book, some people like to travel in groups and have the logistics taken care of for them. That is exactly what the packagers offer.

One thing is for sure: viewing the scenery from a river raft or a mountain bike is a lot more fun than seeing it from a double-decker bus.

US-BASED TRAVEL ADVENTURE PACKAGERS

• **Outer Edge Expeditions**, *Tel. 800/322-5235. Website: www.outer-edge.com*
• **Butterfield & Robinson**, *Tel. 800/678-1147. Website: www.butterfield.com*
• **Country Walkers**, *Tel. 800/638-0291. Website: www.countrywalkers.com*
• **Mountain Madness**, *Tel. 800/328-5925. Website: www.mountainmadness.com*
• **Wilderness Travel**, *Tel. 800/3682794. Website: www.wildernesstravel.com*

STUDY TOURS/LANGUAGE LEARNING PACKAGES

Chilean Spanish is one the more difficult dialects to understand. If you learn Spanish here, Latin Americans will certainly be able to identify your linguistic roots. A good periodical to consult that lists language schools for teaching opportunities as well as learning opportunities is *Transitions Abroad*. It's available on most magazine shelves in big bookstores.

Consider one of these programs:
• **Amerispan Unlimited**. *Tel. 800/879-6640. Website: www.amerispan.com*
• **Berlitz**. *Tel. 800/257-9449. Website: www.adventurequest.com*
• **Council Study Abroad**. *Tel. 888/268-6245. Website: www.ciee.org*
• **CWU Semester in Chile**. *Tel. 509/963-1558. E-mail: zukroff@cwu.edu*
• **Spanish Abroad**. *Tel. 888/722-7623. Website: www.spanishabroad.com*
• **Language Link**. *Tel. 800/552-2051. Website: www.langlink.com*
• **USAC**. *Tel. 702/784-6569. E-mail: usac@admin.unr.edu*

GETTING AROUND CHILE

A good general transportation strategy is to do long-distance travel by airplane, medium-distance by bus, in-town sightseeing on foot and in taxis, and surrounding or out of the way attractions in a rental car. Sometimes you can hit the surrounding attractions in organized tours, but you lose the flexibility to get off the beaten path. Remote parks are usually easier to access by auto rather than public transport.

BY AIR

Due to the great distances to be covered, air travel is the most effective method of reaching the far-flung destinations in Chile. The air service of the national carriers **Lan Chile**, **Ladeco**, and **Avant** is comfortable, efficient, and reasonably priced. You should be able to book round-trip tickets from Santiago to most destinations for $150-$300. One-way tickets are merely one-half of the round-trip, so there is no penalty for continuing overland. Major airports are located in key cities throughout the country. Small plane travel is also possible to access more remote locations.

Lan Chile offers a Visit Chile Pass that costs $350 if you fly to Chile on another airline or $250 if you fly there with Lan Chile. The basic pass consists of three flights anywhere in the country. You have the option of adding up to three additional flights for $80 each at the time of purchase. You must buy the pass outside of the United States and the flights must be used within a 30 day time limit.

Chilean Airlines with Toll Free Numbers in the US
• **Lan Chile** and **Ladeco**, *Toll Free in the US, Tel. 800/735-5526*

BY BOAT & FERRY

The most popular boat trip in Chile is Navimag's four day voyage between Puerto Montt and Puerto Natales. We give details on this trip in the in the Puerto Natales section of the Magallanes-Chilean Patagonia chapter. The Skorpios cruise line offers luxurious trips to Laguna San Rafael that we cover in Austral Region chapter.

With so much coastline and so many lakes and rivers, ferry travel is common. Larger ferries that you might travel on include those that go to Chiloé and to Tierra del Fuego. On a smaller scale, quaint hand-pulled ferries appear wherever they are needed to cross a river.

BY BUS

Bus service is an economical way of seeing the country. Bus lines reach all major towns with direct routes while smaller towns can be reached by local service. The long distance buses are quite comfortable. They usually show American films on video and on the longer runs, even organize activities like Bingo.

BY CAR

Renting a car offers a great deal more maneuverability and time-saving than local buses, especially to get to remote attractions. Rates run about $50-$100 per day. Four wheel drive vehicles are at the higher end of the scale, usually starting at about $75 for the two-door vehicles.

Technically you need an international drivers license to drive in Chile. You can obtain these for $10 from American Automobile Association offices, even if you are not a member. However, we do not know of anyone who has been fined for using a foreign driver's license. The auto rental agencies accept them and do not advise that an international license is required. You can probably get away with your current license, but to be 100% sure you should get the international license.

The Chilean police (*carabineros*) are earnest and honest. Infraction protocol includes confiscating your license, (another good reason to get an international license). The license is returned when you pay the ticket, either on the court date indicated on the ticket in that locality, or in Santiago several weeks after paying the fine there. You can still drive with the receipt that is given to you, but the hassles of regaining your license are obvious. Unlike some other Latin American countries, the Chilean police do not solicit or accept bribes. Attempting to bribe a police officer is a serious offense.

BY FOOT

Crosswalks can be dangerous terrain. You should wait for vehicles to stop before stepping in front of them. There are many aggressive drivers and an equal number of inept ones so you should be wary, especially in Santiago.

BY THUMB

Hitchhiking is still common in Chile, especially among young people and in the rural areas.

BY TRAIN

Because Chile's passenger and freight movement developed by boats that could easily travel the length of the country, train service is inefficient or non-existent. You can take the train from Santiago as far south as Temuco, but the bus lines offer more comfortable and frequent service. Trains depart from the *Estación Central* that can be reached by the metro of the same name. No train service is offered from Santiago to the north of the country, although there is regional service between Arica and La Paz.

ACCOMMODATIONS

The most important note when it comes to lodging is that nearly every hotel charging $50 or more for a double will discount the 18% sales tax (referred to by the acronym IVA, pronounced *ee-vah*). This adds up quickly so you should be sure to ask for the rate without IVA when checking-in, and verify that the tax was not billed at check-out time. To obtain this discount, you must show the tourist card that you filled out for immigration. Cheaper and smaller hotels often aren't set up to do the paper work.

Many room prices include a continental breakfast, which usually consists of bread, jam, cheese, coffee, and juice. Some of the upscale hotels include a breakfast buffet.

We used high season rates in our listings so you should be quoted less than our indications in the off-season. Outside of the months of January and February it is always worthwhile to ask for an additional discount when inquiring about rates. Most establishments earn their bread and butter during the high season and are eager to attract clients in the off-season. We've even had the nicest hotels in some towns offer *un pequeño descuento* without any prompting.

APART-HOTELS

Apart-hotels offer all of the services of a normal hotel but include extra living space, typically a small living room, a bedroom, and a kitchenette. The hybrid name is appropriate because the space isn't big enough to be called an apartment in most cases, but it is spacious enough to eliminate hotel room claustrophobia. Apart-hotels cost about the same as a double room of similar decor and quality. The kitchenettes allow for the advantage of eating a few meals in, or at least grabbing a simple, healthy breakfast on the run.

CABAÑAS

Cabins are another good option for extra space. The facilities are built with big Chilean families in mind, which is why the space and price tags are larger. This is good for families and groups but less attractive for two people traveling together. The management might discount the price if you explain that you want the cabin for only two people. The cabins are usually fully-equipped with cookware and all kitchen appliances. Many have wood stoves or fireplaces. You can find *cabañas* in the snow, in the woods, or at the beach.

CAMPING

Since much of what there is to admire in Chile is contained within the national parks, the parks themselves are great place to stay. The parks charge a fee, normally about $4 per person to enter and sometimes an additional fee to camp. Although high season draws crowds to the parks, especially easy access car camping areas, you can easily transplant yourself to a beautiful piece of serenity with a bit of hiking. You will practically have the park to yourself if you go even a few weeks out of the high season of mid-December to the end of February. Some parks include sites with running water, bathrooms, and showers. All have designated camping areas to minimize environmental damage. White and unleaded gas for camp stoves is widely available in towns.

HOSTALES

The direct translation of *hostal* would be hostel, but these aren't necessarily dormitory sleeping arrangements. Usually, they are the simplest of inns, frequently a private house with the living room and dining room serving as common areas. Other *hostales* are as comfy as bed-and-breakfast inns in North America.

HOTELS

Santiago is host to most of the major international five star hotel chains such as the Hyatt, Sheraton, Radisson, and Intercontinental. You will likely find only one or two such hotels in each of the other major cities. Best Western has an excellent presence that it accomplished by forming an association of outstanding family run hotels.

The most unique Chilean chain is the Explora, which features five star service in the remote and extraordinary locations of Torres del Paine National Park and San Pedro de Atacama. Other national chains include the Panamericana chain, which has four and five star hotels all over the country.

Individual Chilean hotels run the gamut from no star to five star. Sernatur, the national tourism agency, controls the star rating system. It is slightly less demanding than other international standards and is not widely utilized outside of Santiago.

HOSTERÍAS

Hosterías are inns that can range from simple to sumptuous. Usually they are in more remote locations, look like woodsy lodges, and have good country-style restaurants.

MOTELS

Motels in Chile are normally shelters for an illicit rendezvous. They are located in city outskirts and surrounded by high solid fences to protect the identities of those frolicking within.

RESIDENCIALES

Residenciales are private homes that rent out rooms, frequently charging on a per person basis.

YOUTH HOSTELS

The youth hostel system exists in Chile, but is not widely utilized. Solo and budget travelers tend toward *residenciales* and *hostales*.

7. BASIC INFORMATION

BUSINESS HOURS

Santiago: In the area around Santiago most businesses stay open throughout the day. Stores are open Monday through Friday, 10am-7pm, and Saturday from 10am-2pm. Offices are open from 9am-6pm, Monday through Friday, but some may close for lunch from 1pm-2pm. Malls are open Monday through Saturday from 10am-9pm and on Sunday from 11am-8pm. Restaurants are open from 12:30pm-4pm and 8pm-1am. Cafes are open from 8am-11pm. Many restaurants are closed on Sunday evening. There are 24-hour gas station/convenience stores sprouting up around town for late night necessities.

The Rest of Chile: As you travel both north and south from the Central Valley you will notice a change, as entire towns close up for the midday meal.

Banks: Banks throughout the country are open from 9am-2pm, Monday through Friday. They are not open on the weekends.

COMPUTERS & INTERNET SERVICE

The local number for American Online users in Santiago is *Tel. 697-3081*.You must change your network to the "aolglobalnet" at sign-on. Compuserve users can dial *Tel. 252-5899* on the "Chilepack." Be aware there is a surcharge of $12/hour for both services and make sure your computer is set up to handle 220 volts.

The major phone companies offer Internet service for a fee, but you need a phone account for that. Cybercafes are starting to pop up all over Chile for cruising the net or checking your hotmail. They are listed in the *Practical Information* section for each destination.

COST OF LIVING

The US Government lists Chile's costs of living at 112% compared to Washington, DC. It is definitely not a bargain travel country like Bolivia or Peru. Things are going to cost roughly what they do at home.

EARTHQUAKES

It is not unusual to experience the earth tremble during your time in Chile. You should be safe, as the modern buildings are constructed to withstand earthquakes. Remember not to run out of buildings or use elevators, but rather stand under a doorway until the quake is over. Lights will go out automatically to prevent fires if the quake is over a five on the Richter scale.

ELECTRICITY

Voltage in Chile is 220. Be sure to check your computers and hairdryers before you plug them in. If you need to buy a transformer, they are sold in the **Casamusa** chain in Santiago as well as in **Easy**. You will also need an adapter to fit the Chilean outlets.

EMERGENCY PHONE NUMBERS

The following numbers function throughout the country:
- **Conaf** (forest fires) – *130*
- **Ambulance** – *131*
- **Fire Department** – *132*
- **Police** (*Carabineros*) – *133*
- **Coast Guard** – *137*
- **Air Rescue Service** – *138*
- **Roadway Repairs** – *139*

ENGLISH LANGUAGE READING

The *News Review* is an English language paper that comes out in Santiago on Wednesday and Saturday. You can buy it on newsstands or pick in up in major hotels. You can also find international weeklies such as *Time* and *Newsweek* on newsstands. Other English magazines are available but are quite expensive. See our *Recommended Reading* sidebar in the *Land and People* chapter for books to take along for the trip.

ETIQUETTE

In general Chileans are quieter and more reserved than other South Americans you might have met. They tend to dress more formally in cities and restaurants. If you don't want to stand out you should wear slacks and nice shoes. Travelers are granted leeway, however, so if you are comfortable with some of the looks you will receive, go ahead and wear shorts on that hot day in Santiago.

HEALTH CONCERNS

Chile is basically a safe country. The Centers for Disease Control & Prevention (CDC) in Atlanta has up-to-date information about Chile's disease concerns and risks. The CDC will only pass on regional information through their fax-back service *(Tel. 404/332-4564)*. You'll need to give them Chile's country code, which is 56. You can also get the information on-line at *www.cdc.gov*.

Visitors to the high plains may experience some altitude sickness, also called acute mountain sickness or *puna*. Its symptoms include shortness of breath, difficulty sleeping, headache, nausea, and vomiting. These symptoms can last from two to five days. The best things to do if you feel this way are to drink lots of water, avoid alcohol, and take ibuprofen or aspirin for pain relief. To avoid the situation all together, try to climb no more than 2000 meters for the first two days and then add another day for each additional 500 meters.

High altitude pulmonary edema, swelling of the lungs, is a more advanced and dangerous state of altitude sickness. Its symptoms include repeated vomiting, staggering and confusion. It can be fatal within a few hours. If you suspect somebody on your group of pulmonary edema, you must move immediately to lower elevations.

Chile has recently had a few cases of the fatal Hanta virus. It should really be of no threat to tourists, though it is good to be aware of how it is transmitted. The virus, carried by long-tailed rats, is spread by breathing or ingesting dust contaminated with rat urine, feces, or saliva. Basically that means you need to stay away from rat poop. If you camp you should use a tent. You should also avoid eating wild fruits or lounging around anyplace that rats might live. Another good idea is to air out rooms in rural lodging. The symptoms of the illness are flu-like, with headaches, aching muscles, high fever, and increasing difficulty breathing. If you are feeling any of these, go immediately to the nearest medical services.

HOLIDAYS

Chilean businesses are closed for the following holidays:
• January 1, New Years
• Easter, two days to a week
• May 1, Labor Day
• May 21, Navy Day
• May 30, Corpus Christi
• August 15, Asuncion of the Virgin
• September 11, Military Takeover 1973
• September 18,19, Independence
• October 12, Indigenous Peoples Day

- November 1, All Saints Day
- December 8, Immaculate Conception
- December 25, Christmas

If any of these holidays falls on a Thursday, you can bet that many businesses will be closed on Friday. Chileans are accustomed to extending time off to the days that fall between holidays and weekends. They call it a *sanwich*.

MONEY & BANKING

The **current rate of exchange is US $1 = 455 Chilean pesos = Canadian $1.65**. All prices in this book are listed in US dollars. The peso is devaluating at about 10% a year against the dollar, with inflation running at roughly 7%. Coins come in 100, 50, 10, and 5 peso denominations. Distinctly colored notes are issued for 500; 1,000; 2,000; 5,000; 10,000; and 20,000 pesos.

ATMs, on both the Cirrus and Plus systems, are the most convenient way to withdraw money from your home bank account. There is usually a fee for withdrawal, but that is outweighed by the favorable exchange rate and convenience. ATMs are available through out the country with the exception of the smallest towns. Make sure that your card is authorized for international withdrawals and that you know your pin. You can get money off your credit card out of the same machines.

Some Chilean ATMs have an extra step in the withdrawal process at the beginning. Before choosing the language in which you want to do the transaction, you need to choose the option that says, "*estranjero/*foreigner."

Money exchange offices, *casas de cambio,* and banks will take your travelers checks for pesos. In remote places it can be hard to find anybody to cash travelers checks. As another option, American Express offices will cash a personal check if you have one of their cards.

Credit cards are widely used in Chile. When you sign, people may ask for your tax ID number, *número de carnet.* Just give them your passport number.

It's best to travel with a combination of cash, a few traveler's checks, credit cards, and your ATM card.

NEWSPAPERS & OTHER NEWS SOURCES

El Mercurio, although definitely slanted to the right, consistently has the strongest reporting. The Sunday paper is especially enjoyable with its excellent Travel pages. *La Epoca,* founded during the NO campaign against Pinochet is the liberal alternative, but its reporting is just not as complete. Many of its readers have switched to *El Mercurio* now that Pinochet is no longer running the country, so it is constantly in danger of folding due to lack of advertising.

La Segunda is the tabloid paper. You can identify it in the summer because it always has bikini clad women and Marcelo Rio gracing its cover. *La Nación* is the official government paper and *La Estrategia* is the mouth of the business community. The best condensed news source on the web is Chip News at *http://www.chip.cl.*

POST OFFICE

The Chilean mail service, *Correos de Chile,* is dependable. Sending postcards abroad costs around 75¢ and letters just a bit more. As far as packages go, they can easily be sent from the post office, but we suggest using an international courier such as DHL for better security and tracing ability.

You can have general delivery letters held at the post office. They should be marked *lista de correos* and have a hold date. If you are expecting a letter and it's not there, look under your first and last names because you never know how the clerk has filed it.

SAFETY

Chile is considered one of the safest countries in Latin America. Even in Santiago, a city of five million, personal safety is just a minor issue. You don't want to walk alone through the *centro* late at night, but in Providencia and Las Condes you should be okay. Pickpockets are known to work the buses and subways so keep a close eye on your bags.

Even in the safest of cities there is always the chance of a bad egg, so you might want to buy a neck or waist pouch for traveling with your passport and valuables. Once you arrive to a town you should put everything into a safe deposit box, *caja de seguridad,* at your hotel if there is one available. At a minimum you should have copies of your passport, travelers checks, and plane tickets. Just stay sharp and you'll stay safe.

STAYING OUT OF TROUBLE

Many Americans, used to traveling in Mexico and Central America, come to Chile with a cavalier attitude towards the *Carabineros,* police. An attempt to bribe a Chilean officer will land you directly in jail. The Chilean police take their jobs very seriously, but the good news is that they are on the streets to help people, not solicit bribes. If you keep a low profile and don't break the law you should have no problems. Needless to say, but we will anyway, using drugs in a foreign country is stupid.

WOMEN TRAVELERS

We have met many women vacationing alone through Chile. Most of them, including the female half of your writers, consider it a good country for solo traveling. Be smart and don't take chances that you wouldn't take at home.

Chile is a macho country, but sometimes that can work in your favor. Families can't understand why a nice woman would be traveling by herself and will invite you to join them. On the other hand, people will view you as an oddity. Chilean women rarely travel alone, so they will probably ask you many questions about what your parents think about your traveling alone.

Less of a safety issue but more a pain, are the piropos. Even after years of living in Latin America, I find the propositions you get from men on the street irritating. The best thing to do is ignore it, but if somebody really bothers you, a direct look in the face coupled with a loud "perdon?" will usually shame the culprit into silence. You can forget about trying to embarrassment anybody at construction sites however – just walk on the other side of the street.

TAXES

Chileans are subject to a whopping 18% value added tax, IVA. All hotels are supposed to discount the IVA if you show them your tourist card and pay in dollars or with a credit card. Be sure to mention it when you check in, and certainly before you pay, as they sometimes forget. Lower-end hotels, however, are rarely set up to deal with the discount.

TELEPHONES

The competition between phone carriers in Chile is brutal and we are the beneficiaries. Every long distance company has a code. To make a collect call, *cobro revertido*, you dial the company's code and then 182 to get an operator. Entel (123), CTC (188), BellSouth (181), and Chilesat (171) are the most popular carriers. Calls cost about $1/minute to the US.

Entel and CTC phone booths throughout Chile accept coins, cards, or both. A local call costs 100 pesos. If you are using a card, which can be bought at kiosks, the CTC cards are easier because you use a magnetic strip rather than dialing a number and entering a code as you do with Entel.

You can rent cellular phones at the BellSouth offices in Santiago.

TELEVISION

There are 11 broadcast stations that always seem to be showing soap operas or soccer, but cable continues to gain popularity. We highly recommend the nightly soap operas, *telenovelas*, as a way to improve your Spanish and learn Chilean slang. Even at the ends of the earth you can get CNN, ESPN, HBO, and, scarily, *Baywatch*.

TIME

Chile is four hours behind GMT. During the austral winter Chile is two hours ahead of the East Coast of the US, which is on daylights savings time. If it is 6:00pm in New York it is 8:00pm in Chile. During the austral summer, however, when Chile goes on daylight savings time and the US goes off it, Chilean time is the same as Eastern Standard Time.

TIPPING

Non-mathematical people can relax because standard tipping in restaurants is 10%. You generally don't tip cabs unless the change is very small or the cabby has helped you with your bags.

TOURISM OFFICES

Sernatur is the name of the official Chilean tourism department. They have offices throughout the country that offer excellent maps and up to the minute information on things like ferry schedules, museum exhibits, bus routes and the like. Their staff is quite helpful and knowledgeable. Many cities have their own tourist office as well.

WATER

Most Chileans drink their water straight out of the tap, as it is potable. Many travelers, however, don't like the flavor. It's also not worth taking the chance of foreign microbes upsetting your system and losing days out of your trip. Just buy bottled water either with, *con*, or without, *sin*, carbonation, *gas*.

WEIGHTS & MEASURES

Chile uses the metric system. A meter is 1.1 yards, a kilogram is 2.2 pounds, a liter is .26 gallons, and a kilometer is .62 miles. They also use the Celsius as opposed to the Fahrenheit temperature system. An easy way to convert C degrees to approximate F degrees is 2C+30.

8. SPORTS & RECREATION

Chile is an outdoor enthusiast's Shangri-La. The variety of land-scapes, as well as the short distance from mountain to sea, means that you can enjoy a wide range of sports during a trip here. In the same weekend you can hike to hanging glaciers one day and rip along the coast on a windsurf board the next. Or, you can enjoy multiple sports in a single region. One time we rafted down a clear, swirling river; rode horses through fields of corn with a perfect volcano as the backdrop; and played tennis next to a cool lake all on the same day. The single greatest gift that Chile offers visitors is her nature.

Below you'll find an overview of the country's sporting alternatives as well as the best regions of the country to enjoy the different options. The more specific information about where and how is included in the regional chapters.

BEACH ACTIVITIES

Although tanning without sunscreen seems to be the most popular activity, there is lots of other action happening at the beach. Paddleball, played with a tennis ball *a la Chino Rios*, is hugely popular, as is beach soccer. Kite flying and jogging round out the mix.

Best Regions: Central, North.

BOARDSAILING

With so many miles of coastline it is no wonder that Chileans have taken to boardsailing. Devotees tend to congregate in the warmer bays of the north, where Arctic waters have had a chance to be warmed a bit through that hole in the ozone layer.

Best Regions: Central, North.

CROSSCOUNTRY/BACKCOUNTRY SKIING & SNOWSHOEING

These sports are markedly less developed in Chile than in the US. Access is limited, so most people enter the endless miles of backcountry through the ski resorts. Once you're out there, however, it's just you and the silence of winter.

Best Regions: Santiago, Lake District.

DOWNHILL SKIING & SNOWBOARDING

There are numerous ski resorts in Chile. Some, like the French-owned Valle de Nevado, are as glitzy and developed as their European counterparts. Others are much more rustic, reminding skiers of another era. All of them, however, provide enchanting scenery and what can be excellent snow. The season usually runs from June-September, depending on the white stuff, of course. You may even run into the US ski team, which practices here during the Austral winter.

Best Regions: Santiago, Lake District.

FISHING

Though anglers are famous for stretching the truth, it is no tall tale to say that fishing in Chile is some of the best in the world. If fly-fishing alone in a remote, bountiful stream is your idea of heaven, you're at the gates. Trout and salmon are the usual catch. Just carry your rod with you at all times because whenever you pass a river, chances are there's good fishing.

Best Regions: Austral, Lake District.

HIKING & BACKPACKING

Take the longest country in the world, throw in some mountain chains along both sides, and you'll have a hikers paradise. Many travelers come to Chile expressly for the trekking. With scenery that includes desert high plains, forests, lakes, wild meadows, glaciers and icebergs, hikers could spend years tromping all the trails. Conaf, the Chilean forestry service, manages a treasure chest of parks that cover 18% of the national territory.

Best Regions: The Entire Country.

GOLFING

Golf is almost exclusively a country club sport in Chile. There are a few public courses but access comes at private course prices.

Best Region: Central, Lake District.

HORSEBACK RIDING

The same network of trails that is available for hiking throughout the country is also open to horseback riding. Multi-day treks take you to isolated valleys, hidden lakes, and breathtaking mountain passes. Those who are more prone to saddle sores can enjoy rides of just an hour or an afternoon across the Chilean countryside.

Best Regions: Lake District, Austral.

MOUNTAIN BIKING

While many Chileans' idea of mountain biking is riding a bicycle on a paved road in the mountains, there are plenty of gnarly off-road adventures to be pedaled. From surreal desert landscapes in the North to technical, rocky, paths in the foothills of the Central Valley to pine-covered trails further south, Chile has it all.

Best Regions: North, Central, Lake District.

Touring on mountain bike is also very popular. Kilometers of dirt roads, most famously the Austral Highway, connect small towns while skimming the ocean, passing through majestic mountains or skirting azure lakes. The wind can be a bear, but it's great when it's at your back. Riding on the highways and more traveled dirt roads is not recommended, as there is generally very little shoulder.

Best Regions: Lake District, Austral.

MOUNTAINEERING, ROCK CLIMBING, & ICE CLIMBING

Even the most experienced mountaineers can find a challenge in Chile. Geological forces have worked overtime to make Chile a land of high-reaching mountains and volcanoes, steep cliffs, and expansive ice fields. The second tallest mountain in the Americas, *Ojos de Salado* at 6893 meters, is located in Chile as are several other 5000-plus meter peaks. In the south, the granite spires of Torres del Paine attract climbers from around the world.

Best Regions: North, Central, and Chilean Patagonia.

RAFTING & RIVER KAYAKING

If Chile is a long, skinny leg, she has a terrible case of varicose veins from the knee down. Aqua and kelly rivers pulse across the country in mind-boggling abundance. Some of the rivers, the Futulefú for example, are famous in paddling circles around the globe for their fast, technical descents as well as their splendor. The Biobío, once a mighty river, is slowly being humbled by hydroelectric projects.

The casual rafter can find plenty of adventure on rivers like the scenic Trancura in Pucón, or even the Maipo outside of Santiago.

Best Regions: Lake District, Austral.

SCUBA DIVING

Due to the temperature of Chile's waters (Chile is chilly), divers are forced into full-length wetsuits and hoods. Once properly attired, however, you can enjoy a world of strange delights under the sea, though not enough to merit a trip to Chile solely for diving. The best of Chilean scuba lies off the continent in the tropical climes of Easter Island.

Best Regions: Off the Continent, Central.

SEA KAYAKING

As you head south, passing Puerto Montt, the Andes dive into the ocean. Hundreds of kilometers of fjords separate the mountaintops that just barely poke out of the sea. Sea kayakers delight in the silent, sheltered inlets and bays of the region. The island of Chiloé is another paddlers paradise with its distinct ocean-dependent culture and outstanding food.

Best Regions: Chiloé, Austral.

SURFING

Cold water, strong tides, and rip currents channel surfers in Chile to the same tried and true spots. The warmer waters of the north attract most people, but the "Surf Capital of Chile," Pichilemu, on the Central Coast, is another must for shredders. It's a fun spot even if you don't hang ten.

Best Regions: North, Central.

TENNIS

Marcelo Rios' assent to number one on the men's professional tour has sparked a tennis boom in Chile. Even smaller towns now sport public courts. The most common surface is red clay, which is a novel experience for most Americans accustomed to hard courts.

You can also watch tennis in Chile. Latin America Davis Cup matches are famous for being rowdy. Similar to soccer games, with drum banging, flag waving, and continual cheering, it's a great experience if you happen to be in town. Matches are on center court of the National Stadium in Santiago. Call the Chilean Tennis Federation, *Tel. 2/634-2416,* for scheduling and ticket information.

Best Regions: Santiago, Central.

"EL CHINO" RIOS

*It's hard for Americans and Europeans, with a plethora of world class athletes, to understand the national obsession Chileans have with **Marcelo Rios**. Rios, the first Latin American tennis player in history to reach the number one spot, is the only Chilean to reach the pinnacle of any sport. Affectionately called El Chino, "The Chinaman," by his fans due to his Asiatic features, Rios is not Asian. He is, however, the national embodiment of dreams for Chilean ascendancy.*

At 5'8" and 140 pounds, Rios was long dubbed, like his country, too small to make the big time. Snubbing his nose at his critics, Marcelo quit school at age 16 and joined the international circuit where he became the world's top ranked junior in 1993. Four years later at age 22, with a win over Andre Agassi at the Lipton in Florida, he became the top ranked male in the world. The telecast broke all broadcast records as the eyes of the country were fixed on their pint-sized champ trying to topple the American.

No sooner had Agassi's last ball flown long than throngs of Chileans pored into the street from Punta Arenas to Arica. Waving flags and honking their horns, people celebrated in the streets for hours. A swell of euphoria broke over this normally stoic country. Regardless of what they thought about El Chino's sometimes-suspect attitude or off-the-court shenanigans, all was forgiven. Chile had reached the top.

WATERSKIING & WAKEBOARDING

It should come as no surprise that the Lake District is the center of waterskiing activity in Chile. Protected inlets with little boat traffic mean glassy water and hours of fun. Most resorts have both boat and equipment rental. Lakes Aculeo and Rapel, outside of Santiago are closer alternatives.

Best Regions: Central, Lake District.

RODEO

Chilean rodeo is unique in that there is only one event. It started out as a way to separate the cattle in the colonial days and grew from there. The season runs every weekend from September to March in the 300 rodeo arenas, *media lunas*, throughout the country. Participants vie for points, which will allow them to enter the three regional events of the South, Center, and North. The top participants then qualify for the Nationals, which is held every March in Rancagua.

UNDERSTANDING WOODEN STIRRUPS

*Chilean rodeos are a great way to witness the **huaso** culture first hand. Taller than average Chileans (it must be the boots), cowboys ramble around with cool detachment while children scramble for their attention. Beautiful horses are tended to like lovers in an atmosphere similar to that of a country fair.*

The event is really quite simple. Two cowboys work together to guide a cow around the ring. Judges award points based on how the cow is positioned. One huaso rides behind the cow practically kicking it up the rump, hence the wooden stirrups. He controls how fast they go. The other uses his horse's neck to steer the group into the wall. They get one point if he intercepts the bull at the shoulder blade; 3 points at the middle; and 4 points at the flank. It's quite a spectacle.

There are booths set up to buy food and drinks. At the end of the evening a dance with live music tends to get even the most tired cowboys out on the floor.

SOCCER

Soccer is the national sport of choice. As the billboard says, "The Chilean National Team. Eleven players, 14 million coaches." Even if you know nothing about the sport, you should attend a game purely for the spectacle. Your first choice would be to see a National Team game. Fans are decked out to support their boys with passion.

Your next best bet would be a professional game. The professional season runs from March though December. The favorite teams that play in Santiago are:

• **Colo Colo**, named after an Araucanian chief; *Cienfuegos 41, Tel. 695-2251*
• **University of Chile**, *U de C*; *Campo de Deportes 565 in Nuñoa, Tel. 239-2793*
• **Catholic University**, *Catolica*; *Andres Bello 2782 in Providencia, Tel. 231-2777*

9. FOOD & DRINK

The food in Chile varies depending on the region, but there is one constant – the fruit of the sea. If you like seafood, Chile is your land of plenty. On the other hand, you should not expect the exotic flavors and spices that you will find in other Latin American countries. It comes as a surprise to most visitors that Chilean food is rarely spicy. In fact, to the other extreme, Chilean food can be sort of bland.

That's not to say, however, that you won't eat extremely well here. In some categories, such as shellfish, there are so many delicious possibilities that it will be hard to get through them all during the course of your trip. In addition, the quality of raw materials that go into Chilean cooking is extremely high. Chile has been exporting foodstuffs from its Central Valley for years, putting its quality on par with, if not higher than, international standards. This chapter will help you make the most of each of your meal opportunities.

Chileans generally start their day right before work with Nescafe and bread. Most of them will then work until lunch at 1pm without anything else to eat. The custom is that lunch is the largest meal of the day. The typical fixed price *menú* – soup or a salad, an entrée with a vegetable, and dessert – is standard fare. In some circles people will have high tea, called *once*, around 6pm. Otherwise they won't eat again until 9pm. Dinner at home will be something light, like a sandwich, fruit, or cheeses.

Exceptions to the rule are that in some homes, where both partners work, the larger meal of the day is shared as a family at night. Business or social dinners will be as big, if not bigger, than lunch.

Alcohol consumption is generally low with the older Chilean set. A *pisco* sour and a glass of wine will hold them for the evening. Younger Chileans, however, can drink staggering amounts of *pisco* when out on the town or at a party.

> ## SUNDAY DINNERS
> *"The feast alone was a bone-crushing ordeal: seafood appetizers, spicy meat pies, cazuela...or pastel de choclo... torta de manjar blanco – wine and fruit, and a gigantic jug of pisco sours, the most lethal of Chilean drinks."*
> –**Isabel Allende,** *in her memoir* **Paula**, *describing a typical family meal at her grandfather's house.*

SHELLFISH & SEAFOOD
Mariscos y Pescado

Get ready to eat things you have never seen before. With 4,300 km of coastline, Chile hauls in creatures that don't exist in other places. As a rule, they are all pretty tasty, but there are some that shine above the others. Do not leave Chile without enjoying the following:

• *Machas*: These scrumptious cousins of the razor clam come prepared in a variety of ways, but our hands-down favorite food in Chile is *machas a la parmesana*. Served on the half shell and dusted with a coating of baked Parmesan cheese, we usually can't stop with just one order. A cold pisco sour (see "Alcoholic Drinks" below) rounds out the flavor ensemble.

• *Choritos, Cholgas*, and *Zapatos*: Mussels in Chile come in three sizes. The *choritos* are small, the *cholgas* medium-sized, and the *zapatos* (literally "shoe,") prehistoric. We prefer the *choritos*, but we generally like our shellfish smaller than a quarter. Their musky, briny flavor comes out best when they are served *al vapor*, steamed. Clams, *almejas*, are also best when prepared this way.

• *Centolla*: When you're going to splurge on a meal, check and see if the restaurant has fresh *centolla*, Chilean king crab, in season from July to November. This exquisite, sensual treat is so rich you'll dream about the experience for the next four nights.

• *Locos*: If you are an abalone fan, you'll go nuts in Chile. It's huge, tender, and inexpensive.

• *Calamari, Pulpo,* and *Ostiones*: Squid, octopus, and scallops are not to be missed. We prefer all three of them prepared, *al pilpil*, which is in oil with garlic and hot peppers. The sauce is so good that one relative of ours actually drank the leftovers. Try to control yourself and just soak it up with your bread. This is one dish in Chile that is spicy, so beware.

• *Erizo*: Sea urchin is an acquired taste, but Chileans consider it a delicacy. You should test it simply to have a new experience.

• *Congrio*: Is it a fish or an eel? It is called a conger eel, but looks like a skinny fish. A unique food to Chile, it should not be missed. We enjoy it most in a mustard and caper sauce, *mostaza y alcaparra*.

• *Cazuela de Mariscos, Paila Marina*: These are great dishes for trying everything at once. The *cazuela de mariscos* is a shellfish stew so chock full of sea critters that you eat it with a fork. The *paila marina* goes one step further and throws in fish as well. A steaming bowl of either of these will fill and warm you up.

Many visitors to Chile are already aware of the delicious salmon and trout, *trucha*. You should also try some of the following flaky white fish: *lengua*, sole; *corvina*, sea bass; *merluza*, hake; *albacora*, swordfish; or the untranslatable *reineta*.

Chileans tend to deep-fry their fish. We suggest ordering it *a la plancha*, grilled; *al ajillo*, with garlic; or one of the ways mentioned above. Watch out for food *a la mantiquilla*, swimming in butter; *con mayonesa*, drowned in mayonnaise; and *con salsa Americana*, flooded with Thousand Island dressing.

A GUIDE TO CHILEAN EATERIES

• *Fuente de Soda:* Snacks and non-alcoholic drinks
• *Bar:* Snacks and drinks, both with and without alcohol
• *Cafeteria:* Simple meals
• *Hosteria:* Larger meals with a more complete menu
• *Restaurante:* Full range of food and drinks.

In addition to the above choices, there is always the town central market, **mercado central**, which offers mouthwatering, economical choices in numerous food stalls.

SANDWICHES
Sanwiches

When all you want is a sandwich, you are in luck in Chile. Some of these sandwiches are so hearty that light eaters may even want to split them. The basic ingredients are *jamón*, ham; *churrasco*, steak; *ave*, chicken; and *queso*, cheese. If the steak and cheese sandwich is served hot, our favorite way, it is called a *Barros Luco*, after the favorite daily lunch of former president **Ramon Barros Luco**. The *Barros Jarpa*, hot ham and cheese, was facetiously named later for a famous painter. Common add-ons are *tomate*, tomato; and *palta*, avocado. The most inexpensive and ubiquitous food is a hot dog with everything, called a *completo*.

SALADS
Ensaladas

Salads are unique in Chile in that they are rarely served on a bed of lettuce. Instead the plate is divided into thirds or quarters for each of the items. With the *ensalada mixta*, you can usually choose from the following ingredients: *tomate*, tomato; *palta*, avocado; *choclo*, corn; *apio*, celery; *porrotos*, green beans; and *betarraga*, beets. An *ensalada chilena* is a pile of diced tomatoes covered with onion.

SNACKS & PASTRIES
Picadas, Pan, y Pasteles

Empanadas are the official snacks of Chile. They are turnovers stuffed with various ingredients and then either baked, *al horno*; or fried, *frito*. *Empanadas de pino*, filled with meat, onions, hard boiled egg, and one non-pitted olive, are the most common. Also look for *empanadas de queso*, cheese; *mariscos*, shellfish; and *manzana*, apples. We have bought them in upscale bakeries, from small shacks on the side of the road, and on street corners, and can heartily recommend each option.

Chilean bakeries are an excellent option for a quick, inexpensive nosh to get you to the next meal. Not only do they sell *empanadas*, but also scores of different kinds of breads and desserts. Just point at whatever strikes your fancy. Wheat bread is called *pan integral*. If your sweet tooth is demanding to be fed, *kuchen* is a tasty type of German fruit strudel.

MAIN COURSES - PLATO DE FONDO

TRADITIONAL FOOD
Comida Tradicional

Some of the best food in Chile is the traditional country fare. *Pastel de choclo* is a delicious casserole that includes crispy corn niblets, chicken, beef, and sometimes vegetables. *Porotos granados*, another casserole type dish, is a hearty combination of beans and vegetables au gratin. If you are especially hungry, or hung over, you might want to try *lomo* or *bistec a lo pobre*. Imagine a huge hunk of meat slathered in sautéed onions and topped with two fried eggs. Then take that and bury it in a mound of French fries. That's what *a lo pobre* means.

In the far south of the country, lamb, *cordero*, is added to the list of traditional rations. With a plethora of sheep in the region, they have experimented with all sorts of ways to serve it. Some of the best are

FRUIT OF THE EARTH

One of the best snacks in Chile is fresh fruit from the corner store. Fruit is abundant in the oasis of the North, the Central Valley, and the berry-growing Lakes District, but starts to thin out as you go further south. There always seems to be one high quality fruit stand in town however, so seek it out. Here's a list of Chilean-grown fruits to sample:

- *orange – naranja*
- *apple – manzana*
- *peach – durazno*
- *grape – uva*
- *grapefruit – toronja*
- *apricot – damasco*
- *kiwi – kiwi (extremely inexpensive in season)*
- *raspberry – frambuesa*
- *blackberry – mora*
- *watermelon – sandia*
- *cherimoya - chirimoya*
- *sweet cucumber – pepino dulce (tastes like cantaloupe)*
- *melon – melon*
- *quince – membrio*

prepared with rosemary sauce, *romero*; mint sauce, *menta*; grilled garlic, *al ajillo*; or stuffed with mushrooms, *relleno de champiñones*.

The island of Chiloé is the one region of the county where the traditional favorites are decidedly distinct. In our opinion, a trip to Chiloé is merited simply to try some of the dishes below.

- *Curanto* – Chiloé's version of surf and turf consists of a huge pile of shellfish, beef, chicken, and sausage cooked in a hole over hot stones. When it is cooked above ground in a pot, the same dish is known as *pulmay*.
- *Cancato* – A unique but delicious combination of fresh salmon stuffed with sausage, cheese, and tomatoes.
- *Carapacho* – One of the island's best appetizers is a baked mixture of crab and cream topped with toasted breadcrumbs.
- *Milcoas* – These hashbrown potatoes stuffed with pork are filling enough to be a meal.

BEEF & CHICKEN

Carne y Pollo

Chileans serve a lot of beef, but they tend to overcook it compared to American standards. *A la inglesa*, rare; *jugoso*, medium-rare; *medio*, medium; *tres quartos*, medium-well; and *bien cocido*, well done, are the terms for how you like your steak cooked. You might want order it a step less cooked than you do at home.

A *parrillada* is an assortment of grilled meat that virtually offers every part of the cow. Sometimes it also comes with chicken and pork.

Chicken is everywhere. Most restaurants will have *pollo con papas fritas*, chicken and fries; *pollo al horno*, baked chicken; and *pollo con arroz*, chicken and rice on the menu.

BEST RESTAURANTS IN CHILE

In all of these places you'll find excellent food in an atmosphere that perfectly complements the location:
- *Aquí Está Coco* – *Santiago*
- *Azul Profundo* – *Santiago*
- *El Chiringuito* – *Zapallar*
- *Empanadas Las Delicias* – *Concón*
- *La Colombina* – *Valparaíso*
- *Adobe* – *San Pedro de Atacama*
- *Merlin* – *Puerto Varas*
- *Ostras de Caulín* – *Ancud*
- *Don Eladio* – *Castro*
- *El Sacho* – *Castro*
- *Casa de Bomberos* – *Coyhaique*
- *El Mesón del Calvo* – *Punta Arenas*
- *Pergola* – *Punta Arenas*

DESSERTS

Postres

Even though Chile is a country that exports fresh fruit, many times dessert, especially with the fixed meals, is a disappointing canned fruit cocktail. There are, however, some outstanding ways to get a sugar fix. *Manjar*, caramelized goats milk, is delectable right out of the jar, but even better inside a crepe, *panqueque*. *Flan*, caramel custard; *arroz con leche*, rice pudding; and *suspiro limeno*, sweetened egg whites, are all worth the calories. Ice cream, *helado*, varies greatly in quality.

BREAKFAST

Desayuno

Chilean breakfasts are extremely light. Toast, *pan tostado*; marmalade, *mermelada*; butter, *mantequilla*; and tea or coffee, *te o café*, is somehow supposed to get you through until lunch. Occasionally places will serve eggs that you can order scrambled, *revueltos* or fried, *fritos*.

FAST FOOD

Comida Rapida

Chile is not unique in a world with McDonalds, Pizza Hut, Dominos, KFC, and Burger King sprouting up everywhere. The pizza generally has tough, floury crust. If you have to get a Big Mac, you should do it in Puerto Montt, which at least has the distinction of being one of the southernmost McDonalds in the world.

NON-CHILEAN FOOD

Comida No Chilena

Santiago is really the only city that offers a range of ethic foods. Mexican, Thai, Japanese, Italian, Indian, Chinese, and others can all be had ... for a price. Don't expect bargains at any of these restaurants. Economical Chinese restaurants known as *chifa* do exist in the north.

RESTAURANT LISTINGS IN THIS BOOK

In each restaurant listing we include the address and the phone number of the establishment. If the restaurant does not accept credit cards, or only accepts one type of credit card, we tell you that. If the listing says, "credit cards accepted," we mean they accept Visa, MasterCard, Diners, and American Express.

*All listings fall into a price category of inexpensive, moderate, expensive, or very expensive. It's important to note that it is not cheap to eat in Chile, especially if you wander away from the fixed meals, called **menús**, which are served at lunch. We looked at the price of a meal that includes a main course, one drink, and either an appetizer or dessert.*

- *Inexpensive: under $8*
- *Moderate: $8-$15*
- *Expensive: $16-25*
- *Very expensive: $26+*

CHILEAN DRINKS

NON-ALCOHOLIC DRINKS

Bebidas Sin Alcohol

You can buy water and soft drinks everywhere. Chile has all the international brands like Coke and 7-Up, as well as an outrageously sweet national brand called Blitz. Bottled water can be bought with, *con*; or without, *sin*; carbonation, *gas*.

Juices are available throughout the country, but they too tend to be full of sugar. Even the brands in the grocery store that claim to be "natural" have added sugar.

ALCOHOLIC DRINKS

Bebidas con Alcohol

Pisco, a type of brandy, is the national drink of Chile. While the spirit originated in Peru (don't mention that to a Chilean), there is no doubt about its position at the top of the Chilean alcohol hierarchy. It is most commonly served in the form of a *pisco sour*, with lemon juice, powdered sugar, and egg whites. *Pisco sours* are at their best when served cold with fresh seafood. Other common ways to serve *pisco* are the *piscola*, with Coke; and the *chilcano*, with ginger ale.

THE POWER OF THE PISCO SOUR

"Whenever we sip this zesty libation, we recall why it's such a coveted item. Like gin drinks, it has the curious quality of loosening people's tongues while sharpening their wits. We're told that the wife of Alain Touraine, a French social scientist with Latin American interests, likes to serve this drink at the start of an evening to ensure a smooth, easy rapport among guests. Some even say the Sour has hallucinogenic properties."
–Quotation from **hotwired.com's** *cocktail site about pisco*

The best Chilean beer, *cerveza*, is a brand called Kunstmann that is brewed in Valdivia. Unfortunately, it can usually only be found in the Lake District. Royal Guard is a solid choice with national distribution. Another good one, Austral, lighter and with a lower alcohol content, is sold primarily in Magallanes and Aisen. Crystal does the most advertising with women in bathing suits and is therefore the most popular. Guinness is brewed in Chile but has a completely distinct formula from that of its namesake in England. Draft beer, called *choop*, pronounced "shoop," is quite inexpensive.

WINE

Vino

The popularity of Chile's wines is attributed to consistent, superior quality and reasonable pricing. Chile is now the third largest wine exporter to the United States, trailing only the powerhouses of Italy and France. Contributing to its wide acceptance is the fact that Chile's wines are made from grapes that most people are already familiar with: **Cabernet Sauvignon** and **Merlot** in reds, and **Sauvignon Blanc** and **Chardonnay** in whites.

Chile's wine industry was founded in the 1850's by wealthy families who sent their sons to be educated in France and modeled their estates after Bordeaux châteaux. Most of the well-known wineries are located in the Maipo Valley, just south of Santiago, but there are eight wine growing regions stretching from the Aconcagua Valley, north of Santiago, to the Biobío River. The style of Chilean wines more resembles the elegance of Europe rather than robustness of the New World.

Chilean wines are medium-bodied, supple and balanced, most palatable in their youth when the focus is on their delicate fruit flavor. The vintage is less important here because the vineyards are blessed with temperate, semi-arid weather that ripens the grapes consistently from year to year. The reds are distinguished by their refreshing fruitiness, firm acidity, and light tannins. Most reds are ready to drink two or three years after harvest and rarely benefit from longer cellaring. Sauvignon Blanc is the most attractive of the whites, especially those that come from the newest vineyard region of Casabalanca which mix fruit and herb flavors to create exceptional balance.

The vast majority of Chilean wines are priced from $6-$20. The wines in this range are an excellent value for the quality, and you usually you usually get what you pay for as you move up in price. Although the prestige wines, selling for $50 and above, are earning accolades in some circles, these wines are less consistent in quality.

You can find the major labels in most restaurants and supermarkets. For a wider selection consult the specialty wine stores in Santiago listed in the *Shopping* entry in the Santiago destination chapter. Before you haul back several bottles in your carry-on luggage, consider that you can pick up the major labels back home for roughly the same price that you can buy them for in Chile.

CHOOSING CHILEAN WINES

You can hardly go wrong when selecting a $6-$20 bottle of Cabernet Sauvignon, Merlot, Chardonnay, or Sauvignon Blanc from one the following wineries:

- *Canepa*
- *Casablanca*
- *Casa Lapostolle*
- *Concha y Toro*
- *Cousiño-Macul*
- *Miguel Torres*
- *Montes Alpha*
- *Santa Carolina*
- *Santa Rita*

10. CHILE'S BEST PLACES TO STAY

SMALL HOTELS

HOTEL RUGENDAS, *Callao 3121, Santiago. Tel. 2/246-6000. Fax 2/ 246-6570. E-mail: rugendas@netline.cl. 48 rooms. 4 stars. Double $160. Breakfast included. Cable TV. Restaurant. Bar. Gym. Business Center. El Golf metro. Credit cards accepted.*

This small hotel, built in 1996, provides everything you would expect in a top-notch accommodation, in addition to many well-thought extras. The décor is Chilean-country, which creates a warm, informal ambience that welcomes you as you walk in the door. The bright, cozy lobby has some of the most comfortable sofas in town.

The pleasant rooms are appointed with rustic wooden furniture and sunny yellow walls. Small details, like an extra phone jack by the desk for computer hookup, show the thought that went into creating this hotel. The white tile floor in the bathroom sparkles. The rooms high up on the side that face the Club Frances, #903 and #803 in particular, have excellent views and are quieter than the rooms facing the street.

The game room on the top floor has a brand new, full sized pool table as well as numerous card tables. Windows line the walls for a fishbowl look at the city. There are also conference rooms upstairs for the business traveler.

One traditional drawback to staying in small hotels is the size of the gym. That is not the case here. The Rugendas has one of the better-equipped and more spacious gyms in Santiago. Open 24 hours a day, the workout area has Cybex weight machines, free weights, and the standard cardiovascular machines. For half the price of the international hotels, you get everything but a pool.

The restaurant, El Moro, is decorated in the same informal style as the rest of the hotel. The lavish breakfast and lunch buffets will send you back to the gym to work off those extra calories. The El Golf metro stop is just meters away from the hotel and numerous restaurants lie waiting across Apoquindo.

HOTEL ISLA SECA, *On the Road to Papudo, Zapallar. Tel. 33/741224, Fax 33/741228. 38 rooms. Double $150. Breakfast included. Restaurant. Bar. Pool. Credit cards accepted.*

The Isla Seca, a painstakingly decorated retreat perched high on a hill overlooking the sea, is a true treasure of the area. Two side-by-side buildings offer the finest accommodations on the coast.

The main building houses the original rooms and all the common areas. Light bursts through the floor to ceiling windows in the dining room to infuse the lobby and front sitting area with a golden glow. The terrace in front of the dining room leads down to a perfectly manicured garden and comfortable pool. While swimming, you can observe waves pounding on the rocks below or simply float on your back and take in the endless blue sky. Another small pool between the original and new buildings dangles like a nest over the edge of the property.

Almost every room in the Isla Seca is a different shape, which leads to a number of bed configurations. Tasteful decorations are a common factor in all the rooms. Light walls and curtains, large windows, simple pen and ink drawings, and fresh flowers welcome the visitor. Ocean view rooms are preferable, as are the larger center rooms with terraces. The best room is the middle one on the third floor of the original building, which has its own deck.

The dining room terrace is the perfect place for a drink at sunset. Facing directly west, it offers prime views of the huge orange ball submerging into the ocean. The bar and card room are the central gathering areas once darkness falls. Photographs of the Zapallar elite at play in the early 1900s grace the walls, lending the atmosphere of an exclusive club.

The restaurant is solid, though given the high quality of the rooms and service, one would expect a more creative menu. Room service, with a limited menu, prepares delicious sandwiches. The breakfast is one of the best hotel breakfasts on the coast, with fresh squeezed orange juice and fruit.

Although located high above the sea, the hotel has a pleasant walkway down to the ocean. Descending through the fragrant forest, surrounded by flowers, is an Isla Seca ritual that lets you know it's time to relax and enjoy.

BRIGHTON, *Pasaje Atkinson Numbers 151-153, Cerro Concepción, Valparaíso. Tel. 32/223513. Fax 32/213360. 6 rooms. Double $60-88. Breakfast included. Restaurant. Credit cards accepted.*

This lovely, canary yellow Victorian-style home is a jewel of Valparaíso. There is a nascent movement afoot to restore the city to its turn-of-the-century charm, and this hotel is part of it. Six rooms, decked out with antiques gleaned from local markets, await lucky guests. High ceilings, exposed beams, intricate molding, and interesting furniture fill the small but charming rooms. The showers, thankfully, are late 20th century with piping hot water and good water pressure.

Each room is completely unique in terms of size and view. The suite on the first floor has outstanding views of the harbor as well as a small balcony. Others have views of both the sea and hills. The single room is Lilliputian, so look at it before you decide whether to stay.

Downstairs there is a bar and restaurant with one of the most popular patios in the city. Its black and white tiles point out to the sea while Valparaíso wraps around the surrounding hills. At night, mesmerizing lights twinkle below. Excellent *pisco sours* are the specialty of an extensive drink menu.

From the hotel, situating along a rambling lookout point, you can easily walk to most of the important city sights and explore the steep streets with their houses representing all the hues of Joseph's coat.

HOTEL TERRANTAI, *Tocopilla 19, San Pedro de Atacama. Tel. 55/851140. Fax 55/851037. 9 rooms. Double $82. Breakfast included. Restaurant. Pool. Credit cards accepted.*

This is our favorite hotel out of the multiple fine offerings in San Pedro. Made from native materials such as cactus and adobe, this inn blends seamlessly into its environment. Narrow, rock-lined, outdoor passageways lead to spacious, well-designed rooms. Shadows play across these rooms all day, created by tree limbs in front of the floor-to-ceiling glass sliding door that covers one entire wall. The door opens out to a delightful, flower-covered terrace where hammocks and lounge chairs beckon sinfully. At night you fall exhausted into a cozy bed to snuggle under a thick down comforter.

The hotel smells like warm rocks on a sunny day, even in the shower. You truly feel closer to the desert environment it is trying to evoke. The walls of the dining area are covered with strings of *algarrobo, chañar*, and *tamarugo* seeds, the source of much of life in this wilderness.

There is a small, rock-lined pool in the center of the hotel that is about two meters across and two meters deep. It is perfect for a dunk after a day's activity. You won't lack for diversion here, as the hotel can arrange any number of special excursions. In addition to the standard Valley of the

Moon and Atacama Salt Flat, they can more off-the-beaten-track tours such as Laguna Verde in Bolivia or multi-day treks.

HOTEL VOLCÁN PUNTIAGUDO, *Camino Fundo Las Piedras. Tel. 65/421648, Fax 65/421640. 10 rooms. Double $85. Breakfast included. Restaurant. Pool. Credit cards accepted.*

The striking Bauhaus architecture of this luxurious inn will shake up your perception of country hotels. Its location on a grassy five hectare lot atop a bucolic hill above Lake Llanquihue allows each of the rooms to open up to an unparalleled view of the water and volcanoes. Beautifully custom-crafted, wood headboards, end tables, and shelves interplay superbly with walls painted in bold primary colors. Well thought-out details in the rooms include track lighting, highly functional reading lights, and separate wall heaters in the bathrooms. The common areas are equally sleek and comfortable. There is a well-stocked bar in the lounge area as well as a superb wine selection in the dining room.

The stylish hotel is surprisingly recreational and child friendly. Several rooms are outfitted with a loft nesting two small beds to which fascinated kids climb via a wooden ladder. There is a video room, a raised sexagonal pool, hiking trails accessible from the property, and a fishing boat for guest use.

First generation immigrants Heinz and Anna Hermann, who built the hotel in the region they fell in love with while traveling, extend personalized hospitality. You will find it difficult to leave behind their hearty homemade bread served at breakfast each morning.

Low season rates drop to $68, making the Hotel Volcán Puntiagudo one of the best values in the country. There are discounts for stays of three nights or more all year round, except in July when the hotel is closed.

BEST INEXPENSIVE HOTELS
•*Residencial Santo Domingo* - Santiago
•*Don Juan Carrasco* – *Valparaíso*
•*Takha-Takha* – San Pedro de Atacama
•*Ecole* – Pucón
•*Hostal Kolping* – Castro

APART-HOTELS

HOTEL VICTORIA, *Lota 2325, Santiago. Tel. 2/233-0458, Fax 2/233-0574. 16 full apartments. Double $116. Breakfast included. Cable TV. Metro Los Leones. Credit cards accepted.*

The Hotel Victoria is tops in the apart-hotel department. The apartments are in a red brick, beautifully landscaped building on a quiet residential street in Providencia close to El Bosque. There is no sign outside the building, which makes the Victoria a secret hideaway for those in the know.

These are full sized apartments that the owner has thoroughly furnished for guests. The nicely decorated quarters feature large terraces as well as complete kitchens with microwaves. The kitchen opens out to a spacious living room with a sofa bed and stereo. Light walls and natural lighting from outside keep things cheery.

The 24-hour reception office is downstairs in the back to help you arrange trips, send faxes, or answer the phone when you are away. The reception area for the Apart Lota is in the same building, so make sure you are in the right one. These highly recommended apartments come in different sizes and bed configurations to fit any size group.

CABAÑAS DUNAMAR, *on the road to Punta Lobos, Pichilemu. Tel. 72/841576. 25 cabins. Double $55. Breakfast included. Restaurant. No credit cards.*

The Dunamar, out of town towards Punta Lobos, is our top choice for both food and lodging in Pichilemu. If you are fortunate enough to retire to one of these tastefully constructed, two story bungalows for a siesta after lunch, you can fall lazily into a comfortable double bed upstairs. From here, you can gaze out at the endless stretch of beach below. You catch a different angle of the beach at every turn because even the bathroom and shower have outstanding views.

Downstairs there is a small kitchen next to a cozy living area. The Dunamar is especially pleasant because they pay important attention to detail. The interiors are immaculate and finished with varnished pine boards. Basic cooking staples are available at grocery store, instead of minibar, prices. Best of all are the reading lights. So many hotels skimp in this department, but the Dunamar fills the nooks in its cabins with comfortable sofas and strong lights. Room availability is limited so call ahead for reservations.

LODGES

HOTEL ANTUMALAL, *2 km before Pucón on Villarrica highway. Tel. 45/441011. Fax 45/441013. E-mail: antumalal@entelchile.net. Website: hotelantumalal.co.cl. 11 rooms. 1 suite. 1 apartment. 2 chalets. Double $250. Breakfast and either lunch or dinner included. Restaurant. Bar. Heated pool. Tennis court. Beach. Boating. Sailing. Water-skiing. Tours. Credit cards accepted.*

The Antumalal is one of the finest hotels in the country. Built into the rocks and trees, using natural elements in its construction, the hotel's architecture is similar to that of buildings designed by Frank Lloyd Wright. From its garden-covered position above the lake, the hotel offers excellent views, personalized service, and world-class comfort.

The informal lodge atmosphere envelops you as soon as you walk in the door. The common areas include a cozy bar lined with thick planks of araucaria wood as well as a glass-walled living room overlooking Lake Villarrica. Animal skins, plants, tree trunks, and rocks cover floors and walls, in addition to the requisite fireplaces. A large, wisteria-umbrelled deck extends over the gardens where you can order food and drink or simply take in the view. The restaurant, which also enjoys beautiful vistas, offers a limited but delicious international menu. The first-rate breakfast includes locally produced jams on hot slabs of homemade bread.

To make it feel like you are visiting friends at a summer home rather than staying in a hotel, the Antumalal has neither locks on the doors nor room numbers. The rooms themselves all have huge, panoramic windows; comfortable beds with fat cotton coverlets over the blankets; and thick, soft rugs that beg you to plop down in front of your own personal fireplace.

If the weather is nice, chances are you won't be spending much time in your room. You might be walking around the four hectare property admiring the terraced gardens, playing tennis on the court with a large bolder anchoring one of the net posts, or enjoying a range of water sports. The hotel can also help arrange fishing, golfing, rafting, horseback riding, hiking, or soaking in hot springs.

The family-run Antumalal's history is fascinating. The Pollak's, immigrants from Prague in 1945, came to Chile because they loved the mountains. Starting off with a coffee shop in Pucón (it burned), and then a ski-lodge on the slopes of the volcano (it disappeared in an eruption), they put all they had into the creation of this hotel, the name of which means "corral of the sun" in Mapuche. The list of visitors who have discovered this lakeside jewel is an impressive one. Foreign royalty such as Queen Elizabeth, famous politicians, and even actor Jimmy Stewart have all lived the wonderful life here.

TERMAS PUYEHUE, *Ruta 215 km 76. Puyehue National Park. Tel./ Fax 64/232157, Santiago Tel./Fax 2/293-6000. Website: www.puyehue.cl. 175 rooms. Double lakeside with balcony $135. Breakfast included. Full board, add $35 per person. Restaurant. Bar. Game room. Thermal baths. Indoor and outdoor pools. Horse stable. Tennis courts. Day care center. Convention rooms. Credit cards accepted.*

The Termas Puyehue Hotel is a solid, classic resort built of locally quarried stone in 1942 near the entrance of the national park. One end of the expansive edifice houses a magnificent high-ceilinged restaurant, a woodsy bar, and a rustic lounge area with an immense fireplace. Also in this end of the hotel is the game room, the activity center offering outings from horseback riding to easy hikes to fly fishing, and a day care center.

Ambling to the other end of the 27,000 square meter building will take you to the wing with the majority of the rooms. These are outdoorsy in style but with plush linens as a finishing touch. The rooms on the third floor have the best views from their balconies and cost the same as the ones on the second floor.

During the summer the hotel invites a series of speakers so your evenings can be as stimulating as your days. On the other hand if your prerogative is R&R, you can steep yourself in one of the thermal baths or swim under the beautiful wooden beams of the indoor pool. There is a stylish outdoor pool as well.

HOTEL EXPLORA, *Sector Salto Chico, Torres del Paine, Reservations Santiago Tel. 2/2066060 Fax 2284655. E-mail: explora@entelchile.net. Website: http://www.interknowledge.com/Chile/explora. Rooms 30. Paine Massif View Room $1,706 per person, four night package, double occupancy. Price includes transport from Punta Arenas airport, all meals and all tours. Restaurant. Bar. Gym. Pool. Jacuzzi. Gift shop. Library. Video projection room. Day care center during tour hours.*

Staying at the Explora is more than a lodging decision, it is the choice to experience Torres del Paine in the nascent, highly interactive Explora culture. The attentive service begins as a hostess greets you at the Punta Arenas airport while the chauffeur pulls your luggage from the carousel.

Built into the rolling hills on the shore of Lake Pehoe, the elongated, minimalist, yellow edifice takes advantage of its position for mesmerizing views of the *cuernos* from the front, and the Salto Chico waterfall from the rear. The rooms in the hotel optimize the views, not only in the main portion, but even in the bathrooms which are designed with porthole windows so that you can look at the scenery as you brush your teeth. The vibrant springtime colors – bright yellows, greens, and purples – of the bedspreads and curtains, imported from Barcelona, surprise you with their bold elegance.

The hotel offers 16 different excursions. These include hikes to destinations such as the *torres* and Glacier Grey as well as mountain biking and sea kayaking. The excursion groups meet with their bilingual Chilean guides each evening to preview the following day's activities. Slide shows and books in the library provide supplementary information.

The dining room is finished in indigenous beech wood as is the rest of the hotel. It looks out over the extraordinary blues of Lake Pehoe. The meals are fixed-menu style with your choice meat and fish entrees available for lunch and dinner. The hotel also features a lap pool, outdoor jacuzzi, and gym nearly level with the languid Paine River.

LARGE HOTELS

HYATT, *Kennedy 4601, Santiago. Tel. US 800/233-1234, Santiago 2/218-1234, Fax 2/218-2513, www.travelweb.com/hyatt.html. 310 rooms. 5 stars. Double $342. Cable TV. Restaurant. Bar. Pool. Gym. Business Center. Credit cards accepted.*

We know a guy who came to Chile on vacation and stayed at the Hyatt. He had plans to visit the north and the Central Coast, but enjoyed the Hyatt so much, he never left Santiago. While we think it's a crime that he didn't see more of the country, a part of us understands. The Hyatt stands alone as the premier hotel in Santiago. When dignitaries or movie stars come visit, this is always where they stay.

The real draw of the Hyatt is the pool area. Waterfalls, lush gardens, oleanders, and palm trees spillover into the colossal pool and onto guest lounging areas. You won't forget where you are, however, because the Andes, on a clear day, serve as a dramatic backdrop to the greenery inside the property. There is a bar area on one side of the pool, and Anakena, a fiery Thai market restaurant on the other side. In the summer, local expats can be found sipping *pisco* sours on the patio into the extended twilight.

Entering the Hyatt, the open atrium lobby shoots up 24 floors of glassed walls and elevators. The domed roof allows light to fall naturally on the central areas. The rooms are decorated in earthy, comfortable colors. Windows cover the far wall in each room, affording stunning views of the city and the Andes. Try to get accommodations above the 14th floor on the mountain side.

Club Olympus, the Hyatt's gym, is the best-outfitted hotel gym in the city. In addition to the large space allotted for weights and aerobic machines, there is an area for aerobics classes. Two red clay tennis courts give you the chance to exercise outdoors. Afterwards you can luxuriate with a sauna or massage. The beauty salon is also located in the same building.

The breakfast and tea area, in a sunny atrium, overlooks the pool. An Italian restaurant and an English Pub round out the full selection of eateries. Visitors on working trips have every possible resource available at the Business Center. The concierge can arrange tours, cars, accommodations in other cities, or whatever you might need. Before we moved to Chile we used to stay here for as low as $200 with the best business rate.

TERRADO SUITES, *Los Rieles 126, Playa Cavancha, Iquique. Tel. 57/ 488000. Fax. 57/437755. 91 rooms. Double $145. Breakfast included. Cable TV. Restaurants. Café. Bar. 2 pools. Beach. Gym. Sauna. Business Center. Tour service. Car rental. Baby sitting. Credit cards accepted.*

Terrado Suites sits alone at the top spot in the Iquique hotel rankings. Its prime location on the Cavancha Peninsula means that instead of traffic noise, you hear nothing but waves crashing on the beach. The 15-story hotel feels much more intimate than its size would indicate, mainly because of the excellent service offered by its staff.

A walk through the immaculate lobby, past the hotel bar, leads out to a patio above the inviting blue pool. Below the pool, hotel guests enjoy the tranquility of their own private piece of beach.

The rooms are elegant without being ornate. Playful African prints adorn the light walls, sunlight streams in the large picture windows, while comfortable furniture makes it hard to venture elsewhere. All of the rooms have ocean views, and the majority of them, Superior Suites, have large patios overlooking the sea. From this privileged position you can watch fishermen prepare their colorful boats or spy on all the Cavancha beach activity.

For the best views you can head to the French restaurant on the 15th floor. An excellent buffet breakfast is served there daily. On the first floor you also have the option of the Casa Blanca, a more informal, although excellent, Italian restaurant.

Although it is hard to imagine, if you find yourself wanting to leave the grounds and explore the area around Iquique, the hotel's travel service can arrange trips to all the local attractions.

11. SANTIAGO

Almost all who come to Chile are logistically obliged to spend time in Santiago. The main international airport in the country is here as is the hub for all domestic flights. Your impression of Santiago will greatly depend on the time of year you visit and your hotel location. If you arrive in the summer, you'll enjoy the Central Valley's pleasant Mediterranean climate during a time when many of the city's families and vehicles migrate to the beaches. Genial breezes dry-clean the sky to reveal the Andes Range as a spectacular rocky curtain behind the city.

In winter, the rainy season, you will feel as though you've been tossed into a dungeon due to the bone chilling, damp cold and smog that grimly envelope the capital. A strong winter rain, however, is frequently followed by a morning of piercing blue skies that illuminate the snow-crusted, crystalline Andes.

If you stay in the tidy, arboreal uptown, Santiago will appear to be one of the most modern, well-planned cities in Latin America. If you lodge in the downtown historical center, you will be surrounded by old Latin America, a dense jumble of avenues and buildings inspired by the architectural grandeur of Europe. The attitudes of the workers in each of these sectors contrast as well. Those in the uptown sector stride determinedly in pursuit of success while in the downtown you'll find people with time to sit on park benches and chat amidst all the hustle and grind.

Located about halfway down the length of Chile, in the morning shadow of the Andes, Santiago is a city of nearly 5 million inhabitants. Like most Latin American capitals, Santiago is the unchallenged nucleus of the country's industrial, commercial, and political activity. This centralization has spurred dramatic growth. *Santiaguinos* comprise fully one-third of the Chilean population.

The city radiates out from the original **Historical Center** (*centro*), which is composed of grand post-independence public buildings and tall office buildings constructed in the past few decades. The *centro* is a hubbub of activity. During the day, the streets pop and blur with vehicles, vendors, and pedestrians. If you like the whirl and stimulation of a concentrated city center you will find it here. At night the *centro* becomes deserted, however, as the commuters clock out and go home.

Uptown is a sparkling modern area implanted with newly constructed skyscrapers and high-rise condominiums. Many more are in the works as is evidenced by a proliferation of industrial cranes. The lofty buildings taper off into a suburbia of family residences and shopping malls which run up the Andean foothills until blocked by the steeper slopes. The principal uptown neighborhoods include condominium-plotted **Providencia**, middle class **Ñuñoa** and **La Reina**, upscale **Las Condes** and nature-loving **El Arrayan**. The bohemian **Bellavista** is located about mid-town, at the foot of the hill **Cerro San Cristóbal**. Most of the evening dining and nightlife takes place in Bellavista, Providencia, and Las Condes.

You can easily entertain yourself for several days in Santiago with visits to the museums, historical buildings, and seafood market in the Historical Center. Good shopping and the must-visit **Pablo Neruda Museum** can be found in Bellavista. The best views in town are from **San Cristóbal Hill** which you can summit by tram from this bohemian neighborhood. Attractions out a bit further include urban parks and the beautiful artisans market **Los Dominicos**.

Nature is undoubtedly Chile's most spectacular draw. Fortunately natural wonders are easily accessed in day trips from Santiago. You can venture into the Andes to parks like the **Arrayan Nature Sanctuary**, technically in town; **Hierba Loca National Park**, about forty-five minutes up the road; and **El Morado National Park**, just two hours south of the city. Three ski resorts, open roughly from June to September depending on the snowfall, are less than an hour-and-half away. Beach lovers can hit a variety of Central Coast escapes that range from the lively port city **Valparaíso** to the exclusive Monterrey-like retreat of **Zapallar**.

History

Before the arrival of the Spanish, Mapuche natives inhabited the Central Valley region. The area represented the southern end of Inca influence with the six meter wide Inca trail terminating north of here.

The Spanish, led by **Pedro de Valdivia**, founded the city of **Santiago del Nuevo Extremo**, naming it for the apostle Santiago, (Apostle St. James), and for Valdivia's birthplace in Spain – Nueva Extremadura. The founding ceremony took place on February 12, 1541 at the base of **Santa Lucia Hill**. Six months later Santiago would be attacked and destroyed by the Mapuche natives. The Spaniards quickly rebuilt the city, but ignored the town's development to focus on establishing settlements in the Mapuche heartland south of the Biobío River. In 1600 the Mapuches expelled the Spanish from the southern settlements, forcing the colonists to relocate to Santiago and Chiloé.

Two major earthquakes leveled the city completely, one in 1647 and another in 1730. The only structure currently standing that predates those catastrophes is the **San Francisco Church**, built in 1618. One great pre-independence structure was the **Calicanto Bridge**. Finished in 1790, it magnificently spanned the Mapocho River with eight arches. Since the river is nearly dry much of the year, the thirteen-year effort to build the bridge inspired the colonial catchphrase "Either sell the bridge or buy a river!" The bridge is no longer standing but the remains can be seen in the Calicanto metro station.

The capital's development slowed as the country focused on consolidating its territories at the extreme northern and southern frontiers. Two major remodeling phases would occur during the century after independence. The first was in 1872 when **Santa Lucia Hill** was turned into a city park, a public transport service (with horse-drawn wagons) was created on the newly opened avenues, and the **Municipal Theater** was built. Another developmental phase would follow during the centennial celebration of 1910, when the **Fine Arts Palace** was built and the **Virgin Mary Monument** was dedicated on San Cristóbal Hill.

In the twentieth century, urban growth has increased the metropolitan area's population tenfold. The city expands outward in every direction except to the east, where growth is blocked by the Andes.

ARRIVALS & DEPARTURES
BY AIR
The **Arturo Merino Benítez airport** is about thirty minutes southwest of Santiago. The newer international section was built in 1996 and has modern facilities, such VIP lounges and a food court.

Customs clearance and baggage claim is usually very efficient. You can exchange money at the kiosk as you wait for your luggage, or use the ATM machine in front of the customs exit.

Official taxis are parked outside of the terminal building, directly in front of the customs areas. You can either buy a ticket inside or pay the cab driver. The fare is about $20 to most destinations in Santiago. Vans are also available for bigger groups or for those with excessive luggage.

Buses leave the airport to downtown every 15 minutes and cost $2. The line that runs the service is **Tour Express**, *Tel. 671-7380.* The drop off/pick up point downtown is *Moneda 1529.*

The domestic section of the airport is located in a separate building next to the international terminal. It is an older structure so the services aren't quite as good as those next door. There is an ATM machine near the entrance to the gates. Bus and taxi service costs are the same as from the international terminal.

Airlines
- **Aerolineas Argentinas**, *Moneda 756. Tel. 639-3922*
- **Aeroperú**, *Fidel Oteiza 1953. Tel. 274-3434*
- **Air France**, *Aeropuerto. Tel. 601-9419*
- **Alitalia**, *Av. O'Higgins 949. Of. 1001, Tel. 698-3336*
- **American Airlines**, *Huérfanos. Tel. 679-0000*
- **Avant**, *Santa Magdalena 75. Tel. 335-3077*
- **Avianca**, *Santa Magdalena 116. Tel. 690-1051*
- **Canadian**, *Huérfanos 1199. Tel. 688-3580*
- **Iberia**, *Bandera 206. Tel. 678-1716*
- **KLM**, *Aeropuerto. Tel. 690-1364*
- **Lacsa**, *Fidel Oteiza 1921. Tel. 209-7477*
- **Lufthansa**, *Moneda 970. Tel. 630-1000*
- **Ladeco**, *Av. Libertador Bernardo O'Higgins 107. Tel. 661-3131. Toll free 600-600-4000*
- **LanChile**, *Agustinas 640. Tel. 687-2525. Toll-free 600-600-4000*
- **South African Airways**, *Santa Magdalena 75, Of. 407. Tel. 334-0238*
- **United Airlines**, *El Bosque Norte 0177, 19th Floor. Tel. 337-0000*
- **Varig**, *Miraflores 156. Tel. 693-0999*

BY BUS
There are four main bus stations in Santiago serving points as far away as Arica, 28 hours to the north, and Punta Arenas, 48 hours to the south. Since bus companies and destinations are scattered inconsistently throughout the different stations, the best thing to do is to track down the company and route you want by phone (have the front desk person at your hotel do it if your Spanish is not good), then head to the correct station with the information in hand. Be sure to verify the station from which your bus departs.

For bus companies with service to/from Santiago:

To All of Chile & International
- **Tur Bus**, *Tel. 270-7500*
- **Tramaca**, *Tel. 695-7772*
- **Fénix**, *Tel. 235-9707*

To the North
- **Los Corsarios**, *Tel. 235-4810*
- **Los Diamantes del Elqui**, *Tel. 235-9707*

SAMPLE BUS & AIR FARES FROM SANTIAGO

Fares are for one-way travel to the destinations. One-way airfare is half the price of round-trip ticket. The bus prices are for coach service.

Location	Airfare	Time	Busfare	Time
Arica	$120	4 Hours	$30	28 Hours
Calama	$100	3 Hours	$27	20 Hours
Copiapó	$90	2 Hours	$22	12 Hours
La Serena	$75	1 Hour	$12	7 Hours
Mendoza,				
Argentina	$90	1 Hour	$17	8 Hours
Temuco	$75	1 Hour	$12	9 Hours
Puerto Montt	$90	2 Hours	$14	12 Hours
Punta Arenas	$150	5 Hours	$50	48 Hours
				(via Argentina)

• **Flota Barrios**, *Tel. 698-1494*
• **Tas Choapa**, *Tel. 235-2405*

To the Central Coast
• **Condor Bus**, *Tel. 779-3721*
• **Pullman Bus**, *Tel. 779-2026*

To the South
• **Cruz del Sur**, *Tel. 779-0607*
• **Jac**, *Tel. 233-0517*
• **Varmontt**, *Tel. 232-1116*

Bus Stations in Santiago
• **Alameda**, *Av. Libertador Bernardo O'Higgins 3750. Metro Universidad de Santiago*
• **Los Heroes**, *Tucapel Jiménez 21. Metro Los Heroes*
• **Santiago or Buses Sur**, *Av. Libertador Bernardo O'Higgins 3848. Metro Pila del Ganso*
• **San Borja**, *San Borja 184, Metro Estación Central*

BY CAR
North

Access to and from Santiago is via the **Panamericana Norte, Ruta 5**. To uptown destinations follow Las Condes signs on the Avenida Americo Vespucio. To downtown follow Agustinas east from the Panamericana.

South

Access to and from Santiago is via the **Panamericana Sur, Ruta 5**. To uptown destinations, follow the Costanera or Santa Maria east along the river. The Costanera runs one way during weekday rush hours – east to west in the morning, and west to east in the evening. To downtown, follow Agustinas east from the highway.

Auto Rentals

Many of the auto rental companies offer hotel drop-off and pick-up service with no additional charge.
- **A&T Rentacar**, *Av. General Bustamante 280. Tel. 222-7086*
- **Avis**, *Downtown, San Pablo 9900. Tel. 601-9966. In Providencia, Guardia Vieja 255, Of. 108. Tel. 331-0122*
- **Budget**, *Manquehue Sur 600. Tel. 220-8292*
- **Costanera Rent A Car**, *Andrés Bello 1255. Tel. 235-7835*
- **Fama Rentacar**, *Francisco Bilbao 4184. Tel. 208-7797*
- **Hertz**, *Andrés Bello 1469. Tel. 235-1022*
- **Lacroce Car Rental**, *Seminario 298. Tel. 665-1325*
- **National Car Rental**, *Americo Vespucio 800. Tel. 739-0176*
- **Toluka Rent A Car**, *I. La Católica 5019. Tel. 207-3837*
- **Value Rent A Car**, *Apoquindo 5002. Tel. 228-2822*

BY TRAIN

The **Estación Central**, *General Libertador O'Higgins/Matucana, Tel. 689-1825 or 689-5401, Metro Estación Central*, is the departure point for trains. They run only to the southern part of the country from Santiago. You can buy tickets at the train station, at the Escuela Militar metro station, or at the **Galería Libertador**, *Libertador Bernardo O'Higgins 853*.

ORIENTATION

Santiago is located at the base of the Andes in the Central Valley, a fertile sediment-filled agricultural area. It is roughly at the halfway point in the country, with Punta Arenas positioned 3,090 kilometers to the south and Arica 2,062 kilometers to the north. The coast is 100 kilometers west, the closest cities being **Viña del Mar** and **Valparaíso**. The Argentine border is 70 kilometers east as the condor flies, but it is impassable at that latitude. The closest vehicular border crossing point requires a slight jog to the north so it is about 150 kilometers away. From there you descend into the Argentine province of Mendoza.

The city slopes gently east to west with altitudes of 800 meters in the eastern neighborhood of Arrayan and 543 meters in the city center. The **Rio Mapocho** runs through the city on the same slope, slightly tilted on a northeast to southwest axis, just north of the historical center. Two main traffic arterials, **Santa Maria** and **Andrés Bello**, also known as the **Costanera**, run along either side of the river and serve as the quickest vehicle routes from uptown to downtown. The **Andes** can be used to identify east.

Other good geographical features to pick out are **Santa Lucia Hill**, which marks off the eastern edge of downtown and the more prominent, Virgin-adorned **San Cristóbal Hill** at the midtown point where the Bellavista neighborhood is located. The main avenue downtown is **Libertador General Bernardo O'Higgins**, which is usually referred to by its previous, shorter name, the **Alameda**.

GETTING AROUND TOWN

Once you figure out how to use the **metro** (subway), you've gained access to the majority of points of interest in Santiago. The metro is clean, safe, and provides the most efficient means of getting to and from the *centro* during the business day because it cruises along underneath the traffic jams. The central line runs east to west linking uptown and downtown Santiago. There are two other lines that run north to south bisecting the main line at Baquedano and Los Heroes stations.

Entrances to the metro are marked by street signs with three red diamonds. At the bottom of the stairs you will find a ticket kiosk with fast moving lines. Try to have your change or small bill out before you reach the front of the line. Single ride tickets cost about 50¢ depending on the time of day. Tickets are more expensive during rush hours. You can also buy a $2,000 peso denominated ticket that will give you about 10 rides. The cost of each ride is deducted automatically when you use the ticket. To access the trains, first locate the sign indicating the direction you want to go, then insert the ticket into the turnstile beneath it. When you reach your destination station, you can consult the station map showing details of the immediate area to get your bearings. The maps are located near the ticket kiosk in each station.

For destinations far from the metro lines or if you prefer to travel above ground, you can take a bus or a taxi.

Taxis are cheap and efficient. We've found the cab drivers in Santiago to be courteous and honest, traits that seem to be a point of pride for them. If there is trouble finding an address, it is usually due to confusion, and frequently in such a situation the driver will apologize and charge you less than what the meter reads without argument. You can either flag down a yellow and black cab off the street, have your hotel arrange one, or call one of the radio taxi numbers. The drop rate for street cabs is about 50¢ plus a per kilometer and time cost. Hotel and radio cabs will cost slightly more. Tipping is not common unless there is extra effort involved. Rides within the areas normally visited by travelers cost anywhere from $2-$8. You can negotiate an hourly rate in-town or out-of-town starting at about $10-15 per hour.

SANTIAGO RADIO TAXIS

- **Citycar**, *Tel. 632-5822, 632-6682, 632-5976*
- **Congreso Radio Taxis**, *Salesianos 1739. Tel. 551-2500, 522-7082*
- **Radio Taxi Providencia**, *Irrazaval 3054. Tel. 225-1656*
- **Radio Taxi El Golf**, *Apoquindo 5681. Tel. 220-0873*
- **Radio Taxi Chile**, *Nataniel Cox 929. Tel. 699-4303*
- **Radiotaxi Las Condes**, *Badajoz 6. Tel. 211-4470*

Buses run on all the main streets. The best thing to do is to pick a place on the correct side of the street to go in the direction you want then ask a driver or someone waiting which bus to take. The reader boards on the bus display the final destination and some routing points. The cost is about 50¢.

Driving a vehicle in Santiago can be one of the most bewildering experiences imaginable. Behind the wheel, *Santiaguinos* are notoriously impatient, aggressive, and generally unskilled. It is a relatively new phenomenon for the city to be crammed so full of cars. To compensate, resident drivers will tailgate you, cut you off, honk at you, and pull off some of the most inept moves ever witnessed. Just try to keep your cool and practice defensive driving.

WHERE TO STAY

Hotel choices in Santiago run the range from the ludicrously luxurious to bare-bones budget. There are hundreds of places from which to choose, but we have helped narrow your choices by eliminating the unlivable. We would send friends and family, according to their budgetary constrictions, to all of the hotels listed below. Some are better than others, but all are places we can recommend.

The Part of Town for You: Our preference for moderate and upper end hotels are those located in the green, pleasantly-spaced, uptown areas of **Providencia**, **El Bosque**, and **Las Condes**. Our reasoning for this recommendation is threefold. First, *Santiaguinos* don't really live in the *centro*. They work there and then go home at night, leaving the area relatively deserted after business hours. Second, the uptown areas present better opportunities for quiet walks along tree-lined streets as well as offer excellent services. Third, most of the dinner restaurants and nightlife are located uptown. From uptown you can easily ride the metro to make daytime forays into the historical center for intense cultural stimulation, then return in the evening to a more restful city experience.

Budget travelers will necessarily get corralled into the *centro*, but should make the effort to reserve space in advance at the hotels we've recommended to avoid the unsafe Mapocho Station area.

Cost: Santiago is not an inexpensive city. What $20 gets you in some other South American countries in terms of hotel quality is much different than here. Apart-hotels, however, are an excellent option in Chile and a good value. For the cost of a hotel room you get a furnished apartment. This is especially important if you are traveling with other people, because having separate living and sleeping space can do wonders for travel relationships. Having a kitchen is another plus for those days when you are just sick of eating in restaurants.

The services offered with apart-hotels vary widely. Some of them are just like hotels with a front desk to answer phones, send faxes, arrange travel, and the like. Others are more independent and basically just turn the apartment over to you.

Discounts: The prices we have quoted are the walk-up rack rates. If you make your reservation in advance, you should receive a 10-20% business discount. Send a fax on company letterhead requesting the rebate. Many times you can also negotiate a discount when you check in during slower periods.

You should always reconfirm when you are checking in and checking out that you are not being charged sales tax (IVA). The 18% tax, deducted for foreigners, makes double-checking worthwhile. You will be asked to show your tourist card in order to obtain the discount.

Rankings: In each price category, we have ranked the hotels. The first hotel on the list is our top choice for the price category in that neighborhood and we work our way down from there. The hotels at the top of the list are not necessarily the most expensive. Rather they are the hotels that provide excellent accommodations for the category in addition to offering something special. That distinguishing quality may be location, size, décor, friendliness of the staff, or if you're lucky, all of the above.

HISTORICAL CENTER

Lodging in the *centro* is for those who prefer the megalopolis full court press. Historic buildings, skyscrapers, buses, street vendors, and taxi cabs cram both narrow and broad streets to chaotic capacity. Evenings in downtown are almost deserted as the commercial set heads for the residential areas. On weekends the streets fill up with shoppers and amblers.

Expensive

HOTEL CARRERA, *Teatinos 180. Tel. 2/698-2011, Fax 2/672-1083. Toll Free USA Reservations 800/223-6800. 5 stars. 130 rooms. Double $250. Cable TV. Restaurant. Bar. Business Center. Gym. Pool. Retail shops. Credit cards accepted.*

Overlooking the Constitution Plaza, which it shares with the presidential palace La Moneda, the Hotel Carrera is positioned in the heart of the *centro*. Endowed with English style elegance, the hotel offers doubles that are spacious, newly redecorated with tasteful burnt orange bedspreads and drapes, and include a comfortable sitting chair under a reading light.

The hotel can boast of excellent dining locales from top to bottom. Up top is the open air Roof Garden Restaurant, positioned in front of the shimmering pool, with one of the best views in downtown Santiago. The homey pub downstairs is a good place for quaff before a meal. Next door is the Copper Room, one of Santiago's finest prime rib restaurants.

HOTEL PLAZA SAN FRANCISCO, *Alameda 816. Tel. 2/639-3832, Fax 2/639-7826. 5 stars. 156 rooms. Double $260. Cable TV. Restaurant. Bar. Room service. Business center. Gym. Pool. Lan Chile check-in desk. Metro U. Chile. Credit cards accepted.*

The refined Hotel Plaza San Francisco is located on the main broad avenue of downtown Santiago. It is set back off of the street, so the small fountain-graced plaza that the hotel shares with the ancient San Francisco church, is more noticeable than the traffic. The sweeping lobby and reception area expand into a wood-ceilinged bar and lounge area which accents the hotel's spaciousness. Deep blue, green, and purple textured stripes decorate the hallways. The standard doubles are outfitted with king size beds and ample desk space. The business center offers internet access among its services. Quality exercise bikes and treadmills are available in the gym, near the indoor pool. The award winning Bristol restaurant is a favorite of the city's political elite.

HOSTAL DEL PARQUE, *Merced 294. Tel. 2/639-2694, Fax 2/639-2754. 4 stars. 29 rooms. Double $126. Breakfast included. Cable TV. Restaurant. Cafeteria. Bar. Metro U. Católica. Credit cards accepted.*

This is a cheery boutique hotel with views of a park across the street. It is located in a artsy enclave with some good restaurants nearby. The dining area, which is set up for breakfast each morning, opens onto a sunny patio. The rooms are the size and quality of those in the moderate price range so the hotel is somewhat overpriced, but it still a good option.

Moderate

HOTEL VEGA, *Londres 49. Tel. 2/632-2496 or 632-2514. Fax 2/632-5084. 20 Rooms. Double $46. Cable TV. Metro U. Chile. Credit cards accepted.*

The Hotel Vega, housed within a spired, baroque edifice built in 1910, is the best value in the moderate category. The hotel is located in the Bohemian Londres/Paris neighborhood. Recent remodeling has made the large odd-shaped rooms in the old section graceful and comfortable. There are a few rooms that look out onto the peaceful, dead-end Londres street. The staff and services are professional enough for the hotel to be used by businessmen looking for a less expensive option.

RIVIERA HOTEL, *Miraflores 106. Tel/Fax 2/633-5988. 40 rooms. 3 stars. Double $50. Breakfast included. Cable TV. Restaurant. 24 hour room service. Metro Sta. Lucia. Credit cards accepted.*

The Riviera offers clean, medium size, temperature-controlled rooms and superior service which keeps the hotel full of repeat clients. Some of the rooms have views of the beautiful National Library, but with the tradeoff of busy downtown street noise. The interior rooms are quieter. The downstairs restaurant is hopping and has the feel of a local diner. The hotel is located near Santa Lucia Park.

FORESTA HOTEL, *Victoria Subercaseaux 353, Tel 2/639-6261, Fax 2/639-6261. 3 stars. 35 rooms. Double $50. Restaurant. Bar. Metro Sta. Lucia. Credit cards accepted.*

This quirky European-style hotel facing Santa Lucia hill is an anachronistic grab bag of furnishings and color schemes. You might encounter an elegant gold-framed mirror, a tacky modern end table, or an antique telephone, all in the same room. The downstairs sitting room yawns with velvety red upholstery set against a dark mahogany backdrop, while upstairs awaits a suite composed of screaming lime green walls and a palm tree view that is purely Miami beach. On the top floor is a pleasant atrium restaurant offering reasonably priced meals. No problem figuring out which of the restaurant bathrooms is yours. Ken and Barbie, dressed to the nines, perch over their respective gender's door. When booking, ask for a view room, but expect traffic noise. The Foresta fills up with loyal repeat guests so reserve in advance.

HOTEL METROPOLI, *Dr. Sótero del Río 465. Tel. 2/696-1058 Fax 695-2196. 3 stars. 45 rooms. Double $46. Breakfast included. Restaurant. Bar. Coffee shop. Metro Moneda. Credit cards accepted.*

Its location in a narrow building at the end of a dead-end street makes this centrally located hotel relatively quiet. The Metropoli is near the Tribunales garden, a clean, verdant spot to relax after touring the *centro*. A predominantly European client base can be found here. The Metropoli offers ample rooms and closet space, nicely tiled bathrooms, and a small stereo in each room. The hotel has single rooms for $36.

1. Hotel Carrera
2. Hotel Plaza San Francisco
3. Hotel Del Parque
4. Hotel Vega
5. Riviera Hotel
6. Foresta Hotel
7. Hotel Metrópoli
8. City Hotel
9. Hotel Santa Lucia
10. Carlton House
11. Residencial Santo Domingo
12. Residencial Londres
13. Hotel Paris
14. Cervantes Hotel
15. Hotel España

16. Confiteria Torres
17. Donde Augusto
18. Copper Room
19. Jockey Club
20. Gatopardo
21. El Vegeriano
22. Donde Victoriano
23. Roof Garden Restaurant
24. Cafe Santos
25. Les Assesins
26. Cafe Del Bizgaf
27. La Tentación

CITY HOTEL, *Compañia 1063. Tel. 2/695-4526, Fax 2/695-6775. 3 stars. 72 rooms. Double $48. Breakfast included. Restaurant. Bar. Metro U. Chile. Credit cards accepted.*

The City Hotel is a classic 1920's era art deco building enhanced by a jazzy neon outline. The main building is connected to the bar and restaurant by a taught red awning. It is worth stopping by the bar for a drink even if you are not staying here. Senators and other *centro* denizens slap down dominoes and chat among the wood-carved walls, spiral staircase, and elegant wrought iron. The best rooms in the hotel are at the back of the building, away from the street traffic and with views of the cathedral.

HOTEL SANTA LUCIA, *San Antonio 327. Tel. 2/639-8201, Fax 2/6331844. 3 stars. 72 rooms. Double $50. Cable TV. Restaurant. Room service. Metro Sta. Lucia. Credit cards accepted.*

The Santa Lucia is on the 4th floor of a downtown building, centrally located near the active pedestrian street of Huérfanos. Although the reception area is a bit threadbare, all of the rooms have been recently remodeled so they have a new feel to them.

CARLTON HOUSE, *Máximo Humbser 574. Tel. 2/638-3130, Fax 638-2930. 4 stars. 11 rooms, 22 apartments. Double $51. Apartment $60. Some rooms with cable TV. Parking. Metro Sta. Lucia. Credit cards accepted.*

Located near Santa Lucia park, the Carlton House is starting to show its wear. The four star rating seems too high, but you can spread out in the apartment-style rooms. The apartment set-ups include a stove, small fridge, and some tacky furniture.

Inexpensive

RESIDENCIAL SANTO DOMINGO, *Santo Domingo 735. Tel./Fax 2/639-6733. 29 rooms. Double with bath $30, without bath $21. Restaurant. Metro Calicanto. No cards.*

Stepping through the entryway of the Santo Domingo your attention is immediately drawn to the height of the hallways of the 100 year old residence, making you wonder how far up the walls can possibly go. Much of the wall is consumed by extensive, wooden-paned, window squares that suck broad bands of light from the sky to deposit them in the hotel's internal patios and reading areas. After your eyes journey twenty feet they finally encounter the delicate antique molding where the wall meets the ceiling. The rooms, which line one side of the hallway and face an atrium, are simple doubles and triples, and can be a bit drafty due to the high ceilings. The gardens, common areas, and great light are really what make this hotel an exceptional option. It also has a cafeteria that offers economical fixed item lunches and dinners.

RESIDENCIAL LONDRES, *Londres 54. Tel./Fax 2/6382215. Rooms 20. Double $24. Metro U. Chile. No credit cards.*

The management's commitment to "big clean rooms with lots of hot water" is part of the reason that the Residencial Londres is the most popular spot for budget travelers. The *residencial* is located in a baroque building in the Bohemian Londres/Paris neighborhood. Many of the guests are solo travelers who pay for lodging on a $13 per night per person basis, splitting shared rooms with other travelers. Considering the well-maintained quality of the rooms and the low price, the residencial fills up frequently. It is a strongly advised to make a reservation in advance. There are few rooms which have views of the preserved 1920's era buildings on Londres street.

HOTEL PARIS, *Paris 813. Tel. 2/664-0921, Tel/Fax 2/639-4037. 38 rooms. Double $38 with TV, $28 without TV. Cable TV in some rooms. Metro U. Chile. Credit cards accepted.*

This is a good option for a low-end hotel, located in the funky Paris/Londres neighborhood. Its main drawback is that it is somewhat dark, but there are some nice details like exposed wood beams that compensate. Some common areas are curiously set into the stairwells. Rooms on the street side catch a lot of traffic noise.

CERVANTES HOTEL, *Morande 631, Tel. 2/696-7966, Fax 696-5318. 50 rooms. Double $38 w/ TV, $31 w/o TV. Metro Calicanto. Credit cards accepted.*

This hotel is located near the grungy area where most of the cheap hotels are, but is far enough outside of it to make a difference. The rooms are bright with new curtains and bedspreads. There is a good coffee shop style restaurant on the first floor. Single rooms are available for $28.

HOTEL ESPAÑA, *Morande 510. Tel./Fax 2/696-6066. 60 rooms. 2 stars. Double $30. Credit card surcharge of 10%. Metro Calicanto.*

Near the Plaza de Armas, this is an acceptable option because it is clean and bright. The hotel has two singles without baths for $12 and four singles with baths for $18.

BELLAVISTA
Moderate

MONTEVERDE, *Pio Nono 193. Tel. 2/777-3607, Fax 2/737-0341. 12 rooms. Double $49. Breakfast included. Cable TV. Kitchenette. Credit cards accepted.*

Located right at the intersection of Pio Nono and Antonia Lopez de Bello, this hotel couldn't be closer to the center of the bohemian nightlife in Santiago. The Monteverde is a simple place with unadorned rooms, but it's clean and cheery. An unexpected extra is that rooms come with a mini-refrigerator and a microwave for those late night munchies.

If you're a night owl, you'll love it here. The street noise, especially on the weekends, doesn't die down until around 3am, but if you're out on the town until then, it won't matter.

A STEAL OF A DEAL

The hotels on this list cost less than the going price for their neighborhoods yet offer many of the same amenities.

- *Hotel Vega* - *centro*
- *Residencial Santo Domingo* - *centro*
- *Monteverde* - *Bellavista*
- *Diego de Almagro Apart-Hotel* – *El Bosque*
- *Apart Lota* - *Providencia*

PROVIDENCIA
Expensive/Very Expensive
HOTEL VICTORIA, *Lota 2325. Tel. 2/233-0458, Fax 2/233-0574. 16 full apartments. Double $116. Breakfast included. Cable TV. Metro Los Leones. Credit cards accepted.*

The Hotel Victoria is tops in the apart-hotel department. The large apartments are in a red brick, beautifully landscaped building on a quiet residential street in Providencia close to El Bosque. There is no sign outside the building, which makes the Victoria a secret hideaway for those in the know. The nicely decorated quarters feature large terraces, kitchens with microwaves, and a living room with a sofa bed and stereo.

The 24-hour reception office is downstairs in the back to help you arrange trips, send faxes, or answer the phone when you are away. These highly recommended apartments come in different sizes and bed configurations to fit any size group.

Selected as one of our best places to stay – see Chapter 10 for more details.

PARK PLAZA, *Ricardo Lyon 207, Tel. 2/233-6363, Fax 2/233-6668. Website www.integranet.cl/park_plaza. 104 rooms. 5 stars. Double $230. Cable TV. Restaurant. Bar. Pool. Gym. Business Center. Metro Leones. Credit cards accepted.*

The Park Plaza is renowned for its service. The small, European-style hotel offers its guests personalized attention from their highly trained staff. From the moment you enter the elegant lobby, with its polished wood and muted colors, a host of employees is ready to take care of your every need.

King-sized beds and a small sitting area are the highlights of the large and comfortable rooms. Here again, the attention to detail is noted.

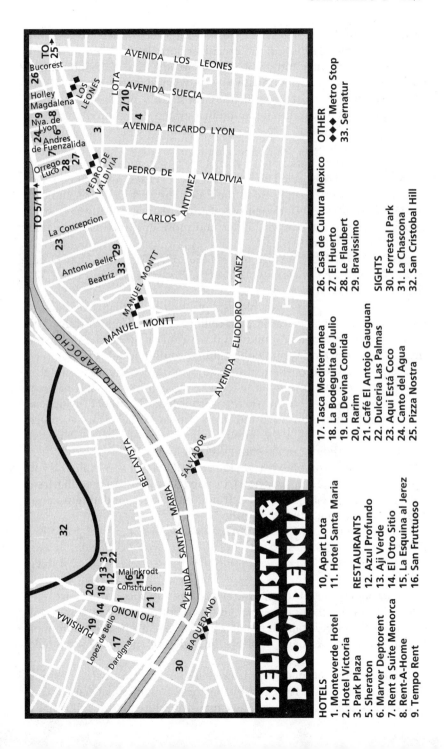

AVENIDA LOS LEONES

AVENIDA SUECIA

AVENIDA RICARDO LYON

PEDRO DE VALDIVIA

CARLOS

RIO MAPOCHO

AVENIDA ELIODORO YAÑEZ

MANUEL MONTT

La Concepcion

Antonio Bellet

Beatriz

BELLAVISTA

SANTA MARIA

AVENIDA

SALVADOR

BAQUEDANO

PURISIMA

ONON Old

Malinkrodt

Constitucion

Lopez de Bello

Dardignac

Bucorest

Holley

Magdalena

Nva. de Lyon

Andres de Fuenzalida

Orrego Luco

LOS LEONES

LOTA

BELLAVISTA & PROVIDENCIA

HOTELS
1. Monteverde Hotel
2. Hotel Victoria
3. Park Plaza
5. Sheraton
6. Marver Deptorent
7. Rent a Suite Menorca
8. Rent-A-Home
9. Tempo Rent

10. Apart Lota
11. Hotel Santa Maria

RESTAURANTS
12. Azul Profundo
13. Aji Verde
14. El Otro Sitio
15. La Esquina al Jerez
16. San Fruttuoso

17. Tasca Mediterranea
18. La Bodeguita de Julio
19. La Devina Comida
20. Rarim
21. Café El Antojo Gauguan
22. Dulceria Las Palmas
23. Aqui Está Coco
24. Canto del Agua
25. Pizza Nostra

26. Casa de Cultura Mexico
27. El Huerto
28. Le Flaubert
29. Bravissimo

SIGHTS
30. Forrestal Park
31. La Chascona
32. San Cristobal Hill

OTHER
◆◆◆ Metro Stop
33. Sernatur

TO 25

TO 2/10

TO 5/11

Double phone lines, voice mail, and an internet connection await all guests. Accommodations on the executive floor are installed with a full multi-media computer and color printer. Nonsmoking and handicapped rooms are also available. As far as views go, you will most enjoy ones from the side of the hotel that faces the San Cristobal hill. For exercise, a small pool and work out area can be found in a sunny, glass-roofed terrace on the top floor of the hotel. The area is unfortunately better for lounging than working out.

The restaurant, Park Lane, is one of the best French dining rooms in Chile. Exquisitely displayed fare satisfies all the senses. Again, the service is as much a part of the appeal as the food. The Park Plaza is located in the heart of Providencia, closer to downtown than any of the El Bosque hotels, so the streets are bit louder and more crowded. Double glass windows help eliminate noise.

HOTEL TORREMAYOR, *Ricardo Lyon 322. Tel. 2/234-2000, Fax 2/ 234-3779. 80 rooms. 4 stars. Double $150. Breakfast included. Cable TV. Restaurant. Credit cards accepted.*

The Torremar, five years old, is a pleasant hotel that covers all the bases. The Mediterranean style, high-ceilinged, lobby is light and airy. The decor carries over to the rooms, which are a tad on the small side for the price. Ones that face Lyon, with numbers ending in a 5 or 4, are the biggest, so be specific when you make your reservation. The hotel is located far enough down Lyon to feel like it is in a residential zone yet it is just a stone's throw from the commercial hustle and bustle of Providencia.

The restaurant is informal and offers standard Chilean fare. As much as the food, you will enjoy the options on its extensive wine list. The staff is helpful and friendly and speaks excellent English.

The Torremayor falls right on the cusp of being a good value. If you want a full restaurant in your hotel, or need the lobby as a meeting area, you are getting exactly that here. If not, one of the moderately-priced apart-hotels may be a better option.

SHERATON SAN CRISTOBAL, *Santa Maria 1742. Tel. 2/233-5000, Fax 2/234-1732. 310 rooms. 5 stars. Double $250. Cable TV. Restaurant. Bar. Pool. Gym. Business Center. Travel agency. Car rental. Beauty salon. Gift shops. Credit cards accepted.*

The Sheraton is the one hotel on this list about which we feel ambivalent. It used to be the best in town, but there are now so many options with better locations that it is hard to give it a hearty recommendation. On the other hand, it offers the high level of service you would expect of a five star hotel.

The location is its main drawback, as it's not close to anything. Sitting on the north side of the river across from the rest of town, you have to take a cab to get almost anywhere. The expansive, white marble lobby has a cold, almost oriental quality that makes it inappropriately impersonal for South America. The architecture is reminiscent of the 70's, which was not a golden age in building design. The rooms are just what you would expect for a hotel of this caliber. The higher you are the better the view.

It does have a pleasant, grassy area around the large outdoor pool with drinking and dining *al fresco*. The indoor pool is just big enough for lap swimming while the gym is quite complete with Nautilus and machines for cardiovascular workouts.

Moderate

MARVER DEPTORENT, *Nueva de Lyon 114. Tel. 2/231-2542, Fax 2/ 231-6068. 12 full apartments. Double $96. Metro Los Leones. Credit cards accepted.*

This is one of the better values in Santiago. The building, with a lovely marble entry, houses large, well-furnished apartments. You know it's different right off the bat because, unlike other apartment buildings in the area, the elevators can hold more than two people.

You'll feel at home in these 80 square meter apartments. The bright, fully furnished kitchen opens out to the dining and living areas. Microwaves are standard in addition to the regular range and oven. The stereo even comes with a CD player for you to listen to your new Chilean music purchases. There is a huge walkthrough closet with a make-up table leading through to the master bath. You may want to take breadcrumbs.

The office, half a block away from the apartment building, will send faxes and provide travel advice. The apartments are on Fuenzalida, which is a quite street right in the heart of Providencia. Ask for an apartment with a view of the San Cristobal hill.

RENT A SUITE MENORCA, *Andres de Fuenzalida 71. Tel. 2/233-3953, Fax 2/233-4030, www.chilnet.cl/menorca. 20 full apartments. Double $100. Metro Leones. Credit cards accepted.*

The apartments are in the same building as the above entry, but have a different owner. They offer all the same amenities as the Marver apartments, but are not quite as nicely decorated. The Menorca office is right next door, however, so if you need to send faxes or talk in person to the receptionist, it is more convenient. They are also set up to help you arrange trips, rent cars, or even find a secretary.

RENT A HOME, *Santa Magdalena 82. Tel. 2/231 0393, Fax 2/233-2266. 34 full apartments. Double $88 or $110. Metro Los Leones. Credit cards accepted.*

Rent a Home actually owns three properties with apartments, but the office is on Santa Magdalena. **San Sebastian II** at *Santa Magdalena 82*, and **San Andres** at *Ebro 2799* are equipped with almost exactly the same interiors. The décor is simple but pleasant. The kitchens are white and clean and all come with microwaves. The apartments here are smaller than those at Marver or Menorca, but some would argue that the location, a few blocks closer to El Bosque, is better. **San Sebastian I** at *Ramon Carnicer 131* is older and not quite as nice, so therefore less expensive.

TEMPO-RENT, *Santa Magdalena 116. Tel. 2/231-1608, Fax 2/334-0374. 65 full apartments. Double $116. Cable TV. Metro Los Leones. Credit cards accepted.*

Tempo-Rent is another solid option for an apart-hotel. The apartments aren't beautiful, but they are certainly more comfortable than a cramped hotel room. The kitchens here are smaller than the above options and don't come with microwaves. The staff is very friendly and the reception area is located right in the building entrance, giving you more contact with the employees than in the other apart-hotels. Negotiate for a business discount – it can be large here.

APART LOTA, *Lota 2325, Tel. 2/233-5906, Fax 2/233-3817. 14 full apartments. Double $72. Cable TV. Metro Los Leones. Credit cards accepted.*

Apart Lota shares the complex with the hotel Victoria. It is in the same red brick building with its attentive landscaping on the same quiet street. It does not have the same quality furnishings however, which is reflected in the price. Apart Lota is still a commendable option both for the space you get and the swanky neighborhood, especially if you get an apartment on one of the higher floors.

HOTEL SANTA MARIA, *Santa Maria 2050. Tel. 2/232-3376, Fax 2/231-6287. 23 rooms. Double $98. Breakfast included. Metro Pedro de Valdivia. Credit cards accepted.*

Sometimes people prefer the communal atmosphere of a rambling hotel to the more private one of apart-hotels. If that's your case, the Santa Maria if your place. This old house, with its high ceilings from a different era, didn't lose its homey charm when it was converted to a hotel. The small restaurant and common sitting areas are idea for hanging out with fellow travelers. The practical rooms are kept spic-and-span. The rooms on the first floor have a terrace in the back yard, the corner suite being especially desirable. Little details like ice machines, peep holes, and security locks show the owner wants you to be as comfortable as possible.

Its location on the north side of the river is not inconvenient because it is just a short walk down Pedro de Valdivia to Providencia.

EL BOSQUE

El Bosque is technically part of Las Condes, but we consider them two distinct areas. In El Bosque you still have access to the subway, which you don't in the rest of Las Condes. This will make a huge difference as far are your mobility is concerned.

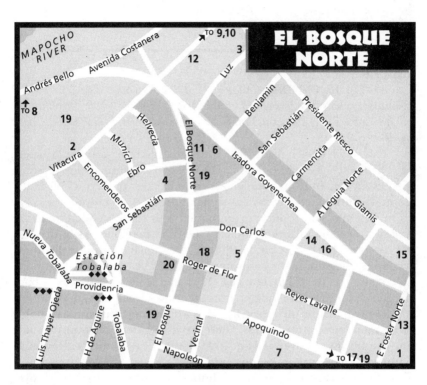

EL BOSQUE NORTE

HOTELS
1. Rugendas
2. The Radisson
3. Hotel Intercontinental
4. Plaza El Bosque
5. Director Apart-hotel
6. Montebianco
7. Diego de Almagro Apart-hotel
8. Los Españoles
9. Hyatt
10. Director

RESTAURANTS
11. Coco Loco
12. El Madroñal
13. Puerto Renato
14. Taj Mahal
15. Shoogun
16. T. G. I. Fridays
17. DaDino
18. New York Bagel Bakery
19. Au Bon Pain
20. Food Garden

OTHER
◆◆◆ Metro Stop

NICEST APART-HOTELS IN SANTIAGO

- *Hotel Victoria* – *Providencia*
- *Marver Deptorent* – *Providencia*
- *Rent A Suite Menorca* – *Providencia*
- *Plaza El Bosque* – *El Bosque*

Expensive/Very Expensive

HOTEL RUGENDAS, *Callao 3121. Tel. 2/246-6000. Fax 2/246-6570. E-mail: rugendas@netline.cl. 48 rooms. 4 stars. Double $160. Breakfast included. Cable TV. Restaurant. Bar. Gym. Business Center. El Golf metro. Credit cards accepted.*

This small hotel, built in 1996, provides everything you would expect in a top-notch accommodation. The décor is Chilean-country, which creates a warm, informal ambience that welcomes you as you walk in the door. The bright, cozy lobby has some of the most comfortable sofas in town. The pleasant rooms are appointed with rustic wooden furniture and sunny yellow walls. Small details, like an extra phone jack by the desk for computer hookup, show the thought that went into creating this hotel. The white tile floor in the bathroom sparkles. The rooms high up on the side that face the Club Frances, #903 and #803 in particular, have excellent views and are quieter than the rooms facing the street.

The game room on the top floor has a brand new, full sized pool table as well as numerous card tables. There are also conference rooms upstairs for the business traveler. The hotel boasts one of the best gyms in Santiago. There is no pool, however.

The lavish breakfast and lunch buffets will send you back to the gym to work off those extra calories. The El Golf metro stop is just meters away from the hotel and numerous restaurants lie waiting across Apoquindo.

Selected as one of our best places to stay – see Chapter 10 for more details.

THE RADISSON, *Vitacura 2610. Tel. US 800/333-3333, Chile 2/203-6000, Fax 2/203-6001. Website www.radisson.com. 159 rooms. 5 stars. Double $266. Cable TV. Restaurant. Café. Bar. Pool. Gym. Business Center. Travel agency. Beauty salon. Tobalaba metro. Credit cards accepted.*

If commerce and money have a pulse, you can feel it here. Attached to the World Trade Center, the Radisson's every detail is focused towards business. The guests who stay here are as cool and smooth as the impressive marble lobby.

Business travelers lack nothing. The spacious rooms come with desks large enough to finish that expense report and sofas for relaxing after a long day. All of the rooms have two lines so you won't miss any phone calls while your computer is connected. Even more impressive, all of the rooms have internet access. If you don't have your laptop, they will lend you one for free. Any guest can also arrange for a fax machine in the room or a cellular phone if that's needed. The Business Center is obviously top notch with such services as secretaries and translators. Lastly, the hotel has small conference rooms that can be reserved without cost.

Entertaining clients is no problem here. The Brick Restaurant features outstanding international cuisine. The café is a good place for a quick bite or a cup of coffee, and we're sure many business deals have been closed in the dark paneled bar.

If you are not traveling for business, the Radisson is still one of the better five star hotels. Its central location puts you within walking distance of many excellent restaurants as well as the metro. The indoor pool is heated, though it is not quite large enough for comfortable lap swimming. The gym may have the best view in Santiago, with all of downtown, El Bosque, and Las Condes laid out before your sweaty eyes.

If you are in a time crunch, the Radisson has a helicopter to sprint you off to the airport in 5 minutes or even get you to the snow covered peaks of Valle de Nevado in 17 minutes. Anything can be had for a price.

HOTEL INTERCONTENINTAL, *Luz 2920. Tel. 2/234-2200, Fax. 2/251-7814, www.interconti.com. 103 rooms. 5 stars. Double $240. Cable TV. Restaurant. Bar. Pool. Gym. Business Center. Metro Tobalaba. Credit cards accepted.*

Location distinguishes the Intercontinental from its peers. Just one block from El Bosque street, there are enough bars and restaurants in walking distance to sate any appetite. The French-style hotel is a perfect size – small enough to feel intimate yet large enough to offer all the services.

The rooms are well appointed and cheerful with extremely comfortable beds. The gym is Lilliputian but adequate with bikes, a treadmill, and a Universal weight system. There is a small pool with eating tables around it that is used more for decoration than swimming.

The bar and restaurant, to the left of the white marble lobby, are where people congregate. Santiago business people, as well as upper class women, meet here for lunch. There is a small gift shop on the other side of the lobby.

The concierge can arrange travel or other types of service you may need. Be aware that this was a Sonesta hotel until recently so many people, including cab drivers, still use that name.

PLAZA EL BOSQUE, *San Sebastian 2800. Tel 2/362-1600, Fax 2/232-7620. 89 full apartments. Double $148. Restaurant. Gym. Credit cards accepted.*

The Plaza's location is tops, just half a block off popular El Bosque Street and very near the metro. The rooms are discerningly decorated with tasteful wallpaper and furnishings. Two-bedroom apartments are equipped with two baths and a sofa bed to sleep up to five. The kitchens include both conventional and microwave ovens and, conveniently, there is a supermarket just a block away to stock the cupboards. For a good view of the Andes try for a room high on the east side of the building. We have gotten them to concede to the corporate price as a walk-in during the slower months.

DIRECTOR APART-HOTEL, *Carmencita 45. Tel. 2.233-2423, Fax 2/ 232-0986, www.nexos.cl/hotelesdirector. 49 rooms. Double $145. Breakfast included. Cable TV. Restaurant. Bar. Kitchenette. Metro El Golf. Credit cards accepted.*

The Director is less an apart-hotel and more a hotel with big rooms and kitchenettes. They offer all the services of a hotel, with the convenience of an apartment. The lobby, restaurant, and bar are up to par with most of the 4 star hotels in Santiago. The reception staff is there to send faxes, arrange trips, or cater to any other need you may have. The difference is the rooms, which include a living and dining space as well as a small kitchen area.

The privileged location of the Director is another plus. It is on the edge of El Bosque in a residential area that is just minutes walking distance from restaurant and nightlife central.

Moderate

MONTEBIANCO, *Isadora Goyenechea 2911. Tel. 2/232-5034, Fax 2/ 233-0420. 33 rooms. 4 stars. Double $107. Breakfast included. Cable TV. Restaurant. Metro Tobalaba and El Golf. Credit cards accepted.*

If you really want to be in the center of El Bosque, you can't get any closer than the Montebianco. This small hotel, decorated in rustic Chilean style, is surrounded by restaurants, bars, and clubs. The rooms are a bit small, but you can extend your space out to the patios. Try to avoid the ones on the ground floor for noise reasons. It might be worth $20 to upgrade to the Montebianco room, which is significantly larger and furnished with an extra table. There is a small restaurant in the hotel, but there is really no reason to have anything other than breakfast here because of your options right out the front door. The Montebianco is all about location.

The hotel has a van for hire that can take you on a city tour or on one of the many day trips around Santiago.

DIEGO DE ALMAGRO APART-HOTEL, *Apoquindo 3397. Tel./Fax 2/335-0787. 20 apartments. Double $65. Cable TV. Kitchenette. Metro El Golf. Credit cards accepted.*

This has to be the most space for $65 in El Bosque. It is not the nicest apart-hotel around, but it is a great deal. The hotel is set off from the sleek, modern buildings on its street by its atrocious pink and blue décor. Luckily, things get better inside. The rooms in the back of the hotel are much quieter than the ones in front. The kitchenette consists of two burners, a sink, and a microwave, which can get you through plenty of meals. The apartments have large beds, ample closet space, and small, but clean bathrooms.

LOS ESPAÑOLES HOTEL, *Los Españoles 2539. Tel. 2/232-1824, Fax 2/233-1048, hotelesp@cepri.cl. 52 rooms, 3 stars, Double $100, Breakfast included. Metro Los Leones. Credit cards accepted.*

Los Españoles is a hotel along the same lines as the Santa Maria. If you want to be around others and it's worth paying more to upgrade from the *centro*, this is a good option. Located in the leafy Pedro de Valdivia Norte neighborhood, it is an older hotel with a venerable air. Both the rooms and bathrooms are spacious.

The restaurant downstairs is decorated like a Spanish cellar. The large bar in the front of the hotel expands your living space. It's a bit like sitting in the den of somebody's home. The front door is on Los Españoles street, though there is an entrance on Santa Maria as well. You should request a room closer to the front as the vista is greener and there is less traffic noise.

A few blocks down Santa Maria at #2828, the same owners have built the **Los Españoles Apart-Hotel**. The traffic noise here is just too loud, which prohibits us from recommending it, even though it is newer.

LAS CONDES
Expensive/Very Expensive

HYATT, *Kennedy 4601. Tel. US 800/233-1234, Santiago 2/218-1234, Fax 2/218-2513, www.travelweb.com/hyatt.html. 310 rooms. 5 stars. Double $342. Cable TV. Restaurant. Bar. Pool. Gym. Business Center. Credit cards accepted.*

The Hyatt stands alone as the premier hotel in Santiago. When dignitaries or movie stars come visit, this is always where they stay.

The real draw of the Hyatt is the pool area. Waterfalls, lush gardens, oleanders, and palm trees spillover into the colossal pool and onto guest lounging areas. There is a bar area on one side of the pool, and Anakena, a fiery Thai market restaurant on the other side.

Entering the Hyatt, the open atrium lobby shoots up 24 floors of glassed walls and elevators. The domed roof allows light to fall naturally on the central areas. The rooms are decorated in earthy, comfortable colors. Windows cover the far wall in each room, affording stunning views of the city and the Andes. Try to get accommodations above the 14th floor on the mountain side.

Club Olympus, the Hyatt's gym, is the best-outfitted hotel gym in the city. In addition to the large space allotted for weights and aerobic machines, there is an area for aerobics classes. Two red clay tennis courts give you the chance to exercise outdoors. Afterwards you can luxuriate with a sauna or massage. The beauty salon is also located in the same building.

The breakfast and tea area, in a sunny atrium, overlooks the pool. An Italian restaurant and an English Pub round out the full selection of eateries. Visitors on working trips have every possible resource available at the Business Center. The concierge can arrange tours, cars, accommodations in other cities, or whatever you might need.

Selected as one of our best places to stay – see Chapter 10 for more details.

HOTEL DIRECTOR, *Vitacura 3600. Tel. 2/207-1580, Fax 2/228-7503. 96 rooms. 4 stars. Double $145. Breakfast included. Cable TV. Restaurant. Bar. Pool. Gym. Credit cards accepted.*

The Director is a miniature, less opulent version of the Hyatt. It is a good choice for people who want either an outdoor pool or to stay in Las Condes, but have a smaller budget. The rooms, decorated in a Mediterranean motif, are large and quiet. As with the Hyatt, the best ones are on high floors with views of the Andes.

The pool is small, but surrounded with greenery. It will be easy to get sucked into spending a few hours relaxing in the sun. The gym is also small but it covers all the bases for getting a workout in while on the road.

Happy hour is a daily event, which you can prolong into dinner at the restaurant. Although the Director's association with Best Western may turn some travelers off, it's really a nice alternative.

WHERE TO EAT

You can find almost any kind of food in Santiago, though some of the things that are inexpensive in many countries (Thai, Mexican, Chinese), are considered exotic here and have a larger price tag. That's not to say it's impossible to find a good meal for those on a small budget.

If you are just in Chile for a short time, you should zero in on seafood and more traditional Chilean fare. If you are spending weeks here however, you'll get to the point where you can't stand to see another mollusk. We have included other food options to get you through when that happens. A smart choice for those that are watching their pennies or in a bit of a hurry is the lunch *menú*. Many restaurants offer this fixed meal that usually consists of soup or salad, a main course with vegetables, dessert, and a drink. It usually costs around $5-8 and gets to your table in minutes.

As a reminder, restaurant hours are generally from 1pm-4pm and 8pm-1am. Restaurants in the *centro* target the workaday lunch crowd. Most are not open for dinner or on the weekends.

Our price categories are broken down as follows:
• Inexpensive: *under $8 per person*
• Moderate: *$8-15 per person*
• Expensive: *$16-25 per person*

See pages 123, 127, and 129 for our hotel and restaurant maps.

HISTORICAL CENTER
Chilean Food in the Historic Center
CONFITERIA TORRES, *Bernardo O'Higgins 1570. Tel. 698-6220. Moderate. Credit cards accepted.*

This century-old establishment still boasts its original bar and furniture. The food is standard Chilean fare, including the delicious cheese and steak sandwich that President Barros Lucos used to eat here and which is named for him. There are live tango and bolero shows in the evenings.

DONDE AUGUSTO, *Central Market Local 166. Tel. 672-2829. Metro Cal y Canto. Moderate. Credit cards accepted.*

The Central Market abounds with cheap seafood stalls, but if you want to get away from the fish odor, you can walk over to the fruit section where Donde Augusto owns the floor. Large Chilean families make it a Saturday tradition to dine here. The *paila marina especial* is the only thing you'll need to order. Chock full of squid, machas, shrimp, mussels, and fish, it offers everything in the ocean except the seaweed.

Other Food in the Historic Center
COPPER ROOM, *Hotel Carrera, Teatinos 180. Tel. 2/698-2011. Expensive. Credit cards accepted.*

The homey pub next to the Copper Room is a good place to start for a quick quaff before a meal. The Copper Room is one of Santiago's finest prime rib restaurants. The daily prime rib lunch includes a trip to the extensive starter bar. The restaurant also prepares seafood confidently featuring entrees such as grilled trout with green olive sauce.

JOCKEY CLUB, *Bombero Salas 1369. Tel. 699-2831. Expensive. Open for lunch only Monday-Friday 12:30-16:00. Credit cards accepted.*

The Jockey Club is a dark, mahogany affair, with international cuisine that attracts the city's business elite. This is very much an upscale club atmosphere with impeccably dressed waiters serving scores of martinis.

GATOPARDO, *Jose Victorino Lastarria 192. Tel. 633-6420. Closed Sundays. Expensive/moderate. Credit cards accepted.*

This is a superb, stylish Mediterranean restaurant with big art hoisted onto yellow stucco walls. Heavy unfinished wood beams support the lofty doorways and ceiling. The floor is checkered with polished white and maroon tiles, which match the waiters' striped shirts. The very reasonably-priced fixed item lunch is among the best in town. The personnel of the nearby French embassy make it a regular part of their lunch routine. It includes a salad bar stocked with items like black beans, sprouts and zucchini, followed by a main course, desert as well as a fresh juice and coffee. A few of the menu items include peanut soup (*sopa de maní*) and ravioli stuffed with smoked salmon (*ravioles donnafugata*). The restaurant is located in the artsy enclave near surrounding the art center Mulato Gil.

EL VEGETARIANO, *Huérfanos 827. Tel. 639-7063. Moderate. Closed Sundays. Credit cards accepted.*

Vaulted stained-glass ceilings and murals adorn the interior of this popular downtown lunch spot. The two narrow floors are crammed with diners, usually 20 and 30-something office workers on their lunch breaks, making for a lively atmosphere. The menu, available in English, is full of creative meatless dishes like vegetable pallea with mushrooms, asparagus, and artichoke hearts. Another savory entree is vegetarian enchiladas. There is usually a daily special such as paprika eggplant rolls. The fresh juices feature exotic flavors like raspberry and chirimoya. The daily fixed item lunch, which includes a appetizer, entree, desert, juice, and coffee is reasonably priced. There are a few meat dishes on the menu too so you can drag along carnivorous friends.

DON VICTORIANO, *Jose Victorino Lastarria 138, Tel. 639-5263. Moderate. Closed Sundays. Credit cards accepted.*

The frivolous decor and eccentric design of Don Victoriano, which has courtyards, balconies, and stairwells where you'd least expect them, makes it popular with the lunch crowd. Located in the same neighborhood as the art center Mulato Gil, the restaurant serves meat, seafood, and pasta and a popular fixed item lunch.

ROOF GARDEN RESTAURANT, *Hotel Carrera, Teatinos 180. Tel. 2/ 698-2011, Fax 2/672-1083. Moderate. Credit cards accepted.*

On the top floor of the Hotel Carrera is the open air Roof Garden Restaurant offering one of the best views in downtown Santiago. This is popular spot for a quick upscale lunch among the city's businessmen and a great break for sightseers weary from crisscrossing the *centro*.

CAFE SANTOS, *Corner of Huérfanos and Ahumada. Tel. 698-5185. Moderate. Closed Sundays. Credit cards accepted.*

Building on a tradition that began in the early part of the century, Cafe Santos serves up enough food to keep the next century satisfied. The downtown office crowd fills the below street- level restaurant to capacity each day to converge on the breakfast and lunch buffets. The lunch buffet includes cheeses, salad, various rice preparations, meat and fish, and desserts.

LES ASSESINS, *Merced 297B. Tel. 638-4280. Moderate. Credit cards accepted.*

Les Assesins offers reasonably-priced French cuisine in a small cafeteria atmosphere. The fixed item lunch is a sumptuous bargain. The restaurant is located near the Mulato Gil art center. If the Les Assesins is full, try the Gatopardo or Don Victoriano, both located nearby on Lastarria street.

CAFE DEL BIZGAF, *Villavicencio 398. Tel. 639-9532. Moderate. No credit cards.*

This is an artsy cafe located between the Cine Biógrafo and art center Mulato Gil. It offers coffee, sandwiches, and a fixed menu meal at lunch. People come here for beers as well.

LA TENTACION, *Huérfanos 1359, Tel. 696-0101. Inexpensive. Closed Saturday and Sunday. No credit cards.*

This is a simple lunch spot with a dining counter forming a square around the cash register as well as lining the window, which looks out onto the hubbub of Huérfanos street. The sandwiches and the plate of the day (*plato del dia*) are cheap and tasty. It would be surprising to see another gringo in this place which caters to loyal lunch regulars. The folks who work here are extraordinarily courteous and emphasize the freshness of their food.

BELLA VISTA

There are three or four restaurants on almost every brightly painted block in Bella Vista. Some of them only stay open a few months before

---

THE BEST CHILEAN FOOD RESTAURANTS IN SANTIAGO

All of the restaurants listed below have excellent Chilean food, but each is unique:

• **Traditional Favorite** – *Aquí Está Coco, Providencia*
• **Ambiance** – *Azul Profundo, Bellavista*
• **Country Fare** – *Hostería Doña Tina, Arrayan*
• **View** – *Gran Vista, La Reina Alta*
• **Rowdy Party** – *La Cuca on the weekends, Departamental*

they are redecorated for another person to take a shot at it. Others, like the ones listed below, consistently offer excellent food in an artsy atmosphere.

Chilean Food in Bellavista

AZUL PROFUNDO, *Constitucion 1111. Tel. 738-0288. Metro Baquedano, Expensive. Credit cards accepted.*

Step off the streets of Santiago into a nautical wonderland. Mast heads decorate the walls and captains' chairs take the place of bar stools. Even the huge wine display is housed in a room with a ship's rounded ceiling. Reminiscent of Pablo Neruda's houses, the poet connection is reinforced by photos of famous bards on the walls of the bar.

Many hip restaurants with cool décor don't seem to bother about the quality of their food. That is not the case here. Azul Profundo is known as one of the best seafood restaurants in Santiago. We especially recommend the *tabua marinho*, which is a overflowing sampler platter of grilled shellfish. Everything is good though, so order whatever strikes your pallet's fancy and wash it down with a chilled Chilean white wine. Reservations are recommended.

AJÍ VERDE, *Constitucion 284. Tel. 735-3329, Metro Baquedano. Expensive. Credit cards accepted.*

Ají Verde offers typical cuisine from all over Chile. While seafood fills most of the menu, you can also sample some of the traditional country dishes like *pastel de choclo* or *porotos granados*. They even offer *curanto*, a surf and turf dish from the island of Chiloé. The rustic, informal décor, with strands of chiles hanging from the ceiling, is cozy and comfortable.

Friday and Saturday nights, as well as Sunday lunch, feature a folkloric dance show. It's a bit touristy, so you may want to visit some other night of the week. The restaurant is set up for tourists, but the food is so good that locals frequent it also. Reservations are recommended.

Other Food in Bellavista

EL OTRO SITIO, *Antonia Lopez de Bello 53. Tel. 777-3059. Metro Baquedano. Expensive. Credit cards accepted.*

It's easiest to think of Peruvian cuisine as spicy Chilean food. This is one of our favorite restaurants to enjoy high quality Chilean seafood with a kick. Both the *ceviche* and the octopus cocktail, *ensalada de pulpo al Otro Sitio*, melt in your mouth. The *picante de camerones*, spicy shrimp, is a fireworks display of flavor. Another of our favorites is the *Ají de gallina*, which is chicken breast in a smooth sauce of nuts, cheese, chiles, and cream. No matter what you order, it should be accompanied by El Catedral. This cathedral sized *pisco* sour, made from Peruvian *pisco*, will really get conversation flowing.

The restaurant is decorated as an informal courtyard. When it gets crowded, service can be slow, especially if you have an upstairs table, but just kick back with another *Catedral* and enjoy the scene. We highly recommend this restaurant.

Flor de Canela, *down the street at #125*, and **Cocao**, *across the street at #60*, offer similar Peruvian fare at lower prices. Take your choice depending on your budget.

LA ESQUINA AL JEREZ, *Mallinkrodt 102. Tel. 777-4407. Metro Baquedano. Expensive. Credit cards accepted.*

Trying Spanish food is another way to enjoy Chilean seafood with a different flavor twist. Many Chileans of Spanish descent relive their roots here on the weekends over long, multi-course meals and bottles of red wine. The rustic décor is similar to that of Ají Verde, with the addition of hanging ham hocks. Anything prepared *a la gallega*, with garlic and peppers, is bursting with flavor. The owner, Jesus, was born in Spain on Chile street, so his adopted country was preordained.

SAN FRUTTUOSO, *Mallinkrodt 180. Tel. 777-1476. Metro Baquedano. Expensive. Credit cards accepted, except Diners.*

Santiago meets Manhattan and Milan in this hip Italian eatery. Exposed brick walls, linen table clothes, giant candelabras, and waiters in matching zoot suits all add to the unruffled air of San Fruttuoso. The food is just as self-possessed. Exquisite green tortellini stuffed with artichokes share top billing with tender, porcini mushroom gnocchi. For dessert try the crepes with ice cream and Chilean raspberries flaming in cognac.

TASCA MEDITERRANEA, *Purísima 161. Tel. 735-3901. Metro Baquedano. Moderate. Credit cards accepted.*

Catalonian food and *tapas* fill the menu at La Tasca. The warm, dark restaurant fills up with romantic couples dining on delicious, fresh seafood.

LA BODEGUITA DE JULIO, *Constitución 256. Tel. 732-0525. Metro Baquedano. Moderate. Credit cards accepted.*

If you've never been to Havana, or even if you have, here's your chance to experience it Chilean-style. La Bodeguita is one of Santiago's hopping hotspots. The lights are low and the walls decorated with voodoo art. The specialties are Cuban food and drinks like *ropa vieja*, Cuban-style beef; and *mojitos,* a rum drink that packs a punch. Don't eat too much so you'll still be light on your feet for salsa dancing in the bar after dinner. There is live music on weekends.

LA DIVINA COMIDA, *Purisma 215. Tel. 737-2300. Metro Baquedano. Moderate. Credit cards accepted.*

A play on words from Dante's Divine Comedy, the Divina Comida offers heavenly pastas. The restaurant, decked out with cheery checkered table cloths, boasts friendly, young waiters. The specialty of the house is a spinach and ricotta stuffed ravioli that makes the angels sing. Wash it down with some of their excellent, yet inexpensive, wine. Another good Italian option is **Divertimento**, *Antonia Lopez de Bello 93*, with an excellent array of Chilean influenced pastas.

RARIM, *Pio Nono 127. Tel. 737-8129. Metro Baquedano. Moderate. Credit cards accepted.*

Directly on the route to San Cristobal, Rarim attracts hot and hungry visitors. Arab food is on the menu, but the real attraction is its location. Next door **Estiatorion Christophoros**, featuring Greek food, is even closer to the park with great outdoor seating so it's packed on weekends. **Tacos Oaxaca**, *across the street, inexpensive, no cards*, is a Mexican-style taco stand serving up Chilean-style Mexican food.

CAFÉ EL ANTOJO GAUGUAN, *Pio Nono 69. Tel. 737-0398. Metro Baquedano. Moderate/Inexpensive. Credit cards accepted.*

You know you are not in El Bosque when you enter this brightly colored café. A giant mural adds to the bohemian air. Sandwiches, especially pitas, are the specialty of the house.

DULCERIA LAS PALMAS, *Antontia Lopez de Bello 0190. Metro Baquedano. Inexpensive. Credit cards accepted.*

This small café packs them in at lunch. With a covered patio that opens on to the street, Las Palmas is a good place to watch life unfold on the streets of Bella Vista. Artists and bands hang notices on the front door of upcoming events and some even hang shows inside. It's a good place to grab a cup of coffee, read the paper, and feel part of the Bella Vista scene. The desserts are delicious.

PROVIDENCIA
Chilean Food in Providencia

AQUI ESTÁ COCO, *La Concepción 236. Tel. 235-8649. Metro Leones. Expensive. Credit cards accepted.*

This renowned seafood restaurant offers the freshest ingredients from Chile's shores, exquisitely prepared and served among playful nautical décor. You can start below deck in the wine cellar bar with the requisite *pisco sour*. *Machas a la parmesana*, razor clams on the half shell, should be next as they are prepared better no where else. For dessert, try the extraordinary chocolate marquise with raspberry sauce. One eccentricity of this upscale eatery is a gift shop selling quality lapis jewelry and aprons imprinted with the *pisco sour* recipe.

CANTO DEL AGUA, *Nueva de Lyon 0129. Tel. 233-1175. Metro Leones. Moderate/expensive. Credit cards accepted.*

Their slogan is that they have the freshest seafood, and you won't doubt it after a meal here. It makes it both easy and hard to decide what to order when you know that everything is going to be good.

Other Food in Providencia
CASA DE CULTURA DE MEXICO, *Bucarest 162. Tel. 334-3848. Closed Sunday. Metro Los Leones. Moderate. No cards.*

Part of the Mexican Embassy, the Casa de Cultura houses a shop with Mexican handicrafts as well as this restaurant. It is the only place in Santiago for authentic, not Tex-Mex, Mexican food. High quality tequila, margaritas, and Mexican beers set the stage for the flavor celebration of well-prepared Mexican food. We recommend the *taquitos*, followed by tortilla soup, and then either the enchiladas or even the mole. *Buen provecho.*

EL HUERTO, *Orrego Luco 54. Tel. 233-2690. Metro Los Leones. Moderate. Credit cards accepted.*

Vegetarians will be happy to know that El Huerto has been servicing the meatless crowd for 18 years. Offering the finest in fruits and vegetables, their specialties of the house depend on what's in season. The whole grain breads, pasta dishes, and vegetable casseroles are all excellent. Freshly squeezed juices are a popular favorite. You can check the bulletin board on your way in for information about upcoming events, yoga, reflexology and the like. **La Huerta**, *next door, inexpensive*, serves the same type food but is only open for lunch.

PIZZA NOSTRA, *Providencia 1975. Tel. 231-9853. Metro Tobalaba. Moderate. Credit cards accepted.*

This upscale Italian restaurant offers a full range of dishes from each region of Italy. We have enjoyed the calamari, pizza, and lasagna. Stay away from the risotto as is it not quite up to par. There are two other branches at *Las Condes 6757 and Luis Thayer Ojeda 019.*

LE FLAUBERT, *Orrego Luco 125. Tel 231-9424. Moderate. Credit cards accepted.*

Dinner on the patio of this small French restaurant is delightful on a summer evening. The service is excellent, the food authentic, and the price extremely reasonable.

BRAVISSIMO, *Providencia 1408. Tel. 235-2511. 8am-11pm, Metro Manuel Montt. Inexpensive. No credit cards.*

There is no better ice cream in Chile. Once you taste it you'll want it every day. Try *manjar* combined with anything.

EL BOSQUE
Chilean Food in El Bosque
COCO LOCO, *El Bosque Norte 0215. Tel 231-3082. Metro Tobalaba. Expensive/very expensive. Credit cards accepted.*

Seafood is the specialty here. The nautical décor is reminiscent of Chilean coastal towns; there is even half of a real fishing boat in the restaurant with tables inside it. The clientele is mainly tourists, but that's due to the price, not the quality of the food. You should try the overflowing *parrillada Coco Loco*, which is a delicious combination of grilled shellfish and fish in a special sauce. Especially noteworthy is the wine list, which includes up and coming Chilean vineyards.

If you've just got to have steak, the **Hereford Grill** down the street at *El Bosque Norte 0355*, serves some of the tenderest beef in town.

EL MADROÑAL, *Vitacura 2911. Tel. 233-6312. Metro Tobalaba. Expensive. Credit cards accepted.*

El Madroñal features Chilean seafood with a Spanish twist. Upper class *Santiaguinos* enjoy the outstanding service at both lunch and dinner. A delicious dish, and one that is fun to see served, is the fish baked in a salt crust. It is not salty, but rather perfectly spiced, flaky and tender.

Other Food in El Bosque
PUERTO RENATO, *Goyenechea 3471. Tel. 231-2798. Metro El Golf. Expensive. Credit cards accepted.*

The kind of almost cheesy, informal décor hides an excellent restaurant underneath. Specializing in both seafood and pasta, Puerto Renato is a favorite of older upper class Chileans for its excellent service, extensive wine list, and scrumptious fare. You know you're living high on the hog when you indulge in the fettuccini with salmon and caviar. Julio Iglesias, amongst other famous Latinos, has dined here.

TAJ MAHAL, *Goyenechea 3215. Tel. 232-3606. Metro El Golf. Expensive. Credit cards accepted.*

While India and Chile may seem incongruous, there's a method to our madness. Lamb, raised by the thousands in Magallanes, is rarely on Santiago menus. The Taj Mahal, however, serves a host of delectable lamb dishes accompanied by curries and other spices. The other dishes are delicious as well. Anup, the general manager, personally takes each table's order. He's a good salesman, so be aware that most dishes are large enough to split.

SHOOGUN, *Enrique Foster Norte 172. Tel. 231-1604. Metro El Golf. Moderate. Credit cards accepted.*

While traditional Japanese food isn't something you would think of trying in Chile, the raw materials are uniquely Chilean. Fresh Chilean whitefish, *lenguado* and *renato*, makes especially fine sushi and sashimi. If you have four or more people you can get a private, Japanese-style room upstairs at no extra cost. The service is excellent and the teak interior calm and relaxing. Reservations are recommended.

If they are full you can try **Sushihana**, *Vitacura 2874, Tel.233-2801, Metro Tobalaba, moderate, credit cards accepted.*

FRIDAY'S, *Goyenechea 3275. Tel. 334-4468, 12pm-2am. Metro El Golf. Moderate/expensive. American Express only.*

We would never eat at T.G.I. Friday's in the US, but sometimes our hamburger cravings in Chile are too strong to overcome. They have numerous televisions in the restaurant and bar tuned to sporting events, if there is an important game you must catch.

DA DINO, *Apoquindo 4228. Tel. 208-1344. Metro Alcantara. Moderate. No credit cards.*

Da Dino's has been a Santiago fixture for over 40 years. Pizza and sandwiches are what they do, and they have gotten the formula right. The pizza, dripping with cheese, has excellent crunchy crust that is baked on the premises. There is an awesome array of desserts in the attached bakery. The downtown branch, at *O'Higgins 737*, is less expensive as it's stand-up only.

NEW YORK BAGEL BAKERY, *Roger de Flor 2894. Tel. 246-3060. 7:30am-9pm. Metro El Golf. Inexpensive. No credit cards.*

This place fits the bill for good, inexpensive bagels and cream cheeses. They also have nice sandwiches, salads, and desserts for dollars less than Au Bon Pain.

AU BON PAIN, *Apoquindo 3575. El Bosque Norte 0181, World Trade Center, and El Bosque Sur 55. Inexpensive/moderate. Credit cards accepted.*

"The Good Pain" as we call it, used to be the only place in town for bagels, for which they charged an arm and a leg. The New York Bagel Bakery changed that. The Au Bon Pain chain still offers great sandwiches, fresh juices, and salads. It's a quick, easy place to get a healthy lunch.

FOOD GARDEN, *Roger de Flor and El Bosque Norte. Metro Tobalaba. Inexpensive.*

This food court serves up a bit of everything. It's a good inexpensive option for the area.

OUR FAVORITE INTERNATIONAL EATERIES IN SANTIAGO

- *Gato Pardo* - *Mediterranean, Historical Center*
- *El Otro Sitio* – *Peruvian, Bellavista*
- *Casa de Cultura de Mexico* – *Mexican, Providencia*
- *Shoogun* – *Japanese, El Bosque*
- *Anakena* – *Thai, Las Condes*

LAS CONDES
Chilean Food in Las Condes
LAS URRACAS, *Vitacura 9254. Tel. 212-0860. Expensive. Credit cards accepted.*

Las Urracas has put together a menu that we call Chil-Mex. While many of the plates are similar to Mexican dishes, they have their own Chilean flare. The appetizers especially focus on Chilean specialties. One dish we recommend is the extremely tasty black bean soup. *Cuecos*, or Chilean yuppies, are the main clientele so it's a good place to people watch. You can enjoy live music on the weekends and there is a disco next door.

HOSTERÍA DONA TINA, *Camino Los Refugios 15125, Arrayan. Tel. 217-1691. Moderate. Credit cards accepted.*

The *Santiaguinos* are slow to the get-go on weekends. When they finally do get rolling, many head out to Arrayan and settle in for a homestyle meal at Dona Tina's. Fresh salsa and bread are set on the table upon arrival. We recommend *bistec a lo pobre* or *porotos granados*, depending on how healthy you feel. There is ample outdoor seating under the ivy-covered trellis during summer and an open hearth inside in the winter.

The owner, Dona Tina, is an inspiration in Chile, a rare example of breaking through the rigid socio-economic strata. As a young woman she emigrated to Santiago from the countryside and worked as a laundress. She began selling homemade baked goods, first to her laundry clients, then from a roadside stand, and finally in her own restaurant. You'll probably see her, shy and successful, as you taste what she does best.

TIP Y TAP, *Las Condes 6851. Tel. 201-2527. Moderate. Credit cards accepted.*

Whenever we go mountain biking nearby we stop afterwards at Tip y Tap and undo all the good we've just done to our bodies. The outdoor seating and huge grassy space in front make it a summertime favorite. The Barros Luco come loaded with steak and melted cheese and the Royal Guard beer is cold so there is no reason to be in a hurry. It's also a good place to stop on the way back from the slopes.

Other Food in Las Condes
ANAKENA, *inside the Hyatt at Kennedy 4601. Tel. 218-1234. Expensive. Credit cards accepted.*

We usually don't recommend eating at hotels, but make an exception for the Anakena. The salad bar overflows with at least 25 options ranging from artichoke hearts to baby corn. The restaurant is set up market-style where you pick out your meat from behind the glass and tell them how you want it cooked. The green curry amps up all the food, but is especially good on the Chilean salmon. Try to get a table outside where you can enjoy the sound of waterfalls and chirping birds while you sip your *pisco* sour or industrial-sized G&T.

MIRADOR LOS FAISANES, *La Pirámide. Tel. 242-7575. Expensive. Credit cards accepted.*

People come here for the view. Set on the side of the hill known as La Pirámide, the restaurant offers international food with the lights of Santiago twinkling below. Romantic couples come to dance to the toned down big band music, while corporate execs choose the Mirador to impress out of town visitors.

SANTA FE, *Las Condes 10690. Tel. 215-1091. Moderate/expensive. Credit cards accepted.*

Owned by a Canadian, Santa Fe is the Tex-Mex locale of choice in Chile (very international.) Crowds of people, Chilean and foreign, enjoy the fajítas and margaritas every night. Reservations are necessary.

QUICK FOOD FIXES

If you are in a hurry and need a quick bite, Chilean bakeries are a great alternative. There are two large chains with outlets all over town – **Fuch's** *and* **La Castaña**, *as well as countless small shops.*

Other parts of town

GRAN VISTA, *La Reina Alta, Talinay 11040 in the Club de Equitación. Tel. 275-0010. 5:30pm-12:00pm Tuesday-Friday, 1:00pm-4:00pm and 5:30pm-12:00pm Saturday, 1:00pm-4:00pm Sunday. Expensive. Credit cards accepted.*

The Gran Vista offers exactly what its name promises – an excellent view. Perched on the edge of the foothills, the restaurant serves Chilean cuisine with all of Santiago spread out below. It is especially lovely at dinner when the lights of town twinkle and shimmer.

The Gran Vista specializes in Patagonian fare like lamb on the spit, king crab, and seafood. The lamb is outstanding, especially when covered with sauce made from *calafate* berries. The *pisco* sours should not be missed and they have an excellent and large array of Chilean wines.

It feels like you are out in the country when you eat here, but it is conveniently only about 15 minutes from El Bosque.

LA CASA VIEJA, *Nuñoa, Chile España 249. Tel. 204-7624. Moderate/Expensive. Credit cards accepted.*

The *parrillada*, or grilled meat, is the specialty here. More than anything, the Casa Vieja is a chance to see the heart of middle-class Santiago and know that you are going to get an excellent meal as well.

DONDE ANA MARIA, *Club Hípico, Club Hípico 476. Tel. 698-4064. Moderate. Credit cards accepted.*

Completely off by itself in a residential neighborhood close to the train station, Ana Maria is famous for serving top quality seafood at an affordable price. The restaurant has grown over the years as has the reputation, slightly boosting prices. Ask the waiter what's the freshest, *mas fresco*, and go with that. Reservations are recommended.

LA CUCA, *Departamental Street at the Vespucio traffic circle. Moderate. Credit cards accepted.*

Middle class Chileans throng to La Cuca to celebrate birthdays, anniversaries, and new jobs. A humongous dancehall with rows and rows of tables covering about half the floor, this place rocks on the weekends. Everybody orders the same thing, the *parrillada*, which comes as heaps of sizzling meat. The salsa dancing cranks up after dinner. This is a place the normally subdued Chileans cut loose. It's most fun if you go in a big group.

EL RINCON DE LA BOTA, *Nuñoa, Jose Domingo Cañas 2229. Tel. 205-2105. Moderate/expensive. Credit cards accepted.*

Hearty Spanish food in a cheery atmosphere is what you get at the Rincón. The rich *fabada*, bean stew, is our favorite dish. Another one to get your mouth watering is the fragrant *pulpo a la gallega*. Cañas is a modest street that sports a number of good restaurants. It's an interesting contrast from the upper class El Bosque street.

SEEING THE SIGHTS

You can fit the most important points of interest in Santiago into one day if you really hustle. You could do it more comfortably in two days, reserving one day for the *centro* and the second day for everything outside of the *centro*. However, you could easily keep busy for a week if you hit every worthwhile attraction in town and added a few day trips.

HISTORICAL CENTER

The best place to begin a *centro* tour is in the lively **Plaza de Armas**. It is not only the center of the city, but also of the country, because it is from here that all distances to other Chilean cities are measured. Pedro Valdivia picked this spot as the town square in 1541 choosing a lot for himself on the northwest corner where the Central Post Office is currently located. The first building erected was a gun powder magazine.

Currently the square is a collage of yellow park benches, balloon animals, historic statues, pigeons, shady palms, old time photographers, caricaturists, raspy, insistent Evangelists, and hustling shoe shiners. A raised amphitheater is the chess playing center, featuring checkered boards painted directly onto the cement tables.

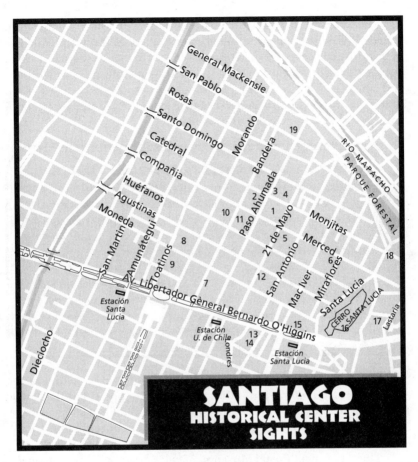

SANTIAGO HISTORICAL CENTER SIGHTS

1. Plaza de Armas
2. Catedral
3. Correo Central
4. National History Museum
5. Casa Colorada Museum
6. Basilica
7. Bolsa de Comercio
8. Plaza de la Constitución
9. Palacio La Moneda
10. Tribunales de Justicia
11. PreColumbian Museum
12. Templo San Francisco
13. Iglesia San Francisco
14. San Francisco Colonial Museum
15. Biblioteca Nacional
16. Cerro Santa Lucia
17. Plaza Mulato Gil
18. Bellas Artes
19. Mercado Cenntral

The **Catedral** is situated on the west side of the plaza. This is the third church built on the site. Earthquakes destroyed the previous two. The current structure was finished by the architect Joaquin Toesca in 1789 in neoclassical style. The primary altar is of white marble inlaid with bronze and lapis lazuli. There are altars dedicated to Santiago, the patron saint of the city and another to Santa Teresa de los Andes, Chile's first saint. A small museum is attached to the cathedral.

SANTIAGO'S ARCHITECT JOAQUIN TOESCA

The Italian born Joaquin Toesca was working in Madrid when he was invited to Santiago by the Chilean government in 1780 to design the La Moneda mint. Toesca would not stop with that extraordinary project, recognized as the supreme example of neoclassic architecture in Latin America. He went on to revamp the plan for the historical center as well as design the Cathedral, Santo Domingo Church, the Governor's House, the Town Council Building, and the Calicanto Bridge. He also built several private houses as well as structures outside of Santiago. After training a legion of disciples to carry on the neoclassical tradition, Toesca died in Santiago in 1799. His remains are encrypted in the San Francisco Church.

The lavish pink building catty-corner from the Cathedral is the **Correo Central**, central post office. It was built in post-renaissance style in 1880 using the partial walls of the two previous buildings situated there, those of the colonial Governor's palace and the later presidential palace. The building's steel-girded, skylit third floor was added in 1908.

There is a small **Postal Museum**, *Monday-Friday 8:30am-5pm*, on the second floor. Take the metal cage elevator up and walk ahead to your right to find the entrance. The museum features an exhibit with stamps from nearly every country in the world as well as antique canceling machines. You should at least step into the ground floor of the building for a look around. Being surrounded by luminescent pink makes you feel like you've returned to the womb. There are post cards and stamps for sale in the lobby so you can take advantage of the plaza benches or nearby cafes to write a few and send them off before losing momentum.

PALACIO DE LA REAL AUDIENCIA, NATIONAL HISTORY MUSEUM, *Plaza de Armas. Tuesday-Saturday 10am-5:30pm, Sunday 10am-1:30pm. Entry $1.50.*

The building that houses the museum was designed by Juan Goyacola, a student of Joaquin Toesca. Built in 1807, it was used as the Supreme Court by the Spanish colonial government for two years, then housed the sessions of the Chilean government beginning in 1810. The 12,000 piece museum, an extensive tribute to dandified white guys with guns, is less interesting than other museums in town. You get a better sense of colonial history by visiting the compact Casa Colorada on the other side of the square. Unless you are on the seven day *centro* tour, we suggest saving your attention span for other exhibits.

Passing the Municipal Building (constructed in 1895) on your left, taking a left on 21 de Mayo and following it for one block to the corner of Santo Domingo, will place you in front of the **Iglesia de Santo Domingo**. There has been bad luck for churches here, with the first three being destroyed by earthquakes, and the current one, finished in 1795, having been gutted twice by fires, most recently in 1963. The neoclassic design with baroque elements was the work of another Toesca disciple, architect Juan de los Santo Vasconcellos, while under the supervision of his instructor.

Return to the plaza, via 21 de Mayo and follow that to Merced Street. Here, on the northwest corner of the plaza, you will see the beautiful **Edificio Eduards**, which currently houses a children's store on the bottom floor. This steel building was prefabricated in France and assembled on this corner in 1893.

CASA COLORADA, MUSEO DE SANTIAGO, *Merced 860. Tel. 633-0723. Tuesday-Friday 10am-6pm, Saturday 10am-5pm, Sunday 11am-2pm. Entry $1.*

The color and height of this colonial home is so subtle among the grandeur surrounding it, that it's easy to walk right by the 230 year old structure. The edifice was built in 1769 as a home for Don Mateo Zambrano y Toro, a shopkeeper by trade and the president of the first creole junta in 1810, a ruling body which preceded Chile's independent government. The bottom floor served as the retail area and the top floor as a residence for his family. Currently it houses the unique **Santiago Museum**. The entertaining display outlines the history of the city utilizing two inch high wood carvings positioned within intricate dioramas. You must see the hundreds of expressive figurines carved by Rodolfo Gutiérrez to appreciate the distinctive craftsmanship that was dedicated to each one. The originality of the exhibit and the well-preserved condition of colonial building makes this one of the worthwhile museums in Santiago. The artist also has exhibits in the Calicanto Metro and at the Galería Histórico in the city of Concepción. If you are interested in his work, you can contact him at *Tel. 321-6151.*

The **Municipal Tourist Office**, *Merced 860, Tel. 632-7785*, is just to one side of the Casa Colorada museum entrance. The office has a helpful bilingual staff which can assist you with any questions about the city. Continue down Merced walking away from the plaza another two blocks until you hit MacIver.

SANTIAGO'S NEOCLASSIC ARCHITECTURE

*Many of Santiago's prominent buildings were constructed in the late 18th century in neoclassical style. **Neoclassicism**, a movement spanning from 1750-1830, rejuvenated ancient Greek and Roman architectural elements. At the time, the emerging science of archaeology uncovered ancient cities such as Pompeii, stimulating an interest in classical antiquity. The newly rediscovered Greco-Roman elements provided the perfect reaction against the decorative Rococo and deceptive Baroque styles which then dominated the architectural scene.*

Although the ruins were in Rome, Italians contributed relatively little to the movement. The center of activity was the French Academy, with the leading designers being French, German, and English. Neoclassical architecture was built throughout South America where initially the most important architects were French. Santiago's most influential neoclassicist, ironically, was an Italian, Joaquin Toesca.

Typical qualities identified in neoclassical buildings include grandeur of scale, strict geometric symmetry, a preference for blank walls, and dramatic use of columns, particularly to articulate interior spaces.

BASILICA MERCED & MUSEUM, *Corner of Merced and Mac-Iver. Tel. 633-0691. Monday-Friday 10am-1pm and 3pm-6pm. Entry $1.*

This is another earthquake-racked site. The third and current church was finished by the hardest working man in Santiago's architecture business, Joaquin Toesca. The most interesting feature inside is the virgin, *Nuestra Señora de La Merced* (Our Lady of Mercy), brought to Chile from Spain in 1548. The neoclassic design is enhanced by the peeling, blood-red paint on the facade and two steeples, one with a clock.

The museum entrance is located to the right of the church entrance. Ring the bell if the door is locked during operating hours. The ground floor opens to a pleasant courtyard garden. The museum, located upstairs on the second floor, is small, but intriguing. One of the rooms has an exhibit of a popular craft from the 18th century. Baby Jesus images, imported from Quito, Ecuador, were placed under room-service size domes of French glass, and decorated by the Chileans with frilly accouterments.

In another area is one of the best Easter Island exhibits in Chile. It includes numerous, severely grinning wooden Maoai sculptures, as well as one of the few original Rongo Rongo tablets engraved with the indecipherable native language of the island. There is a not-so-subtle positioning of a towering Savior statue between the two largest Maoai statues.

From the Basilica Merced walk south one block taking a right on the pedestrian street of Huérfanos. **Huérfanos**, along with **Paseo Ahumada** which it crosses in a few blocks, are the two main pedestrian thoroughfares of downtown Santiago. Blocked to vehicle traffic, the streets fill up with thousands of downtown office workers hustling to their destinations.

COFFEE WITH LEGS

*Along the pedestrian streets of Huérfanos and Paseo Ahumada, you will encounter a distinct coffee culture known as cafe con piernas (coffee with legs), a play on the Spanish cafe con leche. Various chains, including the most popular **Cafe Caribe** and **Cafe Haiti**, feature well-cleaved women in tight, skimpy dresses (risky aesthetics), thick panty hose, and teetering high heels who serve espressos to patrons standing at the coffee counters.*

To initiate the ritual, buy a ticket from the window for an espresso (cafe express), or coffee with milk (cafe con leche). In return for the ticket, one of the heavily eye-lined ladies will serve you a demi-tasse of coffee, spooning in sugar and stirring it for you, along with a side glass of mineral water. It is customary to leave a 50 or 100 peso coin as a tip for the waitress. Although females might feel uncomfortable in some of the more remotely-located coffee bars, Chilean women comprise about one-third of the patrons in the most popular locales.

Continuing west on Huérfanos, take a left on Banderas. At the corner of Banderas and Moneda, you will find a diagonal side street which runs along the **Bolsa de Comercio** (stock market) building. If you want to watch the activity in the trading room, you can leave a piece of identification with the guard in exchange for a visitor tag. Look for the door that says "Sala de Ruedas" and go in. You must arrive before 1pm to observe the trading.

Returning to Moneda street and continuing west will take you to the expansive, austere **Plaza de Constitución**. The overriding astringency of the plaza when compared to any other public square is dramatic. It seems to be an intentional communication on behalf of the former military regime to demonstrate its seriousness of purpose.

The **Palacio de La Moneda** presidential palace dominates the south side of the plaza. Recognized as the finest example of Latin American neoclassical architecture, the Spanish royal mint was designed by Joaquin Toesca, and built from 1784-1799. The edifice served as the colonial mint until President Manuel Bulnes moved in. It functioned as the presidential residence until 1958 and is currently the presidential headquarters as well as the governmental palace. Chilean presidents now reside in their personal homes.

The most poignant day of Chilean history, which marks the La Moneda with infamy, was September 11, 1973. Salvador Allende arrived with a few of his ministers that morning to find the building surrounded by military personnel. Over the course of the morning the coup d'etat forces, led by General Augusto Pinochet, battered the facade with tank fire as well as inflicting a 15 minute bombing from the air. President Salvador de Allende radioed his last address, then committed suicide with the submachine gun he had been using to defend the palace. Fires within building burned throughout the evening.

ALLENDE'S FINAL RADIO ADDRESS

*During the waning hours of the military coup of 1973, one radio station remained on the air broadcasting with an emergency transmitter. President **Salvador Allende** had a direct line to the station from a telephone on his desk. He spoke calmly for about three minutes, ending his speech with this emotional declaration:*

"You, the people, must defend yourselves, but not sacrifice yourselves. You should not allow yourself to be cowed or mowed down, but neither should you be humiliated.

Workers of my fatherland, I have faith in Chile and in its destiny. Other men will overcome this dark and bitter moment that betrayal would impose on us. Continue believing that, much sooner than later, once again the grand promenades will be opened on which free men walk to construct a better society.

Viva Chile! Viva the people! Long live the workers!

These are my last words, and I am certain that my sacrifice will not be in vain; I am certain that, at the very least, it will be a moral lesson that will punish felony, cowardice, and treason."

Although there are no regular tours of the La Moneda building, with luck you can arrange one by filling out an application in the downstairs office at Morande 130. The entrance is actually located on the plaza itself, in a stairwell about halfway down the block the east side. You must apply at least three days before you hope to receive the tour. You can indicate the preferred visit date on the application. The application asks for passport numbers of all people to go on the tour and a contact telephone number (preferably your hotel in Chile) to confirm the time. You can also fax your full name, passport number, telephone number, and preferred visit date to *Oscar Pizarro, Administrative Director, Fax 56/2/690-4096; Tel. 56/2/690-4373.*

Although not major attractions, there are a couple of places on the plaza worth hitting as long as you are there. Step inside the **Intendencia** building on the corner of Morande and Moneda to take a look around. With permission from the reception desk you can walk up the stairs to admire the beautiful stained glass dome and murals. On the opposite side of the plaza is the **Carrera Hotel**. The Rooftop Garden Restaurant in the hotel has great views of the plaza and the city, but it is not a cheap snack stop.

Walking north on Morande street two blocks will take you to the **Tribunales de Justicia**, where Chile's Supreme Court is located. A latecomer to Santiago's neoclassic architectural scene, it was built in 1929 and designed by Emilio Doyere. The building possesses a spectacular interior hall, three stories high, that runs the length of an entire block and is capped by a steel and glass vaulted ceiling. If you leave a piece of identification with the guards, you can wander around inside. It's worth doing.

Across the street from the Tribunales is the **Ex-Congreso Nacional**, where the National Congress met until disolved in 1973, then was relocated to Valparaíso in 1988. The neoclassic building dates back to 1901. A well-maintained public garden surrounds the structure. This is a great place to take a load off your feet if you need a rest.

REAL CASA DE ADUANA, MUSEO CHILENO DE ARTE PRECOLOMBINO, *Bandera 361. Tel. 695-3851. Tuesday-Saturday 10am-6pm, Sunday 10am-6pm. Entry $3.50.*

The neoclassic structure, which houses the Pre-Columbian museum, was built as the Royal Customs House in 1805. The museum exhibits indigenous art of the Americas, covering the area from Mexico to the Southern Andes. With seven exhibit rooms, five of which are permanent displays, the museum is manageable enough to enjoy even if you are not a big fan of indigenous artifacts. The Andean rooms display intricate wood and stone carvings, bug-eyed with lápiz lazuli inlay, including dart shooters and drug paraphernalia. The exhibits are successfully designed to stimulate your imagination and absorb your attention. A single piece is given its own unique space under a spotlight, rather than crowding several objects together. This strategy, along with backdrops of bold colors, makes this one of the most enjoyable pre-Columbian museums you will encounter. On the bottom floor are a good bookshop and a courtyard area with an Au Bon Pain coffee and sandwich kiosk.

From the museum, walk two blocks south on Banderas to Agustinas. Take a left on Agustinas following it two blocks until you reach the brilliant green **Templo San Agustín** with bright yellow pillars. The temple suffered several rounds of earthquake damage since its construction in 1707. The last major reconstruction added the six exterior columns in 1863. The interior of this church is richly adorned with gold trimmed pillars. Sculptured reliefs, surrounded by murals, highlight the ceiling. On the north altar is the Cristo de Mayo whose crown fell to his neck in the May 1647 earthquake. His face reportedly bled as a cause of the accident. The miraculous bleeding was celebrated each May with a procession carrying the sculpture through the streets. There is also an altar with a statue of Santa Rita de Casia, *abogada de lo imposible*, the mediator of the impossible. You will find hundreds of plaques with prayers posted near her altar.

One block to the east on the corner of Agustinas and San Antonio, you will encounter the **Municipal Theater**, originally designed by the French architect Francisco Brunet de Baines in 1857. Ballet and concerts are performed here. *The box office is open Monday-Friday, 10am-6pm, Tel. 633-0752.*

Walk south on San Antonio to cross the broad Libertador General Bernardo O'Higgins Avenue (commonly referred to by its prior name the Alameda). Here you will encounter a wall of the massive Iglesia San Francisco. The church faces west toward a small plaza. Alongside of the church is the San Francisco Colonial Museum.

IGLESIA SAN FRANCISCO, *Libertador General Bernardo O'Higgins 834.*

The oldest church preserved in Chile was built from 1586 to 1618 as a monument for the Virgin de Socorro, the patron saint that Pedro de Valdivia brought from Spain to guide him in his exploration of the new world. Valdivia petitioned the mayor for land on which to build an altar for the virgin and was given this parcel, then considered to lie a great distance from the city center. Upon Valdivia's death, the Franciscan Friar Antonio began construction of the church. The bell tower was added in 1857.

Inside, wide brick archways break the continuity of the church's nave. Valdivia's Virgin de Socorro is the diminutive figure on the main altar. Note the intricately carved, multi-tiered, wood panel which steps down from the ceiling. Among the remains stored here are those of Valdivia's wife Marina Ortiz de Gaete, as well as the Italian architect Joaquin Toesca.

SAN FRANCISCO COLONIAL MUSEUM, *Londres 4. Tel. 639-8737. Tuesday-Saturday 10am-1:30pm/3pm-6pm, Sunday 10am-2pm. Entry $1.*

The **Colonial Museum** is built around a verdant cloister in what was a convent next to the church. The exhibits in the church are eclectic and include an array of religious art such as the fascinating Cristo Chilote, a three foot crucifix featuring a haunting, sinuous Jesus, carved in 1780 on the island of Chiloé. Other interesting exhibits include an antique lock room and a shrine that might cause you to mistake Gabriela Mistral for a saint rather than a poet. There are two rooms full of enormous Cuzco school paintings detailing the life of San Francisco de Asís. You gotta love big art and there are 54 pieces of it in these two rooms alone. The exhibits are much more intriguing than what you would expect from a colonial museum housed in a church.

You might want to walk down Londres street to check out the artsy Bohemian neighborhood of Paris/Londres. Most of the buildings here were built in 1920-1930. Cross the Alameda and head east on it until you reach the National Library.

BIBLIOTECA NACIONAL, *Libertador Bernardo O'Higgins 651, Tel. 630-5259. E-mail memoria@oris.renib.cl. Monday-Friday 9:15am-6pm, Saturday 9:15am-3pm. No admission fee.*

The magnificent National Library elegantly consumes an entire city block. Built in 1925 in French neoclassical style by the architect Gustavo Garcia del Postigo, the library houses 3.5 million volumes making it among the largest libraries in Latin America. Step inside to explore the labyrinth of spiraling marble stairways on your own, or you can call or e-mail ahead of time to arrange a guided tour in English. The walls are decorated with murals by the Chilean painters Arturo Gordon and Alfredo Helsby. Ground floor rooms are separated by impressively hand-crafted wooden window panes that climb twenty feet toward the ceiling. If you investigate the the second floor you will find the expansive Gabriel Mistral reading room at the top of one stairway and at the top of another, the Don Jose Toribio Medina alcove, richly paneled in dark oak and lined with black wrought iron balconies. The library hosts a multitude of free concerts and other cultural events which you can find posted in the entryways or in the Sunday edition of *El Mercurio* newspaper.

Continuing east on the Alameda will take you to **Cerro San Lucia**. The hill was named by Pedro de Valdivia on the December 13th, 1540 for the corresponding saint day of Santa Lucia. Vicuna Mackenna transformed the 69 meter hill into a park in 1874 and initiated the planting of a thousand trees on the premises. Climbing to the replica of a medieval castle gives you a fantastic view of Santiago from which you can see the spires of the city's churches poking up between the aging skyscrapers and utilitarian office buildings. Considering the Chileans' normal penchant for public sanitation and safety, the park is uncharacteristically unkempt and somewhat dangerous. We were hassled repeatedly by shysters and given the willies by solitary, inescapable, foul smelling passageways. The backside of the park is one of the few places in Chile that we've felt uncomfortable walking during the daytime.

There is a good arts and crafts market across the Alameda from Cerro Santa Lucia. The **Centro Artesanal de Santa Lucia** is open everyday from about 11am-8pm. It is clean and has a lively atmosphere accented by Chilean rock music projected from the stalls. You can buy everything from Chilean artisan work to a tattoo to framed photos of the Bee Gees.

A block to the east of Cerro San Lucia on Victorino Latarria you will find several good lunch restaurants including Gatopardo and Les Asseseins which we cover in our *Where to Eat* section. Additionally, the art center **Plaza Mulato Gil** on Victorino Latarria has a pleasant open air cafeteria. On Saturday mornings there is a small flea market in the plaza. The shops in the building surrounding the plaza are mainly bookstores, a few small galleries, and artist studios. Upstairs you will find the **Santiago Archaeological Museum**, *Plaza Mulato Gil, 2nd floor, Monday-Friday 10am-2pm/3:30pm-6pm, Saturday 10am-2pm, Sunday closed.* This small museum is just the right size to present an overview of the Chile's regional indigenous groups. One entertaining exhibit features the fez-like caps worn by the inhabitants of the Atacama desert.

PALACIO COUSINO, *Dieciocho 438. Tel. 698-5063. Tuesday-Sunday 9:30am-1:30pm/2:30 pm-5pm. Entry $2.*

This is a bit removed from the rest of the centro so you should consider taking a taxi, then return to O'Higgins via Calle Dieciocho to admire the turn-of-the-century mansions lining that street.

The Cousiño palace was built in 1878 for Isidora Goyanechea, Luis Cousiño's widow. The family owned carbon mines, silver mines, a commercial shipping company, and a vineyard in Macul that still belongs to the clan. The vineyard sells wine under the respected "Cousiño Macul" label. The mansion was frequently the buzz of Santiago high society at the turn-of-the-century with modern accouterments such as the first elevator in Chile that was operated by water weight. It was also the first building with central heating. Designed by the French architect, Paul Lathoud, much of the colorful tile was imported from Italy. The wood originated from various countries, hallways and rooms were finished with cedar, American oak, ebony, and black walnut. The family's furnishings were donated to the city along with house so it maintains the same ambience as it did a century ago. The walls are adorned with 18th century paintings from European and Chilean artists. Since 1940's the Chilean government has used the house as residence for foreign dignitaries such as Charles de Guale and Golda Meir.

Two expansive parks located just outside of the city center are **Parque O'Higgin's** and **Parque Quinta Normal**. Both parks fill up on the weekends with Santiaguinos looking for a bit of green on which to picnic and kick around a soccer ball. If you are willing to take the time to get to one of these parks, you would probably be much more satisfied by opting for the Nature Sanctuary in Arrayan where you can avoid the crowds.

PARQUE QUINTA NORMAL, *Av. Matucana, 8am-8:30pm.*

This 40 hectare park is located to the west of the Pan-American highway. Along with the lagoons and open picnic areas, the park is home to the **Natural History Museum**, *Tel. 681-4095, Tuesday-Saturday 10am-5:30pm, Sunday 12pm-5:30pm.* Other museums in the park include the **Science and Technology Museum** as well as the **Railroad Museum**.

PARQUE O'HIGGINS, *Metro Line 2, Parque O'Higgin's station. Daily 9am-7pm.*

This is another seemingly endless park, well-worn due to its popularity with the city's residents. There are two small museums in the park, **Mueso del Huaso**, *Monday-Friday 10am-5pm, Saturday-Sunday 10am-2pm* and an **Insect Museum**, *Daily 10am-8pm.* Both of these are located in the **El Pueblito** area, a long corridor of souvenir shops, snack bars, and restaurants. Also located in the park is the popular amusement park **Fantasialandia**, *Tuesday-Friday 2pm-8pm, Saturday-Sunday 11am-8pm. Entry $8.50.*

ONE VERY BUSY DAY IN SANTIAGO

These are the most important spots to hit in a one day Santiago tour. If you fit all this in, you will have earned the right kick your feet up and sip a pisco sour.

- *Plaza de Armas and Cathedral*
- *Casa Colorada Museum*
- *Real Casa De Aduana - PreColumbian Museum*
- *Tribunales de Justicia*
- *Plaza de la Constitución and La Moneda Palace*
- *Iglesia San Francisco and Museum*
- *Taxi to Parque Forestal and Bellas Artes*
- *La Chascona, Pablo Neruda Museum*
- *Funicular to the top of Cerro San Cristóbal*
- *Taxi to Los Dominicos (Graneros de Alba) Artisan Market*

FORESTAL PARK

Starting just a few blocks from Bellavista, this walking tour can be combined with the Bellavista tour if you have stamina. You might want to time it to eat at the Central Market or the Mapocho Station when you finish. Begin at the intersection of Pio Nono and the Costanera. Walking west through the park the tree shaded trails of this inner city refuge lead you past ornate fountains, statues, and monuments as well as couples of all ages making out on the benches.

The park, from 1900, is designed after European public spaces from the same era. The first monument, **The German Fountain**, *Fuente Alemán*, was given to the city by its *Deutsche* residents in 1910 to mark 100 years of Chilean independence from Spain. Try to guess which part of Chile each piece of the sculpture represents.

NATIONAL FINE ARTS MUSUEM AND PALACE, *Parque Forestal. Tel. 633-0655. 11am-7pm. Closed Monday. Entry $1.15.*

Regardless of the current exhibit, the *Palacio y Museo Nacional De Bellas Artes* merits a visit for its beautiful architecture. Opened on the centennial independence day in 1910, the neoclassical French style building houses thousands of works. The iron and glass cupola, designed in Belgium, allows natural light to spill into the central hall. Note the columns upstairs by the permanent exhibit and think about those poor ladies' heads. The gift shop, on the entry level, is stocked with standard museum shop inventory.

CONTEMPORARY ART MUSEUM, *Parque Forestal. Tel. 639-6488. 11am-7pm. Closed Monday. Entry 65¢.*

This museum, *Museo de Arte Contemporaneo*, is housed in the back half of the Bellas Artes building. Less grand than its counterpart on the front side, this part of the building has become a bit run down. Never the less, it shares the impressive iron and glass ceiling. Its exhibits, not surprisingly, tend to be more edgy than those displayed in the national museum.

Continue west in the park for two blocks until you reach bustling yellow market building.

CENTRAL MARKET, *Vergara and 21 de Mayo. Tel. 698-3771. 7am-3pm.*

This beautiful wrought iron structure was bought pre-fab in 1868. It was made in England and shipped to Chile to be used as a national art gallery. Now, transformed to the *Mercado Central*, it is a place of constant activity. You can wander through the stalls to ogle at pigs' heads, get a feel for Chilean seafood, or just head straight to one of the always-crowded lunch stands.

MAPOCHO STATION, *Tel. 361-1761. Hours depend on events.*

Across the bus and people-filled streets, at the end of the block, this cavernous iron building used to serve as the train station to Valparaiso. It now houses rotating events and concerts. The ornate lobby has beautiful stained glass at the ceilings and multiple domes. It's a lovely building and deserves a visit for that alone, but more importantly it serves as a refuge after the noise of the streets and the *mercado*. It is cool even in the heat of summer and is blessedly quiet, unless there is a major event. It houses a giftshop, bookstore, and café.

You can get back to your hotel via the metro or by taxi. The Calicanto metro station is between the market and the train station. You should walk

---

WHAT YOU CAN BUY IN THE METRO

Looking for a thingamajig? If in doubt, try the metro. You'll be amazed at the commerce going on underneath your feet. Passport photos, photocopies, baked goods, computer disks, sets of keys, books, and aspirin are just some of the items offered underground. The Calicanto, Los Leones, and Tobalaba stations are especially well-stocked.

---

down there even if you're not taking the subway to see both a section of the historic **Calicanto bridge** and a fascinating **diorama** by local artist Zerreitug.

BELLAVISTA

Bellavista, with it's older, brightly painted buildings and plethora of galleries and theater companies, is the artistic heart of Santiago. Known as the bohemian district, it offers visitors a distinct view of life in the big city. Things move slower here and are definitely on a different schedule. The numerous restaurants and bars don't fill up until past many people's bedtime. Even if you only have a short time in Santiago, Bellavista should be on your list.

From the **Baquedano metro station**, head north across the river. Pio Nono Street is one of two arteries into the neighborhood. As soon as you cross the bridge, you will see the **hippie market** in the Gomez Rojas Park on your left. Street buskers and groups of young people lend to the carnival atmosphere. Tie-dye clothes, beaded jewelry, and head shop paraphernalia seem to be the biggest sellers.

From there, take a right on Bellavista Avenue to visit the numerous **lapislazuli shops**. Lapis, as it's known in English, is a royal blue, semiprecious stone found only three places in the world. Chile is one of them.

Continuing down the street you will pass the **La Casa Larga Art Gallery**. It's the first of many galleries in this neighborhood that merit a peek. At the next corner, Mallinkrodt Street, take a left to truly enter the community. Charming little houses share walls on the tree-lined street with bars and restaurants. Continue down Mallinkrodt until it dead-ends on Antonia Lopez de Bello. Turn left to wander through the restaurants and art galleries. Take your time, enjoy a drink or cup of coffee in a café, and appreciate the uniqueness of this area.

After wandering through the shops, take a right on Constitución. One block down, the strangely angled Marquez de la Plata Street veers off to the right. Make your way around the corner to the whimsical treat of Pablo Neruda's restored house:

LA CHASCONA, *Marquez de la Plata 0192. Tel. 777-8741. 10am-1pm and 2:30pm-5:30pm Tuesday through Sunday. Entry $6.25 for a tour in English, $3.25 for Spanish.*

To walk through the doors of this residence turned museum is to wander about in the capricious mind of Chile's Nobel Prize winning poet, Pablo Neruda. The house is decorated with a bewildering array of his collections including glass paperweights, Latin American paintings, 19th century pornographic playing cards, wooden fish, clocks, seashells, and Russian dolls. Neruda, also a controversial politician, was recently re-popularized in the film *Il Postino* which touches upon his time in Italy.

The residence is named for Matilde Urratia, Neruda's third wife with whom he built the home. Her nickname La Chascona is an endearing term roughly translated as "Wild Hair." La Chascona will inspire you to explore Neruda's other two houses in Isla Negra and Valparaíso as well as to read his poetry.

WILD HAIR

*In a room of Neruda's Santiago home hangs a portrait of his wife **Matilde** by the Mexican muralist Diego Rivera. Rivera painted a hidden profile of Neruda in her flaming red locks with the explanation, "It is said that men hide themselves in their women. If this is true, then you could best hide yourself in Matilde's hair."*

Returning to Constitución, you continue along to the foot of Cerro San Cristobal. Pio Nono Street ends here as well. You can either enjoy the fare of the many eateries in the neighborhood or keep touring in one of two directions. You can head north, up to the top of Cerro San Cristobal, or south to the Forestal Park.

SAN CRISTOBAL HILL

Some days from the top of this hill you can see the city shining below; and beyond, the immense Andes standing tall. Other days, all you can see is smoggy Santiago. It's worth a trip to the top, even if it is polluted, to get a real sense of the city's layout below and hang out with *Santiguinos* in their backyard.

The entire foothill, *Cerro San Cristobal*, is a public area. There are gardens, restaurants, swimming pools, mountain biking trails, and a zoo all within its confines. This is not just a tourist spot, but rather a place for people from the city to stretch their legs. On weekend mornings the area is crawling with bikers, runners, and baby strollers.

There are three ways to get to the top: 1) the funicular from Bellavista, 2) the cable car from Pedro de Valdivia, and 3) car, taxi, or foot from Pedro de Valdivia. Do whichever fits your schedule logistically, but we recommend coming and going different ways to cover more of the park.

From Bellavista, at the foot of the park, you can buy tickets for the funicular. It runs *Tuesday through Sunday from 10am-8pm*. Take note when you buy your ticket because there are several funicular/cable car *(teleferico)* combinations. The ride is thrilling to some, as the hill gets as steep as 45 degrees. The only stop on the way up is for the **Santiago Zoo**, *Cerro San Cristobal, 10am-6pm, Closed Monday, Entry $3.30 adults, $1.15 children.* There's really not much reason to stop at the *Jardin Zoologico* unless you have kids. The animals, especially the big cats, are in depressingly small cages. If you are interested in species native to Chile, they do have pudus, vicuñas, and rheas on display. The funicular does not stop at the zoo on the way down.

Continue to the top of the funicular, which will let you off at the **Bellavista Terrace**. Literally translated as "beautiful view," it depends on the day as to whether that is true or not. From there it is a short walk to the base of the 14 meter tall **Virgen of the Immaculate Concepción**. This statue, in place since 1908, can be seen from all over the city. There is a restaurant at the top of the hill where you can enjoy cold drinks and decent food. It's a fun place to hang out if the weather is nice.

The cable car, *teleférico*, departs around the corner from the restaurant. Disembark at the **Tupahue Station** to walk around this section of the park. *Tupahue* means "place of God" in the Mapuche language and was their name for the hill. There is a large, public swimming pool uniquely built into the side of the mountain. You might give it a try on an especially hot day.

Camino Real Restaurant is also accessible from this stop. The views from its patio are marvelous and the entire grounds got a face lift in 1998 when all the presidents from the Summit of the Americas dined here. The fixed meal comes with half a bottle of wine. A better value is the wine tasting at $1.50 per shot at the bar in the restaurant. There is a wine museum downstairs which is really just a lame display of Chilean wines.

Another site at the stop is the **Botanical Garden**, *Jardin Botanico Mapulemu*. Admission is free and it's a nice place to wander around for a while.

If you are up for a walk, you can go to the **Antilen swimming pool** from here as well. Most of the **mountain biking trails** start below the pool and behind the playground.

Continuing down in the cable car, skimming tree tops as you drop towards Pedro de Valdivia, you'll be entertained by the views of the neighborhoods in the east of town. Take special note of the **CTC building**, which is the tallest in Santiago. The phone company had to build that awkward looking tower at the top of the sky scraper to earn the distinction.

From the cable car station you walk through the trees to the park entrance at Pedro de Valdivia. You can either jump in one of the waiting cabs or walk a few kilometers down Pedro de Valdivia to the metro.

If you are staying in Providencia or El Bosque, it's a nice morning run to the top of San Cristobal. The skies are usually clear and you share the road with exercising Chileans.

PROVIDENCIA

If you walk from the Pedro de Valdivia entrance of the San Cristobal Hill towards Providencia, you will pass the **Sculpture Garden**, *Avenida Santa Maria between Pedro de Valdivia and Padre Letelier, All hours, No admission fee*. Sandwiched between busy Santa Maria and a river that can be stinky at times, its location is less than ideal. The park itself is beautiful maintained with wide paths branching under the trees to distinct works of art. Many of the benches in the park are themselves works of art. There is an outdoor concert series in the summer, but you might want nose plugs.

Continuing along Pedro de Valdivia, crossing Providencia Avenue, you hit 11 de Septiembre Avenue. On your left is a mansion from the 1930s, now home to the **Cultural Institute of Providencia**, *Tel. 209-4341, Monday-Saturday 9am-7pm, Sunday, 10am-5pm, no admission fee*. Rotating shows impart culture into the neighborhood at the *Instituto Cultural de Providencia*. The old building, with its ornate molding, high ceilings, and huge windows remind visitors of another era. Don't miss the stain glass ceiling upstairs. It's definitely worth popping in for a look at the show if you're in the neighborhood.

NIGHTLIFE & ENTERTAINMENT

BELLAVISTA

Theater

Small theater thrives in this section of town. **Teatro Bellavista**, *Dardignac 0110, Tel. 735-6264*; **Teatro Taller**, *Lagarrigue 191, Tel. 235-1678*; **Teatro El Conventillo I and II**, *Bellavista 173, Tel. 777-4164*; and **Teatro La Feria**, *Crucero Exeter 0250, Tel. 737-7371,* have functions that usually run from March through December. Sernatur has listings of what is currently running.

Bars & Clubs

You must spend an evening eating in Bellavista and walking the street afterwards. Whole blocks come alive as young hippies set up outdoor stalls selling their wares. Throngs of people cruise the streets and stand outside discos hoping to be admitted, while others just stand around looking cool. There's an energy on the avenues that keeps you hopping until early in the morning if you let it.

While people start to hit the streets around ten, the night crawlers of Santiago's bohemian neighborhood don't appear until midnight. These people are on a different schedule than the rest of town. With dinner beginning closer to 10pm in Bellavista, bars don't start to fill until around one or two in the morning.

Manifesto, *0175 Dardignac*, is painfully hip with its stark, iron and copper interior. They have one of the longer beer menus in Chile. If it's dancing you're after, **OZ**, *Chucre Manzur 5, Tel. 737-7066* is a popular disco, but there is a steep cover charge.

PROVIDENCIA
Theater
TEATRO UNIVERSIDAD DE CHILE, *Baquedano 043. Tel. 634-5295. Metro Baquedano.*

This theater, associated with the University, provides a full schedule of ballet and orchestra throughout the year.

TEATRO ORIENTE, *Pedro de Valdivia between Providencia and Bello. Tel. 232-1306. Metro Pedro de Valdivia.*

To buy tickets you must go to *11 de Septiembre 2214, Office 66*. This theater, run by the Beethoven Foundation, invites foreign artists to perform from May through September. Sernatur has listings of what is currently running.

Bars & Clubs
Providencia offers numerous clubs and bars frequented by foreign travelers and young Chileans. Most of the establishments are used to dealing with their patrons in English, so it's not a place to go if you want to be forced to speak Spanish. The concentration of foreigners has created another unfortunate phenomena – flower sellers and beggars, which you won't find in other places in Chile. On the other hand, many find it a fun, convenient place to drink and dance the night away.

The main cluster of night spots is concentrated around the intersections of General Holley with Suecia and Bucarest. Things get going earlier here, as it is a popular spot for drinks after work. Many of these bars are also open for lunch.

BOOMERANG, *General Holley 2285. Tel. 334-5457. Metro Los Leones. Credit cards accepted.*

Known as something of a meat market, Boomerang is one of the most popular bars in this area. With half price drinks from 6pm-9pm and live bands everyday except Sunday, its understandable why. Giant illuminated beverage ads on the floor show you the way to the bar. They have a menu of sandwiches and other finger foods.

CLAVO OXIDADO, *Nueva de Lyon 113. Tel. 234-3673. Metro Los Leones Credit cards accepted.*

In a small pedestrian area behind General Holley known as Plaza del Sol, Clavo Oxidado is a bit different from your typical Providencia bar. While they offer such standards as two for one happy hour and regular bar food, they go a step beyond. Live theater, 16mm films, and domino tournaments keep patrons coming back for more. They try to be cool with a funky mural on the ceiling and in-laid colored stones in the bar, and pretty much pull it off.

There are many other bars and dance spots on these streets that are in favor with the throngs one month and out the next. Just wander around to find the place that looks like it has lots of action and try your luck there.

There are other bars spread out along Providencia. The **Phone Box Pub** at *Providencia 1670, Tel. 234-9972*, has big beers and a happy hour frequented by Brits.

EL BOSQUE
Bars & Clubs

There are plenty of bars tucked in with the restaurants along El Bosque street. Many of them are like pubs, offering moderately priced meals during the day before turning into watering holes at night.

GEO PUB, *Encomenderos 83. Tel. 233-6675. Metro Tobalaba. Credit cards accepted.*

This is really a four shop complex. Catering to the outdoor traveler, there is an expedition center, an outfitter, an internet café, and the comfortable pub. You can pop into **Altue Expeditions** to check out the trips (rafting, sea kayaking, trekking, horseback and mountain bike riding); walk downstairs to **Geo 42** to pick up those last minute clothing or accessory items that you forgot; cruise the net or pick up e-mail at the **Cyber Cafe;** and then dine, drink and hang with fellow travelers in the cozy wood-hewn **Geo Pub**. The pub has daily *menús* for lunch as well as a typical bar menu. At night it's big beers and more big beers.

PUBLICITY, *El Bosque Norte 0155. Tel. 246-6414. Metro Tobalaba. Credit cards accepted.*

Taking the theme bar to new levels, PubLicity's subject is marketing and advertising. The slick 25-40 year old set has made this their headquarters. With an open terrace on busy El Bosque street, it's a place to see and be seen through out the day and night. Be aware that drink prices go up after 9:30pm.

EL CLUB, *El Bosque Norte 0380. Tel. 246-1222. Metro Tobalaba. Credit cards accepted.*
El Club is the PubLicity equivalent for financial directors and general managers. This is one uptight group, but their hang out has a great terrace. It's a good place to have a beer after a day of touring, before the big guys get off work.

LAS CONDES
Bars & Clubs
Las Condes has less to offer in terms of nightlife, but that does not mean it is lacking. **Spy,** *Las Condes 10690, Tel. 217-3130,* is next door to Santa Fe Restaurant and usually crowded on Thursday and Friday when there is no cover for ladies. **Las Urracas,** *Vitacura 9254, Tel. 212-0860* also has an attached disco. **San Damián,** *Las Condes 11271, Tel. 243-1108,* has a number of bars and discos that are open until 5am.

SPORTS & RECREATION
The Santiago area offers abundant options for outdoor activity.

Basketball
There is a public outdoor court behind the Almac supermarket at the corner Las Condes and Vitacura. Hoopsters show up for pick-up games Saturday and Sunday mornings. Otherwise its pretty hard to find a place play because all of the courts are in private clubs.

Biking
Road biking is a hazardous venture in town. We've seen some dedicated triathletes training along the Pan-American highway, but shake our heads in wonder as the trucks zoom by.
There are good mountain biking trails in town. The most centrally located ones are on San Cristóbal hill, on the eastern side of the park. A great set of trails is behind the new housing development in Huinganal, a neighborhood in Lo Barnachea. The housing development will probably consume it in a few years, but for the time being it has a challenging single track loop in beautiful Northern California type landscape with hawks soaring overhead. Another good alternative is the trails in the Arrayan Nature Sanctuary (see *Excursions & Day Trips* section below).
The most popular mountain biking that *Santiaginos* engage in is actually on-road biking. Each weekend morning, hundreds of bikers tackle the steep winding road to the Farallones ski resorts and then whiz back down at furious speeds.

Golf

There are no public courses in Santiago, although there is the private Club de Golf Los Leones on an extraordinary piece of real estate in the uptown area if you can manage to get invited. The closest public course is in Pirque, about an hour south of Santiago.

Gyms

Several good gyms have popped up in Santiago over the past few years. Most of these have state of the art treadmills, bicycles, stairmasters, weight machines and free weights. They charge about $10-$15 per visit for non-members.

- **Powerhouse**, *Ecomenderos 192, El Bosque. Tel. 366-9911* and *Vitacura 3900, Las Condes. Tel. 207-3030*
- **Sportlife**, *Helvecia 280, second floor, El Bosque. Tel. 236-5080*

Hiking

You can hike to the top of **Cerro Manquehue**, 1,650 meters, in about two hours. Cerro Manquehue is the hill on the east side of town which looks like someone lopped off the top of a volcano leaving it with a flat top. You can begin that hike from Los Pyramides, the park east of San Cristóbal hill. The moderate hike has challenging grades at the beginning and the end. Much of the time you are hiking through grassy slopes. On a clear day you will have a good view of the city and of the Andes across the valley.

There are also good hikes just outside of town. We cover **Arrayan Nature Sanctuary**, **Hierba Loca National Park**, and **Cerro Providencia** in the *Excursions & Day Trips* section below and **El Morado National Park** in Chapter 12, *The Central Region*.

Horseback Riding

The best bet in town is at the **Arrayan Nature Sanctuary**, described below in *Excursions & Day Trips*. Outside of town, you can ride below the purple peaks of El Morado Park described in Chapter 12, *The Central Region*. Also offering horseback riding around Santiago is **Cascada Expediciones**, *Orrego Luco 54, 2nd floor, Tel. 234-2274* or *232-7214*.

Kayaking/Rafting

Paddlers head for the **Rio Maipo** in El Cajón del Maipo, about an hour and half southeast of Santiago. We cover the area in Chapter 12, *The Central Region*. For an organized rafting trip, contact **Cascada Expediciones**, *Orrego Luco 54, 2nd floor, Tel. 234-2274 or 232-7214*.

Mountain, Ice, & Rock Climbing

Prime peaks to bag in the area include **El Plomo** (5,424 meters) and **Aconcagua** (6,960 meters), the highest peak outside of the Himalayas, located just across the border in Argentina. Experienced climbers can summit El Plomo without a guide, but crampons are necessary for the glacier. For further information and excursions you can contact **Club Andino**, *Almirante Simpson 3, Tel. 222-1073*. The club organizes expeditions, offers guides for hire, rents equipment, and can give further suggestions for rock and ice climbing.

Skating

There is an in-line skate board park within **Parque Araucano** in Las Condes. There are no rentals there so you have to take your own wheels.

Running

Running near the hotels is unpleasant due to the traffic congestion. If you are staying in Providencia or El Bosque, you can head across the river to **San Cristóbal Hill** where, inside the park, there is almost no traffic during the weekdays. If you can't make it there, you are probably better off going to one of the gyms and using a treadmill.

The **Hash House Harriers**, who describe themselves as "drinkers with a running problem," gather each Sunday at the Almac supermarket where Las Condes meets Vitacura, at 10:30am in the winter, and 9:30am in the summer. This odd group of characters from around the world wholeheartedly welcomes new members and visitors. From the Almac they relocate to a good running location, run at a steady clip for about an hour while on the trail of a human "hare," then drink and sing songs. You have experience it to understand it. Actually, we've participated several times and still don't understand it, but always have fun.

Skiing

There are three very distinct ski areas near Santiago up the Mapocho river valley. The closest of these, **Colorado-Farellones**, is less than an hour from El Bosque. Even the furthest one, **Valle Nevado**, takes only about an hour and a half to reach.

Skiing in Chile can be different than that of the United States or Europe. You are above the tree line here, so everything is wide open. There are rarely long lift lines, except for the most crowded days, and it seems like you can always find an area without people.

Depending on the snow conditions, ski season runs from the middle of June to the end of September. Lift ticket prices go up and down during the season depending on demand, but they generally range between $30 and $40. Half-day tickets are available after 1pm for about a $10 discount.

All three resorts are located at the top of the road to Farellones, which starts near the end of Las Condes. After passing the guard stop and renting chains if necessary, the road climbs the valley in a series of hairpin turns that can make even the driver carsick. The road is one way going up until noon and then changes to one way heading down about two or three in the afternoon.

If you want to spend a few days skiing you might want to get a condominium or hotel room. High season prices can run as much as $300 a night, but at the beginning or end of the season you can find rooms for a low as $80 for a double. If you have a group to share expenses you'll find it much more economical, even though your housemates may come back from the disco yelling about women and Brazilian drinks.

Most people from Santiago do their skiing as day trips. The drive is generally not bad, even if you have to use chains, because you can pay $3 to have somebody else to put them on.

If you're not driving, there is an excellent, inexpensive service to get up and down the mountain. **Ski Total**, *Alto Las Condes and Lo Castillo shopping centers in Los Condes, Tel. 246-0156, 246-6881*, has vans that make the round trip daily from their stores to the mountain for only $12. They leave at 8:45am and return at 5:30pm. Make reservations before you go. If you didn't bring warm clothes, they even rent ski suits and gloves.

Colorado-Farellones Ski Area

We love this ski area. Maybe it's the numerous blue sky, deep powder snowboarding days we've had here, maybe the fact that it's only 32 km from Santiago, or maybe because this is where we got engaged, but whatever the reason, the 22 runs here are always good for a day of fun. **Farellones** and **El Colorado** are actually two separate little hamlets, but they are connected to by ski lifts. Parking and renting equipment in Farellones is the quickest way to the base of El Colorado, but we find it more convenient to go ahead a drive to the top.

El Colorado is a full service ski resort with equipment rental (skis and snowboards), lessons, children's programs, restaurants, hotels, and even a disco. For a snow report or more information about the resort, call *Tel. 220-9501* or *211-0426.*

There are a number of hotels and condos at El Colorado. You can try **Apart-hotel Colorado**, *Santiago Tel. 2/246-0660*, **Monteblanco** or **Edificio Los Ciervos**, *Santiago Tel. 2/233-5501*, or **Villa Palomar**, *Santiago Tel. 2/ 233-6801.*

Valle Nevado Ski Area

Valle Nevado, built in 1988, is the newest and nicest resort. With 800 beds it is also the largest. Valle Nevado's 27 runs include the most difficult of the three ski areas, but there are plenty of options for beginner and intermediate skiers and snowboarders as well. If the runs are too skied out, you might want to try their heli-skiing.

Loads of Brazilians and Argentines charter trips here during the winter. You'll find them filling the resort's three hotels and seven restaurants as well as jamming the floor of the disco at night. Valle Nevado has some of the best rental equipment, along with high quality instruction and children's programs. For snow reports or more information about the resort call *Tel. 206-0027.* For information about lodging in one of the three **Valle Nevado Hotels**, call *Santiago, Tel. 2/698-0103.*

La Parva Ski Area

La Parva is a small, homey resort with no intention of changing. There is only one hotel here. The rest of the people on the slopes are from the same families that rent houses year after year. They come to escape Santiago, which you can see in the valley below at sunset.

The back bowls here make for some great skiing, as does connecting up with Valle Nevado. You can buy a pass good for both resorts. The fondue restaurant, **La Marmita de Pericles**, draws people from all three resorts. La Parva offers equipment rental, lessons, and children's programs. For snow reports or more information about the resort call *Tel. 264-1466.* To make reservations at the **Apart-hotel Condominio Nueva Parva**, call *Santiago, Tel. 2/212-1363, Fax 2/2208510.*

Swimming

There are outdoor public pools at the **San Cristóbal Hill Park** which we cover in the *Seeing the Sights* section above. The **Club de Sport Frances**, *Beltrán 2550, Tel. 212-9696,* usually schedules a few hours each day for lap swimming.

Tennis

Well-groomed clay courts are available at **Parque de Tenis**, *Cerro Colorado 4661, Tel. 208-6589.* The cost per court is about $10/hour. You can usually walk on, but its a good idea to make a reservation in advance on evenings and weekends, especially when Marcelo Ríos is on a hot streak which inspires everybody to dust off their racquets.

SHOPPING
Handicrafts

Chilean handicrafts include some lovely, bargain-priced lapis lazuli jewelry, rugged wool caps and sweaters from Chiloé, and plush alpaca goods from the north. **Los Dominicos**, also known as **Graneros del Alba**, is especially popular because it's set up in a old, white-washed Dominican monastery.

Handicraft Markets
• **Artesanía Nehuen**, *Dardignac 59, Bellavista. Monday-Saturday, 9:30am-7:30pm*
• **Callfucura**, *Bellavista 096, Bellavista. Daily, 11am-7pm*
• **Graneros Del Alba**, **(Los Dominicos)**, *Apoquindo 9085. Tuesday-Sunday, 11am-8pm*
• **Mercado Santa Lucia**, *Bernardo O'Higgins across from Santa Lucia Hill. Daily 11am-8pm*
• **Vitacura Handicrafts**, *Vitacura 6838. Daily, 11am-7pm*

Lapis Lazuli Jewelry
For upscale lapis lazuli jewelry, we recommend **Precolombo** with two locations, one at *Ricardo Lyon 146, Providencia, Tel. 242-0178*, and another in *Parque Arauco Mall, Local 538, Tel. 234-2363*. One of the authors was surprised with an engagement ring made here.

There are a few higher end jewelry shops selling lapis in the Bellavista neighborhood, as well as the Las Condes and Parque Arauco malls. You can find the inexpensive lapis jewelry in all of the handicraft markets and shops in Bellavista.

Wine
A good variety of Chilean wines is available in all of the city's supermarkets. For expert advice on selection, try the **Wine House**, *Vitacura 3446, Tel. 207-3533* or *Vitacura 2904, Tel. 233-4846*. The Wine House also offers wine tasting classes. Another shop with an extensive collection is **La Vinoteca**, *Isidora Goyenechea 3520, Tel. 334-1987*. We cover visits to wineries below in *Excursions & Day Trips*, while giving general information on wine in the *Food & Drink* chapter.

EXCURSIONS & DAY TRIPS

While Santiago can be an interesting, vibrant city, many of the real treasures of the area lie outside the city limits. Hikers will be delighted with the excellent options less than an hour from town. You can trek along an electric blue stream to hanging glaciers, follow a cactus lined trail for days through a nearby valley, summit a 5400 meter mountain, or just wander along a stream until you find your swimming hole.

If it's skiing you like, and the snow gods have been benevolent, you can leave your hotel and be on the slopes in an hour. There are three excellent resort options nestled in the mountains above the city.

Even if you're not in the active mode, the area around Santiago offers some fun diversions. Whether its wine tasting at one of the local vineyards or shopping in a traditional Chilean town, there's something for everyone.

If all this isn't enough, keep in mind that the majority of the locations in Chapter 12, *The Central Region*, are under two hours from Santiago. The beaches, mountains, and lakes of the area could keep you busy for months.

Winery Tours

A few of the most important Santiago area wineries offer tours. It is highly recommended that you call in advance to reconfirm that the winery still offers tours and the hours that it does so. The best way to get to the wineries is to rent a car or hire a taxi by the hour.

The **Santa Rita** winery in Buin has a beautiful, stately restaurant in its 200 year old hacienda. One hundred and twenty patriots, including General O'Higgins, sought refuge there during the struggle for independence. The winery's respected "120" label is named after the patriots. You can enjoy a drink and an appetizer in the splendid garden before indulging in an exquisite lunch. To do both the tour and lunch, you can leave Santiago about 11:30am and be back before 4:30pm.

Concha y Toro, *Subercaseaux 210, Pirque. Tel. 853-0042, extension 7090 or 7040. No admission fee for the one hour tour. Wine tasting $1 per glass. For tours in English, reserve one day in advance.*

Santa Rita, *Buin. For a tours in English or Spanish, contact Roberto Rivas Tel. 821-4211, Fax 821-4163, e-mail rrivas@santarita.cl. No admission fee for the tour. The restaurant is open for lunch Tuesday-Sunday. Lunch reservations, Tel. 821-4211.*

Cousiño Macul, *Quilín 7100. Monday-Friday, 11am-2pm. No admission charge for the tour and the tasting is free as well.*

Undurraga, *Camino a Melipilla Km 34, Talagante. Monday-Friday 10am-4pm. Call Carry Dudman for a tour reservation, Tel. 372-2932. Tours are given in Spanish and English.*

The Arrayan Nature Sanctuary

This nature sanctuary is an excellent option if you're a time constrained outdoors person yearning to set foot in the Andes or if you're simply in need of a quick nature fix. Located in a cactus-dotted canyon only 25 minutes from Providencia, the privately-run park is composed of well-maintained trails meandering along a glacier-fed stream. Most visitors stick close to the parking area to picnic, so within 15 minutes of hiking you are alone in the pristine Andes, with the possible exception of condors spying on you from above.

Horse rentals can be arranged by calling *Tel. 215-1352* in advance. There is also an option of a horseback ride combined with an overnight campout that includes a pack mule to haul your gear. There's good news if your preferred steed is a **mountain bike** because the sweet, sometimes technical single track goes for as long as you can ride it.

The Sanctuary is located east of town in Arrayan at the end of El Cajón. It's an easy cab ride there and is the one park where you can usually hail a cab at the entrance to get back into town. *Entry $2.50.*

Yerba Loca Nature Sanctuary

Yerba Loca, a nature sanctuary situated in a wide valley carved out by the slow movement of a gargantuan glacier, is a gently climbing, beautiful escape a mere 45 km from Santiago.

The Technicolor stream is one highlight of the hike. It's a bright blue swath rushing over smooth, rust-red rocks. As the area receives little rainfall, the color of the sky often matches the intense blue of the stream.

Leaving the picnic area after paying the $1.25 entrance fee, you cross the stream and head up the slowly climbing, well-worn trail. Continuing into the valley, you enter a 5000 meter rock hewn bowl. Back to the right is the peak **El Altar Falso**, straight ahead is **El Altar**, and to the left you sees the spiky pinnacles of **La Paloma**. Continue to follow the stream back until you reach the glacier. Here you'll discover huge ice slabs hanging between sides of deep gorges.

With a loaded pack it takes five hours to walk the 15 km to the glaciers, as you have an altitude gain of 1500 meters. There are numerous places for camping along the way. Day hikers with light packs can do the round trip in about eight hours, but most of them prefer to walk up the river a few hours, picnic, enjoy the sun and blue sky, and head back.

The park is located on Curve 15 on the way to Farellones. You can either rent a car or coordinate your trip with a taxi or hotel driver. Anything you need you will have to take with you, as there are no stores between Las Condes and Farellones. The water in the stream is full of sulfates, so you need to carry your own or bring a water filter.

Rio Clarillo

Blue skies, sun-baked rocks and crystalline pools make this the perfect lazy-day outing. The **Rio Clarillo National Reserve** is part of a deep river basin with an abundance and variety of flora and fauna, but the numerous swimming holes are the best thing here.

A trail runs along the banks of the river beckoning you to discover the pools around the next bend. From the last of the picnic tables it crosses the river a number of times, continuing back into box canyons framed by blue skies. White egrets rise silently in and out of the picture while fish and frogs populate the pools.

The further up the river you go, the more beautiful and isolated the area becomes. All the river crossings, however, mean wet feet, so a dry pair of socks is a good idea for the ride home. You should also be careful while climbing because the trail is challenging to follow in some spots as it meanders over boulders and snakes along steep ledges to climb the Clarillo river basin. Find your perfect swimming hole and then slink out of the water to bask lizard-like on warm, bald, slabs.

The banks of the Clarillo were made for picnicking and Conaf has augmented that capacity by erecting picnic tables and barbecue grills under the shade trees. On less crowded days these sites, especially the ones in the back, are a nice way to enjoy a slice of the river. Otherwise you should pack a lunch and head up stream to find peace and quiet.

The park is not open for camping and costs more than most Conaf sites at $6.75 per person so it makes sense to spend much of the afternoon there. A well-planned day could include a tour of the nearby **Concha y Toro** vineyards.

It is easy to get to the park both in car and via public transportation. If driving, take Vicuña Mackenna south to Puente Alto and then follow signs to Pirque, El Principal, and the park. Bus 32 (El Principal) leaves every few hours from Puente Alto to El Principal. From there the entrance is only a few kilometers away. Hitching or walking will get you the rest of the way.

Cerro Providencia & Vallecito

If you've been to the top of San Cristóbal Hill in Santiago and looked towards Argentina, you've seen Providencia, a high peak beyond the eastern edge of town. You can climb that peak if you wish, or simply hike back to a small, green valley. Although this area is closer to Santiago than the above options, it is usually less populated.

The path is steep at the trailhead, but then starts a gradual climb to the first lookout. The trail splits here, with one path taking the easy accent to Vallecito, and the other following the ridge up to the top of Providencia. **Vallecito** is a small valley with running water most of the year. The majority of day hikers choose this route. **Providencia**, on the other hand, is a 2700 meter peak from which you have outstanding views of the *cordillera* and not so great ones of Santiago's haze.

With loaded packs it takes about ten hours to reach the summit of Providencia. Even with day packs it's at least a seven hour hike to the top, so start early. This hike is best done in the summer and fall. Be aware that there is limited water on the route.

The turnoff to the park is just five km up the road to Farellones. It is marked with a sign of a hiker. Take this dirt road back about a half a kilometer to reach the trailhead and parking area. There is no public transportation up the road to Farellones, so you'll have to rent a car or arrange pick up with a driver. There is no park admission fee.

El Plomo

If you've come to Chile to climb, this is the big daddy of the Santiago-area mountains. At 5430 meters, reaching the solid rounded peak of **El Plomo** is a true accomplishment. The route itself is not too technical, but rather a long haul. You do need ropes and crampons at the top to cross the glacier, so unless you are an experienced climber you should go with a guide. See the adventure tour company information below.

Pomaire

If you're into searching out bargains, head straight to **Pomaire**. About an hour outside of Santiago, this sleepy little village is a gold mine of inexpensive, unusual pottery. The whole town is filled with artisans who work the clay from the surrounding hills. Hundreds of shops stand wall to wall filled with pots, serving dishes, piggy banks, decorations and miniatures. There's a pig theme running through every store in town. Some of it is a bit tacky, but there are some real treasures to be found if you dig around.

Pomaire merits a visit even if you're not a shopper. Dirt sidewalks line the town's four streets while vineyards dot the surrounding hills. There are a number of excellent traditional Chilean restaurants in town. **San Antonio**, with two locations, is one of the best. You can try such typical casseroles as *pastel de choclo, cazuela de chanco,* and *porotos granados.* The pleasant **El Parrón de Pomaire** *on Prat* serves *empanadas* the size of newborn babies.

Weekends are crowded here. It's best to visit on a weekday, but not on Monday, as that's the day the entire town closes down.

Pomaire is located on Highway 78 to San Antonio and Santo Domingo three km before Melipilla. You can rent a car, hire a driver, or take the bus. Buses Melipilla from the San Borja Terminal in Santiago makes the trip a few times as day.

The Central Valley

Almost every one of the locations in the Central Region chapter is also a day or weekend trip from Santiago. There are a number of wonderful places along the coast, like **Zapallar**, **Valparaíso**, or Pablo Neruda's home at **Isla Negra** that could end up being highlights of your trip to Chile. The ski resorts at **Portillo** and **Chillán** certainly give the ones in the Santiago area a run for their money, while the hikes at **La Campana** and the **Cajón del Maipo** rate up with some of the best in the country. Don't forget to thumb through that chapter as well before deciding how you want to spend your time.

Adventure Tour Companies in Santiago
All of the companies listed below lead trips in the Santiago area. Most of them have excursions to many other parts of the country as well.
• **Altue Expediciones**, *Encomenderos 83, Las Condes. Tel. 232-1103. Fax 233-6799*. Rafting, kayaking, trekking, horseback riding.
• **Cascada Expediciones**, *Orrego Luco 054, Providencia. Tel. 234-2274. Fax 233-9768. E-mail: cascada@ibm.net*. Rafting, horseback riding, mountaineering, trekking, mountain biking, kayaking. Offer one day and weekend trips as well as longer outings.
• **Chiltue**, *Murta 1381, Estación Central. Tel./Fax 776-4288*. Trekking.
• **Act Tourismo**, *O'Higgins 949. Tel. 696-0391. Fax 672-7483*. Mountaineering, trekking, skiing.
• **Evasion**, *Santa Beatriz 84A, Providencia. Tel. 236-1325. Fax 235-5225*. Mountaineering, trekking.
• **Pared Sur**, *Juan Montero 5497, Las Condes. Tel. 207-3525. Fax 207-3159*. Mountain biking, trekking, rafting, skiing, horseback riding, kayaking.

PRACTICAL INFORMATION
Banks
You can throw a stone in any direction in Santiago and hit a bank. Nearly all of them have ATM machines that accept one or more of the cards from Cirrus, Star, Plus, MasterCard, and Visa. There are many freestanding ATM's in convenience stores and other locales as well. Banks are open from 9am-2pm.

Bookstores with Books in English
• **Feria Chilena de Libros**. Two branches in the *centro* are located at *Huérfanos 623, Tel. 639-6758* and *Agustinas 859, Tel. 639-5354*. In Providencia, *Sta. Magdalena 50, Tel. 232-1422*
• **Librería Inglesa**, *Pedro de Valdivia 47, Providencia. Tel. 231-6270*
• **Librería Zapping Book**, *Parque Arauco Mall. Tel. 201-5556*
• **World Book Center**, *Alto Los Condes Mall. Tel. 213-1076*

Business Hours
Business hours generally run from 9am-6pm with an hour-long lunch at 1pm or 2pm. Retail hours are from 10am to 8:30pm. Most retailers do not close for lunch. Supermarkets stay open as late as midnight.

Church Services in English:
- **Baha'i Faith**, *Tel. 273-1581 or 209-7692*
- **International Bible Church**, *Hotel Kennedy 2nd floor, Av. Kennedy 4570, Vitacura. Tel. 218-1526, Pastor Hamilton. Sunday Worship and Children's Church 9:30am*
- **Lutheran Church**, *Tel. 211-5398 Pastor Karl Kuenzel*
- **San Marcos Presbyterian Church**, *Corner of Hualtatas and Manquehue, Las Condes. Tel. 202-0397. Services Sunday 9:30am*
- **St. George's College Chapel**, *Tel. 243-6041 Vicky Tanco. Catholic Mass Sunday 10:30am*
- **Santiago Community Church**, *Av. Holanda 151. Tel. 232-1113. Sunday Service 10:30am. Sunday School 10:30am. Holy Communion Thursday noon*
- **Understanding Islam**, *Tel. 216-6200, Roeeda Khalil or 274-5295, Fatim*
- **Victoria en Cristo Baptist Church**, *Roberto Peragallo 6678. Tel. 229-6920 or 209-5038. Bible study in English*

Currency Exchange
It's hard to beat the exchange rates and convenience of ATM machines, but for those packing cash or traveler's checks, there are several currency exchange houses in each of the major hotel neighborhoods.
- **Andino Ocho**, *Agustinas 1062, Centro. Tel. 360-1313*
- **Cambios Azul**, *Metro Los Leones, Providencia. Tel. 233-2394*
- **Guinazu**, *El Bosque Norte 0192. Tel. 334-3690*
- **Manquehue**, *Huérfanos 1160, Centro. Tel. 698-3875*
- **Pedro de Valdivia**, *Pedro de Valdivia 059, Providencia. Tel. 231-9933*

Embassies
- **Argentina**, *Miraflores 285, Centro. Tel. 633-1076*
- **Australia**, *Gertrudis Echenique 420. Tel. 228-5065*
- **Brazil**, *Alonso Ovalle 1665. Tel. 698-2486*
- **Canada**, *Ahumada 11, Centro. Tel. 696-2256*
- **Ecuador**, *Providencia 1979, 5th Floor. Tel. 231-5073*
- **Britain**, *El Bosque Norte 0125, 3rd Floor. Tel. 231-3737*
- **Peru**, *Andrés Bello 1751, Providencia. Tel. 235-2356*
- **US**, *Andrés Bello 2800, Las Condes. Tel. 232-2600*

E-Mail Service
- **Cafe Virtual**, *Alameda 145, 2nd floor, Centro. Tel. 638-6846*
- **Geo Pub**, *Encomenderos 83, Las Condes. Tel. 233-6675*

Laundry

Ask the front desk of your hotel for the nearest laundromat (*lavandería*) or dry cleaner (*lavaseco*). The full-service laundromats charge about $8 per load to wash and dry.

Medical Service

Two of the best private hospitals are **Clínica Las Condes**, *Lo Fontecilla 441, Tel. 210-4000,* and **Clínica Alemana**, *Vitacura 5951, Tel. 212-9700.* For non-emergency medical services, contact the **American Embassy**, *Tel. 232-2600.* The embassy provides a recommendation list for the type of specialist you need.

National Parks

• **Conaf**, *Bulnes 285, Centro, Tel. 390-0000,* or at *Eliodoro Yañez 1810, Providencia, Tel. 205-2372*

Post Office

Correos de Chile. In the centro, *Plaza de Armas 989* or *Libertador O'Higgins 2350.* In Providencia, *Pedro de Valdivia 1781* or *Providencia 1466.* In Las Condes, *Metro Tobalaba* or *Isidora Goyenechea 3372.*

Supermarkets

Supermarkets located throughout the city include **Almac**, **Unimarc**, and **Jumbo**. All of these stores carry standard Chilean brands and widely distributed imported brands. For the largest selection of imported foods, try **Jumbo**, *Alto Las Condes Mall.*

Telephone/Fax

The area code for Santiago is 2. There are many CTC, Entel, and other long distance offices throughout Santiago. Contact the front desk of your hotel for the nearest one. Cellular telephone rentals are more reasonable than you might expect. Try **Bellsouth**, *El Bosque Norte 0134, Tel. 339-5000,* or **Entel**, *Andrés Bello 2687, Tel. 360-0123.* These or other cellular companies might have offices closer to your hotel, so consult the front desk.

Tourist Office/Maps

• **Sernatur**, *Providencia 1550. Tel. 251-8496*

12. THE CENTRAL REGION

If Chile consisted of nothing more than the slice of land around Santiago from **Zapallar** in the north to **Chillán** in the south, it would still be a worthy place to visit. The 650 km stretch hosts two mountain chains, fertile valleys, sparkling beaches, roaring rivers, ski resorts, vineyards and interesting cities.

Head out in any direction from Santiago and you'll be delighted and intrigued by the number of travel options. The most visited area, the **Central Coast**, offers a variety of beach experiences. From the lifestyles of the rich and famous to simple fishing villages, you can find just the place to fit your mood or manner.

To the northeast you have **Portillo**, one of the best ski resorts in Chile, along with one of the most spectacular drives in the country that winds up and over the Andes to Argentina. To the northwest you'll find the sleepy weekend retreat of **Olmué**, and a prime perch for viewing the entire width of the country in **La Campana National Park**.

To the southeast, **Cajón del Maipo** is filled with adventures. Rafting, skiing, hiking, and mountain climbing are all accessible just a few hours from Santiago. The more sedentary can enjoy the view from a summer cabin after a session at the hot springs.

When you head south, vineyards, lakes, and national reserves compete for your time before you reach the smoking volcanoes of **Chillán**.

Traveling to any of these areas, you plough through the fertile farmland that brings a cornucopia of goods to the Chilean table. Fresh produce stands dot the highways and will undoubtedly entice you to stop and sample the merchandise.

THE BEST OF THE CENTRAL REGION

*Most travelers to Chile usually end up having a day or two to spend in or around Santiago. We recommend getting out of the city to one of the places below. We would also have to include **Yerba Loca Nature Sanctuary**, which is found in Santiago Excursions & Day Trips.*

*•**Zapallar** – Excellent seafood lunches on the most beautiful stretch of central Chilean coast*

*•**Valparaíso/Isla Negra** – Turn-of-the-century architecture, funiculars, museums and a unique ambiance along with Pablo Neruda's most creative home*

*•**Cajón del Maipo** – Country towns, river rafting, hiking, and a glacier*

THE CENTRAL COAST

Santiaguinos love their Central Coast. A large number of upper-class Chileans owns homes or condos along the beach. The middle class, instead of buying, will rent apartments for weeks at a time. Even the lower income workers get their beach escapes by piling on to buses and crowding into hotel rooms. Chilean society being as stratified as it is, each income level frequents its own beach towns.

Parts of Santiago become almost deserted in the summer as entire neighborhoods pack up and head for the littoral. One newspaper estimated that 20% of town, 1 million people, leave for the beach during the peak month of February. The typical pattern is that upper-income mothers and children go for the entire summer while the fathers stay in Santiago working during the week. Those men and their working class compatriots jam the highways on Friday nights in a slow crawl to their weekend retreats.

You should be aware of this pattern as you plan your trip. The hotels, restaurants, and beaches are packed and rocking during the summer months of January and February, especially on the weekends. As soon as school goes back in session, at the beginning of March, order is restored and the beaches are calm again until December 15th.

Keep in mind that there are dangerous undertows and riptides along the entire coast. Just because someone has built a hotel on the beach does not mean that the water is safe. Ask around and study the water before taking the plunge.

THE BEACH PHENOMENA

"My childhood summers were spent at the beach, where our family owned a huge, rundown old house by the sea. We left in December, before Christmas, and returned at the end of February, black from the sun and stuffed with fruit and fish."
— **Isabel Allende** *in her memoir* **Paula**

History

By the 1600's, all the land in Central Chile, including the coast, had been ceded to the most prominent Spanish colonists. The beaches were mostly empty until the turn of the century because the landowners erected their houses inland, next to fresh water, instead of on the shore. In the late 1800's they began to build summer houses near the coast for friends and family. **Viña del Mar**, the first of the beach resorts, was founded in 1874. There are now over 25 resort towns along the Central Chile coastline.

THE VIÑA DILEMMA

The road most traveled these days is the highway from Santiago to Viña del Mar. Santiaguinos adore Viña and have crowded into it so much they have created a city of 300,000 people.

Our idea of the perfect beach spot, however, is not a metropolis with multiple high rise condos. We prefer the smaller towns along the coast or the rambling, quirky Valparaíso.

People from Santiago will exert incredible pressure to have you stay in Viña del Mar and visit some of the smaller towns as day trips. We recommend you give the smaller towns the attention they deserve and maybe visit Viña as a day trip.

ZAPALLAR

This gorgeous little town with its intimate beach and outstanding restaurants is our favorite spot on the coast for R&R. Large yet subtle houses snuggle into a hillside that spills down to a small oyster bay. Around the bay, profuse terraced gardens threaten to burst over their fences and vault the footpath to cover black rocks below. The ambiance is comfortable and relaxed, while the scenery is similar to Carmel, California.

History

Olegario Ovalle, the original land owner, founded Zapallar in 1893. He gave property to his friends for free as long as they would build a house within two years. Many of them took him up on the offer. In a spirit of cooperation, they connected their beautiful homes with a hike and bike trail that runs along the ocean the entire length of the town.

ARRIVALS & DEPARTURES

By Bus

There are no direct buses from Santiago. You must take a bus to Valparaíso and then catch a Sol del Pacifico bus north to Zapallar. You can board at either the Sol del Pacifico office in Valparaíso, *Galvarina 110, Tel. 32/288577,* or the bus terminal. You can also hail the Sol del Pacifico buses in Valparaíso on *Avenida Errazuriz.*

By Car

Take the Panamericana north to Catapilco where you turn left at the sign to Maitencillo and Zapallar after passing through the Cuesta el Melon tunnel. This road runs into the coastal highway where you turn right and go 13 km to Zapallar. The whole trip takes about two hours with the highlight being the last ten minutes along the seashore.

ORIENTATION

The town is nestled between the highway and the bay. The main artery to the beach is not obvious. It is down the hill to the right once you enter town. The upper section of Zapallar is the commercial center, with small grocery stores and bakeries. Visitors spend most of their time along the shell-shaped bay where a pleasant footpath connects the homes, the beach, and seafood restaurants.

WHERE TO STAY

Zapallar has a reputation for exclusivity based on its dearth of hotels. There are only three, so be sure to reserve in advance.

HOTEL ISLA SECA, *On the Road to Papudo. Tel. 33/741224, Fax 33/741228. 38 rooms. Double $150. Breakfast included. Restaurant. Bar. Pool. Credit cards accepted.*

The Isla Seca, a painstakingly decorated retreat perched high on a hill overlooking the sea, is a true treasure of the area. Two side-by-side buildings offer the finest accommodations on the coast.

The main building houses the original rooms and all the common areas. Light bursts through the floor to ceiling windows in the dining room to infuse the lobby and front sitting area with a golden glow. The terrace in front of the dining room leads down to a perfectly manicured garden and comfortable pool. While swimming, you can observe waves pounding on the rocks below or simply float on your back and take in the endless blue sky. Another small pool between the original and new buildings dangles like a nest over the edge of the property.

Almost every room in the Isla Seca is a different shape. Tasteful decorations are a common factor in all the rooms. Light walls and curtains, large windows, simple pen and ink drawings, and fresh flowers welcome the visitor. Ocean view rooms are preferable, as are the larger center rooms with terraces. The best room is the middle one on the third floor of the original building, which has its own deck.

There is a great dining room terrace, perfect for that sunset drink. There is also a bar and card room. The restaurant is good but not overly creative, but breakfasts are first-rate.

Selected as one of our best places to stay – see Chapter 10 for more details.

CABAÑAS AGUAS CLARAS, *Avenida Zapallar 125. Santiago Tel. 2/ 232-0766. 6 full cabins. $180. No credit cards.*

These cozy cabins with full kitchens sleep six. There are two bedrooms downstairs, and another in the loft above, though there is only one bath. The kitchens are well stocked and have enough space for you to be relatively comfortable when cooking. The central rooms are great for hanging out and even have fire places for cooler evenings. The big front porches have snatches of views of the ocean, which is just a short walk away. Aguas Claras is a wonderful option for families and groups of friends.

RESIDENCIAL RESTAURANTE LA TERRAZA, *Del Alcalde 142. Tel. 33/711409. 9 rooms. Double $60. Breakfast included. No credit cards.*

This *residencial* is not a good value. You would expect to pay only half of what they charge, but it is the least expensive option in town. It is located up the hill, in the middle of the commercial section.

WHERE TO EAT

L'HERMITAGE, *on the highway between Cachagua and Zapallar. Tel.33/ 771100. Expensive. No credit cards.*

The ten foot silverware sculpture at the entrance makes most people just drive on by this delightful French restaurant located in Cachagua. Once you have had the food, however, you'll be willing to drive around, over, or though the sculptures for a return visit. Located in an old house tucked down below the hill, the restaurant seats only a few patrons a night. There is no menu because the chef only buys the freshest seafood in the market each day. For $28 you get an appetizer, main course, dessert and coffee. There are usually about five or six appetizer and dessert alternatives as well as three main course options. They are open for dinner only and you must make reservations.

EL CHIRINGUITO, *on the point of the bay next to the fish market. Moderate. No credit cards.*

Some of our best afternoons in Chile have been spent under the umbrellas on Chiringuito's patio. Hunky tables and chairs made of tree trunks sit solidly on the edge of the bay. Small fishing boats pass by with their catch, while seals occasionally bask on the rocks below. The sun sparkles as it warms your arms, while a cold pisco sour gives everything a rosy hue.

And then there is the food. The *machas a la parmesana* are consistently baked to golden perfection. The fish comes prepared a variety of ways, but the caper sauce, *alcaparra*, on the fresh catch of the day makes our mouths water just writing about it. All of this should be washed down with a cold bottle of Chilean wine and followed by a long afternoon nap.

RESTAURANTE CESAR, *on the beach. Moderate. Credit cards accepted.*

Restaurante Cesar was started as a small kiosk 60 years ago by the current manager's grandfather. It is a place of strong traditions with thatched roofs offering shade to long tenured, red-coated waiters. The current chef was young Cesar's nanny when he was growing up and his favorite dinner recommendation is sole cooked in her special sauce. It's delicious. This should be preceded, of course, by a Cesar salad and followed by Cesar crepes.

HOTEL ISLA SECA, *On the Road to Papudo. Tel. 33/741224, Fax 33/741228. Moderate. Credit cards accepted.*

The high quality of the hotel, the gorgeous dining setting, and the well-trained staff lead you to expect an out of the world dinner. The food is good but not unforgettable. You'll get a solid seafood meal in an outstanding atmosphere. Sunset drinks, however, are a must.

SEEING THE SIGHTS

Relaxation is the name of the game in Zapallar. Lounging on the beach and hanging out under an umbrella at one of the restaurants are the main activities of the day. There are however, some other rituals of the visit. One of these is walking the shaded footpath from end to end. The *rambla*, as it is called, winds under large trees with the crashing ocean on one side and spectacular houses and gardens on the other.

The *rambla* ends at the fish market, but you can continue around and up to the top of **Cross Hill** with its solitary tree. From there you enjoy wonderful views of the bay. If you continue around past the hill you can scramble about on boulders to explore tide pools filled with iridescent sea grass, star fish, and strange growths.

If you head up Porto Seguro Road, by the fish market, and turn right at the top you will find the **Mar Bravo Plaza**, where groups gather each night for sunset. From here you can walk the streets of town to enjoy more of the splendid architecture. You'll tend to turn in not long after dinner as they roll up the streets here at night.

SPORTS & RECREATION

The beach in Zapallar is mainly used for sunbathing and paddleball. **Cachagua**, down the road, has a much larger beach with more sporting activity. You can run along the *rambla*. There are tennis clubs in both Zapallar, *on the highway to Papudo*, and Cachagua, *at the lower town entrance*, that allow non-members to play when the courts aren't full. To arrange scuba diving in the area you can call **Centro Buceo Octopus** in Viña del Mar, *Tel. 32/973857.*

EXCURSIONS & DAY TRIPS
Cachagua

It is said that Cachagua plays the country cousin to the exclusive and shiny Zapallar. The two places actually have much more in common than that comparison would imply. Cachagua is simply younger, founded in 1956, and a bit more laid back. There are no hotels here so some people just pass it by, but it definitely merits a visit. Cachugua's main points of interest are the powdered sugar croissant of a beach and **Penguin Island**.

The wide beach stretches down as far as you can see. The location is an ideal spot for beach sports, with throngs of teenagers playing soccer, rugby and volleyball. The ocean in front is one of the rare places to surf

---

CACHAGUA ISLAND NATIONAL MONUMENT

The island is home to a population of around 2,000 **Humbolt penguins***. This type of penguin can be found along the Humbolt current from northern Peru down to Chiloé, but is a threatened species in Chile. Chicks are born twice a year, from September through November and again in April and May. Both times are ideal for viewing, although the fall period is usually less successful as autumn rains can pummel the dens, breaking eggs and drowning chicks.*

CONAF, the Chilean forestry service, conducts a number of counts and studies on the island and its personnel are the only ones allowed access. The birds can be seen from land with the bare eye, but binoculars add greatly to the experience of studying this fascinating ecosystem.

on this part of the coast as well. Next to the parking lot, groups of horses sit saddled and ready to be rented by the hour.

A real treat of the area is the small rock island just 75 meters off the coast. Hundreds of penguins sit basking in the sun in weather far different from the polar climes you think of them inhabiting. Pelicans and black terns also enjoy the tranquillity of a preserved habitat while sea otters frisk around in the rocky pools between the beach and the island.

Apart from the main Cachugua beach there is a hidden cove, **Playa Las Cujas**, further into town. You descend a series of stairs when suddenly a beautiful blue lagoon unfolds below. A wooden statue of Saint Peter, the guardian of fisherman, casts his protective and reassuring glance over the small inlet where families set up umbrellas to spend the day.

Papudo

If the hotel options in Zapallar are too steep, or if you just have to go to a disco, Papudo is only ten km north of Zapallar. The town itself is sort of run down and it's one of the only places along the coast that we have seen piles of trash in the road. Concha and Corillos streets have the highest concentration of inexpensive *residenciales*.

PRACTICAL INFORMATION

Banks: The one bank in town is on Ovalle just a few blocks in from the highway. There is no ATM so bring plenty of cash.
Business Hours: Monday-Saturday 10am-2pm, 5pm-9pm.
Supermarkets: There are a number of small markets at the town entrance. They carry surprisingly wide inventories for such a small place.
Telephone/Fax: The area code is 33. There is a phone center on Riesco next to the gas station.

MAITENCILLO TO HORCÓN

This section of coast, south of Zapallar, offers a range of accommodations from the 5 star resort at **Marbella** to simple cottages in fishing villages. Buses run continually along the coast from **Papudo** to **Valparaíso**. You just have to stand at a bus stop and hail one to carry you to the next town. Hitchhiking is also common in the summer.

MAITENCILLO

Maitencillo is a laid-back town with a long stretch of beach know as **Playa Larga**. It's an affordable place to stay that has retained much of the feel of its fishing village past, yet offers a complete infrastructure for vacationers. From much of town your views are of beautiful sheer cliffs and crashing waves instead of the stacked condos that you find further south. There are a number of hotels and cabins available.

The more affordable accommodations here are at the **Cabañas Hermansen**, *Avenida del Mar 592. Tel./Fax 32/771028. 14 cabins. Double $60. No credit cards.* These wooden cabins, our favorites, are so integrated into the landscape that they are difficult to see even from the parking area. Trees and flowers surround you as you walk to your cabin. Once you are inside you still feel like a part of nature, as the interiors are finished with wooden walls and decorated with rough hewn log furniture. It's very comfortable and earthy. The fireplace in the den keeps you warm on those chilly Chilean nights and a well-stocked kitchen allows you to cook up the fresh seafood you buy from the fishing boats.

At the southern end of Playa Larga, **Caracola** serves up good, moderately priced seafood in a restaurant overlooking the sea. **Las Rocas Restaurant**, across the street, has an outstanding location, but it has become a bit run down.

Continuing down *Avenida del Mar*, you come to many rocky cliffs where the waves smash dramatically, sending spray dancing into the air. You can sit and watch this show for hours at the **Pajarera**, a blue and white restaurant that offers incredible views. The food is some of the best in Maitencillo because it is actually part of the **Marbella Resort**. It has a funicular that runs to the property. If you'd like to stay at the resort, here's the information:

MARBELLA RESORT, *Km 35 on the Coastal highway, Tel. 33/931155. 55 rooms, 22 suites. Double $180. Two restaurants. Bar. Pool. Spa. Tennis. Golf. Polo. Horse rental. Bike rental. Credit cards accepted.*

This resort is a 280 hectare property above Maitencillo. Its fresh-scrubbed yet elite atmosphere is unique among Chilean beach resorts. Surrounded by an 18 hole golf course on a bluff overlooking the ocean, the white-washed Spanish style hotel offers a variety of facilities for activity and inactivity. In addition to playing golf, guests can swim, play tennis, or take walks along the beach accessed by a funicular descending steeply to the surf. There are both indoor and outdoor pools. For further relaxation, the spa offers a full menu of body pampering services. Well thought-out extras like a complete video shop, daycare, and fireplaces in the rooms make the Marbella a great option for those yearning for a carefree escape.

HORCÓN

If you continue south, the next turn-off on the coastal road leads to Horcón. *The Old Man and the Sea* meets *Electric Kool-Aid Acid Test* in this small fishing village. Hippies found the place years ago and have managed to live in harmony with the local residents. The town's informal atmosphere, simple lodgings, and excellent seafood attract a younger crowd. Be forewarned — it is almost too crowded on summer weekends to be enjoyable, but any other time of the year you'll find it a nice place to spend a day or two.

There is only one true hotel in town, but many Horcónians hang shingles on their doors and turn their homes into *residenciales* as demand dictates. Consider the **Hosteria Arancibia**, *Avenida Playa. Tel. 09/324-1986. 10 cabins. Double $44. Restaurant. Credit cards accepted.* These cabins, at the far end of the line-up of restaurants and shops along the sea, are basic but passable. The grounds are pleasant and both the lobby and restaurant nicely decorated. It is necessary to make a reservation in advance in the summer.

The seafood in Horcón is fresh, cheap, and tasty. **La Ancla**, on the beachfront, is the traditional favorite, but **El Balcón** is another strong choice. From its balcony you have prime people watching position.

While Horcón's main beach, **Playa Larga**, is not very appealing, there are some exceptional beach coves on both sides of town. **Quillliruca Beach** is four km north of Horcón at the very end of Playa Larga. You can camp on the beach, which is protected from the wind, or just picnic for the day.

Cau-Cau Beach, accessed from a marked road in town, is also excellent. You descend what feel like hundreds of stairs before arriving to the small cove. After spending the morning on the beach, lunch at **Caballo de Mar**, the seaside restaurant, is a must.

The area from **Horcón** to **Quintero** has been sacrificed to industry. This section of coast houses the largest industrial complex in Chile, complete with the highest smoke stack in South America. A copper

WHY YOUR TOES ARE BLUE

*The beach experience in Chile is different than elsewhere as people spend about 95% of their time outside the water. Just dipping your feet in the ocean is enough to cool the rest of your body. Why is the water so cold? Blame it on the **Humbolt current**.*

The Humbolt current, running up the entire coast of Chile, can be thought of as a huge oceanic river. It is 600 km wide and over 400 km deep. The average water temperature varies from 48°-66°F depending on how close you are to its source in the frigid water of Antarctica.

If you curse the current while you're in the water, you'll bless it when you go to lunch. The temperature is ideal for marine organisms, explaining Chile's abundance of fish and other sea creatures.

refinery, petroleum terminal, and thermoelectric plant make an ugly trio. Our advice is to keep moving. Windsurfers skim across the water in Quintero's main bay, but you wonder if they are selectively blind to the other activity there.

The next section of coast, south of Quintero, is greatly influenced by the Aconcagua River. The river empties large amounts of sediment into the sea, which has washed ashore creating mountain-sized sand dunes all the way to Concón.

VIÑA DEL MAR

Viña is the largest beach resort in Chile. Founded in 1874, it was originally a weekend retreat for the rich industrialists of Valparaíso. When the Grand Hotel was built in 1880, a steady stream of *Santiaguinos* started pouring into town. That stream has yet to be dammed.

Chileans love Viña. They gush about it so effusively that you'll wonder what all the fuss is about when you finally get there. There is a "Viña state of mind" that you have to reach before your visit, or you will be disappointed. You have to prepare yourself for the urban beach experience, which includes traffic, tall buildings, and lots of people. It also includes an interesting, high energy scene, gambling, and dancing until the wee hours of the morning.

ARRIVALS & DEPARTURES

By Boat
You can make the short ride from Viña to Valparaíso in boats that leave constantly from the Vergara Dock, *Muelle*, on Playa Acapulco for $3.

By Bus
Most of the long distances buses that stop in **Valparaíso** make a stop in Viña as well. The bus station is located two blocks from the Vergara Plaza at the intersection of Valparaíso and Quilpue streets.

Bus Companies
• **Buses JM**, *Tel. 883184*; east to Los Andes
• **Fenix Pullman Norte**, *Tel. 883489*; north to Arica, south to Valdivia, east to Mendoza, Argentina
• **Pullman**, *Tel. 680424*; north to Arica
• **Sol del Pacifico**, *Tel. 883156*; north along coast to Papudo, south to Los Angeles
• **Tramaca**, *Tel. 690195*; north to Antofagasta, Calama
• **Tur Bus**, *Tel. 882661*; Santiago every 15 minutes from 6am-9pm, south to Puerto Montt
• **Zambrano**; *Tel. 883942*; north to Arica

Buses run almost non-stop between Viña de Mar and Valparaíso. Any one that says *Puerto* or *Aduana* is headed to Valparaíso. Sol del Pacifico buses run along Avenida Libertad and connect to all the towns up the coast to the north.

By Car

It's a straight shot from Santiago to Viña on the toll road 68. Probably the best highway in the country, it is four lane almost the entire way. With no traffic, the ride takes 90 minutes. On Friday evening, it could take three hours. You won't use a car to get around Viña, but you might want one to explore the coast. The drive to Concón is spectacular and having your own car gives you the luxury of creating your our schedule.

Rental Car Agencies
• **Anditour**, *Viana 31, Tel. 32/690817*
• **Automoviles Setien**, *15 Norte 1119, Tel. 32/970451*
• **Bechan**, *Arlegui 102, Tel 32/906117*
• **Flota Verschae**, *Libertad 1030, Tel. 32/971184*
• **Hertz**, *Calle Quillota 656, Tel. 689918*
• **Heros y Heros**, *San Martin 458, Loc 13, Tel. 695119*
• **Morris**, *Libertad 1075, Tel. 32/970451*

By Train

The efficient commuter train, Mervel, runs between Viña and Valparaíso. There are two train stations in Viña:
• **Estación Viña del Mar**, *Plaza Sucre on Alvarez*
• **Estación Miramar**, *Alvarez and Agua Santa on the southwest side of town*

By Plane

LanChile and Ladeco have offices in Viña:
• **LanChile**, *Ecuador 289, Tel. 680560*
• **Ladeco**, *Ecuador 80, Tel. 979089*

ORIENTATION

Viña, just a few kilometers north of Valparaíso, runs along the ocean. The town is divided by the Marga Marga Stream, over which there are a number of bridges. The beach scene is on the north side of the bridge and downtown on the south.

Running roughly parallel to the beaches, three to six blocks back, is the main artery Liberty Avenue, *Avenida Libertad*. Streets to the east of it are *oriente*, and streets to the west of it, *poniente*.

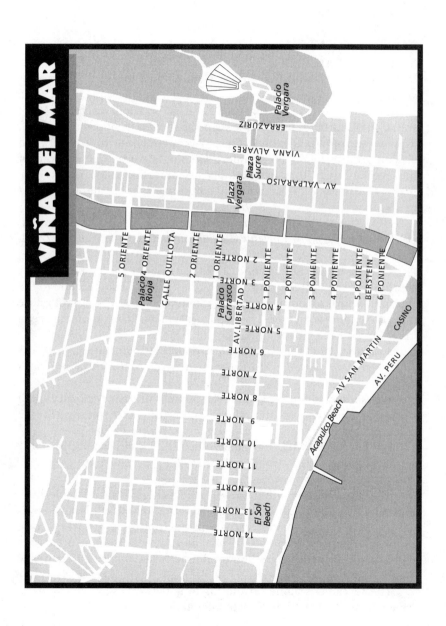

VIÑA DEL MAR

Palacio Vergara

ERRAZURIZ

VIANA ALVARES

Plaza Sucre

Plaza Vergara

AV. VALPARAISO

5 ORIENTE

Palacio 4 ORIENTE
Rioja

CALLE QUILLOTA

2 ORIENTE

1 ORIENTE

Palacio
Carrasco

AV. LIBERTAD

2 NORTE

3 NORTE

4 NORTE

5 NORTE

6 NORTE

7 NORTE

8 NORTE

9 NORTE

10 NORTE

11 NORTE

12 NORTE

13 NORTE

14 NORTE

1 PONIENTE

2 PONIENTE

3 PONIENTE

4 PONIENTE

5 PONIENTE

BERSTEIN

6 PONIENTE

CASINO

AV. SAN MARTIN

AV. PERU

Acapulco Beach

El Sol
Beach

GETTING AROUND TOWN

Once you get into town you will probably walk every where. Cabs are available on the streets if you need one.

WHERE TO STAY

CAP DUCAL, *Marina 51. Tel. 32/626655. 25 rooms Double $110. Restaurant. Bar. Discotheque. Sauna. Gym. Ocean water pool. Credit cards accepted.*

If it weren't for the fact that Cap Ducal has been a class act since 1936, you might think that a hotel in the shape of a boat is flamboyant gimmick. The subtle, rusty red hues of the linens, lacquered beech wood beams, and elegant terraces solidify its premiere standing. Be sure to reserve one of the several rooms with yellow-canopied balconies that extend out over the sea. The Cap Ducal's restaurant and coffee shop bar are among the best in Viña.

HOTEL SAN MARTIN, *San Martin 667. Tel. 32/689195. Rooms 172. Double with a view $110. Cable TV. Restaurant. Bar. Gym. Sauna. Credit cards accepted.*

This big brown hotel is one of the few options for lodging directly overlooking the beach. Unfortunately, they need to take this one to the Atacama desert to dry out for a while as musty odor sneaks into your nose from the minute you enter. The Cap Ducal is a much better on-the-ocean hotel for the same price.

ANKARA HOTEL, *San Martin 476. Tel. 692085. Rooms 50. Double $117. Restaurant Cable TV. Stereo. Room service. Sauna. Parking. Credit cards accepted.*

This slick, centrally-located hotel is popular with *Santiaguinos* visiting the beach. The rooms are new, clean, slightly frilly, and a bit small for the price. It stays full even in the low season, so people do like it.

HOTEL OCEANIC, *Avenida Borgoño 12925 on the road to Reñaca. Tel. 32/830006. Fax 32/830390. 30 rooms. Double $90. Restaurant. Bar. Gym. Sauna. Pool. Credit cards accepted.*

The Hotel Oceanic is the "house on the rock" of biblical parable. Built on a solid foundation jutting out in the sea, it withstands crashing of waves all around it. Spray from whitecaps keeps you cool as you sit on the terrace or float in the pool. As you would imagine, the view from the ocean-side rooms is spectacular. The restaurant Rendez vous, also with a wonderful view, serves delicious seafood.

The Oceanic is alone on the highway between Viña and Reñaca, which means that you'll be isolated if you don't have a car.

HOTEL O'HIGGINS, *Plaza Vergara. Tel. 32/882016. Fax 32/883537. 265 rooms. Double $93. Restaurant. Bar. Pool. Credit cards accepted.*

Many people visit this humongous hotel year after year. The hotel has enjoyed a reputation of excellence in Viña for over 75 years, with attentive service and rooms that are the nicest in the downtown area. We particularly like the old elevators with their uniformed attendants guiding us from floor to floor. While the downtown location turns some away, others prefer this historic section of town over the modern area by the beach. The restaurant is top quality and they even have baby sitting services.

HOTEL QUINTA VERGARA, *Errazuriz 690. Tel. 32/685073. Fax 32/691978. 15 rooms. Double $49. Breakfast included. Credit cards accepted.*

This maroon and white hotel backs up to the large park after which it is named. This means that if you have a room in the rear of the hotel, you'll be treated to leafy, green views. The hotel is clean and cheery and its proximity to Quinta Vergara gives you the chance to roam about tree-lined paths. Again, you're not by the beach, but you have the Garden of Eden in the backyard.

HOTEL ALBAMAR, *San Martin 419, Tel. 32-975274. 30 rooms. Double $70. Restaurant. Cable TV. Parking. Credit cards accepted.*

The Albamar is a solidly built, comfortable hotel and a nice value. It has a good central location to boot.

CANTAMAR HOTEL, *5 Norte 230. Tel. 32/884900. 30 rooms. Double $60. Breakfast included. Cable TV. Parking.*

This hotel, as long and thin as Chile itself, is only a few blocks from the beach and is often full. Like the Albamar and Crown Royal, it is a good value considering its quality and the upscale prices of the digs surrounding it.

CROWN ROYAL HOTEL, *5 Norte 655. Tel. 32/682450. 70 rooms. Double $50. Breakfast included. Cable TV. Credit cards accepted.*

The hallways and walls of this hotel are painted in all of the colors of a pastel rainbow - peach, pink, and lime green. The rooms are newly decorated with functional furnishings similar to US motel chains. Its location, several blocks off of the beach, allows it to offer reasonable prices that you might be able to negotiate even lower during non-peak season visits.

HOTEL ESPAÑOL, *Plaza Vergara 191. Tel. 32/685145. Fax 32/685146. 25 rooms. Double $50. Restaurant. Breakfast included. Credit cards accepted.*

The Hotel O'Higgins looms down the street, but you might prefer this downtown hotel because of its manageable size. The rooms of this colonial-style house are large, ceilings high, and banister polished to a glowing sheen. The quarters on the second floor are the best, as the third floor rooms are not as big. The place is fading a bit, but is still comfortable.

The restaurant offers the classic Chilean menu, but we like the breakfast churros and coffee.

RESIDENCIAL BLANCHAIRD, *Avenida Valparaíso 82-A. Tel. 32/ 974949. 20 rooms. Double with bath $27. Breakfast included if staying more than 2 nights. No credit cards.*

This old house is a little threadbare, but it's clean and the staff is friendly. Down an alley off Valparaíso, it's quieter than many hotels in the area and is really a good value. The rambling turn-of-the-century home has hard wood floors and high ceilings, giving the place a touch of class.

RESIDENCIAL 555, *5 Norte 555. Tel. 32/972240. 14 rooms. Double $40. Breakfast included. Cable TV. Credit cards accepted.*

This residencial is one charming piece of work. Vibrant purple, red, and yellow flowers provide a brilliant flash of color in the front yard. The rooms are comfortable, quite tasteful, and reminiscent of an American B&B ambience. The owners are extremely courteous. The homey atmosphere of the 555 is the perfect alternative if you want to avoid Viña's glitz.

WHERE TO EAT

CAP DUCAL, *Marina 51. Tel. 32/626655. Expensive. Credit cards accepted.*

The Cap Ducal's restaurant, located at the base of a ship-shaped edifice, has been a favorite in Viña del Mar since 1936. The dining room is a tastefully outfitted with desert-red tablecloths and napkins. Most of the tables are stationed alongside the windows overlooking the ocean. There is a second level balcony that lines both walls, also with excellent window views. The house specialties include simple dishes like salmon baked in the traditional clay bowl, to the bold conger eel in sea urchin sauce. There is also a bar and coffee shop where newspaper readers frequently lounge as they sip their morning java.

LAS DELICIAS, *San Martin 459, Tel. 901837. Expensive. Credit cards accepted.*

This sassy international restaurant is decked out in sultry red tablecloths. The specialty of the house is seafood and Marilyn Monroe. No less than thirty photographs of the legendary film idol line the walls. The menu is divided into to two sections – *Sabores Suaves* (Smooth Flavors) and *Sabores Acentuados* (Accented Flavors). Among the smooth dishes is *Salmon Gratinado*, salmon with a shrimp and Parmesan sauce accompanied by asparagus. One of the accented favorites is *Congrio Pimentón*, conger eel prepared in a sauce of red bell peppers, golden-baked garlic, tomatoes, and white wine.

CAFE SANTA FE, *Corner of Av. San Martin and 8 Norte. Tel. 691719. Expensive/moderate. Credit cards accepted.*

A mustard-colored adobe houses Viña's Santa Fe Cafe, a Tex-Mex restaurant spun off from one of the same name in Santiago. Santa Fe is famous for its shrimp, chicken, and beef fajitas which are served sizzling on the pan, accompanied by multiple tortilla stuffing extras like sour cream, jalapeños, tomatoes, and lettuce. The restaurant also offers other Mexican fare and several creative variations of Cesar salads but our experience in with those is limited since we order the fajitas time and time again.

GURIS BRASILEIROS, *San Martin 304, Tel. 881215. Expensive/ moderate. Credit cards accepted.*

Its hard to imagine Brazilians not having fun, and so, it is hard to imagine not having a good time in Guris. Samba-playing Brazilian musicians set the lively tone Friday and Saturday nights so you can work off the decadent calories while shaking your *bunda* to the acoustic beat. The featured fare is Brazilian *churrasco* barbecue, a meat-lover's dream. Waiters appear constantly at your shoulder to serve succulent pork, steak, chicken, sausage, and sweet meats directly from the skewers onto your plate. An ample salad bar accompanies the meat-fest.

DON TITO, *Arlegui 857. Tel. 684451. Moderate. No credit cards.*

Just down from the Hotel O'Higgins, Don Tito's packs in the lunch time crowd. Downtown workers are the regulars at this simple restaurant that specializes in seafood but offers the full Chilean spread.

RISTORANTE SAN MARCO *San Martin 597. Tel. 975304. Moderate. Credit cards accepted.*

San Marcos has a long list of pasta loving fans to whom the restaurant has been serving up delicious Italian cuisine for over fifty years. Vines curtain the windows from the inside while white tablecloths dress up the locale. Specialties like home-style lasagna keep the place going strong. Two other Italian eateries that can be recommended are **Fellini**, *Tel. 975742,* and **La Cucina de Veracruz**, both on *3 Norte near the corner of San Martin in front of the casino.*

FOGON CRIOLLO, *5 Norte 476. Tel. 973312. Moderate/inexpensive. Credit cards accepted.*

The Fogon Criollo serves delicious, traditional Chilean fare such as *porotos granados, pastel de choclo,* and spit-roasted meats. The ambience is family-oriented featuring a decor of pine-finished walls and furniture. The daily lunch special is the best bargain in Viña.

Fast Food

Fast food abounds in Viña. **Pizza Hut**, *San Martin 604, Tel. 687000,* **Domino's**, *San Martin 570, Tel. 691010,* and **Pan de Diego**, *San Martin 636, Tel. 838934 or 689512* are all located within a block of one another. Pan de Diego has a big screen TV if you are seeking sports with your pizza. There are **McDonalds** at *San Martin 298, Avenida Valparaíso 912, and 15*

Norte 961. If you want ice-cream, **Bravissimo**, *San Martin 302, Tel. 681862,* serves some of the best in Chile.

SEEING THE SIGHTS
The Grand House Tour

Viña enjoyed its heyday about seventy years ago. Right after the turn of the century, a number of wealthy industrialists and shipping magnates built extravagantly beautiful mansions on huge lots. The finest of these have been preserved, and a few of them house outstanding museums.

QUINTA VERGARA, *Errazuriz and Libertad. Tel. 684137. Tuesday-Sunday, 10am-2pm, 3pm-6pm. Entry $1.*

For the price of a Coke you can walk through one of the prettiest gardens in all Chile, tour a turn-of-the-century mansion, and visit the Fine Arts Museum.

Francisco Alvarez, the founder of Viña, built his original residence on this spot. His wife had a green thumb that she put to work planting hundreds of types of trees, shrubs, and flowers. Their son, who often traveled to the Orient, brought exotic plants for his mother from all over Asia and Australia. This garden is a monument to the family project. You can wander through it paths and see well-marked trees and plants from around the world.

Francisco's granddaughter built the mansion, which is as much a work of art as the paintings it houses. Designed by an Italian architect, the walls of the home are now covered the work by such masters as Rubens and Tintoretto. The room on the far right as you enter is full of portraits of the Vergara family.

Leaving the Quinta Vergara, walk two blocks north along Libertad to the small **Plaza Sucre** and the larger **Plaza Jose Francisco Vergara**. Some of the more important buildings in town are found along the sides of these two plazas.

Continue north, crossing the Libertad Bridge over the stream. Three blocks after the bridge, you'll see the Palacio Carrasco on the right.

PALACIO CARRASCO, *Libertad and 3 Norte. Tel. 883154. Monday-Friday, 9am-1pm, 2pm-8pm. Saturday 10am-1pm. No admission fee.*

Built in 1912 by a French resident of Valparaíso, the palace now houses the Cultural Center, the Vicuna Mackenna Library, and the Historical Archives. You can walk in and see the upstairs exhibit, but it is usually kind of weak. It's interesting just to admire the house from outside.

On the corner of the same block, at 4 Norte, take a right to visit the:

FONCK SOCIETY MUSEUM, *4 Norte 784. Tel. 686753. Tuesday-Friday, 10am-6pm, Saturday-Sunday, 10am-2pm. Entry $1.*

Very few museums in Chile have collections that include artifacts from Easter Island, *Isla de Pascua*. The Fonck, however, houses one of the largest and most varied displays on the Rapanui culture in Chile. The museum provides the rare opportunity to see a traditional Moai statue with its red lava topknot in place. Although the Moai with the topknot is only about a foot tall, it helps you imagine how it would look on the full-sized carving outside of the museum.

The natural history section upstairs includes admirable collections of insects, butterflies, hummingbirds, and a few oddities like a giant armadillo and a two-headed sheep. If you continue two blocks down 4 Norte street, the lane will dead end in the gardens of:

PALACIO RIOJA, *Quillota 214, Tel. 689665, Monday-Sunday, 10am-2pm, 3pm-5pm. Entry $1. Movie theater, Tel. 883322.*

In a bit of dramatic gesture, a Spanish banker bought 40,000 square meters in 1906 and charged his architect to build a masterpiece. Part of the "Belle Epoch" of Viña, the interior of the mansion is restored as it was then. This property used to comprise four entire blocks, but has been scaled back to cover just one. The gardens of the palace are immaculately groomed and include gargantuan ferns, palm trees, and a wisteria plant climbing up and summitting a fifty foot high tree.

Movies are shown through out the year in a theater in the back of the house. The theater specializes in art house movies, which are hard to find in Chile.

The Beach Tour

It is doubtless that you will make this trek during your time in Viña. You can start at the southern-most end of the beach at the **Castillo Wulff** on the left, sticking out over the ocean. The building, constructed in 1906, was the home of nitrate baron Gustavo Wulff. It currently houses the **Museum of Sea Culture**, *Tel. 625427, Monday-Friday 10am-1pm, 2:30pm-6pm. Saturday-Sunday, 10am-1pm.* You can walk on the glass floor, where you actually see the waves breaking beneath you. On the other side of the street is the **Presidential Palace**, built in 1930.

Cross the stream at the Casino bridge, and take a left, which will lead you to **Peru Avenue**, the main beach drag. The street begins with the **Municipal Casino** and its gardens. Full of life and activity in the afternoon, the gardens are prime people watching spots.

This street used to be lined with beach chalets, all of which have been mowed over and replaced with tall buildings. Peru takes a big curve in front of the **Hotel San Martin**. From here you can either walk on the beach, **Playa Acapulco**, or continue on the street, which changes names to **San Martin Avenue**. Both are packed with people in the summer. The **Vergara Dock**, *muelle*, down the beach, has a number of restaurants, but most of them are overpriced.

THE NATIONAL BOTANICAL GARDEN, *From downtown, take a left on Valparaíso and then veer to the right on Lichame which runs into the park. Tel. 672566. Monday-Sunday, 10am-6pm.*

This park, founded by a local industrialist, is now administered by Conaf. Home to over 3,000 plant species, it's an impressive display. One of the trees, the Toromiro, is extinct on its natural home, Easter Island, but alive in the park. There are a number of trails through the grounds, some of which lead to lakes and picnic grounds.

NIGHTLIFE & ENTERTAINMENT

MUNICIPAL CASINO, *Avenida San Martin 199. Tel. 689200, Winter 6pm-2am, Summer 7pm-4am.*

The casino is one of the social centers of Viña. The dress code includes a tie for the game room, which features black jack and craps. For slot machines and bingo you can dress casually.

Most of the discos are inexplicably, and dangerously, located on the curvy road between Viña and Reñaca.

SPORTS & RECREATION

In the summer, the in-town beaches are the ones hopping with activity. They are also the most crowded and littered. The further north you go towards Reñaca, the cleaner the beaches. They stay crowded all the way up however. If you want to be a part of the scene, park yourself right on Acapulco beach and watch the world revolve around you.

LAGUNA SAUSALITO, *End of Los Castanos Avenue. Pools. Tennis. Boat Rental. Entry fee depends on activity.*

Laguna Sausalito is filled with people practicing different water sports. There is skiing, row boating, and jetskiing. Around the shores of the lake there are 12 tennis courts and four swimming pools. All of it is open to the public for different prices.

THE SPORTING CLUB, *Los Castanos Avenue. Sunday races throughout the year, weekday races in the summer.*

The city's horse race track holds live races as well as satellite feeds from Santiago and Concepción.

SHOPPING

There is an **Artisan's Fair** downtown on the Cousiño walkway off Valparaíso Avenue between Libertad and Quinta. There are some nice buys amongst all the junk, but you have to look for them. There is another **Artisan's Market** across the street from the Hotel Oceanic on the road to Reñaca.

EXCURSIONS & DAY TRIPS

Reñaca

Reñaca, once a suburb of Viña, has grown into a self-sufficient, over-crowded town. It is a hot spot on the Chilean coast right now. Building after building angle for views, but most of them just view their neighbors.

Concón

The drive from Reñaca to Concón is a beautiful, curving jaunt along the shore similar to California's Highway 1. There are a number of spots for watching waves and enjoying seafood with great views of the ocean. Each of these places is lined with restaurants serving almost identical food. If you are just out for lunch and a drive, we recommend driving all the way up to La Boca, checking out the sights and restaurants along the way, and then eating at one on your drive back.

The first of these restaurant congregation areas is two km out of town at **Cochao beach**. After passing through Cochao you'll come to two *miradores*, or lookout points. Both are worth a stop; the first one is a prime place for viewing sea lions and the second is an excellent spot for photos of the coastline and winding road.

Further down the road you pass through **Higuerilla**, with its pelicans and gulls surrounding the fishing boats. **Albatros**, **Mar Azul**, and **Bella Mar** are all good restaurants here. The last town before the Aconcagua River is **La Boca**. The restaurants here are not quite as nice as some of the others on the route, but **Empanadas Las Delicias**, on the right side of the road, is a must. People come from all around for these hot pastry treats. The hot *machas* and cheese *empanadas* are otherworldly.

THE BEST EMPANADAS IN CHILE

Here's our list of personal favorites:
- *Machas and cheese empanada:* **Empanadas Las Delicias**, Concón, Central Coast
- *Apple empanada:* **Casa de Empanadas**, Road to Futulefu, Austral Region
- *Seafood empanada:* **Central Market**, Dalcahue, Chiloé

Valparaíso

It would be a waste to be in Viña and not visit Valparaíso for sightseeing or a meal. See the *Valparaíso* entry below.

Olmué

Olmué and La Campana National Park are an easy drive from Viña.

You might want to combine the country and the beach in one excursion. See the *Olmué* entry in this chapter.

Lake Peñuelas National Reserve
This lake on the highway from Santiago to Viña is one of the few reserves in Chile that does not really merit a visit. Most of the park it closed to visitors, and the part that's not is crowded with picnicking families.

PRACTICAL INFORMATION

Banks: BCI, *Valparaíso 193*; **Banco Edwards**, *Libertad 770*; **Santander**, *9 Norte 781*

Business Hours: Monday-Saturday 10am-2pm, 5pm-9pm

Currency Exchange: Cambios Andino, *Arlegui 646*; **Intercambios**, *1 Norte 655-B*

Laundry: Laverap, *Libertad 902*

Medical Service: Hospital Fricke, *Alverez 1532*

National Parks: Conaf, *3 Norte 541*

Post Office: Correos de Chile, *Valaparaiso 846*

Supermarkets: Santa Isabel, *Arlegui and Etchevers*

Telephone/Fax: The area code is 32. **CTC**, *Valparaíso 628*; **Entel**, *Valparaíso 510*

Tourist Office/Maps: Municipal Tourist Office, *Libertad and Arlegui by Plaza Vergara. Tel. 883154.* Monday-Friday 9am-2pm, 3pm-7pm. Saturday 10am-2pm **Sernatur**, *Valparaíso 507, 3rd floor.* Monday-Friday only

VALPARAÍSO
Valparaíso is a fascinating jumble of streets and houses stacked on forty hills and spilling over the edges of cliffs that look out to the sea. Chileans like to say that Valparaíso was never founded, but rather grew spontaneously over hills and in ravines from the moment of its discovery. During the colonial period, all the production that entered or left the country, mainly in trade with Peru, was under legal obligation to go through this port.

Over time, as the trade activity of the country grew, so did Valparaíso ("Valpo" to Chileans.) In the 1840s, Valparaíso was the main financial, commercial, and business center of the country. It wasn't until the 1920s that businessman and their companies moved inland to Santiago.

ARRIVALS & DEPARTURES
By Bus
The bus station is located across from the National Congress building

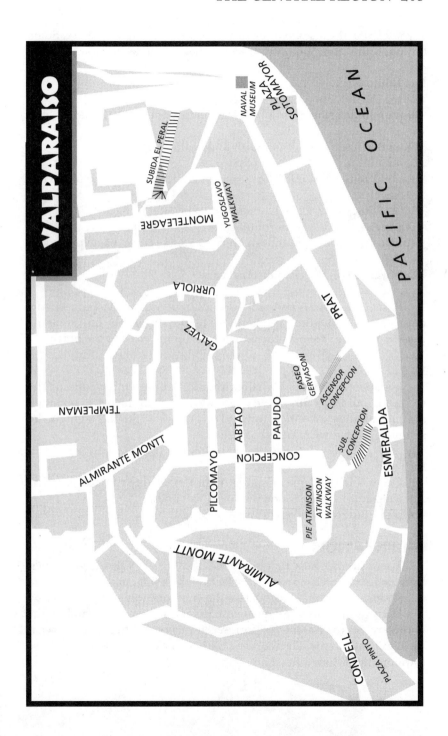

at *2800 Pedro Montt*. All of the lines listed below leave from there. Some buses pass through Viña on the way to their listed destination.

Bus Companies
- **Buses JM**, *Tel. 253161*; east to Los Andes
- **Fenix Pullman Norte**, *Tel. 257993*; north to Arica, south to Valdivia, east to Mendoza, Argentina
- **Flota Barrios**, *Tel. 253674*; north to Arica
- **Pullman**, *Tel. 256898*; north to Arica
- **Sol del Pacifico**, *Tel. 213776*; north along coast to Papudo, south to Los Angeles
- **Sol del Sur**, *Tel. 252211*; south to Concepción
- **Tramaca**, *Tel. 250811*; north to Antofagasta, Calama
- **Tur Bus**, *Tel. 212028*; Santiago every 15 minutes from 6am-9pm, south to Puerto Montt
- **Zambrano**; *Tel. 258986*; north to Arica

Buses run almost non-stop between Viña de Mar and Valparaíso. Any one that says *Viña* is headed there. Sol del Pacifico buses run along the road to Viña and connect to all the towns up the coast to the north.

By Car
It is about an hour and a half drive from Santiago to Valparaíso. The toll road, four lanes almost the whole way, is one of the better highways in Chile. It can be extremely crowded on Friday and Sunday nights in the summer, so plan your trip accordingly.

By Train
There is an efficient commuter train, Mervel, that run between Viña and Valparaíso. There is one station in Valparaíso:
- **Estación Puerto**, *in front of Plaza Sotomayor*

ORIENTATION
There are 45 hills that surround the bay in Valparaíso proper. Stairways and funiculars run up the faces of these hills, making pedestrian travel much easier than negotiating the crazy one-way streets in car.

Many of the sights and older restaurants and bars are found on the lower levels of town along the port. A central point in this part of town is the **Plaza Sotomayor**. The walkways, with their excellent views, are above town on the various *cerros*, hills.

THE UPS & DOWNS OF VALPO

The funiculars are a unique aspect of the city. The steeply pitched tracks and the trams that climb them make it much easier to negotiate Valparaíso's many hills. Here's some ammunition for Ascensor Trivia.
- *Total in town: 15*
- *Oldest: Concepción, 1883*
- *Steepest: Cordillera*
- *Longest: Mariposa, 160 meters*

GETTING AROUND TOWN

For much of the sightseeing, it is better to walk than drive; a route that is a simple funicular ride on foot is a circuitous excursion in a car. *Paseos*, or pedestrian walkways are another good way to cut through streets. Lastly there are the endless stairways that carve a zigzag path up the face of all the hills in town.

If you have a car, you might want to park it and use your feet and public transportation. Parking is difficult and the unmarked one-way streets can lead to comical as well as dangerous situations. Buses are clearly marked with their destinations, as are the collective taxis. There are no individual taxis.

WHERE TO STAY

There are just not that many nice places to stay in Valparaíso. We can highly recommend the Brighton and the Don Carrasco, but beyond that the options are not that great because even the passable hotels are in less-than-desirable neighborhoods.

Moderate

BRIGHTON, *Pasaje Atkinson Numbers 151-153, Cerro Concepción. Tel. 32/223513. Fax 32/213360. 6 rooms. Double $60-88. Breakfast included. Restaurant. Credit cards accepted.*

This lovely Victorian-style home is a jewel of Valparaíso, within walking distance from the important city sights. Six rooms, decked out with antiques gleaned from local markets, await lucky guests. High ceilings, exposed beams, intricate molding, and interesting furniture fill the small but charming rooms. The showers are modern and efficient.

Each room is unique. The suite on the first floor has outstanding views of the harbor as well as a small balcony. Others have views of both the sea and hills. The single room is very small, so look at it before you decide to stay here.

Downstairs there is a bar and restaurant with one of the most popular patios in the city. Its black and white tiles point out to the sea while Valparaíso wraps around the surrounding hills. At night, mesmerizing lights twinkle below. Excellent *pisco sours* are the specialty of an extensive drink menu.

Selected as one of our best places to stay – see Chapter 10 for more details.

LANCASTER HOTEL. *Chacabuco 2362. Tel. 32/217391. 11 rooms. Double $50. Breakfast included. Secure parking. Credit cards accepted.*

The Lancaster has large, clean rooms that give you plenty of space to spread out. The bathrooms are small, but make up they for it by having tubs with lion's claws. Unfortunately, they are located in a part of town filled with car showrooms and repair shops – good if you need a car part, but bad for the ambiance.

HOTEL CASA BASKA, *Victoria 2449. Tel. 32/234036. Fax. 219915. 16 rooms. Double $50. Breakfast included. Credit cards accepted.*

Two colonial homes, combined and converted into a hotel, retain some of the grandeur of their earlier years. Marble steps at the entry lead you to simple rooms with high ceilings and intricate molding. The rooms away from the street are quieter, but the ones over Victoria Avenue have small balconies. The neighborhood, close to the Congress Building, is not the best, but the hotel is a decent, clean option.

Inexpensive

DON JUAN CARRASCO, *Abtao 668, Cerro Concepción. Tel. 210737. $10 per person. 14 rooms. Shared bathrooms. No credit cards.*

This *residencial*, our favorite cheap sleep in Chile, is a 140-year-old house, converted into an inn for budget travelers. The towering facade is painted lime green while the window frames are eye-lined in a striking compliment of purple. Its soul is a varnished helix of a staircase with squeaky, polished, wooden slats. A reading nook at the top of all of those stairs shares the altitude with a church steeple looking out over Valparaíso's bay and forty-plus hills. The best rooms are the two on the third floor that have almost the same view as the reading nook. All of the rooms are extra large with 15-foot ceilings and usually have a table and reading chair in addition to the beds. A fully equipped kitchen is available for the *residencial* guests to use. There is no sign posted outside identifying it, so just ring the bell.

HOTEL PRAT, *Condell 1443. Tel. 32/253081 or 253082. 120 rooms. Double $20. Credit cards accepted.*

The Hotel Prat offers big clean rooms in a building showing its wear. The interior is a bit gloomy because all of the interior tones are brown. The hotel is centrally located in the principal commercial district. The bottom floor of the building is composed of shops so keep an eye peeled for the reception window about 50 meters to your right as you enter.

HOSTAL KOLPING, *Vergara 622 in front of Plaza Italia. Tel. 32/ 216306. Fax 32/230352. 8 rooms. Double with bath $31. Breakfast included. No credit cards.*

The Kolping is clean and well maintained inside and the staff is friendly, but the thick burglar bars tell the story about the neighborhood.

The three other best *residenciales* in Valparaíso are **Señora Venegas**, *Argentina 322-B, Tel. 215673;* **Señora Villaciencio**, *Capitán M. Jarpa 529, Playa Ancha, Tel. 287098;* and **Señor Tesser**, *Quebrada Verde 192, Tel. 288873.* . They all charge about $10 per person. The last two are bit outside of town.

WHERE TO EAT

LA COLOMBINA, *Pasaje Apolo Numbers 91-77. Tel. 236254. Closed Monday. Restaurant-expensive. Pub-inexpensive. Credit cards accepted.*

Sitting on a small passageway below the Belles Artes museum, this house-turned-pub-and- restaurant is another example of Valparaíso's renaissance. The food is so good that we can say if you only have one meal in Valparaíso, you should eat it here. The pub, with its long bar and high ceilings, is a coffeehouse during the day and a bar at night. Lovely stained-glass windows offer slivers of glimpses of the harbor below. There is even a working model of a funicular on the wall. The menu consists of sandwiches and coffee, which fits the budgets of the student clientele.

The restaurant, on the other hand, draws the thicker-walleted set. China and linen tablecloths are the standard here. Tables are set up in what would be the drawing and living rooms of the house. Antiques are the norm, including a hundred year old dresser from a local pharmacy that holds 56 drawers of labeled and dried spices.

La Colombina distinguishes itself from other restaurants in town, and even the country, with its artful sense of presentation. Even the hot sauce arrives to the table decorated with flowers from the garden outside.

Seafood, it comes as no surprise, is the specialty of the house. The *machas a la parmesana* are unforgettable, as is the catch of the day prepared with cheese and tomatoes. For dessert, we recommend the chocolate mousse even if you're not hungry. Washed down with a fine wine, it is sure to be a memorable experience.

CAFE TURRI, *Templeman 147, Cerro Concepción. Tel. 252091. Expensive. Credit cards accepted.*

Valparaíso's most renowned restaurant offers extraordinary, panoramic views of the city and bay. We are disappointed that the food doesn't live up to expectations. One entrée, sea bass in cream sauce topped with bacon and Parmesan cheese, sounds like it should be a flavorful preparation. Unfortunately, everything on the plate is bland in color and flavor.

The restaurant is located in a beautiful building with an outdoor dining area on the first floor. The third floor has a wall of windows to maximize the view potential. It's probably more worthwhile as a stop for coffee on the patio. If you do go there for dinner, opt for the *pil-pil*, chile and garlic, recipes when ordering seafood to guarantee some flavor. Call ahead to reserve one of the five tables alongside the third floor window.

BOTE SALVAVIDAS, *Muelle Prat. Tel. 251477. Moderate/Expensive. Credit cards accepted.*

This is a popular seafood restaurant with a 50 year tradition, right on the waterfront next to the Prat Pier. It is a good option if you prefer your ocean views up close rather than from high in the hills. The specialty of the house is conger eel prepared in a variety of styles.

BAR INGLES, *Cochrane 851 or Blanco 870. Tel. 214625. Moderate. Credit cards accepted.*

Darkened wood composes the lengthy bar and walls of this century old institution. We enjoy the tasty chicken sandwiches with tomato and avocado for lunch, but the restaurant also offers a complete international menu. Many of the patrons simply stand at the bar for a beer or espresso. Men's self-esteem can be enhanced in the restroom where a concave mirror, strategically positioned at waist level next to the urinals, is guaranteed to change your perception of how you measure up.

BRIGHTON, *Pasaje Atkinson Numbers 151-153, Cerro Concepción. Tel. 223513. Moderate/Inexpensive. Credit cards accepted.*

Even if you're not staying in this hotel, you should stop by for a drink or sandwich. The views from the black and while tiled patio are some of the best in town. The remodeled Victorian-style building puts you in another era. If you have enough of their excellent pisco sours, you might really believe you're in turn of the century Valparaíso.

ART CAFE BAR MIRADOR, *Estación Alta Ascensor Artillería. Tel. 280944. Inexpensive. No credit cards.*

If you are visiting the Maritime Museum, this precocious view cafe is worth a visit. The fare is coffee, including flavored coffee drinks, and sandwiches. Our favorite piece in the gallery is *Swimming Nudes*, which shows hundreds of plump skinny-dippers plunging into the ocean with bright orange life buoys around their waists.

EL HAMBURG, *O'Higgins 1274. Tel. 597037. Moderate. Credit cards accepted.*

This bar/restaurant is owned by a German ex-merchant marine who decided that Valparaíso was the place for him to lay anchor. He has decorated the bar with hundreds of objects related to the sea. The food here is simple but good. We recommend lunch here on the weekends.

J. CRUZ MALBRAN, *Condell 1466, down an alley. Tel. 211225. Moderate. No credit cards.*

The restaurant is down a stinky alley, but it's worth it once you get there. The odor is replaced with wonderful, rich smells of typical Chilean food. The cozy, pub-like atmosphere is accented by the low lights and dark wooden panels. Thousands of people from all over the world have signed their names on J. Cruz's walls. We recommend the *menu* for lunch; hearty food that won't break the bank.

CAFÉ RIQUET, *Plaza Anibal Pinto 1199. Inexpensive. No credit cards.*

The décor of this café is less than inspiring, but the hot chocolate is a Valparaíso tradition. Snacks and desserts are the specialty here, as they are at **Cioccolata**, *Condell 1235,* right around the corner.

SEEING THE SIGHTS

LA SEBASTIANA, *Calle Ferrari 692. Tel. 256606. Tuesday-Sunday 10:30am-2:30pm, 3:30pm-6pm. Until 7pm in January-February. Entry $3.*

This is the least known of Pablo Neruda's houses-turned-museums. Smaller and simpler than the others, it never-the-less merits a visit. Reaching up five stories, it teeters like a bird-cage on the edge of a cliff. The sea wraps around the house and all of Valparaíso can be seen below.

The décor is classic Neruda. Colored glass, an outstanding map collection, see-through bathroom doors, embalmed birds, and a ceramic pig for serving punch all hint at this famous Chilean's personality and sense of humor. Don't miss the bar, where the "over-intellectual or cultured" were banned.

One of the best things about this house it that you can work through it at your own pace instead of having to go on a tour. You can get a guide sheet in English at the entrance, where there is also an interesting display on Neruda's life.

You can get their by bus on Bus Verde Mar "O" or "D" or by collective taxi "Plazueta Ecuador."

Valparaíso Walkways

There are three important walkways or *paseos* in Valparaíso that take you through the most historical hills and houses. The first of these, **Paseo Yugoslavo**, can be accessed by the **El Peral** funicular close to **Plaza Sotomayor**. Strolling along the walkway, you'll enjoy stunning views of the port below. There are several interesting houses up Monte Alegro Street, but the most important one, the Baburizza Palace, is at the end.

PALACIO BABURIZZA FINE ARTS MUSEUM, *end of Monte Alegro Street on Paseo Yugoslavo. Interior closed for two years for remodeling.*

This building, built in 1916 by a Yugoslavian nitrate baron, houses the town Fine Arts Museum. Even if the museum is still closed for remodeling, the building is worth a look. Built in art nouveau style, the mansion showcases impressive wooden balustrades and balconies. Kissing couples from the school next door punctuate the Paseo.

The **Gervasoni Walkway** starts at the top of the **Constitución funicular**. Just down from the funicular is the entrance to the:

MUSEO LUKAS, *Paseo Gervasoni 448. Tel. 221344. Tuesday-Sunday 10:30am-1:30pm, 3:00pm-6:30pm. Entry $1.25.*

Every once in a while someone comes along who is able to capture the spirit of his times with a few lines of pen and ink. These satirical cartoonists offer wonderful insight into the people around them. Renzo Pecchenino, "Lukas," did just that for Chile. In addition to his cartoons, he created volumes of pen and ink drawings of life in Valparaíso as well as sketches, watercolors, and other paintings. Many of these hang of the walls of this wonderful museum.

To your right as you face the sea is the famous **Café Turri**. If you continue up Templeman you come to another vestige of English influence in Chile.

ST. PAUL'S CHURCH, *Templeman and Pilcomayo. Organ recitals at 12:30pm on Sundays. No admission fee.*

This church looks pretty boring from the outside. That's exactly as it was planned. When the first English in Valparaíso collected enough money to erect a place of worship, any non-Catholic services were illegal under Chilean law. They purposely left off the steeple and bell tower to keep a low profile

The inside, however, is beautiful. Carved oak beams support a lovely wooden roof, while colored light dapples down from stained glass windows. The organ is the *piece de resistance*. Brought over from England, it has 1604 pipes, which we highly recommend you hear at work in the weekly organ concert. One block down and over you can see the spire of the Anglican church, built ten years later after the law against Protestant worship was repealed.

From here you return towards Café Turri, but take a right on Papudo and then a left on Constitución to arrive to the **Atkinson walkway**. This simple *paseo* takes you past a group of similar houses with large shutters and flower-covered lawns. It ends at the Brighton Hotel and café where you can sit over a drink and enjoy the view.

Downtown walk

The **Prat Pier**, (Muelle Prat), features a short boardwalk from which you can view freighters being loaded, colorful fishing boats bobbing in the bay, and proud gray navy vessels tied up to the harbor wave break. You can hire the fishing boats to take you for a cruise in the harbor for a few dollars per person. To do so, either ask the guys sitting on the cement rail or look longingly at the boats and they will soon approach you. A replica of the Santiaguillo, the boat in which Juan de Saavedra discovered Valparaíso Bay in 1536, serves as a monument. You will also find near the pier, a helpful tourist information office, a seaside restaurant called Bote Salvavidas, and a few souvenir stands.

Walking away from the bay you will encounter **Sotomayor Plaza**. The Heros of Iquique Monument is the centerpiece of the plaza, below which lie the remains of Arturo Prat, and other heroes of the War of the Pacific. (A complete oxymoron because Prat is the only one you ever hear about.) At the back of the plaza stands the ornate, gray and white Victorian edifice that houses the **Navy Command Headquarters**. Built in 1910 as the provincial government's seat, it also served as the president's summer residence until that was moved to Viña del Mar.

Follow Cochrane Street with the bay to your right. In about five blocks you will pass the pleasant **Echaurran Square**, landscaped with a small fountain, plum, and palm trees. On the next block, on the right hand side of the street, is the **Port Market**, *Mercado Puerto*, sheltering fruit and vegetable stalls. The interior of the building features an intriguing, blockish, spiral walkway leading up to a skylight. Unfortunately, piles of trash inside the market attract more flies than customers.

Continue a few more blocks down Cochrane street until it ends. Across a cement triangular plaza you will see the grayish blue, American colonial style **Customs House**, *Edificio de la Aduana*, which was built in 1854. To the right of the Customs House is the Artillería funicular, built in 1893, which will take you up to **21 de Mayo Walkway**, *Paseo de 21 de Mayo*. The bright orange funicular car creaks and groans as it is pulled up the rails which are visible through gaps in the floorboards. To the right of the funicular exit is a gazebo built out over the edge of the cliff which provides an awesome view of the city and harbor. If you need a break, grab a seat in the frivolous Cafe Arte Mirador on the other side of the funicular exit.

NAVAL AND MARITIME MUSEUM, *Paseo 21 de Mayo, Cerro Artillería. Tel. 283749. Tuesday-Sunday, 10am-6pm. Entry $1.*

Even if you are normally put off by maritime museums, the effort and resources that went into this one makes it worthwhile. The courtyard features an anchor composed of purple and yellow flowers in a lush green lawn. The two stories that surround the courtyard are lined with support posts and a two-tone natural wood balustrade. There are several rooms that feel like the Navy Hall of Fame, featuring smart displays of Chilean admiral's swords, uniforms, and medals. You can push through those until you make it to the Arturo Prat room. This room is filled with items salvaged from the wooden Esmeralda war ship that was sunk near Iquique by the armor-plated Peruvian battleship Huáscar in the War of the Pacific.

Prat, the captain of the Chilean vessel, valiantly boarded the Huáscar along with one other sailor, after promising his men he would fight until his death if necessary. His martyrdom proved to be the inspiration that turned the momentum in the war to Chile's advantage. One item on display is the salvaged clock which shows the time of ship's sinking on a face covered with barnacles.

You can descend to the bottom of the hill on the funicular, or the by the steps in snaking alleyway, twenty meters to its right. Walk past the so-called sailor's discotheque on Bustamante Street, the street to the right of the gas station, until you reach the **Iglesia Matriz del Senor**. The first church in Valparaíso was built on this site in 1559. At that time the church was located on the water's edge and sailors could land their vessels at its doorstep. Land reclamation has resulted in the current church, built in 1842, being located several blocks from the bay. Its wooden steeple, bright yellow like the rest of the church, tilts precariously to one side.

Continue in the same direction on Pascal street until arriving to the Echaurren Plaza that you already passed. From the plaza, take Serrano two blocks until you reach the Ascensor Cordillera funicular. You can either take this up or walk the 160 steps to reach the **Lord Cochrane Museum**, *Merlet 191, Cerro Cordillera, Tuesday-Sunday, 10am-6pm, free.* This isn't much of a museum, just a few small rooms with paintings and models of ships, but it is located in a nicely-restored colonial house, built in 1842, with a pleasant garden and view.

NATIONAL CONGRESS BUILDING, *Avenidas Argentina and Montt. Tours arranged at Tel. 230995, extension 2138. No admission unless with tour.*

There are many lovely building in Valparaíso, but this is not one of them. This ultra-modern behemoth was built after Pinochet moved the congressional branch of the government away from Santiago in 1980. He had it built on the site of his boyhood home. Marble blocks, glass and concrete cylinders, and repeating intertwined circles come together in the shape of the mathematical *pi*.

If you have at least ten people you can arrange your own tour. If you have a small group you can ask the receptionist at the Victoria Street entrance the time of the next tour and tag along with them.

The park next to it, **Plaza O'Higgins**, hosts an antique market on weekends. The **Municipal Theater**, directly across the park from the Congress Building, hosts interesting performances from time to time. Any bus that says *Congreso* will drop you here.

PALACIO LYON NATURAL HISTORY MUSEUM, *Condell 1546. Tel. 257441. Tuesday-Friday 10am-1pm, 2pm-6pm. Saturday 10am-6pm. Sunday 10am-2pm. Entry $1.25.*

This under-funded museum offers a partial look at Chile's history from a naturalist's perspective. Kids will like the displays of birds and animals, but there's not much interesting for adults besides the stuffed albatross.

There is a wonderful art gallery next door. The **Galaria Municipal de Arte**, *Condell 1550, Monday-Saturday 10am-7pm,* was built in the basement storage area of a turn of the century Palacio Lyon. They built decidedly larger basements back then. The interconnected brick cellars are surprisingly great places to display art.

Just behind the Palacio Lyon is the **Open Air Art Museum**, *Museo a Cielo Abierto.* The concept of having Chilean artists paint murals on large sections of walls following snaking stairways is a good one. Unfortunately, the reality is large sections of urine-covered steps and graffitied paintings.

NIGHTLIFE & ENTERTAINMENT

Valparaíso is one of the few cities in Chile with a vibrant and unique nightlife. Bar hopping has been perfected to a sort of recreation here. The old warehouse district on the 1100 block of Errazuriz has been converted into the hippest bars. Try La **Piedra Feliz**, **Barlovento**, **Roland Bar**, or **Bulevar**.

Emile Dubois, *Ecuador 144, Tel. 213486*, is more of a discotheque, but its style is unique and worth a visit. Dubois was the first person in Chile to receive the death sentence and a small morbid cult has grown up around him. You can order drinks with names like "strangulation," and "murderer."

If you can't get to Argentina, but are dying to hear tango, **Cinzano**, *Esmeralda facing Plaza Anibal Pinto*, is part of a 105 year old *porteño* tradition.

SHOPPING

Valparaíso is the city of antiques. European immigrants who arrived to the port ended up leaving much of their furniture here. The area around Plaza Victoria and the Congress building is the best place for nosing around. **El Abuelo**, *Independencia 2071*, is the oldest. Pablo Nerudo rooted through its wares almost weekly. **La Casa Lagazio**, *Independencia 1984*, and **El Reastro**, *Victoria 2722 in front of Plaza O'Higgins*, are two other well known stores. On weekends from 10am-2:30pm there is an antique fair on Plaza O'Higgins next to the Congress Building.

EXCURSIONS & DAY TRIPS
Algarrobo & Isla Negra

There is little road access to the beaches south of Valparaíso until the town of Algarrobo. From there, the coastal road follows the shore all the way south to Santo Domingo. The small towns along the way are not much, but you shouldn't miss **Pablo Neruda's house** in Isla Negra. Isla Negra is not an island at all, but rather a town between El Quisco and Las Cruces.

This road is packed to a standstill on the weekends during the summer, so if all possible, try to plan your trip to avoid the crowds. A nice schedule would be an early morning drive to Isla Negra for a tour of Neruda's house and then a stop for lunch in Algarrobo. Another option would be to continue on from Isla Negra to Santo Domingo.

To get here by bus, take one of the buses heading south to San Antonio, which pass through both Algarrobo and Isla Negra. See the Valparaíso *Arrivals & Departures* section for more details. By car from Valparaíso, head back towards Santiago on highway 68. After 40 km you will see the turn off to Algarrobo on the left. Take the turn and drive south along the coastal road, passing through El Quiso before arriving to Isla Negra.

Unfortunately, there is wide-scale condominium construction underway in Algarrobo, which is changing the make-up of this once tranquil vacation spot. Sailing is a popular sport here and the town hosts many summer regattas. The main draw however, is a simple restaurant called **Los Patitos**. It is located on the northern entrance of town along the coastal road. Families drive here for lunch from Santiago year round, so there is a crowd even when all the vacation homes are boarded up for the winter.

PABLO NERUDA'S HOUSE, *Isla Negra. Tel. 35/461284. Tuesday-Sunday. Summer 10am-8pm, Normal 10am-2pm, 3pm-6pm. Entry $2.50.*

Even if you have already seen his other houses in Santiago and Valparaíso, you should not miss a visit to Isla Negra. Taking some of the same themes he had touched upon in his other homes, he let them run wild in this oceanfront refuge. He filled the house with "a collection of small and large toys I can't live without" in order to "play in it from morning 'til night."

A WRITER'S REFUGE

"I needed a place to work. I found a stone house facing the ocean, in a place nobody knew about, Isla Negra. It's owner, a Spanish socialist of long standing, a sea captain, Don Eladio Sobrino was building it for his family but agreed to sell it to me...Isla Negra's wild coastal strip, with its turbulent ocean, was the place to give myself passionately to the writing of my new song."

–Pablo Neruda, in his Memoirs

The house is really a hodgepodge of rooms that were added on a few at a time whenever the poet's whims and financial circumstances were in alignment. His prolific collections, many with a nautical theme, run from scores of ships in bottles to real mastheads off sailing vessels. Neruda gave each of the mastheads its own story and personality. His favorite, the Maria Celeste, sheds tears every winter. Other fantastical furnishings include a life-sized horse, as well as a boat where he would sit and have cocktails.

Call ahead to arrange a tour in English. Even if you speak Spanish, this is the best option as the English tours are always smaller than those in Spanish. Take note that they are closed on Monday.

PRACTICAL INFORMATION
Banks: BCI, *Prat 801*; **Banco Edwards**, *Cochrane 785*; **Santander**, *Esmeralda 939*
Business Hours: Monday-Friday 9am-1pm, 4pm-8pm. Saturday 9am-1pm
Currency Exchange: **Ascami Ltda**, *Esmeralda 940*; **Intercambio**, *Plaza Sotomayor 11*
Medical Service: **Hospital van Buren**, *Colon and San Ignacio. Tel. 254074*
Post Office: **Correos de Chile**, *Plaza Sotomayor and Prat*
Telephone/Fax: **CTC**, The area code is 32. *Esmeralda 1054*; **Chilesat**, *Brasil 1456*; **Entel**, *Muelle Prat*
Tourist Office/Maps: **Municiple Tourist Office**, *Muelle Prat*. 10am-2pm, 3pm-7pm

SAN ANTONIO & SANTO DOMINGO
San Antonio is a working class port city that was opened when the Spanish blockaded and bombarded Valparaíso in 1865. Most visitors go to Santo Domingo, its sister city across the Maipo river.

Formally known as Rocas de Santo Domingo, the resort's name comes from the Dominican order that originally owned the land. In 1942, two Santiago businessmen developed the community from scratch, making sure to include plenty of parks and other green space. Modeled after Palo Verdes, California, Santo Domingo is now a pleasant if rather planned community.

ARRIVALS & DEPARTURES
By Bus
Regular bus service connects San Antonio to both **Valparaíso** and **Santiago**. From the San Antonio bus station, local buses go to Santo

Domingo. You can also catch a bus from Santiago to Pomaire and then from **Pomaire** (see Santiago *Excursions and Day Trips*) to San Antonio.

By Car

If you are coming from up the coast, the coastal highway runs from **Algarrobo** to Santo Domingo. If you are coming from **Santiago**, the excellent toll road 78 is a straight shot, though you should stop in **Pomaire** (See Santiago *Excursions and Day Trips*) to look around.

ORIENTATION

The streets of Santo Domingo are not laid out in the standard grid, but rather twist around in confusing curves, changing names along the way. The Gran Avenida del Mar runs along the beach, while the Avenida del Parque cuts straight through town. Interestingly, the streets do not have the standard Chilean hero names, but more poetic names of trees and flowers as they were all named by a Spanish writer.

WHERE TO STAY & EAT

CABAÑAS PIEDRA DEL SOL, *Avenida del Pacífico 10. Tel. 35/44301. 8 cabins. Double $100. Restaurant. Credit cards accepted.*

These simple cabañas at the northern end of the beach fill up quickly in the summer. They are nothing special, but fulfill your basic needs. Their beach location is what makes them popular. The restaurant serves a fixed lunch menu that is a good value.

HOTEL ROCAS DE SANTO DOMINGO, *La Ronda 130. Tel. 35/444356, Fax 35/444494. 20 rooms. Double $65-120. Breakfast included. Restaurant. Pool. Conference rooms. Credit cards accepted.*

The hotel's bright pink exterior has faded a bit, but it's still hard to miss. Inside, smooth finished wood and a comfortable living room lend a calm dignity that the exterior lacks. Foosball and Ping-Pong, as well as a playground, make it a good place for kids.

The rooms are not a great value, as they are in need of redecoration and on the small side, but the hotel can get away with it because there are only two places to stay in town. The place is located in the higher part of town, above the beach. The restaurant is a solid choice for the local seafood.

SEEING THE SIGHTS

Santo Domingo is known as a family beach town. Children run and play on the wide beach under the watchful eyes of their nannies until sunset, when the whole family comes down to catch the view. Adults divide their time between the links and the shore. The country club is private, so unless you can finagle an invitation, you'll have to be content with the beach.

A walk or drive through town is worthwhile to admire the lovely homes and carefully tended private and public gardens.

PRACTICAL INFORMATION

Bank: The closest banks are in San Francisco.

Phone: The area code is 35. The public phone is next to the municipal building at Plaza del Cabildo on the Gran Avenida Arturo Phillips.

PICHILEMU

Pichilemu is a beach town that has always wanted to be important. Fortunately its dreams of grandeur have not materialized and it remains a homespun ocean-side village offering affordable seafood feasts and rustic cabins.

Agustín Eduard Ross founded the town in 1885 with hopes that the coastal site would evolve into a major port city. He built the grand Hotel Ross, which housed a casino that was a major tourist attraction until 1932, when it was surpassed by the one in Viña del Mar.

These days the mayoral candidates sound just as determined as Ross was in pushing the cozy town toward celebrity, this time as a Viña-like beach resort. Happily, it's all talk. Pichilemu has the soul of a surfer town and that's hard to change. It will stay *Ciudad de Olas*, Wave City, as is proudly highlighted on its welcome sign, for the foreseeable future.

ARRIVALS & DEPARTURES

By Bus

Buses depart on a regular basis from **San Fernando** to Pichilemu. See the Santiago section for information on buses to the south. San Fernando is on the route to **Puerto Montt**.

By Car

People debate over which of these two routes is faster. The simplest is to head south on the Panamericana until reaching San Fernando, and then to take the highway west to Pichilemu. The other route is via Melipilla and Litueche, which includes a stretch of dirt road. The Pichilemu locals argue that the Melipilla route is 70 km shorter, but the truth is that both routes involve just over three and half hours driving.

ORIENTATION

Pichilemu, due east of San Fernando, sits on a stretch of coast that is refreshingly undeveloped when compared to its northern neighbors. The commercial part of town is above the beach, centered around Ross Avenue and Ortuzar. For recreational purposes, the Costanera, running along the beach, is the main artery. Most of the cabins are located at the far end of this road where to beach curves to a rocky point.

WHERE TO STAY

Pichilemu can get crowded during January and February. You might want to make reservations before arrival during these months. At other times of the year, you should really bargain for lower room rates.

CABAÑAS DUNAMAR, *on the road to Punta Lobos. Tel. 72/841576. 25 cabins. Double $55. Breakfast included. Restaurant. No credit cards.*

The Dunamar, out of town towards Punta Lobos, is our top choice for both food and lodging. Accommodations are two story bungalows featuring comfortable double beds. From your room, you can gaze out at the endless stretch of beach below. Downstairs there is a small kitchen next to a cozy living area.

The Dunamar is especially pleasant because they pay important attention to detail. The interiors are immaculate and finished with clear varnished pine boards. Basic cooking staples are available at grocery store, instead of minibar, prices. Best of all are the reading lights. So many hotels skimp in this department, but the Dunamar fills the nooks in its cabins with comfortable sofas and strong lights. Room availability is limited so call ahead for reservations.

Selected as one of our best places to stay – see Chapter 10 for more details.

CABAÑAS WAITARA, *Costanera 1039. Tel. 72/841331. 5 cabins, 6 rooms. Double $40. Restaurant. Breakfast included. Surf shop. No credit cards.*

These simple cabins are one of the places that water sports *aficionados* patronize. They offer kayak and windsurf rentals as well as a surf shop with basic gear at reasonable prices. One of the main surf breaks is right out their front door. They also offer inexpensive rooms, though they are threadbare at best. The restaurant here is quite good and has an excellent view.

LAS TERRAZAS, *La Marina 201. Tel. 72/841708. 9 cabins, 7 apartments. Double $44. Breakfast included. No credit cards.*

Las Terrazas, across the street and a little above the Waitara also offer well-kept, clean cabins with a good beach location.

GRAN HOTEL ROSS, *Marina 136. Tel 72/841038. 30 rooms. Double $18. Breakfast included. Restaurant. Credit cards accepted.*

This historic hotel is up from the beach in front of the verdant Ross park. The restaurant is only average.

HOTEL CHILE-ESPAÑA, *Ortuzar 255. Tel. 72/841270. 18 rooms. Double $20. Breakfast included. Credit cards accepted.*

The Hotel Chile-España is a hip place popular with the younger surfing crowd. It is right in the commercial part of town, but is constantly full. An open inner courtyard, strewn with surfboards, is the communal gathering place

WHERE TO EAT

For the late risers who were not up to meet the fishermen in the morning, there is an array of excellent restaurants catering to the seafood connoisseur's palate.

CABAÑAS DUNAMAR, *on the road to Punta Lobos. Tel. 72/841576. Moderate. No credit cards.*

This cozy restaurant, looking out to the sea, sits above the black sand dunes that separate Point Lobos from town. Both the items off the menu and the daily specials are delicious. Their savory fare includes a rich *jaiba* crab cake and *carbonata*, a hearty beef and potato soup.

PALDOA, *across from Las Terrazas cabins. Moderate. No credit cards.*

The Paldoa sits high above the town's main bay. Both the food and the views are excellent. Their bubbling seafood chowder, *paila marina*, is a perfect warmer after any time in the Humbolt current. Daily specials are fresh and succulent.

CABAÑAS WAITARA, *Costanera 1039. Tel. 841331. Moderate. No credit cards.*

The restaurant at the Waitara is not as highly respected as the options above, but it still offers great seafood with a view.

HOSTERIA LA GLORIA, *Prieto 432. Tel. 841052. Moderate. No credit cards.*

This hostel is on the side of town opposite the beach, but the seafood still does not have to travel very far to arrive fresh on your plate.

NIGHTLIFE & ENTERTAINMENT

As with most small beach towns, nocturnal life is barely single-celled. With energy spent on sun and sea, most visitors tend to be wiped out earlier than usual. **La Ventana**, *Ross and Gaete*, is a fun pub stop. The **GiGi** bar, *one block down from the Chile-España*, attracts a younger crowd.

SEEING THE SIGHTS

Other than water sports, the thing to do is Pichilemu is take walks along the black sand beaches. Try to be on the beach around 10am, when brightly painted fisherman's boats are dragged to rest upon the sand. Crowds emerge to peer over the edge of the boats to see what's been netted. The fish are segregated by species and await suitors to barter and tote them off to be cooked up for the evening's meal.

Your walk should include a stop at the Ross Park, towards the end of the beach. The well-tended park, with its large trees, is a reminder of Ross' dreams of grandeur.

SPORTS & RECREATION

Pichilemu earns its surf reputation in part by hosting an international surf competition each year. The most popular surf spots are along the **Playa Principal** and off the rocks on **Playa Caletilla**. Six km south of the town is **Punta Lobo**. Here the surfers have erected a park to contemplate the waves, a sort of a surf meditation point. There is also a wooden halfpipe for skateboarding or in-line skating that stands in stark contrast to the rocky point dotted with flowering cactus.

PRACTICAL INFORMATION

Bank: **Banco del Estado de Chile**, *Errázuriz 397*
Phone: The area code is 72. **Centro de Llamados**, *Ortuzar 446*
Post Office: **Correos de Chile**, *Ortuzar 544*
Tourist Office: **Municipal tourist office**, *Gaete 365*

THE ACONCAGUA VALLEY TO PORTILLO

This gorgeous valley, which runs the width of Chile, passes through prime agricultural land before climbing to the top of the Andes. The rich soil, fed by silty run off from the Aconcagua River, faithfully nurtures Chilean produce every year.

The area is best known to travelers for its outstanding ski resort, **El Portillo**. The resort sits in a 2800 meter rocky bowl with a lake at its base. The curvy road up the mountains, along the river, is unforgettable. From Portillo you can continue on to the pass through the Andes, alongside the magnificent 6900 meter Aconcagua Mountain, which leads to the verdant Argentine city of **Mendoza**.

The valley's small, colonial towns, with their adobe buildings and thatched roofs, seem to be from another age. Old churches and monasteries abound in the region, as does the influence of Teresa de Los Andes, the first Chilean saint.

The quaint city of **Los Andes** is the commercial center of the area. The citizens live their lives on its streets. The central plaza, with its park and bandstand, is always crammed with families, couples, and dogs. The streets around the park are lined with small restaurants and shops where the whole valley seems to congregate.

Zapallar

Portillo

Los Andes

Olmué

Viña del Mar

La Parva

Valparaiso

Valle Nevado

SANTIAGO

ARGENTINA
CHILE

San Antonio

El Morado
National Park

Los Lingues

Pichilemu

San Fernando

ARGENTINA
CHILE

Chillan

CENTRAL
CHILE

History

This valley was already highly populated before the arrival of the Spanish, thus it was a natural spot to begin conversion exercises. In 1553 the missionaries arrived, followed soon after by colonial land-owners.

The valley has been important in the cultivation of foodstuffs ever since. It was not until the 1920s, however, that large-scale cultivation really took off. The Aconcagua Valley is now important not only for Chilean exporters, but also for Argentines in the Mendoza Valley who use Chilean ports as their quickest route to the rest of the world.

ARRIVALS & DEPARTURES

By Bus

There is regular international bus service from Santiago's Los Heroes terminal to Mendoza, Argentina. These buses pass through both Los Andes and Portillo. The bus will stop in Los Andes at the bus station, *Membrillar one block east of the plaza*, but you'll have to tell the driver if you went to get off anywhere else along the route. If you continue on into Argentina, you will need your passport at the border.

The ski resort provides transportation for guests in small buses and vans directly from the airport in Santiago to the slopes. This must be arranged in advance.

To explore the smaller towns around Los Andes, it is necessary to take local buses from the Los Andes bus station.

By Car

There are two routes to Los Andes from Santiago. The most direct route is to take the Panamericana north 53 km to the highway 57 turnoff. 57 runs straight to Los Andes where you turn east on highway 60 to Portillo and the border. You can also take 57 all the way from Santiago. Cabs from the airport are willing to make the drive to Portillo, but it's costly.

ORIENTATION

The Aconcagua Valley is located north of Santiago in the 5th region. It is the last transversal valley in this part of Chile. From Santiago you travel almost directly north to Los Andes, where you then take a sharp right and head east up the mountains. You climb from 820 meters in Los Andes to almost 3200 meters at the international border.

If you continue across the border, the steep climb on the Chilean side is followed by a slow, easy decent through painted mountains down the Argentine side to Mendoza.

WHERE TO STAY & EAT

The best location during the ski season is the Portillo Lodge at the foot of the mountain. Some skiers, however, opt to stay and dine in the less expensive Los Andes. The quality of hotels is nothing great, but you can at least get a comfortable bed and a hot shower. You should reserve in advance if you are traveling during the ski season.

In Los Andes

HOTEL PLAZA, *Rodriguez 368. Tel. 34/421929. 40 rooms. Double $54. Breakfast included. Restaurant. American Express only.*

Located right on the main plaza and built decades ago, this hotel is past its prime but still serves its purpose. The location puts you in the center of the town's activity, but you can get a good night's sleep if you ask for one of the quieter rooms in the back.

The moderately priced restaurant has the typical Chilean menu. The food is not out of this world, but it is some of the best in town.

HOTEL DON AMBROSIO, *Freire 472. Tel. 34/425496. 11 rooms. Double $43. Breakfast included. Restaurant. Credit cards accepted.*

Located two blocks from the plaza area, this small hotel is much quieter than most. It is also just a few blocks from both the O'Higgins park and the footpath to the top of the hill of the virgin.

There are a number of cafes around the plaza for quick bites. The patio at the corner of *Esmeralda and Santa Rosa* is a popular place to grab a drink and watch the town pass by.

The entire valley is filled with small restaurants, called *picadas*, where the locals stop to fill up on traditional fare. The most famous is *chancho*, pork, as well as excellent *empanadas*. Try **Donde El Guaton** in Los Andes at *Sarmiento 240*. Another good option for traditional food is **Restaurante Entre Parras**, *Calle Larga, Parcela 9, Tel. 461038*.

On the Way to Portillo

HOTEL RIO COLORADO, *Camino Internacional kilometer 18. Tel. 34/481062. Double $45. 15 rooms. No credit cards.*

Tucked off the left hand side of the road 17 km from Los Andes, the hotel sits along one of the Aconcagua's tributaries. Many skiers prefer to stay here because you can get a jump on the crowds coming up from Los Andes.

Portillo
   PORTILLO SKI LODGE, *Route 60, km 59. Santiago Tel. 2/263-0606, Fax 2/263-0595. 135 rooms, 8 cabins. Double $220. Breakfast included. Restaurant. Bar. Disco. Heated pool. Sauna. Massage. Gym. Game room. Ice skating. Credit cards accepted.*

   This classic lodge sits at the foot of a lake surrounded by high mountains. There is a real communal feel here because most of the people stay for a week and eat all their meals together. You get to know people on the lifts and then see them again at dinner or at the disco.

   The prices change almost every month depending on how deep you are into the ski season. Most rooms are booked in packages from Brazil and Argentina, but call the week before you want to go to see if there is availability. If you have a group, the cabins are a good alternative.

SANTA TERESA DE LOS ANDES

   *Revered on altars and churches throughout Chile, Santa Teresa's influence is perhaps strongest in this valley she called home. The first Chilean recognized as a saint, **Santa Teresa** was a pious girl who entered the Carmelite nunnery at age 19 and died six months later. Soon after her death numerous miracles were attributed to her intercession and a popular cult began to grow up around her figure. The Pope beatified her in his 1987 visit to Santiago.*

SEEING THE SIGHTS

   Los Andes is a small, relaxed town with a pleasant square. Besides this, it is known primarily for two things, ceramics and Santa Teresa.

   CERÁMICA CALA, *Freire and Rancagua. Monday-Friday 9am-12:30pm, Saturday 10am-2:30pm. Free admission.*

   There are a number of ceramic shops in town, but here you can watch the artisans at work. Follow their creations through the entire operation as they produce lovely ceramics by hand. They also have items for sale.

   ESPIRITU SANTO MONASTERY, *Avenida Santa Teresa and O'Higgins. Saturday, Sunday, and holidays 10:30am-6:30pm.*

   The original building where Santa Teresa was a nun in 1919 was been destroyed, but this museum gives visitors a taste of her monastic lifestyle. The second floor houses the **Museum of Religious History**, which is full of relics and pictures of the saint.

   THE HILL OF THE VIRGIN, *By road, at the top of Avenida de la Fuente. On foot, via trail that begins at Avenida Independencia and Freire.*

   Hike or drive to the top of the hill for excellent views of the town and the Andes beyond.

SPORTS & RECREATION

Hiking

Once you get used to the altitude, the mountains around Portillo offer excellent hiking opportunities in the off season. From the resort there are hikes for all ages and abilities. On the Argentine side of the pass, there are also numerous hikes around the foothills of Aconcagua.

Horseback Riding

There are some beautiful rides in the area around Los Andes. **Desnivel Chile Expediciones** at *Tel. 34/424339* in Los Andes can arrange guided tours of the area.

Mountaineering

A huge feather in any mountaineer's helmet is summitting Aconcagua, the tallest mountain in the Americas. Although the 6959 meter mountain is in Argentina, the easiest access is from Chile. The climb is for experienced mountaineers only. Santiago adventure tour companies arrange trips.

Skiing

Skiing at Portillo is delightful. You never know when you'll be sharing the mountain with top US and European ski teams as they keep in shape for the up-coming season. With slopes for all abilities, heli-skiing, ice-skating, and a full spa, the whole family should be happy. Twelve lifts, snow making machines and a fully equipped ski shop with equipment rental are the proper ingredients for a great ski week. Portillo is known for its excellent, dry powder.

While the ski area has runs for all abilities, international skiers come to enjoy the famously steep blacks. You can buy lift tickets for the day for $33, but lodging is usually booked by the week. (See *Where to Stay*.)

There is another ski resort on the Argentine side, about four hours from Los Andes, called Vallecitos.

SHOPPING

Ceramics are the most famous artisan works out of Los Andes. In addition to **Cerámica Cala**, *Freire and Rancagua*, there's **Cerámica Razeto**, *General de Canto 1514*, **Cerámica Engobada**, *General del Canto 500*, and **Cerámica Manque**, *Maipú 475*.

EXCURSIONS & DAY TRIPS

There are a number of quaint villages, thermal baths, and religious sites around Los Andes that make for interesting day trips or even overnight stops.

•**Mendoza, Argentina** – Mendoza is a lovely five-hour drive from Los Andes. Crossing the pass brings you into another world in Argentina, as all the rain falls on the Chilean side of the mountains. Aconcagua sits like a fat toad above the inspiring desert mountains that lead down to vineyards and verdant Mendoza.

• **Santa Teresa of the Andes Sanctuary** – Pilgrims come from all over Chile to pay homage to the bones of their first saint. Small plaques and offerings outside witness to the strength of her intercessions. The Sanctuary is located in Auco, on the route to Los Andes from Santiago.

• **Santa Rosa Convent in Curimón** – This convent is one of the purest examples of colonial architecture in Chile. Stop for a traditional lunch at **La Ruca** *on the road from Curimón to Rinconada.*

•**Termas el Corazon** – A comfortable resort alongside the Aconcagua River, El Corazon has thermal pools and a spa. The pools are open to the general public. *Tel. 34/481371.*

• **Termas de Jahuel** – This resort is more upscale than El Corazon. Darwin visited these thermal pools in his travels through Chile in 1834. The pools are open exclusively to resort guests. *Tel. 34/582320.*

PRACTICAL INFORMATION

Banks: **BCI**, *Esmeralda 347*; **Banco del Chile**, *Maipu 350*, **Santander**, *Centenario 68*

Medical Service: Hospital Los Andes, *corner of Argentina and Clark*

Post Office: Correos de Chile, *corner of Esmeralda and Santa Rosa*

Telephone/Fax: The area code is 34. **Centro de Llamados**, *Cambate de las Coimas 214*, **Entel**, *Esmeralda 463*

Tourist Office/Maps: There is a tourist information kiosk on the plaza.

OLMUÉ & LA CAMPANA NATIONAL PARK

Olmué, northwest of Santiago, is a jewel on one of the fingers of the Quillota valley. Streams and rivers paint broad green streaks through terrain that without them, would be coughing up dust devils. Instead greenhouses, fruit orchards, and vineyards abound in this valley. Roses creep through fence gaps, decorate roadside memorials, adorn lattices, and tangle toward the sky like the arms of a belly dancer. Vibrant wildflowers also abound. Look for the national flower, the *copihue*, a magenta champagne flute tipped over on its vine.

Decorating the middle of this corsage is **La Campana Hill** at 1900 meters. Surrounded by an 8000-hectare national park of the same name, La Campana offers a glimpse of how skinny Chile really is. From its peak you can see the Argentine border to the east and the Pacific Ocean to the west.

La Campana, which means "The Bell," has long been known for its outstanding views. When Charles Darwin came through the area in August of 1834 he climbed to the top and camped overnight. There is now a gold plaque under a small waterfall near the peak that commemorates his visit

DARWIN'S DELIGHT

"We spent the day at the summit, and I never enjoyed one more thoroughly. Chile, bounded by the Andes and the Pacific, was seen as in a map."
— **Charles Darwin**, *describing the view from La Campana*, **Voyage of the Beagle**

ARRIVALS & DEPARTURES

By Bus

From Santiago: **Buses Golandrina**, *Tel. 778-7082*, leaves from the Borja Bus Station in Santiago directly to Olmué.

From Viña del Mar: **Ciferal Express**, *Tel. 953317* heads to Olmué every couple of hours.

By Car

From Santiago: Take the Panamericana north. For the scenic route, take a left hand turn where signs point to Tiltil, then follow the unpaved road, navigable in a two wheel drive vehicle, over the crest of the pass which leads to Olmué. There is a roadside natural food shop selling fig treats and home-cured olives, as well as wonderful views of the valleys on this route, which takes two and half to three hours.

The quicker option is to continue on the Panamericana Norte until the highway 60 turnoff to Viña del Mar after Hijuelas. Follow this for 15 km and then take the turnoff to Limache/Olmué after passing Quillota. This route takes about two hours, all on good highway.

From Viña: Take the road to Limache where, after passing through town, you head east 8 km to Olmué. It is about an hour drive.

ORIENTATION

Olmué is situated in a narrow spur of the fertile Quillota valley. Almost surrounded by mountains, it sits in the middle of the coastal range, *El Cordon de San Pedro*. Northwest of Santiago, Olmué is almost on the same latitude as Argentina's **Aconcagua Mountain**, the highest peak outside of the Himalayas at 6962 meters, which can easily be seen from the top of La Campana.

WHERE TO STAY & EAT

The typical lodgings in Olmué are tourist retreats. These consist of cabins and suites centered around a swimming pool and other sport courts such as tennis and volleyball. There is usually a large grassy area for lounging and games. Most of the compounds don't have more than ten cabins, which creates a relaxed, familiar atmosphere. They also offer some of the town's best dining in their restaurants. During the summer is it best to have reservations. Other times of the year you can just show up and take your pick.

Because the cabins are designed to sleep from four to six people, most of them are in the $50-$100 range. You should definitely bargain in the off-season. If you're on a tight budget, your best option is probably camping at **La Campana National Park**. Even if you are not on a budget, a night in La Campana is a wonderful option. Darwin loved it.

CT PARAISO, *Eastman 2761. Tel./Fax 33/441643. 10 cabins, 8 suites. Double cabin $68. Breakfast included. Restaurant. Heated pool. Tennis. Credit cards accepted.*

This is one of the nicest places in town. The heated pool makes it a good option any time of year and the restaurant is popular too.

LAS MONTANAS DE OLMUÉ, *Avenida Granizo 9139. Tel. 33/441253. Fax 33/441374. 6 cabins, 4 room. Double cabin $67. Pool. Tennis. No credit cards.*

While the cabins here are nothing special, the playground is out of this world. Even adults can't resist the Alice in Wonderland bridges and swings.

HOSTERIA AIRE PURO, *Avenida Granizo 7672. Tel. 33/441381. 6 cabins. $48. Breakfast included. Restaurant. Pool. Credit cards accepted.*

The Aire Puro is tucked in against the Ganizo Creek with Olmué Hill serving as a backdrop. One of the highlights here is the frog game on the patio, the Chilean version of pitching washers.

HOSTERIA EL COPIHUE, *Diego Portales 2203. Tel./Fax 33/441544. 32 rooms. Double $49. Breakfast included. Restaurant. Pool. Tennis. Credit cards accepted*

This hostería has both rooms and cabins, which makes it a less expensive option for solo travelers and couples.

For a home-style meal away from your hotel, the best is **Parador de Betty**, one block behind the plaza on Eastman, with funky interior decor as well as outdoor seating and ample yard space for kids to frolic.

SEEING THE SIGHTS

There is not much to see in Olmué, which is why it is such a perfect place for relaxing. You should however, walk the streets to get a feel for the easy rhythm of life here. The square is one of the quaintest imaginable without being cheesy. It is the perfect place to enjoy an afternoon or evening snack. Try the coconut macaroons at Pasteles Venezia

Walking down Avenida Granizo, in front of the square, you can also stop by the **Huaso museum**, which offers insight into the Huaso culture. The one room museum displays the Chilean cowboys' saddles, clothing, and handicrafts. Continuing up Granizo from the museum the local park is filled with animated children circling on tame plodding horses and equally tame go-carts.

LA CAMPANA NATIONAL PARK, *Tel. 33/441342. 8am-7pm, September-April all days; May-August, Sunday only. Entry $1.75.*

There are three sections of the park. Two of them, El Granizo and Cajon Grande, are accessed from Olmué. The other sector, Palmas de Ocoa, the Chilean Palm Reserve, is on the other side of the park

Granizo: This is the most frequently hiked sector of the park. It leads to the top of La Campana in about three and half hours. The trail from the Conaf station winds steeply through the shady pine and beech tree mountainside up to granite walls used for challenging rock climbing. You skirt the walls by scrambling around on boulders to the other side of the mountain. As you cross the high ridge leading to the summit, the great Aconcagua Mountain leaps into view, a stunning spectacle with the Chacabuco basin laid out below. The one negative note is that the rocks at the summit have been repeatedly painted with graffiti, tarnishing the otherwise well-maintained park. The view that inspired Darwin's description, however, is absolutely spectacular. Go early in the morning so you have time to linger at the top.

Cajón Grande: This entrance accesses an easier hike through a relatively flat path shaded by native trees. The pleasant walk follows the Granizo Stream through a canyon where descending pools form for dipping your toes. On this tour you might spot a degú, a Doolittlean cross between a rabbit and a field mouse.

Palmas de Ocoa: The last sector is directly on the other side of the La Campana Peak from Olmué. You can either hike through the park to get there, an overnight trip, or approach it by car from the Panamericana Highway. You get there from Santiago by taking Highway 5 north through Llaillay. Right after passing through the La Calavera tunnel there is an almost hidden sign to Los Maitenes and Palmas de Ocoa on the left. Turn here and continue on the dirt road 10 km to the park entrance.

The hike from the Ocoa to the Granizo sectors follows a 14 km trail through the Rabuco Creek Canyon. The highlights of the hike are the hundreds of fat and hardy Chilean palms, as well as the views from the pass to the other side. You must take your own water on this hike, as this section of the park is extremely dry.

There is another pleasant trail in this sector which is a 6 km path to the La Cordadera Waterfall. You follow a double-track road for about 4 km to the trail turn-off. The trail leads to two viewing spots. The first is above the falls, with the impressive valley of palms laid out below. The second leads down a steep embankment to the bottom of the falls where you can cool off on the wet, black rocks.

CHILEAN PALMS

Chilean Palms, with their fat midsections, used to cover this entire part of Chile. The trees take decades to reach maturity and can live over one hundred years. In Darwin's journal he talks about an estate where they tried to count the palms, but gave up after having counted several hundred thousand. They are now an endangered species.

It was the palm's sap that almost brought about its demise. Thousands of the palms were felled every August to collect the sap for syrup production. As the trees take so long to grow, felled trees were not replaced with new ones. The Palmas de Ocoa Park is one of only two areas in the country where palms still grow as they did in Darwin's day.

SPORTS & RECREATION

There are multiple hiking trails and options for all athletic bents in the La Campana National Park. If you prefer to use animal power, horses are for rent at the local park. You can ride them through the fields around Olmué, or into La Campana. There is also excellent trail running in the hills above the northern edge of town. Just pick a route and be prepared to work up a sweat.

Tennis courts grace almost every one of the cabin complexes. Be sure the check out the courts before you rent your cabin, as some are in much better condition than others.

PRACTICAL INFORMATION

Banks: There are no banks in Olmué. Bring your money with you.

National Parks: There are two Conaf ranger stations in La Campana. One is in the Granizo sector, and the other in Ocoa.

Supermarkets: The best supermarket in town is across the street from the square. You can get all your fixings for a picnic at the top of La Campana.

CAJÓN DEL MAIPO

Cajón del Maipo, or Canyon of the Maipo River, is a natural playground just a short drive from Santiago. In the not too distant past, political dissidents used the valleys around the Cajón as a route to freedom in Argentina. Now, *Santiaguinos* and visitors alike escape to the same area for a sensual revival. The mountain air, stunning vistas, glacial rivers, and clear night sky are a treat for any body numbed by urban existence.

The centerpiece of the canyon is **El Morado National Park**. This easily accessible preserve, nuzzled in the valley below El Morado Mountain, "The Bruised One," offers visitors impressive views of the purple peak for which it is named. In addition to soaking in the sights, you can quaff fresh mineral water from natural springs, go for a dip in a small lake, or contemplate up close a crevasse crammed glacier that would have enchanted Georgia O'Keefe.

While this trip can be done in a day from Santiago, we like to spend a night in the park.

The route winds along the banks of the Maipo River. On the first section, from Vertientes to San Jose de Maipo, you will pass by the green lawns of many private picnic and camping areas. We recommend continuing on, as crowds thin out the farther you get from Santiago.

From San Jose, the road passes through San Alfonso, where the mountains become striped with reds and greens and the landscape becomes drier as you gain altitude. There is a *carabinero* guard spot about 11 km outside of San Alfonso where you are registered and given a piece of paper that you must present upon leaving the area.

You then continue through El Volcán on to Baños Morales, which is where you'll find the trailhead for the park. Across the river from Baños Morales is Lo Valdes, with its excellent restaurant.

ARRIVALS & DEPARTURES

By Bus

On the weekdays you can take the buses that leave on the half hour from the Parque O'Higgins metro station in Santiago to San Jose de Maipo. From there, *colectivo* buses continue on to Baños Morales. During the weekend, buses go directly from Plaza Italia (metro Baquedano) to Baños Morales.

By Car

It is roughly a two hour drive from Santiago to Baños Morales. Take Avenida La Florida towards Las Vizcachas. Follow this road all the way to San Jose de Maipo. To continue to Baños Morales, go through San Jose de Maipo and follow the signs to San Alfonso. About 20 km after the guard spot there is a fork in the road. Take the left fork to Baños Morales or the right fork to Lo Valdes and Baños Colina.

ORIENTATION

The Cajón de Maipo lies southeast of Santiago. The Maipo River, fed by runoff and glacial melt from the Andes, has cut a wide valley through the mountains on its run to the sea.

WHERE TO STAY & EAT

EL MORADO NATIONAL PARK, *Baños Morales. Camping only. $2.50 per person.*

As far as we're concerned, this is the premier place to stay in the canyon. A friendly, non-intrusive community of all ages and ilks can be found at the campsite. Domed tents dot the area like giant beetles while new restrooms and potable water mean you don't have to go completely natural. Experienced glacier climbers share the views and campfires with groups of enthusiastic teens and leave romantic couples to stargaze in solitude.

If you don't have camping gear or prefer a roof over your head, there is another good option.

REFUGIO ALEMAN, *Lo Valdez, Tel./Fax 2/220-7610. 11 rooms. $53 per person. All meals included. No credit cards.*

We highly recommend lunch or dinner in this alpine-style lodge. The delicious fixed meal should be followed by an Andes-watching-space-out-session on the front porch. Clean, cheery bunk bed rooms are available if the urge to nap or stay the night becomes too strong.

Other lodging can be found in the numerous cabañas and hostelries on the road between San Jose de Maipo and San Alfonso.

In addition to the restaurants in town, both sides of the road from San Jose de Maipo are peppered with places to stop for *empanadas* and other delights. Small flower-laden stands and restaurants seduce you into slowing the pace while enjoying homemade *kuchen*, German pastry, in the shade of their awnings.

SEEING THE SIGHTS

San Jose De Maipo

Founded in 1792, upon discovery of silver in the surrounding hills, San Jose is now a weekend retreat for families from Santiago. You should stop at the main square for a visit to the **Parochial Church**, which has been declared a Chilean National Monument.

Lagunillas

After passing through San Jose, there is a turn-off to the left to Lagunillas Ski Center. The dirt road curves up and around the mountain for 16 km, where it reaches the open fields of the ski area at 2500 meters. Mountains surround the small resort area offering up endless trails for hiking and mountain biking when there is no snow. The **Club Andino de Chile**, *Santiago Tel. 552-8095*, and the **Refugio Suizo**, *Santiago Tel. 205-5423*, offer simple food and lodging.

Baños Morales

There are three thermal pools here as well as a couple of hostelries and a small store selling drinks. The pools are overrun with people in the summer, but are much nicer in March. They are generally only open from December to March, but if you have ten or more in a group, they will open for you any time during the year. *Santiago Tel. 226-9826.*

El Morado National Park

This park reveals a 360-degree, surrealistic array of colors and landscapes. Ocher and red mineral-painted hills contrast with purple, snow-covered mountains and grassy banks.

A single trail leads to the campground and beyond to the glacier. After about an hour of steep climbing, the **Aguas Panimavidas** mineral springs make a perfect resting spot. Every person that hikes by will sample the water, and though almost everyone puckers at the mineral laden taste, it is a ritual of the hike not to be omitted.

The climb is more gradual for the second hour up to the spring fed pond where the peak of El Morado, 5060 meters, becomes the central focal point. Small tarns along the way are homes for various waterfowl, while birds of all types flit about during the entire hike.

The imposing heft of El Morado cradles a glacier in its lap. The chance to experience this slow-motion river is just another hour's upward clamber. You can hear the movement of the ice and see, in its blue crevasses, the rapids it has formed. The sensual cleaves of this frozen-yet-living water are mesmerizing. Be careful to stay to the side of the glacier as each crevasse represents danger to the untrained.

The celestial show that starts once night creeps in is a South American treat. Arguably the most famous constellation of this hemisphere, the southern cross, dangles kite-like over the bottom of the valley. The toucan, another treasure of this half of the world, perches somberly above, balanced by his gigantic beak. Even if you don't have a star map, the shooting stars make for an excellent show.

The rangers insist that the water out of the taps at the top is potable, but we filtered it anyway. There are large temperature swings in a day (from 50F to 80F in the summer) so bring layers. Firewood is not available along the route, though many people hike in with their own. You'll need a camp stove for cooking dinner. *Entry $2.50 per person.*

Baños Colina
Twelve km into the Andes past Lo Valdez, these thermal springs are less visited than the ones at Baños Morales. Open from October through April, the facilities are less crowded, and there is a small restaurant. They also have horse rental available. *Santiago Tel. 850-1173.*

SPORTS & RECREATION
Hiking
El Morado has a wonderful trail. If you're comfortable heading out into the Andes on your own, Las Lagunillas is a less traveled hiking area.

Horseback Riding
There are horses for rent in Baños Morales to take you to the glacier at El Morado. The approximately four hour round-trip trail ride costs $13 per group for the obligatory guide and then another $13 per person for the horse.

Horse rental is also offered at Baños Colina.

Mountain Biking
From the ski center at Las Lagunillas you can head out for miles on your bike. The trails are steep and the oxygen is thin, but the views are stellar.

Rafting
Paddlers take advantage of the snow melt from September through April to run the Maipo. While not as technically challenging as the Futulefú, the Maipo offers plenty of excitement with its class III and IV rapids in the stunning scenery of the canyon. **Altue Expediciones** in Santiago, *Encomenderos 83, Tel. 232-1103*, runs half-day trips. If you have your own kayak, you can put in at El Melocoton and take out at Parque Los Heroes.

Skiing
Lagunillas, while touted as a ski center, is only open during big snow years. The small resort has three runs with rope tows. If good skiing is your main objective, you should head to the ski centers around Santiago. If, however, ambiance counts in your decision making, Lagunillas deserves a weekend simply for its laid back atmosphere. Groups of young people gather around the fire to pass the night hanging out.

PRACTICAL INFORMATION

National Parks: The Conaf hut is at the El Morado trailhead. There are no maps available, but the ranger will point out the route on a three dimensional scale model of the area. He makes it sound more complicated than it is as there is only one trail leading to the camping area and glacier.

Supermarkets: If you need camping supplies, San Jose de Maipo is the best place for stocking up.

The land south of Santiago, from **Rancagua** to **Chillán**, is famous throughout Chile for its agricultural production. From the highway you see acres and acres of fields and orchards, huge buildings that house international fruit packing operations, and a score of billboards advertising the latest in harvesters and pesticides. To the east the Andes, and to the west the Coastal Chain, run parallel to the highway.

The cities along the route, **Rancagua**, **San Fernando**, **Curicó**, **Talca**, and **Linares** have grown up as agricultural centers to handle the fruit production in the valley. They are peaceful places, but unless you want to buy a tractor, your time will be best spent away from these population areas.

History

Wandering Native Americans gradually settled in the valley as they mastered animal domestication and farming techniques. Around 1400, these groups came under the military and cultural domination of the Inca empire, based out of Peru.

The Incas had retreated northwards, due to internal power struggles, before the Spanish arrived. By the mid-1600s, the land in the valley was being used mainly for pastoral purposes.

The 17th century saw the rise of the hacienda system. Each hacienda was run like a fiefdom, being practically self-sufficient through the use of *peón* labor. The *peón*, or day laborer, was a resident of the estate where he worked. Another group, the *inquilinos*, were tenant farmers who paid their rent through labor at the hacienda. The *huaso*, or Chilean cowboy culture grew out of the *inquilino* tradition. It wasn't until 1964 that the system was changed and agrarian reform became a reality.

LAKE RAPEL

Lago Rapel is not a natural lake, but rather an extremely large reservoir created in 1968. People from the Central Valley flock to its shores for parties and picnics while enjoying the water for swimming, boating, and other aqua sports. There are no sights to see, no cities to tour, just relaxation and fun in the excellent climate.

ARRIVALS & DEPARTURES

By Bus

You can catch a bus from Santiago to Lago Rapel at the San Borja Terminal, *Alameda 3250.*

By Car

The ride is 145 km, or about two and a half hours from Santiago. Take toll road 78 towards the coast and exit at Melipilla. Go through Melipilla and head southwest towards the Y in the road at Cruce Las Arañas. At the Y, take the left fork towards El Manzano. Before reaching El Manzano you will cross the El Durazno bridge over the northern arm of the lake. At El Manzano, take a right on the gravel road towards Punta Verde to access most of the lodging options.

A lovely route back is to continue on 66, going southwest, until you reach the Panamericana. If it is clear, the Andes are in sight for much of the drive as you wander along fecund fields.

ORIENTATION

There are two sections, or arms, of the lake. The southernmost one, the Llallauquen section, is less developed for tourism but has excellent fishing and numerous campgrounds.

The northern arm offers cabins, hotels and campgrounds. Most of the aquatic activities take place here. It is the most pleasant and lush area of shoreline, which explains its development.

The sections come together off of Punta Verde and serpentine through the hills for 20 km before reaching the Rapel Hydraulic Center.

WHERE TO STAY & EAT

Lodging alternatives run the range from full service tourist complexes to campgrounds in a field next to the lake. The most common type of lodging is the cabin complex designed to house large Chilean families. Most of the cabins come equipped with kitchens where many people fix all their meals during their stays. The tourist centers also have restaurants, which are generally quite good.

PUNTA VERDE RESERT AND MARINA, *Punta Verde. Santiago Tel. 2/688-1198, Fax 2/688-6184. 30 apartments. Double $110. Restaurant. Piano bar. Pool. Sauna. Disco. Boat and other equipment rental. Credit cards accepted.*

The Punta Verde is one of the largest and most upscale complexes on the lake. With a full lineup of water sports, there is hardly any need to go inside your well appointed apartment. The restaurant is one of the best on the lake. During the slow season they offer up to a 20% discount.

HOSTERÍA MARINA RAPEL, *On the road from Estero to Punta Verde. Tel. 72/571139. 15 cabins. Double $60. Restaurant. Credit cards accepted.*

The Hostería Marina Rapel is equipped for the boater, with gas, a mechanic, and a guard service. The hostería has a boat for hire for water-skiing. The cabins are utilitarian, but not uncomfortable. The restaurant has sandwiches and cold beer that are especially delicious on hot days.

CABAÑAS AND CAMPING NAVIOCAR, *On the road from Estero to Punta Verde. Tel. 2/5227805. 10 cabins. Cabin $100. Credit cards accepted.*

You can either camp or rent a cabins here. The services are basic, but the atmosphere is homey and casual. The campground can get very crowded during the summer.

There are also cabins and campgrounds on the part of the lake around Llallauquen.

SPORTS & RECREATION

People go to Lago Rapel to enjoy water sports. Almost all of the tourist complexes have equipment for rent, ranging from ski boats with drivers, to sail boats, to windsurfers and canoes. Sailing is best during midday, while skiers will find the calmest water early in the morning and around sunset.

The hills around the lake are ideal for hiking and trail running. From their summits you can enjoy some outstanding views of the area.

PRACTICAL INFORMATION

Melipilla is the closest town of the size to offer services other than the most basic food and gas.

LOS LINGUES HACIENDA

HACIENDA LOS LINGUES, *30 km south of Rancagua off the Panamericana near Pelequen. Santiago Tel. 2/235-5446. 15 rooms. Double with full board for two $434. Pool. Tennis courts. Fly fishing. Horseback riding. Mountain Biking. Transfer from Santiago available. Credit cards accepted, but cash preferred.*

If you want to get a taste of last century's country good life, you have the chance here. This working hacienda is as much about the past as the present. About two hours south of Santiago, Los Lingues is replete with museum quality art, Queen Ann furniture, sterling silver, and other riches.

The estate has been in the family for over 400 years, with some of the existing buildings, like the simple yet moving chapel, dating back almost that long. The "new" buildings of the hacienda have been around for 200 years, and even the snooker table has seen 15 decades of use.

The colonial guestrooms, sheltered from the sun by wide, shaded porches, are built around a garden patio. The patio, with umbrellaed tables, is a favorite gathering spot for guests. Lunch and happy hour are traditionally served here in nice weather. Each room, with high ceilings and antique furniture, is decorated differently. They are not fancy, but rather, authentic. The Los Lingues experience is not about large bathrooms, fluffy towels, and king-sized beds.

Guests sup together around the grand table in the formal dining room. Silver candelabra, crystal glassware, and sterling place settings from 1790 set the tone for the delicious meal. The white-coated waiters serve Chilean specialties with international flair. If the house wine is not to your liking, you have over 2000 other bottles from which to choose in the wine cellar. After dinner you move to the great hall for nightcaps. In the same room where the leaders of the Chilean independence movement plotted their strategy, you can scheme about the next day's activities.

The grounds of the hacienda are spacious and open to guests. Gardens, pathways, huge lawns, orchards, and hilltops await your discovery. Sporting opportunities abound, with biking, horseback riding, year-round fishing, hiking, and tennis heading the list, though there is an additional charge for each of these activities. Swimming in the large, fresh water pool is free.

Los Lingues is also a prestigious horse-breeding farm. Some people spend much of their time around the stables and corrals watching the impressive horses go through their paces.

A recommended excursion from Los Lingues is the **Colchagua Museum**. A small, well-funded museum founded by an arms-dealer giving back to the world, it houses excellent indigenous artifacts.

LOS CIPRESES NATIONAL RESERVE & CAUQUENES HOT SPRINGS

Wild parrots fly through the canyon to nest in tall cliffs gold-plated by the setting sun. Trails meander through the forest leading to waterfalls, petroglyphs, or areas with guanacos. Foxes investigate your camp as you cook your evening meal. Los Cipreses, named after the local Cypress trees, is an enchanting, off-the-beaten-path national reserve.

After a day or two of camping and hiking, you can rest your weary bones, just as the Chilean liberators San Martin and O'Higgins did, at the Cauquenes hot springs.

ARRIVALS & DEPARTURES

By Bus

Buses go directly from **Rancagua** to Termas Cauquenes. From there, you can either hike or hitch the 15 km dirt road to the park entrance. You can also try to arrange a ride with Conaf in Rancagua, *Tel. 72/297505.*

By Car

The trip is 140 km, or about 2.5 hours from Santiago. Take the Panamericana south to Rancagua. Exit there and, from Rancagua, find the Presidente Frei highway to Coya. From Coya, follow the signs to the gravel road to Termas Cauquenes, which connects by dirt road to Los Cipreses.

ORIENTATION

Los Cipreses, east of Rancagua covers nearly 37,000 hectares. There is an Administration Office at the entrance, where you pay your fee, and camping area six km into the park. You must speak with the rangers to enter the heart of the park, but they are fairly liberal with allowing access and pointing out good trails. Termas Cauquenes is just north of the park entrance.

WHERE TO STAY & EAT

Los Cipreses is a wonderful place for camping. The official camping areas have small barbecue pits and picnic tables. The canyon cliffs change color continually and parrots are constantly chatter overhead. Backcountry camping is more spectacular, as you are alone.

If you don't want to camp, you could visit Los Cipreses for a day trip and then relax at the Cauquenes Hotel and Hotsprings. If you just want to enjoy lunch before hitting the road, Cauquenes serves excellent meals.

HOTEL TERMAS DE CAUQUENES, *Termas de Cauquenes. Tel. 72/297226. 50 rooms. Double $185. All meals included. Restaurant. Thermal pools. Credit cards accepted.*

This large gothic-style hotel, first established in 1885, still has some of its original structures. The original marble pools imported from Europe have been kept, but don't worry, there are also more modern spa facilities. Meticulously maintained gardens invite you to sprawl out and spend the afternoon after a relaxing bath. The restaurant is known throughout the region for its excellent food, so be sure to fit in a meal between all that bathing and sprawling.

SPORTS & RECREATION

Aside from hiking in Los Cipreses, it is also possible to arrange horseback rides. You must call Conaf in Rancagua in advance, *Tel. 72/297505*, to organize a trip.

You can hike or ski, depending on the snow, at the **Chapa Verde Ski Area**, 38 km north of Coya. They do not allow cars during the ski season, so you must take a bus from the Hipermercado Independencia, *Avenida Miguel Ramizer in Rancagua*. There are three pommel lifts and one chair lift for the eight runs, as well as a café, restaurant, rental shop and ski school.

PRACTICAL INFORMATION

Rancagua is the closest town to offer services other than the most basic food and gas. Spring and fall are the best times to visit both the park and the springs.

SIETE TAZAS NATIONAL RESERVE & CURICÓ AREA WINERIES

Siete Tazas, meaning Seven Cups, takes its name from the park centerpiece, a series of waterfalls that tumble in succession through a narrow gorge from beakers hewn by the force of the water. Other hikes lead you from the sunny banks along the river to the high, narrow canyon walls above.

After your visit to the park, you can stop to taste the goods at two of Chile's world famous vineyards, Miguel Torres and Viña San Pedro.

ARRIVALS & DEPARTURES

By Bus

It takes some time to get to Siete Tazas by bus, but it is certainly doable. From Santiago, take any of the bus companies that run the route south down the Panamericana to the bus station in Curicó. From there you will have to walk or take a *colectivo* to the regional bus station, which is at the end of Prat Street across from the railroad station. At the regional station, buy a ticket to Molina. From Molina, Buses Hernandez connects directly to Parque Ingles inside Siete Tazas.

The wineries are on the road to Lontué, which is just 13 km outside of Curicó. You can take either a taxi or *colectivo*.

By Car

It is 250 km from Santiago to the park. The route south to Molina is a straight shot on the Panamericana, but the road from Molina to the park is a narrow, bouncy, dirt track. The whole trip takes about 4.5 hours.

There is a signed exit on the Panamericana, just after Curicó, that will take you to the bodega Miguel Torres. From there you continue towards Lontué where you will find the Viña San Pedro. It is just a few kilometers from Lontué on to Molina.

ORIENTATION

Although access to the reserve is from Molina, it actually lies due east of Talca along the Rio Claro. Three chains of mountains cut through the park, two run from northeast to southeast along the banks of the river, and the third runs directly north to south.

There are two main sections of the park, Radal and Parque Ingles. The rangers office is found in the Parque Ingles sector of the park, which is nine km beyond the park entrance at Radal.

The wineries are between Curicó and Lontué.

WHERE TO STAY

There is camping in both the Parque Ingles and Radal sectors of the park, but Parque Ingles is closest to the falls. The Parque Ingles campground has numerous sites along the river on both sides of the road. There are toilets for public use, but they are not kept as clean as they could be.

HOSTERÍA FLOR DE LA CANELA, *Parque Ingles. Tel. 75/491613. 10 rooms. Double with bath $50. Breakfast included. Restaurant. No cards.*

The Flor de la Canela enjoys a prime location right on the banks of the Rio Claro. It also enjoys a monopoly as the only hotel in the park, so their prices reflect that. The rooms are small, but some have very nice views of the river. If you don't want to camp, this hostel is a good option, but they close in the winter and fall.

WHERE TO EAT

HOSTERÍA FLOR DE LA CANELA, *Parque Ingles. Tel. 75/491613. Moderate. No cards.*

Catering to the needs of campers, this is both a restaurant and a small store. Again, the prices reflect their monopoly, but you can find just about anything you need here. Checkered tablecloths cover the small tables inside, and there is a wonderful sitting area on the river outside. Pizza is the specialty, but you can also get sandwiches to eat there or pack on a hike.

VIÑA SAN PEDRO, *Lontué, Tel. 2/235-2600. Expensive. No cards.*

Viña San Pedro sometimes offers lunch as part of its tours. The meal is, of course, accompanied by their excellent wines. They require a group of 20 to fix the meal, but if you call ahead you can sometimes arrange to tag along with somebody else's group.

CABAÑAS DE LA LAGUNA, *Pan-American Highway by Lontué. Moderate. No cards.*

If you can't eat at the Viña San Pedro, this is a decent option before hitting the road.

SEEING THE SIGHTS

SIETE TAZAS. Within the park there are a few sights that are almost required viewing. The first is the Siete Tazas waterfall. Another is the **Velo de la Novia**, or Bride's Veil fall, that plunges 50 meters into a Blue Lagoon-like pool.

BODEGA MIGUEL TORRES, *Outside Curicó. Tours Monday-Friday at 12:30pm, 3:00pm, 5:30pm. Free entry.*

Miguel Torres, a subsidiary of the famed Spanish winery, offers tours of their making process and the chance to taste the goods. Keep in mind that it is not open on weekends.

VIÑA SAN PEDRO, *Lontué, Tel. 2/235-2600. Tours Tuesday-Thursday. Call ahead for appointment or to arrange lunch.*

San Pedro's tradition of wine-making goes back to 1701. It is the third largest winery in the country.

SPORTS & RECREATION

There are a number of **hiking** trails in Siete Tazas. The main one, which leads to both the Seven Cups and Bride's Veil falls, continues down past the cascades to the river. Another trail heads up the river from the Hostería Flor de la Canela. You'll pass transparent pools, perfect for swimming, before heading up along the canyon walls. You can practically touch both sides of the canyon as the water screams through narrow gorges below. A longer hike heads up to the top of Cerro el Fraile. For a multiple day excursion, you can trek all the way to **Gil de Vilches National Park.**

Terracota Excursions has put together three to 11 day **horseback riding** trips that originate in the Siete Tazas area. You can arrange these through their office in Santiago at *Agustinas 1547, Tel./Fax 2/6961097, e-mail terracot@intercity.cl.*

PRACTICAL INFORMATION

Molina is the closest town to offer services. Spring and fall are the best times to visit the park as it is very hot and crowded in the summer.

CHILLÁN

Chillán, set amongst smoking volcanoes, has a long history of destruction and rebuilding. The last major earthquake, in 1939, flattened about 90% of the town, meaning that there are few buildings over 60 years old. Today, thankfully, most of the buildings are built to withstand seismic activity.

Highlights of a visit to the area include one of Chile's best artisan fairs, Mexican murals, and the renowned ski area.

ARRIVALS & DEPARTURES

By Bus

Numerous bus lines run trips from both the Terminal Santiago and Terminal Alameda in Santiago to the bus terminal in Chillán, *Avenida O'Higgins 010*. Regional buses connect Chillán to the surrounding area from the rural bus terminal, *Maipón 890*.

By Car

Chillán is about 400 km south of Santiago on the Panamericana highway. The drive takes about 5.5 hours. You can rent a car in Chillán at **First Rent A Car**, *18 de Septiembre 380, Tel. 42/211218*.

By Plane

Airfare from Chillán to Santiago is around $80 one-way. **Ladeco**, *Tel. 42/224857*, has one flight a day. The airport is seven km from town. Small Ladeco buses shuttle people into town as do taxi cabs.

By Train

The train runs from Santiago to Puerto Varas, stopping in Chillán. The extremely slow service is rarely on time as it leaves from the train station, *Avenida Brasil 520* in Chillán, *Tel. 42/222424*.

ORIENTATION

Chillán sits on a plain between the Andes and the Coastal mountain chains. The ski area, Termas de Chillán, lies to the south-east of town on the flank of the Chillán Volcano.

The city is divided between Chillán and Chillán Viejo (old Chillán) to the southwest. Chillán was created after an earthquake in 1835 destroyed old Chillán. Some residents did not move from old Chillán, however, so the cities have grown side-by-side.

Chillán's streets are laid out in the standard Spanish grid with the Plaza O'Higgins in the middle.

WHERE TO STAY

In Chillán

HOTEL LAS TERRAZAS, *Constitución 664, 5th floor. Tel. 42/227000. Fax 42/227001. 37 rooms. Double $86. Breakfast included. Cable TV. Parking. Credit cards accepted.*

This relatively new hotel on the fifth floor of a downtown professional building has a nice, open feel. A large, light sitting area opens to the banistered stairway, which leads to the breakfast nook. The rooms are simple but nicely decorated. This is the best in-town option in the price category.

GRAN HOTEL ISABEL RIQUELME, *Arauco 600. Tel. 42/213663, Fax 42/211541. 75 rooms. Double $85. Breakfast included. Cable TV. Restaurant. Bar. Credit cards accepted.*

The elegant green blockish hotel overlooking Chillán's central square begs a remodeling job to transform it into a classic hotel. A jerky elevator ride and dark hallways lead to rooms that are sub-par. You will be more comfortable staying on one of the newer mid-priced hotels a few blocks away.

PASO NEVADO, *Libertad 219. Tel. 42/221827, Fax 42/237666. 15 rooms. Double $55. Breakfast included. Cable TV. Credit cards accepted.*

This new hotel is conveniently located a few blocks away from the plaza. It features tastefully selected wooden furniture and a small, grassy, interior courtyard where you can enjoy a quiet drink. This is an excellent option for a quick comfortable stay in Chillán. You'll be happiest avoiding the noise of the street level rooms.

HOSTAL DE LA AVENIDA, *O'Higgins 398. Tel./Fax 42/230256. 8 rooms. Double $52. Breakfast included.*

This small, clean hotel is a pleasant choice as the comfortably furnished rooms are built around a garden courtyard. The only negative is the curtain-less showers that spray all over the bathroom. Get a room off O'Higgins for less noise.

On the Way to the Ski Area

PARADOR JAMON, PAN Y VINO, *Kilometer 73 on the road to Termas de Chillán. Tel. 42/222383. Fax 42/220018. 40 rooms. Double $180. Breakfast included. Restaurant. Bar. Pool. Sauna. Credit cards accepted.*

Just eight kilometers from the ski area, this is an excellent choice if you don't want to pay the really big bucks of the Gran Hotel. The Spanish-style lodge is a good option in both winter and summer. The rooms are comfortable, the staff friendly, and the food good.

CABAÑAS LOS NIRRES, *Kilometer 72 on the road to Termas del Chillán. Tel./Fax 41/587652. 5 cabins, 4 apartments. Double $50. Sauna. Game room. No credit cards.*

These cabins are a favorite of families escaping from Santiago. With covered garages and big porches they are well equipped for any season. Other popular cabins are the **Cabañas El Leñador**, at *kilometer 71, Tel. 42/224176*, and the more economical **Cabañas La Baita** at *kilometer 70, Tel. 41/226887*.

At the Ski Area

GRAN HOTEL TERMAS DE CHILLÁN, *Termas de Chillán. Santiago Tel. 2/233-1313. Santiago Fax 2/231-5963. 150 rooms. Double $235. 5 Restaurants. Bar. Minimarket. Clubhouse. Disco. Game room. Spa. Thermal springs. Babysitting. Skiing. Tennis. Mountain bike rental. Horseback riding. Rock climbing. Credit cards accepted.*

This large hotel on the edge of the slopes at Chillán is certainly the most convenient for skiers. You can spend the day schussing away, ski right to the hotel entrance, and then work out any soreness in the thermal spa.

While this is a great hotel during the ski season, we like it even more in the summer. There are so many things to do that you'll run out of time before you run out of options. The rooms are nothing special, but they are comfortable and well decorated.

There is a smaller two star hotel next to the Gran Hotel that costs about $120 a night. Reservations are made through the same telephone number. In the summer there is camping as well.

WHERE TO EAT

In Chillán

The food options in Chillán are less than stellar. There are only a few that we recommend.

CENTRO ESPAÑOL, *Arauco 555 on the plaza. Tel. 216212. Moderate. Credit cards accepted.*

This is the best restaurant in town. With a standard Chilean menu sprinkled with Spanish influence here and there, you won't walk away hungry or disappointed.

Most of the other restaurants in Chillán are of the café or more informal variety. For coffee, desert, or a light lunch, try the **Cafe Paris**, *Arauco 658, Tel. 212773*. If it's full you can try the similar **Fuente Alemana** or **Aladino's** across the street. **Pizzeria Venecia**, *Prat 348, Tel. 210105*, is the best option in town for pizza.

On the Way to the Ski Area

PARADOR JAMON, **PAN Y VINO**, *Kilometer 73 on the road to Termas de Chillán. Tel. 42/222383.*

This restaurant inside the hotel is another with Spanish influence. The *chorizo* is good, as is anything prepared *a la gallega*.

At the Ski Area

GRAN HOTEL TERMAS DE CHILLÁN, *Termas de Chillán. Tel. 2/ 233-1313. 5 restaurants with different price levels. Credit cards accepted.*

There is a restaurant for every price level here on the ski slopes. It is usually just resort guests that frequent the more expensive and formal restaurant at night, while hungry hoards hit the sandwich shop and cafeteria.

SEEING THE SIGHTS

PLAZA DE ARMAS, *Between Libertad, 18 de Diciembre, Constitución, and Arauco streets.*

Sitting on a bench at the Plaza O'Higgins, surrounded by trees and flowers, is a good way to get a feel for the town. Much of Chillán's informal social activity takes place in front of you.

SIQUEIROS MURALS AT THE ESCUELA MEXICO, *O'Higgins 250, Tuesday-Friday 9:30am-12:30pm and 3-6pm. Monday and Saturday 9:30am-12:30pm. No admission fee but donations requested, and they need them.*

The school, a gift from the country of Mexico after the earthquake of 1939 razed the city, has a powerful mural in the library by the famous Mexican painter Siqueiros. The work, titled *Death to the Invader*, stars both Chilean and Mexican resistance heroes. The Mexican wall features Cuauhtemoc, Hidalgo, and Zapata amongst others. The Chilean mural includes the famous Mapuche Lautaro and, of course, O'Higgins.

SIQUEIROS & NERUDA

David Siqueiros and Pablo Neruda became close friends while Neruda was Chile's consul to Mexico. Siqueiros was in jail at the time, but that didn't stop the two from going out together. Siqueiros, with his greasy-palmed warden, would meet Neruda in out-of-the-way bars where they would drink and talk late into the night.

Neruda personally attached Siqueiros' Chilean visa to his passport, allowing him to leave jail and travel to Chile with his wife. It was then that Siqueiros painted the murals in Chillán. As Neruda says in his Memoirs, "The government of Chile repaid me for that service to our nation's culture by suspending me from my consular duties for two months."

Xavier Guerrero, a Chilean muralist, painted the staircase leading to the library with a work titled Mexican Brothers. The condition of the forceful works is sadly starting to decline due to both human and weather elements. It is well worth the visit to see a Siqueiros mural in such an out of the way place.

PARQUE MONUMENTAL BERNARDO O'HIGGINS, *Chillán Viejo on Avenida O'Higgins. Open all week from 8am-6pm (8pm in summer.) No admission fee.*

Large gardens, a museum, and a 60 meter mural depicting O'Higgins' life are the centerpieces of this park. For real O'Higginsphiles there is also a stone from his birthplace as well as his mother and sister's remains. It's almost Libertador over-load.

CONVENTO SAN FRANCISCO, *Aldea and Vega de Saldias. Open all week from 10am-1pm and 4-6pm. $0.50 to enter museum.*

This convent has an important history in the area, starting in 1835, when it was the headquarters for 15 Franciscan missions in the region. The museum inside houses both religious and historical artifacts that relate to the original convent and private school which were founded in 1585.

SPORTS & RECREATION

Most of the outdoor activity takes place up the mountains around the Termas de Chillán.

Hiking

During the summer the most talked about hike is to the crater of the 3100 meter Chillán Volcano. Guided trips are arranged out of the Gran Hotel at the ski area. There are other less rigorous hikes around Termas de Chillán such as the one to Los Pangues Cave.

Horseback Riding

You can organize anything from a half-day outing to multiple-day excursions. Contact Sr. Rivas at the **Cabañas Las Ananucas**, *km 72, Tel. 51/215881*, about day trips. The **Parador Jamón, Pan y Vino**, *El Roble 580, Tel. 42/222682*, arranges longer horseback rides into the mountains, as does the Gran Hotel Termas de Chillán.

Mountain Biking

There are bikes for rent at the ski area during the summer. You can take your bike up the mountain on the lift and bomb back down.

Skiing

The most practiced sport in Chillán is skiing. The resort has 28 runs and 9 lifts. The standard restaurant, café and equipment rental shop can be found here, along with deluxe lodgings. The runs actually hug the side of the smoking Chillán volcano. It is really something to see vents in the snow letting out sulfuric plumes as you ride up the chairlift. The views of the Andes are gorgeous and, depending on the snow, the skiing can be excellent.

Other Sports

There is a snowmobile track at the resort in the winter and tennis courts in the summer.

SHOPPING

FERIA DE CHILLÁN, *Maipon and 5 de Abril, Open daily*. Chile, compared with Peru, is not known for its colorful handicrafts. Most of its crafts are more ingenuous, keeping to natural colors and less complex designs. If you keep this in mind, you'll be delighted with the finds at this, one of Chile's best collections of *artesania*. Sweaters and other weavings, alpaca rugs, hats, ceramics, woodwork, baskets, and leather fill the stalls to overflowing. You're expected to bargain here, but don't anticipate prices to come down much.

Coihueco, about 25 km to the east of Chillán, is famous for its wood carvings and weavings. **Quinchamalí**, known for its ceramics, lies about 25 km to Chillán's west.

EXCURSIONS & DAY TRIPS

Termas De Chillán

Before its fame as a ski resort and summer sports heaven, Termas de Chillán was known for its namesake thermal baths. These still exist and can be used throughout to year to ease sore muscles. Nine pools and full spa services will get you back in working order. The scenery alone puts more spring in our steps.

The drive from Chillán takes about an hour. Signs in town mark the way. Buses Loyola, *Tel. 217838, 5 de Abril 594*, will get you up there if you don't have a car.

PRACTICAL INFORMATION

Banks: BCI, *Libertad 601*; **Santander**, *Arauco 595*

Business Hours: Monday-Friday 9am-1pm, 3pm-7pm. Saturdays 9am-2pm

Currency Exchange: **Cambios**, *Constitución 550*

Medical Service: Hospital Herminda Martín, *corner of Avenida Ramirez and Argentina. Tel. 212345*
Post Office: Correos de Chile, *Libertad 501*
Telephone/Fax: Chillán's area code is 42. CTC, *Arauco 625;* Entel, *18 de Septiembre 746*
Tourist Office/Maps: Sernatur, *18 de Septiembre 445. Tel. 223272.* It is open through lunch in the summer, but closes for lunch the rest of the year. The local tourist office can be found on the plaza at *18 de Septiembre 580*

13. THE NORTH

Kilometer after kilometer of shoreline broken by beaches and bays; hot desert plains, dotted with geoglyphs and rifted by deep fissures; Amerindian farmers terracing the land and raising llamas and alpacas; flamingo-filled lakes ringed with smoking volcanoes...and that's just one day in the striking and varied North.

The geography of the north changes so dramatically from east to west that you have the chance to pack a week's worth of experiences into a few days. There are five main traveler's hubs in the north. Each of these centers is located on or near the coast. From these cities you can travel east across the country for a stunning display of diversity.

The northern-most hub, **Arica**, lies just a few kilometers from the border with Peru. From this pleasant ocean-side city you cross fertile valleys and stop by lovely pre-colonial villages as you climb to **Lauca National Park**. These vast, isolated high plains, broken by green lakes and purple volcanoes, teem with fascinating bird and wildlife. Semi-nomadic Amerindians herd their alpaca as their ancestors have done for hundreds of years.

Iquique, the next center, has transformed itself from a city whose richest days have passed to a hopping beach metropolis. The nitrate kings of yesteryear left their mark, from the ornate architecture of the city's center to the haunting nitrate ghost towns. From Iquique you can follow geoglyphs through the **Atacama Desert**, the world's driest, to reach the *sierra* on the western edge of the Andes. Oasis villages, such as **Pica**, offer welcome shade and fresh swimming holes.

From the hub of **Antofagasta**, a working class port city, you cross the desert to marvel at the sight of the Andean Depression covered by vast salt flats. An even more popular access point is the mining city of **Calama**. The area around funky **San Pedro de Atacama** is a spot where natural wonders are literally overwhelming. Foreign lunar landscapes and spouting geysers are continually backed by a brilliant, blue sky. Hiking, mountain

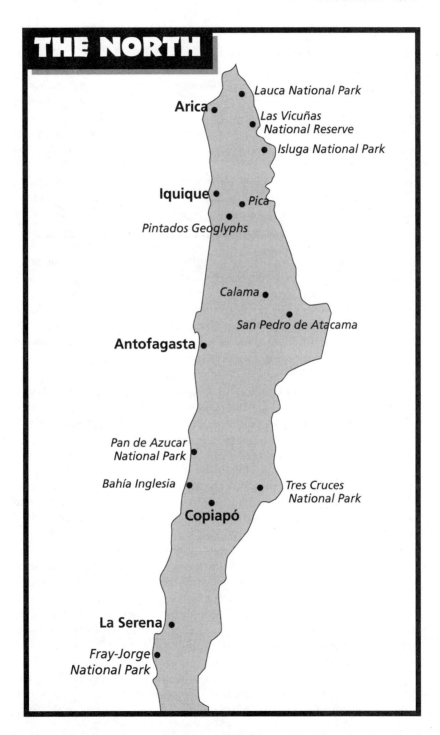

THE NORTH

Lauca National Park

Arica

Las Vicuñas
National Reserve

Isluga National Park

Iquique

Pica

Pintados Geoglyphs

Calama

San Pedro de Atacama

Antofagasta

Pan de Azucar
National Park

Bahía Inglesia

Tres Cruces
National Park

Copiapó

La Serena

Fray-Jorge
National Park

YOUR TIME IN THE NORTH

How do you best use your time to cover the thousands of kilometers that make up northern Chile? We have a couple of suggestions. If you only have a few days we recommend one of two options. You make the decision based on your priorities:

• San Pedro de Atacama – Incredible natural wonders; well-developed, yet laid-back infrastructure; multiple sporting options; comfortable temperatures.

• Arica and Lauca National Park – Overwhelming beauty; colonial villages; geoglyphs, abundant wildlife; Aymara Altiplano culture; less infrastructure; high altitudes.

biking and horseback riding are popular ways to experience this land. Many people prefer to access San Pedro by plane via **Calama**.

The mining city **Copiapó** is unique among the hubs as it sits about 70 km inland. From here you can head towards the sea to explore the strange coastal landscape at **Pan de Azúcar National Park** or relax in the quiet bay of **Bahía Inglesa**. Chile's highest mountain, **Ojos de Salado**, and remote high mountain lakes await discovery to the west.

The last hub, **La Serena**, is close enough to Santiago to be a favorite beach getaway. To the east you'll find lush green valleys, such as **Elqui**, backed by purple desert hills; internationally famous observatories; and, if it's been a rainy winter, a profusion of wildflowers blanketing the desert.

History

Three groups of people inhabited this area until the arrival of the Spanish. Roaming the Altiplano, working the sides of the Andes, and fishing the coast, the groups lived in relative harmony for years. The **Inca Empire**, out of Peru, extended its reach over these peoples in the 1400's. Upon arrival of the Spanish in 1536, the entire zone was under Inca control.

Arica was founded in 1545 with the discovery of a large silver mine in Potosí, Bolivia. For hundreds of years the town supplied the mine's workers and shipped out the mine's bounty. Terrible malaria in Arica obliged the Spanish to develop other cities along the route. Another silver mine close to Iquique, as well as guano export, attracted fortune seekers and laborers and opened up more of the region.

The Atacama Desert is the world's only source of natural sodium nitrate. After Independence the desert was split between Chile, Peru and Bolivia. The **War of the Pacific** in 1879 consolidated the entire region under Chilean rule. This bounty was Chile's great source of wealth until synthetic nitrates were invented in the 1930s. The stamp of this Golden Era can be seen on the central plazas of all the cities in the region.

Mining, especially copper, continues to fuel the north's economy.

ARICA

Arica is unique in this part of Chile, as water from the Andes reaches all the way to the coast, creating fertile, green valleys and allowing wide-scale farming in the Azapa Valley. Serving as the main tourist hub for visitors to the small, pre-colonial villages dotting the Sierra and Altiplano, Arica also is a required stop for those who want to visit the impressive national parks, such as Lauca to its east.

ARRIVALS & DEPARTURES

By Bus

Arica's bus terminal, *Diego Portables 948, Tel. 241390,* is the departure point for buses making connections to cities in Chile as well as many other countries in South America. Some of the international routes run only in the summer.

Buses leave throughout the day for points south of Arica, as well as Tacna, Peru; Lima, Peru; Quito, Ecuador; La Paz, Bolivia; Asuncion, Paraguay and Salta, Argentina.

Bus Companies
- **Fenix Pullman Norte**, *Tel. 223837*, south to Santiago
- **Geminis**, *Tel. 241647*, Calama, south to Santiago, La Paz, Asuncion, Salta
- **Buses Carmelita**, *Tel. 241591*, Iquique
- **Buses Zambrano**, *Tel 241587*, south to Santiago
- **Tur-Bus**, *Tel. 222217*, Calama, south to Santiago
- **Tramaca**, *Tel. 221198*, Calama, south to Santiago
- **Flota Barrios**, *Tel 223587*, Santiago
- **Adsubliata**, *Tel. 241972*, Tacna, Peru
- **Taschoapa**, *Tel. 222817*, Lima, Peru; Quito, Ecuador; Bogota, Colombia; Caracas, Venezuela

Shared taxis, called *colectivos*, are a fast, reasonably priced alternative for getting to both Iquique and Tacna.

Regional buses run to **Lauca National Park** (**Buses Martínez**, *Pedro Montt 620, Tel. 232265;* **Transportes Cali**, *Pedro Montt 636, Tel. 255361*), and the Colonial villages of **Socoroma**, **Belén**, and **Putre**, (**Buses Paloma**, *Riesco 2071, Tel. 222710.*)

By Car
Arica is at the northern-most end of Chile's section of the Pan-American highway. It is a four hour drive from Iquique.

Rentals are an excellent option for exploring the area around Arica. You can travel on your own schedule and get to places not served by public transportation. The road to Lauca National Park is paved, so you don't need 4WD, but for most other points in the area you do.

Rental Car Companies
• **American**, *General Lagos 559,Tel. 252234*
• **Avis**, *Chacabuco 180, Tel. 232210*
• **Budget**, *21 de Mayo 650, Tel. 252978*
• **Hertz**, *Hotel El Paso, Velásquez 1109,Tel. 231487*
• **Klasse**, *Velásquez 762, Local 25, Tel. 254498*
• **Reinco**, *Baquedano 999, Tel. 251121*

WHEN YOU RENT

As we've said before, we highly recommend renting cars in Chile because you have greater control over your itinerary. There are some extra cautions you need to take in this region, however, before you hit the road. The extreme isolation of the area means that the AAA tow truck is not going to be handy. Be aware of the risk of getting stranded. Always check in with carabineros and park rangers to let them know your destination, carry extra gas, and bring food, water, and warm clothes.

Make sure you rent from a company prepared for you to venture off into the wild. ***American,*** *for example, equips its 4WD vehicles with two spare tires and three extra gas tanks. We've found them to be an excellent, high quality renter with lower prices than the multinational chains.*

By Plane
Lan, *21 de Mayo 345, Tel. 251641;* **Ladeco**, *21 de Mayo 443,Tel. 252021;* and **Avant**, *21 de Mayo 227, Tel. 232328* have a couple of daily flights from Santiago to Arica, some stopping in Antofagasta and others in Iquique.

Lan flies to La Paz and Santa Cruz, Bolivia as does the Bolivian airline, **Lloyd Aéreo Boliviano**, *Patricio Lynch 298, Tel. 251919.* **Aeroperu** and **Iberia**, *Edificio Empresarial 78, Tel. 251937* share an office in Arica although they have no flights from here.

The airport is 18 km north of Arica near the Peruvian border. **Radio Taxi Arica**, *Prat 528, Tel. 250340*, will take you door to door in a shared ($4) or private ($10) cab.

By Train

The La Paz-Arica train, *21 de Mayo 51, Tel. 231786,* departs from Arica twice a week on Tuesdays and Saturdays. For $52 your meals are included on the 12 hour ride. Take warm clothes and make sure you can pay in US dollars.

There is another train from Arica to Tacna, Peru. It leaves twice daily, noon and 5pm, from *Maximo Lira 889, Tel. 231115.*

ORIENTATION

Arica, on the Pacific Ocean, is a mere 54 km from the border with Peru. The town is bounded by the sea to the west and El Morro Hill to the south. Most of downtown is between El Morro and the San Jose riverbed. 21 de Mayo, closed to car traffic between Prat and Baquedano, is the main commercial street with restaurants, banks, pharmacies, bookstores, airline offices and more.

The streets of town are laid out in a grid pattern, but instead of having one central plaza, city life unfolds on the plazas, on 21 de Mayo, and on the beaches.

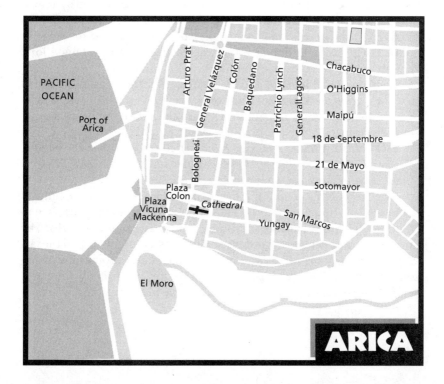

GETTING AROUND TOWN

Collective taxis are a good way to get from points that are not within walking distance of each other. If you know the route to take, just look for the cab with that route number on the roof and flag him down. If you don't know the route, an empty *colectivo* will go off its route to take you anywhere in town for $2.50.

WHERE TO STAY

Most of the hotel choices in Arica are less than wonderful. There are a plethora of shabby residenciales and mediocre moderate hotels. There are, however, some pleasant places to stay, which we have listed below.

Expensive

HOTEL ARICA & RESORT, *Comandante San Martín 599. Tel. 58/ 254540, Fax 58/231133. 114 rooms, 14 suites, 20 cabins. Double $115. Restaurant. Bar. Cable TV. Swimming pool. Tennis and volleyball courts. Private beach. Business center. Meeting rooms. Credit cards accepted.*

The Hotel Arica & Resort dominates the business and upscale segment of Arica because the Chilean Panamericana chain possesses the ideal location and offers enough amenities to it make it tough to beat. The tastefully decorated rooms with white stucco walls are extended by a small sitting area, which leads to an ocean view balcony or patio. The two person cabins front the hotel's small, tame, private beach and cost the same as doubles. The bar and dining room's decor has been maintained long enough that it has come back into style.

Racy simulated leopard and tiger skins cover the seats in the ocean view bar, a good place for a cocktail even if you aren't staying here. Activity options include a game of tennis on hotel's clay court, but be aware that any balls over the fence are probably ocean bound.

HOTEL EL PASO, *Velásquez 1109. Tel. 58/231041. Fax 58/231965. 60 rooms. Double $105. Breakfast included. Restaurant. Bar. Cable TV. Pool. Tennis courts. Bike rental. Credit cards accepted.*

The Hotel El Paso does not have a beach or an ocean view, but it is the best of the upper end hotels in town. It is within walking distance of all of the sights, yet harbors a tranquil, green oasis within its walls. The hotel has three hectares of gardens and trees as a buffer between the city and you. The rooms spread out in wings that center around the "mini-zoo" garden complete with multiple parrots and two friendly monkeys. The rooms are well appointed and comfortable with furnishings that have been recently updated.

Moderate

HOTEL GENOVEVA, *Maipu 455. Tel. 58/232870 or 232863. 12 rooms. Double $50. Breakfast included. Cable TV. Minibar. Credit cards accepted.*

Featuring the most modern black and pink furniture that money can buy, the recently opened Genoveva utilizes all possible nooks and amenities to make their guests comfortable. Easily the best value in town in the mid-price range, the big rooms all include well-designed closets, a make-up table, comfortable beds, and a charming petite patio. The hotel also boasts a good central location. The owners are friendly and can point you in the right direction to any of the local points of interest.

HOTEL SAVONA, *Yungay 380. Tel. 58/232319. Fax 58/231606. 32 rooms. Double $57. Breakfast included. Credit cards accepted.*

The Savona has by far the most pleasant ambiance of any downtown hotel. A small garden outside leads to the lobby, which in turn opens out to a flower-filled patio. Greenery and blooming plants are everywhere. Located just a few blocks from Plaza Colón, the hotel is quiet and removed from the main traffic routes. The rooms are frayed at the edges however, and not up to the same quality as the common areas.

HOTEL AMERICANO, *General Lagos 571. Tel. 58/252234, Fax 58/252150. E-mail servituri@entelchile.net. 25 rooms. Double $60. Breakfast included. Cable TV. Minibar. Gym. Sauna. Credit cards accepted.*

This new entrant is scheduled to open by the publication date of this book. The brick facade will be complimented by a glass and aluminum inset. Planned extras include a small gym and sauna. The management will set aggressive introductory rates and is confident that the hotel will outclass higher-priced competitors. After reviewing the architectural plans, we are sure that the Hotel Americano will be among the best options in town.

HOTEL BAHÍA CHINCHORRO, *Luis Beretta Porcel 2031. Tel. 58/241068. Fax 58/245217. 32 rooms. Double $71. Breakfast included. Restaurant. Bar. Pool. Cable TV. Credit cards accepted.*

If you want to stay on the beach in Arica, this hotel at the end of *Playa Chinchorro* is the best option in the moderate range. All of the stucco rooms have ocean views and the shore is right off the porch or patio. The flower-covered grounds include a small pool and an outdoor restaurant. The room furnishings, unfortunately, have been allowed to decline, but listening to waves break instead of traffic can make up for that. This is not a fancy resort, but rather a well-worn family place. You can talk to the parrot in the garden on your way to the ocean.

HOTEL PLAZA COLÓN, *San Marcos 261. Tel. 58/254424. Fax 58/ 231244. 35 rooms. Double $50. Breakfast included. Cable TV. Parking. Credit cards accepted.*

You cannot miss this bright pink and baby blue hotel with its faux Colonial exterior. There are two sections to the hotel. You can stay in the older one with large rooms and aged furniture, or the newer one with small rooms and new furnishings. Neither choice is perfect, but the newer section does has small balconies.

HOTEL DIEGO DE ALMAGRO, *Sotomayor 490. Tel. 58/224444. Fax 58/221240. 55 rooms. Double $53. Breakfast and parking available at extra charge. Credit cards accepted.*

Don't be too put off by the hotel's late communist-period exterior. Once you're inside, the décor is that of a modern, mid-priced hotel almost anywhere in the world. The rooms are decent sized and have small patios to expand your space. The furniture is a bit dated, but the hotel is in the midst of an ownership swap, so that could change soon.

HOTEL CENTRAL, *21 de Mayo 425. Tel. 58/252575. 34 rooms. Double $61. Breakfast included. Cable TV. Bar. Restaurant. Credit cards accepted.*

The Hotel Central is part of the Best Western chain. Currently the rooms are worn around the edges and have sagging beds. The management says that a complete renovation is in the works.

Inexpensive

HOTEL LYNCH, *Patricio Lynch 589. Tel. 58/251959. 25 rooms. Double $40. Breakfast included. Restaurant. Credit cards accepted.*

The Lynch is an aging, lovely hotel with a mural of vicuñas and flamingos covering one entire wall in the reception area. There is a brilliant blue interior courtyard and several good common areas. The hotel has been open since 1973 and some of the fixtures and furnishings show their age. A coffee shop style restaurant is connected to the hotel. This is a good option in this price range.

In a pinch you could also try **Hotel Tacora**, *Sotomayor 540, Tel. 251240, Double $30.*

There are many run-down *residenciales* in Arica appropriate only for lodging bedbugs. Three clean and hospitable ones we found, however, are **Residencial America**, *Sotomayor 430, Tel.58/254148*, **Residencial Arica**, *18 de Septiembre 466, Tel. 58/255399*, and **Residencial Lima**, *San Marcos 443, Tel. 256721*. All of these charge about $10 per person in rooms without baths. The scarce double rooms with baths go for about $25. Because these are the few good budget options, they fill up quickly, so it is worthwhile to get there early or call to reserve a spot.

WHERE TO EAT

You'll find a Peruvian influence in much of the food here, as it has more sauces and spice than that of the rest of Chile. There are also some Peruvian imports on the beverage side. You should try both Cerveza Ariquipeña, an excellent beer; and Inka Cola, a bubble-gum tasting soft drink that is a continual thorn in Coke's can. The climate nourishes fresh tropical fruit year round.

Most of the meals in Arica are low priced when compared to the rest of Chile. Don't let that fool you on the quality though. There is some excellent food to be had here.

RESTAURANT MARACUYA, *Av. Comandante San Martín 0321. Tel. 227600. Expensive. Credit cards accepted.*

Perched on the edge of the Pacific Ocean, the Maracuya enjoys both a literal and figurative privileged position in Arica. Although the rich, burnt-orange décor is not formal, the service and the prices are. This restaurant is expensive for Arica, but the outstanding menu offers creative, complex dishes rarely seen in Chile. We recommend starting your meal with *alcachofa nautica*: two fist-sized artichoke hearts covered with shrimp and crab in a creamy, rich cheese sauce. Another outstanding dish is the *lenguado a lo macho*, a fillet of sole topped with spicy white wine sauce featuring octopus, clam, *machas*, peas, and chilies. You can enjoy your meal outside on the patio if you wish.

BAR CASANOVA, *Baquedano 397. Tel. 231550. Expensive/moderate. Credit cards accepted.*

The Bar Casanova offers an ample outdoor dining area overlooking the 21 de Mayo pedestrian street. The menu is composed of an extensive listing of fish, meat, and pasta dishes which you can combine with any of the sixteen sauces such as caper, mustard, curry, or mushroom. The drink list is almost as long as the menu. The decor includes a brilliant pattern of yellow and green tiles and a ceiling exuding a 70's disco flashback aura.

CYCLO, *Patricio Lynch 224. Tel. 232823. Moderate. Credit cards accepted.*

Cyclo offers surprisingly moderate prices considering its creative menu and decor. This spin-off of a Santiago eatery is located within long walls adorned with local crafts. The house favorites are two steak dishes - *Carne Plateada* prepared with carrots, garlic, and onions in a light beer sauce, and the *Carne Mechada,* basked in a sauce of crushed tomatoes, garlic, and bacon. Check out the salad bar before ordering. It includes savory chilled offerings such as *ceviche*, stuffed tomatoes, and whole grain salads.

LOS ALEROS DE 21, *21 de Mayo 736. Tel. 232636. Moderate. Credit cards accepted.*

Los Aleros de 21 offers traditional Chilean cuisine in a *huaso* ambience. Idyllic paintings of haciendas adorn the white-washed walls along with protruding thatch that serves as roofing on rustic huts. The menu includes an extensive selection of seafood and meat dishes along with traditional favorites like *pastel de choclos*. If you are headed here on a Saturday night, you can stop by the Tango-Tan social club next door to dance a few tangos after 10pm.

CHIFA SHAO-LIN, *18 de Septiembre 601. Tel. 231311. Moderate. Credit cards accepted.*

Godzilla eating with chopsticks overwhelms the outside wall of this small, red-lanterned restaurant. *Chifa* is a Peruvian-style Chinese cuisine popularized by Chinese immigrants in Peru. Hunan stuffed pepper works deliciously as an appetizer. The reasonably-priced, spicy Mongolian duck with an accompaniment of vegetable-laced rice is an excellent choice for an entree. We found one appetizer, one rice dish, and one entree to be enough for two of us.

Another option for *chifa* is the **Kon-Chau**, *General Lagos 659, Tel. 232275*, which one local resident insists is the best in town.

CASINO LA BOMBA, *Colón 367. Tel. 232323. Inexpensive. No credit cards.*

We loved visiting the fire station as kids, as we love eating there now. It's so fun to walk between the shiny, red hook and ladders to the dining room in the back of the station. Simple red and white tablecloths and chairs go well with the simple, but delicious food. From the flavorful chile sauce made from crisp *ají* to the fresh fruit for dessert, everything about your meal is high quality. Order the daily *menú*, not because it's inexpensive, which it is, but because it's good.

CAFE SAM, *21 de Mayo 571-A. Tel. 255529. Inexpensive. No credit cards.*

This small coffee shop offers the cheapest sandwiches around. It is always full of locals so try to squeeze in there somewhere.

The entire block of Maipu between Colón and Baquedano is lined with inexpensive fast food spots called *fuentes de sodas*, (soda shops), offering sandwiches and quarters of roasted chickens for just over a buck. A few of them include **San Fernando**, *corner of Maipu and Baquedano*; **Pollos al Spiedo**, *Maipu 388*; and **Patricia**, *Maipu 351*.

The pedestrian walkways on and around **21 de Mayo** have the highest concentration of restaurants in town. Most are inexpensive sandwich or coffee shops. Many have tables and chairs set up outside that are great places to sit on a sunny day and people watch. If you really like activity, try to be here around 2pm when everybody gets off work and the streets literally come alive. These are some of our favorites.

DI MANGO, *21 de Mayo 244. Inexpensive. No credit cards.*

Di Mango's pink chairs and white wrought iron tables are some of the most popular outdoor seating in town. They are deservedly known for having some of Arica's best ice cream and coffee. Friends meet here after work in groups that are constantly expanding as people they know walk by and join them. **La Fontana**, down the block at *21 de Mayo 221*, is another good choice for ice cream if Di Mango's is full.

SCHOP 21, *21 de Mayo 211. Inexpensive. No credit cards.*

As the name suggests, this is the place for draft beers under their colorful outdoor umbrellas. If you prefer to be healthy, they also offer fresh juices. The menu covers the fast food spectrum from sandwiches to pizzas, but the real specialty is beer.

SCALA, *21 de Mayo 201. Inexpensive. No credit cards.*

Right on the corner of Bolognesi and 21 de Mayo, Scala is the place to sit and watch all of Arica pass by. Pizza, empanadas, sandwiches and ice cream are the standard fare here.

GOVINDAS, *Bolognesi 454. Tel. 231028. Delivery. Inexpensive. No credit cards.*

If your body rejects the idea of another steak sandwich, it can find relief here. This small restaurant, adorned with East Indian decorations including a poster touting "Krishna es amor," is an excellent vegetarian option. The lunch *menu* is a delightful array of tastes including salad, soup, and fresh squeezed fruit juice. Squash stuffed with beans and spinach is an example of the types of entrees they serve. Go here at lunch because the dinner options of pastas, pizzas, and soyburgers don't compare to the delicious and well-rounded lunches.

MERCADO, *corner of Colón and Maipu. Inexpensive. No credit cards.*

As with the markets in almost every other town in Chile, the one here is a traditional favorite for an inexpensive meal with the masses. Dive in and pick your favorite stall for a meal or just a quick bite. **El Caballito del Mar** has tables for a sit-down meal.

SEEING THE SIGHTS

EL MORRO, *Sotomayor street by car, or the path at the end of Colón by foot. No admission charge.*

Start your tour of Arica at the top of this sandy peak to get a lay of the land. The pathway is unfortunately sprinkled with litter, but the view from the peak is worth it. You can see the plazas, beaches, lighthouse, and colorful, boat-filled port. The **History and Arms Museum**, *8am-8:30pm, Entry $1*, sits at the top of the knoll. The museum pays tribute to a Chilean offensive that overtook the hill during the War of the Pacific. Unless you are a battle *aficionado*, the museum is weak. There are old uniforms, flags, firearms, and a vase with the ashes of some of the fallen heroes.

Walking Tour From Plaza Vicuña Mackenna

At the foot of **El Morro**, you can enjoy a quick tour of the downtown sights. Take a left on San Marcos after passing the lovely blue and white **ex-consulate of Peru**. You'll come to the gothic **San Marcos Cathedral**. The cathedral was ordered pre-fab from the Gustave Eiffel company, of Eiffel tower fame, by a Peruvian president. Arica's original cathedral was destroyed in an earthquake, so the president opted to place Eiffel's church here. As the War of the Pacific changed national boundaries, the Peruvian treasure became Chile's. While it is rusting a bit on the outside, the inside is quite a sight. The orange and yellow interior is done almost entirely in iron. The playful ceiling struts are beautiful, as are the columns.

From the church you can look out at all three of the plazas below. **Plaza Colón**, with its bougainvillea-covered sitting areas, is a perfect spot for lounging. The tiny **Plaza del Roto Chileno**, to the right, has a sculpture of the downtrodden Chilean for which it is named. Large palm trees housing equally large birds surround **Mackenna Plaza**. You might want to cover your head as you walk through here. Arica's plazas are especially pleasant because they are open and not surrounded by tall buildings.

Continuing north through the Mackenna Plaza, you will see the peppermint-striped **Ex-Aduana**, built in 1874. Once the city's important customs house, it is now the **Casa de Cultura**. It too was pre-built in Eiffel's shop and is worth stepping inside for a visit. The wooden ceiling, iron supports, and intricate staircase are works of art.

North of the Ex-Aduana, on 21 de Mayo and Manual Montt, is the **Arica-La Paz train station**, built in 1913. The **locomotive** in front used to haul trains along the mountainous route. From here you should stroll along the pedestrian walkway on **21 de Mayo**.

Tour Companies

If you do not want to deal with renting a car, there are some good tour companies in Arica that offer trips to the Azapa Valley; Tacna, Peru; Lauca National Park; and other destinations. If you are going on one of the day trips to Lauca or any other high altitude destination, make sure your tour company has oxygen in the vans. Some of the better companies are:

- **Ecotour**, *Bolognesi 460, Tel. 250000*; all its guides are history or geography professors.
- **GeoTour**, *Bolognesi 421, Tel. 253927, Fax 251675, Email* geotour@mail.entelchile.net; one of the largest and a solid choice for a quality tour.
- **Globotour**, *21 de Mayo 260, Tel. 232909, Fax 231085*; offers the standard tours as well as books plane tickets and makes other travel arrangements.

NIGHTLIFE & ENTERTAINMENT

CASINO DE ARICA, *Costanera. Monday-Thursday 9pm-3:30am. Friday-Saturday 9pm-4am. Entry $4. No tie necessary.*

With slot machines as well as gaming tables, you can pass the night away gambling if you're not too tired out from touring or fun in the sun.

If you want to dance, try the **Sun Sat Disco**, *km 3.5 on the road to Azapa*, or **Soho** at *Buenos Aires 509* near the beach.

SPORTS & RECREATION

Beach

Arica's popularity as a beach spot is not undeserved. Sunny skies, comfortable temperatures, and the warmest water in Chile (not that that's very warm) all beckon you. Unfortunately, so do strong currents and rip tides. Be extremely careful about where you swim.

There are nice beaches both north and south of downtown. They all have small restaurants and outdoor bars, which are good hangouts in the summer. Both **Playa El Laucho** and **Playa La Lisera**, to the south, are fine for swimming. **Playa Bravo**, is not. **Playa Chinchorro**, just north of downtown, is good for swimming and sports on the beach. There is surfing off its docks and a skate park on its shores.

Bicycling

Bikes are for rent at *Sotomayor 540*. You can use them to tool around town or head to the beach. There are no mountain bike rentals, which is unfortunate, because mountain biking the hills and valleys around town is becoming popular here.

Birding

Birders can take a tour with Birding Altoandino in Putre. They arrange area walks as well as trips to **Lauca**, the **Salar de Surire**, and **Isluga**. Contact them at *Tel. 58/300013* or *Fax 58/222735*.

Climbing

You can hire a guide and equipment for climbs in the Lauca area at the military base outside of Putre. You must have a license, which is free from the municipal building in Putre with a 24-hour wait

Fishing

You can get a fishing license at Sernap, *Serrano 1856*. The local tour agencies can arrange boats.

Hiking

The best hikes are out of town, in area national parks such as **Lauca**. See *Day Trips & Excursions.*

Surfing

Playa Chinchorro and **Playa Las Machas**, both north of downtown, are the closest spots for surf. **Isla Alacrán** has bigger, but more dangerous waves. Talk to one of the many shops on 21 de Mayo about other breaks. Unfortunately there is no board rental in town, but El Gringo, Surfing Sun, and Solari all have boards for sale.

Swimming

There is a beautiful Olympic-sized pool at the Parque Centenario which is open from Tuesday-Saturday from 8:30am-6:30pm. Entry costs $1.50.

SHOPPING

POBLADO ARTESANAL, *Hualles 2825 on the way to the Azapa Valley. Tuesday-Sunday, 9:30am-1pm, 3:30pm-7:30pm.*

A model of an Indian pueblo, the town has resident artisans who have set up workshops and market areas. Weaving, ceramics and woodwork are all for sale. There is also a restaurant with a folkloric dance show.

There is also an artisan's market in town north of Plaza Colón between Sotomayor and 21 de Mayo. **Pasaje Bolongnesi**, as it is called, offers leather crafts, sweaters, hats, and other items from the Altiplano.

EXCURSIONS & DAY TRIPS

If you can afford it, we recommend renting a vehicle for these excursions. You'll gain the freedom to explore at your own pace. On the other hand, public transportation or tour companies can get you to all but the most remote sites.

Azapa Valley

This fertile valley, just a few kilometers east of Arica, offers a wonderful archaeological museum as well as views of ancient geoglyphs and plentiful olive orchards, tomato fields, and banana plantations. The river only runs in the summer, but the greenery stays throughout the year.

There are a number of excellent geoglyphs just outside of Arica on the south side of the San Jose River. Entire llama caravans march around the sides of hills. **Cerro Sagrado**, Sacred Hill, was thought to be a ritual site because of its ethereal array of designs.

At **Pukará San Lorenzo**, you'll find the remains of a 12th century fort. The ruins are only so-so, but the spot offers excellent views of the valley, where you can see that there is no transition zone between the sandy hills and the fertile farmland.

SAN MIGUEL DE AZAPA MUSEO ARQUEOLOGICO, *12 km down the road to San Miguel. Tel. 205555. Daily 9am-6pm. Open until 8pm in January and February. Entry $1.25.*

This museum, one of the best in the North, has a solid collection of artifacts that spans several centuries. The simple but powerful displays show how the local people lived, dressed, worked and worshiped while highlighting how these things changed through successive periods of development. The Chinchorro mummies on display are the oldest in the world. There is information available in English if you ask for it at the front

---

CHINCHORRO MUMMIES

Why are these puckered little guys so important? They have basically shifted our understanding of world prehistory. For many years the planet's oldest civilizations were presumed to be from Egypt and Babylon. These mummies, however, date back 10,000 years: to times before ancient Egypt.

*You can see from the museum displays that the **Chinchorros** were a fairly advanced culture. Their mummification methods were even more highly evolved than those of the Egyptians. The discovery of this culture on the Chilean coast put into doubt the entire theory of human migration from Asia to the Americas, because they could not have come so far in so little time.*

Colectivos leaving from Chacabuco between Baquedano and Lagos will get you to the museum. If you want to stop at the sights along the way and you don't have a car, we suggest booking a tour. It costs less than going in taxi and the guide is much more informative than your cab driver will be.

Lluta Valley To Putre

This trip over the desert and up the sierra is a stunning voyage back in time. Putre, a sleepy Colonial town, is an excellent place to spend a night acclimatizing to the altitude before heading up to **Lauca National Park**. It is also an easy base from which to explore the Colonial cities **Socoroma** and **Belén**, which can also be investigated from Arica.

From Arica, you pass the **Lluta Geoglyphs**, large designs that stand out on the southern hillside 13 km out of town. These llamas and human figures are similar to the ones seen on the way to the Azapa Valley. We

> ## BIG ART
>
> As you travel throughout the north, you will run across a number of **geoglyphs**. They were created between 1000-1400 AD, when there was much travel and social interchange between the peoples of the area. It is believed that most of the geoglyphs were constructed as giant roadside markers, indicating routes from the sierra to the sea. Others seem to have been produced for ritual purposes.
>
> The works were created in communal effort by two different processes. On the light sand around Arica, darker rocks were placed in mosaic fashion on the sand. On the dark, oxidized sand around Iquique, the top layer of earth was scratched away, leaving the lighter under-layer in the shape of the object.

think the **Lluta Valley**, green to its edges where it harshly turns to barren sand, is the most striking watershed in the area.

As the road climbs, you arrive to **Ponconchile**, the first of many Colonial towns with charming churches from the turn of the 17th century. Don't miss the graveyard behind the church, which spreads like a colorful, cross-orchard across the desert. There are outstanding views of the valley as you continue to gain altitude until the condors are soaring beneath you.

Once you leave the valley, a rocky desert of fantastic oranges and pinks surrounds you. Strange candelabra cactus dots the landscape. After 90 km of climbing, you reach the **Pukará (Fort) de Copaquilla**, from the 12th century. In much better shape than its San Lorenzo counterpart, this fort affords prime views of the deep canyon below, still lined with ancient terrace work.

Belén and **Socorama** are both justifiably famous as excellent examples of Colonial architecture. The road to Belén, however, is a rough and curving 34 km as opposed to the short six km track to Socorama. Unless you are just crazy about Colonial churches, we recommend sticking to Socorama's canal-lined, cobblestone streets.

As you descend into Socorama from the dry sierra, the verdant valley strikes your senses with its huge, fragrant eucalyptus trees. Don't miss the timeless church, with its thatched roof and separate bell tower, perched on the edge of the valley. The town square with its small garden is the perfect place for a relaxing afternoon picnic. Silver laden mule trains used to pass through here in a constant stream to Arica, but now the streets are eerily empty.

Continuing on the main road, you come to **Putre**, backed by purple and gold twin volcanic peaks. There is not much happening here, but you can wander the streets to see the 17th century stone doorways and visit the plaza. At 3500 meters it's an effort, but worthwhile, to walk down to the green ravine on the edge of town It will take all your strength to dodge the goats bleating by you. By spending the night here you not only have some time to acclimatize, but you also get a jump on all the day trips to Lauca from Arica. If you're really feeling strong you can take a birding walk with **Birding Andino**, *Tel. 58/300013.*

There is one hotel in town and a few hostels. There is also a CONAF office where you should check in with your itinerary if you are driving through the parks of the Altiplano.

HOSTERÍA LAS VICUÑAS, *O'Higgins. Tel. 58/224466. Fax. 58/222166. 30 rooms. Double $75. Dinner and breakfast included. No credit cards.*

It's unfortunate that the only hotel in town looks more like military barracks than a tourist retreat. The rooms are plain, with old furniture, but they are heated. You won't be living in luxury here, but you'll have a warm room and decent food so you can spend the night getting used to the altitude.

HOSTAL CALI, *Baquedano 399. Tel. 58/221220. 5 rooms. Double $22. Shared kitchen. No credit cards.*

Clean and simple, this hostel is a fine place to spend the night if just to use the kitchen. The restaurant opportunities in Putre are so limited that being able to prepare your own meal is a huge plus. The attached store sells all your basic staples as well as fresh fruit and vegetables. The rooms are cold at night, but there are plenty of blankets.

Codpa Valley

Codpa, a tribal government center long before the arrival of the Spanish, is a weekend getaway for the people of Arica. Located in the hills along-side the Vitor River, the temperate climate and clean water make it an excellent location for fruit cultivation. Don't miss the local wine, *vino pintatani.*

The variety of landscapes makes the excursion especially enjoyable. Vast deserts are replaced, as you climb eastwards, by hills backed with snowcapped mountain chains. Codpa itself is nestled in a lush, thin strip of valley. Walk the streets and visit the church, one of the prettiest in the region, before moving on. From Codpa you can make a loop to Belén, visit the smaller towns of Guanacagua and Chitita, or, head back to Arica.

Tacna, Peru

Tacna, a Peruvian border town, is a fun visit if you want to get another stamp in your passport, drink Peruvian *pisco*, and buy handmade textiles. The market specializes in woven, especially alpaca, handicrafts. Both buses and *colectivos* connect Arica to Tacna. The down-side of the *colectivo* is it takes longer than the bus to cross the Peruvian border.

Desert Drive To Iquique

The drive from Arica to Iquique, about four hours, is an intense desert crossing that takes you through four immense fractures in the earth. At the largest canyon, **Cuesta de Chiza**, you dive over 850 meters to the bottom of the fissure and drive kilometers along the wind-whipped floor before surfacing on the other side. There are some excellent mosaic geoglyphs at the bottom of the *cuesta*.

Eighty five km before arriving to Iquique you pass the turn to **Pisaqua**, an important nitrate port. Many of its buildings, constructed from proceeds of the nitrate trade, are now national monuments. See Iquique's *Excursions & Day Trips* for more information on Pisaqua.

PRACTICAL INFORMATION

Banks: 21 de Mayo Street is strewn with banks and most of them have ATMs. **Banco de Chile**, *21 de Mayo 330*; **Banco Santander**, *21 de Mayo 403*; **Banco Santiago**, *21 de Mayo 212*; **Banco Sud America**, *21 de Mayo 187*

Business Hours: Monday-Friday 9am-1:30pm and 4:30pm-9pm, Saturday 9am-1:30pm

Currency Exchange: **Concha y Cia**, *Chacabuco 300*; **Marta Daguer**, *18 de Septiembre 330;* **Yanulaque**, *21 de Mayo 175*

Laundry: **La Moderna**, *18 de Septiembre 457*; **Niko's Laundry**, *18 de Septiembre 188-A*

Medical Service: **Dr. Juan Noé Hospital**, *18 de Septiembre 1000*

National Parks: **Conaf**, *Vicuña Mackenna 820, Tel. 250570,* Monday-Friday 9am-1pm, 2pm-5pm. Closes at 4:30pm on Fridays

Post Office: **Correos de Chile**, *Prat 305*

Supermarkets: **Ekono**, *Portales 2291* (best selection in town); **Super Azul**, *18 de Septiembre 299, 401, 799*

Telephone/Fax: The area code is 58. **Chilesat**, *21 de Mayo 372*; **CTC**, *Colón 476*; or **Entel**, *21 de Mayo 345*

Tourist Office/Maps: **Sernatur**, *Prat 305, Tel. 254506, second floor of Municipal Building*, Monday-Friday 8:30am-1pm and 3pm-7pm

LAUCA NATIONAL PARK

Thermal springs, emerald lakes, delicate vicuñas, snow-capped volcanoes, and strange green growths are only the highlights of this unforgettable, high-altitude national treasure. Covering almost 140,000 hectares, Lauca has room for all this and more. Known for its variety of Chilean flora and fauna, the park offers you the chance to see all four cameloids as well as over 130 species of birds, including flamingos and ñandus. Four volcanoes over 6000 meters and hundreds of lower peaks mean plenty of hikes and climbs for those accustomed to the altitude.

The Andean culture of the Altiplano still thrives in these remote reaches. Aymara descendents graze llamas and alpacas just as they have for hundreds of years. Adobe structures and stone corrals dot the landscape, while the beautiful Colonial village **Parinacota** sports one of the most intriguing churches of the region.

PUNA

That nausea and pounding headache don't necessarily mean you had too much pisco last night. With an average elevation of about 4000 meters, the altitude of the high plains is enough to make almost anyone feel ill. Altitude sickness, also called **acute mountain sickness** *or* **puna**, *is a condition of cellular swelling caused by a reduction of atmospheric pressure due to rapid ascent to high elevations.*

Some people feel the effects of puna as low as 2000 meters. Its symptoms include shortness of breath, difficulty sleeping, headache, nausea, and vomiting. These symptoms can last from two to five days. The best things to do if you feel this way are to drink lots of water, avoid alcohol, and take ibuprofen or aspirin for pain relief. To avoid the situation all together, try to climb no more than 2000 meters for the first two days and then add another day for each additional 500 meters.

High altitude pulmonary edema, swelling of the lungs, is a more advanced and dangerous state of altitude sickness. Its symptoms include repeated vomiting, staggering and confusion. It can be fatal within a few hours. If you suspect that somebody in your group has pulmonary edema, you must move that person to lower elevations immediately.

ARRIVALS & DEPARTURES

By Bus

Regional buses run daily between Arica and the park. Tour companies also offer both one and multi-day trips. See the Arica section above.

By Car

It is about a four and a half hour drive from Arica to **Lake Chungará**. The road is paved the entire way, making it one of the few easy trips off the Panamericana. Many people travel from Arica to **Putre** in one day, visiting sights along the way, and spend the night before continuing on to the park. Not only do they get to see some other treasures of the area, but they also give themselves a day to get used to the altitude. We recommend doing this if you have the time.

Be aware that there is no sure gas available once you leave Arica. It is sometimes available at the Hostal Cali in Putre, but don't count on it.

ORIENTATION

Lauca lies directly east of Arica on the border with Bolivia. The park ranges in altitude from 3200 to 6300 meters, which can take some getting used to. The road from Arica runs directly through the park and continues on into Bolivia. **Parinacota** lies about 36 km into the park.

Lauca's southern border is the northern edge of the **Las Vicuñas National Reserve**, which in turn borders the **Surire Salt Flat National Monument**.

WHERE TO STAY & EAT

Choices are few and simple within the park. The **Chungará ranger station** has basic bunk beds. Check with the Conaf office in Arica to make reservations, *Tel. 250570*.

Several families in **Parinacota** accept people in their homes for a few dollars a night. You can arrange this at the market in front of the church. **Chucuyo**, on the route to Parinacota, has a small restaurant.

SEEING THE SIGHTS

Las Cuevas

Enter the park early to truly experience its remoteness. At the **Las Cuevas Ranger Station** a few kilometers past the entrance, you should stop to see the sunbathing vizcachas. These squirrel-tailed rabbit relatives are excellent photo subjects. There is a trail from the ranger station that allows you to walk along the moist *bofedal,* an area of wet grasslands used by the animals of the Altiplano for grazing. You can make a stop on your way out at **Las Cuevas thermal springs** for a relaxing dip in the naturally heated water.

As the road climbs through the open plains you should be able to spot llamas and their kin against the dramatic twin peaks of the Pomerape and Pirinacota volcanoes.

Parinacota

Parinacota is a brilliant ritual village whose population only comes to town for important festivals such as the celebration of the Virgen de Natividad on September eighth. The rest of the year the streets are empty except for a few old women and people selling crafts at the center of town.

CAMELOID PRIMER

Domesticated Cameloids

Llamas, with their inward curving ears, are the largest cameloids. They are ordinarily brown with a black face, but can also be white or black. Llamas can be characterized as the utility player, as they are used for their meat, wool, and ability to carry loads. They were an important factor in the expansion of the Inca Empire.

The **alpaca**, on the other hand, is smaller and its fame comes from its long, thick, soft wool. They are the rag-tag adolescents of the family with shaggy coifs and a rebellious tuft of hair on the top of their heads that hangs down into their eyes. They too have been domesticated since before Inca times.

Wild Cameloids

The **guanaco** is the larger of the two wild species. While they used to range over much of South America, they are now found mainly on the Altiplano and in Patagonia. They can be characterized as homebodies because they live in marked territories in family groups that consist of one male, several females and their young. If you see a herd of slackers in the wild, lying around on their bellies or munching on grass, chances are it's a family of guanacos.

The rarest and most delicate-looking of the family is the **vicuña**. They are ephemeral flower children with huge eyes and fringes of chest hairs that curve down to bellies atop long, slender legs. Vicuña wool is one of the softest and most valuable that exists. They were almost hunted to extinction by the European invasion but are now protected and beginning to recover. They are still rare enough, however, for a vicuña-wool sweater to cost upwards of $1000.

Surrounded by mountains in the middle of the high plains, it is reminiscent of Tibetan villages. The 17th century church is a work of art. Its whitewashed outer walls, decorated with thatch and carved volcanic stone, blaze against the blue sky, while excellent examples of Cuzco crafts can be found inside.

Conaf has a small museum a few hundred yards behind the church as well as a three km trail. The walk takes you past a lagoon filled with birds that nest on mud islands in the middle of the water. The trail leads up to a ridge from which there are excellent views of the town and area volcanoes.

Cotacotani Lagoons

Before arriving to Chungará, you pass these aquamarine lagoons, edged in white and tucked between large brown heaps of volcanic soil. Here you'll also see the strange, green, hundred-year-old cushion vegetation known as *llaretas*. As these tiny plants grow they slowly cover the surrounding rocks to form bulbous, green lumps. There is a four km trial around the lagoons that starts at the Parinacota ranger station.

Lake Chungará

This emerald lake, completely ringed by volcanic peaks, is one of the most stunning sights in the park. Pink flamingos balance on one leg at the edges of its cold waters, while ducks, geese and other birds enjoy their protected status. There are over 130 bird species in the park. A short trail wraps along the lakeshore, which is about all you can handle at 4570 meters.

SPORTS & RECREATION

Hiking is the main sport in the park. With the extremely high altitudes it is important to remember to take it easy as you hike and wear plenty of sunscreen.

EXCURSIONS & DAY TRIPS

Altiplano Route To Iquique

From Lauca, it is possible to head south on dirt roads through **Las Vicuñas National Reserve**, visit the **Surire Salt Flat National Monument**, travel to **Isluga Volcano National Park** and return to the Pan-American highway near Iquique. This incredible two or three day trip through extremely isolated and beautiful portions of the country can only be accomplished in four wheel drive vehicles.

Make sure you have a good map and plenty of extra gas, food, and water. The Conaf office in Arica can tell you about road conditions, as well as reserve beds for you at the various ranger stations along the route. A few trucks hauling borax out of the Salar de Surire pass along the road each day if you do break down.

Las Vicuñas National Reserve

Check in at the Las Cuevas ranger station in Lauca before heading southeast on the road to **Guallatiri** and the Las Vicuñas National Reserve, home to thousands of caramel colored vicuñas. The reserve is populated by semi-nomadic Aymarans who move from site to site grazing their llamas and alpacas just as their ancestors have done for hundreds of years. Guallatiri, named after the smoking volcano that looms over it, is a small pre-Hispanic village used only during celebrations.

Surire Salt Flat

From Guallatiri the road, sprinkled with borax, leads south to Surire. You meander through along the Altiplano until you turn the corner to a sparkling valley filled with salt. The Salar de Surire, whose name means "he who is adorned with ñandu feathers," is actually covered with ñandus, geese, three types of flamingos, and cameloids. Sunset over the flat is absolutely spectacular. This is the best place to spend the night on the route as the Conaf station has bunk beds, a kitchen, and hot water.

ODD EXTRACTIONS

What are these elements offered forth from the lands of the north that have helped Chile prosper over the years? You'll hear people talk about them and now you'll know what they are:

*• **Borax**: Borax is a soft, crystalline substance found in saline lakes and salt flats. It is used in glass and pottery glazes, as a fertilizer additive, soap supplement, disinfectant, mouthwash, and water softener.*

*• **Nitrates**: These naturally occurring inorganic compounds are found only in Chile's Atacama Desert. Chile had a nitrate monopoly until synthetic nitrates were first produced during WWI. Nitrates are used as explosives, solvents, and raw materials in chemical processing.*

*• **Guano**: Guano is the accumulated excrement and remains of birds, bats, and seals. It is used as a fertilizer.*

Isluga Volcano National Park

After leaving Surire, the road climbs across a barren pass on the Bolivian border and drops down to the Isluga Volcano National Park. The park is the most remote yet, as the borax trucks from Surire do not come this far. There is less wildlife here, but more traces of the Aymara culture. At **Enquelga**, with its arched church wall, there is a Conaf ranger station and the **Aguas Calientes** campsite and hot springs. Further down the road, there is a hiking trail from the road three kilometers to the Fort, *pukará*, at Isluga. The Moorish looking church in Isluga, with its blue door, is the last of the colonial churches along this route.

To the Panamericana

From Isluga the road twists and turns, climbs and falls before crossing the desert to **Huara** on the Pan-American Highway. The road is partially paved and it looks like work is being done to finish the job, but at the moment there are some rough, deserted stretches. At the same time, there are some of the most bizarre landscapes of the route. The lifeless, red rocks would be the perfect place to film a movie set on Mars. Deep canyons line the side of the road, so it can be a stressful drive. It is extremely rewarding, however, to do this entire loop.

PRACTICAL INFORMATION

There are phones, food, and sometimes gas available in Putre, but the best idea is to stock up in Arica.

IQUIQUE

Iquique, the capital of the region, has long been an important commercial city. During colonial times, and even before, guano was collected off its shores. In the 1700's it was silver, from a mine above town, which filled its coffers. At the end of the 19th century, the nitrate business took off, causing Iquique's population to grow from 2,500 to 10,000 in 12 years. It was during these years that most of the city's important buildings were constructed. Today Iquique is the beach hotspot of the area.

Big cities on the beach are hard to make appealing unless they're Rio or Miami, but Iquique is extremely popular with both Chileans and neighboring Argentines. The town and beaches are absolutely packed in the summer. Floodlights illuminate Cavancha Beach until the wee hours of the morning and it's not uncommon for revelers to hit the water after a couple of hours at the disco.

ARRIVALS & DEPARTURES

By Bus

Iquique's bus terminal, *Tel. 426492, Patricio Lynch and Souper*, is the departure point for buses making connections to cities in Chile as well as other countries in South America. Most of the bus companies also have offices by the market, which is a more convenient spot both for buying tickets as well as departing.

Buses leave throughout the day for points north and south in Chile as well as La Paz, Bolivia; Oruro, Bolivia; Jujuy, Argentina and Salta, Argentina. Many lines make bus changes in Antofagasta and Topcopilla.

Bus Companies
• **Fenix Pullman Norte**, *Anibal Pinto 531, Tel. 412423*, north to Arica, south to Santiago
• **Geminis**, *Labbe 151, Tel. 413315*, Oruro, Boliva, La Paz, Bolivia, Salta, Argentina
• **Buses Carmelita**, *Barrios Arana 841, Tel. 412237*, north to Arica, south to Santiago
• **Cuevas y Gonzales**, *Aldea 850, Tel. 412471*, Arica

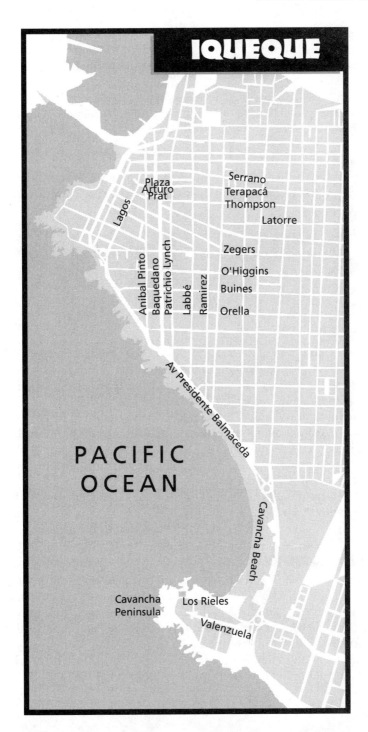

IQUEQUE

Plaza
Arturo
Prat

Lagos

Serrano
Terapacá
Thompson
Latorre

Anibal Pinto
Baquedano
Patrichio Lynch
Labbé
Ramirez

Zegers
O'Higgins
Buines
Orella

Av Presidente Balmaceda

PACIFIC
OCEAN

Cavancha Beach

Cavancha
Peninsula

Los Rieles

Valenzuela

• **Buses Zambrano**, Aldea 742, *Tel 413215*, Valaparaiso and Viña del Mar
• **Buses Evans**, *Vivar 955, Tel. 413462,*south to Santiago
• **Flota Barrios**, *Aldea 987, Tel 426941*, south to Santiago, Calama

Regional buses run to Colchane (**Mass & Kiss**, *Martínez 398, Tel. 417106*), and the colonial villages of Pica and Mamiña, (**Transporte Tamarugal**, *Aldea 781, Tel. 412981*, **Turismo Mamiña**, *Latorre 779, Tel. 420330.*)

By Car

Iquique is connected to the north via the Panamericana highway, and to the south by both the Panamericana and the more popular Coastal Highway 1.

Rental Car Companies

• **Budget**, *O'Higgins 1361, Tel. 422527*
• **Hertz**, *Souper 650, Tel. 420213*
• **Procar**, *Serrano 796, Tel. 413470*
• **Senort**, *Souper 796, Tel. 413480*

By Plane

Lan Chile, *Vivar 675, Tel. 600-600-4000 or 414128*, has up to three flights a day to Santiago. Many of the planes from Santiago either stop in Antofagasta on the way to Iquique or in Arica upon leaving. From Arica flights continue on the La Paz and Santa Cruz, Bolivia.

Ladeco, *San Martín 428, Tel. 413030*, also has three flights a day to Santiago. Again most in-bound planes stop in Antofagasta and outbound ones in Arica. Ladeco's prices are similar to Lan's.

Avant, *Serrano 430, Tel. 407007*, follows the same flight structure, but they have more flights per day.

The airport is 40 km south of town on the coastal highway. Radiotaxi Aeropuerto, *Pinto 595, Tel. 413368*, offers door to door service for $15. You can also take a *colectivo* taxi from Plaza Prat to the airport.

ORIENTATION

Iquique, 1800 km from Santiago, is jammed on a skinny strip of coastal platform. The sandy coastal range looms over the city, limiting growth to the east and forcing the town to spread north and south.

The main historic area is on and around Baquedano street leading to the **Arturo Prat Plaza. Costanera**, the street running along the coast, is flanked with long sidewalks for miles along the beaches. The best hotels are found along the Costanera and on **Cavancha Peninsula**.

GETTING AROUND TOWN

Private taxis are a good way to get to points that are not within walking distance of each other. They are always available on Plaza Prat and along the *costanera*. Collective taxis also troll the streets.

WHERE TO STAY

Expensive

TERRADO SUITES, *Los Rieles 126, Playa Cavancha. Tel. 57/488000. Fax. 57/437755. 91 rooms. Double $145. Breakfast included. Cable TV. Restaurants. Café. Bar. 2 pools. Beach. Gym. Sauna. Business Center. Tour service. Car rental. Baby sitting. Credit cards accepted.*

Terrado Suites sits alone at the top of our Iquique hotel rankings. Its prime location on the Cavancha Peninsula means that instead of traffic noise, you hear nothing but waves crashing on the beach. The 15-story hotel feels much more intimate than its size would indicate, mainly because of the excellent service offered by its staff.

A walk through the immaculate lobby, past the hotel bar, leads out to a patio above the inviting blue pool. Below the pool, hotel guests enjoy the tranquility of their own private piece of beach.

The rooms are elegant without being ornate. Playful African prints adorn the light walls, sunlight streams in the large picture windows, while comfortable furniture makes it hard to venture elsewhere. All of the rooms have ocean views, and the majority of them, Superior Suites, have large patios overlooking the sea. For the best views, head to the French restaurant on the 15th floor. An excellent buffet breakfast is also served there daily. You also have the option of Casa Blanca, a more informal although excellent Italian restaurant.

If you want to explore the area, the hotel's travel service can arrange trips to all the local attractions.

Selected as one of our best places to stay – see Chapter 10 for more details.

HOTEL TERRADO CLUB, *Avenida Aeropuerto 2873, Playa Brava. Tel. 57/437878. Fax 57/437755. 104 suites and apartments. Double $103. Breakfast included. Cable TV. Restaurant. Café. Bar. Pool. Gym. Sauna. Massage. Business Center. Tour service. Car rental. Bike rental. Babysitting. Credit cards accepted.*

The Terrado Club, held by the same owners as the Terrado Suites, is another fine hotel. One block from Playa Brava, the Terrado Club offers small apartments instead of rooms. The clean, new Mediterranean style hotel has some things in common, however, with its sister hotel, such as excellent service and a high level of professionalism.

The hotel offers five types of apartments from the basic room with kitchenette to large, two-bedroom apartments. All of them are light, spacious, and airy with well-stocked kitchens and tasteful furnishings. If you want to spread out in style, this is the place for it.

The pool area and patio restaurant are perfect spots for lounging. If exercise is in your daily plan, this hotel is an excellent choice. The long pool is ideal for lap swimming and the Playa Brava boardwalk is a runners paradise.

HOSTERÍA CAVANCHA, *Los Rieles 250, Tel./Fax 57/434800. 53 rooms. Double $100. Breakfast included. Cable TV. Restaurant. Bar. Pool. Beach. Tennis. Travel agency. Car rental. Credit cards accepted.*

Once the best hotel in town, the Hostería Cavancha has been displaced by the newer Terrado entrants. It remains, however, a fine hotel with an excellent location. While the building's style is out of the 1970s, the room furnishings have been recently updated. All of the rooms have surprisingly large patios with prime ocean views. The hotel has a relaxing, open feel that immediately helps you get into the vacation mode.

APART-HOTEL CASABERMEJA, *JJ Perez 44. Tel. 57/412533. 24 apartments. Double $100. Breakfast included. Cable TV. Credit cards accepted.*

The Casabermeja offers large apartments for a reasonable price. With a full kitchen opening out to a comfortable living area, you could stay here a while and not feel cramped. The location is not as ideal as that of the resort properties above, but you have ocean views and are in walking distance of both downtown and Cavancha beach.

SUNFISH HOTEL, *Amunategui 1990. Tel. 57/419000, Fax 57/419001. 45 rooms. Double with ocean view $140. Double without view $95. Buffet breakfast included. Cable TV. Restaurant. Pool. Conference rooms. Business center. Credit cards accepted.*

The bright blue and yellow coloring on the Sunfish makes it as attractive as a tropical fish. Inside, classic wood tables with brilliant floral arrangements add to the hotel's allure. The rooms are also smartly outfitted with fresh flowers and tasteful, yet vibrant decor. The highlight of the hotel is the pool located on the top floor in which guests can swim while looking out over Iquique's most popular beach. For all of its pluses, the one negative that the Sunfish can't remedy is that a main traffic arterial lies between it and the beach, making car noise more audible than the surf.

ARTURO PRATT HOTEL, *Aníbal Pinto 695. Tel. 57/427000, Fax 57/429088. 80 rooms. Double $81 and $107. Breakfast included. Cable TV. Restaurant. Bar. Pool. Beauty salon. Credit cards accepted.*

Overlooking the town square with its turn of the century buildings, the Pratt is both historical and modern. The front section of the hotel, a historic edifice, hooks around a street corner. The modern addition, seen only after passing through the elegant lobby, is a colorful array of steel support poles tilted like pick-up sticks. The new rooms are comfortably outfitted and more expensive. Favorite guest escapes are the rooftop pool and the cozy wood-paneled bar.

THE HAMPTON INN, *Costanera 3939, Tel. 57/381188, Fax 57/ 380434. $120.*

A new entry to the upper level hotels, the Hampton Inn sits on the rocks south of town towards the airport. It's a nice hotel with good views, but it's just out there in the middle of the desert with nothing around it.

Moderate

HOTEL CHUCAMATA, *Avenida Balmaceda 850. Tel./Fax 57/435050. 45 rooms. Double $85. Breakfast included. Cable TV. Restaurant. Pool. Credit cards accepted.*

Located at the beginning of the Cavancha Peninsula next to the Casino, this hotel offers prime location in the moderate price range. The plain, well-used rooms, in small cottages scattered around the property, all face the interior lawn and pool area. This is an ideal spot for families because of the large pool, volleyball, and ping pong tables just 50 meters from the beach.

HOTEL ATENAS, *Los Rieles 738. Tel. 57/433021. Fax. 57/431100. 40 rooms. Double $75. Breakfast included. Cable TV. Restaurant. Café. Bar. Pool. Credit cards accepted.*

The Atenas is the least expensive option on Cavancha. The rooms in the old house in front are smartly decorated in classical turn-of-the-century style. The newer addition in back, however, is no longer so new after housing countless groups of vacationing students throughout the summers. There is a small pool in the garden where hotel guests tend to congregate.

HOTEL CARANI, *La Torre 426. Tel. 57/413646. 25 rooms. Double $67. Breakfast included. Credit cards accepted.*

This is one of the better values downtown. A green atrium in the center of the hotel is a pleasant change from the bustle of the streets, as is the patio in the back. The rooms are plain but comfortable. Make sure your room does not face La Torre as the traffic noise can be disturbing.

HOTEL BARROS ARANA, *Barros Arana 1330. Tel. 57/412840, Fax 426709. 60 rooms. Double $50. Breakfast included. Cable TV. Pool. Credit cards accepted.*

The Barros Arana is the traditional mid-price favorite of Iquique. The addition of a side building has doubled the number of rooms available, all of which overlook a swimming pool in the interior courtyard. The hotel is several blocks from the beach, but still within walking distance. There is nothing extraordinary about the motel-style rooms, but they are the cleanest and most functional that you will find in this price range.

HOTEL ANAKENA, *Orella 456. Tel. 57/426509, Fax 57/422126. 30 rooms. Double $50. Breakfast included. Credit cards accepted.*

The Anakena is located towards Cavancha beach in a bright yellow Victorian building. An addition behind the original house has expanded the number of rooms, but all guests enjoy breakfast in the airy dining room of the main edifice. The rooms are simple and clean. This is a good option in this price range.

Inexpensive

HOTEL PHOENIX, *Aníbal Pinto 451. Tel. 57/429983, Fax 57/411349. 30 rooms. Double $30. Breakfast included. Credit cards accepted.*

The aging, but steadfast Phoenix is located above a pool hall between the fishing docks and the main square. After walking up the tunnel-like stairwell you emerge into the rustic white reception area which seems vast due to a wooden, stained glass-lined, box top expanding the ceiling space. The big rooms look out over active streets filled with port workers and sailors.

It is a great place to people watch or to write a novel, except you would probably be so distracted by the urge to observe the street commotion that not a page would be written. The downside is the noise from the pool hall and the neighborhood as well as furniture past its prime.

Hostels

In the budget category, we culled these three clean, homey options. All cost about $15 per person with a shared bath which is a good deal for solo travelers, but if you want a double with a private bath, it is worthwhile to bump up to the Anakena or the Barros Arana.

The **Hostal Catedral**, *Obispo Labbe 253, Tel. 57/412184, Fax 57/412360, per person $15, double with bath $40,* is located downtown, across the street from the cathedral and has an pleasant interior courtyard.

The **Hostal Cuneo**, *Baquedano 1175, Tel/Fax 57/428654, per person $12, double with bath $35,* is close to Cavancha beach and is run by a nice family. The **Hostal Iljal**, *Obispo Labbe 1560, Tel. 57/425175, per person $17, double with bath $40,* is just a block away from Cavancha beach in a pink Victorian building with new, simple, carpet and furnishings.

WHERE TO EAT

ENTREMARES, *Terrado Suites 15th floor, Los Rieles 126. Tel. 488000. Expensive. Credit cards accepted.*

For a special night, Entremares can't be beat. With bird's eye views of Cavancha beach and the lights of Iquique, this 15th floor restaurant's ambiance is the most romantic in town. All of the tables have outstanding views, but you should ask for a seat next to the window when you make your reservation. The chef uses the choicest ingredients from the region prepared in haute French cuisine.

ALOHA, *11 de Septiembre 1727. Tel. 448313. Expensive. Credit cards accepted.*

Located right on Playa Brava, this restaurant offers excellent views of the crashing waves. It's a strange combination of Polynesian décor and Italian food with an international twist, but somehow it works.

CLUB NAUTICO CAVANCHA, *Los Rieles. Tel. 431864. Expensive. Credit cards accepted.*

This restaurant shaped like a ship is one of the town favorites for seafood. The options cover all of the standard Chilean specialties, such as *machas a la parmesana* and *congrio*, served well enough to have created a faithful clientele. Its location at the tip of Cavancha is another plus.

CASA BLANCA, *Terrado Suites 15th floor, Los Rieles 126. Tel. 488000. Expensive/moderate. Credit cards accepted.*

This Italian restaurant over the pool at the Terrado Suites offers excellent food in an informal atmosphere. The antipasto bar is a meal in itself with delights such as sautéed eggplant, mozzarella and tomato salad, and a full array of delicious cold shellfish. Only in the finest Italian restaurants do we have enough faith to test the chef by ordering risotto. We did it here and the result was ambrosia. The Casa Blanca is especially nice because you can enjoy outdoor seating next to the sea.

CASINO ESPAÑOL, *Plaza Pratt, near corner of Tarapacá. Tel. 423284. Expensive/moderate. Credit cards accepted.*

Inspired by the Alhambra Palace in Granada, every square inch of the restaurant in the Club Español is richly adorned in Moorish patterns and tiles. As we sipped pisco sours while seated in the sofa-chairs of the bar, we searched for spots that hadn't been embellished, but failed to find any. Every corner we thought might have been overlooked, even the space beneath the stairwell, was painstakingly painted in intricate detail. The archways above all of the doors are mosque tower cut-outs. The finely finished wooden handrail of the stairway leads up to the second floor the walls of which display oil paintings of Spanish women in regional dress such as that from Valencia and Sevilla.

The spectacular club opened its doors in 1904 without pomp or inaugural festivities. Its menu features a long list of seafood and fish in a variety of preparations. To gain access to the dining room or bar, you'll first have to slip past the armor-clad soldiers guarding the entryway.

CROATA RESTAURANT, *Plaza Pratt 310. Tel. 416222. Moderate. Credit cards accepted.*

Next door to the Club Español on the main square, the Croata is overshadowed by its more opulent neighbor but is still a good option for international cuisine in an old-style European grandeur. The specialty of the house is fish and seafood, which comes straight off the dock just a few blocks away.

RÍNCON MEXICANO, *Patricio Lynch 751. Tel. 422301. Moderate. Credit cards accepted.*

Mario Maldonado, a famous Chilean soccer player, spent most of his career playing and coaching in Mexico. This native son has returned to Iquique with his Mexican wife and opened a restaurant. While newspaper clippings of his glorious past adorn the walls, it's the famed fish prepared Yucatan-style that caught our attention. It stands up there as one of the best fish dishes we have tried in Chile. The homemade tortillas are also excellent.

TACO TAQUILLA, *Thompson 123. Tel. 427840. Moderate. Credit cards accepted.*

Located near the main square, Taco Taquilla is another choice for Mexican food. On weekends, a *mariachi* band accompanies the lively decor and savory north of the border cuisine. The margaritas convert everyone who tries them into renowned *mariachi* singers.

BISTRO 221, *Valenzuela 221 on Cavancha. Tel. 433366. Moderate. Credit cards accepted.*

This Bistro is a perfect place to grab a quick sandwich, enjoy an afternoon coffee and dessert, or start your evening with a cold pisco sour. With outdoor seating under the trees, the pleasant atmosphere tempts you into ordering another. Across the street at *Valenzuela 270*, the log cabin **Nuevo Arriero**, *moderate, credit cards accepted*, is a good option for dinner after drinks at the Bistro. Barbecued beef is their specialty.

CASINO BOMBA, *Serrano 520. Tel. 422887. Inexpensive. No credit cards.*

As is the case in many towns in Chile, the fire station offers some of the best inexpensive meals in down. This restaurant is next door to, as opposed to inside of the station, but you still pass the green fire trucks as you enter.

Other good inexpensive options are **Bavaria**, *Pinto 926*, with its complete range of Chilean salads and sandwiches, as well as **D'Alfredo**, *Vivar 631*, for pizza. For inexpensive seafood, try the **Mercado Centenario**, *at Barros Arana and Aldea.*

For outdoor cafes with sandwiches, coffee, and beers, there are several places on Plaza Pratt as well as the popular **Vizzio Bar**, *corner of Lynch and Tarapacá*. **Mascarrieles**, just off of Plaza Pratt, attached to the Hotel Arturo Pratt, offers sandwiches with train names, such as the "Dining Car" and "Double Rail," in a pub atmosphere.

SEEING THE SIGHTS

Historic Baquedano Avenue

Iquique's unique architectural style can be attributed to its enormous wealth and large concentration of foreigners during the height of the nitrate monopoly. Begin your tour at the northeast corner of O'Higgins and Baquedano.

PALACIO ASTORECA, *Patricio Lynch and O'Higgins. Tel. 425600. Tuesday-Friday 10am-1pm, 4pm-7:30pm. Saturday 9:30am-1:30pm. Sunday 11am-2pm. Entry $1.50.*

No amount of reading can make the riches of the nitrate days as real as a quick walk through this lavish, neoclassical mansion. The 37-room house, built in 1903, displays the rooms as they were almost 100 years ago. Notice details like the stain-glassed ceiling and thick wooden doors. The Palacio is now a cultural center with rotating displays upstairs.

Heading north on Baquedano, you see wall to wall Georgian-style homes painted in decidedly non-English hues. The scrimshaw work in front comes in a variety of interesting colors and patterns.

REGIONAL MUSEUM, *Baquedano 951. Monday-Friday 8am-1pm, 3pm-6:30pm. Saturday-Sunday 10am-1pm. Entry $0.50.*

Housed in the old courthouse, this admirable museum covers the history of the area from 4000 BC through to the nitrate days. Each room focuses on a different time period. Mummies are used as mannequins to show off the high fashion of the Chinchorro era, while the Aymara display includes an entire house brought from the Altiplano.

Further up Baquedano, **Plaza Arturo Pratt** serves as Iquique's town square. In the center of the plaza, is the **clock tower** built in 1877, which is now the official symbol of Iquique. The most important buildings on the plaza are located on its south side. The **Municipal Theater**, erected in 1890, once drew performers from around the world but now its downstairs gallery displays works by regional artists. At night its steps are covered with socializing students. Next door, the **Tarapacá Employees Union Building** (*Sociedad Protectora de Empleados de Tarapacá*) was erected in 1911. The Moorish-style **Spanish Club**, also on the plaza, is another must see.

Continue down Baquedano Street north for three blocks until you encounter the sturdy gray **Aduana Customs Building**, built in 1871 when the Iquique was part of Peru. The building houses the **Naval Museum**. On the ocean in front of the customs building is the **covered passenger pier**. From here you can take tours of the bay for a closer look at the resting place of the submerged Esmeralda. Fishing boats dock here, which attracts hoards of pelicans. You may also see sea lions on the dock as big as grizzly bears.

NAVAL MUSEUM, *north end of Baquedano. Tuesday-Saturday 9:30am-12:30pm, 2:30-6pm. Sunday and holidays 10am-1pm. Entry $1.*

There is not much to see in the neglected one-room museum that has some salvaged items from the sunken Esmeralda and photos of its martyred captain, Arturo Pratt. The naval museum in Valparaíso displays the better part of the relics, though the historic battle occurred off of Iquique's shores.

From the Aduana building, follow the train tracks to Sotomayor Street and walk east for two blocks. The Georgian style **old-train station**, built with Oregon pine in 1883, is located on Sotomayor, opposite of Ramírez. The historic buildings surrounding the courtyard are now utilized as judicial offices.

The Beach Tour

CAVANCHA BEACH, *along Balmaceda street.*

This is where Iquique comes to play. The most popular beach in town, it is also the site of the casino, disco, and many restaurants. You should walk along the boardwalk from Cavancha to Brava Beach for excellent people watching. There are youths playing soccer, volleyball, and paddleball; others surfing or shredding the skate park; couples of all ages strolling along; and a line-up of people eyeballing the passing crowds. Cavancha is lit at night during the summer so the fun never stops.

BRAVA BEACH, *along Balmaceda street.*

Playa Brava's strong currents make it inappropriate for water sports, but people enjoy its broad boardwalk interrupted by pleasant palm trees and fountains. The sidewalk is inlaid with designs of geoglyphs discovered in the area, which makes running along it quite entertaining.

MARINER'S POINT, *Puntilla del Marinero.*

Located north of the city, the monument to every-mariner stands facing the sea. More importantly for Chileans, from here you can see the buoy marking the site of the shipwrecked Esmeralda. The little ship, captained by national hero Arturo Prat, took on the larger and better equipped Peruvian navy. Though the Esmeralda was sunk and Prat killed, their heroic battle was a rallying point for Chileans throughout the War of the Pacific, much like Texas' Battle of the Alamo. You can go to **Punta Gruesa**, south of town, to see where the other part of the battle was played out.

NIGHTLIFE & ENTERTAINMENT

In addition to the **Casino** at *Balmaceda 2755, Tel. 431391*, the **Pub Barracuda**, *Gorostiaga 601* is a year round draw. The most popular discos are the **Pink Cadillac**, next to the Casino at *Balmaceda 2751*, **Faro's** at

Camino Costero Sur, and **Bank's** at *Luis Uribe 330*. Movies are shown nightly at **Cine Tarapacá**, *Serrano 206, Tel. 422329*.

SPORTS & RECREATION

Beach sports are the most popular ones in Iquique. As is the case with most of the Chilean coastline, strong undercurrents can make swimming in many beaches unsafe. **Cavancha Beach**, Iquique's most popular, is safe for swimming and surfing, unlike **Brava Beach** to the south (as a rule, most beaches named "Brava" are unsafe).

The beaches north and south of town are less crowded, but not free from signs of people. The southern beach **Huaiquique** has nice waves for surfing. Check the shop **Surf Animals**, *619 Ramíriz*, for more surf news.

There are two tennis clubs in town, the **Club de Tenis Tarapacá**, *Bulnes 140, Tel. 412489*, and the **Club de Tenis Chile**, *Concepción and Portales, Tel. 433288*.

Golfers will get a kick out of the **Club de Golf Playa Blanca**, south of town towards the airport. The entire course is sand. The out of bounds and tee boxes are drawn in the sand with white lines like a type of modern geoglyph, while the "greens" are made of a different kind of darker sand.

Those in search of more adventure can try paragliding with the Franco-Argentine **Escuela de Parapente Manutara**, *Tel. 418280, 18 de Septiembre 1512*. Iquique is known as one of the best places in the world to practice this sport.

SHOPPING

ZOFRI, *north on Amunátegui. Monday-Friday 10am-1:30pm, 4:30pm-9pm. Saturday 10am-2pm, 5pm-9pm.*
With the proud distinction of being the largest duty free shopping area in South America, Zofri offers goods free of Chilean duties or value-added tax. Americans and Europeans are not likely to find much of interest, but people come from all over Chile as well as the neighboring countries to take advantage of the savings. They really shop like mad. If you do find some electro-domestic item you just can't live without, keep in mind you will have to pay taxes if you buy over $1000 worth of merchandise.

ARTISAN FAIRS, *11 de Septiembre on Plaza Brava; Plaza Prat.*
Both of these fairs sell local handicrafts such as sweaters, alpaca rugs, and leather items.

EXCURSIONS & DAY TRIPS

There are a number of interesting trips from Iquique. Some of the sights can be seen in the same day for nice variety. Common combinations include Humberstone, Pica, Cerros Pintados Geoglyphs, and the

Tamarugal Pampa; or Humberstone and Mamiña. You can take public transportation, rent a car, or join one of the tour groups such as **Surire Tours**, *Baquedano 1035, Tel. 411795.*

Oficina Humberstone

47 kilometers east of Iquique, where Route 16 meets the Pan-American Highway. Open daily during daylight hours. Entry with a donation, suggested $1.50 per person.

This ghost town, once a community and plant for a nitrate company, is one of the most interesting man-made attractions we've run across in the North. Well-preserved by the arid climate, the sixty-five year old buildings lining the lifeless streets are as beguiling as an old-time movie set. The expansive site is fun to explore and provides a provocative setting for photographs. If you can get an early start on a weekday, you will have the entire town to yourself.

The operation was originally established in 1872 by the Peruvian Nitrate Company that dubbed it "La Palma". The property passed through a series of owners until it was eventually acquired by the British-owned Nitrate Company of Tarapacá and Antofagasta in the 1930's. The company completed construction of most of the prominent buildings and employee housing in 1934. The complex was named "Oficina Salitrera Santiago Humberstone," after the Englishman James T. Humberstone, who worked in the industry for over sixty years and was known as the Father of Nitrate. The mine went broke and was abandoned in 1960.

From the entry, walk up Avenida Baquedano past the two buildings on your right, then take a right on Calle de la Recova. You will soon encounter the **central plaza**. From here you can identify several of the principal buildings erected in 1934. The **church**, restored in 1989, is off the southwest corner of the plaza. Directly south of the plaza, is the **recova**, which occupies most of the block. This structure housed commercial establishments such as the Paulo Photography Studio, the Saavedra Soda Shop, and the beauty salon run by Japanese immigrant Manuel Etisidaki. A clock tower, which held speakers that filled the square with recorded music, projects out of the *recova*. The **theater**, the tall building directly north of the plaza, hosted touring theater troupes, national performers, and projected movies. Be sure to go inside. The seats are still there. On stage, you can rehearse your favorite Shakespearean monologue that will echo off the theater walls. The *pulpería* **town store** is on the west side of the plaza, and the **hotel** is to the east.

Two other great venues to check out are the sporting areas. You can just imagine these dilapidated facilities once brimming with activity and voices. If you face north on the plaza, then walk to the left of the hotel, down Esmeralda street, you will encounter the **swimming pool** on the right hand side of the street. The pool, made from an old ship's hull, is constructed of thick steel sheets and rivets. A three level high dive, a rusty skeleton of steel tubing, graces one side, while the wooden grandstand is on the other. Underneath the grandstand, you can see the electric pumps that extracted water from 45 meters below the surface. To reach the **tennis club**, walk back down Esmeralda Street, across the square, heading northeast between the theater and town store. If you see the Victorian musicians' kiosk in front of the soccer field, you are going in the right direction. Just beyond that you will find the tennis courts complete with overhead lights and a crumbling judge's stand.

Humberstone is currently being renovated so that it can serve as a permanent museum. Hopefully, the improvements will be slow, so that it can maintain its ghost town allure a while longer.

Pica to Pintados Triangle

Orchards of citrus and mangos surround **Pica**, a lovely oasis in the desert. The paved road takes you through other pre-Hispanic towns before arriving to this small paradise. From the Panamericana south you take the road east to **Tirana**. Tirana is a sleepy little town of 558 people most of the year – but from July 12-18, 80,000 faithful flood the town for the **festival of the Virgen del Carmen**. Crosses mark the highway every kilometer, acting as road signs for the pilgrims. Wearing masks and dressed in costume, the devout leave offerings for the Virgin and dance in the streets. Both the large church, with its pretty blue ceiling, and expansive plaza overwhelm the town any other time of year.

Continuing on to Pica, you'll come to the small villages of **La Guaica**, which enjoyed its finest hours as agricultural supplier for the nitrite mules, and **Matilla**, once a wealthy wine-growing suburb of Pica. Matilla's **San Antonio church** is completely different from others in the region. With a neoclassical façade and domes that are almost Moorish, it's stylistically unique. Don't miss the chance to buy homemade *alfajores*, a sweet mash of caramelized milk and cinnamon sugar stuffed between crackers, before continuing on to Pica.

Pica has been a settlement for hundreds of years as it was once a stop on the famous Inca trail. The first Spaniard in Chile, Diego de Almagro, was forced to fight when he first passed through here, but later many Spanish settled in the area. During the 19th century Pica was an agricultural supplier for the nitrate *oficinas*. As business fell off, Pica re-outfitted itself as a weekend retreat, which it is today. Its fragrant orchards still provide luscious fresh fruit to the region.

Stroll around the plaza and visit the church before heading off to the pools for which Pica is famous. The plaza, amazingly overflowing with flowers in the middle of the desert, is a true oasis. Bougainvillea-burdened lattice work provides shade to welcoming benches.

Pica's main selling point is the cooling waters in the outdoor pool at **Cocha Resbaladero**. An underground spring flows out to a natural rock pool surrounded by bamboo. The fresh water is the perfect temperature after a drive through the desert. You can have the place to yourself if you visit in a morning during the off-season.

There are a number of restaurants in town, but we highly recommend the **Café and Hostal Suizo**, *Ibañez 210, inexpensive, no credit cards,* for a delicious sandwich and fresh juice on their pleasant, shady patio. The desserts are all homemade and all delicious.

Instead of going back the way you came, make a triangle to visit the geoglyphs:

CERROS PINTADOS GEOGLYPHS, *45 kilometers south of Pozo Almonte. Daily 9:30am-6pm. Entry $2.50.*

Over 350 enormous, stone-laid and earth-etched figures decorate the side of the Cerros Pintados hills. The impressive figures are thought to be part of an ancient Tiwanaku system of trail signs indicating the caravan routes from the high plains to the coast and vice versa. It is theorized that the geoglyphs informed travelers about the location of vital water sources along the desert routes. The figures, created in different phases from 500-1450 AD, include 137 geometric forms, 121 animals, and 97 human shapes. It takes just over an hour to reach the geoglyphs from Iquique and the visit can be combined with a day trip to the Humberstone nitrate ghost town and the Pica oasis. There is no public transportation once you leave the Panamericana, but tours regularly visit the sight.

TAMARUGAL PAMPA NATIONAL RESERVE.

The *tamarugo*, a native tree, is well adapted to its environment. Not only can it grow in highly saline soil, it can also capture atmospheric humidity and use it for water. Once covering parts of the pampa, the trees were gradually depleted as the nitrate industry used them for fuel. Conaf began this reforestation project in the 1960s, and now you have the chance to see a forest in the middle of the desert. It does not merit a visit on its own, but you pass through it on the way back to Iquique from the Cerros Pintados Geoglyphs.

Atacama Giant Geoglyph

About an hour and a half from Iquique, 14 km directly east of Huara on the way to Tarapacá, you can see one of the largest existing geoglyphs. The titanic **Atacama Giant** stands 86 meters tall on the side of the a hill. You'll recognize the rays coming out of his head from all the postcards in town. Take a tour or taxi to the sight because if you have a bus drop you off it could be a day or two until another passes by.

Isluga Volcano National Park

Isluga has some similarities with the more famous Lauca National Park near Arica. Although not home to as many species of animals, Isluga harbors a wide variety of interesting fauna, such as vicuñas, vizcachas, flamingos, and ñandus. The park is extremely remote, which can be rewarding if you put in the work to get there. Semi-nomadic Aymara people share the land with their llamas and alpacas against a backdrop of snowcapped volcanoes. The park is difficult to access without a car. There is a Conaf ranger station inside the park at the tiny village **Enquelga**. There are beds there as well as a campsite and hot springs at **Aguas Calientes** a few kilometers from there.

It is possible most of the year to drive the stunning albeit rigorous loop from Isluga to **Surire Salt Flat**, **Las Vicuñas National Reserve**, **Lauca National Park** and **Arica**, but you must have a four wheel drive vehicle and plenty of extra fuel, food, and water. (See *Excursions & Day Trips* in the Lauca National Park section above.)

Mamiña

The hot springs at **Mamiña** reputedly cured an Incan princess of blindness, but you don't have to be royalty to enjoy their soothing effects. Pre-Hispanic ruins dot the landscape around town and the local church is unique in Andean architecture with its double towers. A path leads to the *pukará*, old fort, at the top of **Cerro Ipla**. Try the **Refugio del Salitre**, *Tel. 57/751203*, for food and lodging. Other excursions include the more isolated village **Tarapacá** or the hot springs at **Chusmisa** further to the east.

Pisagua

The turn-off from the Pan-American Highway to **Pisagua** is 80 km north of the turn-off to Iquique. A forty km journey east over the Coastal Range is required to reach the small fishing village, nitrate port, and military outpost. The drive is the most spectacular part of the adventure as the pavement dips down between towering sand walls and finally turns into a dirt road that zigzags precariously as it descends to the ocean. The town itself has a few decaying buildings from the late 1800's, including a municipal theater and a hillside clock tower.

The public jail in Pisagua was utilized by the Pinochet regime as a detention center for political prisoners and was frequently crammed with as many as 500 captives at a time. In 1990, the Rettig committee's investigation led to the discovery of nineteen bodies in a mass grave alongside the community cemetery. Families of thirteen of the victims had been previously informed by the regime their relative had died and been given a Christian funeral. The regime claimed to have no knowledge of the other six casualties and has listed them "disappeared." In a macabre-tourism development, the public jail has been turned into the town's only hotel.

The excursion requires a three-hour time investment once making the turn from the Panamericana, so it is only worthwhile if you are hard-pressed for something to do in the area.

Coastal Road To Antofagasta

This scenic drive along Chile's Highway 1 takes you past numerous beaches, ghost towns, and a large salt mine at the **Salar Grande** salt flat. It is the preferred route to Antofagasta by private and commercial traffic alike. The road hugs the shoreline and curves along beaches and bays while the sandy coastal chain looms off the other side of the road. The best swimming on the route can be found at the **Playa El Aguila Turtle Sanctuary**, and **Playa Ike-Ike**. These are also the best places to camp.

You must make reservations in advance, *Tel. 57/411267*, to visit the **Punta de Lobos Salt Mine** at the Salar Grande. It is 26 km off the highway on a road made of salt.

After you pass through **Tocopillo**, the main route to **Calama**, you come to the ghost villages at **Gatico** and **Cobija**. Cobija, now in ruins, played an important role in the development of this part of Chile. Originally a Chango water station, it was transformed in 1825 when it was declared Bolivia's main port. The founders of the region's important cities, as well as many of the first explorers of the desert, hailed from this lonely place. **Hornitos** is one of the nicest beaches on this stretch of highway.

Desert Drive To Arica

See *Day Trips and Excursions* in the Arica section above for a description of this drive through desert canyons.

PRACTICAL INFORMATION

Banks: You can find many ATMs both downtown and in the free trade zone. Try Luis Uribe street with **Banco del Estado, Banco Santiago, Banco Edwards, Banco Santander**, and **Banco Sud Americano**.

Business Hours: Monday-Friday 9am-1pm, 4pm-9pm. Saturday 9:30am-1:30pm

Currency Exchange: AFEX, *Lynch and Serrano*; **Free Zone Exchange**, *Zofri*; **Fides Ltda**, *Zofri*, **Operadora de Cambio**, *Galaria Lynch local 18*

Laundry: Autoservicio, *San Martín 490*; **King Service**, *Thompson 666*; **Central**, *Serrano 772*

Medical Service: Hospital Regional Doctor Torres, *Avendia Héroes de la Concepción 502, Tel. 412695*

Post Office: Correos de Chile, *Bolívar 458*
Supermarkets: Santa Isabel, *Plazuela Héroes de la Concepción*; **Ekono**, *Héroes de la Concepción 2653*
Telephone/Fax: The area code is 57. **Chilesat**, *Tarapacá 520*; **CTC**, *Serrano 620*; **Entel**, *Gorostiaga 287*
Tourist Office/Maps: Sernatur, *Econorte Building, Serrano 145, Office 303, Tel. 427686*

ANTOFAGASTA

Antofagasta is the fifth largest city in Chile and an important industrial center. In addition to handling its own bustling port and mining activity, Antofagasta acts as Bolivia's principal port. There are some nice beaches in the southern part of town, but no hotels, so you get stuck staying in the generally overpriced and grimy downtown. If you are traveling to San Pedro de Atacama, we recommend flying to Calama and avoiding Antofagasta all together.

History

The Spanish holdings in South America were fractured during the wars of Independence, with most of the area being named part of Bolivia. When Bolivia raised taxes on nitrate exports, the numerous Chilean nitrate companies in the region objected, which started the **War of the Pacific**. After the war, Bolivia lost its ocean access, as the whole area became Chilean territory.

ARRIVALS & DEPARTURES

By Bus

Unlike Arica and Iquique, Antofagasta does not have a central bus terminal. Instead, each company's buses leave from its main office. Buses leave throughout the day for northern and southern Chile as well as Calama, San Pedro de Atacama, and Argentina.

Bus Companies

- **Tramaca**, *Uribe 936, Tel. 200124*, Tocopilla, Maria Elena, Taltal, Calama, Argentina
- **Flota Barrios**, *Condell 2764, Tel. 268559*, Tocopilla, Maria Elena, Calama
- **Tur-Bus**, *Latorre 2751, Tel. 266691*, Tocopilla, Calama, San Pedro de Atacama, south to Santiago
- **Geminis**, *Latorre 3055, Tel. 251796*, Calama
- **Pullman**, *Latorre 2805, Tel. 262591*, Calama, south to Santiago
- **Feptsur**, *Requelme 513, Tel. 222982*, Mejillones

By Car
Antofagasta is connected to Iquique in the north by both the coastal road and the Panamericana. Most people prefer the more scenic coastal road for the eight hour drive. To the south only the Panamericana runs through the desert the six hours to Copiapó.

Calama is about a two and a half hour drive to the east, and San Pedro is another hour and a half from there.

Rental Companies
• **Avis**, *Balmaceda 2499, Tel. 221073*
• **Budget**, *Prat 206, Tel. 251745*
• **First**, *Bolivar 623, Tel. 225777*
• **Hertz**, *Balmaceda 2492, Tel. 269043*
• **IQSA**, *Balmaceda 2575, Tel. 268323*

By Plane
Lan, *Washington 2507, Tel. 221730*, has flights to Santiago and Iquique, as does **Ladeco**, *Washington 2589, Tel. 269170*. **Avant**, *Prat 266, Tel. 284412*, has these flights as well as one to Calama.

By Train
You can buy tickets for the train from Calama to Oruro, Bolivia in Antofagasta at *Uribe 936, Tel. 200124*.

ORIENTATION
Antofagasta, 14 km south of the Tropic of Capricorn, fits on a spit of coastal platform wedged between the mountains and the sea. Corralled by the mountains behind, the town has extended to the north and south. Baquedano and Avenida Argentina, in a triangle with the sea, form the historic area. Further to the south, the tourist area Avenida Grecia runs along the ocean, as does the longest boardwalk in Chile.

GETTING AROUND TOWN
Collective taxis abound on the streets with their destinations written on the sign on the roof. Private taxis are also available on the streets around the plaza.

WHERE TO STAY
There is a dearth of suitable hotels in Antofagasta. Many are over-priced and an astonishing number of them are dirty and ragtag. We have ferreted out the few good ones.

Expensive

HOLIDAY INN EXPRESS, *Avenida Grecia and Antonio Puopin. Tel. 800/366666. 120 rooms. Double $100. Breakfast included. Cable TV. Pool. Gym. Credit cards accepted.*

We usually don't recommend cookie-cutter hotels, but the Holiday Inn Express has the best location in town. Away from the noise and dirt of the *centro*, the hotel looks out on the ocean near the best in-town beaches. The facilities are clean and new, which is more than can be said for many Antofagasta establishments.

HOTEL ANTOFAGASTA, *Balmaceda 2575. Tel. 55/228811. Fax 55/ 264585. 163 rooms. Double $97 for city view and $111 for ocean view. Breakfast included. Cable TV. Restaurant. Bar. Pool. Beach. Parking. Credit cards accepted.*

Filled mostly with business travelers, this huge hotel overlooking the sea is the traditional high end choice in town. The rooms, accessed by wide hallways, are comfortable and well appointed. It's worth the extra money for the tranquility of an ocean view room. The pool is inexplicably surrounded by Astroturf, but it's still a nice place to relax. The restaurant is one of the best choices in town for seafood, while the outdoor café/bar is a good bet on a sunny day.

Moderate

HOTEL ANCLA INN, *Baquedano 516. Tel. 55/224814. Fax 55/ 261551. 63 rooms. Double $77. Breakfast included. Cable TV. Restaurant. Heated pool. Credit cards accepted.*

This is one of the better values in the category. The rooms are comfortable, the staff friendly, and the location central. One of the nice surprises here is the heated rooftop pool that allows you to relax above and away from the bustle below.

APART-HOTEL DON LUIS, *Prat 819. Tel. 55/227787. Fax 55/ 262599. 12 apartments. Double $69. Parking. Car Rental. Credit cards accepted.*

Every once in a while a hotel will really surprise you. Walking up to the third floor reception area, past the government office on the second floor, you don't expect much here. Enter one of the mammoth apartments, however, and your opinion instantly changes. If you need space, this is the place. These are true apartments with large kitchens, patios, bedrooms, and living areas. You are a few blocks away from the main concentration of hotels, but it's worth it for the square footage. Ask for an interior apartment because of street noise.

APART-HOTEL EL ARRIERO, *Condell 2644. Tel. 55/264371. Fax 55/268759. 20 apartments. Double $56. Restaurant. Café. Parking. Credit cards accepted.*

These conveniently located units are more like suites that apartments. There is no kitchen, but they all have a microwave and small refrigerator in the den/bedroom. The apartments are clean and light, which is unique in Antofagasta. We consider this place a good value.

Inexpensive
HOTEL SOL DEL HORIZONTE, *Latorre 2450. Tel./Fax 55/221886. 12 rooms. Double $45. Restaurant. No credit cards.*

Because so many places in Antofagasta are run down, new is an important adjective. This new hotel is a good, moderate option because it hasn't had time to get shabby yet. The rooms off the street are quiet, clean, and comfortable.

HOTEL NIKYSAN, *La Torre 2743. Tel. 55/221297. 15 rooms. Double $45. Credit cards accepted.*

This is more like a *residencial* than a hotel. The place has recently been redecorated, but with thin carpet that already shows some water stains. It is clean, at least, and the owners are nice.

WHERE TO EAT

The good restaurant options are as slim as the hotel choices. Your best bests are those listed below.

HOTEL ANTOFAGASTA, *Balmaceda 2575. Tel. 55/228811. Expensive. Credit cards accepted.*

With its privileged position sitting out over the ocean, the restaurant here is a consistent winner. Seafood is the logical specialty, and they do it well. The *machas a la parmesana* are savory here, as is the catch of the day.

CLUB DE YATES, *Balmaceda 2705. Tel. 263942. Expensive. Credit cards accepted.*

The Club de Yates features indoor and outdoor seating with excellent views of the boats in the harbor. As would be expected, seafood and fish specialties dominate the menu. The decor is nicely done in subtle, olive green. The dinner plates are stamped with the nautical anchor logo of the restaurant while the bread plates are painted with the debonair, bearded face of the owner, Carlos Flambeau. Butter his forehead for fun.

MEXALL, *Poupin and Orchard. Tel. 223672. Moderate/expensive. Credit cards accepted.*

This restaurant is stylish enough to make you forget you are in Antofagasta. Blue lights under the darkened bar, Santa Fe furnishings, and nicely dressed young waiters all add to its hipness. The food, while overpriced for Mexican, is quite tasty. We recommend the *tacos tinga de pollo*, a flavorful mixture of chicken and spices, or the heaping plate of *fajitas*.

BAVARIA, *Ossa 2424. Tel. 266567. Moderate. Credit cards accepted.*

We usually don't recommend chains, but this popular Chilean one is a good choice in Antofagasta. You'll get hearty sandwiches in a clean place.

D'ALFREDO, *Condell 2539. Tel. 261643. Moderate. Credit cards accepted.*

This restaurant would probably not make our list in any other city, but because it is clean and reasonably priced, it's a winner here. Known for their pizza, the pasta *al pesto* is also quite good. Save the sandwiches for Bavaria.

PIZCA BAR, *O'Higgins 1998. Tel. 265273. Moderate. Credit cards accepted.*

Downtown workers frequent the Pizca at lunch, where you can join them for a good sandwich at a reasonable price. The same workers can be found there after work lifting a round or two before heading home. You can join them then also.

FUENTE DE SODA ALEMANA, *Condell 2644. Tel. 264371. Inexpensive. No credit cards.*

Clean is a key adjective in here. Many of the sidewalk eateries are not up to par in this sense, but Fuente Alemana is. Offering sandwiches and a daily menu, this is a quick, inexpensive option.

SEEING THE SIGHTS
Historic Downtown

The old port, diminutive compared with the current one, handled the early days of the nitrate trade. The original dock, the **Muelle Salitrero** is the only one that is still standing. It is a good place to begin a tour of the historic section. Just to the south of the dock on Pinto are a number of interesting buildings from the beginning of the century – the **Old Naval Defense Building**, *Ex Resguardo Maritimo*; the **Old Department of the Interior**, *Ex Gobernación Marítima*; and the **Old Customs Building**, *Ex Aduana*.

REGIONAL MUSEUM, *Corner of Bolivar and Balmaceda, Tuesday-Saturday 10am-1pm, 4pm-7pm. Sunday 11am-2pm. Saturday closed. Entry $1.*

This small museum is located in the old customs building. The edifice was originally built in Mejillones in 1866 as a mining administrative office and later moved to its current location. The museum has a collection of historic odds and ends upstairs, such as the tokens the mine workers were paid and required to use at the company stores. Downstairs are rooms dedicated to basic regional anthropology and geology overviews.

Looking toward the waterfront from the museum, you can see two historic buildings across Balmaceda Street. Both were built in 1910 and served as **Coast Guard facilities**. Across Bolivar Street, a few blocks away, is the **old railway station** and neoclassic administrative buildings constructed by the Compañía de Salitre y Ferrocarriles in 1887. From there, walk across the street to the **Fisherman's Market**, *Féria y Terminal Pesquero*, to inspect the day's catch.

ANDRÉS SABELLA MUSEUM, *Baquedano 574. Monday-Friday, 10am-1pm, 4pm-9pm. Saturday 10am-1pm. Sunday- closed. Entry - donation.*

This museum is dedicated to Andrés Sabella, who is renowned as the regional writer that accomplished the most in promoting the North's causes and culture. He is most well-known for his novel, *Norte Grande*, and his extensive anthology of poetry. The museum dedicates one room to his personal belongs, such as his writing desk and book shelf. Another room is adorned with fine-line paintings and drawings composed by Sabella. The main gallery features artwork from his personal collection. There is also space devoted to another Chilean poet known as the Doctor of the Poor. The display includes his humble personal affects and antiquated operating instruments, which make you thankful for modern medical advances.

PLAZA COLÓN, *Intersections of Prat, Washington, Sucre, and San Martín.*

The town's main plaza benefited from the riches of Europeans who made their fortunes in Chile. It is still quite a pleasant place, with flower-covered trellises covering the benches below in shade. The **Watch Tower**, a gift from the English settlers, is a replica of London's Big Ben. The **Orchestra Kiosk**, donated by the Slavic community, has pretty ironwork. The **Cathedral**, currently being refurbished, rounds out the sights on the plaza.

The Boardwalk

The 20-km boardwalk, the longest in Chile, is the most pleasant part of the Antofagasta scene. Locals and tourists fill the restaurants, bars, discos and beaches to see and be seen along Avenida Grecia.

NIGHTLIFE & ENTERTAINMENT

The most popular discos, especially in the summer are found along Grecia. The **Pub Discotec Contutti**, *Grecia 421, Tel. 247582*, is a year round favorite. Another popular one is the **Disco Vox Sitis**, *on the road to Caleta Coloso, Tel. 238708*, which has a dance area as well as pool and foosball.

SPORTS & RECREATION

Recreation in Antofagasta centers on the beach and boardwalk. Runners, in-line skaters, and bikers take advantage of the long, protected strip while soccer players gather on the beaches. The currents and undertow can be dangerous along the Chilean coast, so make sure an area is safe for swimming before diving in.

The surf can be decent some times of the year. Try the surf shop, **El Lugar Secreto** on *Condell 2532*, for information on the best breaks.

There are two hikes, one easy and one a more difficult scramble, in the **Chimba National Reserve**. See *Day Trips and Excursions* below.

SHOPPING

PLAZA DEL MERCADO, *Intersections of Matta, Maipú, Ossa and Uribe*.

The **Artisan Fair** within the central market is a good bet for hats, sweaters, and other local crafts.

EXCURSIONS & DAY TRIPS

La Portada Natural Monument

This is the singular most popular image of Antofagasta. A natural arch off the coast, La Portada is especially impressive at sunset. You can hike around the cliffs or enjoy a pisco sour in the restaurant at the view point. If you are coming in from the airport, have your cab detour the three km to the lookout. It's worth it.

You can combine a stop to La Portada with a visit to **Juan Lopéz**. Small houses line the shore at this pleasant beach getaway, 36 km north of Antofagasta. The protected cove is ideal for a swim, as the sea is calm and inviting. Most visitors come for the day to enjoy the ocean and feast on a tasty seafood lunch. If so moved, however, you can also stay the night at the town hotel or camp on the beach.

La Chimba National Reserve

La Chimba is a relatively untouched reserve with little in the way of infrastructure. Though there are no rivers or lakes on the property, its many ravines are filled with desert life. There are two longer hiking trails in the park through the Chimba and Cactus Ravines that are a nice change of pace from the normal beach activities. Bus 29 will drop you off on the highway, almost four km from the park's entrance.

Mejillones

Mejillones is slated for an enormous project to make it the largest port in South America. Currently, however, it's a small industrial and fishing city with an interesting history as an important Bolivian port. The town has some engaging port and municipal buildings from the turn of the century.

From Mejillones you can continue north along Highway 1 to the **Hornitos**, the finest beach around Antofagasta. It stays clean by not allowing camping or even picnicking. There aren't even any restaurants, but the beach is worth the bother. Be sure to bring lots of water.

Baquedano

Baquedano's glory days are long past, but the trains remain. The Northern Longitudinal Railway, known as the Longino, used to pass through here, connecting diverse private rail lines. All that is left of those days are the old train station, the water towers, and the Railroad Museum. The museum, set outside, displays train cars and locomotives from the turn of the century. Baquedano, 69 km north of Antofagasta on the way to Calama, merits a stop if you are passing through, but is not worth going out of your way to visit.

Taltal

During the nitrate days, Taltal boasted 20,000 inhabitants and a vibrant port. There are now 9,500 people living here and fishing and mining keep the city alive. The main plaza, on Prat, has most of the historic buildings such as the church, municipal building, and theater. The **Taltal Museum**, with displays on the Chango natives and the nitrate industry, is a half a block up Prat from the plaza. Further to the north, at the foot of the **Hill of the Virgin**, you can explore the old buildings of the defunct Railway Company.

Just south of Taltal you'll find the beautiful beach at **Cifuncho**. Known as one of the best beaches in all the North, it can get crowded in the summer. Crowded is a relative term, however, as it's a pretty isolated spot. It is a great place for camping, but you have to pack everything you'll need in with you. Even if you just go for the day, take more water than you think you'll need.

Coastal Road To Iquique

See *Day Trips & Excursions* in the Iquique section for a description of this drive along the coast.

PRACTICAL INFORMATION

Banks: There are many banks with ATMs around the plaza. **BCI**, *Washington 2683;* **Banco Edwards**, *Prat 461*; **Banco de Chile**, *Prat 356*; **Santander**, *San Martín 2600*

Business Hours: Monday-Friday 9:30am-1:30pm, 5:00pm-9:30pm. Saturday 10am-1:30pm

Currency Exchange: Casa de Cambio, *Baquedano 516*
E-Mail Service: Intitour, *Baquedano 460, Tel. 266185*; $1.50/15 minutes
Laundry: Clean Clothes, *Lorca 271, Tel. 244903*. **Laverap**, *14 de Febrero 1802, Tel. 251085*
Medical Service: Antofagasta Regional Hospital, *Avenida Argentina 1962, Tel. 269009*
National Parks: Conaf, *Avenida Argentina 2510. Tel. 227804*
Post Office: Correos de Chile, *Washington 2615, by Plaza Colón*
Supermarkets: Maxi-Market, *El Huascar, Tel. 274174*
Telephone/Fax: The area code is 55. **Chilesat**, *Uribe 645*; **CTC**, *Uribe 746*; **Entel**, *Baquedano 751*
Tourist Office/Maps: Sernatur, *Maipú 240, Tel. 264044*. Monday-Friday 9:30am-1pm, 3:30pm-7:30pm. Weekends in summer 10am-2pm. Information booth at Balmaceda and Prat

CALAMA

Although Calama existed before the arrival of the Spanish, and had an important history as a Bolivian government seat, the town is alive today to serve and feed the nearby **Chuquicamata Copper Mine**. Many travelers just glimpse Calama's bad side as they travel from the airport to San Pedro de Atacama. It's really not a bad town, but San Pedro is so much better that most people just pass on through. From Calama you can visit nearby oasis cities or, if your tastes run more towards the gigantic and industrial, tour the world's largest open pit copper mine.

ARRIVALS & DEPARTURES

By Bus
There is no central bus station in Calama, so you need to go to the offices listed below to buy tickets for the various destinations. You can, however, go to the sub-station to catch the first bus to Antofagasta that has space.

Bus Companies
- **Tramaca**, *Granaderos 3048, Tel. 340404*, Antofagasta, San Pedro de Atacama, Arica, Iquique, Santiago
- **Buses Frontera**, *Antofagasta 2041, Tel. 318543*, San Pedro de Atacama, Toconao
- **Buses Atacama**, *Abaroa 2105-B, Tel. 314757*, San Pedro de Atacama
- **Buses Morales y Moralito**, *Sotomayor 1802, 342671*, San Pedro de Atacama, Toconao
- **Flota Barrios**, *Ramirez 2298, Tel. 341497*, Antofagasta, Arica, Iquique, Santiago

- **Tur-Bus**, *Ramirez 1802, Tel. 316699*, Antofagasta, San Pedro de Atacama, Arica, Iquique, Santiago
- **Geminis**, *Antofagasta 2239, Tel. 341993*, Antofagasta; Salta, Argentina; Asuncion, Paraguay
- **Pullman**, Sotomayor 1808, Tel. 311410, Antofagasta, Arica, Iquique, Santiago

By Car

The 105 km drive from Calama to San Pedro takes about an hour and a half. The road is paved and well marked. The 215 km drive from Calama to Antofagasta takes a little over two hours. If you rent a car it's a good idea to rent a 4WD truck so that you can get to all the area sites. If you are flying into town you can arrange for any of these companies to meet you with your car at the airport.

Rental Companies

- **Avis**, *Balmaceda 2499, Tel. 319797*
- **Budget**, *Granaderos 2925, Tel. 341076*
- **Hertz**, *Latorre 1510, Tel. 341380*
- **Rent a Car Iam**, *Vivar 1980, Tel. 312412*

By Train

The train leaves every Wednesday at 11pm from Calama to Oruro, Bolivia. There is one class of service and the ride takes 32 hours. Take warm clothes and a sleeping bag if you have one. Tickets are available at *Balmaceda 1777, Tel. 342004*.

ORIENTATION

Calama, situated right in the middle of the country on the Tamarugal Pampa, is one of the few large population centers in the North not located on the coast. Originally kept alive by the Lao River, Calama gained access to even more water when the Salado River was rerouted for use at Chuquicamata.

The town is centered around its plaza at Ramírez and Abaroa streets, with Ramírez being the main commercial artery.

GETTING AROUND TOWN

Calama is small enough to walk almost anywhere of interest, but there are taxis waiting at all bus offices if you need one. Collective taxis leave from Plaza 23 de Marzo.

WHERE TO STAY
Expensive
HOTEL LICAN ANTAI, *Ramírez 1937. Tel. 55/341621. Fax. 55/341308. 50 rooms. Double $140. Breakfast included. Cable TV. Restaurant. Credit cards accepted.*

This hotel is overpriced, but it is one of the best in its category nonetheless. It has an interesting minimalist desert-industrial décor and nice photos of the region on the walls. You would think that all rooms would come with a tub, but some only have showers. It's not a good value, but it's still a nice hotel.

HOSTERÍA CALAMA, *LaTorre 1521. Tel. 55/341511. Fax 55/342033. 50 rooms with a 60 room addition in process. Double $118. Breakfast included. Cable TV. Restaurant. Pool. Credit cards accepted.*

All the mining business in the area has led the Hostería Calama to double in size. The construction is loud and irritating, but when it is done this should be an okay option. As with most of the hotels in town, it is overpriced, but having a pool in the desert can make up for a multitude of sins.

Moderate
HOTEL EL MIRADOR, *Sotomayor 2064. Tel./Fax 55/340329 or 55/310294. 15 rooms. Double $60. Breakfast included. Cable TV. Credit cards accepted.*

The Hotel Mirador isn't only the best deal in town, it is the best hotel. The light wooden lookout tower signals a charming, comfortable inn with its own distinctive style. Beyond the rough hewn doors awaits a lovely sitting room adorned with black and white photographs depicting the region's settlement. Hardwood floors lead the way to the rooms, all subtly decorated in desert colors. The largest room in the hotel features an antique, free-standing tub. The patio is a good place to read among the greenery. The hotel offers full day tours to San Pedro and the regional points of interest such as the Tatio Geysers.

HOTEL ALFA, *Sotomayor 2016. Tel. 55/342496. 40 rooms. Double $95. Breakfast included. Cable TV. Credit cards accepted.*

The Hotel Alfa is new, clean, and can almost pull off being able to charge what they do in this overpriced town, except that they scrimp on certain details. The TVs in each room, for example, sit on a wobbly metal stands. In terms of quality, the hotel lags behind the more reasonable Mirador. There is a monster TV in the sitting area if you've got the big screen need.

HOTEL QUITOR, *Eleuterio Ramírez 2116. Tel. 55/314159. 30 rooms. Double $85. Breakfast included. Restaurant. Bar. Credit cards accepted.*

The Quitor is located on the main plaza and has big rooms, but its excessive wear makes the hotel overpriced.

Inexpensive

HOTEL EL LOA, *Abaroa 1617. Tel. 55/341963. 20 rooms. Per person $12. No credit cards.*

Located a few blocks away from the main square, the Hotel El Loa is the best budget and solo traveler option. Regional maps hang on the corridor walls, which lead to the clean, simple rooms. There is a fully equipped kitchen and a big living room that can be utilized by guests. Being one of the few livable bargain spots, this hotel always fills up, so call ahead to reserve a room.

RESIDENCIAL SAN SEBASTIAN, *Pinto and Ramirez. Tel. 55/318279. 12 rooms. Double $25. Breakfast included. No credit cards*

This clean, family-run *residencial* is a decent option in the budget category.

WHERE TO EAT

The restaurant options here are almost pathetic. Miners don't seem to be too picky about what they eat.

HOTEL LICAN ANTAI, *Ramírez 1937. Tel. 341621. Expensive. Credit cards accepted.*

Like the hotel, the restaurant here is not a good value, but it's still good food. The informal dining room serves some of the best seafood in Calama.

BAVARIA, *Sotomayor 2093. Tel. 341496. Moderate. Credit cards accepted.*

The locals consider this national chain restaurant the best in town, which is a strong commentary on the choices here. The upstairs restaurant serves solid home-style meals with a view of the square. The downstairs coffee shop offers sandwiches.

HRVATSKI DOM CLUB CROATA, *Abaroa 1869, Tel. 342126. Inexpensive/moderate. Credit cards accepted.*

The Club Croata is a cheery locale with red tablecloths. The main draw is the bargain-priced fixed menu lunch.

PIZZERIA D'ALFREDO, *Abaroa 1835 Tel. 319440. Moderate. Credit cards accepted.*

Sandwiches, pizzas, and pastas are available in this outlet of a regional chain. The pizza is the most popular, but we also like the pasta *al pesto*.

The **Chaxas Cafe**, *Sotomayor 2020,* is a coffee bar that serves great java and a chewy coconut macaroon with each shot.

SEEING THE SIGHTS

You can quickly cover all there is to see in Calama proper. Start at the plaza and then take a stroll down Ramírez. There is a large park in the south of the city, **Parque El Loa**, which is where you'll find an **artisan market**, a swimming pool right on the river, and the town museum.

ARCHAEOLOGY MUSEUM, *Parque El Loa. Tuesday-Sunday 10am-1pm, 3pm-7:30pm. Entry $1.*

After a complete remodeling, the museum is slated to be bigger and better than its original version. It will highlight the indigenous cultures with displays on how the people lived, dressed, worked, and worshipped.

EXCURSIONS & DAY TRIPS

Chiu Chiu & the Lasana Fort

Chiu Chiu, 33 km northeast of Calama, is a beautiful oasis town with a long history. As early as 1,000 BC nomadic peoples of the area began to settle here on the banks of the Loa River. Later, during the days of the Inca reign, Chiu Chiu was on the trade routes bringing goods from as far away as Brazil. The first Spanish conquistadors stayed here as they traveled south, followed by other Spaniards who settled the town. The main attraction in town is the church, built in the late 1600's.

IGLESIA SAN FRANCISCO, *Chiu Chiu. Tuesday-Sunday 9am-1pm, 3pm-7pm.*

The adobe walls, over a meter thick, keep the interior pleasantly cool. Notice the lovely cedar doors lined with cactus when you enter. There are some interesting works from the Cuzco school inside, including a passion scene painted on both sides of the canvas.

Heading north along the Loa River from Chiu Chiu, you pass orchards suckled by the river. Keep an eye on the cliffs above, where there are over 70 pictoglyphs from as early as 400 AD. After 12 km you come to the **Pukará de Lasana**. This fort, a government center populated until the arrival of the Spanish, is an interesting look at Amerindian architecture. There are over 110 buildings on the site.

You can take a taxi to Chiu Chiu for $25, but most of the tour groups in town do the trip for $12 per person.

Loa River Villages

This trip, further east than Chiu Chiu, takes you to small pre-Hispanic villages, some of which are empty most of the year. A small part of the population stays in town year-round, overseeing and protecting the houses and buildings, while the rest of the village works in the countryside. Only during religious holidays and festivals does the entire community come together.

Caspana, the first village, is populated year-round. The people of the village provide produce and flowers for Calama. An **artisan fair**, specializing in alpaca wool products, is one of the town's highlights, as is its **San Lucas church**.

Toconce, east of Caspana, is famous for its terraced agriculture. You can climb up the hillside for a first-hand view of this interesting technique. Just north of Toconce is the **Pukará de Turi**, the largest fort-city in the Atacama region. Made from volcanic stone, the city includes plazas, houses, streets, and administrative buildings.

The last stop on the route, **Aiquina**, is a beautiful village made of stone. The houses are lined up together leading to the church with its red stucco tower. Only on the seventh and eighth of September, during the Festival of Guadalupe, do the streets fill with people.

Chuquicamata Copper Mine

This area has been mined for over six centuries, but it wasn't until 1915 that the Guggenheim brothers produced the zone's first bar of fine copper. Since then, the mine has become one of the largest companies in the world, producing over 600,000 tons of fine copper annually. It is so large that over 12,000 people live in the company town, complete with schools, soccer stadiums and shopping malls. You should take a walk around the **plaza** or stay for lunch after a mine tour to see it all. **El Arlequín**, on O'Higgins and Cochrane close to the plaza, is one of the best places to eat.

A guided tour of the mine takes about an hour and a half. Big is the overriding adjective here. The main pit is four km long, two and a half km wide, and over half a kilometer deep. The extraction trucks look like Tonka toys in the pit, which blows your mind when you see one of them up-close. Each truck has tires that are over three meters tall. Even the tailings, many of which are now being reprocessed, are the size of small mountains.

Tours are available in English and Spanish Monday-Friday at 9:45 am. Sign up in the company town at the Sede Chuqui Ayuda a la Infancia, which is on the corner of Avenida Carrera and Tocopilla. You need to have a passport or some other sort of ID and dress in long pants, long-sleeved shirt, and closed toe shoes. You can get to the mine in collective taxi from the plaza for less than $1.

Maria Elena & Pedro De Valdivia Nitrate Towns

For all the influence that the nitrate companies and their money had on the area, only a few of them still operate today. Seventy km west of Calama, Maria Elena is one of them. The town of 7600 is supposedly laid out in the shape of the union jack, but even on a map that is hard to make out. A walk through the company town should include the main plaza, theater, and archaeological museum. Plant tours are available, but must be arranged a week in advance by calling *Tel. 55/632903*.

Further south at the **Oficina Pedro de Valdivia**, the plant still functions but the city was abandoned in 1996. Its plaza and surrounding buildings have all been named national monuments.

El Tatio Geysers

These geysers, one of the most impressive sites in the region, can be reached from either Calama or San Pedro de Atacama. See *Day Trips & Excursions* in the San Pedro de Atacama section.

PRACTICAL INFORMATION

Banks: BCI, *Sotomayor 2002* and **Banco Santiago**, *Sotomayor 2026* have ATMs.

Business Hours: Monday-Friday 9:30am-1:30pm, 5:00pm-9:30pm. Saturday 10am-1:30pm

Currency Exchange: Moon Valley, Sotomayor 1818

Laundry: Lavexpress, *Sotomayor 1889, Tel. 315361*; **Autoservicio**, *Hoyos and Abaroa*

Medical Service: Hospital Carlos Cisterna, *Granaderos and Hoyos, Tel. 342347*

Post Office: Correos de Chile, *Mackenna 2167*

Telephone/Fax: The area code is 55. **CTC**, *Abaroa 1987*; **Entel**, *Sotomayor 2027*

Tourist Office/Maps: Municipal Tourist Office, *Latorre 1689, Tel. 242742. 9am-1pm; 3pm-7pm*

SAN PEDRO DE ATACAMA

San Pedro and its surrounding sites are a highlight of any visit to Chile. The surreal landscapes, interesting archaeological monuments, funky little town, and vast blue skies will stay on your mind long after you have left the country. The clarity of the light in San Pedro is phenomenal and there aren't many places in the world where you have a perfect conical volcano at the end of the main street.

San Pedro was an important regional center from the time of the original peoples of the Atacama on through the nitrate days. Over the last century, however, many of its residents have moved to follow jobs in the mining industry. It is now greatly dependent on the non-stop flow of tourists to support its economy.

While there are many tourists in San Pedro, especially during the summer, the town has maintained its totally laid-back atmosphere. It's

SAN PEDRO DE ATACAMA

worth a visit any time of year to experience the myriad natural wonders in every direction.

ARRIVALS & DEPARTURES

By Bus

All buses depart across from the artisans market on Licancabur on the way out of town to Calama. You can get information on departure times and buy tickets from there. Tramaca has the only bus that goes to Antofagasta without having to change in Calama.

By Car

The 105 km drive from San Pedro to Calama takes about an hour and a half. The road is paved and well marked. If you are going to explore on your own, rent a truck in Calama, as the options are limited in San Pedro. **Nativa Expediciones** on *Caracoles* sometimes has trucks for rent.

ORIENTATION

Located on the eastern edge of the widest part of Chile, San Pedro is just 45 km from Bolivia and 215 km from Argentina. The town sits on the northern tip of the Salar de Atacama, the largest salt flat in the country, with great views of 5000+ meter volcanoes to its east. Most people access the town from Calama.

Founded at the outlet of the Rio Grande, the largest river on the salt flat, San Pedro is a small oasis town. Adobe walls, some whitewashed, line the few streets of town. There may be a hotel behind one wall or a field of alfalfa behind another, so it can be confusing at first. Caracoles is the main commercial street, but be aware that many establishments do not have street numbers. The Lascar Volcano can be seen straight down Caracoles.

San Pedro currently has electricity in the evenings only, though that is slated to change soon. The more expensive hotels have generators, but you might want to carry a flashlight to make your way through the streets late at night.

WHERE TO STAY

Expensive

HOTEL EXPLORA, *Ayllú Larache. Santiago Tel. 2/206-6060. Santiago Fax 2/228-4655. US Fax 800/858-0855. 50 rooms. 3 day minimum. 3 days full room, board, open bar, activities, and Calama airport transfer $1296 per person. Restaurant. Bar. Pool. Sauna. Massage. Hiking. Biking. Horseback riding. Tours. Credit cards accepted.*

We couldn't feel more ambivalent about the Explora's entrance into the San Pedro market. It's a high quality, first class hotel, but it's overdone. Instead of trying to fit in with its surroundings, it almost feels like the Explora is trying to outdo the desert itself. That hubris is a turn-off. The hotel's ambitious design looks like an airport, and its use of primary colors are out of place in a world of understatement and pastel hues.

Having said that, the buildings' interiors could not be more comfortable. The main building houses a large sitting area and bar. Cushy furniture is placed to aid conversation while at the same time allowing for plenty of personal space. Large, pyramid-shaped wooden statues are scattered throughout this area along with displays of artifacts from the region. A spacious bar looks out over the 14-hectare grounds and horse stables, while an upstairs terrace offers amazing views of Lascar Volcano. There is a TV room downstairs so that the guest rooms are free of such earthy distractions. Nightly meetings are held here to talk about the next day's activity options.

The buildings housing the rooms spread out like rays from the main edifice. The rooms are tastefully decorated and each comes with its own feather duster to deal with desert sand. The bath rooms all have shower heads the size of frisbees hanging over the middle of the tub to confer the luxury of an abundance of water in middle of the dessert.

Along these same lines, four swimming pools dot the property. Next to each of these pools is a sauna and massage area. It will be hard to find the time to slow down and sit by one of the pools however, with so much to do. Along with the excursions to area attractions, the Explora offers hiking, biking, and horseback riding.

Moderate

HOTEL TERRANTAI, *Tocopilla 19. Tel. 55/851140. Fax 55/851037. 9 rooms. Double $82. Breakfast included. Restaurant. Pool. Credit cards accepted.*

This is our favorite hotel in San Pedro. Made from native materials such as cactus and adobe, this inn blends seamlessly into its environment. Narrow, rock-lined outdoor passageways lead to spacious, well-designed rooms. Shadows play across these rooms all day, created by tree limbs in front of the floor-to-ceiling glass sliding door that covers one entire wall. The door opens out to a delightful, flower-covered terrace where hammocks and lounge chairs beckon sinfully. At night you fall exhausted into a cozy bed to snuggle under a thick down comforter.

There is a small, rock-lined pool in the center of the hotel that is perfect for a dunk after a day's activity. You won't lack for diversion here, as the hotel can arrange any number of special excursions. In addition to the standard Valley of the Moon and Atacama Salt Flat, they can offer more off-the-beaten-track tours such as Laguna Verde in Bolivia or multi-day treks.

Selected as one of our best places to stay – see Chapter 10 for more details.

HOSTERÍA SAN PEDRO, *Solcor. Tel. 55/851011. 42 rooms. Double $71. Breakfast included. Restaurant. Pool. Credit cards accepted.*

The Hostería features white adobe cabañas with the distinctive thatched roofs of the Altiplano. Spread out over the large grounds, each room has its own small patio. The furnishing are a bit worn, but the hotel is in the midst of remodeling. In the southwest part of town, the Hostería feels removed from city, but is just three blocks from the plaza. The real selling point here is the swimming pool, which is heaven on a hot afternoon.

HOTEL TULOR, *Domingo Atienda. Tel/Fax 55/851027. E-mail: tulor@chilesat.net. 20 rooms. Double $75. Restaurant. Bar. Credit cards accepted.*

This hotel is owned by the Chilean archaeologist Ana Maria Baron who discovered Tulor, the oldest known village in the Atacama desert. The bar is a circular-shaped adobe edifice, inspired by the structures she uncovered on the dig. Photos of the excavation, jewelry, and textiles adorn the bar. The rooms are in optimal condition because the hotel is new.

HOTEL TAMBILLO, *Antofagasta. Tel. 55/851078, Fax 55/319967. 15 rooms. Double $50. Restaurant. Credit cards accepted.*

The Tambillo is a newly built hotel finished in gray stucco with wooden window frames. The rooms are smartly adorned with striped bedspreads and comfortable furnishings. This is a strong hotel option in this price range.

HOTEL KIMAL, *Corner of Caracoles and Atienda. Tel. 55/831152, Fax 55/851030. 5 rooms. Double $85. Breakfast included. Restaurant. Bar. Credit cards accepted.*

Mud and hay adobe brick walls provide shelter in the comfortable rooms at the Kimal. Several of the rooms have patios that serve as good areas to relax at the end of the day. The hotel's attractive Atacama desert design is a few flowers short of keeping up with many similar competitor's in the area, but is still a good option.

HOSTERÍA CASA DE DON TOMAS, *Tocopilla. Tel./Fax 55/851055. 12 rooms. Double $80. Breakfast included. Credit cards accepted.*

This hotel was the newest and best in town just a few years ago. It is now outclassed by the more recent entrants into the market.

Inexpensive

TAKHA-TAKHA, *Caracoles, west of Domingo Atienza. Tel. 55/851038. 15 rooms. Double $45. 4 campsites. Camping $7.50 per person. No credit cards.*

We are enchanted by the laid-back atmosphere of the Takha-Takha. The rooms are simple and clean with comfortable beds. An expansive, healthy three-hectare garden spreads out in front of all of the rooms. The inviting lawn chairs provide an advantageous position from which to observe the cactus and towering flowers lengthen their afternoon shadows. We pondered the half dozen foosball tables scattered about the yard when suddenly it struck us – "takha-takha" is the sound of the ball clacking around a foosball table, and the name of the game in Chile. Fortunately, the place is a mecca for mellow itinerants, rather than avid takha-takha players.

HOSTAL KATARPE, *Domingo Atianza. Tel. 51/851033. 10 rooms. Double $40. Credit cards accepted.*

This is another good, clean option in this price range, but it lacks the common areas and courtyards that some of the other hotels offer.

Both the **Residencial Florida**, *Tocopilla, Tel. 851021* and the **Residencial Rayco**, *Antofagasta. Tel. 55/851008* are good budget options. They charge about $12 per person with shared bath.

CAMPING GUNZA, *Antofagasta. $5 per person. No credit cards.*

Camping Gunza is a social hot-spot for outgoing campers. If you are looking to meet a youthful crowd of Chileans and other travelers, pitch your tent and belly up to the rustic bar, centered around a rock hearth.

WHERE TO EAT

PAACHA, *Corner of Caracoles and Domingo Atienda. Tel. 851152. Expensive. Credit cards accepted.*

The Paacha has utilized regional materials to create the most charming dining area in town. The exposed beams are hewn from local *chañaral* wood. Sticks from the same tree dangle around the ceiling lights to form Flinstonian chandeliers. The house specialty is a *Pollo Cacique*, chicken in a creamed curry sauce over a bed of rice and fruit. Another good dish, the pasta with Roquefort and walnut sauce is a stinky-cheese-lover's dream. The food is excellent, but service can be slow. *Peña* musicians play Andean-style music during weekend nights in the high season.

ADOBE, *Caracoles. 851089. Moderate. Credit cards accepted.*

The Adobe is run by a pack of gregarious Chilean slackers. Your waitress will probably sit at your table and chat a while as she takes your order. The grin and red eyes of the reggae-grooving chef may make you wary, but the kitchen comes through with delicious fare. Although the Adobe is best known for its pizza, the chicken in paprika sauce is also outstanding. The outdoor tables are aligned to form a square around an open bonfire. Many of the patrons linger long after their meals are finished, sipping wine or beer, mesmerized by the crackling flames.

LA ESTAKA, *Caracoles. Tel. 851038. Moderate. No credit cards.*

La Estaka is one of the town hangouts. The outdoor bar, painted with a wild mural, fills up during dinner and keeps going long into the night. The indoor tables are lined up in an open room anchored by a busy kitchen. The restaurant offers set nightly meals with a choice of appetizer, meat or veggie entrée, a side dish, and dessert. It is deservedly crowded nightly, so you might want to make a reservation.

LA CASONA, *Caracoles 26. Tel. 851004. Moderate. Credit cards accepted.*

The La Casona is the town's favorite restaurant for vegetarian fare. The white stucco dining room is always packed with hungry herbivores, but the menu includes several items for carnivorous companions.

TIERRA TODO NATURAL, *Caracoles. Inexpensive. No credit cards.*

If you need to pack a meal for a hike or mountain bike ride, this is the place to get it. The Tierra Todo Natural features delicious vegetarian sandwiches on homemade whole wheat bread. They also serve fresh juices and desserts.

SONCHEK, *Calama between Licancabur and Antofagasta. Inexpensive. No credit cards.*

This simple one room restaurant, owned by Czech immigrants, offers reasonably priced sandwiches and veggie specials.

SEEING THE SIGHTS

Walking through the adobe-fronted streets of San Pedro you are immediately struck by its uniqueness as far as Chilean towns go. Vegetarian restaurants and crystal-selling new-agers share the sidewalk with adventure tour companies and small grocery stores. Mellowness just oozes out of the residents, making you slow down and enjoy the fantastic sights at their pace.

SAN PEDRO CHURCH, *Plaza de Armas.*

Surrounded by a white, geometrically decorated adobe wall, the church at San Pedro is one of the largest of the region. A parish since 1641, this building dates from 1744. Notice the rustic ceiling beams, made of cactus, and the hand carved and painted icons.

FATHER LE PAIGE ARCHAEOLOGICAL MUSEUM, *Padre Le Paige street. Monday-Friday 9am-12pm, 2pm-6pm. Weekends 10am-12pm, 2pm-6pm. Entry $2.50.*

Father Le Paige, a Belgian priest, took over the parish in 1955 and began to study and collect artifacts of the native peoples. By the time he died in 1980, he had helped put together one of the best collections of pre-Colombian artifacts in this part of the world. This assemblage is now housed in the modern museum with eight wings that walk the visitor through the history of the Atacama.

Some of the more memorable pieces are a well-preserved mummy of a young woman known to many as "Miss Chile;" a human bone imbedded with an arrowhead; and all sorts of pipes and straws that were used with ceremonial hallucinogens.

SPORTS & RECREATION

The parade of tourists has brought an infrastructure that makes it easy to participate in all sorts of outdoor activities. We highly recommend getting active in the desert in addition to the standard Valle la Luna, Tatio Geyser tours. San Pedro is at 2400 meters, which you might feel a bit when first exercising.

Biking

There are bikes for rent all over town, but the best, along with good maps, can be found at **Pangea Expediciones** on *Tocopilla, Tel. 851111*. The Devil's Gorge is an excellent ride through a twisty canyon that goes back for about 45 minutes of amazing singletrack. You can also arrange guided rides to out of the way points on the Salar de Atacama or Death Valley. Valle de la Luna is another popular mountain bike destination.

Climbing

Many tour companies offer climbs up the 5300 meter Lascar Volcano or the 6000 meter Sairecabur Volcano. A good outfit, such as **Desert Adventure** (see below under *Excursions & Day Trips)*, brings oxygen.

Hiking

One of the most popular hikes is the 6 km round trip to the Pukará Quitor fort. It is very worthwhile. Tour groups also offer hikes in the Valle de la Luna.

Horseback Riding

You can rent horses across the street from the Hostería San Pedro. The 16 km round trip to Catarpe is a good ride.

SHOPPING

There is an artisan alley just off the main plaza filled with handicrafts from all over the north. San Pedro also has a few art galleries with crafts and some jewelry on Caracoles.

EXCURSIONS & DAY TRIPS

Many people find it easiest to visit the incredible sights around San Pedro in group tours. You can usually arrange your next day's activity by signing up for a trip with one of the tour offices that evening. Be aware that tour companies pop up in San Pedro like weeds. Many of them are here today, gone tomorrow, Although you might be tempted to save a few dollars and go with the cheapest company, we would urge you to consider otherwise. While having your van break down at the Valley of the Moon might not be critical, having an inexperienced guide while climbing Lascar could be very dangerous.

A few companies have stood the test of time. We can highly recommend both **Cosmos Andino Expediciones**, *Caracoles, Tel. 55/851069* and **Desert Adventure**, *Caracoles, Tel. 55/851067*. Cosmos Andino is starting to put together longer, more unique trips to differentiate themselves from the crowd. It's worth calling before you arrive or stopping by to see what they have on tap during your stay.

Valley Of The Moon

The *Valle de la Luna*, with good reason, is one of the most visited sights around San Pedro. The wind has sculptured the area into bizarre formations that look more lunar than of this earth. You can hike up the side of the hill and walk out a thin ridge for the best view of the area. There is also a 8 km trail that runs parallel to the road that crossing the valley. Sunset and full moons are especially popular times to visit. Almost every tour company in San Pedro offers the trip for less than $10, but mountain bike is another excellent transportation alternative. Camping is not allowed.

Flamingo National Reserve & Toconao

This reserve is actually made up of seven noncontiguous protected sectors. Designed to safeguard nesting areas of the local flamingo population, each sector is either a lake or salt flat. The one exception is the Valley of the Moon, which also falls under the Flamingo National Reserve's administration, as it sits on the edge of the Salar de Atacama.

Heading south from San Pedro you quickly come upon the **Salar de Atacama**, the largest saline deposit in Chile. The clarity of the air and pureness of the light are phenomenal. The lack of humidity allows you see extreme distances over the flat to the blue and purple volcanoes beyond.

Thirty-three km south of San Pedro you arrive to the desert oasis **Tocanao**. Tocanao is famous for its fresh water, its stonework, and its orchards. The **San Lucas church** is an excellent example of the kind of masonry for which Tocanao is known. It's worth walking through the entire town, but don't miss the stone workers hewing away at the volcanic rock along 18 de Octubre street. Just north of town is the **Quebrada de Jerez**, or Jerez Ravine, where you'll find the orchards full of apples and grapes and other fruits.

Heading southwest of Tocanao you will come to **Lago Chaxa**, an important flamingo breeding area. The bizarre sight of thousands of flamingos here in the driest of deserts is unforgettable. A few kilometers further down the road, **Lago Barros Negros** is another excellent sight for spotting flamingos. Take binoculars for the best views.

It is possible to circle the entire Salar de Atacama by continuing south from Tocanao. You can visit small oasis towns, such as **Camar** and **Peine**; see other flamingo nesting sights at **Lagunas Salada** and **La Punta**, walk on the Inca trail south of Camar; and catch incredible views of the flat.

Most tours visit the Salar, Toconao, and Jerez for about $12.

THE INCA TRAIL

*Four km south of Camar, on the left, you'll see a cross sticking out of the ground. Rather than marking the site of a traffic accident, as many highway crosses do, this one marks the **Inca Trail**. Although the Inca were headquartered in Cuzco, Peru, they built an impressive network of roads throughout their empire, including northern Chile. Their system was made up of two north-south roads, one running along the coast for about 3,600 km, the other inland along the Andes for a comparable distance, with many interconnecting links.*

Use of the system was strictly limited to government and military business. In a type of human pony express, a well-organized relay service carried messages up to 240 km a day. Ironically, this same road system that helped them govern and control their large territory played a vital role in their conquest. The Spanish were able to gain access to the entire Inca empire along the trail.

Tatio Geysers

This geyser field, one of the highest in the world, is another must-see for anybody visiting San Pedro. It is best to get there at sunrise, around 6am, when you can best see the steam of the geysers rising against the dark mountain backdrop. The strange formations and colors of the hundreds of thermal pools are mesmerizing, as are the bubbling, steaming waters.

It is important to watch your step, as the edges of the pools can be extremely fragile. Breaking through can mean horrible burns.

Most of the tour companies leave San Pedro for the geysers at about 4am. Even if you have your own car, that is the best time to depart so that you can be there at sunrise. It is very cold at the geysers that early in the morning, so dress appropriately.

It is possible to go straight to Calama from Tatio if you have your own vehicle. If you are returning to San Pedro, you can stop at the **Puritama** thermal pools on the way back. For $20 the tour company itinerary includes both the geysers and the thermal pools.

Pukará De Quitor

This fort, just three km from town, is an easy walk or mountain bike ride away. Perched on top of a hill, the fort offers wonderful views of the oasis below and desert beyond. The stone structure, which blends in with the surrounding rocks, dates from the 12th century. The Spanish overran it in 1540 in a bloody battle that left the local chiefs headless. You can also visit the Inca ruins at **Catarpe** three km further down the road.

Tulor

This ancient village, nine km from town, was buried in sand years ago and preserved intact until its discovery by Chilean archaeologist Ana Maria Baron. Dating from between 800BC to 200AD, it's the oldest trace of human settlement in the area. A small portion of the find has been excavated. Just as interesting are the artistic forms of the tips of the walls sticking out from the sand in the other areas.

Laguna Verde, Bolivia

If you want to get off the beaten path, this is an excellent alternative that takes you past the impressive Licancabur and Juriques volcanoes before entering into Bolivia. The Laguna Verde, or Green Lagoon, is a beautiful emerald colored lake filled with flamingoes. Because nebulous border regulations, it is best to take this trip with a tour company.

PRACTICAL INFORMATION

Banks: There are no banks in San Pedro and it is difficult to cash travelers checks. Come with plenty of pesos.

Business Hours: Few towns in Chile shut down as completely in the afternoon between 2pm-4pm. You should plan on taking a nap during that time as that is what everybody else seems to be doing.

Currency Exchange: **Cambios Atacama**, *Caracoles*

Laundry: **H2O**, *Caracoles*

Medical Service: **Posta Médica**, *Toconao by the plaza, Tel. 851010*

National Parks: There is no Conaf office in San Pedro, but there is a Conaf Information Center on the road to Toconao. It is a good idea to check in there and let them know where you are going if you're traveling independently so they can look for you if you don't come back.

Post Office: **Correos de Chile**, *across from the museum on Padre La Paige*

Supermarkets: There are no supermarkets per say, but plenty of small shops on Caracoles.

Telephone/Fax: The area code is 55. **CTC**, *Caracoles off the plaza*; **Entel**, *on the plaza.*

Tourist Office/Maps: **Tourist Information Office**, *bus terminal.* Monday-Friday 10:30am-2:30pm, 4pm-7:30pm. Weekends 9am-1pm

CHAÑARAL

Located in the Salado River Valley 165 km north of Copiapó, this mining port of 12,000 owes its livelihood and deterioration to the copper mines of the Atacama desert. The town served as a fishing village and a fruit port for the Chañaral oasis until famous explorer Diego de Almeyda discovered copper and made Chile's first export of the mineral from its port.

The copper mines proved to be quite profitable and as they grew, water waste from their operations was transported along the Rio Salado and dumped into the sea. During 68 years, more than 320 million tons of copper-contaminated earth was washed down to the coastline, considerably broadening Chañaral's beach as well as those north of the town. In 1988 the community successfully sued the state-owned copper company, Codelco. In response to the suit the company first diverted the waste north of the town via a canal and now deposits the water in the desert.

Although the residents insist that the copper waste does not constitute a threat to human health, it is impossible not to ponder this while looking out at the broad beach tinted green by the deposit of copper sulfates.

The main reason most people come to Chañaral is to transfer to **Pan de Azúcar National Park**, 29 km north of town. If you get stuck overnight in Chañaral, it has a surprisingly good mid-range hotel, the **Hostería Chañaral**.

ARRIVALS & DEPARTURES
By Bus & Car
Chañaral is on the Pan-American highway 165 km north of Copiapó and 400 km south of Antofagasta. There is direct bus service from both Copiapó and Antofagasta.

To get to **Pan de Azúcar** you can take the one local bus that leaves from the Costanera, the street along the beach. The bus charges $2.50 one way and offers continuous service from 8:30am to 7pm during high season. During the low season, the service is more erratic. If there are too few passengers during low season, the bus simply won't go. Taxis charge $18 one way or about $30 for drop-off and previously arranged pick-up. We suggest contacting the courteous and informative taxi driver, Richard Grenet, *Tel. 480844.*

WHERE TO STAY & EAT
HOSTERÍA CHAÑARAL, *Muller 268. Tel. 52/480050, Fax 52/480554. 25 rooms. Double $50. Credit cards accepted.*
If you can't time our arrival to make it directly out to Pan de Azúcar you'll be pleasantly surprised with the comfortable facilities at this hotel. The rooms line a smartly tiled courtyard over which trellises suspend vines and flowers. The common areas include a game room with a pool table, a bar with a big screen TV featuring hundreds of movies and sports channels via direct satellite, and the best restaurant in town.

If you are looking for a less expensive place than the Chañaral, try the **Hotel Mini**, *San Martín 528, Tel. 480079,* or the **Hotel Nuria**, *Av. Costanera 300, Tel. 480903,* both with doubles for about $25.

Eateries, other than the Hostería Chañaral, are located at the intersection of the Panamericana and Merino Jarpa. Four restaurants are located here - **Nayo**, **El Carro**, **La Querencia**, and **Mi Casita**.

EXCURSIONS & DAY TRIPS

Pan de Azúcar National Park can easily be done as a day trip. Details are listed in the next entry.

You can visit a piece of the **Inca Trail** by traveling about two hours east. The remains of the ancient road are near Portal del Inca.

Another option is contacting amateur archaeologist and professional taxi driver Richard Grenet, *Tel. 480844.* He has been digging around in Inca and Chango sites since boyhood and has a small personal collection of arrowheads, pottery, and a beautiful stone pipe. He doesn't speak English, so take your Spanish dictionary if you need it. You can visit a few spots on the way out to Pan de Azúcar if you use his services for transportation.

PRACTICAL INFORMATION

Banks: **BCI**, *Maipu 319, Tel. 480121.* There are no banks with ATM's.
Laundry: There are no laundry mats. Hotels have laundry services.
Post Office: **Correos del Chile**, *Comercio near the Hostería*
Supermarkets: **Supermercado**, *Corner of Freire and Merino Jarpa*
Telephone/Fax: The area code is 52. **Entel**, *Merino Jarpa 1197*
Tourist Office/Maps: **Municipal Tourist Office**, *Corner of Conchuela and Merino Jarpa*

PAN DE AZÚCAR

The Pan de Azúcar National Park is a 44,000-hectare piece of desert on the sea. It is blessed with distinct and varied cactus life, some nice sandy beaches, and an island that serves as a sanctuary for Humboldt penguins, sea lions, and the otter-like *chungungo*.

On the road to the park, you will encounter numerous natural caves that the native Changos utilized as shelters. Many of these are blocked with makeshift walls of loose stone that served to further protect the shelters from the elements.

The majority of the plant life is cactus and other rugged flora, which present beautiful blossoms during the spring months of September and October. During times of abundant precipitation, roughly every five years, the entire hillside is covered in a carpet of wildflowers. Given the arid and rocky landscape of most of the park, you will be surprised to encounter plant life transforming the upper elevations of the park into verdant terrain. The foliage extracts water from the coastal fog known as *chamanchaca*.

The Conaf visitor's center located inside of the park just above the Caleta Pan de Azúcar fishing village, features a cactus garden to created to familiarize visitors with the distinct varieties of cactus found in the park. The center has a large wall map of the park as well as displays with other supplementary information on the flora and fauna.

The park is open year-round. The Conaf registration office at the entrance of the park charges $4 per person. There is an additional fee for camping.

USING THE CHAMANCHACA

The same fog that nourishes the flora of the park may have far more applications in the future. Scientists have found a way, using giant nets, to capture the fog and turn it to potable water. In Chungungo, north of La Serena, fog collectors have worked well enough to provide bath and drinking water for the village.

ARRIVALS & DEPARTURES

The park is located 29 km north of Chañaral on a dirt road running along the coastline. It takes about a thirty minutes to get there by car.

See the Chañaral *Arrivals & Departures*, immediately above, for transportation information.

WHERE TO STAY & EAT

PAN DE AZÚCAR CAMPING AND CABINS, *Juan Tamblay Silva Concessionaire. Tel. 52/480551, Fax 52/480539. Camping $30/site. Cabins $100. No credit cards.*

The sole concessionaire has set up 65 campsites along the beach. The most remote are about two km south of the small fishing village, Caleta Pan de Azúcar. Most of the sites are set up north of the village, just below the camping reception office. Each site is equipped with a cooking grill and 20 liters of potable water. There are bathrooms but no showers. You should reserve in advance during the high season. There are only two cabins so you must reserve in advance if you are planning on staying in these. The cabins have six beds and fully-equipped kitchens.

There is a restaurant, open during the high season, on the road just before the fishing village. The green house on the beach in the fishing village sells sandwiches and empanadas. The hygiene is questionable, but the fish sandwiches that the *señora* makes are tasty.

There are two mini-markets in the fishing village, open during the high season, with very basic supplies. You are better off buying food and supplies before coming to the park.

EXCURSIONS & DAY TRIPS

Rodrigo Carvajal runs the Conaf-approved boat service to Isla Pan de Azúcar, which is home to a **Humboldt penguin sanctuary**. You can also see sea lions and *chungungos*, a type of nutria. He prefers boatloads of four to six people but is flexible. The cost per person is about $8. You can find him in the fishing village at the white house marked "Transporte a Isla Pan de Azúcar". If necessary, ask the Conaf rangers to direct you there.

There are two good day hikes. **El Mirador** is a six hour round-trip hike to a look-out point. The trail ascends through a fertile valley made green by cactus and plant life. An easier and closer hike can be done up through the **Aguada Los Sapos Canyon** in about two hours. You have a good opportunity to observe the park's flora and fauna on this short hike. You also get a great view of the beaches and the island. Consult the visitor center map and the Conaf rangers for specifics of the routes.

BAHÍA INGLESA

Bahía Inglesa is a small beach town and fishing village, four km south of Caldera, and about 80 km west of Copiapó. Beach houses and an apart-hotel cluster around a miniature, white sand beach with a shallow green swimming area hemmed in by rocks. The inlet's waters are tame enough to have earned the nickname *la piscina* (the pool).

Further out on the bay, strings of buoys from the scallop and seaweed harvesting operations bob about like Styrofoam beads. The bay is surrounded by a long beach of crushed shell and sand, the hard-packed, wet portion of which is good for long runs or walks.

Bahía Inglesa is a tranquil escape during the low season and a beach-loving family-fest during the high season and holiday weekends. Families love it here because it offers one of the best places on the entire coast for kids to play and swim. Two apart-hotels and several cabins, all built with families in mind, serve as the accommodations.

The nearby, more industrialized town of Caldera, offers a greater number of services and more restaurant options if the need arises.

ARRIVALS & DEPARTURES
By Bus

Bus service from cities in the area such as Copiapó or Chañaral arrive to Caldera. You can either take a local bus or a taxi the remaining four kilometers to Bahía Inglesa.

By Car

From Copiapó, you should take the exit to Bahía Inglesa before reaching Caldera. From Chañaral, the quickest route is through Caldera.

WHERE TO STAY & EAT

APART-HOTEL ROCAS DE BAHÍA, *Av. El Morro. Tel./Fax 52/ 316005 or 52/316032. 27 apartments. Double bed apartment with kitchen and dinning room $85. Swimming pool. Restaurant. Bar. Game room. Credit cards accepted.*

The Rocas de Bahía is the best option in Bahía Inglesa. All rooms have terraces, complete with patio furniture and wet clothes racks, which overlook the principal beaches and the bay. The comfortable apartments are in excellent condition and boast fully equipped, tidy kitchens. Families can opt for one of the apartments that sleep up to six. The off-season rates drop to $55 per apartment making it an excellent option for a tranquil escape. The pool, game room, bar, and restaurant are located on the top floor. It is the best spot in town to gaze at the orange-streaked sunsets under which fishing boats rock in the tide.

Other lodging possibilities include the well-worn, family-friendly cabins at **Jardines de Bahía**, *Copiapó 100, Tel. 52/315359*, or the less centrally located, new **Apart-Hotel Bahía Blanco**, *Camino de Martín 1300, Tel./Fax 52/316044 or 316468*, both with two-person lodging at $80. There is also year-round camping at **Camping Bahía Inglesa**, *Tel. 52/ 683177*.

The best restaurant in town is **El Corral**, *El Morro 564, Tel. 315331*, featuring scallops (*ostiones*) pulled from the waters of its front yard. You can travel to Caldera for several other restaurant options which include **New Charles**, *Ossa Cerda 350, Tel. 315348*, **Mystic Pizza**, *Carvallo 350, Tel. 315033*, **El Pirón de Oro**, *Cousiño 218, Tel. 315109*, and the popular seafood *picada* (small restaurant), **El Macho**, *corner of Vallejos and Circunvalación*.

EXCURSIONS & DAY TRIPS

Granito Orbicular Nature Sanctuary, with its strange mineral formations, is a geological fluke. Just 11 km north of Caldera, this stunning sight was formed by the weathering of highly fractured rocks.

Inland excursions to salt flats, thermal baths, and the parks can be arranged through **Avernturismo**, *Tel. 316305*. **Sr. Montero**, *Tel. 316206*, offers boat rides to visit sea lion dens as well as diving trips. **Puerto Viejo**, south of Bahía Inglesa, is an ever more laid back beach town.

PRACTICAL INFORMATION

Banks: **BCI**, *Ossa Cerda 127, Caldera*
Post Office: **Correos de Chile**, *Edwards 325, Caldera*
Supermarket: **Minimarket**, *two blocks behind El Coral, Bahía Inglesa*
Tel./Fax: The area code is 52. **CTC**, *Edwards 360, Caldera*

COPIAPÓ

Copiapó means "cup of gold" in the indigenous language. It was silver, however that led to the city's development during the heady mining days of the mid-1800's. As the silver petered out so did the population. Over time other mining booms, mostly in copper but also gold and marble, brought this town of 98,000 people back to life.

History

The nomadic Chango Amerindians occupied the coastal area before the arrival of the Spanish. Excellent mariners, they developed boats out of inflated sea lion skins and traded dried fish with the peoples of the interior. When the Spanish arrived in 1540, the fertile areas such as the **Copiapó** valley received most of the conquistadors' attention, leaving the coast more-or-less untouched.

In the mid-1800s, many of Chile's elite lived in and around Copiapó. These wealthy mining families constructed beautiful homes and public buildings. With the growth of mining came the need for transportation and in 1851 the first railway in Chile was built from Caldera to Copiapó. Many of the sights in the region are related to this affluent time in Norte Chico's past.

Today mining is still the most active sector of the economy, with agriculture, fishing, and tourism filling in the gaps.

ARRIVALS & DEPARTURES

By Bus

Regular bus service connects Copiapó with other points north and south along the Panamericana Highway as well as further up the Copiapó valley. All buses leave from the terminal at *Chacabuco 112*, with the exception of Pullman, which leaves from its own terminal at *Colipí 109*.

Bus Companies

- **Inca Bus**, *Tel. 213488*, Caldera
- **Tramaca**, *Tel. 213979*, Chañaral via the Panamericana and Inca de Oro routes
- **Pullman-Bus**, *Tel. 212629*, Chañaral via the Panamericana and Inca de Oro routes, south to Santiago

Colectivos leave about every 15 minutes from the corner of *Chacabuco and Rodriguez* for Tierra Amarilla. **Gather** buses leave from the main bus terminal four times a day up the Copiapó Valley.

By Car
Copiapó is located on the Pan-American Highway about six hours from both La Serena to the south and Antofagasta to the north. It is only one hour from Caldera and Bahía Inglesa on the coast.

Rental Companies
•**Avis**, *Peña 102. Tel. 213966*
•**Budget**, *Freire 466. Tel. 216030*
•**Hertz**, *Copayapu 173. Tel. 213522*
•**IQSA**, *Copayapu 1233. Tel. 214722*

By Plane
The only flights to Copiapó are from Santiago and La Serena. **Lan**, *Tel. 213512*, **Ladeco**, *Tel. 217406*, and **Avant** *Tel. 219275*, all located on the plaza on *Colipi Street*, have daily flights.

ORIENTATION
Copiapó runs northwest through a transversal valley created by the river of the same name. The town lies on the river's northern bank, about 70 km inland from the ocean. In town, the main tourist zone is bounded by tree-lined Alameda Matta to the west, and Plaza Prat to the east.

GETTING AROUND TOWN
Collective taxis ply the streets with their destinations marked on the roofs of their cabs. Private taxis can be found on the plaza or in front of the Miramonti Hotel.

WHERE TO STAY
Moderate
HOTEL MIRAMONTI, *Ramon Freire 371. Tel./Fax 52/210440. 45 rooms. Double $85. Breakfast included. Cable TV. Restaurant. Bar. Billiard room. Room service. Two handicap-equipped rooms. Conference rooms. Credit cards accepted.*

The Hotel Miramonti is nostalgically embellished by its Italian owners with prints and paintings that hearken back to the homeland. The spacious rooms are tastefully decorated with large wooden end tables and desks. The suites include details such as whirlpool jets in the baths. The upstairs salon features a large billiards table with the smallest pockets in

Chile. The versatile conference facilities make Miramonti a popular choice for business people. Both its bar and restaurant are the among the town's favorites, the latter featuring exquisite Italian cuisine. We recommend the Miramonti as the best option of the upper end hotels.

HOTEL DIEGO DE ALMEYDA, *O'Higgins 656. Tel./Fax 52/212075. 60 rooms. Double $98. Breakfast included. Cable TV. Restaurant. Bar. Parking. Pool. Credit cards accepted.*

Hotels on the plaza in Chile are usually old and frayed at the edges. That is not the case with the Diego de Almeyda. Decorated in informal country style, this hotel is a good option. The room furnishings have been recently updated as have the bathrooms. The especially pleasant pool is surrounded by a lush garden bursting with bougainvillea. Street noise is an issue if you get a room facing the plaza, so try to get one in the back of the hotel.

LA CASONA, *O'Higgins 150. Tel./Fax 52/217277 or 52/217278. 10 rooms. Double $55. Breakfast included. Cable TV. Credit cards accepted.*

The La Casona is located in an elongated, one story, historic house, painted hot pink. It is singularly the most "bed-and-breakfasty" hotel we've encountered in Chile. Antiques such as a century old coffee grinder adorn the breakfast area. Overstuffed couches line the sitting room. There are two separate patios in the garden on which to lounge. All of the rooms are lovely with little details like the minibar items displayed in baskets. The rooms vary slightly in price according to size and location. It is better to avoid the cheapest ones, which are exposed to street noise.

CHAGALL HOTEL, *O'Higgins 760. Tel. 52/213775. Fax 52/211527. 45 rooms. Double $76. Breakfast included. Cable TV. Restaurant. Bar. Parking. Credit cards accepted.*

Our only real complaint about the Chagall is its color scheme – lime green exterior and fufu purple rooms. If you can get past that, or if you are color blind, it's a decent place to hang your bag. The rooms are newly furnished, the bathrooms sparkling white, and the restaurant one of the better choices in town. Its location, a block off the plaza, is another plus.

Inexpensive

MONTECATINI I, *Infante 766. Tel. 52/211363. 25 rooms. Double $37. Breakfast included. No credit cards.*

Many hotels in Copiapó have nice gardens, but the Montecantini takes it to another level. You walk through the front door and out to a profusion of delightful colors and scents. Pretty and quiet, this hotel is also an excellent value. The rooms are nothing special, but they are clean and comfortable. This is the top choice for a mid-level hotel.

PALACE HOTEL, *Atacama 741. Tel. 52/212825. 30 rooms. Double $42. Parking. No credit cards.*

The Palace is built around a pleasant garden patio. The rooms have basic furnishings, but they are clean.

HOTEL EL SOL, *Rodriguez 550. Tel./Fax 52/215672. 30 rooms. Double $40. Breakfast included. Parking. Credit cards accepted.*

There are a number of inexpensive hotels and *residenciales* along Rodriguez Street, and this is the best of the bunch. You walk through the doorway to an open, bright, sunny interior complete with chirping birds. The rooms are clean and simple, as are the bathrooms.

HOTEL INGLES, *Atacama 337. Tel. 52/212797. Fax 52/211286. 15 rooms. Double $25. Credit cards accepted.*

If you are looking for a bargain hotel with personality, this is it. Established in 1897, the Hotel Ingles claims to be the oldest continually operating hotel in Chile. The simple cream facade has been defaced with some graffiti. You should step inside to see the quaint garden gracing the courtyard. We're sure the wooden planks on the open air walkway could tell some great stories if they could talk. The downside is that the fixtures and furnishings show a great deal of wear.

RESIDENCIAL BENBOW, *Rodriguez 541. Tel. 52/217634. 35 rooms. $13 per person. Restaurant. No credit cards.*

The Benbow, run by a family, is refreshingly pleasant and clean for the price. Small details such as bouquets of plastic flowers hanging from each doorway and satiny bedcovers show that these owners have pride in their establishment. The attached restaurant is solid as well.

RESIDENCIAL TORRES, *Atacama 230, Tel. 219600. Per person $8. No credit cards.*

The Torres is family run with the family almost overrunning it. It is clean, homey, and cheap.

WHERE TO EAT

While Copiapó can brag about a surprising number of quality hotels, the restaurant options are less than superb. We found a few good ones, though:

HOTEL MIRAMONTI, *Ramon Freire 371. Tel. 210440. Moderate/ expensive. Credit cards accepted.*

The Italian dining room in the Miramonti features sumptuous cuisine in a convivial atmosphere. Turquoise walls are set off by red tablecloths and intricate blue tiles. Sheer drapes cover large windows on each wall, one that shows off the kitchen where the chef and assistants can be observed hard at work at their art. The restaurant features a extensive list of Chilean and Italian wines. The lasagna, which is one item we try in nearly all Italian restaurants, was the best we've had in Chile. This is, hands down, the best restaurant in Copiapó.

HOTEL DIEGO DE ALMEYDA, *O'Higgins 656. Tel. 212075. Expensive. Credit cards accepted.*

Location is the key with this restaurant. Looking directly out on the tree covered plaza, the Diego de Almeyda is a favorite choice for visiting mining execs. The décor is informal, with café-style seating and a long wooden bar, but the price tag isn't. The menu is limited to the standard Chilean fare.

EL QUINCHO, *Atacama 109. Tel. 214647. Moderate/expensive. Credit cards accepted.*

The El Quincho is where Copiapó's carnivores converge to munch steaks seared over an open flame. The restaurant is located in a historic neighborhood and surrounded by settlement era houses.

EL CORSARIO, *Atacama 245. Tel. 215374. Moderate. Credit cards accepted.*

The Chilean cuisine at El Corsario ranks at mediocre, but the bizarre atmosphere makes it worth mention. The historic building is somewhat crumbing and bright green walls surround the outdoor seating area. There's a raised pond with turtles and fish swimming in florescent yellow water at one end of the dining area. Your service will be provided by an aging but enthusiastic staff.

HAO-HWA, *Yerbas Buenas 334. Tel. 215484. Also at Colipi 340, Tel. 213261. Moderate. Credit cards accepted.*

The Hao-Hwa has two locations serving up its town favorite *chifa*-style Chinese food. Both feature a variety of reasonably-priced duck plates such as Peking duck, duck with bamboo, and duck in pineapple. Several of these same dishes are also prepared with turkey.

BRAMADA, *In mall at O'Higgins and Colipi, Tel. 236288. Inexpensive. Credit cards accepted.*

This sandwich and coffee shop is located in the courtyard of a small, two-story mall and surrounded by artisan shops, antique booths, and a bookstore. The locale offers a variety of hefty sandwiches loaded with ingredients like avocado, onions, and sliced green beans as well as a fixed-menu lunch that is a bargain considering its tastiness.

SEEING THE SIGHTS

Plaza Prat, at the center of town, is a shady, tree-lined refuge. A marble statue from Paris sits in the fountain at its core surrounded by large, blue pools. The neo-classical **Cathedral**, designed by an Englishman, anchors the western side of the plaza. Opposite the cathedral is the Plaza Mall.

MINERALOGICAL MUSEUM, *Rodríguez and Colipi. Monday-Friday 10am-1pm, 3:30pm-7pm. Saturday 10am-1pm. Admission fee $0.75.*

The most complete collection of minerals in Chile, this museum is designed to showcase Chile's underground riches. The colorful displays help you understand what's happening in those rocky hills all around you. The rocks under ultraviolet light are especially striking. It is one block off the plaza up Colipi.

You can take a nice stroll in the historic district by walking down Atacama Street in a northwesterly direction beginning from Chacabuco. It's worth taking a look in the **Hotel Ingles**, *Atacama 337*. Built in 1897, it is reported to be Chile's oldest continually functioning hotel. Just after crossing Rancagua, you'll encounter the **Casa Matta Regional Museum**, *Atacama 98, Tuesday-Saturday 9:30am-12:45pm, 3pm-7:15pm (Fridays closing at 6:15pm). Sundays and holidays, 10am-12:45pm. Entry $1.* The museum is well-organized, featuring local artifacts such as mine workers animal-bladder shoes and a room with the household furnishings of the Matta Goyenacheya brothers who built the house in the 1840's.

Continue down Atacama until reaching the tree lined Alameda street. Here, you have the option of continuing down the same street, which changes names to Juan Martínez, several long blocks until you reach the **train museum** located in the old station. The museum, which houses a collection of old railcars, is supposed to be open in the afternoons, but isn't always reliable.

If you want to skip the trains, turn left on Alameda street which has several buildings from the 1800's, one of which is the maroon **Iglesia de San Francisco**, built in 1872. In front of that is a statue in the image of the hammer-wielding Scot, **Juan Godoy**, outfitted in shorts and animal-bladder shoes.

When you reach the end of Alameda street, turn right on Avenida Kennedy. After nearly a kilometer of walking, you will see the Italian-style **Villa Viña de Cristo** on the opposite side of the street. The mansion, built in 1860, was once the fanciest in the province. It now belongs to the University of Atacama. The interior has been converted into offices and is open almost all day. You can climb the stairs until reaching the narrow, wooden, spiral staircase that leads to the look-out cupola. From here, the easiest way back is to cross back to the smaller auxiliary street and catch a bus with a sign marked "centro."

SPORTS & RECREATION

Hiking and climbing are the main sporting activities in the region. See *Excursions & Day Trips* below.

SHOPPING

Handicrafts are for sale on the corner of Maipú and Atacama. Anything else can probably be found in the Plaza Mall. With banks, restaurants, pharmacies, and a department store, it's one stop shopping.

EXCURSIONS & DAY TRIPS

Nevado Tres Cruces National Park & Laguna Verde

Some of the most beautiful scenery in the entire region lies between Copiapó and Argentina. The Andes is actually split into two ranges in this part of Chile, the **Domeyko** and **Claudio Gay**, with large salt flats formed between the two. These flats, dotted with flamingos and other birds, are surrounded by snowcapped mountains.

Heading east, you climb and cross the Domeyko range before dropping down to Nevado Tres Cruces National Park. On the left, after passing the Conaf hut, you'll see **Laguna Santa Rosa** sitting on the southern tip of the **Maricunga Salt Flat**. The lagoon is home to over 40 species of birds, including the three types of flamingos that live in Chile.

The road climbs again until reaching the Altiplano. Here, over time, the mountains were filled in with lava with the exception of the peaks of the tallest volcanoes. One of these, **Ojos de Salado**, is the highest peak in Chile at 6893 meters. As you drive you climb to 4300 meters before reaching the **Laguna Verde**, or Green Lagoon. This gorgeous, remote

CLIMBING OJOS DE SALADO

Ojos de Salado is the highest active volcano in the world and highest mountain in Chile at 6893 meters. It is a cold and windy, but not a particularly technical mountain. The time of year to attempt to summit is from October to March.

There are two rustic shelters on the mountain, the Atacama at 5100 meters and Tejos at 5750. If the roads permit, you can drive to the Atacama shelter in 4WD vehicle. You should plan on around five days of acclimatization hikes before attempting the summit. It is about an eight hour push from the Atacama shelter to the peak.

Talk to your guide about these details, but currently if you plan to climb the mountain you need to get a permit from Difrol, the government department in charge of the border, at Bandera 52, 4th floor, Santiago, Tel. 2/671-4110, Fax 2/697-1909. You can send them a fax with your name, address, nationality, passport number, and expected date of assent and they will send you the permit. You should also check in with both the carabineros and Conaf in Copiapó.

lake, high on the plain, with huge volcanoes looming all around it, is one of the most stunning sights in Chile.

You must speak to the Conaf rangers in Copiapó if you plan to make this trip on your own, as road conditions vary from poor to impassable depending on the time of year. The ranger station at Nevado Tres Cruces is normally about a five-hour drive from Copiapó in 4WD vehicle.

Erik Galvez Romero at **Mountain Guides Copiapó**, *Tel. 319038*, is an excellent guide who can lead all levels of trips from hikes in Pan to Azucar to the summit of Ojos de Salado. **Turismo de Aventura Expediciones Puna Atacama**, *Arredonode 154, Tel. 212684*, and **Aventurismo Expediciones**, *Casilla 134 in Caldera, Tel. 316395, E-mail eventurismo@mixmail.com*, also run trips to the mountains regularly.

Copiapó Valley

This pleasant half-day trip winds up the Copiapó river valley past vineyards and other agriculture. It is the green valley spreading below as much as the sights along the way that make this drive worth your while. Grapevines surround **Tierra Amarilla**, just 16 km from Copiapó. Its small church is a national monument. **Nantoco**, built by a successful miner as his country home, is a beautiful example of neoclassical architecture.

A little further up the road **Jotabeche**, the home of the famous Chilean miner, politician, and essayist José Joaquín Vallejo, is also worth a stop. Continuing through the valley, **Los Loros** is a pleasant village with lovely houses and a nice place for an outdoor lunch. If you prefer older monuments, the Inca copper foundry **Viña del Cerro** sits atop a hill another 17 km up the road. The 15th century structure contains 26 hearths strategically located at the windiest point on the hill, which accelerated the firing process.

Chañarcillo Silver Mine

Discovered by the explorer Juan Godoy, Chañarchillo was the third largest silver mine in the world and the source of Copiapó's wealth in the 1800s. Today both the mine and the town that serviced it are nothing but dusty ruins. The ghost town has a strong impact, however, and the drive across the remote plain is interesting if you haven't already put in a lot of time on the road. There is no public transportation and you need a four wheel drive vehicle to make the drive.

Bahía Inglesa To Chañaral

The Pacific coast is only an hour away and can be visited in a day trip from Copiapó. See the *Bahía Inglesa* and *Chañaral* sections.

PRACTICAL INFORMATION

Banks:. **BCI**, *Chacabuco 449*, **Banco Concepción**, *Chacabuco 485,* **Banco O'Higgins**, *O'Higgins 555*, **Santander**, *O'Higgins 539*. There is also an ATM just inside the front door of the plaza mall.

Business Hours: Monday-Friday 9:30am-1:30pm, 5:00pm-9:30pm. Saturday 10am-1:30pm

Currency Exchange: **Banco Concepción**, *Chacabuco 485*

Laundry: There is a dry cleaner and laundry service on the corner of Chañarcillo and Chacabuco cattycorner from the Ekono.

Medical Service: The hospital is 10 blocks east of the plaza on the corner of O'Higgins and Vicuña.

National Parks: **Conaf** , *Corner of Atacama and Salas. Tel. 212571*

Post Office: **Correos de Chile**, *Los Carrera 691 on the plaza*

Supermarkets: **Ekono**, *Chañarcillo and Chacabuco*, is the best stocked store.

Telephone/Fax: The area code is 52. **CTC**, *Plaza Prat*; **Entel**, *Colipí 500*

Tourist Office/Maps: **Sernatur** has a regional office next to the post office on the north side of the plaza at *Los Carrera 691*. You can get maps and information on the entire region.

THE FLOWERING DESERT

*Only four times in the last 20 years has there been enough rain to provoke one of the most stunning sights in all Chile – the **desierto florecido**. Unusual amounts of precipitation cause seeds and bulbs that have lain dormant for years or decades to germinate and blanket the normally arid desert with color.*

This sparks an entire ecosystem of insects, birds, and mammals, which come from afar to enjoy the bounty of the flowering desert. It's worth a trip to the Norte Chico area to catch a glimpse of foxes playing amid the colors of the rainbow.

The most stunning profusion of color is found between Vallenar and Copiapó, but flowers line the highway from Chañaral to La Serena. September and October are the prime months for viewing the phenomena.

LA SERENA

The Spanish founded **La Serena**, the second oldest city in Chile, in 1544. Downtown has maintained the feel of another time as many of its 29 churches date from the previous centuries. Other buildings, constructed in the 1940s during the "Plan Serena," only look as if they are from the Colonial era. The beach, on the other hand, is a completely modern resort area with cabañas, hotels, bars, and restaurants lining the six km boardwalk.

A short distance from La Serena, the Elqui river valley is especially suited for the production of *pisco*, the national liquor of Chile. The green valley was also the birthplace of Gabriela Mistral, one of Chile's two Noble Prize-winning poets, and there are many reminders of her time in the area. Lastly, the clear skies over this part of the country are some of the best in the world for gazing into galaxies. You can visit a number of important observatories that sit on the tops of area hills.

La Serena undergoes complete transformation in the summer and on holidays. What is normally a laid back town becomes party central. Cars and people jam the road along the sea, restaurants are packed, and the nightlife goes on and on. Keep that in mind as your plan your trip.

ARRIVALS & DEPARTURES

By Bus

The La Serena bus station is in the middle of town on the Panamericana Highway just past the Francisco Aguirre traffic circle. Buses go both north and south on the Panamericana as well as to Valparaiso and the Elqui Valley.

Bus Companies
• **Fenix, Pullman Norte, Inca, Tramaca,** *Balmaceda 594, Tel. 226148*; north to Copiapó, Iquique, Arica
• **Los Corsarios,** *Panamericana and Aguirre, Tel. 225157*; south to Santiago
• **Pullman,** *O'Higgins 663, Tel. 225284*; south to Santiago, Viña del Mar, Valparaiso
• **Tramaca,** *Aguirre 375, Tel. 226071*; south to Santiago

All buses to the Elqui valley leave from the *Plaza de Abastos between Pení and Colo-Colo streets*. From here buses leave on the hour for Vicuña and three times a day to Pisco Elqui. *Colectivo* taxis also cover the route.

By Car

La Serena is about a six hour drive from Santiago or a five hour drive from Copiapó on the Panamericana.

Rental Companies
• **Avis,** *Aguirre 068. Tel. 227171*
• **Budget,** *Freire 466. Tel. 216030*
• **La Serena Rent a Car,** *Balmaceda 2884. Tel. 226333*
• **Florida Rent,** *Colo Colo 4450. Tel. 217029*

By Plane
   Lan, *Eduardo de la Barra 435A, Tel. 225981*; **Ladeco**, *Cordovez 484, Tel. 225753*; and **Avant**, *Tel. 219275* all fly out of the small La Serena airport. Maybe it's just bad luck, but every time we have flown out of La Serena our plane has been delayed by over an hour, making us wish we had just driven the six hours to Santiago.

ORIENTATION
   La Serena, on the coast, sits at the mouth of the fertile Elqui river valley. The older part of town, with museums and important buildings, is situated around the town plaza. Most of the tourist infrastructure however, runs along Avenida del Mar/Costanera de Coquimbo in front of the long, flat beach. These two areas are connected by the tree and statue-lined Francisco Aguirre Avenue.

GETTING AROUND TOWN
   Taxis regularly troll Avenida del Mar, which can be helpful getting from one end of the six km boardwalk to the other. Around town, there are always taxis on the plaza as well as along Francisco Aguirre.

LA SERENA

WHERE TO STAY

Chileans will tell you that if you go to La Serena you must stay in a cabaña or apart-hotel along the beach. We are inclined to agree. There are some nice hotels around downtown, but why stay near the traffic and noise when you can be in front of the ocean? You should only stay in town if you are looking for a hotel in the inexpensive category.

The prices listed below are high season rates; off-season rates are almost half of the listed price, especially if you bargain a little.

ON THE BEACH
Expensive

JARDIN DEL MAR, *Costanera 5425. Tel. 51/242835. Fax 51/242991. 17 cabañas. 24 apartments. Double $140. Cable TV. Restaurant. Bar. Pool. Sauna. Squash court. Game room. Baby sitters. Ceramics studio. Car rental. Credit cards accepted.*

Located on the most popular stretch of the Costanera, these white stucco, thatched roofed cabañas are the best of the bunch. On a large, grassy property punctuated with palm trees, the Jardín del Mar offers top quality lodgings and more.

The cabins are spacious and comfortable, with fully appointed kitchens, newly remodeled bathrooms, large living areas, and two or three bedrooms. Details like double refrigerators (one for the beer), a small patio with lounge chairs and a table, covered parking, and a barbecue grill on request give it that extra edge.

The large pool in the middle of the compound is a popular gathering area. There are swing sets for the kids, as well as Ping-Pong, foosball, and billiards for the kid in all of us. The glass-walled Spanish restaurant, with an excellent view of the ocean, offers some of the best *calamari* in town.

LA SERENA CLUB RESORT HOTEL, *Avenida del Mar 1000. Tel. 51/221262. Fax 51/217130. 96 rooms. Double $160. Cable TV. Restaurant. Bar. Pool. Tennis court. Business center. Credit cards accepted.*

This seven story resort complex merits attention for its well-landscaped pool and attached bar. It's easy to imagine yourself enjoying umbrella drinks by the cool, boulder-surrounded water while pondering the palm tree growing out of its middle. The rooms are well decorated with large patios and the restaurant is excellent. Its drawback, however, is its size. With almost 100 rooms, it can get very crowded in the summer.

Moderate

APART-HOTEL LA FUENTE, *Avenida del Mar 5665. Tel. 51/245755. Fax 51/241259. 10 apartments. Double $93. Cable TV. Credit cards accepted.*

This small complex has modern apartments for two to six people. Kitchens open out to comfortable, light, living areas that are attached to one, two, or three bedrooms. You don't have a lot of bells and whistles on the grounds, but the location is excellent, as is the value.

CANTO DEL AGUA APART-HOTEL, *Del Mar 2200. Tel. 216630. 25 apartments. Double apartment $80. Breakfast buffet included. Restaurant. Pool. Credit cards accepted.*

This mid-range apart-hotel offers you the opportunity to spread out a bit. Considering the space and location, it is one of the better deals on the beach strip. An ample buffet breakfast is included with price of the room. There are a number of beach side restaurants and pubs nearby.

Other good options for apartments and cabañas are **Camino del Sol**, *Avenida del Mar 1500, Tel./Fax 51/215681*; **Apart-Hotel Mar Serena**, *Avenida del Mar 4900, Tel. 51/241855*; and **Campo Marino**, *Avenida del Mar 2900, Tel. 51/222223.*

IN TOWN
Expensive
HOTEL FRANCISCO DEL AGUIRRE, *Cordovez 210. Tel./Fax 51/222991. 60 rooms. Double $100. Restaurant. Bar. Pool. Credit cards accepted.*

If you're absolutely averse to staying at the beach, this is the nicest hotel in town. It's not the newest, but it is the classic, large downtown hotel. The rooms furnishings are not brand new, but they are up to par.

Moderate
HOSTERÍA LA SERENA, *Francisco de Aguirre 0660. Tel./Fax 51/225745. 85 rooms. Double $90. Breakfast included. Cable TV. Restaurant. Pool. Gym. Sauna. Tennis courts. Credit cards accepted.*

The Hostería La Serena is a good compromise for those who want to be on the beach, yet within walking distance of town. The hotel is located next to La Serena's most familiar landmark, the red light house at the beginning of the beach. The hotel is new so all of the rooms and furnishings are in top condition. The Olympic size swimming pool is the favorite lounging area.

Inexpensive
HOSTAL DE TURISMO CROATA, *Cienfuegos 248. Tel. 51/224997. 15 rooms. Double $25. Breakfast included. Cable TV. Credit cards accepted.*

The Croata is a popular place and good value for low-end accommodations. An open stairway and hall overlook a nice courtyard lined with plants.

HOTEL PACIFICO, *Eduardo de la Barra 252. Tel. 51/225674. 25 rooms. Double $20. No credit cards.*

This rambling old house turned hotel is another good low-end value. Tall ceilings and big rooms are the norm here, even if they are a bit dark.

The location, a block and a half off the plaza, is central for exploring downtown.

RESIDENCIAL SUIZA, *Cienfuegos 250. Tel. 216092. 10 rooms. Double $25. Breakfast included. Credit cards accepted.*

The spotless rooms of the Residencial Suiza are located within an attractive, multi-colored courtyard.

RESIDENCIAL CHILE, *Matta 561. Tel. 51/211694. 10 rooms. Double with shared bath $22. No credit cards.*

This clean, flower-laden option is just a half block from the plaza. Honeysuckle sweetens the air on the pleasant back patio, off of which you'll find the best rooms. Olga, the owner, does a good job making your stay enjoyable. If she is full, you can try the **Residencial Lido**, next door, which is no where near as clean, but will do in a pinch.

WHERE TO EAT

EL CEDRO, *Prat 572. Tel. 219501. Moderate/expensive. Credit cards accepted.*

Arab food may not be something that you think about in La Serena, but this pleasant downtown restaurant is worth a visit. The sampler platter, with fat stuffed peppers and grape leaves is almost enough for dinner for two, especially if accompanied with one of the delicious side dishes. We think the eggplant is especially tasty. They also offer an international menu.

ANDALUCIA, *Costanera 5425. Tel. 242835. Moderate. Credit cards accepted.*

There's not a bad seat in the house, as the entire ocean-side restaurant is walled in glass. Spanish cuisine is the specialty here, and you won't find it better anywhere else in town.

EL CLUB, *Avenida del Mar 1000. Tel. 221262. Moderate. Credit cards accepted.*

This hotel is always packed in the summer, as is its popular restaurant. Although they offer an international menu, most people are here for the seafood. Try the sea bass cooked in chiles and garlic covered with a rich shellfish sauce.

ZAPOTECO, *Los Pescadores 63. Tel. 243611. Moderate. Credit cards accepted.*

Although there's a big sombrero on the sign outside, the food here is more a fusion of Chilean and Mexican. This restaurant, with its cheery Santa Fe-style décor, doesn't really get going until about 10pm. The *fajitas* are remarkably tender and will get you through a Mexican craving, especially if you cover them in some of their delicious homemade salsas. **El Atajo Pub**, on Avenida del Mar offers a similar menu in a bit rowdier environment.

LA MIA PIZZA, *Avenida del Mar 2100. Tel. 212232. Moderate. Credit cards accepted.*

La Mia Pizza is not your typical pizza joint. More of an Italian restaurant specializing in pizza, the décor and ambiance are a step above what you'd expect. The pizza is delicious as well.

CAFÉ DEL PATIO, *Prat 470. Inexpensive. No credit cards.*

For a laid-back meal in town we recommend the Café del Patio. Its inviting, plant shrouded courtyard is a good place to rest your weary dogs. Sandwiches and coffees are standard during the day. On weekend nights the café turns into a jumping jazz joint.

BRAVISSIMO, *Balmaceda 545. Inexpensive. No credit cards.*

Ice cream is very popular in La Serena, and we think this is the best option. We love the combo of a scoop of *manjar* and a scoop of bitter chocolate.

For more inexpensive seafood you can head in town to the market, **La Recova**, *Cantournet and Cienfuegos*, where there are a plethora of good, cheap options.

There are about twenty inexpensive, informal restaurants and bars lining the beach side of Avenida del Mar. Some are better than others. **Crepes La Brisa** is a good one offering almost every kind of crepe you can imagine. Just down from there, **La Tabla** is the most popular spot for a quick bite. It is nothing fancy, but the outdoor seating is a prime place to see and be seen. Further south, **El Muelle** is one of the sites where they film the popular nighttime soap opera "Borrón y Cuenta Nueva." Young people crowd the bar both on the show and in real life. At the end of the boardwalk you'll find **La Pica del Lupa**, the best of the *picadas*, informal seafood restaurants. Many of the people who work here eventually leave to start up their own places, but the original is still the best.

SEEING THE SIGHTS

The flower and tree-covered town **plaza** is a natural place to start a tour of the city. There are several important buildings overlooking its streets, such as the eye-catching, red and white **municipal building**. The **cathedral**, dating from the mid-1800s, is worth a walk-through for the surprisingly subtly painted ceiling and the excellent Virgin de Guadalupe.

On the opposite site of the square you'll find the town museum:

GABRIEL GONZALES VIDELA HISTORIC MUSEUM, *Matta 495 on the plaza. Tel. 215082. Tuesday-Saturday 9am-1pm, 4pm-7pm. Sunday 9am-1pm. Entry $1.25. No admission fee on Sunday.*

Gabriel Gonzales, a La Serena favorite son, was president of Chile from 1946-1952. He lived in this house on the plaza, which is now a museum with displays about his life. During his presidency Chile undertook various large public works, claimed a slice of Antarctica, and gave

LA SERENA'S LUCK

Although many of La Serena's buildings look as if they date from Colonial times, many of them were built in the 1940's. A string of bad luck did away with many of the most important structures from earlier times.

La Serena was founded in 1543 only to be destroyed by Indians in 1549. In 1578, the town was attacked by Sir Francis Drake. Things went by more or less smoothly until 1680, when it was plundered by Bartholomew Sharp, another English pirate. This seems to have inspired pirate Edward Davis, who repeated the favor in 1686. Any repairs were later undone by an earthquake in 1730 that leveled much of the town.

women the vote, all of which are highlighted in the museum. Another part of the museum is an art gallery showcasing various Chilean artists. It's worth a visit if you are near the plaza.

JAPANESE GARDENS, *Pedro Pablo Muñoz. Daily 10am-6pm. Entry $1.25.*

These tranquil gardens, below the plaza, were designed by Japanese specialists to commemorate the city's 450th year. They are a nice escape, especially during the chaotic summer season. Bonsai trees, goldfish ponds, and calm pools line the curving paths. One of the oldest churches in the area **Iglesia De San Francisco** is on the corner of *Eduardo de la Barra and Balmaceda*. Built over the years from 1585 to 1627, the church and the small **Religious Art Museum** inside are in the process of being restored.

MUSEO ARQUEOLÓGICO. *Casilla 617. Tel. 224492. Tuesday-Friday 9am-1:30pm, 4pm-7pm. Saturday 10am-1pm, 4pm-7pm. Sunday 10am-1pm. Closed Mondays. Entry $1.*

This small archaeological museum displays regional artifacts such as a seal skin canoe, good samples of Diaguita tools and pottery, and the requisite mummies. The most interesting piece is a skull from an extinct American horse that once roamed the area. There is also good Easter Island exhibit that includes one of the big Moai statues.

IGNACIO DOMEYKO MINERALOGICAL MUSEUM, *Muñoz 870. Weekdays only 9am-12pm. Entry $2.*

Chile is a country with a plethora of minerals, and you can see around 2,000 samples of them in this small museum. It's worth a walk through even if you're not a rock hound.

On your way back to the beach, take the time to walk down **Francisco de Aguirre Avenue**. With its large, green trees and multiple statues, it is one of the trademarks of the city.

NIGHTLIFE & ENTERTAINMENT

After the pubs on Avenida del Mar slow down, everybody heads to the discos on Avenida Cuatro Esquinas. This street connects the Panamericana to Avenida del Mar and has a rotating line-up of hopping night spots.

SPORTS & RECREATION

All sporting activity takes place on the beach and along its boardwalk. Joggers, in-line skaters, and power walkers own the sidewalk, while beach soccer and paddle ball are the sports of the sand.

SHOPPING

The central market, called **La Recova**, *Cantournet and Cienfuegos*, is an excellent spot for buying *artisanía* or just people watching. The homemade candy and white *manjar* are La Serena specialties.

If you didn't make it to the Elqui valley, you can buy pisco at the showrooms of the **Pisco Control Pisquero de Elqui**, *Rengifo 240*.

EXCURSIONS & DAY TRIPS

Elqui Valley

It's worth going to La Serena simply to visit the **Elqui river valley**. The scenery alone, hectares of fertile orchards banked up against purple and blue mountains, justifies the drive. You can also mosey through charming country towns, visit internationally famous observatories, tour and taste area pisco plants, and learn loads about favorite daughter Gabriela Mistral.

From La Serena you head due east up the valley towards Vicuña. After passing through a number of typical country towns you arrive to the turn off for the **Cerro Tololo Observatory**. The observatory, 36 km up the road, runs tours on Saturdays from 9am-12pm and 1pm-4pm. On the tour you walk through the grounds, see the large telescopes, and learn about the work taking place at the observatory. The telescopes are some of the largest in the world and scientists wait years for a chance to use the facilities for one or two nights. The scenery on the drive up is outstanding, but the tour itself is a bit dry. Call *Tel. 51/225415* to make reservations.

If you continue up the highway you'll come to **Vicuña**, famous for its **Gabriela Mistral Museum**. The plaza is a good place to begin a tour of the town. Both its parochial church and strange German castle/tower date from the turn of the century. Across the plaza from the church you can study bugs at the **Entomological Museum**, *Monday-Friday 10:30am-1:30pm, 3:30pm-7:00pm; Weekends 10:30am-7:00pm, entry $0.75*. Head east from the plaza down Gabriela Mistral street to visit the town's most famous museum.

GABRIELA MISTRAL MUSEUM, *East end of Gabriela Mistral street. Tuesday-Friday 10am-1pm, 2pm-6pm. Saturday 10am-1pm, 3pm-6pm. Sunday 10am-1pm. Open Monday in summer. Entry $1.25. No admission fee on Wednesday.*

This simple museum, with the Noble Prize winning poet's letters and personal effects, helps you realize what an ascetic life Mistral led as compared to Chile's other famous poet. Mistral, born Lucila Godoy Alcayaga, was a shy woman who channeled her energies into education. Her love of and efforts to help the country's children have endeared her to all Chileans.

Throughout your drive you will have seen signs of the huge *pisco* business in the valley. The Muscatel grapes from Elqui are used to make the brandy Chileans so adore. Outside of Vicuña, the **Pisco Capel** plant gives free tours every day from *10am-1pm*, but are closed on Monday. On weekdays they also give afternoon tours from *2:30pm-6:00pm*. Not only do you get to walk through the entire distillation process, but you also get to taste free samples at the end.

From Vicuña you continue on the paved road towards Mistral's birthplace **Monte Grande**, where you can visit her tomb on the outskirts of town. There is also a small museum in what was her first school.

PISCO 101

Pisco, the national treasure, is made from fermented grapes. You'll see on your tour that the fermentation process takes place in large steel containers. The liquid is then removed through distillation. Water is added to dilute the alcohol to the proper proof and then the mixture is aged in oak barrels.

The Capel plant is the largest producer of pisco in the country. If you buy a souvenir, pay attention to the proof indication on the bottle, as pisco can range from the manageable 35% alcohol to the staggering (i.e., you'll be staggering) 50%.

Pisco Elqui is the town at the end of the paved road. The town's name, originally Unión, was changed in 1939 to block a Peruvian effort to internationally register the "pisco" trademark. The town now houses **Solar de Pisco Elqui**, makers of RRR, one of the higher end *piscos* on the market. Tours here are interesting, but most importantly, end with a free *pisco* tasting.

Buses from La Serena cover the 104 km route to Pisco Elqui, but we suggest renting a car or hiring a cab to have the freedom to stop and go as you wish. There is no public transportation to the Tololo Observatory.

FRAY JORGE NATIONAL PARK, *Two hours southwest of La Serena. December-March: Thursday-Sunday 8am-4:30pm, April-November: Weekends only 8am-4:30pm. Entry 50¢.*

It's difficult to believe, but there is a Valdivian rain forest here in this semi-arid land. Roughly 120 km southwest of La Serena, Fray Jorge showcases a fascinating rain and fog-fed woodland. As you drive through the desert you won't believe that this park exists. After turning off the Panamericana you climb a curvy, dusty dirt road 20 km towards the sea. The land, filled with cactus and rocks, is basically hard scrabble until you come around a corner and see the one cloud in the sky perched on the highest hill in the park. You climb up into the cloud and the environment changes drastically. Dense forest and dripping ferns replace the cactus. A one kilometer hiking trail takes you through this wet, green anomaly.

There is another trail in the park that goes down to the ocean, but the rangers prefer that only organized groups make the hike. Conaf can provide a guide for either horseback or hiking trips to the shelter by the sea. Call Conaf in La Serena, *Tel. 225686,* to arrange a trip.

PRACTICAL INFORMATION

Banks: Banco de Chile, *Balmaceda 481;* **Banco del Estado de Chile,** *Balmaceda 506;* **Banco O'Higgins,** *Balmaceda 458*

Business Hours: Monday-Friday 9:30am-1:30pm, 4:30pm-9:00pm. Saturday 10am-2:00pm

Currency Exchange: Giratour, *Prat 689;* **Cambios Fides,** *Balmaceda 460;* **Intercam Turismo,** *Eduardo de la Barra 435*

Laundry: Lavarap, *Aguirre 447*

Medical Service: Hospital Juan de Dios, *Balmaceda 916*

National Parks: Conaf, *Cordovez 281. Tel. 225686*

Post Office: Correos de Chile, *Prat and Matta on the plaza*

Supermarkets: Las Brisas, *Corner of Cienfuegos and Cordovez*

Telephone/Fax: La Serena's area code is 51. **CTC,** *Cordovez 446;* **Entel,** *Prat 571*

Tourist Office/Maps: Sernatur, *Prat and Matta on the plaza. Tel. 882285*

14. THE LAKE DISTRICT

The **Lake District** could have just as easily been named the Volcano District, as it is home to a majority of Chile's majestic, snow-capped volcanoes. The cones are so abundant that it is not unusual to turn your head on a sunny day to see four of five distinctly shaped volcanoes posing beyond the quilted pastureland. The fertile valley that parallels the *cordillera* is reticulated by hundreds of rivers, flowing directly from the range or from the magnificent lakes for which the region is named.

Although the area was once the heart of the indigenous Mapuche nation, which held onto the territory until 1880, that culture has by and large been assimilated into the Northern European influenced, Chilean society. The *huaso* culture remains strong, however. It is common to encounter a pancho-clad horseman heckling a pair of oxen, begrudgingly yoked with a rough beam of timber. Travel adventure seekers form the burgeoning new clique as they flock to the region eager to hike, climb, horseback ride, ski, raft, kayak, and fish to their hearts' desires.

The most sought-out destinations are the Villarrica and Llanquihue lakes due to the variety of natural attractions that surround them. **Lago Villarrica**, at the base of the perfectly shaped volcano of the same name, is located toward the north end of the district, and is best explored from the outdoor adventure epicenter of **Pucón**. The closest airport is in the larger city of **Temuco**. Similarly, at the southern end of the Lake District the best base from which to access the environs of **Lago Llanquihue** and its flawless cone, **Volcán Osorno**, is the town of **Puerto Varas**. The nearby airport is associated with the larger city and seaport, **Puerto Montt**.

A highly recommended outing is to pick one of the less frequented, intimately beautiful lakes, and spend the day driving around it to make your own discoveries of unexpected waterfalls and crystal clear streams. Several of the lakes remain almost completely undeveloped including some of the **Siete Lagos**, south of Villarrica, as well as **Lago Rupanco**, and the east side of the expansive **Lago Ranco**. If you choose to stay at one of the less well-known lakes during the off-season, it will feel like you have the lake all to yourself.

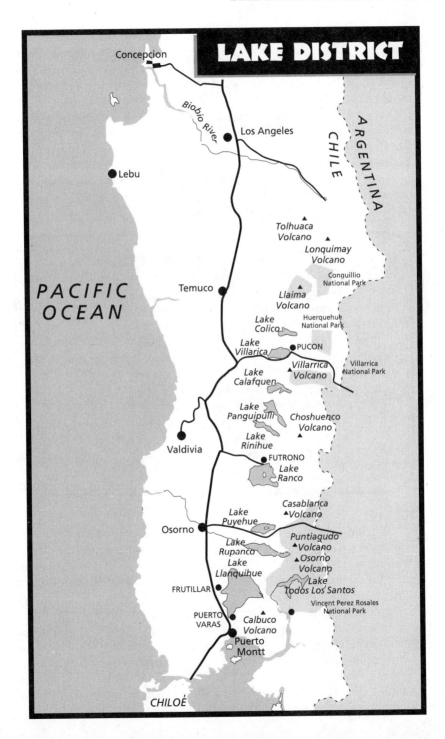

The Lake District is home to magnificent, verdant national parks. Several of these, such as the extraordinary **Conguillío National Park**, northeast of Temuco, and the enchanting **Huerquehue National Park** near Pucón, serve the additional role of protecting the umbrella-shaped monkey puzzle tree, known as the *araucaria*. Hiking in a forest of this peculiar species is an unforgettable experience. **Puyehue National Park** is famous for its thermal baths and comfortable lodging. **Vicente Pérez Rosales**, near Puerto Varas, contains the emerald green waters of Lago Todos Los Santos which visitors ferry across to the Argentine border.

In addition to the Andean destinations, there are two attractive river cities near the coast which are noted for their universities, forts, and German influence - **Concepción** and **Valdivia**.

A FEW DAYS IN THE LAKE DISTRICT

If you have only a few days scheduled for the Lake District, you should decide between exploring the areas around Pucón or Puerto Varas. Both towns have excellent infrastructure to make you comfortable and to facilitate activities in the surrounding natural beauty.

***Pucón** is close to the two best national parks in the Lake District – Conguillío and Huerquehue – both of which are endowed with remarkable araucaria forests. The town is smaller and more remote than Puerto Varas and is close to the less developed area of Siete Lagos.*

*To explore the **Puerto Varas** area, you can either base in that town, in Frutillar, in the cabins near Ensenada, or in the Vicente Pérez Rosales Park's lodge. The panoramic scenery is more expansive than in Pucón and there are good national parks nearby. A big bonus is that you can get to Chiloé in two hours.*

History

When the Spanish began to explore the area south of Santiago, they encountered fierce resistance from the native inhabitants who they called **Araucanos**. The 500,000 natives, who referred to themselves as **Mapuches**, were a semi-nomadic people who sustained themselves through fishing, agriculture, and the collection of the araucaria pine nut. They did not gather in large communities but rather lived in clans of extended families.

In an attempt to capture more slaves and to establish a foothold in Mapuche territory, **Pedro de Valdivia** founded the settlement of Concepción on the northern bank of the **Biobío River** in 1550. Four years later the Mapuches besieged the city, at the same time capturing and killing Valdivia. In the ensuing years the Spanish reclaimed the city and commenced seven new settlements to the south. The Mapuche added

Spanish-introduced horses to their army and became skilled riders. In 1598, the Mapuche warriors began an offensive that routed the recently built seven cities. The Spanish would never succeed in bringing the Araucanian territory under control during their three hundred years of rule in Chile, and for most of that time were forced to respect the frontier line of the Biobío River.

A few decades after Chilean independence, the new government turned its energies to adding the Araucanian territory to the nation. Government troops began to make headway toward the interior from fortifications in Concepción, Valdivia, and Puerto Montt. The objective took on added importance in 1860 when a Frenchman, Orelie-Antoine I, made the fantastic claim to be the King of Araucania and Patagonia. The government immediately launched a military offensive that squeezed the territory from three sides, subduing the majority of Mapuches and driving the rest over the Andes into the Argentine pampas. The annexation of Araucania was complete with the capture of Temuco in 1881, and Villarrica in 1882, by forces led by **General Urrutia**.

As soon as the territory had been absorbed, the government initiated land incentive programs to attract European immigrants. Four thousand immigrants arrived in the 1880's, mostly from Switzerland and Germany, stimulating agricultural and industrial growth that made the Lake District among the most prosperous areas of the country.

Forestry, fishing, aquaculture (particularly farm-raised salmon), and agriculture, led by dairy and export-quality berries, are the primary economic forces today.

MAPUCHE HEROES

The Mapuche warriors achieved military triumphs over the Spaniards through the leadership of three great chiefs whose glory is remembered via street signs, statues, names of the newborn, and the jerseys of a professional soccer team.

*The Mapuche chief **Lautaro** was captured by Pedro de Valdivia's forces in 1551, and forced to work for the Spanish army. For three years he maintained communication with his people awaiting the appropriate moment for ambush and revenge. That moment came in the historic Battle of Tucapel, when two other renowned chiefs, **Colo Colo** and **Caupolicán** laid siege to Valdivia's fort. Valdivia was one of two survivors. Although the great chiefs were in favor of sparing the conquistador's life, another warrior killed him with a blow to the neck. All three of the chiefs beleaguered the Spaniards for many years to come by constantly attacking their fortifications and settlements.*

CONCEPCIÓN

Concepción, Chile's second largest metropolitan area with 320,000 inhabitants, is fifteen times smaller than the front runner, Santiago. The city serves as the Biobío Region's capital, as well as a commercial center for the area's timber, fishing, and mining industries and as the home of the **Universidad de Concepción** campus. Although it isn't Chile's most renowned visitor's destination, the city is pleasant enough, boasts a lively university atmosphere, two excellent small museums, and an extraordinary number of coffee shops.

Concepción was one of Chile's original seven cities of the south, from which the settlers were expelled by Mapuche warriors in 1600. The city was the only one to be immediately reestablished and would serve as the southern frontier outpost during its early history.

In Concepción's main plaza, General Bernardo O'Higgin's declared Chile's independence to the Southern Army on January 1, 1818.

ARRIVALS & DEPARTURES

By Bus

There are several bus stations, each of which handles separate destinations. The two long distance bus stations, unfortunately, are not that centrally located.

• **Terminal Collao**, *Tegualda 860, Tel. 316666*
• **Terminal Chillancito**, *Camilo Enríquez 2565, Tel. 473405*

If you prefer to buy your ticket in advance nearby, instead of going to one of the bus stations, we suggest trying the company with the most frequent departures, **Tur-Bus**, *Tucapel 530, Tel. 315555*.

The terminals which handle departures to local destinations are:

• **Terminal Costa Azul**, *Las Heras 530. Tel. 237562.* To Tome, Dichato, Cobquercura
• **Terminal J. Ewert**, *Arturo Pratt 535, Tel. 229212.* To Lebu, Cañete, Contulmo

By Car

There is a new toll road about ten km south of Chillan that links Concepción to the Pan-American Highway. The four lane highway is 82 km long with beautiful, rolling hills covered with dairy farms and forest. A more spectacular way in or out, which makes the most sense to or from the south, is along the Ruta de Madera, a forested, winding road which hugs the southern bank of the Biobío.

In town, you should take care to note that almost all of the streets are one way.

Car Rentals
• **Fama's Rentacar**, *O'Higgins 1154. Tel. 41/248300*
• **Flota Versache Rentacar**, *Las Golondrinas 1556. Tel. 41/410594*
• **Localiza Rentacar**, *Tel. 41/482705*

By Plane
Lan Chile, Ladeco, and Avant all fly to Concepción. The airport is about five kilometers from town on the way to Talcahuano. A shared micro-bus will cost you about $4 to town, while a taxi costs about $8.

Airlines
• **Avant**, *O'Higgins 734, Locale 19. Tel. 252732*
• **Lan Chile**, *Barros Arana 451. Tel. 229138, Toll free 600-600-4000*
• **Ladeco**, *O'Higgins 533. Tel. 248824, Toll free 600-600-4000*

ORIENTATION

Although Concepción is on the riverbank of the Biobío, you won't see the river in your normal wanderings since it is separated from the city center by railway tracks and an industrial area. You will see it and cross its expansive mouth if you head south to the beaches. The central plaza is crossed by two pedestrian walkways that run for several blocks - Barros Arana and Aníbal Pinto. The main natural orientation point is the woodsy hill, Cerro Caraol, which is the southeastern border of the city. At its base is the **Parque Ecuador**, with the **Galería de Historia** at the south end, and the **university** at the north end.

GETTING AROUND TOWN

All of the main points of interest in town are within walking distance. There is a taxi stand on the main square, across the street from the university, and in front of the museum. Many of the taxis in town are *colectivos*, which means they have routes like buses, and charge $200 pesos to anyone who jumps in on their route.

WHERE TO STAY

Expensive
HOTEL ALBORADA, *Barros Arana 457. Tel./Fax 41/242144. 70 rooms. Double $120. Buffet breakfast included. Cable TV. Bar. Business center with internet access. Meeting and conference rooms. Credit cards accepted.*
The Hotel Alborada, part of the Best Western chain, is the premiere hotel in Concepción. From the reception desk, you walk through a greenhouse hallway, ceilinged with glass, and overflowing with greenery. At the end of this hall is a dining area where the breakfast buffet is served,

which includes a variety of delicious fresh juices. The standard double rooms are among the biggest we have encountered in Chile, all outfitted with king-size beds. The bathrooms are impressively expansive as well. All rooms are subtly decorated and feature excellent working space, including a separate phone jack for modem connection. The rates drop to $90 for a double in the off-season, which makes this an upscale bargain.

HOTEL EL ARAUCANO, *Caupolicán 521. Tel. 41/230606. Fax 41/230690. hotel.araucano@chilnet.cl. 120 rooms. Double $92. Breakfast included. Restaurant. Bar. Pool. Sauna. Massage. Business center. Car rental. Credit cards accepted.*

Once the premiere hotel in town, the El Araucano has now slipped a notch below the Alborada. Located right on the plaza, it remains a solid option. The rooms on the upper floors have excellent views of the city and environs, especially those facing the Biobío. The comfortable quarters are generally what you would expect for a hotel of this caliber.

Moderate

HOTEL DELLA CRUZ, *Aníbal Pinto 240. Tel./Fax 41/240016. 12 rooms. Double $55. Breakfast included. Cable TV. Credit cards accepted.*

The Hotel Della Cruz is located in a classic, gray stucco building and offers small, cheery functional rooms. There is a quaint sitting area on each floor if you need some lounging space. For a quick, affordable stay, this hotel will get the job done.

HOTEL ALONSO DE ERCILLA, *Colo Colo 334. Tel. 41/227984, Fax 41/230053. 70 rooms. Double $75. Breakfast included. Cable TV. Bar. Restaurant. Credit cards accepted.*

The Hotel Alonso de Ercilla is the classic choice among Concepción's mid-range hotels. The rooms are average-sized with comfortable furniture. The hotel is popular with regional businessmen and is frequently full so it is a good idea to call ahead for reservations.

HOTEL EL DORADO, *Barros Arana 348. Tel. 41/229400. Fax 41/231018. 100 rooms. Double $82. Breakfast included. Cable TV. Credit cards accepted.*

The marble-floored lobby and glass elevator give a good first impression here, as do the friendly reception staff. The rooms, however, are on the small side with extremely narrow bathrooms. This is a decent choice in the price range, but not an exceptionally good value.

Inexpensive

For cheap digs, two good *residenciales* are **Residencial Domingo**, *Freire 243, Tel. 812553, $17 per person, breakfast included* and the **Residential O'Higgins**, *O'Higgins 457, Tel. 41/228303, Double with bath $25, breakfast included.*

WHERE TO EAT

LE CHATEAU, *Colo Colo 340. Tel. 229977. Expensive. Credit cards accepted.*

Next door to the venerable Alonso de Ercilla Hotel, this French restaurant is sought out for its savory steaks. There is also a good selection of fowl with such entrees as pheasant stuffed with olive or orange sauce. The sophisticated ambience is highlighted by crimson table cloths set against advocado colored walls.

EL RANCHO DE JULIO, *Barros Arana 337. Tel. 228207. Expensive. Credit cards accepted.*

This Argentine restaurant is renowned as a carnivore's paradise. As Argentine tradition dictates, we suggest starting with a baked wheel of *provaleta* cheese before cutting into the *bife de lomo*. As any *che* will tell you, this should be washed down with a bottle of red wine and followed up with a stiff shot of espresso.

CASINO ALEMÁN, *West end of Plaza Ecuador. Tel. 238569. Moderate. Credit cards accepted.*

This German chalet-style firehouse, located at the end of the Plaza Ecuador Park, is the most upscale of the firehouse dining rooms we've encountered. As usual, the main attraction is the economical fixed item lunch, but the restaurant includes an extensive menu of international fish and meat plates. If you haven't eaten in a fire station while in Chile, definitely give this one a try. You can combine it with a visit to the unique Galería de Historia next door.

PIAZZA, *Barros Arana 631. Tel. 240229. Moderate. Credit cards accepted.*

This Italian bistro specializes in pizza and pastas. Dark and intimate, with small round tables, it's a good place to spend a quiet evening, (as long as the TV on the bar is not blaring). The plaza location, on the second floor, is prime for watching the goings-on below.

L'ANGELO, *Rengo 494. Tel. 244061. Moderate. Credit cards accepted.*

You might as well be in Buenos Aires in this café. The small tables, crowded with gossiping friends, are reminiscent of Argentina. The nondescript choices of sandwiches, ice cream, and beers pull the people in at lunch and after work. Students seem to hang around all day. People in Concepción like to lounge and talk and this is one of their favorite places to do that.

HUPU'S, *Lincoyán 465. Moderate. No credit cards.*

Touting itself as a bar, café, and pub, this place is trying to cover all the bases. It pretty much does that with a menu of sandwiches, beers, and coffee drinks. The pleasant, well lit interior is a change from some of the other dark, smoky cafes.

FUENTE ALEMANA, *O'Higgins and Rengo. Inexpensive. No credit cards.*

There are no tables in this popular coffee shop. Instead, patrons prop themselves on stools that wrap around the walls of the restaurant as well as along the long bar. A sandwich and a shot of double expreso will fuel you for an afternoon of sightseeing.

CAFETERIA GERMANÍA, *Barros Arana 368. Inexpensive. No credit cards.*

A combination bread store and café, this is a great choice for a quick sandwich. The bread is always fresh and its scent fills the restaurant.

Among fast food options, there is a **McDonalds**, *corner of Barros Arana and Rengo*, and **Pipón**, *Barros Arana 890*, a popular roasted chicken joint.

SEEING THE SIGHTS

GALERÍA DE HISTORIA, *Corner of Lincoyán and Lamas in Parque Ecuador. Tel. 236555. Monday 3pm-6:30pm; Tuesday-Friday, 10am-1pm and 3pm-6pm; Saturday and Sunday 10am-2pm and 3pm-7pm. No admission fee.*

The delightful History Gallery features dioramas with miniature wood carvings by Rodolfo Gutiérrez. The artist, who signs his name backwards, is the same whimsical creator of the exhibit on Santiago history in that city's Casa Rosada museum. This exhibit on Concepción's history is no less enjoyably portrayed by hundreds of tiny figurines, each with its own distinct outfit and facial expression.

See how many humorous situations you can find transpiring in the University of Concepción model. Start with Mr. Cool wearing a leather jacket, smoking a cigarette, and leaning up against the university building. Look closely and you will see that there is a "wet paint" sign next to him. You can imagine the artist sitting in front of the university observing the passersby for inspiration - easy pickings.

There are also a few good indigenous artifact exhibits. Ask for the plastic placards in English to assist with full explanations of all exhibits.

CASA DEL ARTE, *University of Concepcion, corner of Chacabuco and Larenas. Monday closed. Tuesday-Friday 10am-6pm, Saturday 10am-2pm, Sunday 10am-1pm. No admission fee.*

This museum features one of the country's best collections of Chilean paintings, spanning from colonial to modern times. One wall of the entrance hall is covered with an explosive mural entitled *Presencia de America Latina*, painted by the Mexican muralist Jorge Gonzalez in 1965. The mural alone makes the museum worth a visit. The museum is next to the front gate to the university campus so you can stroll through the grounds during the same visit.

NATURAL HISTORY MUSEUM, *Plaza Acevedo. Entry$1. Tuesday-Saturday 10am-6pm, Sunday 3pm-5:30pm.*

In addition to zoological specimens, this natural history museum features Mapuche artifacts and photographs of the city's resettlement.

NIGHTLIFE & ENTERTAINMENT

There are several good cultural centers and theaters that offer concerts and other performances. Ask your hotels front desk to check the local listings for you.

SHOPPING

Artisan markets include **Feria Artesanal**, *Freire 757*, **Mercado Central**, *Corner of Freire and Caupolicán*, and **Galería Alessandri**, *Aníbal Pinto 450*. You can check out antiques at two locations, **Almacén Antigüedades**, *Maipu 1011* and **Sala Strauss**, *Barros Arana 340*.

EXCURSIONS & DAY TRIPS

The Huáscar Battleship

Talcahuana Naval Base. Entry $1.00. Tuesday-Sunday 9:30am-12:00pm and 1:30pm-6pm. Closed Monday.

The historic naval can be visited in Talcahuano, about 30 minutes east of Concepción. The ship was built in 1865 in England for the Peruvian Navy. The Huáscar sunk the Esmeralda, captained by Arturo Prat, in a historic battle in Iquique in 1879, but was eventually captured by the Chilean Navy.

Other excursions from Concepción include spending the day at one of the area's beaches, the favorite of which is **Dichato**, about 40 kilometers north of the city. Another day trip is traveling 40 kilometers south to the seaside mining town of **Lota**, which is home to the popular **Isidora Cousiño Park**. In one of the park's attractions, you don a hard hat and tour two kilometers of underground tunnel in a mine cart. If you are traveling from Concepción in a car, or just feel like taking a nice drive, we suggest the **Ruta de Madera**, which is a beautiful, wooded road that winds southeast along the Biobío river. To raft the once great Biobío, now tamed considerably by a hydroelectric dam, contact **South Expeditions**, *Guesswein 44, Tel. 44/331084*.

PRACTICAL INFORMATION

Banks: There are several banks with ATM's on the main plaza.
Bookstores: **Libros**, *O'Higgins 680, locale 7. Tel. 239978*
Business Hours: 9am-1pm and 3pm-6pm
Currency Exchange: **Afex**, *Barros Arana 565, Locale 57. Tel. 239618;* **Inter Santiago**, *Barros Arana 565, Locale 58. Tel. 228914;* **Varex**, *Barros Arana 565, Locale 54. Tel. 228334*

E-Mail Service: Cyber Cafe, *Caupolicán 553. Tel. 238394*
Laundry: Santa Barbara, *Barros Arana 565, Locale 52*. **Masterclean**, *Rozas 1620*
Medical Services: Hospital Regional, *Corner of Roosevelt and San Martin. Tel. 237445*
National Parks: Conaf, *Serrano 529, 3rd Floor. Tel. 237272*
Post Office: Correos, *Corner of O'Higgins and Colo Colo*
Supermarkets: Santa Isabel, *Aníbal Pinto 534* and **Unimarc**, *Chacabuco 70*
Telephone/Fax: The area code is 41. Long distance calls centers include **Chilesat**, *O'Higgins 799* and **CTC**, *Caupolicán 649*
Tourist Office/Maps: Sernatur, *Aníbal Pinto 460. Tel. 227976*

TEMUCO

The Temuco of which Pablo Neruda writes adoringly in his autobiography, *Memoirs*, has pretty much disappeared. Of course, he grew up here in the early 1900's, only twenty-odd years after the territory was wrested from the Mapuche natives. Now the traffic hubbub of the narrow, noisy streets is only matched by the humdrum of what to do after visiting the *artesanía* market. The principal attractions of the city are the airport and bus station, which are utilized as transfer points to access the extraordinary national parks to the east, as well as the resort towns of Pucón and Villarrica.

Temuco lasted 280 years under the control of the Mapuches after they forced the Spanish out of the settlement in 1600. In 1882, during a major push by the Chilean government to absorb the Auracanian territory into their own, the army was able to establish a fort in Temuco. Shortly after a train link to Puerto Montt was completed and the city grew rapidly. A forestry and agricultural base propelled the economy and continues to do so today. The current population of Temuco, which is located 670 km south of Santiago, is 210,000.

ARRIVALS & DEPARTURES

By Bus

The regional bus terminal, located at the corner of Balmaceda and Pinto, is best used to access closer destinations such as Pucón, Villarrica, Conguillío National Park, and smaller communities around Temuco. The long distance companies have independent offices downtown. You can use their services for the most popular regional points like Pucón and Villarrica, in addition to the long distance destinations.

Bus Companies

• **Cruz del Sur**, *Mackenna 671. Tel. 210701*

- **JAC**, *Vicuña Mackenna 586. Tel. 213094*
- **Lit**, *San Martin 894. Tel. 211483*
- **Longitudinal Sur**, *Lagos 694. Tel. 213140*
- **Tas Choap**, *Antonio Varas 609. Tel. 212422*
- **Tur Bus**, *General Lagos 576. Tel. 212613*

By Car

There is no missing the turn-off to Temuco because the *Panamericana* runs right through town at which point it is called Caupolicán. The Plaza de Armas is on the east side of the highway. Claro Solar will take you to the plaza. Antonio Varas will take you back out to the highway.

Auto Rentals

- **Avis**, *Mackenna 448. Tel. 237575. Airport Maquehue Tel. 337715*
- **Christopher Car**, *Antonio Varas 522. Tel. 215988*
- **Dollar**, *Airport Maquehue. Tel. 336512*
- **Explorer**, *Lynch 471. Tel. 215997. Airport Maquehue Tel. 335792*
- **First**, *Varar 1036. Tel. 233890. Airport Maquehue Tel. 335793*
- **Hertz**, *Las Heras 999. Tel. 318585. Airport Manquehue Tel. 337019*

By Plane

The airport is just south of Temuco so it is a convenient entry point for either Temuco, about ten minutes away, or the Pucón-Villarrica area, about an hour and a half away. There is no direct bus transport to Pucón-Villarrica from the airport so you would have to go into to Temuco to catch the onward bus. Major airport links to and from Temuco include, Santiago, Concepción, Valdivia, and Puerto Montt.

Airlines that fly here are **Ladeco**, *Arturo Pratt 565 Loc. 102, Tel. 213180, Toll free 600-600-4000, and* **Lan Chile**, *Bulnes 687, Tel. 211339, Toll free 600-600-4000.*

ORIENTATION

The Pan-American highway cuts a diagonal through Temuco with the majority of the town's services being concentrated around the Plaza de Armas, five blocks the southeast of the highway. Temuco is small enough that you can walk to almost everything in town. Everything is sandwiched between the creek-like Cautín River and Ñielol Hill.

Points that are distant enough from the plaza that you might consider taking a taxi to include Cerro Ñielol Park, the Araucano Museum, and the Temuco Mall.

WHERE TO STAY

Expensive

HOLIDAY INN EXPRESS, *Ortega 01800, North Entrance to Temuco. Tel. 45/223300, 800/36666. Fax 45/224100. 40 rooms. Double $95. Breakfast included. Cable TV. Credit cards accepted.*

Perfectly generic and meant to be that way, this hotel offers a comfortable bed in a nice clean room. Located on the highway at the edge of town, this is the choice for those who have already seen Temuco and are just using the hotel as a place to sleep before moving along.

NUEVO HOTEL DE LA FRONTERA, *Manuel Bulnes 726. Tel. 45/ 210718, Fax 45/212638. 80 rooms. Double $110. Breakfast included. Cable TV. Restaurant. Bar. Credit cards accepted.*

Built by the same owners as the old La Frontera hotel across the street, the Nuevo La Frontera is angling to retake the top end market that it lost as its classic hotel deteriorated. The modern building is blase architecturally, but the rooms suitably outfitted to its price. It is centrally located, about a half a block from the Plaza de Armas.

Moderate

HOTEL CONTINENTAL, *Antonio Varas 708. Tel. 45/238973, Fax 45/233830. 40 rooms. Double $50. Restaurant. Bar. Credit cards accepted.*

Although showing signs of wear, the Continental survives as a classic hotel dating back to 1890. This is the place to stay if you have one night in Temuco, and prefer character with a few inconveniences, like luke warm water, over absolute comfort. The expansive first floor is consumed primarily by the hotel's timeless restaurant located in its center and partitioned off by high window-paned walls. If you yearn to rest your head where Chile's elite did, then reserve room number nine to snore where Pablo Neruda snored; room number ten to yawn where Gabriela Mistral yawned; and room number eleven to dream where Salvador Allende dreamed. Hotel lore says these were the Chilean heroes' favorite rooms and they cost no more than the others. You should visit the hotel bar and eat at the restaurant even if you don't stay here.

APART HOTEL TIERRA DEL SUR, *Manuel Bulnes 1196. Tel./Fax 45/232439. 15 rooms/apartments. Double $45. Breakfast included. Cable TV. Café. Bar. Pools. Jacuzzi. Sauna. Credit cards accepted.*

This cornflower blue complex is one of the most comfortable in Temuco. The location is only five blocks from the square, but it feels much further as you sit by the serene pool overlooking a quiet field. The scent of eucalyptus fills the air and you forget about the blasting horns and buses in town. The rooms are cozy and tastefully decorated, as are the two bedroom apartments. The reception building also houses the spa, which includes an indoor pool, saunas, and hot tubs.

HOTEL AITUE, *Antonio Varas 1048. Tel. 45/211917, Fax 45/212608. 25 rooms. Double $75. Breakfast included. Cable TV. Credit cards accepted.*

The Aitue is the among the most comfortable options in the moderate range. It won't win any awards for distinctiveness, but it is quiet and well-maintained.

HOTEL DE LA FRONTERA, *Manuel Bulnes 733. Tel. 45/212638. Rooms 65. Double $50. Cable TV. Credit cards accepted.*

Not to be confused with the new La Frontera across the street, the old La Frontera is being allowed to deteriorate. Try the Continental instead, which is a more interesting hotel for the same price.

Inexpensive

APART-HOTEL LUANCO, *Aldunate 821. Tel. 45/213749, Fax 45/ 214602. 8 apartments. Two-person apartment $40. Breakfast included. Cable TV. Credit cards accepted.*

Although a bit dark and worn, odd-shaped expansiveness makes these apartments a bargain. The kitchens are fully-equipped.

Other inexpensive options include **Hostal Casablanca**, *Manuel Montt 1306, Tel. 45/212740* and the **Hostal Argentina**, *Aldunate 864, Tel. 237841.* Both offer double rooms with breakfast for about $30.

WHERE TO EAT

LA ESTANCIA, *Rudcindo Ortega 2340. Tel. 221385. Expensive. Credit cards accepted.*

This is the place to go if you need a steak. From the cowhide chairs and menu covers, ham hocks hanging from the ceiling, and trophy goat's heads on the walls, you know they take meat seriously here. The grilled steaks and *parrilladas* are delicious, as is the *serrano* ham. You can order fish and chicken as well, but you might get a raised eyebrow from the waiter. Set up like a country home on large, garden-covered grounds, you can join the rest of the clientele relaxing for hours over lunch.

CLUB ESPAÑOL, *Bulnes 483. Tel. 238664. Expensive/Moderate. Credit cards accepted.*

Temuco's Spanish Club is a pleasant one, opening out to an airy interior patio and garden. The food is the basic Chilean seafood and meat selection, but some of it is spiced up with Spanish top notes. Next door, but sharing the same patio, **El Mezón**, is a barbecue restaurant that is also part of the club. After a meal in either restaurant you can waddle down to the public bowling alley in the club's basement.

HOTEL CONTINENTAL, *Antonio Varas 708. Tel. 45/238973. Moderate. Credit cards accepted.*

The classic atmosphere of the Hotel Continental's restaurant is highlighted by high window-paned walls, bronze lamps, and Vienese chairs all within a French interior design dating back to 1890. The specialties of the house include an out-of-this-world cheese soufflé (it requires forty-five minutes to prepare, so go before you're hungry), scallops in Parmesan cheese (*ostiones a la parmesana*), and corn and chicken pie (*pastel de choclo*). This should be the restaurant you hit in Temuco if you eat one meal here.

QUINCHO DE LA EMPANADA, *Varas and Aldunate. Tel. 216307. Moderate-Inexpensive. No credit cards.*

Although they have a full range of Chilean-country cuisine, it's the *empanadas* that steal the show here. You won't be able to order just one of the warm turnovers filled with your choice of beef, seafood, ham, cheese, chicken and peppers, mushrooms and onions, or corn. The décor is welcoming and rustic, with cattle yokes above the bar. The staff is quite friendly here and occasional live music is an extra treat.

DINO'S, *Bulnes 360. Tel. 213660. Moderate. Credit cards accepted.*

This popular restaurant is full through out the day. During meal-times, Temuco's downtown workers frequent both the upstairs restaurant and street level café. In the off hours, the café stays full with coffee drinking friends meeting for a chat, harried salesmen grabbing a quick sandwich, or teenage couples taking their time over an ice cream float. There is nothing fancy here, but that is part of its appeal.

MUNICIPAL MARKET, *Aldunate and Portales. Inexpensive/Moderate. Credit cards accepted.*

As is the case with most cities in Chile, the local market is an excellent place for inexpensive seafood and *empanadas*. What makes Temuco different is how pleasant and clean the restaurants in its market are. **La Caleta**, **El Criollito** and **El Chilote** are three of the best stands in town.

There are fast food restaurants like **Pizza Hut** and **Lomito'n** in the Temuco Mall.

SEEING THE SIGHTS

MUSEO REGIONAL LA ARAUCANA, *Alemania 084. Tel. 211108. Tuesday-Friday 10am-5:30pm, Saturday 11am-5:30pm, Sunday 11am-2pm. Entry $1.*

This museum is dedicated to the history and culture of the Mapuche Indians. Exhibits include textiles, weapons, and maps showing the natives' resistance of the Spanish attempts to conquer their territory. This is a worthwhile museum if you have the time to spare.

For a view of Temuco, you can hike the hill in **Cerro Ñielol Park**, located on the north side of the Pan-American highway. *Entry $1. 8:30am-12:30pm and 2:30-6:00pm.*

SHOPPING

Temuco has one of the region's biggest handicraft markets which is located at the corner of Adunate and Portales. The market includes Mapuche musical instruments, wooden odds and ends, wool sweaters and hats, and jewelry. There are several small seafood restaurants here as well. The **mercado** is open *Monday-Saturday 9am-8pm, Sunday 9am-3pm.*

You can also buy handicrafts at the **Casa de La Mujer Mapuche**, *Prat 283. Monday-Friday 9am-1pm. Saturday 9am-1pm in January and February.* Part of the proceeds from their sales are used to support Mapuche community programs.

EXCURSIONS & DAY TRIPS

Temuco is the closest large town to several national parks and reserves. The easiest way to get to these is in a car. Getting there by bus is more work and usually leaves you short of the park, at the closest small town. Another alternative is to contact one of the tour agencies listed and go for the day with a group.

CONGUILLÍO NATIONAL PARK. We cover this park, one of our favorites, in a separate section after Temuco.

TOLGUACA NATIONAL PARK, *105 km northeast of Temuco. Open December-April. Entry $4.*

This 6,400 hectare park has several good trails through araucaria and laurel trees. One 12 km-long trail goes to Mescura and Lagunillas Lakes. Another runs along the Malleco River and is highlighted by a 50 meter waterfall. Camping is possible in a campsite run by Conaf designated concessionaire. The only practical way to get to the park is by four wheel drive vehicle. From Temuco, drive the 84 km of paved road to Curacautín. From there, proceed 21 kilometers north to the Tolguaca thermal baths. There is a hotel, campsite, and public thermal baths here. By taking the road west from the baths, you will arrive to Malleco Lake where the campsites with bathrooms, running water, and fire pits are located.

NAHUELBUTA NATIONAL PARK, *35 kilometers west of Angol, 170 kilometers northwest of Temuco. Entry $4.*

This 6,900 hectare park in the remnants of the coastal mountain chain has two short walking trails. The 4 km Piedra de Aguila trail goes up through beech forest to a lookout point from which you can see the width of Chile, from the cordillera to the ocean. Another trail, Cerro Anay, winds through denser forest which includes ancient araucaria trees. It is possible to camp in the park in the Conaf designated areas. To get here on public transport, you can take the Buses Biobío bus from the Temuco terminal to Angol, then take a bus from there to Vegas Blanca. This will still leave you about 7 km short of the park, which you will have to do by taxi or hitching.

Travel & Tour Agencies
• **Delsur**, *Bulnes 655. Tel. 232021*
• **Gira Viajes**, *Bello 870. Tel. 272041*
• **Tursimo Club**, *Bello 785. Tel. 273704*
• **Turismo Sur de America**, *Antonio Varas 924. Tel. 235036*
• **Viajes del Sur**, *Bulnes 677. Tel. 230021*

PRACTICAL INFORMATION

Banks: There are several banks with ATM's around the Plaza de Armas.
Business Hours: *9am-1pm; 3pm-6pm*
Currency Exchange: **A. Pascual**, *Claro Solar 780, local 4, Tel. 270615;* **Turcamb**, *Claro Solar 733, Tel. 237829;* **Global**, *Bulnes 655, Tel. 213699*
Laundry: *Manuel Montt 1099 and Aldulante 842*
Medical Service: **Hospital Regional**, *Manuel Montt 115, Tel. 212525*
National Parks: **Conaf**, *Bilbao 931, 2nd floor. Tel. 211912*
Post Office: **Correos de Chile**, *Corner of Prat and Diego Portales*
Supermarkets: **Ekono** in the shopping mall
Telephone/Fax: The area code is 54. Long-distance center **Entel**, *Portales 541* and *Mackenna 515*
Tourist Office/Maps: *Corner of Bulnes and Claro Solar, Plaza de Armas*

CONGUILLÍO NATIONAL PARK

This park is one of the prettiest in the country. Created to protect its stands of **araucaria trees**, it also features a smoking volcano, small lakes, and a snowy mountain range. The drive to the park alone is stunning as you view volcanoes in every direction. Once inside, it's the centuries-old araucarias with their tall, moss covered trunks and dark green, waxy branches that leave a lasting impression.

ARRIVALS & DEPARTURES

There are three ways to enter the park. The first, into the area called **Los Paraguas**, is 112 km from Temuco. This road, paved for all except the last 21 km from **Cherquenco**, ends on the west side of the 3,100 meter Llaima Volcano. There is a small, rustic ski center here in the winter. This is also the area from which climbers begin assaults on the volcano.

The other two entrances, the northern and southern access points, are connected by a dirt road that winds through the park. The campgrounds, cabins, and best hikes are along this artery. The northern access point is a few km further from Temuco than the southern one, but more of the route is paved.

The route to the northern access point leads up the *Panamericana* to Lautaro, where it heads east to **Curacautín**, the last city before the park. From Curacautín there are 27 km of dirt road to the information center and camping areas.

To enter from the south, you head southeast from Temuco to Cunco, where you then catch the dirt road to **Melipeuco**. From the park entrance at the small town of Melipeuco, you have another 30 km to the visitor's center. Many people like to make a loop through the park. It is gorgeous along the route, but keep in mind you must cover over 90 km of bumpy, dirt roads.

By Bus

Los Paraguas: Flota Erbuc, *Tel. 212939*, runs buses a few times daily from the rural bus terminal in Temuco to Cherquenco. There is no public transportation the last 21 km into the park, but many people try to hitch rides.

North Entrance: Flota Erbuc, *Tel. 212939*, also manages the route from Temuco to Curacautín. A few times a week in the summer they have buses that go all the way to the park entrance. Other times of the year you will have to arrange a taxi in Curacautín.

South Entrance: Narbus, *Tel. 211611*, has regular daily service from Temuco to Melipeuco. Again, from there you will have to hire a taxi to get into the park.

By Car

Car rental is a good option for seeing this park. It is a little over a two hour drive from Temuco to the visitor's center in a four wheel drive vehicle with good clearance. If you rent a car, clearance is more important than four wheel drive, but neither are absolutely necessary. We have seen plenty of standard rental sedans in the park.

If you are not going to do the loop, we recommend the northern access point, as more of the route is paved.

ORIENTATION

The 61,000 hectare park, northeast of Temuco, ranges in altitude from 900 to 3100 meters. The most prominent feature of the park is the conical smoking volcano in the park's southwestern sector. It has erupted 22 times in this century, the latest being 1994. You can see the legacy of these eruptions throughout the park.

Most of the tourist infrastructure is around the backside of the volcano. It is six kilometers from the northern ranger station to the visitor's center and Lago Conguillío. All of the campgrounds are around the lake, as is the cafeteria.

East of the park, there are three national reserves, the **China Muerta**, **Galletue**, and **Alto Biobío**, between Conguillío and the Argentine border.

WHERE TO STAY & EAT

There are seven campsites on or near the shores of Lago Conguillío. The rangers open the sites as demand dictates, so they will tell you what your options are when you arrive. **Los Nirres**, on the lake, is the largest with 44 sites. **El Estero**, with just 10 sites, has some great *araucaria*-surrounded options on the south side of the creek. Prices vary from $10-30 per site depending on the campground and the time of the year. Back country camping is not permitted within the park.

CABANAS LA BAITA, *southern park entrance. Temuco Tel./Fax 45/236037. 6 cabins. Four person cabin $85. Café. Small store. No credit cards.*

These rustic cabins include a kitchen and sitting area. They are simple, but will suffice if you don't have a tent. During the summer they have mountain bike rental and guided hikes. Be sure to call ahead for reservations if you are planning on staying here.

SEEING THE SIGHTS

This park is absolutely beautiful, rain or shine, but if you are blessed with a clear day you will be overwhelmed with its elegance. Even on a cloudy day, however, the most important physical features of the park are observable.

The **Llaima Volcano**, a giant smoldering barnacle, is almost always in view. While the top of the volcano's cone may be shrouded in clouds, the interesting patterns of snow against its red and black volcanic shoulders is hypnotic.

The blunt presence of the volcano is contrasted throughout the park by thousands of graceful **araucaria trees**. Like long-limbed dancers they wave their spindly arms to the wind's beat. The trees, Chilean National Monuments, are known in English as money-puzzle trees. Generally found in cold places with volcanic soil, they thrive between 2000-3000 meters. The tree's excellent quality lumber almost led it to its demise before it was declared to be a protected species.

Other features of the park are the lakes and lagoons; many formed by lava tongues cutting off the river, and the **Sierra Nevada**, a surprising snow covered mountain anchoring one side of Lake Conguillío. Just inside the southern park entrance the **Truful Canyon and Waterfalls** are a short hike away.

The **visitor's center** has excellent displays on the park's volcanic activity, flora, and fauna. In the summer the rangers host daytime excursions and evening talks on such topics as the formation of the volcano and the importance of the araucaria trees.

HANGING AROUND ARAUCARIAS

It's humbling to think about the life span of the araucaria trees around you. Taking roughly 200 years to reach reproductive states, they are not fully adult until they have been alive for half a millennium. That's a lot of volcanic eruptions. Some mature trees have lived for over 1200 years.

Their nuts, piñones, were the primary stable of the Pehuenches, a regional Mapuche tribe. Living only in places where the araucarias grew, the Pehuenches would collect the nuts in the fall and warehouse them underground. From these stores they would make a pemmican-type bar that got them through the winter providing an amazingly balanced diet (pemmican is a food used by South American Indians made of lean dried meat and melted fat).

SPORTS & RECREATION

Climbing

Climbers heading up the volcano start from the ski center at Los Paraguas.

Hiking

The moderate **Sierra Nevada Trail**, leading up the backside of the mountain on Lake Conguillío, is one of the best day hikes in the region. The route starts up crunchy, shimmering, volcanic soil from the beach on the eastern end of the lake before entering the wind-protected forest. Coigue trees shoot up around you as you climb the soft trail under canopies of bamboo. After about ten minutes the trail comes around to the front of the mountain for a view of the lake below before returning back to the trees. The second lookout point, about 40 minutes later, is high enough to offer a spectacular panorama of the lake, volcano, and mountain. Ancient araucarias frame perfect photo opportunities. From here you continue to climb along the ridge for about another hour or until the snow line, whichever is first.

The trailhead is four km south of the Estero campground. It is marked by signs for Playa Linda and Sierra Nevada.

Skiing

Conguillío receives an unusual amount of snowfall in the winter. Cross and back-country skiers, along with snowshoe enthusiasts, enjoy the park during this time of year. Alpine skiers head to **Los Paraguas** with its small ski center. There are two lifts on the side of the volcano. Rental equipment is available and tickets cost $20 for a full day on the weekends.

Swimming
The black, volcanic beaches around **Lake Conguillío** heat you up enough in the summer to make its cold, clear waters a welcome antidote.

PRACTICAL INFORMATION
There are no services other than those mentioned above within the park. You can get gas and supplies in Curacautín, Melipeuco, or Temuco.

PUCÓN
In the shadow of the cantankerous Villarrica Volcano, on the shores of the enormous lake of the same name, Pucón was begat by adventure seekers and now prospers by sating their needs. The first hotel in town, the Gudenschwager, and the first ski lodge on the volcano were established in the 1920's, when the only way to reach the settlement was by boat. These days, 70,000 vacationers burst the town at the seams in the high season months of January and February. The rest of the year, however, it is sleepy a mecca for connoisseurs of outdoor activity and lovers of nature.

Pucón has developed a dynamic infrastructure to cater to visitors drawn by the awe-inspiring natural surroundings such as magnificent araucaria forests and fish-brimming, raft-tipping rivers. The town offers excellent lodging in all ranges, from cozy backpacker hostels to family-sized cabins to the exclusive, unique Antumalal Hotel, built in 1945 by a Czech immigrant blessed with the vision thing. Tour agencies organize packages chock full of every type of outdoor romp you could hope for – skiing, climbing, rafting, hiking, fishing, mountain biking, horseback riding and more.

This is not a town in which to shift to idle and contemplate. It is a town to get out of, to interact with the forests, rivers, lakes, and volcanoes that surround it.

ARRIVALS & DEPARTURES
By Bus
Several companies are located in the main bus station at Palguín 383 and others nearby. The companies service regional destinations like Valdivia, Puerto Montt, and Concepción, as well as Santiago.

Bus Companies
• **Lit**, *Palguín 383. Tel. 441055*
• **Tur-Bus**, *Palguín 383. Tel. 441965*
• **JAC**, *O'Higgins 492. Tel. 442069*

By Car
Heading south on the *Panamericana*, the turn-off at Freire is well-marked. Travel southeast for 55 kilometers through Villarrica, then 25 km more to Pucón. Heading north on the *Panamericana*, take the turn-off just past Loncoche. You will go for 40 km until passing through Villarrica, then 25 km more to reach Pucón.

Car Rental Companies
• **Hertz**, *Tel. 441664*
• **Christopher**, *Tel. 449013*
• **Pucón Rentacar**, *Tel. 441992*

By Plane
The closest major airport is Temuco's, just over an hour away. There is no direct transport from the airport to Pucón so you would either need to go by car from the airport or by bus from downtown Temuco.
You will enter Pucón via Caupolicán. The main commercial street is Bernardo O'Higgins which you can access by taking a right turn off of Caupolicán.

Airlines
• **Ladeco**, *Tel. Toll free 600-600-4000*
• **Lan Chile**, *Tel. Toll free 600-600-4000*

ORIENTATION
Pucón is located on the northern shore of Lago Villarrica near the base of the Villarrica Volcano. In addition to these beautiful natural attractions, there are several good parks to the east, and several lakes within an hour's drive that are intriguing destinations in themselves. Pucón is a small town. The main commercial street is O'Higgins which is only seven blocks long. The majority of hotels and restaurants are in the area four blocks to the north and two blocks to the south of O'Higgins.

GETTING AROUND TOWN
You can walk to everything in town. The reason you might want a car here is to get to the surrounding destinations, such as Huerquehue Park, more efficiently and independently than would be possible on a tour or with public transport.

WHERE TO STAY
Expensive
HOTEL ANTUMALAL, *2 km before Pucón on Villarrica highway. Tel. 45/441011. Fax 45/441013. E-mail: antumalal@entelchile.net. Website:*

hotelantumalal.co.cl. 11 rooms. 1 suite. 1 apartment. 2 chalets. Double $250. Breakfast and either lunch or dinner included. Restaurant. Bar. Heated pool. Tennis court. Beach. Boating. Sailing. Water-skiing. Tours. Credit cards accepted.

The Antumalal is one of the finest hotels in the country, yet it retains an informal lodge atmosphere. Built into the rocks and trees, using natural elements in its construction, the hotel's architecture is reminiscent of Frank Lloyd Wright's designs. From its garden-covered position above the lake, the hotel offers excellent views, personalized service, and world-class comfort.

The common areas include a cozy bar lined with thick planks of araucaria wood and a glass-walled living room overlooking Lake Villarrica. Animal skins, plants, tree trunks, and rocks cover floors and walls, in addition to the requisite fireplaces. A large, wisteria-umbrelled deck extends over the gardens where you can order food and drink or simply take in the view. The restaurant, which also enjoys beautiful vistas, offers a limited but delicious international menu. The first-rate breakfast includes locally produced jams on hot slabs of homemade bread.

The rooms all have huge, panoramic windows; comfortable beds with fat cotton coverlets over the blankets; and thick, soft rugs that beg you to plop down in front of your own personal fireplace. Reinforcing that homey feel, there are no keys or room numbers.

The hotel features terraced gardens, a tennis court, and a range of water sports. The hotel can also help arrange fishing, golfing, rafting, horseback riding, hiking, or soaking in hot springs.

The list of visitors who have discovered this lakeside jewel is an impressive one. Foreign royalty such as Queen Elizabeth, famous politicians, and even actor Jimmy Stewart have all lived the wonderful life here.

Selected as one of our best places to stay – see Chapter 10 for more details.

GRAN HOTEL PUCÓN, *Holzapfel 190. Tel./Fax 45/441001. E-mail ghp-sk@entelchile.net. 90 rooms. Double $148. Breakfast and buffet dinner included. Restaurant. Bar. Beach snack bar. Two pools. Racquetball. Paddle tennis. Beach. Nightly shows. Children's activities. Credit cards accepted.*

Completely distinct from the Antumalal, the stately green and white Gran Pucón is none the less a fine hotel. It is big and bustling with people and activity. Extensive remodeling in the last two years has significantly upgraded the facilities. New bathrooms and bedroom furniture make your quarters a nice place to spend time, especially if you have a lakeside view.

The common areas of this venerable resort, with high ceilings and wooden floors, have been spruced up but not altered. You half expect Dolly and Gatsby to come strolling through the lobby out to the beach.

The Gran Pucón is full of life in the summer. With children's programs, nightly movies, a long, black beach, and many other activities, it's a great place for families.

ALMONI DEL LAGO, *Kikometer 19 Camino Villarrica. Tel. 45/ 442304. Four person cabin $200. Pool. Credit cards accepted.*

Almoni del Lago is a collection of five modern cabins on a small private beach, located ten minutes outside of Pucón on the way to Villarrica. This option is ideal for those who want to stay on the lake in a more remote location rather than in the middle of one of the resort towns. Each cabin comes with a fully equipped kitchen and a balcony just 10 meters from the lake shore. To cool off, you can choose to dive into the lake from the dock out front or into the swimming pool.

If these particular cabins are too pricey for your budget, there is a slough of options on the road between Pucón and Villarrica. Unfortunately most are situated so that the highway is between your cabin and the

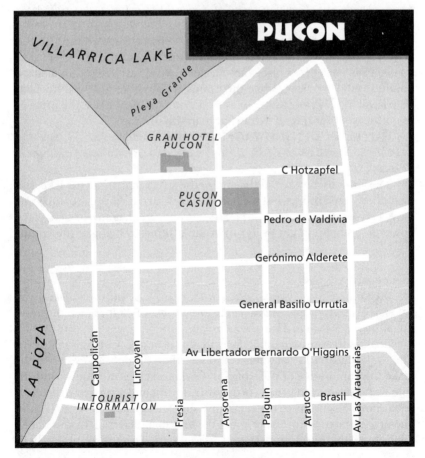

lake, or on a narrow strip between the lake and the highway, so that the highway is at your back door. We like the Almoni set-up because the cabins are located at the bottom of a precipice, a good distance from the highway, and right on the lake.

LA POSADA PLAZA PUCÓN, *Pedro de Valdivia 191. Tel. 45/441088. Fax 45/441762. 19 rooms. 4 cabins. Double $109. Breakfast included. Cable TV. Restaurant. Bar. Pool. Credit cards accepted.*

Located on the garden-covered plaza, just a block off the beach, this hotel is another popular option. Built in the style of an old house, many of the rooms have interesting nooks and layouts. The rooms are very close to each other, which means you get to know your neighbors, but the garden and pool in the back offer ample spillover space.

Moderate

HOTEL ARAUCARIAS, *Caupolicán 243. Tel./Fax 45/441286. 25 rooms. Double $93. Breakfast included. Cable TV. Central heat. Credit cards accepted.*

This pleasant hotel, with its thick wood décor, is a good option for the price range. The comfortable common areas, big upstairs deck, and strategically located fireplaces are nice extra touches. The rooms all have porches with lake views, while the cabins are spacious and well-stocked. Use of the indoor pool and saunas next door are included in the price in the off-season but has an extra charge in the summer.

HOTEL GUDENSCHWAGER, *Pedro de Valdivia 12. Tel./Fax 45/ 441156. 20 rooms. Double $83. Breakfast included. Restaurant. Credit cards accepted.*

The Gudenschwager, at the end of the street in front of the lake, has nicely decorated rooms, but the hallways are a bit dark and the bathrooms have seen some wear and tear. The restaurant patio has an excellent view, however, and you might prefer the calm offered by being at the end of road.

Inexpensive

¡ECOLE!, *General Urrutia 592. Tel. 45/441675. E-mail: trek@ecole.mic.cl. 15 rooms. Double $24, shared bath. Per person $12. Breakfast included. Restaurant. Excursions. No credit cards.*

Ecole is the overwhelming favorite in the budget category in Pucón. The social backpacker ambience and well-thought out services are what make this diminutive hostel a big hit. Common areas include a comfortable living room with green corduroy furniture and a garden patio. The restaurant, which features vegetarian dishes and back-home breakfasts, is one of the best in town. There is an excellent small selection of new books on Chile-related and regional topics, as well as a used book swapping shelf.

Among the excursions that Ecole organizes are hiking, horseback riding, and nocturnal visits to the thermal baths. The rooms are small and tidy with wood-planked walls. Call or e-mail ahead for a reservation because its always full.

LA TETERA, *General Urrutia 580. Tel/Fax 45/441462. 6 rooms. Double $35 with bath, $25 shared bath. Breakfast included. Restaurant. Tour services. Credit cards accepted.*

La Tetera is a Swiss-Chilean couple's charming bed and breakfast lodge. Finished in beautiful varnished pine, the rooms are cozy and well-maintained. Le Tetera's cafe serves a wide selection of herbal teas, coffee, pastries, and healthy breakfasts. While the Ecole next door gains more acclaim, the rooms at the La Tetera are roomier and better equipped. The owners provide personal, insightful customer service.

HOSPEDAJE SONIA, *Lincoyán 485. Tel. 45/441269. 10 rooms. $12 per person, shared bath. Breakfast included. No credit cards.*

The Sonia is a homey option. The rooms are average sized and show some wear, but this is still a decent option in this price range. A similar place is **Hospedaje Lucia**, *Coyán 565, Tel. 441721.*

WHERE TO EAT

HOTEL ANTUMALAL, *2 km before Pucón on Villarrica highway. Tel. 45/441011. Expensive-Moderate. Credit card s accepted.*

If you don't have the luxury of staying at the Antumalal, you should at least stop by for a drink or a meal. This wonderful, rustic lodge built into the hillside on the edge of Lake Villarrica offers excellent meals in an unforgettable setting. You can take advantage of warm weather by dining on the wisteria-covered deck.

Dinner can start with a carrot and poppy seed soup, to be followed by flaky, local trout or a rich fettucini with cream sauce, nuts, and cheeses. The fare is sumptuously accompanied by one of the Chilean wines from the extensive wine list. Finish it off with *copa de las flores*, special house desserts decorated with flowers from the garden.

EL FOGÓN, *O'Higgins 480. Expensive/Moderate. Credit cards accepted.*

The El Fogón is the town's carnivore center offering a variety of grilled meat, including an *asado* special combination of chicken, steak, pork, and sausage for two people. The menu also includes an impressive array of seafood, the star of which is trout prepared in ten different recipes.

EL MESON, *Corner of O'Higgins and Arauco. Expensive-Moderate. Credit cards accepted.*

This folksy restaurant situated in a pink Chilote-style house offers a wide variety of meat and fish specialties.

MARMONCH, *Ecuador 175. Tel. 441972. Moderate. Credit cards accepted.*

The Marmonch serves stick-to-your-ribs regional dishes like hot corn and chicken pie (*pastel de choclo*) and three types of hearty stews - chicken, roast beef, and turkey. The menu also includes a long list of fish entrees including succulent, fresh trout. The kitchen has one wall open so you can observe the chefs hard at work on your meals. The dining room is nicely done in natural wood.

ALTA MAR, *Fresia 301. Tel. 442294. Moderate. Credit cards accepted.*

This nautically decorated restaurant has the best seafood in town. Its deck is a popular spot for drinks in the summer, but the food is the real draw. Anything prepared *al pilpil*, sautéed in garlic and hot peppers, is delicious here. The *centolla*, king crab, are a special treat when they're in season. Another popular seafood restaurant is **Milla Rahue**, *O'Higgins 460. Tel. 441610.*

PUERTO PUCÓN, *Fresia 246. Tel. 441592. Moderate. Credit cards accepted.*

This popular Spanish restaurant, with its long wooden bar and large deck is another strong choice for seafood. The octopus fixed *gallego* style is one of our favorite dishes. Puerto Pucón is also known for its extensive selection of wine, which you can see makes up much of the interior's décor.

LA MARMITA DE PERICLES, *Fresia 300. Tel. 441114. Moderate. Credit cards accepted.*

If you're looking for a change of pace, this restaurant is a good option. Specializing in fondues and *raclettes*, you get to be involved in cooking your food here. It's always fun to go in a group so you can fight over who dropped their bread in the cheese.

BUONATESTA PIZZERIA, *Fresia 243. Tel. 441434. Moderate. Credit cards accepted.*

The Buonatesta prepares craving-satisfying pizza as well as pastas, salads, and fresh juices. The intimate restaurant is decorated with black and white photos of Mapuche culture gone by.

¡ECOLE!, *General Urrutia 592. Tel. 45/441675. Moderate-Inexpensive. No credit cards.*

The restaurant in the Ecole hostel borrows recipes from around the world to spice up its vegetarian dishes. Among the tantalizing menu items are vegetarian burritos, eggplant with Parmesan, cauliflower baked in cheese sauce, and Greek salads. The restaurant is also packed at breakfast serving up home-style specialties like waffles and pancakes covered in fresh fruit. It is best to plan not to be in a hurry here.

TIJUANA'S, *Miguel Ansorena 303. Tel. 441891. Moderate-Inexpensive. Credit cards accepted.*

The best strategy at this restaurant is to avoid the pseudo-Mexican food and opt for the inexpensive fixed item lunches like the locals do.

TRABUN, *Palguín 348. Tel. 441815. Inexpensive. No credit cards.*

Serving Chilean specialties and cheap fixed item lunches, indoors or out, the Trabun is the most popular place in town for low-priced meal.

Other places for inexpensive fare include **Coppakabana**, *Urrutia 407, Tel. 449033* which is a good spot for sandwiches and **Club 77**, *O'Higgins near Palguín*, serving pub food and beers.

NIGHTLIFE & ENTERTAINMENT

The best that the town has to offer is the casino in the **Gran Hotel Pucón**, *Ansorena 23, Tel. 441873*. It is one of the better casinos in Chile, so if you are going to lay your pesos down somewhere, this is a good place to do it.

SHOPPING

There are handicrafts available at the **Feria Artesanal**, *O'Higgins 255*, as well as in a few shops around town.

EXCURSIONS & DAY TRIPS

The reason people come to Pucón is to venture into the extraordinary outdoor playground that surrounds it. The town has developed admirable infrastructure to accommodate visitors in copping adrenalin-laced and nature-inspired buzzes.

We recommend two outdoor adventure companies over the others, **Sol y Nieve** and **Trancura**. We've had satisfying experiences with these companies as well as strong recommendations from the hotel owners in the area. If you are simply looking for a convenient round-trip bus ride to Huerquehue park, then it is probably OK to price shop. For higher risk excursions like rafting and climbing, you are better off sticking with these two agencies.

Huerquehue National Park

35 km northeast of Pucón. Entry $4.

Huerquehue is a beautiful 12,500-hectare jewel with several small lakes surrounded by the umbrella-shaped pines, known as araucarias in Spanish, and as monkey puzzle trees in English. You shouldn't miss the four hour round-trip hike which winds through the monkey puzzle trees up to three enchanting small lakes - Lago Chico, Lago Toro, and Lago Verde. This is one of our favorite day hikes in Chile. The trail is extremely

STRAP ON YOUR SAFETY HELMET

Keep in mind that the litigation framework in Chile is less punitive than in the United States. It allows for more "adventure" in organized adventure travel, which means more risk. Ultimately you should consider yourself responsible for your own safety, and analyze the hazards involved rather than simply assuming that your guide and the agency are 100% flawless. You will find many skilled, informative guides in Chile; it's the occasional neophyte to beware of.

well-cut and marked, an easy hike, but with enough elevation gain to give you some exercise.

If you want to stay in the park, Conaf runs a camping area on Lago Tinquilco which has 18 sites and a bathroom. The cost is $5 per night per person. A superb new possibility is to stay in the **Refugio Tinquilco**, a beautiful cabin near Lake Tinquilco erected by three Chilean nature lovers - an architect, an engineer, and a writer. The hostel portion costs $15 per person, a double room $50, and a full day's meals $10. For reservations, call in Santiago, *Tel. 2/777-7673, Fax 2/735-1187,* or e-mail *tinquilco@lake.mic.cl.*

To get to Huerquehue by car, follow O'Higgins or Brasil out of town going away from the lake. When the road forks, veer left toward Lago Caburga. The pavement ends near Lago Caburga, but a two wheel drive vehicle can handle the dirt road to the park with only the lowest of suspensions bottoming out a few times along the way. Buses leave you in Paillaco, 8 kilometers short of the park, so it is better to arrange transport through one of the tour agencies.

Rafting the Trancura River

The rafting trip along this beautiful green river is highly recommended as a way of experiencing the region's splendor while getting good adrenalin jolt. You should wear a swim suit, sport sandals or sneakers, and bring a change of clothes. The agency will provide the necessary gear. There are two river rafting options according to difficulty level.

The Lower Trancura is the easier of the two, rated as a class III. Any capable swimmer should be able to handle it. The season for the lower Trancura runs from September through April, priced at $35 per person in January and February, and $17 per person during the other months. The descent takes about an hour and a half.

The Upper Trancura is rated as class III with several wild sections rated as class IV. The season is shorter, from December to March. The cost for the upper Trancura is $60 per person. If you want to do this trip, you should be confident in your swimming skills and have a strong sense of adventure. The descent takes three hours.

Climbing the Villarrica Volcano

This is a full day outing in which you climb up the nearly perfect cone of the 2840-meter Villarrica Volcano to peer into its crater of bubbling lava. The climb begins at the ski lodge and takes about seven hours round-trip. It is a non-technical climb through loose volcanic rock then up the snowy top with crampons (spikes which attach to climbing boots), and includes spectacular views of the surrounding volcanoes.

The outfitters will supply everything you need including backpack, boots, crampons, ice axe, wind-breaking pants and coat, gloves and eye protection. You should wear a warm base layer of clothes, preferably non-cotton long underwear and fleece pants and jacket. The cost of the climb is $55 in January and February; $40 during the rest of the year.

Mountain Biking

Bicycle rentals start at $3/hour or $10 for a half day. If you want to maximize your time on single track, the best thing to do is to go out with a guide. It will cost extra, about $15 for the ride, but it is worth it to avoid wasting time looking for a decent trail.

Horseback Riding

Horseback riding can be arranged easily for a short ride of an hour or more at the beginning of the road going up to the Villarrica Volcano. This will cost about $8/hour with a guide. Half day and full day excursions to destinations like the Termas de Huife thermal baths can be arranged through one of the tour agencies.

Thermal Baths

There are eight thermal baths in the mountains around Pucón. The most popular of these are Huife, Palguín, Menetué and San Luis. You can either swim in one of the large steaming pools or reserve a private cabin. The folks at the **Ecole Hosteria** organize a night visit to the baths, a soothing response to a day of rigorous outdoor activity.

Snow Skiing

The slopes on the Villarrica Volcano often have snow when the resorts around Santiago do not. The ski center has a beautiful lodge, four chairs, and two rope tows. There are nine advanced runs and four short moderate runs. Villarrica won't wow you if you are used to Colorado resorts, but when you consider that you are skiing on the side of a burping, nearly conical volcano in the Andes, it scores some points for novelty. The season runs from July through mid-October. Lift tickets cost $25. The lodge charges $135 for a double, but also offers multi-day packages. Contact the Gran Hotel Pucón (reviewed above in *Where to Stay*) at *Tel. 45/441001* for more information and reservations.

Volcanic Caves

5 km up road to Volcán Villarrica. 10am-6pm. Admission $6.50.

These caves are in one of the Villarrica Volcano's craters that extinguished over two million years ago. It's a good rainy day activity because you spend your time, after you get your hard hat, out of the elements, though the caves are cold and humid. The half-kilometer path leads past solidified rivers of magma, as well as stalactites and other mineral incrustations. Outside you can see "*bonsai coigues*" (bonsai beech trees), that were trapped in the lava and prevented from continuing to grow.

Explore the Siete Lagos

If you want to get out into some really remote areas rarely explored in the off-season by passers through, rent a car, pick a few lakes in the Siete Lagos area and drive around them. We describe this pristine area completely in a separate entry.

Other Lakes, Trails, and ... Wild Boar Hunting

Other possibilities in the Pucón area include fishing expeditions and lake sports. Turismo Trancura even offers a two day outing to hunt *jabalí*, a native wild boar.

Tour Agencies

- **Sol y Nieve**, *Corner of O'Higgins and Lincoyán. Tel./Fax 45/441070. E-mail solnieve@entelchile.net*
- **Trancura**, *O'Higgins 211 or O'Higgins 575. Tel. 441189*
- **Ecole Hosteria**, *General Urrutia 592. Tel. 441675*
- **Anden Sport**, *O'Higgins 535, Tel. 45/441236*
- **Conexión**, *O'Higgins 472. Tel. 449030*

Bicycle Rentals

- **Politur**, *O'Higgins 635. Tel. 441373*
- **Off Limits**, *Fresia 275. Tel. 441210*
- **Trancura**, *O'Higgins 211. Tel. 441189*
- **Anden Sport**, *O'Higgins 535, Tel. 45/441236*
- **Conexión**, *O'Higgins 472. Tel. 449030*
- **DaSki**, *Fresia and Alderete*

PRACTICAL INFORMATION

Banks: Banco Edwards on *O'Higgins* and **BCI**, *corner of Alderete and Fresia*, have ATM machines.

Business Hours: 9am-1pm; 3pm-6pm. Tour agencies stay open late, many until 9pm

Currency Exchange: Turismo Christopher, *O'Higgins 335, Tel. 449013;* **Conexión**, *O'Higgins 472, Tel. 449030*

E-Mail Service: Cyber Bar Brink, *Ansorena 243*

Laundry: Automática, *Fresia 224, Tel. 441106;* **Magala**, *Colo 478, Tel. 441078* – Dry cleaning service too; **La Esperanza**, *Colo Colo 469, Tel. 441379*

Medical Service: Hospital San Francisco, *Uruguay 325. Tel. 441177*

Post Office: Correos de Chile, *Uruguay 325*

Supermarkets: Eltit, *O'Higgins 336*

Telephone/Fax: The area code is 45. Long distance call centers include **Entel**, *Ansorena 299* and **CTC**, *Palguín 348*

Tourist Office/Maps: Oficina de Turismo, *Brasil 115. Tel. 441671*

VILLARRICA

Villarrica lies on the western shore of Lake Villarrica and boasts a spectacular view of the Villarrica Volcano. You would think that would be enough to make it the star of the region, but it has lost the role to neighboring Pucón because it is 25 kilometers farther away from the natural wonders. The town of 23,000 bulges in the summer when Chilean families fill the town's cabins and hotels.

ARRIVALS & DEPARTURES

Villarrica is located 82 km southeast of Temuco, which has the closest convenient airport. To get here in car, heading south on the Panamericana, the turn-off at Freire is well-marked. Travel southeast for 55 km to reach Villarrica If you are heading north on the Panamericana, take the turn-off just past Loncoche. You will hit Villarrica in 40 km. Villarrica has bus connections to and from most regional cities as well as Santiago.

WHERE TO STAY

CABANAS MONTE NEGRO, *Pratt and Montt. Tel. 45/411371. 8 cabins. Six person cabin $112. No credit cards.*

These solidly built, new cabins on the point are the nicest places to stay in town. Across from the lake, they are the also on a prime location. If they are full, try **Bugalolandia**, *Tel. 45/411035*, next door.

CABANAS MILILAFQUEN, *General Korner 250. Tel. 45/411562. 10 cabañas. Double $45. Credit cards accepted.*

Located on the shores of Lake Villarrica, these a-frame cabins are a credible option. The comfortable, wood paneled den stays nice and warm because of its stove, but the bedrooms can get cold when it's chilly outside. Well-tended gardens brighten up even the cloudiest of days.

HOSTERIA KIEL, *General Korner 153. Tel./Fax 45/411631. 12 rooms. Double $50. Breakfast included. Restaurant. Credit cards accepted.*

This attractive option is also one of the better places to eat in town. The rooms are close to each other, which can be loud when there is a full house, but they are also very pleasant. Large baths and new bedding are two of the highlights. Private porches allow you to sit and look across the street to the park on the lake.

HOTEL VILLARRICA, *General Korner 255. Tel. 45/411641. 14 rooms and cabins. Double $33. Breakfast included. Restaurant. Credit cards accepted.*

This informal hotel across the street from the lake is architecturally reminiscent of the hotels of the 60's. The rooms, with varnished wood exteriors, have been updated inside but the bathrooms have not. It's a decent value for the price simply because of its location.

Two good low-end accommodation options are **Maravillas del Sur**, *Francisco Bilbao 821. Tel. 45/412830* and **Las Brasas**, *Pedro Valdivia 533, Tel. 45/411854.* Both charge about $12 per person, breakfast included.

WHERE TO EAT

EL REY DE MARISCOS, *Letelier 1030, Tel. 412093. Moderate. Credit cards accepted.*

The chef, Daniel Leighton, cooked at some of the finer hotels and restaurants in the country before opening up shop here. Located at the end of the street with large windows overlooking the lake, this place has business on even the slowest days. In the summer it is hard to get a table. His specialty is seafood, but the hot *empanadas* are also a tasty starter.

HOSTERIA KIEL, *General Korner 153. Tel./Fax 45/411631. Moderate. Credit cards accepted.*

Almost all the seats in the house look out on Lake Villarrica in this popular restaurant. On clear days there are wonderful panoramic views of the volcano at the foot of the lake, which makes anything taste better. The standard Chilean menu of shellfish appetizers with fish, meat or chicken entrees is done well here.

THE TRAVELLERS, *Valentin Letelier 753. Tel. 412830. Moderate. No credit cards.*

The Traveller's is a cafe hangout with a far-ranging fusion of international cuisine, the vastness of which is only matched by the territory roamed by the group of young owners. The menu reads like their travel journals with dishes from Thailand, Indonesia, China, Greece, and Mexico. There is a big area for outdoor seating to cool down with beers in the summer sun or you can play board games inside while taming a winter chill with one the extensive selection of teas and coffee.

EL FOGÓN DE LUCHO, *General Korner and Letelier. Tel. 411232. Moderate. No credit cards.*

Specializing in mixed grill barbecues, this is the place to go if you've had your fill of seafood. The steak *a lo pobre* will easily carry you over to, if not through, your next meal.

For light lunches and sandwiches try the pub-style **El Viejo Bucanero**, *Henríquez 552.*

SIETE LAGOS

The seven lakes are located in Valdivia province, south of Lago Villarrica and north of Lago Ranco. There are four large lakes covering 70-120 square kilometers each: **Calafquén, Panguipulli, Pirehueico,** and **Riñihue** and three smaller ones – **Neltume, Pellaifa,** and **Pullinque.** The lakes are popular with fishermen seeking tranquil waters into which to cast, as is the system of tributary rivers that flow from the lakes to later form the Valdivia River. If you go to this area during the off season you will have many trails, much shoreline, or perhaps a whole lake entirely to yourself. By far the easiest way to explore the isolated, pristine areas that are the attraction of this region is in a rental car.

Lago Calefquén is a lush, tadpole-shaped lake only thirty kilometers south of the town of Villarrica. **Lican Ray** is the principal visitor area, a town of 1,500 people. The town has some nice lakeside beaches and a small peninsula that has been converted into a park. There are campgrounds and several places to stay including the **Hotel Refugio Inaltulafquen**, *Cacique Punulef 510, Tel. 63/431115* on Playa Grande and the **Hotel Becker**, *Felipe Manquel 105, Tel. 63/431156* on Playa Chica. Both hotels charge about $50 for a double. For a meal the best bets are the **Refugio Inaltulafquen** on Playa Grande or **Ñaño's** and **Guido's** on General Urrutia.

If you drive 20 km east along Calafquén's shores to the tail of the tadpole you will see some spectacular views of the backside of the Villarrica Volcano before reaching the town of **Coñaripe**, the petite **Pellafa Lake**, and the **Coñaripe Thermal Baths.** If you want to stay in Coñaripe, try the **Hotel Entre Montanas**, *Ramberga 496, Tel. 63/317298, Double $35.*

Lake Panguipulli is the largest of the seven lakes stretching for 25 km toward the *cordillera.* The town of the same name which anchors the lake to the west has a population of 8,000 and all services you might need including ATM's, grocery stores, and good tourist office on the plaza. Most of the lodgings in and around town are 2-6 person cabins. We stayed in a great small set of cabins outside of town, **Cabañas La Riconada**, *km 5 in Chauquen, Tel. 311225, Two Person Cabin $60.* The set-up is four new cabins overlooking the lake, each with a good piece of terrain around them as a buffer; all with fully equipped kitchens and wood burning stoves. You should pick up provisions in the grocery store before going out there. It is a ten minute taxi ride from town or you can call them to come and pick you up. In town, there are three groups of cabins up the street from Etchgaray on Carrera Pinto – **Tío Carlos**, *Tel. 63/311215*, **El Mirador**, *Tel. 63/311106*, and **Villa Los Encinos**, *Tel. 63/311043*. The preferred restaurants are **La Plaza**, on the square, and **Cafe El Central**, *Martinez de Rosas 880.*

If you drive the 35 km of unpaved road along the north side of the Lake Panguipulli toward the Choshuenco Volcano you can visit the enchanting **Lake Neltume**, the gorgeous **Saltos de Huilohuilo** waterfall, and the elongated **Lago Pirihuelco**. The latter lake has twice a day ferry service to the Argentine border crossing point called Huamhuam that leads to Junín de los Andes. You can also drive 30 km along the twisting, rattling road up to the rustic ski resort on the Choshuenco Volcano. The road runs along the Enco River and has extraordinary views of Lago Riñihue as it goes up.

Lago Riñihue is a pristine, almost completely undeveloped lake, its narrow body fed by the glacial run-off of the lounging Choshuenco

---

ON TOP OF OLD SMOKEY

Most of Chile's 55 active volcanoes are in the Lake District. Some of them are a little too active. Llaima and Villarrica, both near Temuco, have tallied about 20 eruptions each since the Spanish arrived. The worst recent volcanic destruction was the burying of the town of Coñaripe in Villarrica's lava in 1971. Frequently mud and debris washed down in melted snow from the volcano top is more of a threat than lava. This was the case when the mud flow from Villarrica wiped out its ski lodge in 1948.

If you are wondering what makes some of the volcanoes perfect cones, and others a bit contorted, the reason lies in consistency. The perfect cones like Osorno are stratovolcanoes that have long records of eruptions from their summits. The overlapping tongues of lava and ash from succeeding eruptions form the cone. The lumpy guys owe their poor posture to fickleness. They spew from one vent then another located elsewhere, and may also change eruption type.

Volcano. If your goal for your time in Chile is to stay in a remote, comfortable Chilean lodge on an beautiful, almost unknown lake, Lago Riñihue is a great choice. About the only structures on the lake are the two enticing lodges. We hesitate in calling these fishing lodges, which is what they are set up for in season, because they have a broader appeal than that, and can be a base for several other activities such as hiking and horseback riding, in addition to fishing.

RIÑIMAPU HOTEL, *End of Lake Riñihue. Tel. 63/311388. Santiago fax 2/696-1786. 16 rooms. $100 per person with full board. Restaurant. Bar. Tennis. Fishing. Horseback riding. Credit cards accepted.*

This beautiful lodge hidden away at the end of Lake Riñihue on the headwaters of the San Pedro River is about two and half hours from Temuco. Remote, natural, pristine, and relaxing, the value of your stay lies in the ambiance. The Choshuenco Volcano fills the valley at the far end of the lake, while flowers explode around the sides of the lodge.

The hotel itself is absolutely welcoming, with spacious sitting areas, warm fireplaces, picture windows, and a well-trained staff. Constructed of unfinished stone and wood, the lodge setting is rustic yet refined. The rooms are simple and comfortable with the preferred location being the larger rooms downstairs.

You can join the mostly foreign clientele in world class trout fishing, tennis, horseback riding, hiking, and even croquet. You could also find a quiet nook by a fireplace and spend the day reading if that's what you prefer.

Another option is the **Hosteria Huinca Quiñay**, *Lago Riñihue. Tel. 09/643-1248 or 09/642-1252* which is a four star lodge on the opposite side of the lake with fourteen 4-6 person cabins.

VALDIVIA

Valdivia is arguably Chile's most beautiful city, an engaging collection of old Spanish forts and German style mansions set along riverbanks. Known as the **City of Rivers**, it is situated at the meeting point of the **Cau Cau** and **Calle Calle Rivers**, which combine here to form the **Valdivia River**. The quality of life is enviable. Rowing skulls cruise silently down the languid current, inhabitants amble about the area's gardens, parks, and beaches, then quench their thirsts with **Kunstmann**, a tasty local brew.

Pedro de Valdivia founded the city in 1552 perceiving its strategic importance as a military stronghold. The Spaniards could not keep it for long though, as the settlement was lost in the Mapuche uprising in 1599. A year later, the Dutch corsair Sebastian Cortes took possession of the city as would his countryman Elias Erckmans in 1643, but neither of them could defend the town against the Mapuche natives and were forced to abandon it. The Spanish reclaimed the terrain in 1645 and utilized it as a base of operations from which to seize territory from the Mapuches. The city would be one of the last remaining Spanish encampments during the war of independence, and was finally taken by the Chilean-employed British mercenary, **Lord Cochrane**, in a daring surprise attack in 1820.

Valdivia was populated by a continuous flow of German immigrants from 1850-1875 that created one of the most prosperous communities in the nation. A devastating earthquake almost completely destroyed the city in 1960, a disaster that would also consume three meters of the land along the waterfront. Valdivia recovered. Several of its turn-of-the-century mansions remain in tact. In fact a few of them have been converted into hotels, such as the intriguing **Hotel Jardín del Rey**. Valdivia currently earns its keep through logging, fishing, and tourism, is home to a population of 130,000, and is the provincial capital.

ARRIVALS & DEPARTURES

By Bus

There is a central bus terminal is located at Anfión Muñoz 360, about eight blocks east of the Plaza de Armas. All buses arrive and depart from here. The bus companies service all regional destinations and Santiago.

Bus Companies
• **Cruz del Sur**, *Tel. 213840*
• **Lit**, *Tel. 212835*
• **Pirehueico**, *Tel. 218609*
• **Tal Norte**, *Tel. 213544*
• **Tas-Choapa**, *Tel. 213124*
• **Tur-Bus**, *Tel. 226010*

By Car

If you are traveling south on the Panamericana, Valdivia is 50 kilometers southwest of San Jose de la Miriquiná. If you are traveling north on the Panamericana, Valdivia is 30 kilometers northwest of Paillaco. You will enter the city via Ramon Picarte which will take you directly into the city center. You depart via the same road, Ramon Picarte.

Car Rental Agencies
• **Andes**, *Runca 582. Tel. 213838*
• **Assef y Méndez**, *General Lagos 1335. Tel. 213205*
• **Autovald**, *Camilo Henríquez 610. Tel. 212786*
• **Hertz**, *Picarte 640. Tel. 218317*

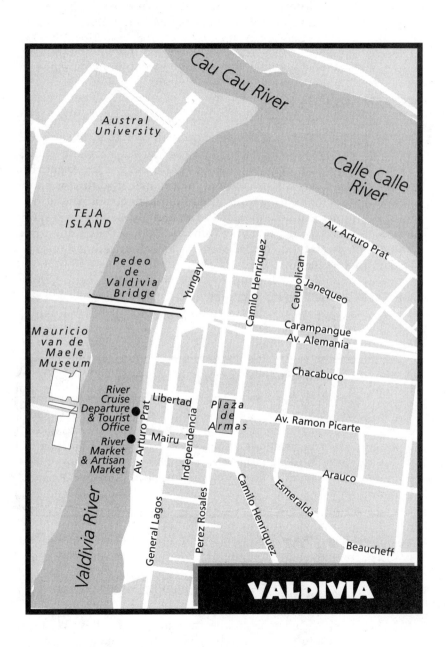

By Plane

The Valdivia airport is located 30 kilometers northwest of town. Taxi transport to the city center is $10 and bus transport is $2.

Airlines that fly here are: **Avant**, *Chacabuco 408, Local 27, Tel. 251431;* **Ladeco**, *Caupolicán 364, Local 7 & 8, Tel. 213392, Toll free 600-600-4000;* and **Lan Chile**, *O'Higgins 386, Tel. 218841, Toll free 600-600-4000.*

ORIENTATION

The Valdivia River and its largest tributary, the Calle Calle, which will appear to be one and the same, wind through town to divide it in half. There are several other rivers west of the city which flow into the Valdivia River. The most important of these are the **Cruces** and the **Angachilla**.

The Plaza de Armas and most of the commercial district is on the eastern bank of the Valdivia River. The landmass directly across the river from the Sernatur office, Fluvial Market, and Muelle Schuster is **Teja Island**, which can be reached by crossing the Valdivia Bridge downriver. The university and the Austral Museum as well as several hotels are located on Teja Island.

GETTING AROUND TOWN

You can reach almost all destinations in town on foot or by taxi, which will be rarely needed.

WHEN IT RAINS, IT POURS

The reason that the Lake District is so green is because it rains here, a lot. Concepción and Temuco receive 25% more annual rainfall than Seattle. Valdivia, amazingly, receives twice as much. Fortunately the majority of rain is concentrated in four soggy months, May through August. You can greatly increase the odds of enjoying blue skies and sparkling lakes by planning your travel during the driest months, November through March.

WHERE TO STAY

Expensive

HOTEL NAGUILAN, *General Lagos 1927. Tel. 63/212851, Fax 63/219130. 45 rooms. Double $135 . Breakfast included. Cable TV. Restaurant. Bar. Pool. Meeting rooms. Credit cards accepted.*

The Hotel Naguilan is another example of the Best Western's distinctive hotels in Chile. This classy hotel, beautifully illuminated at night, offers elegant rooms overlooking the Calle Calle River. The reception area leads into a cozy piano bar, an excellent place to relax with a drink. The first class restaurant serves Chilean and international specialties. An ample lawn and garden surrounding the hotel accommodates the pool and stretches down to the hotel's dock. The hotel is slightly more distant from the city center than most others, but the any logistical inconvenience is more than compensated for by the tranquil surroundings.

HOTEL PUERTA DEL SUR, *Los Lingues 950. Tel. 63/224500. Fax 63/211046. Rooms 85. Double $135. Breakfast included. Cable TV. Restaurant. Bar. Pool. Meeting rooms. Business Center. Credit cards accepted.*

The newly constructed Puerta del Sur is the only five star hotel in Valdivia and serves it role competently. The hotel is located across the river from the city center on Teja Island. Most of the rooms, all smartly decorated, look out onto the pool and several have views of the river. Recreational facilities include the pool, sauna, spa, tennis and volleyball courts. The hotel also offers canoe rentals so you can paddle to some of the town's attractions.

Moderate

HOTEL JARDÍN DEL REY, *General Lagos 1190. Tel. 63/218562. Rooms 30. Double $60. Breakfast included. Cable TV. Credit cards accepted.*

The Jardín del Rey boasts a magnificent structure for a moderately priced hotel as it situated in a nineteenth century mansion. The solid grey neoclassic edifice is set back from the street and is accessed through an expansive, well-manicured garden. The rooms are simple, but remodeled recently enough to make the furnishings cheery and functional. The hotel is four long blocks from the central plaza, but it is a pleasant walk that takes you past several other turn-of-the-century buildings.

DI TOLBASCHI APART-HOTEL, *Yerbas Buenas 283. Tel. 63/224103, Fax 63/224003. 16 apartments. $83 two person apartment. Credit cards accepted.*

If you are in need of some extra space to spread out, this apart-hotel, which offers condominium-like cabins, is our recommended option. All of the units come with fully equipped, well-organized kitchens. The living rooms are homey areas, highlighted by exposed wooden beams and cream-colored walls. The low-season price of $72 makes this apart-hotel a bargain.

HOTEL PEDRO DE VALDIVIA, *Carampangue 190. Tel. 63/212931. Fax 63/203888. 77 rooms. Double $90. Breakfast included. Restaurant. Bar. Cable TV. Credit cards accepted.*

This classic large pink and black hotel sits up on a grassy knoll above the river. Extremely popular with business people and conventions, it's a solid choice for the price category. The room furnishings are a bit dated, but are in top condition. The large grounds and pool are the real highlights of the hotel, as is the location.

HOSTAL CENTRO TORREÓN, *Pérez Rosales 783. Tel. 63/212622. Fax 63/203217. 13 rooms. Double $55. Breakfast included. No credit cards.*

This turn-of-the-century home is an extremely popular choice for the price range, and deservedly so. Large rooms, comfortable common areas, a friendly owner, and a hip bookstore next door make it one of the best in its class. Prices are discounted considerably in the off-season.

Inexpensive

VILLA BEAUCHEFF, *Beaucheff 844. Tel. 63/216044. 15 rooms. Double $35. Breakfast included. Credit cards accepted.*

The Beaucheff is a good option in the inexpensive category. It is on the hill overlooking downtown and the Calle Calle river. The accommodations are simple, but well-maintained and clean. They also have a few independent cabins for rent behind the main building.

HOSTAL ESMERALDA, *Esmeralda 651. Tel. 63/215659. 12 rooms. Double $40. Breakfast included. Cable TV. Credit cards accepted.*

The Hostal Esmeralda is an old, colorful, two-story house with oversized rooms and high ceilings. Slightly too soft beds seem to be the only significant flaw of the place. It is well-located, a block away from the plaza in the heart of the Beaucheff-Esmeralda area, so it is surrounded by good restaurants. You can probably negotiate a lower rate or a per person rate here.

Another good low-end accommodation, charging about $15 per person with breakfast is the **Residencial Germanía**, *Picarte 873, Tel. 63/ 212405.*

WHERE TO EAT

CAMINO DE LUNA, *Costanera north of the Carampangue bridge. Tel. 213788. Expensive. Credit cards accepted.*

This floating restaurant has some of the best views of the river and passing boats in town. The wide range of seafood is all good, but you're really paying for the view. It's worth the splurge for a special night.

CLUB DE LA UNION, *Camilo Enríquez 540. Tel. 213377. Moderate. Credit cards accepted.*

The Club de La Union is the traditional favorite, located on the town's Plaza de Armas. The second floor restaurant is surprisingly bright for an old social club, highlighted by big windows looking out onto the square. Black and white photos line the adjoining bar and game rooms. In addition to Chilean seafood specialties a la carte, the club offers two reasonably priced fixed item lunch options.

NEW ORLEANS, *Esmeralda 682. Tel. 218771. Moderate. Credit cards accepted.*

The New Orleans is a sleek, brick-walled restaurant with a menu loosely based on Cajun specialties, and all named after motion pictures such *Moby Dick*, *Valley of the Dolls*, and *One Fine Day*. The restaurant is one of the anchors of the Esmeralda-Beauchef neighborhood. For seafood you can try the **New Babor** next door.

LA CALESA, *Yungay 735. Tel. 213712. Moderate. Credit cards accepted.*

La Calesa is a homey restaurant located in an beautiful old building overlooking the river. The restaurant offers good fixed item lunches daily as well as a net full of Peruvian-style seafood options. Closed on Sundays.

APPROACH TEMPO PIZZA, *Esmeralda 675, Tel. 219447. Moderate. Credit cards accepted.*

This is a popular pizzeria done up in a golf decor, located amid the restaurants in the Esmeralda-Beauchef neighborhood.

CAT'S CLUB, *Esmeralda 657. Tel. 207546. Moderate. Credit cards accepted.*

This is a great pub, set up in an old yellow and red house that is brimming with bossa nova and jazz tunes. There are only a few pub-style food selections on the menu like sandwiches and hamburgers, but the hip ambience and surrounding restaurants, make it an excellent spot for a pre or post dinner drink.

ENTRELAGOS, *Pérez Rosales 640. Tel. 218333. Moderate-inexpensive. Credit cards accepted.*

This café just off the square is one of the best places in town for desserts any time of day. While they have a complete menu, a look at the cake selections or ice creams may make you skip your main course to get to the good stuff. The atmosphere is casual. Their shop next door, **Mazapanes Entrelagos**, has a good selection of the candies and marzipan for which Valdivia is famous.

CAFÉ HAUSSMANN, *O'Higgins 394. Tel. 213878. Inexpensive. No credit cards.*

This Valdivia institution is famous for its nut *kuchen* pastries and *crudos*, steak tartar. It's amazing to see every person in the small restaurant eating plates of raw meat on toast with onions, lemon, and yogurt sauce. We have to admit that we're not big fans of uncooked beef, but the rest Valdivia can't get enough, the tiny locale is always packed. Even if you're not up for the *crudos*, the sandwiches here are delicious. Try the Barro Luco, which is served with pork instead of beef.

For a fast food fix, the world's nearly southernmost **McDonald's** is located on the corner of Chacabuco and Independencia, (Wellington, New Zealand beats it out by a few degrees). **Dino's**, *Maipu 191,* is a reliable chain for a light meal and sandwiches.

SEEING THE SIGHTS

The Valdivia waterfront is what makes this one of the prettiest and most pleasant cities in Chile. Crew boats skim along like river bugs while cruising ships tie up along the waterfront area known as **Schuster Dock**. North of the passenger sightseeing ships is the **Floating Market**. This colorful jumble of vendors selling both seafood and agricultural products fills the docks and stalls daily from 8am-2pm, although Tuesdays and Thursdays are the most active.

Across the street from the floating market is the regular **City Market** with its cheap upstairs seafood stalls. Take note of the Shell gas station right below the bridge where you can either fill your car from the street-side, or your boat from the river-side.

If you follow Prat south past Schuster Dock to where it ends, you will find a small **artisan market**. From there take a left on San Carlos, then a right on Yungay which will turn into General Lagos. **General Lagos** runs for a few kilometers along the river, and features a few old German style mansions over the first several blocks.

VALDIVIA HISTORY AND ANTHROPOLOGICAL MUSEUM, *Los Laureles 47. Tel. 212872. Admission fee $1.50.*

Located on Teja Island in the lovely yellow house that belonged to Carlos Anwandter, one of Valdivia's first German immigrants, this museum houses a collection of period furniture and knickknacks as well as Mapuche *artesanía*. Some of the highlights include excellent dated maps of Chile, along with a stunning display of indigenous silver work. The grounds of the museum are worth a walk-through, as is the **Contemporary Art Museum** next door. The waterfront scene when looking from the museum back over to town is one of the classic shots of Valdivia. The museum lies directly across the river from the Schuster Dock and floating market so you might want to make the trip over in boat.

UNIVERSIDAD AUSTRAL BOTANICAL GARDEN, *End of Los Laureles, Teja Island.*

The university's botanical garden features native flowers and plants and a lovely pond covered with water lilies. There is a small cafe so you can enjoy the surroundings while sipping whatever beverage the weather dictates.

KUNSTMANN BREWERY, *Route T-350 number 950. Tel. 292969. Noon to midnight daily. Admission fee $2.00.*

Found mainly in the Lake District, the German-style Kunstmann beer is the best brew in Chile. Here at the brewery you can visit the beer museum, take a tour of the processing facilities, buy some souvenirs, eat a meal, or best of all, sample the wares. They usually have four types of beer on tap. The chocolatey, dark beer, *negra*, is our personal favorite.

You'll no doubt find yourself agreeing with the label to proclaim, "*Das gute bier.*"

SPORTS & RECREATION

During summer, there are kayak rentals on the riverfront near Muelle Schuster on Avenida Prat. Several short hikes can be done on the trails of the **Parque Oncol**, north of Niebla, but you need a four wheel drive vehicle to get there.

SHOPPING

There are several stalls selling *artesanía* at the corner of Prat and San Carlos, south of the Muelle Schuster. To buy some of Valdivia's renowned chocolate, go to **Marzipanes & Salon de Te Entrelagos**, *Pérez Rosales 640.* They have a counter selling chocolate and pastries, as well as popular coffee shop where you can nibble on the delicacies with a cup of java.

EXCURSIONS & DAY TRIPS

Boat Excursions

A great way to explore the area around Valdivia is by boat. There are several boat excursions offered to the rivers, parks, and forts around Valdivia. All of the boat tours leave from the Muelle Schuster on Avenida Prat. More than likely you will be approached by touts trying to sell you tickets as soon as you get close. The tours range from a simple hour and half boat ride to a six hour outing exploring several points of interest. The cost for these is from $20-$40 per person depending on sailing time, if lunch is included, and if the attraction entrance fees are included. The boat tours will offer combination of the destinations listed below.

If you prefer to visit destinations without a tour group, you can reach Niebla by bus or car, and Corral and Mancera by small boat from Niebla for about a dollar.

Mancera

The principal attraction of this small island, located in the mouth of the Valdivia River in Corral Bay, is the **San Pedro de Alcántara Castle**. The castle was originally built in 1648, with additions in 1680 and 1762. It includes a small chapel and several canons. You can also reach this island from Niebla in a small boat for $1 per person.

Corral

Corral is a small port town of 3,500 people on the southern bank of the Valdivia River mouth. Its castle, **San Sebastian de la Cruz**, was originally built in 1645 and reconstructed in 1764. There is also a small regional history museum in Corral open daily from 9am-1pm and 2pm-6pm. It is possible to reach Corral from Niebla in a small boat for $1. Vehicles can cross for $10 on the ferry that goes once per day in the low season, and three times per day in the high season.

Niebla

Niebla is the port town on the northern bank of the Valdivia River mouth, 17 kilometers west of Valdivia. The principal fort here is the **La Pura y Limpieza Concepción de Mondfort de Lemus Castle**, named for Count Lemus, a viceroy of Peru. This castle houses a museum that focuses on the colonial history of Valdivia. There are several seafood restaurants to choose from along the shorefront of Niebla, the most popular of which is the **Cafe Restaurant Alemán**. If you would like to stay in Niebla, we recommend the **Hotel El Castillo**, *Antonio Duce 750. Tel. 282-2061. Double $50.* The is a comfortable bed and breakfast style hotel with a swimming pool.

Santuario de la Naturaleza del Rio Cruces

This nature sanctuary is accessed via the Cruces river which the park surrounds on both sides. There is abundant bird life and waterfowl to be seen, such as the black neck swan and *tagua*, a Chilean duck.

Isla Huapi

Isla Huapi is an eight hectare island nature reserve owned by one of the tour companies, H.E. Tours. Their cruise gives you the option of having lunch on the island.

Beaches

There are several good beaches on the road heading north from Niebla, including the white sand beaches of **San Ignacio** and **Curiñanco**, and the pink sand beach called **Playa Rosada**. You can reach these beaches by taking the buses in front of the Valdivia Municipal Market on Prat.

PRACTICAL INFORMATION

Banks: There are several banks with ATM's around the Plaza de Armas and on Esmeralda.

Bookstore: Libros Chiloé, *Corner of Caupolicán and Chacabuco*

Business Hours: 9am-1pm; 3pm-6pm

Currency Exchange: Arauco, *Galería Arauco 331, Local 24, Tel. 212177;* **La Reconquista**, *Carampangue 325, Tel. 213305;* **Banco Santander**, *Pérez Rosales 585, Tel. 213066*

E-Mail Service: Internet Public Access, *Letelier 236, Of. 202. Tel. 294-4300*
Laundry: Lavandería Azul, *Chacabuco 280*
Medical Service: Regional Hospital, *Bueras 1003. Tel. 214066*
Post Office: Correos de Chile, *O'Higgins 575*
Supermarkets: Las Brisas, *east side of the Plaza de Armas*
Telephone/Fax: The area code is 63. Long distance call center **Entel,**
    Arauco 601.
Tourist Office/Maps: Sernatur, *Prat 555, Tel. 215739*

LAGO RANCO

Lago Ranco, an enormous lake of 41,000 hectares, is one of the least visited lakes in the Lake District for the simple reason that it does not have a snow-capped volcano reflecting into its waters. Instead, visitors must be content with gorgeous folds of verdant mountains layered into infinity. A four hour drive around the lake will take you to translucent green streams traversed by hand-pulled ferries, to sweeping viewpoints, and to the hidden **Salto de Nilahue** waterfall. Most of the houses on the lake are vacation homes, but there are a couple of interesting lodging options.

Bahía Coique, *Tel. 63/481264,* is a set of condominiums on an isolated beach front property near the town of Futrono. The condominiums vary in size and can accommodate 6-15 people. They are extremely popular with families, especially during the high season. The resort features a good restaurant, a golf course, tennis courts, a pool, fishing, and horseback riding. Prices start at $200 per condominium with weekly rates available. Another lodging possibility is the **Thule Hotel,** *km 2 Camino Puerto Lapi, Tel. 63/491293, Double $85.* The towns of **Lago Ranco** on the south side of the lake and **Futrono** on the north side are simple agricultural communities which service the tour industry during the high-season.

PUYEHUE-RUPANCO-OSORNO AREA

This area consists of two large lakes – **Puyehue** and **Rupanco** – and **Puyehue National Park,** which is sandwiched in between the eastern end of the lakes. **Osorno** is the region's commercial center, founded to serve as an intermediary settlement between Chiloé and Valdivia.

Most people will travel the 47 km from Osorno on highway 215 to **Lago Puyehue** only to pass alongside of the lake en route to the park. **Entre Lagos** is a simple town on the western shore of the lake. On the town's main road there are a few small grocery stores and a country-style restaurant, **Cafe El Fin,** which fixes any kind of meat desired *a lo pobre,* that is, covered in grilled onions, french fries, and fried eggs.

Continuing up the highway along the shoreline you will encounter an array of cabins and restaurants. A good choice for a restaurant is the Chilean *asado*-style barbecue **Fogón Las Leñas** featuring a huge deck circling the restaurant with impressive views of the lake. Up the highway is the best place on the lake for recreational lodging, the **Cabañas Ñilque**, *km 65 Lago Puyehue, Tel. 64/231177*. The cabins are set up in a huge lakeside field for kids to romp in and fishing boats are available.

If you continue on highway 295 toward the Argentine border rather than entering the park, you will reach a Conaf station where two a kilometer long trail can be hiked to the **Salto del Indio** waterfall. Another alternative is a to pack your gear to hike a 16 kilometers trail to the **Puyehue Volcano**.

LAKE MAKING

The vast majority of Chile's lakes were created by glacial activity. Glacial tongues descended from the Andes carving out depressions and transporting sediment en route. Glacial melting began 17,000 years ago, leaving behind walls of moraine sediment that dammed up water runoff in the depressions.

A few of the lakes formed when a volcanic eruption sealed off a valley with volcanic rock. An example is Lago Todos Los Santos in Vicente Pérez Rosales National Park, formed by an eruption of the Osorno Volcano.

The 107,000-hectare **Puyehue National Park** is endowed with extraordinary multiple volcano views, thermal baths, numerous small lakes, and a rambunctious waterfall, it seems, around every turn. The reason Puyehue is the most frequented national park in Chile is because of the extensive road access for motorists and the large number of beds available in three large lodging centers, which include the notable **Termas Puyehue Hotel** and the ski resort's **Hotel Antillanca**. Despite the number of visitors it receives, the park is mellow in the off-season. During the high-season months of January and February, however, you are more likely to encounter traffic line-ups than happy trails.

There are a couple of good but steep hiking trails and a thermal bath complex near the visitor center. The bath consists of a large indoor and a large outdoor pool and cost $15 and $10 respectively. There are also 4-6 person A-frame cabins available here for $50 in low season and $95 during the high season. Below the cabins is an appealing restaurant designed with the tables centered around a open circular kitchen area. For cabin reservations, call **Aguas Calientes**, *Tel. 64/231177 or 64/236988*. The camping area is across the stream from the cabins and baths.

If you follow the road 22 km to the Antillanca Ski Resort, you will pass several small waterfalls and lakes. There is some of the most reliable snow skiing here even during the driest of winters. If you are in the area during a clear day, you should make it a priority to drive to the top of the Casablanca Volcano. Continue past the hotel four kilometers to reach the **Mirador**. The black road, made of crunchy volcanic soil, snakes under ski lifts, up the side of the volcano, and past an ancient plugged crater to the top of the world. The green Puyehue valley stretches below, as the tops of surrounding volcanoes come into sight. You climb the last, lunar mound and suddenly there are volcanoes and lakes in every direction. It is one of the most spectacular views in Chile on a clear day and it is amazingly accessible by car. It is also rewarding to reach on foot.

Two notable hotels in the region include one of our best places to stay in Chile:

TERMAS PUYEHUE, *Ruta 215 km 76. Puyehue National Park. Tel./Fax 64/232157, Santiago Tel./Fax 2/293-6000. Website: www.puyehue.cl. 175 rooms. Double lakeside with balcony $135. Breakfast included. Full board, add $35 per person. Restaurant. Bar. Game room. Thermal baths. Indoor and outdoor pools. Horse stable. Tennis courts. Day care center. Convention rooms. Credit cards accepted.*

This is a classic resort built of locally quarried stone in 1942 near the entrance of the national park. One end of the expansive edifice houses a magnificent high-ceilinged restaurant, a woodsy bar, and a rustic lounge area with an immense fireplace. Also in this end of the hotel is the game room, the activity center offering outings from horseback riding to easy hikes to fly fishing, and a day care center.

Rooms are rustic but with plush linens as a finishing touch. The rooms on the third floor have the best views from their balconies and cost the same as the ones on the second floor.

During the summer the hotel invites a series of speakers so your evenings can be as stimulating as your days. On the other hand if your prerogative is R&R, you can steep yourself in one of the thermal baths or swim under the beautiful wooden beams of the indoor pool. There is a stylish outdoor pool as well.

Selected as one of our best places to stay – see Chapter 10 for more details.

HOTEL ANTILLANCA, *Puyehue National Park. Tel. 64/202001. Fax 64/235114. 137 rooms. Double $129. Breakfast included. Restaurant. Bar. Pool in summer. Alpine skiing. Babysitting. Boutique. Credit cards accepted.*

Located at the bottom of the Casablanca Volcano, this lodge features skiing in the winter and hiking in the summer. The rooms are well-furnished and cozy, as is the entire lodge. The cafeteria has a huge deck that fills up with resting skiers or sunbathers depending on the season.

The hotel is rustic, with columns made from trees that still sport limbs, and giant fireplaces where everyone gathers at night. There is also an attached 30-room hotel, called the **Refugio**, which offers nice rooms for about 30% less.

Lago Rupanco is one of the most undeveloped of large lakes in the Lake District. The lake can be reached only by unpaved road either by traveling 13 kilometers south from Entre Lagos on Lago Puyehue or by traveling 20 kilometers north from Puerto Octay on Lago Llanquihue. The going is rough on these roads but the payoff is the exceptionally lush, remote environs. The southern lake shore offers excellent views of the Casablanca Volcano across the water. Two lodging options on this lake are **El Paraíso**, *Tel. 09/6433272* at the west end of the lake, and **Hosteria Rupanco**, *Tel. 64/235861* at mid-lake on the south side. There is a fly fishing lodge at the far east end of the lake, **Hotel Bahía Escocia**, *Tel. 64/ 371352.*

Osorno is sometimes confused as a destination of interest with its namesake the Osorno Volcano. The town is actually a regional agricultural commercial center. With the scores of attractive options within a few hours of it, there is no reason to stay here. If you do get stuck here overnight in transit, try the **Hotel Del Prado**, *Cochrane 1162, Tel. 64/ 235020, double $95*, or the **Villa Eduviges**, *Eduviges 856, Tel. 235023, double $40.*

FRUTILLAR

Frutillar is the quintessential, charming Lake District berg on **Lago Llanquihue**. Surrounded by dairy fields and a wrap-around view of the majestic Osorno Volcano, it exudes bucolic tranquility and German cultural influence. The German Club is the town's most popular restaurant, the German Museum is the town's primary attraction, and *leiderhosen* must be worn by all who visit. OK, the dress code isn't strictly enforced.

ARRIVALS & DEPARTURES

Frutillar is 30 km north of Puerto Varas and 50 km north of Puerto Montt. The exit from the Pan-American Highway will deposit you in Frutillar Alto so you have to take Carlos Richter Road down to the lake to reach the hotel area in Frutillar Bajo.

The bus companies that service Frutillar have their offices in Frutillar Alto so you have to take a taxi the kilometers between there and the hotel area in Frutillar Bajo. The bus companies with offices in Frutillar are **Cruz del Sur**, *Pedro Montt 2333, Tel. 671218*, and **Tur-bus**, *Diego Portales 150, Tel. 421390.*

ORIENTATION

The town of 5,000 people is divided into two parts - Frutillar Bajo and Frutillar Alto. **Frutillar Bajo** (Lower Frutillar) is the charming lakeside neighborhood, while **Frutillar Alto** (Upper Frutillar) is the comercial center almost two kilometers away. The two sections are connected by Carlos Richter Road. Almost all of the hotels, restaurants, and shops are located on Phillipi which runs along the lake, or on Vicente Pérez Rosales, a parallel street one block toward the hill.

WHERE TO STAY

Expensive

HOTEL AYACARA, *Avenida Philippi 1215. Tel./Fax 65/421550. 8 rooms. Double $115. Breakfast included. Restaurant during summer. Fishing trips. Babysitting. Open September-April. Credit cards accepted.*

If you want to stay across from the beach right in lower Frutillar, this is an excellent choice. The charming old house, built in 1910, looks no different than the scores of others along the main drag from the outside, but once inside you realize that it has been completely and competently remodeled. High ceilings, large windows, and blond wood let in loads of light.

All of the rooms are large and comfortable with beautiful furnishings. The front ones with lake views are especially impressive. The rooms are so well-furnished and inviting, it might be hard to pull yourself out of repose to enjoy the adventures to be had in the area. The hotel specializes in trout and salmon fishing trips, but can also organize other activities.

BADENHOFF APART-HOTEL, *Pérez Rosales 673. Tel. 65/421649. 12 apartments. Four person apartment $160. Breakfast included. Credit cards accepted.*

The centrally-located Badenhoff offers split level units with two bedrooms, well-equipped kitchens, and newly furnished, homey living areas. The hotel offers a two person rate of $75 for the same units during the low season.

HOTEL SALZBURG, *Road to Playa Maqui, Lower Frutillar. Tel. 65/42589. Fax 65/42599. 25 rooms. 15 cabins. Double $105. Breakfast included. Restaurant. Bar. Excursions. Credit cards accepted.*

This hotel is very popular with Chilean families. The cutesy pseudo-German building, complete with geese embroidered on lace curtains, is a bit overdone for us, but some people really like this style. The well-landscaped property a few kilometers out of town is perfectly situated for prime views of the lake and area volcanos from both the common areas as well as the rooms. Both the cabins and the rooms and clean and comfortable.

HOTEL KLEIN SALZBURG, *Philippi 663. Tel./Fax 65/421201. 8 rooms. Double $118. Breakfast included. Credit cards accepted.*

A sister hotel to the Hotel Salzburg, this remodeled gray and white German home in front of the beach is a Frutillar landmark. A bit saccharine, but airy and well-maintained, this hotel offers location, location, location for those that want to be in the center of things. The restaurant, open for lunch and *onces*, offers some of the best desserts in town.

HOSTAL CINCO ROBLES, *Camino Los Bajos km 3. Tel. 65/339130. 20 rooms. Double $100. Breakfast included. Restaurant. Credit cards accepted.*

A white gravel driveway lined with enormous elms leads the way to this family run cabin-style hotel. The rooms are somewhat worn but not overly so, in fact, the wear seems appropriate in the woodsy surroundings. The front side view from the rooms is of the lake and the Calbuco Volcano. There is extensive acreage out back where families play volley-ball and soccer. Larger rooms are available for families. Note that the Cinco Robles is located three kilometers out of town so it is more convenient if you have a car.

Moderate

HOTEL VOLCÁN PUNTIAGUDO, *Camino Fundo Las Piedras. Tel. 65/421648, Fax 65/421640. 10 rooms. Double $85. Breakfast included. Restaurant. Pool. Credit cards accepted.*

The striking Bauhaus architecture of this luxurious inn will shake up your perception of country hotels. Its location on a grassy five hectare lot atop a bucolic hill above Lake Llanquihue allows each of the rooms to open up to an unparalleled view of the water and volcanoes. Beautifully custom-crafted wood headboards, end tables, and shelves interplay superbly with walls painted in bold primary colors. Rooms also feature track lighting, highly functional reading lights, and separate wall heaters in the bathrooms. There is a well-stocked bar in the lounge area as well as a superb wine selection in the dining room; breakfasts are noteworthy here.

The stylish hotel is surprisingly recreational and a good choice for those of you traveling with children. Several rooms are outfitted with a loft nesting two small beds to which fascinated kids climb via a wooden ladder. There is a video room, a raised sexagonal pool, hiking trails, and a fishing boat for guest use.

Low season rates drop to $68, making the Hotel Volcán Puntiagudo one of the best values in the country. There are discounts for stays of three nights or more all year round, except in July when the hotel is closed.

Selected as one of our best places to stay – see Chapter 10 for more details.

RESIDENZ AM SEE, *Avenida Philippi 539. Tel. 65/421539. Fax 65/421858. 12 rooms. Double $86. Breakfast included. No credit cards.*

During the high season you're better off at one of the top tier hotels for roughly the same price, but a low season price of $43 makes this an excellent value the rest of the year. Right on the beach in lower Frutillar, this spotless, light hostal is the best choice in its class. The rooms are tidy and the owners are nice. The **Hosteria Winkler**, *down the street at Philippi 1155, Tel. 65/421388*, is a decent second alternative in the same price range.

Inexpensive

Inexpensive accommodations running about $35 for a double with breakfast are the **Hosteria Trayén**, *Philipi 963, Tel. 65/421346* and the **Hosteria Arroyo**, *Phillipi 1155, Tel. 65/421560.*

WHERE TO EAT

MERLIN, *Martinez 584, Puerto Varas. Tel. 233105. Reservations needed. Expensive. Credit cards accepted.*

Although this restaurant is in the neighboring town of Puerto Varas, we consider it worth the trip from Frutillar. See the *Puerto Varas* section.

CLUB ALEMÁN, *San Martin 22. Tel. 421249. Moderate/Expensive. Credit cards accepted.*

With Frutillar's reputation as the town with the best preserved German heritage, you can't miss the chance to eat at the German Club. With excellent views of Osorno and simple décor, the restaurant offers a mainly Chilean menu with German influence. The *longaniza a lo pobre*, sausage with grilled onion, french fries, and fried eggs, is an outstanding dish that can easily feed two. Wash it down with a cold Kunstmann. As the label says, *"Das gute bier."*

SELVA NEGRA, *Antonio Varas 24. Tel. 421408. Moderate/Expensive. Credit cards accepted.*

The name means Black Forest in English, referring of course to Germany. The German influence is mainly in the name, but that doesn't preclude this from being one of the best spots in town for a meal. The chilote-style hut is a cozy place for both meats and seafood.

PARRILLA DON CARLOS, *Balmaceda and Philippi. Tel. 09 643-5909. Moderate/Expensive. Credit cards accepted.*

If you want steak, this is the place for it. The recently remodeled log cabin with views of the lake and volcano is owned by an Argentine. The grilled meats are cooked to perfection as only the *ches* can do. The grilled chicken is also tasty.

SALON DE TE TRATEN, *Philippi 963. Tel. 421254. Moderate. No credit cards.*

This is one of the better places in town for afternoon tea. The restaurant is plainly decorated, but have nice views. While kuchen is the specialty, they serve a full menu. **Bauerhaus**, just down Philippi, is another popular spot at tea time, as the **Hotel Klein Salzburg** at Philippi 663.

CASINO DE BOMBEROS, *Philippi 1065. Tel. 421588. Inexpensive. No credit cards.*

Even though the hook and ladder is in the garage around the corner, it's still fun to eat at the fire station cafeteria. The economical fixed lunch is one of the best in town at any price.

SEEING THE SIGHTS

MUSEO COLONIAL ALEMÁN, *Independencia 641. Open Tuesday-Sunday 9:30am-2pm, 3:30pm-6pm (open until 8pm in the high season). Entry $3.*

A visit to the German Colonial Museum begins with a walk through the well-manicured flower garden with plants native to Germany. There are several buildings on the hillside property replicating life as it was during the settlement of the Lake Region. The first is a watermill which demonstrates the workings of the mechanism and houses a collection of black and white photos. There is a blacksmith shop set up alongside a furnished house that would have been typical of such owned by a craftsman. On top of the hill is the larger *casona* stuffed with imported furnishings of the era and other luxuries such as antique musical instruments and a telescope.

RESERVA FORESTAL EDMUNDO WINKLER, *End of Caupolicán Street. Open 10am-7pm. Entry $1.*

This small park provides a good opportunity to acquaint yourself with the typical flora of the Lake District or just to enjoy a walk in the fresh air. If you wish to lengthen your stroll, you can walk to the reserve by following Avenida Phillipi north along the lake until reaching Caupolicán. Walk up Caupolicán about a kilometer until reaching the park at the end of the road.

Cemetery

You can enjoy some of the best views in town from this well-maintained cemetery. It is interesting to walk through the older plots on the back rows to study the names and relationships between the German families. There are so many Winklers you expect to see a plot for the Fonz. Just follow the main lake front road, Philipi, north up the hill to get here.

Summer Music Festival

Frutillar is host to the region's most popular music festival which is held each year during the last week of January and first week of February. Classical orchestras and solo artists from around the world are invited by the town to play in the 1,000 seat Municipal Gymnasium, then play a few other locations such as Termas de Puyehue and Lago Ranco. You should book your lodging well in advance if you plan on attending.

The Other Side Of The Lake

For other activities in the area, such as activities in the **Vicente Pérez Rosales National Park**, consult the *Seeing the Sights* section of the *Puerto Varas* entry. All activities can be initiated from Frutillar with a half-hour earlier start.

PUERTO VARAS

The perfect cone of the **Osorno Volcano**, magnificently rising 2,650 meters from Llanquihue Lake, dominates the mesmerizing view from Puerto Varas. Meanwhile, Osorno's less renowned sister, the rugged **Calbuco Volcano** to the south, makes up for her symmetrical deficiency by dressing up in illuminated fire tones at sunset.

Like Pucón in the northern section of the Lake District, Puerto Varas has developed to provide comfortable amenities for travelers seeking out the splendors in the southern section. Nature's masterpieces near PuertoVaras include **Vicente Pérez Rosales National Park**, one of the most popular in Chile; the emerald waters of **Lago Todos Los Santos** located in the park, which many cross in boat en route to the Argentine resort town of Bariloche; and the **Rio Petrohue**, which thrills with white water rafting surrounded by three distinctly-shaped volcanoes. Opportunities for outdoor activity are extraordinary. If you engaged in a different outing each day, you could easily fill a month without rest.

The "Puerto" in Puerto Varas' name sometimes leads to confusion as a "Port" reference is normally utilized for seaports. It gained the distinction by serving as the transportation funnel, beginning in 1854, for goods flowing to and from towns around the 86,000 hectare lake. Overland transport to the nearby seaport of Puerto Montt allowed the goods to be shipped onward. The town was populated by German immigrants in the late 1800's. In-town attractions include century old Germanic mansions in the hills above town, a popular black sand beach, and a pleasant boardwalk which runs from town to the beach area. Of culinary note is **Merlin**, an unassuming restaurant that prepares the most creative and savory Chilean cuisine in the country.

ARRIVALS & DEPARTURES
By Bus
Buses all operate out of individual offices. They have direct service to most Lake District destinations as well as to Santiago.

Bus Companies
• **Cruz del Sur**, *Del Salvador 237. Tel. 233008*
• **Lit**, *Walker Martinez 227. Tel. 233838*
• **Tas Choapa**, *Walker Martinez 230. Tel. 233831*
• **Varmontt**, *San Francisco 666. Tel. 232592*

Buses offering service to Ensenada and Petrohue National Park:
• **Andina del Sur**, *Del Salvador 257. Tel. 232511*
• **Buses Erwin**, *San Pedro 210*

By Car
Puerto Varas is 110 kilometers south of Osorno and 20 kilometers north of Puerto Montt on the Panamericana. Access to and from the north is via Del Salvador Street; to and from the south is via San Francisco Street. Both roads lead you into the heart of the *centro*.
• **Auto Rental: Turismo Nieve**, *San Bernardo 406. Tel. 232299*

By Plane
The Puerto Montt airport is 25 kilometers from Puerto Varas. Flights to and from Santiago, Concepción, Balmaceda, and Punta Arenas are serviced by the large national airlines You can reach Puerto Varas by cab for about $20 or take a bus into the Puerto Montt Bus Terminal, then catch another bus to Puerto Varas which will cost about $5 total.

Airline Offices in Puerto Montt (not in Puerto Varas):
• **Avant**, *Benavente 305, Tel. 278317*
• **Lan Chile**, *San Martin 200. Tel. 253141. Toll free 600-600-4000*
• **Ladeco**, *Benavente 350, Tel. 253002. Toll free 600-600-4000*

ORIENTATION
Puerto Varas is located at the southwestern point of the semi-triangular Llanquihue Lake, 20 kilometers from Puerto Montt. The town's commercial center is set up on and around Del Salvador Street. The Plaza de Armas is just a half block away from the lake. From the commercial center you can walk along the boardwalk or drive one kilometer to the beach area.

GETTING AROUND TOWN

Everything in the commercial area is within walking distance. You might want to take a cab between the centro and the beach area establishments on Vicente Pérez Rosales street, but this can also be pleasantly strolled on the boardwalk.

WHERE TO STAY

Expensive

HOTEL COLONOS DEL SUR, *Del Salvador 24. Tel. 65/233369. Fax 65/232080. E-mail: htlcolal@entelchile.net. 54 rooms. Double $130. Breakfast included. Restaurant. Bar. Swimming pool. Sauna. Cable TV. Credit cards accepted.*

This hotel, built in the German colonial style, boasts the best location in town. Positioned on the waterfront with excellent views of Volcán

Osorno, it is also just blocks from the center of town. Both the rooms and the hotel are decorated with period antiques such as the map of Chile hanging in the stairway that we coveted each time we passed it. The rooms are large enough to have space for a small table with chairs in addition to the standard bedroom furniture.

The bar overlooking the lake is an excellent place to spend some time watching the sunset while you sip your complementary welcome *pisco* sour. The hotel restaurant offers an international menu with both southern Chilean and German cuisines.

HOTEL CABANAS DEL LAGO, *Klenner 195. Tel. 65/232291. Fax 65/232707. E-mail calago@entelchile.net. 55 rooms. 21 cabins. Double $105. Restaurant. Bar. Swimming pool. Sauna. Cable TV. Baby sitting. Credit cards accepted.*

This hotel sits above the lake and the rest of town with outstanding views of both the Osorno and Calbuco volcanoes across the lake. The rooms are decorated with lovely blonde wood, floral prints on the walls, and light bed covers. The fully furnished cabins are a bargain as they cost less than the rooms. This is a good place if you have kids, as there is a play area with swings in the middle of the grounds as well as an indoor playhouse for those rainy days.

BELLAVISTA, *Pérez Rosales 060. Tel. 65/232011. Fax 65/232013. 40 rooms. Double $100. Breakfast included. Cable TV. Restaurant. Credit cards accepted.*

The Bellavista is a strong option for a waterfront hotel. The rooms are warmly decorated with exceptional views that look out to Lago Llanquihue and the Osorno Volcano. The boardwalk is just across the street. A restaurant on the ground floor which specializes in seafood also shares the excellent views. The ambience, view, and prices at the nearby **Hotel Licarayén**, *San Jose 114, Tel. 65/232955* are quite similar but the Bellavista is in superior condition.

LOS ALERCES HOTEL AND CABANAS, *Avenida Vicente Pérez Rosales 1281. Tel. 65/232070. Fax 65/233394. 44 rooms, 10 cabins. Double $100. Breakfast included. Restaurant. Bar. Swimming pool. Sauna. Cable TV. Baby sitting. Credit cards accepted.*

This hotel is an excellent option if you want to be on the beach away from downtown. Just twenty meters from the shore, with views of the volcano, you are still just a few minutes in taxi from the center of town. The comfortably furnished rooms, almost all with lake views, are located around a sunny atrium. The fully outfitted *cabañas* sleep up to six and all come with a grill for outdoor barbecues.

Moderate

HOTEL WESTFALIA, *La Paz 507. Tel 65/235555. Fax 65/234446. 19 rooms. Double $50. Breakfast included. Cafeteria. Cable TV. Credit cards accepted.*

This hotel in a quiet residential neighborhood above downtown is an exceptional value. Built in an old colonial home, the hotel offers excellent lodging for the price. Floral bedspreads cover solid furniture, while each room has a distinct, but enjoyable view. We highly recommend this hotel for its price category.

LOS TILOS, *Pérez Rosales 1057. Tel. 65/233126. Rooms 15. Double $95. Breakfast included. Cable TV. Restaurant. Credit cards accepted.*

This bed and breakfast style hotel is housed in a tall Victorian mansion across the street from the beach. While the hotel ratchets up its prices to $95 in January and February, the rooms are less than half that price during the rest of the year making it an excellent value during low season at $45. Details like serpentine wooden handrails and rich floral wallpaper accentuate the hotel's splendid interior.

HOTEL MERLIN, *Martinez 584. Tel. 65/233105. Fax 65/234300. E-mail Merlin@entelchile.net. 6 rooms. Double $50. Breakfast included. Restaurant. Credit cards accepted.*

We think that staying here would be sheer torture because of the temptation to eat every meal in the best restaurant in Chile, which happens to be just downstairs. If you think you are strong enough to ignore the seduction, this is a nice hotel. Simple yet spacious and comfortable rooms are standard. You can take the money you save by staying here and at least allow yourself a few dinners downstairs.

Inexpensive

There are many inexpensive accommodations ranging from $10-$20 per person with shared bath, including several that are in classic German-style homes such as **Hospedaje Rincón Alemán**, *San Francisco 1004, Tel. 232087*, and **Residencial Germanía**, *Senora del Carmen 873, Tel. 233162*.

A highly recommended place with heaps of character in the center of town is **Colores del Sur**, *Santa Rosa 318, Tel. 65/338588, $12 per person*. A few other good options in this category are **Hostal Opapa Juan**, *Arturo Prat 107, Tel. 232234* and **Hospedaje Amancay**, *Walker Martinez 564, Tel. 232201*.

WHERE TO EAT

MERLIN, *Martinez 584. Tel. 233105. E-mail Merlin@entelchile.net. Reservations needed. Expensive. Credit cards accepted.*

This is the best restaurant in Chile. Nothing else comes close. Those are strong words, but we can confidently say that this one comes out on top. Located in the downstairs portion of a small hotel, the two-room restaurant holds only eight tables. There is nothing special about the décor, but its intimate, candle lit simplicity lets you focus on the most important thing – the food.

Our main complaint with most Chilean restaurants is their lack of creativity. Given all the wonderful raw materials the country offers, most items are prepared the same way in almost every restaurant in the country. Things are different here. The German chef has searched out the most uniquely Chilean ingredients and combined them with international flavors to create a sunburst in your mouth.

The traditional *pisco* sours are excellent here, but we recommend branching out and trying the fresh raspberry sour. For appetizers nothing can beat the succulent razor clams, *machas*, in curry vinaigrette. Other excellent choices include another type of clam called *navahuelas* in tart ginger sauce, or the tender asparagus wrapped in smoked trout.

One of the most sublime, as well as popular, main courses is the conger eel and spatzel covered with rich, wild mushroom sauce. We also find ourselves craving the lamb with cilantro and garlic, or the flavorful rabbit cooked with oysters and covered in a delicate white wine sauce. The owner/chef will frequently suggest wine to accompany your fare. One excellent option he showed us was the Casa de Toqui Cabernet Sauvignon, one of the more sumptuous wines in Chile, yet rarely found on menus.

We highly recommend dessert whether you have room or not. The ice creams are made daily on the premises. The berry sorbetes are so fresh you almost have to check for prickers. One of the best is the blackberry sorbete with white chocolate mousse bathed in fresh kiwi sauce.

You cannot be in a rush when you dine here. The owner/chef personally takes each order and it is not unusual to spend two and a half to three hours over your meal. With only one seating an evening, there is nobody rushing you out of the restaurant. Sit back, relax, and give your taste buds the royal treatment.

IBIS, *Vicente Pérez Rosales 1117. Tel. 232017. Expensive/Moderate. Credit cards accepted.*

It's easy to drive right on by this small restaurant in front of the lake, but the food here warrants a stop. The decor is highlighted by delightful middle-eastern dolls and puppets. The menu is international with a Chilean traditional plates offered as well.

MAMUSIA, *San Jose 316. Tel. 233343. Moderate. Credit cards accepted.*

The hardest part about eating at the Mamusia is getting past the desert counter to order your meal. The front-line impediment is staffed by an infantry of chocolates armed with nuts, fruit, and creams. Next you must dodge an entire line of baked delicacies such as fruit tarts, cheese-cakes, and flaky pastries. If you actually make it to the peach-colored dining area, an enticing menu awaits with a long list of salads, main courses, and sandwiches on homemade bread.

DONDE EL GORDITO, *Mercado Municipal, Corner of San Bernardo and Del Salvador. Tel. 233425. Moderate. Credit cards accepted.*

This family-run establishment is a perennial favorite for those seeking seafood. The restaurant offers a wide variety of fish and seafood, including *curanto*, the regional surf and turf dish from Chiloé. If you can't make it to Chiloé to order it, do so here.

RESTAURANT EL MERCADO, *Del Salvador across from Las Brisas. Tel. 232876. Moderate. No credit cards.*

This small restaurant is an excellent option a for a traditional seafood meal. Totally informal, yet clean and cheery, they offer the standard seafood menu along with some interesting twists. Sea urchin quiche and octopus soup are two of the more distinct dishes that we've tried.

CAFE DANES, *Del Salvador 441. Tel. 232371. Moderate. Credit cards accepted.*

The Cafe Danes offers hearty meals in a pleasant Scandinavian ambience. It is most popular at lunch time for its fixed item lunch, usually a meat and potato combination that can satisfy the most ravenous of diners. The locale is also host to a variety of newspaper readers and other idlers sipping espresso and lattes.

PIM'S PUB, *Los Colonos 1005. Tel. 233998. Moderate. Credit cards accepted.*

The Old West ambles into Puerto Varas with this Chilean style Tex-Mex entrant. The pub is among the most popular night spots.

For a pizza fix, try either **Aníbal Pizza**, *Corner of Del Salvador and Santa Rosa* or **El Retorno**, *Del Salvador and San Pedro*. The **Open Cafe** on San Pablo serves sandwiches and other light fare.

SEEING THE SIGHTS

There is some good walking to be done in Puerto Varas. The boardwalk along the lake front is a popular stroll. Start from the **Paseo Dock**, a small isthmus with park benches located a half block from the Plaza de Armas. **Canoas Tour Kayak Excursions** sets up kayaks rentals from a truck here or you can call them at *Tel. 233587*.

Turn to your right as you face the Paseo Dock. About a kilometer along the way you will reach the town's black sand beaches.

To see the early twentieth century German mansions in the hills, walk south on San Francisco Street from the centro. Take a right on Maria Braun street where you will see the immense **Iglesia del Corazón Sagrado**, built in 1915. Continue up Purrisima. On the corner of O'Higgins you will encounter Casa Wetzel (1930); on the corner of San Luis, Casa Yunge (1932); on the opposite side of San Javier, Casa Horn

(1925); and at the end of the road Casa Kashel (1930). Here you have the option of turning right on Del Salvador and returning to town or taking a left and continuing to Arturo Prat. Take a right on Prat, then another right on Senora del Carmen.

On that corner you will see Casa Hischfel (1930), then Casa Schwerter housing the Residencial Germanía. Walking down to Senora del Carmen to the next corner you will see Casa Anguilo (1910), then Casa Alemana (1914). Take a left going up a block. Take a right on Decker. To return to the *centro*, take a the next right on Estación. Continuing on Decker you will pass the Casa Emhart (1920) on the corner of Independence, and Casa Binder (1932) on the corner of San Martin. You can continue on Decker to **Phillipi Park** which has a nice viewpoint. To return to town, work your way down by following Bellavista then cutting right to Turismo which will take you to the waterfront.

NIGHTLIFE & ENTERTAINMENT

The main nightlife activity is gambling at the **Municipal Casino** on San Francisco Street in the old Gran Hotel Puerto Varas. **Pim's Pub**, *Los Colonos 1005, Tel. 233998,* is a popular watering hole. **Burlizzer Pub**, *Ruta 5 Sur km 1007, Tel. 232270* is a dance club located five kilometers south of PuertoVaras.

EXCURSIONS & DAY TRIPS

You can find pretty much any outdoor activity you desire in the area surrounding Puerto Varas. We recommend **Aqua Motion** as a well-organized and respected tour operator. They offer a long list of excursions spanning the entire range of difficulty levels. Another good company is **Turismo Nieve**. An excellent website to check out before going is *http://travelhouse.cl* which highlights the vast array of outdoor activities in the region.

VICENTE ROSALES NATIONAL PARK AND TODOS LOS SANTOS LAKE, *70 kilometers east of Puerto Varas. Entry $2.*

Chile's oldest national park is this 250,000 hectare protuberant beauty, dominated by the 36 kilometer long **Todos Los Santos Lake**, and three volcanoes - **Osorno**, **Puntiagudo**, and **Tronador**. Due to the steep mountainsides which surround the lake, there is not as much terrain dedicated to hiking trails as one would assume for a park of this size. Most of the time spent here is on the lake, ferrying across its emerald waters on a half day trip to **Margarita Island** or to reach **Peulla** on the east side, with many visitors continuing overland to the Argentine lake resort of **Bariloche**.

On the way into the park, five kilometers before reaching the lake's edge, there is a turn-out to the gorgeous **Saltos de Petrohue**, (Petrohue Falls), which dazzle with frothy turbulence as they crash over and through the rocks, and flow translucent emerald green in between and beyond. After paying a $3 entry fee, you walk down a short trail that leads you to a series of bridges leading you out to and over the water.

A two hour round-trip boat ride to the Margarita Island costs $10. The three hour lake crossing to Peulla costs $30. **Andina del Sud** sells tickets at the park's dock and in Puerto Varas, *Del Salvador 72, Tel. 232511.* The excursion is an enjoyable experience when the vibrant hued water of the lake is calm, and the sky is clear enough to see the surrounding volcanoes.

The hiking and horseback riding trails which are easily accessed in the park climb the backside of the Osorno volcano. Camping is not permitted along this route due to a lack of fresh water and sanitary facilities. Another route takes you along the western end of the lake end.

If you have a few days and the proper camping gear to dedicate to an adventure, there is an excellent multi-day hike that begins at mid-lake and cuts behind the Puntiagudo Volcano. You must first hire a boat for the $50, ninety minute lake crossing to El Rincón. There are several small boat operators below the Petrohue Lodge that can accomplish this. The first day's hike of four hours will take you to the **Callao thermal baths**, the second day's hike of four hours to small mountain lake, **Laguna Quetros**, and the third day's hike of three hours to the road that runs along **Lago Rupanco**. Stop by the Conaf ranger station for details on these hikes.

HOTEL PETROHUE, *Vicente Pérez Rosales National Park. Tel./Fax 65/258042. 30 rooms. Double $105. Breakfast included. Restaurant. Bar. Adventure tour company. Credit cards accepted.*

Located at the end of the road into Petrohue National Park, this lodge is sandwiched between the perfect cone of the Osorno Volcano and the emerald waters of Lake Todos Los Santos. Many travelers use it as a base to take advantage of the myriad activities available in and near the park. With comfortable rooms, good food, and an excellent on-site adventure tour company ready to plan any outing, you could easily stay occupied for a week.

The wooden lodge is simple, but welcoming. A cozy bar and informal restaurant are reliable spots to meet other travelers. The restaurant does a good job of using local ingredients to spice up the meals, such as the delicious smoked salmon spread at breakfast. The hotel is powered by a noisy generator and the floors are squeaky, so try to get a room at the end of the hallway facing the lake.

The adventure company located here, **Expediciones Vicente Pérez Rosales**, offers treks, climbs, canyoning, mountain biking, and rafting. All of the excursions originate and end at the lodge.

HOTEL PEULLA, *Peulla, Vicente Pérez Rosales National Park. Tel. 65/ 258041. 45 rooms Double $115 . Breakfast included. Restaurant. Credit cards accepted.*

The Hotel Peulla is similar to the Hotel Petrohue, but with fewer crowds surrounding it due the more remote location. Those who travel between the Argentine resort town of Bariloche and the Lake District frequently use this hotel as a stopover.

Rafting the Petrohue River

Several adventure tour organizers offer a half-day rafting trip down the Petrohue River for about $40 per person. This is a relatively tame rafting trip made up of Class III rapids. The guides will direct the raft to the biggest holes to add to the excitement, but really what makes this trip worthwhile is the spectacular scenery. Depending on which way the raft is spinning, you will be looking at one or more of the three volcanoes which surround the river. This is a great way to see the region's wilderness while getting a workout at the same time.

You can book the trip with an adventure tour office in the park or in Puerto Varas. From a logistical stand-point, the park is closer to the drop-in and take-out points so it is better to do it from there if you are staying out there anyway. The tour companies will provide transportation, all necessary gear including wetsuits, and a snack at the take-out point.

RAFTING SPANISH 101

We've rafted with a few Chilean guides who preferred giving paddling instructions in their native tongue rather than attempting to accommodate a polyglot crew. It might be helpful to take note of the specialized Spanish to assist you in your white water adventure:

raft: balsa
paddle (n): remo
paddle (v): remar
life jacket: chaleco salvavidas
helmet: casco
wetsuit: traje de neopreno
rapids: rápidos
hole: hoyo
forward: adelante
back: atrás
high side: high side

Climbing the Osorno Volcano

This is a full day outing departing at 5:30 in the morning from Puerto Varas. The ascent to the 2,650 meter summit takes four hours from the La Burbuja ski center, half of that through volcanic rock, half through the snow at the top of the cone. The descent takes about two hours. Tour companies will provide all necessary gear. It is always recomendable to take extra water on excursions like this to assure proper hydration. Climbing trips up the 2,015 meter Calbuco Volcano are also possible.

Horseback Riding
There are several different horseback riding excursions including an excellent full day ride to the turquoise waters of the sixty meter El Caliente Falls.

For a weekend outing at a remote ranch, contact **Campo Aventura**, *Tel. 65/232910, Fax 65/232910, E-mail outsider@telesur.cl.*

Other Excursions
You can also arrange fly fishing, multi-day hiking trips, mountain biking, and canyoning (climbing up through a river and canyon walls) through the adventure tour organizers.

Adventure Tour Agencies
• **Aqua Motion**, *San Pedro 422. Tel/Fax 232747. E-mail: aquamotn@telsur.cl.*
• **Expediciones Vicente Pérez Rosales**, *Vicente Pérez Rosales Park. Tel./Fax 258042.*
• **Turismo Nieve**, *San Bernardo 406. Tel. 232299. Fax 232399. E-mail: turnieve@entelchile.net*

PRACTICAL INFORMATION
Banks: BCI, *Del Salvador 305.* BCI has an ATM as do others on the plaza.
Business Hours: 9am-1pm; 3pm-6pm. Some tour organizers stay open as late as 9pm
Currency Exchange: Exchange, *Del Salvador 257, Local 11*
Laundry: Center, *Gramados 1090* and **Schnee**, *San Pedro 26-A*
Medical Service: Clínica Alemana, *Dr. Bader 810. Tel. 232336*
Post Office: Correos de Chile, *Corner of San Pedro and San Jose*
Supermarkets: Las Brisas, *Corner of Del Salvador and San Bernardo*
Telephone/Fax: The area code is 65. Long distance call center at *Santa Rosa and Del Salvador*
Tourist Office/Maps: Municipal Tourist Office, *Plaza de Armas, Corner of San Jose and San Juan*

PUERTO MONTT
Puerto Montt, the waterfront capital of the Tenth Region, is utilized as the primary transportation hub at the southern end of the Lake District. Although not really worth planning into your trip as a destination in itself,

many travelers wind up passing through here en route to other destinations. Puerto Montt is at the southern end of the *Panamericana* in the Lake District; at the northern end of the **Austral Highway**; the port of departure for the ships which cruise through the **Chilean fjords**; and just north of the dock from which ferries cross to island of **Chiloé**.

The Puerto Montt airport is located 12 kilometers from Puerto Montt, but it is important to note, only 30 kilometers from Puerto Varas, a pleasant resort town on the edge of Lago Llanquihue and the southern Lake District center for outdoor excursions. Although Puerto Montt isn't the type of town that should be avoided like the plague, the point is, you can probably conveniently spend your time in the more attractive town of Puerto Varas unless an early morning departure from Puerto Montt precludes you from doing so.

Puerto Montt was founded by the Chilean government's agent appointed to colonize the area, **Vicente Pérez Rosales**. Rosales colonized the area with German immigrants who celebrated the founding of the town in 1852 by singing songs in their native tongue while decked out in traditional dress from the homeland. The town was named for President Manuel Montt. Although construction of the larch church was finished six years later (and still stands today), the town's growth lagged until a railroad link was established in the early 1900's. It's commercial expansion accelerated as it became a logistical hub linking the territories of Chiloé, Aisén, and Magallanes to Santiago. In addition to logging, the area has recently added a number of salmon farms to support the regional economy. Puerto Montt's current population numbers at 110,000.

ARRIVALS & DEPARTURES
By Boat

Puerto Montt is the arrival and departure point for the popular Navimag cruise through the Chilean Fjords to and from Puerto Natales. The four day/three night cruise navigates through the verdant islands and fjords along the southern Chilean coast. For full details see the *Puerto Natales* section of the *Magallanes* chapter.

Another option is to take the shorter, more upscale Skorpios cruise to Laguna San Rafael to see the San Valentín Glacier. We cover this cruise in the *Coyhaique* section of the Austral Region chapter.

The ferry boats to the island of Chiloé arrive and depart from Paragua, 60 kilometers southwest of Puerto Montt. There are two boats running continuously and the wait to depart is rarely more than twenty minutes. The crossing takes about one half hour. Buses to Chiloé will cover the boat transport in the price of the ticket.

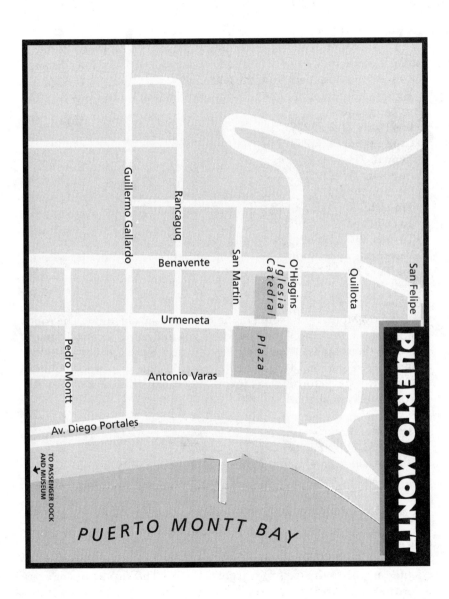

Guillermo Gallardo

Rancaguq

Benavente

San Martin

O'Higgins

Iglesia
Catedral

Quillota

San Felipe

Urmeneta

Plaza

Pedro Montt

Antonio Varas

Av. Diego Portales

TO PASSENGER DOCK
AND MUSEUM

PUERTO MONTT

PUERTO MONTT BAY

Passenger Boats
• **Crucero Skorpios**, *Angelmó 1660, Tel. 252996*
• **Navimag Puerto Eden**, *Angelmó 2187. Tel. 253318*

By Bus
    Puerto Montt has a central bus terminal located on Diego Portales, about a kilometer west of the Plaza de Armas. All local and long distance buses arrive and depart from the terminal

Bus Companies
• **Bus Norte**, *Tel. 252783*
• **Cruz del Sur**, *Tel. 254731*
• **Tepual**, *Tel. 254999*
• **Intersur**, *Tel. 259320*
• **Lit**, *Tel. 254011*
• **Transchiloe**, *Tel. 254934*
• **Tas Choapa**, *Tel. 254828*
• **Turbus**, *Tel. 253329*
• **Varmontt**, *Tel. 254410*
• **Via Tur**, *Tel. 253133*

By Car
    Puerto Montt is just south of the Panamericana highway. The route to the city center is well marked with signs indicating "centro". Follow Petorca, then take a left on Benavente. To access the Carretera Austral, follow the coastal road, Diego Portales toward Pelluco. To head to Chiloé, leave town via Petorca, then follow the Panamericana south to the Paragua ferry dock.

Car Rental Agencies
• **Autovald**, *Diego Portales 1330. Tel. 256355*
• **Budget**, *Gallardo 450. Tel. 254888*
• **Fama**, *Diego Portales 506. Tel. 258060*
• **Hertz**, *Antonio Varas 126. Tel. 259585*
• **Salfa**, *Urmeneta 1036. Tel. 255000*

By Plane
    The Puerto Montt airport is the best entry point for accessing the southern part of the Lake District and Chiloé. The airport is almost as close to Puerto Varas as it is to Puerto Montt, in case you prefer to utilize that town as a base. Flights to and from Santiago, Concepción, Balmaceda, and Punta Arenas are serviced by the large national airlines. Many regional destinations can be accessed by the regional airlines. The bus

from the airport cost $1.50 to the Puerto Montt bus terminal. Taxis cost $11 to downtown Puerto Montt and $22 to Puerto Varas.

Airlines
• **Avant**, *Benavente 305, Tel. 278317 or 228312 or 228322.*
• **Lan Chile**, *San Martin 200. Tel. 253141. Toll free 600-600-4000*
• **Ladeco**, *Benavente 350, Tel. 253002. Toll free 600-600-4000*
• **Aero Chaiten**, *Quillota 127. Tel. 253219*
• **Aero Sur**, *Urmenta 149. Tel. 252523*

ORIENTATION

The Plaza de Armas looks out to the **Bahía Puerto Montt**. The commercial area around extends for several blocks on the other three sides, until running into a steeply graded hill on the back side. Many travelers end up spending time on the eastern side of town where the museum, bus terminal, and the dock where the Skorpios and Navimag cruises depart are all located. The coastal road Diego Portales, which eventually becomes Angelmó, is the best link between the two areas. A boardwalk runs along most of Diego Portales, far enough from the street to make it a pleasant foot route.

GETTING AROUND TOWN

You can walk to most places in town but you might want to use a taxi between distant points of the city such as the Plaza de Armas and the dock.

WHERE TO STAY

Most of the hotels are located in the commercial sector around the Plaza de Armas, including the area along the waterfront. The cheaper hotels are located in the older part of town near the bus station and the dock. Good moderately priced hotels are scarce.

Expensive

DON LUIS GRAN HOTEL, *Corner of Urmeneta and Quillota. Tel. 65/ 259001, Fax 65/232707. 60 rooms. Double $105. Breakfast included. Cable TV. Restaurant. Bar. Sauna. Conference rooms.*

The Don Luis is an excellent choice among the top end hotels in Puerto Montt and is particularly suited for business people. Conveniently located, a block away from the main square the hotel is designed with several conference rooms. Those guests traveling for pleasure will also find the hotel quite comfortable. The hotel features a dry sauna and cozy bar warmed by a fireplace. Several of the smartly decorated rooms have views of the bay.

VIENTO SUR, *Ejercito 200. Tel. 65/258701. Fax 65/258700. 27 rooms. Double $110. Breakfast included. Restaurant. Bar. Cable TV. Parking. Car Rental. Credit cards accepted.*

High on a hill over the water, this yellow and blue German-influenced building houses our top choice in town. The style is turn of the 20th century, while the comfort and service are turn of the 21st. The warm and inviting interior is decorated with a mixture of antiques and clean, modern lines. Woods native to the region cover the walls and floors, while huge picture windows peer down over Puerto Montt's bay.

The bright lobby entrance is on one of the upper floors, as the hotel's rooms are built into the hill below. Each of the rooms is painstakingly decorated with such details as stained glass windows inlaid in the doors. The quarters are a bit small, but the view makes up for it.

The hotel is only four blocks from the town's plaza, but that's two blocks over and two blocks straight up. Be prepared either to get a good workout or take a cab.

HOTEL VICENTE PÉREZ ROSALES, *Antonio Varas 447. Tel. 65/252571. Fax 65/255473. 83 rooms. Double $105. Breakfast included. Restaurant. Bar. Tea Salon. Cable TV. Credit cards accepted.*

The first thing to catch your eye as you enter the large lobby of this hotel is the masthead literally busting out of the fireplace. This figure has been a symbol of the establishment since it was built in 1962. Long the best hotel in town, it is still a traditional favorite, which offers good food and service in a privileged location. The rooms are larger than in some of the other options in town, and most have been recently redecorated.

Moderate

COLON APART HOTEL, *Pedro Montt 65, 7th floor. Tel. 65/264290. Fax 65/264293. 29 apartments. Double $93. Breakfast included. Cable TV. Parking. Credit cards accepted.*

These comfortable apartments are a great option if you want to be in the middle of things in town but also want space. Located on the top floors of a professional building, the apartments are central to just about everything with restaurants, shopping, tour offices and other services all in a two block radius. Most of the units have excellent views of the bay, while all have kitchenettes with both a microwave and a small range. A number of the apartments have Jacuzzi bathtubs, the perfect way to start an evening of R&R after a day of exploring.

HOTEL MONTT, *Antonio Varas 301. Tel. 65/243651, Fax 65/253652. 45 rooms. Double $60. Breakfast included. Cable TV. Restaurant. Credit cards accepted.*

The Hotel Montt offers ample rooms, some with balconies, overlooking the waterfront. The hotel's redecorated reception area is expansive, but the hallways are a bit dark and are decorated with nature mural wallpaper. It is appropriately priced and close to the Plaza de Armas.

Inexpensive

HOSPEDAJE POLZ, *Jose Mira 1002. Tel. 65/252851. 9 rooms. Double $25. Breakfast included. Cable TV. No credit cards.*

This is the most solid budget accommodation to be found near the bus station. The narrow two-story German style townhouse contains a spiral staircase to the upper floor. The senora who has run the inn for 14 years, keeps it in impeccable shape.

RESIDENCIAL NAVE, *Corner of Antonio Varas and Ancud, Tel. 65/ 253740. 12 rooms. Double $25. $10 per person with shared bath. Breakfast included. No credit cards.*

This is a good option if the Polz is full and is just around the corner from it. Located near the bus station, the *residencial* is two story dwelling decked out in blue, and is a popular spot so a reservation is suggested.

HOSPEDAJE SUIZA, *Independencia 231. Tel. 65/252640. 10 rooms. Double $30. Breakfast included. No credit cards.*

Although somewhat removed from the center of activity, which you can take as a pro or con, depending on your objectives, the Suiza overlooks the harbor a few blocks north of the cruise dock. In addition to providing a bed and breakfast atmosphere, the Swiss artist owner organizes painting and Spanish classes.

HOSPEDAJE PEDRO MONTT, *Pedro Montt 180, Tel. 252276. Rooms 25. Double $30. Breakfast included. No credit cards.*

This low end option is more centralized the others we have listed, but a slight notch down in quality. It is the best budget option outside of the bus station area anyway.

WHERE TO EAT

MERLIN, *Martinez 584, Puerto Varas. Tel. 233105. Reservations needed. Expensive. Credit cards accepted.*

Although this restaurant is in the neighboring town of Puerto Varas, we consider it worth the trip from Puerto Montt. See the *Puerto Varas* section.

BALZAC, *Urmenta and Quillota. Tel. 259495. Expensive. American Express only.*

This is the top choice in town for excellent quality seafood prepared in ways that go beyond the run of the mill "fish baked in butter." Excellent appetizers such as garlic sautéed eels, or Chardonnay crab go down especially well with a cold *pisco* sour. You can't go wrong with anything on the menu, but don't forget to ask about the daily specials.

CLUB DE YATES, *Juan Soler S/N. Tel. 263606. Expensive. Credit cards accepted.*

The Yacht Club is an upscale locale built on a pier over the Puerto Montt bay about a kilometer east of the Plaza de Armas. The elegant restaurant serves traditional Chilean seafood dishes such as conger eel and scallops. Outdoor seating is available in the summer.

CLUB ALEMÁN, *San Felipe and Antonio Varas. Moderate/Expensive. Credit cards accepted.*

While menu at the German Club has become decidedly Chilean over time (no spatzel or schnitzel here), you'll still get a good meal in an impeccable restaurant. You can try the German-brewed Kunstmann beer out of Valdivia for a touch of the Teutonic.

HOTEL VICENTE PÉREZ ROSALES, *Antonio Varas 447. Tel. 65/ 252571. Moderate/Expensive. Credit cards accepted.*

Known as one of the better restaurants in town, the Vicente Pérez Rosales offers a traditional menu of Chilean seafood specialties along with a wide selection of non-marine choices. The main draw is the view as well as the solid service.

DI NAPOLI, *Gallardo 119. Tel. 254174. Moderate. Credit cards accepted.*

The food here is sure to warm you up if the Puerto Montt weather turns foul. The smell of baking pizza envelops you when you enter the small restaurant. There are over twenty topping options, but our favorites are the *calabria*, with excellent sausage; and the *pinta*, which includes such up-town veggies as artichoke hearts and heart of palm.

AMSEL, *Pedro Montt 56. Tel. 253941. Inexpensive. Credit cards accepted.*

This bi-level café near the plaza is a town gathering spot. Sandwiches, coffees, and desserts are shared over gossip, but the draw is more the downtown location on the water than the food. **Dino's**, at Varas 550, offers similar fare in a comparable environment.

CAFE REAL, *Rancagua 137. Tel. 253750. Inexpensive. Credit cards accepted.*

The Cafe Real offers sandwiches and quick lunches in a coffee shop atmosphere. You can also try the **Cafe Central** next door which offers the same fare. For fast food, go to the **Paseo del Mar Mall** on the corner of Antonio Varas and Talca. The third floor food court includes **Pizza Hut**, **Kentucky Fried Chicken**, and several Chilean outlets like **Lomiton**.

SEEING THE SIGHTS

JUAN PABLO II MUSEUM, *Diego Portales S/N, Tel. 261822. March-December, daily 9am-12pm and 2pm-6pm. January-February, daily Sunday 9am-7pm. Entry $1.*

The museum is named for the Pope John Paul II, who visited Puerto Montt in 1987, and there are a few photos of the visit, but most of the museum displays a hodgepodge of regional artifacts. The museum is in dire need of additional funding and a make over. Although you shouldn't go out of your way to see the museum, it is worthwhile if you are trying to kill time waiting for onward transportation. The museum is close to both the bus station and the dock.

There are a couple of interesting exhibits in the collection. One small area is dedicated to the local archaeological dig at the location of the 12,000 year-old community of Monte Verde. The discovery of this site on the nearby Maullín River, forced archaeologists to adjust their time line estimates of the crossing of the Bering Strait and the migratory populating of the Americas. Also of interest is the Chilote crucifix in the religious iconography section. The artists of the Chilote school used lean, muscled fishermen for models which is evidenced by the sinewy forms of their Christ figures.

DIEGO RIVERA GALLERY, *Corner of Antonio Varas and Quillota. Entry free.*

Named for the Mexican muralist Diego River to commemorate Chilean-Mexican brotherhood, the gallery features temporary art exhibitions. There is not always an exhibition in progress so be prepared for a hit or miss experience.

There is a theater on the ground floor showing art films on the weekends. We caught a fun Jim Jarmusch flick here, *Dead Man*. The top third of the giant screen was slightly out of focus, but it seemed appropriate considering the movie's quirky style.

SHOPPING

There is a large *artesanía* area along Avenida Angelmó past the bus terminal going away from the city center. It is nearly in front of the dock where the Navimag and Skorpios cruises depart.

EXCURSIONS & DAY TRIPS

ALERCE ANDINO NATIONAL PARK, *50 Kilometers southeast of Puerto Montt, 12 kilometers from Chaica. Entry $2.*

The drive out to Alerce is a beautiful adventure featuring fishing villages set on picturesque inlets. The drive follows the northernmost segment of the **Austral Highway**, a winding rubble rock road, with inherent risks of sometimes out-of-control oncoming traffic. The park itself is a mountainous 40,000 hectares covered with a beech forest and the old growth larch (*alerce*), for which it is named, starting at elevations of over 400 meters. Many of the gigantic larch trees are thousands of years old.

The principal walk from the **Chaicas Sector** entrance is along the crystal clear Rio Chaica. From the park entrance, if the road to the campground is closed, you hike the two and a half kilometers to the campground, an additional 500 meters to the waterfall trail, and perhaps 500 meters more through dense rain forest on a well-cut trail until reaching the waterfall. One of the great larches, estimated to be 3,000 years old, is fenced off just above the principal viewing point of the falls.

This hike will take about two hours round-trip from the entrance or only about a half an hour round-trip from the campground. You can also continue up to **Lago Chaiquenes**, an additional three kilometers up the path from the campground. Here, the larches are more abundant and surround the small lake. Another three kilometers of hiking from Lago Chaiquenes will take you to through higher elevations until reaching **Lago Triangulo**.

Camping was not permitted in the park at the time of our last visit, but was okay in the past, and might be permitted again in the future, depending on Conaf's negotiations with a private concessionaire. If you are planning on camping, we suggest, before heading out, that you contact **Conaf** in Puerto Montt, *Ochagavia 464, Tel. 254882.*

The best way to get to the park independently is in a car. Follow the coastal road out north out of Puerto Montt which heads to the Pelluco beach area. Once across the Pelluco Estuary, take the obvious left on Avenida Gallardo to the Austral Highway. The loose gravel road signifies the start of the Austral Highway and it doesn't get any smoother the rest of the way, only more extraordinary in its scenic beauty. The turn-off to the park is about 40 km down the road in the town of Chaica. If you cross the Chaica Bridge (Puente Chaica) then you've gone too far. The left turn to the park is about 500 meters before the bridge. From there, it is 12 km on a sometimes severe road to the park entrance. You should be able to make it out in a two wheel drive, but if its been raining heavily you might opt for a four-wheel drive.

The other independent option is to take a bus from the terminal to Chaica, but from there you are on your own for 12 km. It is a lot easier to try to arrange shared transportation all the way to the park through one of Puerto Montt's travel agencies which offers excursions here, rather than trying to do it with public transport.

ALERCE MOUNTAIN LODGE, *Kilometer 36, Austral Highway. Tel/ Fax 65/286969. E-mail* smontt@telsur.cl. *3 cabins. 6 rooms. Double with full board $230. Bar. Restaurant. Game room. Satellite TV. Sauna. Jacuzzi. Guided hikes. Fishing. Credit cards accepted.*

This lodge, finished in 1998, sits in the middle of 2,000 hectares of forest just a few kilometers from Alerce Andino Park. Constructed from local materials, the rustic-style inn offers a complete escape from the world. Whether you are looking for active days full of trekking, or relaxing ones reading around the fire, you'll be satisfied here.

After turning off the Austral Highway, you still have to cover 12 km of bumpy, dirt road and board a boat to cross *Laguna Reflejos* before arriving to the tree-shrouded lodge. The interiors, decorated with unfinished logs and local *artesanía*, are warm and welcoming. Both the rooms and cabins are decorated in a comfortable, yet first class manner. Don't worry about bringing slippers as each guest is given a pair of wool ones upon arrival to protect the fine wood floors.

Other Excursions Near Puerto Montt

Pelluco is frequently mentioned as an excursion option. This is a beach area about four kilometers east Puerto Montt with a few seafood restaurants. The beach is less than desirable at low tide because exposes trash that has washed ashore.

We cover excursions like climbing the **Osorno Volcano**, rafting the beautiful **Petrohue River**, and visiting **Vicente Pérez Rosales Park** in the *Puerto Varas* section. Travel agencies in Puerto Montt also offer trips to these destinations and are covered below. The Navimag cruise to Puerto Natales through the **Chilean Fjords** is covered in the *Puerto Natales* section of the Patagonia chapter. The Skorpios cruise to the **San Rafael Glacier** is covered in *Coyhaique* section of the *Austral Region* chapter.

Travel Agencies
• **Andina Del Sud**, *Antonio Varas 437. Tel. 257797*
• **Islas del Sur**, *Pacheco Altamirano 2513. Tel. 317526*
• **Travelers Patagonia**, *Angelmó 2456. Tel. 258555*

PRACTICAL INFORMATION

Banks: There are several banks with ATM's on Urmeneta east of the plaza. Other ATM's are located in the Paseo del Mar shopping center and in the supermarkets across from the bus station.

Business Hours: 9am-1pm; 3pm-6pm

Currency Exchange: Exchange, *Antonio Varas 595, Local 3;* **Passport**, *Diego Portales 514, Local 9, Tel. 253811;* **La Moneda de Oro**, *Bus Terminal, Local 37, Tel. 255108;* **Turismo Los Lagos**, *Antonio Varas 595, Local 3, Tel. 259644*

Laundry: **Narly**, *San Martin 167. Tel. 311528*

Medical Service: **Hospital Regional**, *Seminario S/N. Tel. 253992*

National Parks: **Conaf**, *Ochagavia 464. Tel. 254882.*

Post Office: **Correos de Chile**, *Rancagua 126252719*

Supermarkets: The best supermarket downtown is **Full Fresh**, *Paseo del Mar Shopping Center, Corner of Antonio Varas and Talca.* There are two big supermarkets across the street from the bus terminal and near the dock, **Las Brisas** and **Full Fresh**, both on Diego Portales.

Telephone/Fax: The area code is 65. Long distance call centers include: **Chilesat**, *Talca 70*; **Entel**, *Antonio Varas 567*; **CTC**, *Pedro Montt 112.*

Tourist Office/Maps: There is a regional **Sernatur** office on the Plaza at the *corner of San Martin and Antonio Varas*. There are two **municipal tourist kiosks**, one is located across the street from the Plaza toward the waterfront, and another is in the bus terminal.

15. CHILOÉ

The island of Chiloé, along with the smaller islands to the east that complete the archipelago, is one of the most intriguing destinations in Chile due to a rich, distinctive culture developed during centuries of isolation. The landscape of undulating pasture-covered hills is surrounded by the sea on all sides. The family vehicle is as likely to be a motorboat as a car. You will find the diminutive vessels transporting the most unwieldy of cargo, from furniture to farm animals. The inhabitants, known as *Chilotes*, are friendly, hardworking folks, proud of their hearty, flavorful cuisine and colorful legends.

The main island is the second largest in South America, outsized only by Tierra del Fuego. It measures 180 km lengthwise and about 60 km across. The island and archipelago are actually the peaks of the submerged southern end of the Coastal Range. Off the islands' eastern shores are what would be the Central Valley, but here the depression is covered by the ocean, and is known as the **Golfo de Ancud**. Beyond that body of water, the majestically blue Andes Range is visible on the occasional clear day. The islands are frequently socked in below dense cloud cover. The summer months are the best time to visit to avoid rain.

The primary cities of the island are **Ancud**, at the northern extreme, **Castro**, roughly at the halfway point, and **Quellón**, at the southern end. Of these destinations Castro has the most to offer with excellent options for hotels, restaurants, worthwhile attractions, and a centralized location for day trips.

A QUICK TRIP TO CHILOÉ

*A short trip to Chile should include two nights in **Castro**, with a day trip to **Dalcahue** and other small towns, then adding a night in **Ancud** if possible. Additional time could be spent in the more remote locations, perhaps lodging with Chilote families that participate in the Agroturismo program.*

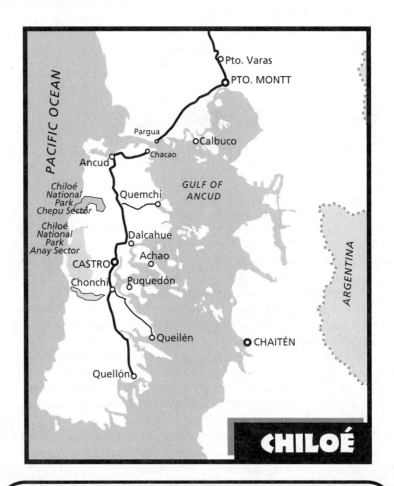

QUELLÓN

Quellón is the southernmost town on Chiloé, the transit point for ferries to and from the Austral Region. Although the town doesn't merit a visit other than in-transit, it is pleasant enough with colorful fishing boats on its dock and a good artisan market. Call ahead to confirm the ferry schedule and buy tickets in advance when possible, especially if you have a vehicle. There are several crossings per week during high season and as few as one per week or one per month during low season. Approximate ferry travel times are six hours to Chaiten, eight hours to Puerto Chacabuco, and nine hours to Puerto Montt.

• Navimag, RR Alejandro, Costanera Pedro Montt across from ferry dock; in Puerto Montt, Angelmo 2187, Tel. 65/253754; in Santiago, El Bosque Norte 0440, Tel. 2/2035030.

• Transmarchilay, B Pincoya, Costanera Pedro Montt by ferry dock, Tel. 65/680511; Ancud Tel. 65/624801; Puerto Montt Tel. 65/270420.

History

Chiloé's original inhabitants were a mixture of the northern Mapuche and the Chonos, a seafaring people from the coastal region of Aisén. The natives lived in sedentary collections of families ruled by a chief. Their staples were potatoes, corn, and fish. As many as 12,000 native people lived on the island when the Spanish arrived. Many died in a succession of epidemics while the rest were assimilated into the European population composed almost entirely of Spaniards. This resulted in Chiloé's regionally distinct mestizo population.

The Spanish settlers easily subdued the natives when they took possession of the island in 1567. They divided up the terrain and natives for labor, which yielded exports of wood and textiles. The Spanish survivors of the mainland Mapuche uprising of 1600 relocated to Chiloé. The local government reported directly to the Spanish Audiencia in Lima, not to Santiago. For most of its early history one ship each year would call on the island from Lima to exchange goods from an extremely advantageous bargaining position. Other visits to the island came from Dutch corsairs who occupied and destroyed its cities on two different occasions.

Chiloé was the last Spanish stronghold in Chile and almost the last one on the entire continent. The Chileans finally wrested the island from the Spanish in 1826, eight years after independence.

The island remained isolated from the rest of the country even after independence. Although contact became more prevalent after Puerto Montt was founded in 1852, the island was not truly linked with the rest of the world until the advent of modern communication. Chiloé's cultural heritage is distinct from the rest of the country due to this isolation. Impoverished and inclement conditions are the norm of this rugged island. *Chilote* migrant workers have earned a reputation for diligence as they've traveled to southern Chile and Argentina to seek jobs in the mines and ranches there.

Agroturismo

Agrotursimo (Agricultural Tourism) is a program run by **Fundación de Todos.** The foundation organizes and maintains a network of countryside *Chilote* family homes in which travelers can lodge. The opportunity to meet and interact with the rural families whose homes we had previously admired from afar was one of the most memorable and insightful travel experiences we had in Chile.

One of our stays was on a small dairy. The host took us fishing in his motorboat up a narrow, serpentine river hidden in the dense wilderness. We were awed by the serene beauty of this languid stream so anonymous that it would never have occurred to us to plan it in an itinerary. We stayed at another home high on the hills overlooking a shallow bay, the water of

EAT LIKE A CHILOTE

One of the great pleasures of Chile is eating in Chiloé. Restaurants prepare a variety of savory fare unique to the island. Make sure you try these delicacies while you are here.

• **Cancato** – *This delicious salmon preparation features a broiled filet stuffed with tomato, cheese, and spicy sausage.*

• **Carapacho** – *One of Chiloé's best appetizers is a mixture of crab meat, bread crumbs, and cream baked in a crab shell.*

• **Chapaleles** – *These are fried flour and potato cakes normally served with curanto.*

• **Curanto** – *Chiloé's version of surf and turf consists of a huge pile of shellfish, beef, chicken, sausage, and potato creations cooked over hot stones in a earthen hole. Curanto is commonly offered in restaurants, but more difficult to encounter cooked in the traditional fashion. When it is cooked above ground, the dish is sometimes called* **pulmay**. *Either way it is delicious.*

• **Licor de Oro** – *This is a line of indigenous fruit-flavored liqueurs.*

• **Milcoas** – *This dense ball of hash brown-like potatoes filled with seasoned pork is a hearty snack.*

• **Roscas** – *This lightly sweetened croissant-pretzel hybrid is usually sold six or more to the bag in the markets.*

Castro's **Festival Costumbrista**, *celebrated the weekend closest to February 15 each year, provides the opportunity to sample tasty fare from fifty booths in the municipal park while enjoying folkloric music and entertainment.*

which ebbed dramatically at sunset. On the muddy flats appeared rubber-booted neighbors who gathered shellfish and one couple who pitched long, intensely green strands of algae into an ox-drawn cart. Our meals with the families were enlightening affairs highlighted by rib-sticking cuisine.

Keep in mind that these are humble rural homes, not hotels. You give up a lot of control because you can't fine-tune the attention you receive. Some people might feel smothered in one home or perhaps ignored in another. You will share your meals and living space with the hosts who more than likely speak little or no English. Typically you should expect accommodations that are equal to good quality *hospedajes*, but with hospitality that is much more family-like than commercial.

Fundación de Todos is managed by the Archbishop of Chiloé in Ancud. The foundation selects households that meet their cultural criteria, then assists them with loans to add heat, hot water, and additional rooms as necessary to make the household comfortable for guests. They also provide basic managerial training in areas such as program objectives, meal preparation, and accounting so that host family has a better chance of success.

The cost per person is $10 with breakfast or $20 with three meals. For more information or to make a reservation contact **Fundación de Todos**, *E. Ramírez No. 207, 2nd floor. Tel./Fax 65/622604 or 65/624062. E-mail contodos@chilesat.net.*

ANCUD

Ancud is a town of 23,000 inhabitants located in the northern end of the island. Although it is not as dynamic as the capital of Castro, Ancud is a pleasant community endowed with the regional hospitality, food, and culture that makes Chiloé a great place to spend time.

ARRIVALS & DEPARTURES
By Boat
Ferry service between Pargua and Chacao runs continuously with boats leaving every twenty minutes or so.
• **Transmarchilay**, *Libertad 669. Tel. 622289*
• **Naviera Cruz del Sur**, *Chacabuco 672. Tel. 622508*

By Bus
There is no central bus terminal. The bus companies all have separate locations. All offer service to Castro, Puerto Montt, and Santiago (including the ferry crossing). Trans-Chiloé is the best company for the smaller local destinations.

Bus Companies
• **Cruz del Sur**, *Chacabuco 650. Tel. 622265*
• **Trans-Chiloé**, *Chacabuco 750. Tel. 622876*
• **Turbus**, *Dieciocho S/N. Tel. 622289*
• **Varmontt**, *Errazuriz 330. Tel. 623049*

By Car
There is ferry service between Chacao on the island and Pargua on the mainland. The *Panamericana* south will take you directly to Ancud.

The exit to Ancud from the Panamericana South or North will deposit you onto Aníbal Pinto which then turns into Almirante Latorre. To reach the main plaza you should take a left on Baquedano, a slight right onto Arturo Prat, then take a left on Libertad.

By Plane

There is no air commercial service to the island. You must fly into Puerto Montt's **Maquehue Airport**, then do an overland/ferry combination to get here.

ORIENTATION

Ancud is located at the northern end of Chiloé island, 27 km from the Chacao ferry dock. The town is on a northern pointing peninsula in the **Golfo de Quetalmalhue**. Almost all of the hotels and restaurants are concentrated on a few blocks around the square.

GETTING AROUND TOWN

Everything in town is within walking distance.

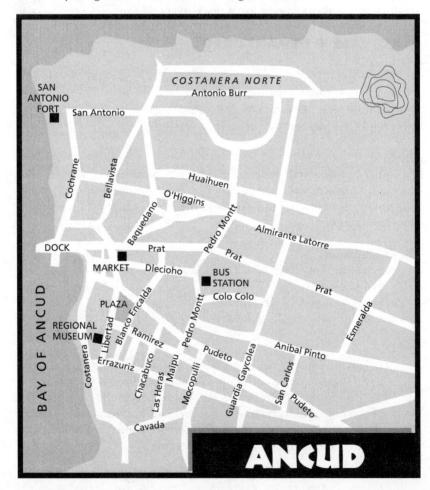

WHERE TO STAY

Expensive

HOSTERÍA ANCUD, *San Antonio 30. Tel. 65/622340. Fax 65/622350. 60 rooms. Double $90. Breakfast included. Restaurant. Bar. Cable TV. Credit cards accepted.*

This hotel, part of the Panamericana chain, is a solid option if the Galeón Azul is full. Roosting over the remnants of Fort San Antonio, with the sea extending beyond that, the Hostería Ancud is renowned for its views. The interior is a bit dark, but the *Chilote* woodcarvings adorning the walls are a nice touch. The rooms are comfortable and upscale, on par with expectations for a hotel of this quality.

Moderate

GALEÓN AZUL, *Libertad 751. Tel./Fax 65/622543. 16 rooms. Double $55. Breakfast included. Cable TV. Restaurant. Bar. Credit cards accepted.*

This capricious bright yellow edifice seems to have run aground atop a hill because from behind it protrudes the mast of a ancient boat in the Regional Museum. To take full advantage of the shared property line, the hotel has a windowed wall which looks out to the museum's sculpture garden.

The interior of the hotel is finished in a bright nautical motif featuring details like port hole windows and antique ship fixtures. High ceilings and walls of varnished blonde wood accent the rooms and second floor hallway. Ocean views can be enjoyed from all of the rooms, as well as from the bar, restaurant, and a hillside terrace with lounge chairs. The beach and boardwalk are located just at the bottom of the hill.

Inexpensive

HOSTERÍA AHUI, *Costanera 906. Tel./Fax 65/622415. 25 rooms. Double $40. Breakfast included. Restaurant. Bar. Credit cards accepted.*

This comfortable, old hotel stands alone down the Carrera Pinto boardwalk towards Ancud's beach. Built with traditional *Chilote* shingles, it definitely fits in with its surroundings. The rooms in front on the third floor have the best views of the beach.

HOSTERÍA LLUHAY, *Cochrane and Aldea. Tel. 65/622327. 8 rooms. Double $30. Breakfast included. No credit cards.*

This house looks like it was designed for the Brady Bunch, but that doesn't interfere with its noteworthy views. Set on a hill between the docks and the fort, the location is also a good one for exploring the town.

HOTEL LYDIA, *Chacabuco 360. Tel./Fax 65/622990. 25 rooms. Double $43. Restaurant. Credit cards accepted.*

While this older hotel is nothing special, it is centrally located by the plaza, clean and well-run. The rooms, with wooden floors, are all acceptable, but the ones facing Avenida Chacabuco are quieter than the ones facing Pudeto. The restaurant is popular not only with guests, but also with the locals. Try the smoked salmon.

HOTEL LACUYA, *Pudeto 219. Tel. 65/623019. 17 rooms. Double $45. Breakfast included. Cable TV. Restaurant. Credit cards accepted.*

Like the hotel Lydia, the Lacuya is a comfortable, nicely finished hotel and a good place to stay for the price. It is centrally located near the square.

HOSPEDAJE BELLAVISTA, *Bellavista 449. Tel. 65/622384. 10 rooms. Double with bath $25. Breakfast included. No credit cards.*

Just one block from the market and three from the plaza, the Bellavista is conveniently located, yet above all the commotion of town. The cute red and green building, perched on the side of a hill, is a clean, pleasant Ancud option. It is not fancy, but offers a basic room in a cheery environment.

WHERE TO EAT

HOSTERÍA ANCUD, *San Antonio 30. Tel. 65/622340. Expensive. Credit cards accepted.*

Although it boasts the same elegant atmosphere of the hotel, the restaurant hides behind a disappointingly bland "international" menu rather preparing its seafood with savory *Chilote* recipes.

OSTRAS CAULÍN, *Caulín, 25 km from Ancud. Tel. 09-6437005. Moderate. Credit cards accepted.*

We stumbled onto this fantastic dining experience by disembarking from the Chacao ferry quite ravenous. Hoping to find the nearest restaurant we followed the signs that appeared every few kilometers promising fresh Chilean oysters. The road immersed us into the Chiloé countryside, past the curious disc-protruding spire of the Caulín chapel, and finally to the charming restaurant on a tranquil inlet. Black-necked swans coasted beyond the shoreline and *Chilote* mythological creatures stood sentry in the yard.

Ostras Caulín features a daily fixed item lunch that is as delightful as the drive to get to it. The meal begins with a plate of fifteen delectable oysters on the half-shell. That's fifteen oysters per person. Chilean oysters are smaller than most varieties. They are now rarely found even in Chile because the government supports harvesting a larger variety for export sales. The gold-rimmed plate of fifteen is a gorgeous bounty of delicate morsels to behold and consume. This wonderful appetizer is followed by a creamy, piping hot bowl of oyster chowder, a tender piece of roast beef, and dessert.

The atmosphere of the small restaurant is surprisingly sophisticated, yet homey. The walls are decorated with wooden replicas of Chilote churches. You can expect cordial, attentive service from the owner who proudly harvests and serves the rare Chilean delicacies himself.

GALEÓN AZUL, *Libertad 751. Tel. 65/622543. Moderate. Credit cards accepted.*

The Galeón Azul's diminutive restaurant and bar is a pleasant place for unpretentious fare with a relaxing ocean view.

HOSTERÍA AHUI, *Costanera 906. Tel. 622415. Moderate. Credit cards accepted.*

This restaurant is a good one to combine with a stroll down the boardwalk along the Gulf of Quetalmahue. With excellent views, a bar made of *Chilote* shingles, and a menu full of treats from the sea, you can't go wrong here. They even have *curanto*.

EL SACHO, *in the market. Moderate. Credit cards accepted.*

Crammed in next to the other market stalls, El Sacho is one of the most popular places for a reasonably priced seafood orgy. Don't miss the chance to try *carapacho*, one of our favorite appetizers. It's a delicious combination of crab and cream sauce baked to golden perfection. If El Sacho is overflowing you can try **La Pincoya**, down the street at *Prat 61*, for similar fare.

SEEING THE SIGHTS

AUDELIO BORQUEZ CANOBRA REGIONAL MUSEUM, *Libertad and Ramírez. Monday-Friday, 10am-1pm, 3pm-6pm; Saturday-Sunday 11am-4pm. Entry $1.25.*

This small museum is an excellent showcase of and introduction to *Chilote* culture. A large courtyard, complete with a sailing ship, affords superb views of the Gulf of Quetalmahue. Around the courtyard, during the summer, local artisans peddle their crafts. Upstairs there are interactive exhibits about life on Chiloé. The displays are well-designed and will probably hold even children's attention. Downstairs, temporary displays based on some aspect of the island's culture are exhibited on a rotating basis.

FUERTE SAN ANTONIO, *Corner of San Antonio and Cochrane. No admission fee.*

The remnants of the San Antonio Fort are situated on a grassy terrace overlooking the ocean. It is here that the last flag of the Spain flew in Chile, eight years after the country's recognized independence. There is not much here to see except a nice view and perhaps some kids playing soccer between the rusty canons.

SHOPPING

There is a small market with typical *Chilote* handicrafts where Ignacio Carrera Pinto runs into Arturo Prat.

EXCURSIONS & DAY TRIPS

Caulín

Caulín is a quaint fishing settlement on the shores of the Chacao Channel, 24 km northeast of Ancud. It has an enchanting seaside chapel and a cemetery as well as one of the best restaurants on the island – **Ostras de Caulín**. You can see flocks of black-necked swans swimming along the shoreline from October through March and pink flamingoes poking out from the tide flat from March through August.

Tour Agencies

• **Turismo Huaihuén**, *Pudeto 135, 2nd floor. Tel./Fax 623800*. This company offers excursions all over the island.

PRACTICAL INFORMATION

Banks: There are banks with ATM's on the Plaza de Armas.
Business Hours: 9am-1pm; 3pm-6pm
Currency Exchange: There are no *Casas de Cambio* in Ancud.
Laundry: **Pat Very**, *Pudeto 45. Tel. 623241*
Medical Service: **Hospital**, *La Torre 405. Tel. 622356*
National Parks: **Conaf**, *Pudeto 358, Of. 4. Tel. 622630*
Post Office: **Correos de Chile**, *Corner of Pudeto and Blanco*
Telephone/Fax: The area code is 65. Long distance centers: **CTC**, *Chacabuco 640* and **Entel**, *Pudeto 219*
Tourist Office/Maps: **Sernatur**, *Libertad 665. Tel. 622800*

CASTRO

Castro should be considered one of the top city destinations on every traveler's itinerary. The hillside city overlooking the **Castro Fjord** boasts great hotels in all price categories, excellent restaurants showcasing Chilote cuisine, an extraordinary church, Chile's most exceptional modern art museum, and a good selection of day trips.

Castro, founded in 1600, is the third oldest continuously occupied city in Chile behind Santiago and La Serena. It has served as the capital of the archipelago for most of its history, except for a brief interruption in the late 1800's when the capital was relocated to Ancud. Castro's current population is 21,000.

ISLAND MYTHS

Chiloé has a rich tradition of mythology, very much alive today. The characters are not only an inspiration to storytellers, but to artists as well. You will find artisan markets full of the mythological creatures carved from stone and wood or woven from reeds. Here are the Chilote pantheon's who's who short list.

Pincoya *is the most well-known of the mythological beings. The sensual blonde goddess dances nude at the ocean's edge, gently swaying her hips, her hands raised in search of the stars. If she dances facing the sea, there will be a plentiful catch; if her partner is the hills, the nets will be empty.*

Trauco *is a repugnant, forest-dwelling dwarf who is strong enough to fell even the largest of trees with three swings of his wooden hatchet. His loathsome appearance is not helped by his fashion choice of a grass tunic and matching conical hat. Nonetheless, his charm is irresistible, and those who don't give in to his dalliances, he curses with erotic dreams. If an unmarried woman becomes pregnant, there can be no doubt that Trauco's to blame.*

Basilisco *has snake's body with a rooster's head. He slithers into bedrooms at night to suck the saliva from his sleeping prey. His victims awaken with a dry throat, begin to cough, then frequently die. Basilisco is not satisfied until all in the house are dead. Only a witch can exorcize the beast, by sacrificing the aging hen or the discolored rooster that spawned it.*

The ***Caleuche*** *is a ghost ship resounding with the festivities of witches partying and dancing on board. When someone follows the sound coming from the ship, it simply transforms into a log or a rock to fool the pursuer. Those presumed lost at sea have really been captured by the witches to work as slaves on the Caleuche.*

ARRIVALS & DEPARTURES

By Bus

The bus terminal is located on the corner of San Martin and Sotomayor. Most of the other bus companies are located nearby. Island destinations such Quellón, Chiloé National Park, and Dalcahue are all serviced from the bus station.

Bus Companies
- **Buses Arroyo**, *Bus Terminal, Tel. 635604*
- **Cruz del Sur**, *San Martin 486. Tel. 632389*
- **Trans-Chiloé**, *Bus Terminal. Tel. 635152*
- **Queilen Bus**, *Panamericana Sur 1822. Tel. 632594*
- **Varmontt**, *Balmaceda 289. Tel. 632776*

By Car

Castro is 146 km south of Ancud and 99 km north of Quellón. If you are heading south into town you take O'Higgins to the plaza and heading north into town you take San Martin to the plaza. The Pan-American highway connects into these streets.

By Plane

There is no commercial air service to the island. You must fly into Puerto Montt's **Maquehue Airport**, then do an overland/ferry combination to get here.

ORIENTATION

Castro is located roughly at the mid-point of the island. It looks out to the Castro Fjord to the west. The main streets are San Martin which runs north, and O'Higgins which runs south. Lillo and its continuation, Costanera, run along the waterfront.

GETTING AROUND TOWN

Everything in town is within walking distance except the Modern Art Museum. You should drive or take a taxi out there.

WHERE TO STAY

The best hotel options in each category are clear here: **Las Araucarias** as the upscale choice, the **Unicornio Azul** as the moderately-priced best, and the **Hostal Kolping** as the superlative option in the economical segment. All are excellent values and brimming with personality.

Expensive

HOSTERÍA CASTRO, *Chacabuco 202. Tel. 65/632301. Fax 65/635688. 35 rooms. Double $100. Breakfast included. Cable TV. Restaurant. Bar. Credit cards accepted.*

The Hostería Castro is a masterful, unassuming piece of work. A two story picture window displays the Castro Fjord with a towering monkey puzzle tree in the foreground. The lobby floor shares this magnificent view with the open-ceilinged Las Araucarias restaurant on the floor below. There is a cozy bar on the lobby floor as well as a nice selection of color photographs with scenes from around the island. If you are looking for the restrooms, women should use the one adorned with the image of the skinny-dipping goddess Pincoya on the door, and men, the one with the wily, pint-sized lumberjack Trauco.

The stairwell to the rooms ascends through the center of the floors. Lush indoor gardens spill out from the ends of all of the hallways. The roof of the building is steeply pitched and a vertical line of windows runs down

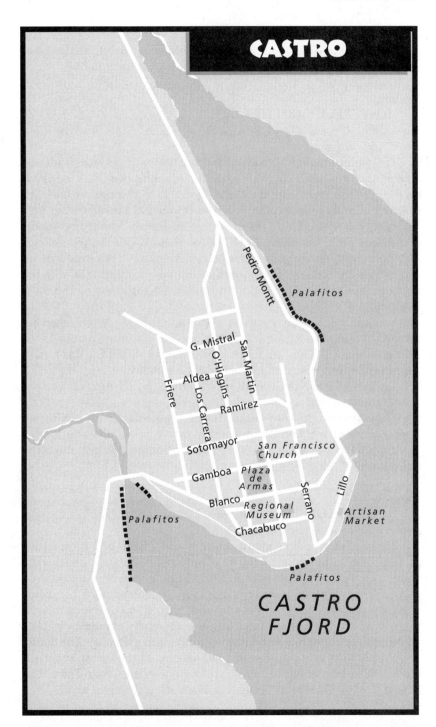

CASTRO

Pedro Montt

Palafitos

G. Mistral

San Martín

O'Higgins

Aldea

Friere

Los Carrera

Ramirez

Sotomayor

San Francisco Church

Gamboa

Plaza de Armas

Serrano

Lillo

Blanco

Regional Museum

Artisan Market

Chacabuco

Palafitos

Palafitos

CASTRO FJORD

either side. These serve as skylights to brighten up the hallways. The rooms are standard in size and decor for an upper end hotel, but they have excellent views, especially those on the east side of the building.

Moderate
HOSTERÍA UNICORNIO AZUL, *Pedro Montt 228. Tel. 65/632359. Fax 632808. 17 rooms. Double $70. Breakfast included. Cable TV. Restaurant. Bar. Credit cards accepted.*

This whimsical pink Victorian structure begins at the waterfront and ambles up the hillside. There are a handful of rooms that share the perch on the hillside overlooking the Castro Fjord, so it is best to call ahead to reserve one of these. Each of these hillside rooms has a small balcony with chairs to enjoy the fresh ocean breeze with your view. The rooms themselves are a geometry book full of shapes with slanted ceilings juxtaposed with doors, walls and windows where you'd not expect them. The owners turned several random spaces into common areas, with the best one being a well-lit reading nook on the top floor of the main building.

You will enjoy your meals in a charming dining room featuring hardwood floors, photographs of old Chiloé, and a grand piano. As for the blue unicorns, they are there to provide the kitsch for this hotel's charm, effectively enhancing its singular personality.

CABAÑAS PLENO CENTRO, *346 Carrera. Tel. 65/635122. 3 cabins. Double $80. No credit cards.*

These spacious in-town cabins are really more like condos. With two floors, ample space, and new furniture, this is an excellent option for groups of four or more. If you want to have your own kitchen, this is the place for it.

Inexpensive
HOSTAL KOLPING, *Chacabuco 217. Tel. 65/633273. 11 rooms. Double $25. Breakfast included.*

This enchanting lime green *casona* is one of the best inexpensive places to stay in the country in terms of personality, comfort, and quality. Constructed of indigenous larch in 1925, the house was relocated in 1960 utilizing the traditional *minga* collaboration. Neighbors pool their labor and oxen to assist the owners in uprooting their home and then move it to another lot. The house's interior was completely remodeled in 1994 and stands out for its fine wood finishing and warm wallpaper. The dining room and common areas are particularly cheery. There are two rooms on the top floor with small balconies that look out to the Castro Fjord. The Hostal Kopling is centrally located, a block off of the main sqaure.

HOTEL CASITA ESPAÑOLA, *Los Carreras 359. Tel. 65/635186. 15 rooms. Double $40. Breakfast included. No credit cards.*

This cute little hotel looks like a cabin. The rooms are decorated with the worst of the 1970's color combinations, but the hotel is clean and economical. Its location just two blocks from the plaza is also a plus.

HOSPEDAJE CHACABUCO, *Chacabuco 449. Tel. 65/635735. 9 rooms. Double $20. Shared bath. Breakfast included. No credit cards.*

This house has a great location for views of the Castro Fjord and its brightly colored *palafitos*. On a corner lot, you can see water and rolling hills out of all but the back rooms. The rooms are what you would expect for the price. The **Hotel Chilote**, around the corner, is a pretty orange house on a quiet residential street is just a block and a half from the plaza. Well maintained and clean, it is a good option in the same price range

For other inexpensive lodging, there are several popular *hospedajes* on the hillside pedestrian street Barros Arana including **El Mirador**, *Barros Arana 127, Tel. 633795*, with a nice sitting area out front, and the **El Molo**, *Barros Arana 140*. These run about $17 for a double, with breakfast.

WHERE TO EAT

LAS ARAUCARIAS, *Chacabuco 202. Tel. 65/632301. Expensive/moderate.*

Las Araucarias, located in the splendid Hostería Castro, is named for the Araucaria trees in the foreground of its sweeping view of the Castro Fjord. The upscale locale offers a variety of hearty seafood chowders as appetizers. In addition to traditional *Chilote* fare such as *cancato* and *curanto*, the restaurant offers some delicious non-seafood preparations such as the *pollo arvejado*, chicken simmered in a sauce of white wine, tomatoes, and green peas.

OCTAVIO, *Pedro Montt 261. Tel. 632855. Moderate/Expensive. Credit cards accepted.*

This restaurant, set over the ocean on *palafitos*, is an excellent place to sample the varied and delicious cuisine of Chiloé. With large windows looking out at the sea and *Chilote* handicraft decorations, there is no mistaking where you are. Try the *almejas*, clams, covered with fragrant melted cheese to start. For your main course you'll be torn between the *curanto*, a giant wooden trough overflowing with seafood, meat, and potatoes; and the *cancato*, an unusual yet mouth-watering combination of salmon stuffed with sausage, tomatoes, and cheese. The service here is a bit erratic, but it's worth sticking with them because the final result is scrumptious.

SACHO, *Thompson 213. Tel. 632079. Moderate. Credit cards accepted.*

Named for the unique Chilote wood and stone anchor, this restaurant is among the best for typical island cuisine. The restaurant is decorated with wood sculptures that protrude from frames you'd expect to hold paintings. You will also find mythological creatures lurking about. The upstairs portion of the restaurant has a cheerful ambience and views of the Castro Fjord.

For an appetizer, try the tantalizing *carapacho,* a mixture of crab meat, bread crumbs, and cream baked in a crab shell. The octopus prepared *al pil-pil,* with oil, garlic, and red pepper is excellent as well. The restaurant is most famous for its *curanto* as well as for its *congrio papillote,* conger eel with ham, onions, and mushrooms baked in a paper bag.

HOSTERÍA UNICORNIO AZUL, *Pedro Montt 228. Tel. 65/632359.*

The intimate restaurant of this flamboyant pink hotel is a solid option for seafood prepared with traditional Chilean recipes such as fresh steamed salmon and scallops *a pil-pil*. For desert, treat yourself to the decadent *panqueque* Unicornio Azul, crepes wrapped around ice cream and covered with *manjar* carmel sauce.

LA BRÚJULA DEL CUERPO, *O'Higgins 308. Moderate. Credit cards accepted.*

This is probably the most popular restaurant on the plaza. Any day of the week both locals and tourists meet here for sandwiches, coffee, or beers. The food is pretty good, if not creative, and the atmosphere is nice. Catty corner from the Brújula is the more upscale **Café del Mirador**, specializing in seafood.

CAFE TORREONES, *Gamboa 387. Tel. 635894. Inexpensive. No credit cards.*

This small restaurant is on the second floor the shopping mall across the street from the plaza. It is a popular stop for snacks like *empanadas* and waffles or a cold beer.

Perhaps the best noshes in Chile are the *milcaos* sold out of baskets in front of the bus terminal at *San Martin and Sotomayor*. Unique to Chiloé, these hash brown-like potato snacks stuffed with pork are reason enough to visit the island.

SEEING THE SIGHTS

One of the focal points of town is its large, verdant **plaza**. A purple obelisk pierces the sky declaring Castro unique from the rest of Chile. Restaurants and shopping areas ring its sides, but the real eye catcher is the local *iglesia*.

IGLESIA DE SAN FRANCISCO, *on the plaza. No admission fee.*

It's impossible to miss this purple and orange edifice with its twin towers projecting over the city. Built in 1906, it is now a national monument. Originally constructed from local timber, the church is now armored in molded sheet metal to prevent erosion. Even if you've had your fill of churches, you must walk inside this one. The interior, done entirely in wood, is breathtaking. Huge wooden columns shoot up to delicate carved arches. Keep an eye out for the avenging statue slaying a devil that looks curiously like a figure from the pantheon of *Chilote* mythology.

MUSEO REGIONAL DE CASTRO, *San Martin between Blanco Encalada and Chacabuco. Monday-Saturday 9:30am-1:30pm and 3pm-6:30pm; Sunday 10:30am-1pm. No admission fee.*

This small, well-organized museum is worth a visit to observe the *Chilote's* ingenuity in crafting anything they needed from resources found on the island. This includes a wooden scooter-like bicycle, a sledgehammer carved from a single piece of wood, and an example of the now iconic *Chilote* anchor, a *sacho*. There are also exhibits documenting the life of the native Chonos and the devastation of the island's earthquakes.

Palafitos

There four areas where you can see the *palafitos*, colorful, traditional Chilote houses built on stilts over shallow water or mud flats, depending on the tide. There are two good sets for photographs. The best is on the Pan-American highway, just north of town. You can walk here by following either San Martin or Pedro Montt north. Another good point to snap photos is from the small park at the corner of Freire and Gamboa. The market on Lillo includes some restaurantes on *palafitos*. There is one last set on Pedro Montt just beyond the Unicornio Azul Hotel. You would mistake these for ordinary houses if you didn't look closely because you approach them from the street side.

MUSEO DE ARTE MODERNO DE CHILOE, *Parque Municipal, about 5 km west of town. Open seasonally, usually December-March. Monday-Sunday 10am-6pm. Tel. 645454.*

We were blown away by this avant guard museum located in the sleepy hills above Castro, extraordinary both in its design and content.

The *tejuela*-sided structures that compose the museum include one old traditional *Chilote* house and new sections attached to it, which won the architects Rojas and Feuerhake a national architecture award. Huge wall-consuming windows integrate the *Chilote* countryside into the museum as though it were one of the pieces in the gallery. In utilizing the old structure, the designers chose not to fill in the gaps running along the tops of the walls, so blackberry vines creep in from above, then inch down the walls between the artwork.

It is as if Chilean artistic freedom of expression has all been funneled to this unlikely focal point. Not that we want to hang all of this stuff on our walls at home, but with the political controversy that has broiled in Chile, it is refreshing to see someone vent on canvass. The themes are not exclusively political, but all approach their subject manner in radical form rarely, if anywhere else, seen in a Chilean institutional gallery of this caliber.

One collection of works is prepared for each season and the artists frequently utilize the space and structure of the buildings to display their work. We walked up a makeshift stairway to one exhibit, located in the compact attic space, to find that the artist had adopted the building's crisscrossed framework of two-by-fours by wrapping them in cellophane.

We recommend that you call the museum ahead of time to confirm that an exhibition is running and verify the hours of admission. If you are in Castro during the off-season, you can probably get in to see the gallery without an exhibition, which would be worthwhile for architecture and design fans.

SHOPPING

There is a good *artesanía* market on the waterfront street of Lillo. Some of the shops across the street from the market are worth poking your head into as well. **Libros Chiloé**, *Blanco Encalada 202,* in addition to good regional books, has a few interesting collectibles like a series of high quality, black and white photographs of *Chilote* churches suitable for framing.

EXCURSIONS & DAY TRIPS

PARQUE NACIONAL DE CHILOÉ, *54 kilometers southwest of Castro. Entry $4.*

If you are hoping for a sunny day in the park, this is not the one to visit. We were thrilled by the prospect of our outing as we drove to the park on a spectacular day of blue skies, because we had skipped going on previous, overcast days. As we crested a hill, the park came into view in the distance. Its territory alone was covered by a massive, elongated cloud.

The southern section of the 43,000-hectare national park is situated across the narrow portion of Lake Cucao from the town of the same name. Cucao is 43 km from Castro on a good unpaved road. It is the most frequently visited section because access to the northern part of the park is so difficult. The park preserves the majority of the island's indigenous trees including great larches at higher elevations. You can hike or horseback ride endlessly along undeveloped beach dunes or into the hills above the Pacific Ocean. It should be noted that the park receives 2,200 millimeters of rainfall at lower elevations and nearly 3,000 millimeters at higher elevations. That is about as wet as it gets in Chile. Wind can also be a comfort-altering factor, especially on the beach.

HOW DO YOU DO MR. PUDÚ!

One of the island's non-mythical creatures is the **pudú**, *a miniature deer that grows to a height of about 40 centimeters. Pudús roam from the Biobío River to Magallanes, but Chiloé is the most likely place to see one. The few we've seen were not in the national park, but rather poking their heads out from the underbrush alongside the highway from Ancud to Castro. We dream of seeing two males doing battle with toothpick-like antlers to win the love of their diminutive mate for life.*

Camping sites and a few cabins are available in the park. There are several *residenciales* in Cucao. One interesting lodging alternative is Parador Darwin, near the entrance of the park. It is endowed with a hippie ambience, cozy, immaculate rooms with shared baths, and a restaurant that offers seafood, pizzas, and sandwiches. **Parador Darwin**, *Public Tel. 65/633040 in Cucao, Santiago Tel. 2/272-8854. E-mail quirland@mail.excite.com. Double $25.*

Dalcahue & Quinchao

Dalcahue is a fishing village of 2,500 people located 40 km northeast of Castro. It is most well-known for its artisan market in which the local crafts people display baskets, wool sweaters, strings of dried mussels, and other wares for amblers to ponder and buy. The market operates Sundays and Wednesdays. This is one of the highlights of the island and shouldn't be missed.

On one side of the market, you will find a permanent collection of open kitchens sheltered under one roof cooking up everything that lives in the sea in huge bubbling pots. You really have to put aside your hygienic reservations and dig in here. One delicious snack is the seafood *empanadas*. The folks who run the kitchens aren't shy and neither should you be - if there is something you see that you can't identify, ask for a taste, *una prueba*.

Dalcahue has one of the larger typical Chiloé-style chapels, built in 1858. There is also a small ethnic museum, **Museo Histórico Arqueológico Etnográfico**, *open daily from 8am-6pm*. All of the points of interest are on or near the waterfront.

Quinchao Island can be reached on a ten minute ferry ride from Dalcahue. It is a pleasant place for a drive, with sinuous fertile terrain. Located on the island are the towns of **Achao**, which has the Chiloé's oldest church, Santa Maria, built in 1767, and the town of **Quinchao** with the Chiloé's largest church. The towns are 25 and 35 km away from the ferry dock respectively.

THE TEJUELA WAY

Regional architecture shows marked German influence and is distinguished by **tejuelas**, *long slats of indigenous larch, overlapped on the sides of the buildings like elongated shingles. The tejuelas are shaped and placed to form a variety of patterns. The tejuelas of homes are frequently painted in bright colors but fade as they are battered by the elements. The numerous, quaint, tejuela-sided churches of Chiloé are one of the island's main attractions.*

Other Small Towns

Going to the small towns in Chiloé provides panoramas of lush countryside on the way there, short visits to quaint *Chilote* churches, and the inevitable unplanned discoveries. The towns are far enough apart that it is worthwhile to rent a car to visit several in a day, rather than putting in a huge time investment in public transport to get to one, then wanting to move on after seeing the church.

In addition to Dalcahue and Quinchao, other towns you can visit include **Chonchi**, built on a steep seaside hill, **Huilnco**, on the way to the national park, and **Queilén**, located 46 km along an isolated peninsula.

Tour & Travel Agencies

• **Altue Expediciones**, *Encomenderos 83, Santiago. Tel. 2/232-1103.* Altue organizes sea kayaking expeditions in the area's fjords. Contact their office in Santiago.
• **Pehuén Expediciones**, *Blanco 299. Tel./Fax 635254.*
• **Queilén Travels**, *Gamboa 502. Tel. 632594*
• **Turismo Quelcun**, *San Martin 581. Tel. 632396*

PRACTICAL INFORMATION

Banks: Banco de Chile, *corner of Encalada and Barros Arana*, has an ATM.
Bookstore: Libros Chiloé, *Blanco Encalada 202*
Business Hours: 9am-1pm; 3pm-6pm
Currency Exchange: Julio Barrientos, *Chacabuco 286. Tel. 635079*
Laundry: Lavandería, *corner of Gamboa and Freire*
Medical Service: Hospital O'Higgins, *O'Higgins 807*
National Parks: Conaf, *Gamboa 424. Tel. 632289*
Post Office: Correos de Chile, *O'Higgins 388*
Supermarkets: Supermercado, *Corner of O'Higgins and Ramírez*
Telephone/Fax: The area code is 65. There are several long distance call centers near corner of Gamboa and San Martin.
Tourist Office/Maps: Tourist Kiosk, *Plaza de Armas, across from the church*

16. THE AUSTRAL REGION

The **Austral Region**, also called **Aisén**, is often compared to Alaska. While this is an appropriate comparison due to the area's wild forests, rugged mountains, roaring rivers, giant glaciers, and unforgiving remoteness, it falls short. The Austral Region is this and much more. Running from just below Puerto Montt in the north, to the end of the **Southern Ice Field** in the south, its Alaskan features are complemented by painted deserts around **Chile Chico**, fertile valleys by **Cochrane**, the raw rain forest of **Quelat National Park**, and golden pampa along parts of the border with Argentina.

Once you leave **Coyhaique**, the main hub, you are immediately struck by the isolation of the region. This remoteness is both a curse and a blessing for travelers. Getting to and moving within the territory is certainly not as convenient as touring other parts of the country. On the other hand, you have the opportunity to be one of a handful of visitors in vast national parks, alone in a trout-crammed stream, or the only group for miles on a horseback ride to electric blue glaciers. The reward far outweighs the effort it takes to tour this isolated area.

History

With the last of its pioneers still alive, the region's history is recent. It's this unique aspect of the area, so shortly removed from its frontier days, which makes it especially interesting to visitors.

Distinct native peoples populated the islands, shoreline, and pampas when Spanish explorers first arrived in 1794 looking for the "City of the Caesars," an El Dorado-type goose-chase. Other adventurers and cartographers passed through the region in the 1800s with many, like Darwin's Beagle, looking for a connection between the Pacific and Atlantic. It was not until 1894, over 450 years after the Spanish began to colonize the

Central Valley, that the Chilean government even sent a geographer to map the uncharted territory.

The most important early influence in Aisén was the large cattle and sheep companies that were leased state-sized tracts of land in the first part of the 20th century. This handful of outfits wielded immense power as they enjoyed shared concessions to the entire region.

The news of arable land drew pioneers from afar. In the early 1900s, groups of men and their families moved onto the land from three distinct zones. There were the settlers from central Chile who came like nomads via Argentina; the islanders from Chiloe who arrived by boat, hacking their way into the forest; and the Argentines themselves. This mixture created a hybrid culture and folkloric identity very distinct from that of the rest of the country. The intriguing thing for you is that it has managed to stay that way.

WHAT MAKES AISÉNITES UNIQUE

While some of the things that make people from the Austral Region unique in relation to their compatriots may be hard for the traveler to catch, they are like flashing red signs to other Chileans:
- *The Way They Talk: Aisénites speak much more slowly and with a completely distinct, almost Argentine accent.*
- *What They Drink: Mate, tea in a gourd sipped through a special straw, is the national drink of Argentina. Many Chileans wouldn't be caught dead drinking it, but Aisénites love it and have adopted it as their own.*
- *What They Eat: Tortas or sopiapillas, fried bread, are a standard morning and evening starch with meals.*
- *What They Play: Truco, meaning trick, is a card game played in pairs. The "trick" is to let your partner know what's in your hand through facial gestures and R-rated plays-on-words.*

Geography

The geography, more than any other single factor, has shaped the region. Cut off from the rest of Chile by ocean, fjords, and two gigantic ice fields, the people who live here have traditionally felt little influence from Santiago. Even until the mid-1980s, most of the towns in Aisén were supplied out of Argentina because that was the easiest ways to get goods into the region.

Augustín Pinochet, during his dictatorship, felt the hot breath of Argentina on the Chilean neck of land here and determined to unite the region with the rest of the country. Thus was born the dream of the

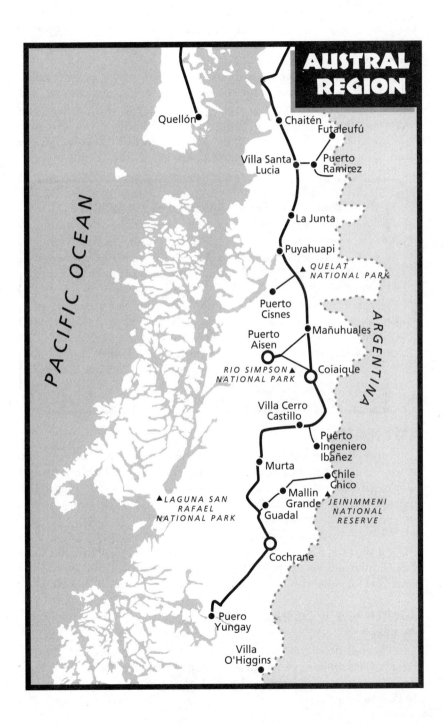

Carretera Austral or Austral Highway. Millions of dollars and tons of dynamite later, the Austral highway, really a 1,130 km two lane gravel road, is now a reality.

The geography continues to shape the lives of the people today. Although now connected to the rest of the country by road and sea, the region is still astonishingly remote. While Coyhaique is a thriving commercial center that is slowly being integrated into the rest of Chile, traveling to the far-flung towns of the north or south is like going back in time.

HOW TO SPEND YOUR TIME IN AISÉN

To get the most out of the Austral Region you need to away from cities and into the remarkable natural wonders it has to offer. There are literally hundreds of outrageously beautiful places here, but we highly recommend:
• Jeinimeni National Park for hiking, fishing, and camping in a sunny microclimate
• Bertrand for horseback riding to the ice fields and rafting and fishing on the Rio Baker.
• Quelat National Park for primordial forests and hanging glaciers.
• Villa O'Higgins for true remoteness in raw, wild country.
*   If you're a zealous adventure seeker consider the Futulefú River for stunning scenery and class V rapids.*

COYHAIQUE

Coyhaique (also spelled Coihaique) means "the camp between the rivers." The town of 44,000 sits above the confluence of the **Simpson** and **Coyhaique Rivers** surrounded by strangely shaped, striated hills. The most prominent hill, **Cerro MacKay**, is a basalt massif anchoring the end of town like a paperweight.

Coyhaique was founded in 1929 as a support center for the megalith Aisén Industrial Society (SAI) which had concession to all the land from Lake Fontana to Port Chacabuco. Today it is the capital and commercial center of the area with over half the population of the XI Region.

ARRIVALS & DEPARTURES

By Boat

There is no direct boat access, but many visitors arrive to nearby Puerto Chacabuco via ferry. In the summer **TranMarChilay**, *21 de Mayo 417, Tel. 231971*, and **Navimag**, *Ibañez 347, Tel. 233306*, connect Chacabuco to Puerto Montt.

By Bus

In the summer you can connect by bus from Coyhaique to the entire region. It can be confusing because different companies have the routes different days of the week, and only a few leave from the bus terminal.

There are connections to Cochrane, Puerto Ibañez, Puerto Aisén, Balmaceda, Puerto Cisnes, La Junta, and Chaiten. If you're up for the long haul, there are also connections from Puerto Montt and Punta Arenas (via Argentina).

Bus Companies
- **Turibus**, *Baquedano 1171. Tel. 231333*, Puerto Montt
- **Emanuel**, *Simpson 829. Tel. 231555*, Chaiten
- **B&V**, *Bus Terminal. Tel. 237949*, Chaiten
- **Munoz, Basoli/Artetur**, *Parra 337. Tel. 232167*, Puerto Cisnes, Chaiten
- **Buses Suray**, *Prat 265. Tel. 238387*, Puerto Aisén, Chacabuco
- **Buses Dong Feng**, *Bus Terminal. Tel. 230627*, Puerto Aisén
- **La Cascada**/Sur, *Lillo 134. Tel. 231413*, Puerto Aisén, Punta Arenas
- **Transportes Morales**, *Bus Terminal. Tel. 232316*, La Junta
- **Acuario**, *Bus Terminal. Tel. 237949*, Cochrane
- **Los Nadis**, *Bus Terminal. Of. F-1*, Cochrane
- **Pudu**, *Bus Terminal. Tel. 231008*, Cochrane
- **Don Carlos**, *Cruz 63. Tel. 231981*, Cochrane, Puerto Aisén

By Car

Coyhaique is the central hub of the Austral Highway. It can be reached in about ten hours from Chaiten and nine from Cochrane. Many people arrive to Coyhaique by air or water and then rent a car to further explore Aisén. Four-wheel drive vehicles average around $115 a day. The following companies have autos available for rent:

Auto Rental Companies
- **Rent a Car Aysen**, *Bilbao 926. Tel. 231532*
- **Auto Club de Chile**, *Bolivar 194. Tel. 231649*
- **Hostal Bon**, *Condell 162. Tel. 231189*
- **Traeger**, *Baquedano 457. Tel. 231648*
- **Automundo**, *Bilbao 510. Tel. 231621*
- **Neumann Rent**, *Carrera 330. Tel. 231010*
- **Ricer Rent a Car**, *Horn 48, Tel. 232920*
- **Carrillo Rent**, *Balmaceda 455. Tel. 231362*
- **Travel Car**, *Colón 190-B. Tel. 236840*

Those who arrive in their own cars often access the area from border crossings with Argentina, as Argentine roads are generally paved and in

NEGOTIATING RUBBLE ROCK ROADS

*The Austral Highway has its own set of **driving rules**. Keep these things in mind as you head out:*

• Maintain control of your vehicle – Your pace should depend on road and traffic conditions, regardless of posted speeds, but as a rule it is not wise to go much above 40 km/hr. In some sections you will go only half as fast. Ruts in the road can flip cars in the blink of an eye, so be extremely careful.

• Use 4-wheel drive on excessive washboards – Having each wheel give you traction can really make a difference when you are bouncing all over the road.

• Help a stranger – The rules of the highway say you stop and help anyone, regardless of that ferry you want to catch. It's the Golden Rule thing that can come in handy if you're in need.

better condition. The most popular route from the south is through Chile Chico, which includes taking a ferry to Puerto Ibañez and driving up from there. People coming from northern Argentina often cross at Futulefú. There is also a pass near Balmaceda.

By Plane

Planes are the easiest and fastest way to access the Aisén region. Both Ladeco and LanChile have daily direct flights from Santiago, Puerto Montt, and Punta Arenas. Larger planes land in Balmaceda, a 50-minute drive from Coyhaique. It's a small but well equipped airport with a black strip of runway cutting the golden pampa.

Buses, minivans and taxis are there to meet every flight and transport you to Coyhaique. Just walk outside and make your choice. If your plane leaves from Balmaceda you can catch a bus in Coyhaique in front of your airline's office a few hours before departure.

Charter flights and small aircraft from Transportes Don Carlos fly to Villa O'Higgins, Cochrane, and Chile Chico from the smaller Teniente Vidal airport in Coyhaique.

Airlines
• **Ladeco**, *Prat 188. Tel. 231300*, flights to Santiago, Puerto Montt, Punta Arenas
• **LanChile**, *Parra 215. Tel. 231188*, flights to Santiago, Punta Arenas
• **Don Carlos**, *Cruz 63. Tel. 231981*, flights to Chile Chico, Cochrane, Villa O'Higgins

ORIENTATION

Coyhaique is in the middle of the Aisén region. It is a little over an hour both east to Argentina and west to the Pacific Ocean. It is also about half way between Cochrane and Chaiten.

The town itself is laid out in the normal grid system except for the area around the plaza. The town "square" is actually a pentagon with ten streets poking out from the center. It is confusing at first and just when you think you've got it down, you find yourself completely disoriented.

GETTING AROUND TOWN

The best way to tour the town is the ten-toed method. The main area of interest centers around the plaza and the distances are not far. Shared taxis called *colectivos* can get you from one side of town to the other. They have signs on their roofs with their route numbers and the streets they follow. Just flag one down and squeeze in with everybody else. Regular taxis are metered and can be hailed from the street or the plaza.

There is no need to rent a car just to see the town. If you are going to explore the surrounding area or head out on the Austral highway, however, renting a car is highly recommended for the freedom you gain.

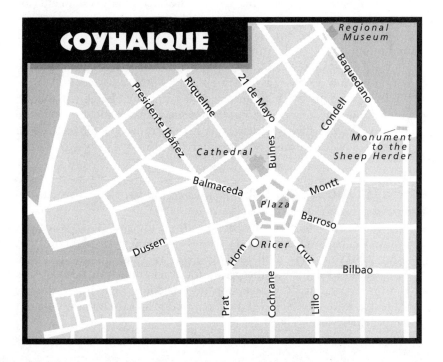

WHERE TO STAY
Expensive
HOSTAL BELISARIO JARA, *Bilbao 662. Tel.67/234150. 6 rooms, 1 apartment. Double $83. Breakfast included. Cable TV. Credit cards accepted.*

You know the Belisario is special as soon as you walk on the property. Your eyes are immediately drawn to the unusual angles of the wooden building, the prominent cupola, and the wrought iron dancing-fish weather vane. You expect Pablo Nerudo to stroll out to the flower filled garden and invite you to a hand of cards in front of the adobe fireplace.

The curious angles outside translate to a maze-like interior. The hotel only has seven rooms though, so you can't get too lost. The walls are clean and white with wooden accents and simple, artisan decorations. The rooms themselves are on the small side, but there is plenty of comfortable spill over space in the breakfast nook and game room. Central heat keeps you warm in any season. This is by far the most intriguing and comfortable hotel in Coyhaique.

HOSTERÍA COYHAIQUE, *Magallanes 131. Tel. 67/231137, 233274. Double $112. Cable TV. Restaurant. Bar. Pool. Credit cards accepted.*

This is the classic stately hotel with large, well-kept grounds and a venerable air. The wood paneled lobby and bar hark back to a different era. All the rooms have been redone, though some have clashing decor. The doubles on the outside with views of the hills are larger than interior ones. The restaurant offers the standard Chilean menu, but prepares everything well. Take a drink in the bar before dinner to properly kick off the ritual.

HOTEL PATAGONIA, *Parra 551. Tel. 67/236505. Double $110. Breakfast included. Cable TV. Restaurant. Bar. Credit cards accepted.*

The Patagonia is a high quality, well-maintained hotel with a light, wooden interior and airy feel. The bathrooms are large and the rooms are comfortable, but the hotel leaves us lukewarm because it feels like a generic US hotel. Upstairs is better than downstairs for noise reasons.

Moderate
APARTHOTEL TRAEGER, *Baquedano 457. Tel.67/231648. 3 apartments. Double $70. Cable TV. Credit cards accepted.*

Because these are true apartments, this is the place to go when you need space. Full, well appointed kitchens allow you take a night off from eating out if you desire. Both the large living area and separate bedroom are open and bright. For the price of a hotel room you can have the comfort of a home. The reception desk is confusingly inside the car dealership next door. Some of the auto repairs can get a bit noisy, but not overbearingly so.

CABINS WITH NO NAME, *Colón 155. Tel. 67/250193. 3 cabins. $65. No credit cards.*

The place is so simple it does not even have a name, but Ana, the owner has created a little oasis. The large, grassy yard surrounded by flowers is the reason you stay here; it's simply pleasant. Ana will prepare meals at your request. The cabins sleep five and have kitchenettes.

CABAÑAS Y HOSTAL SAN SEBASTIAN, *Freire 554. Tel. 67/231762. 5 cabins, 5 rooms. $65 for cabin, $30 for double room. Breakfast included. Cable TV. Kitchenette in cabins. Credit cards accepted.*

These cabins, just two blocks from the plaza, are tucked away on a quiet street to ensure good sleeping. A highlight of the two-level cabins is a floor to ceiling window for excellent natural daytime lighting, while the two A-frames have fireplaces. Stick with the cabins as the rooms are cramped and not a good value.

HOTELERIA SAN SEBASTIAN, *Baquedano 496. Tel. 67/233427. 6 rooms. Double $65. Breakfast included. Cable TV. Credit cards accepted.*

Not to be confused with the previous listing, this is the place if you're a sucker for views. The entryway is dark and the carpet in the hallway overused, but this is forgiven and forgotten when you enter your room and look out at the hills. Poised on the edge of the snaking Coyhaique river with panoramas of cliffs and valleys, this hotel is all about location.

HOSTAL AUSTRAL, *Colón 203. Tel./Fax 67/232522. 10 rooms, 5 apartments. $88 apartment, $55 double room. Cable TV. Credit cards accepted.*

The Austral's homey sitting area with its wood burning stove is a nice place to spend an afternoon reading while petting the family dog. The rooms are clean and well maintained, though the walls are thin. The apartments offer much more space. Because of its location perched four blocks above the plaza, you get views of the hills from all but room five.

HOSTAL LIBANES, Simpson 367. *Tel. 67/234242. 26 rooms, Two types of doubles, $50 and $60. Breakfast included. Cable TV. Credit cards accepted.*

Although ugly from the outside, the spacious common areas and large executive rooms make this a good option if you need to have a private phone. Other details include blow dryers in the rooms and 24-hour message service.

HOTEL LOS NIRES, *Baquedano 315. Tel. 67/232261, Fax 233372. 20 rooms. Double $60. Breakfast included. Cable TV. Restaurant. Credit cards accepted.*

The entry and hallways of the Nires are spacious, but the rooms are not. It's a poor value when you consider you can have an apartment or cabin for about the same price.

HOSTAL BON, *Condell 162. Tel. 67/231189. 10 rooms. Double $65. Breakfast included. Cable TV. Café. Credit cards accepted.*

Its location on the second floor of a loud shopping area make the small rooms seem even tinier. You should look elsewhere.

LUIS LOYOLA, *Prat 455. Tel./Fax 67/ 234200, 234201. 18 rooms. Double $60. Breakfast included. Cable TV. Credit cards accepted.*

This schizophrenic hotel has a dark entry staircase that leads to a white, sun drenched hallway anchored by a fun house mirror. The rooms are spacious but have terrible shag carpet. Save this as a last choice as the street is loud also.

Inexpensive

CABAÑAS MIRADOR, *Baquedano 848. Tel. 67/233191. 2 cabins, 3 rooms. $125 for cabins, $38 for double rooms. No credit cards.*

If you have a big group you should try here first, as Juan's cabins sleep eight. The rooms too are one of the better values in town. The well-tended yard and gardens lead to the edge of a canyon on the Coyhaique river for an absorbing view of the valley. Try to get the room on the end. It is absolutely spotless like the others, and has a huge picture window.

HOSPEDAJE VENTISQUEROS, *Serrano 368. Tel. 67/234620. 2 rooms, 1 apartment. $38 double rooms, $63 apartment. TV. No credit cards.*

Both the rooms and the apartment are set back off the street with a rose-filled garden to buffer any noise. The accommodations are not fancy, but are a good choice for a quiet place to rest.

RESIDENCIAL PUERTO VARAS, *Serrano 168. Tel./Fax 67/235931. 14 rooms. Double $20 shared bath, $30 private bath. No credit cards.*

One of the better budget options with a cheery entry and sitting area, this hotel is frequented by the backpacker crowd. The walls are thin, but what do expect for the price?

If you need to go cheaper try **Residencial Gallardo**, *Barroso 752. Tel. 67/233341. 5 rooms with 1 shared bath. $11. Breakfast included. No credit cards.* The TV is ubiquitous, but the friendly owners invite you to join them to watch in the kitchen if the TV in the common area is on a channel you don't like.

Out of town

LA PASARELA, *Km 2 to Puerto Aisén. Tel. 67/234520. 13 rooms, 4 cabins. $90 for double room, $135 for cabins. Breakfast included. Credit cards accepted.*

Only two km out of town on the banks for the roaring Simpson River, the Pasarela feels a world away. Just getting here is an adventure as you cross the creaking and swaying suspension bridge. Roll down your window to get the full effect. The best rooms are those on the second floor of the newer building with spellbinding views from the porches.

The Pasarela is set up for fly-fishing. Once you arrive, all the logistical details are in their hands. Using the lodge as a base, you can fish a different area everyday for a month. They can also arrange rafting and horseback trips for a change of pace.

Relaxing after a long day is not a problem. The living room, with its big stone fireplace and deep sofas, is so comfortable that people come from town just to have a drink here. The tiny restaurant serves delicious local specialties in an intimate atmosphere. It's the quintessential full service lodge experience.

CABAÑAS RIO SIMPSON, *Km 3 to Puerto Aisén. Tel. 67/232183. 13 cabins, $55 without, $77 with kitchenette. No credit cards.*

More rustic than the Pasarela, these cabañas share the same views. The two small cabins with queen beds and no kitchen have the prime bluff location.

WHERE TO EAT

LA PASARELA, *Km 2 to Aisén. Tel. 234520. Moderate. Credit cards accepted.*

For good food in a comfortable lodge setting, this one is a must. A drive across the creaky suspension bridge starts your visit to this prime real estate. Begin your evening with a drink in the living room around the stone fireplace before moving to the small dining area. Local specialties and candlelight await you there. Reservations are required for dinner but you can always pop in for a drink.

RESTAURANTE CAFÉ RICER, *Horn 48. Tel./Fax 232920. Moderate. Credit cards accepted.*

Practically sitting on the plaza, this café is consistently a good choice. It has a frontier ambiance with log interiors, plank tables, and wood burning stoves. The Ricer offers some regional specialties, though you can find a bit of everything on the menu. It's one of the few places that serves *sopiapillas*, the traditional fried bread. The dining room upstairs is quieter than downstairs. The tables outside are ideal for drinking big beers on a sunny day.

LA OLLA, *Prat 176. Tel. 234700. Moderate. Credit cards accepted.*

You know something good is happening when you walk in this small, log restaurant. The delicious smells lead you right to your table. The fixed meal at lunch is popular with the locals but they also have a full menu.

HOSTERÍA COYHAIQUE, *Magallanes 313. Tel. 231137. Moderate. Credit cards accepted.*

The Hostería Coyhaique has one of the more formal dining rooms in town. They offer standard Chilean fare in a pleasant environment.

CAFÉ ORIENTE, *Condell 201. Tel. 231622. Moderate. Credit cards accepted.*

While the only thing oriental about the place is its bizarre display of Japanese fans on the wall, it's still a good spot for a quick meal. The large sandwiches practically spill over the sides of the plate. The *barro luco* or *ave completo* could be the only meal you'll need for the day. The **Cafeteria Alemana** right down the street at *Condell 119*, serves similar food in a half-step more upscale environment. **Café Kalu** at *Prat 402* is another good choice for the same type food with the addition of hamburgers and fries on its menu.

EL GALPON, *Aldea 31. Tel. 232230. Moderate. Credit cards accepted.*

It only takes being a little above the city to get great panoramic vistas. The Galpon perches on a rise and lets you take it all in while enjoying steak and seafood in the comfortable dining area.

LITOS, *Lautrero 147. Tel. 234361. Moderate. Credit cards accepted.*

You don't know what to expect when you push through the swinging doors of this off-the-main-drag restaurant, but the intimate interior is a nice surprise. They serve a bit of everything, but their specialty is *parrillada*, the mixed grill.

RESTAURANTE ATICOS, *Bilbao 563. Tel. 234000. Moderate. Credit cards accepted.*

The food here is creditable but there are so many irritations that the general experience is negative. On different occasions you might get inattentive service, a blaring 72" TV, the owners' children banging on table legs, or out of stock items on the menu.

CASINO DE BOMBEROS, *Parra 365. Tel. 231437. Lunch only. Inexpensive. No credit cards.*

Who wouldn't want to eat at the fire station? As the sign outside says, "The firemen's lunchroom is everybody's lunchroom." Go at 1:00 or expect to wait for a table at this popular daytime spot. It is possible to order a la carte, but almost everyone asks for the *menú. Empanadas* are sold on the weekend.

RESTAURANTE LOBERIAS DE CHACABUCO, *Prat 386. Tel. 239786. Inexpensive. Credit cards accepted.*

The stark, utilitarian décor looks like nothing fancy and that is exactly the case, but it's one of the best places in town for good, inexpensive seafood and beers.

KAKAREUS, *Bilboa 231. Tel. 235551. Inexpensive. No credit cards.*

This is a great place for those with tight budgets and no cholesterol worries. The smell of roasted chicken will draw you in from the street, but you have to try a cone of their tasty French fries. Sandwiches and *empanadas* are also available.

LA FIORENTINA, *Bilboa 574. Tel. 238899. Inexpensive. Credit cards accepted.*

Good pizza is hard to find in this part of Chile, although it is excellent just a stone's throw away in Argentina. This place is pretty good if you've got the hankering. Try the salmon pizza for something different.

EL BUEN PAN, *12 de Octubre 27. Inexpensive. No credit cards.*

This is the best bakery in town. They are known for their *empanadas*, but also have whole-wheat rolls.

SEEING THE SIGHTS

RESERVA NACIONAL COYHAIQUE, *3 km from town on the road to Puerto Aisén. 8:30am-6pm, Entry $1.50.*

When the sky is clear you should scoot up to this reserve to enjoy fantastic views of Coyhaique and the surrounding country. Yellow, white, and green striped hills stand in front of glacier weighted, gray mountains. There are designated picnic and camping areas, but to enjoy the park and get away from any people you should hop on the six km *Sendero Las Piedras* that takes you to a 1360-meter lookout on the summit of **Cerro Cinchao**.

A taxi ride to the park entrance from town is less than $5. To return to town, you'll either have to arrange pick up, hike, or hitch back. **Aventura Turismo**, *12 de Octubre 253, Tel. 234748*, offers a 2.5-hour trip to the park that includes a walk around Laguna Verde.

MUSEO REGIONAL DE PATAGONIA, *Baquedano 310. Monday-Friday 9am-1pm. Free admission.*

This small museum houses one natural history room and another with a photographic history of the area. There is an interesting display of the making of the Austral highway. From the museum you should walk a few blocks *up Baquedano* to see the statue called the **Monument to the Sheepherder**. Even if the wind is not blowing you'll feel its force howling back at the shepherd and his caravan.

CERRO MCKAY, *2 km from town.*

After even just a day in town the solid peak of McKay beckons those of us who have been using it as a landmark. There are no formally marked trails, but animal paths suffice. The access is obviously not up the steep face but rather from the hill to its left when you are facing McKay. It's a four hour rigorous climb to the top, but not technical. Take appropriate clothing as the weather can change quickly.

City Tours

To hit many of these sites in two hours, you can take one of the city tours offered by **Tours Australis**, *Moraleda 589, Tel. 239696* ($10). They take you to the Indian Rock, on a tour across the pampa, to the plaza, the regional museum and the Monument of the Sheepherder.

NIGHTLIFE & ENTERTAINMENT

There are a number of pubs in town. The **Bar West Pub** at *Bilbao 110* is a good place to hang out in spite of its cheesy cowboy décor. Across the street at *Bilbao 125*, the **Corhal Discotheque** is an option for boogying the night away. **El Bulin** at *Lillo 134* and **El Puesto** at *Moraleda 229* are both intimate spots with live acoustic sets most weekends and some weekdays. The **Quilantal** at *Baquedano 791* has a folkloric dance show on Friday and Saturday nights at 10pm.

SPORTS & RECREATION

Biking

Figon at *Simpson 805, Tel. 234616*, rents mountain bikes. If you have your own rig that's even better. There are all sorts of horse and cattle trails on the outskirts of town. Just head into the hills and have fun.

Fishing

Fly-fishing is a huge draw to the Austral Region. Even if you are just an occasional fisher, you should take the opportunity to cast a few because you are in Mecca. Trout tend to live in magnificent places, so whether you catch any fish or not, you're in for a treat. There are a number of options for fishing in the region:

Full Package Lodge: A handfull of lodges are set up with the international angler in mind. You let them know you want to fish when you make your reservation and they take care of everything from there. They arrange the guides, the transportation, and help you get your license.

Lodge Day Trips: Many lodges will also arrange guides for drop-ins. If you see a sign outside of a place that says *guías de pesca*, just stop by and see if they have anybody available.

Travel Agencies: Some of the travel agencies also arrange fishing trips. They can put together an afternoon or a weeklong trip depending on your druthers. **45 Sur Expeditions**, *Lillo 194, Tel. 233216* can fix trips with Mackenzies or tubes and bilingual guides. They can also prepare a fishing/horseback combo. **Aventura Turismo**, *12 de Octubre 253, Tel. 234748*, arranges fantastic trips to any of the southern hotspots such as General Carrera, Lago Bertrand, and Rio Baker. Their trips, with fish guaranteed, include lodging, meals, transportation, guides, and boats for $280 per day with a three fisher maximum.

Sernatur: Another option is to stop by the Sernatur tourist office and read the business card postings. Some guides put their cards up for direct contact. They change from season to season, but Julio Meier at **Expediciones Coyhaique**, *Portales 195, Tel. 232300* is a good bet.

Signs on the Road: Occasionally you will be bumping past a home with a sign on the fence that says *guía de pesca*. You can stop in and check it out. This is the least expensive and least guaranteed option.

The fishing season runs from November through April. Brown and rainbow trout are the main event in streams, with rainbow, salmon and steelhead found in the area lakes. You must have a license to fish.

WHERE TO GET YOUR FISHING LICENSE

Thoughout the Austral region you can get a fishing license at the town municipal offices:

• **Coyhaique**: *Municipalidad de Coyhaique, Bilbao 357, Tel. 232100.*
• **Puerto Aisén**: *Sernapesca, Bustos 181, Tel. 333134.*
• **Cochrane**: *Municipalidad de Cochrane, Esmeralda 398, Tel. 522115.*
• **Chile Chico**: *Municipalidad de Chile Chico, O'Higgins 333, Tel. 411268.*
• **Futulefú**: *Municipalidad de Futulefú, O'Higgins 596, Tel. 258633.*
• **Chaiten**: *Municipalidad de Chaiten, Libertad 297, Tel. 731310.*

Horseback Riding

You should take the opportunity to get into the backcountry on a horse while you are in the area. Horses are an integral part of the culture as many places are still not accessible by car. A day in the saddle will take you into forests, to crystal lakes and glaciers, and through mountain passes of incredible beauty.

Almost any of the adventure agencies can arrange horseback rides but **45 Sur**, *Lillo 194, Tel. 233216* has some of the best trips. They have half day, full, and overnight trips to the **Coyhaique Reserve** ($25-$150 per person) that include transportation and all meals. They also have a 3-5 day trip into the **Cerro Castillo Reserve** that is a great way to get further south.

Hunting

Hunting is less popular in Chile than in neighboring Argentina. Game birds are in season from April though July as are some mammals. The mammal selection is limited with beaver, wild pigs, and hares being the only legally hunted animals. There are many endangered bird and deer species in Chile.

Mountaineering
    El Puesto Expediciones, *Moraleda 229, Tel. 233785*, runs two weeks trips to **San Lorenzo** and the **Northern Ice Field**. They can also arrange shorter trips if people are interested. Sam, the American partner, has lived and adventured in the area for four years and knows it inside out.

Rafting
    The Simpson is a less impressive river to run than the Baker or the Futulefú, but it's still a fun option if you are sticking close to Coyhaique. **Aventura Turismo**, *12 de Octubre 253, Tel. 234748* is a good bet for arranging it.

Skiing
    There is both downhill and cross-country skiing at the **Centro de Esqui El Fraile**, 29 km southeast of town. There are two rope tows and five runs. Lift tickets are $23 for the day and full equipment rental costs $20. The season usually runs from June through October. Trips can be arranged through **Aventura Turismo**, *12 de Octubre 253, Tel. 234748*.

Spectator Sports
    There are two soccer stadiums in town. The **Estadio Regional** at *Victoria between Baquedano and 21 de Mayo* and the **Estadio Municipal** at *Ejercito and Vaispas*.

SHOPPING

    There are three artisan markets in town. The **Artisans Fair** is in front of the plaza between *Horn and Dussen,* and the **Cema Chile Artisan Gallery** to one side of the plaza *between Barroso and Montt,* feature mostly leather and wood items. **AGROTEC Limitada**, *Dussen 360,* also carries locally made handicrafts.

EXCURSIONS & DAY TRIPS
LAGUNA SAN RAFAEL NATIONAL PARK
    This 1.74 million-hectare park is the single biggest draw in the area and all that many visitors to Aisén see outside of Coyhaique. It is the largest park in the region and a UNESCO biosphere reserve. The 45-km long glacier is stunning, with frequent explosions from calving sections that drop dramatically up to 70 meters into the sea. The trip takes you through the densely vegetated canals of the archipelago, past numerous waterfalls and smaller glaciers before gliding into sight of the massive, 30,000 year old ocean glacier with its glowing blue icebergs.
    There are a number of ways to see the spectacle, from budget to super-deluxe, from air or sea, and in trips that can last a few hours or a few

days. There are several things to keep in mind when making your decision about how to go. If you go by sea, size does matter, as smaller crafts can dock and unload near a path that will take you to the base of the glacier. It's also important to find out whether your boat will sail through the night. If it does you will miss much of the forest-covered hills along the fjords. (Depending on the weather, you might miss them even if you sail through the day.)

As far as weather goes, the area has prodigious amounts of rainfall so chances are you will get wet on deck. After all, something has to feed the glacier and the Northern Ice Field. Even though you are wet, you shouldn't be too cold because the temperature is usually a bearable 58F.

The trip is long, up to 16 hours one way, and expensive, even if you go the budget route. Keep in mind, however, that it is a 400-km round trip to some of the most spectacular scenery in the world. If you have not been to the **Perito Moreno** glacier in Argentina or seen **Glacier Grey** in Torres del Paine, you should not leave the continent without visiting San Rafael.

Seeing the Park By Boat

SKORPIOS I, II, AND III. *70,160,110 passengers. $850, $1200, $1400. Santiago: Leguia Norte 118 in Las Condes. Tel. 2/2035030, Fax 2/2035025. Puerto Montt: Angelmo 1660, Tel. 65/253754, Fax 65/25840. Credit cards accepted.*

The Skorpios has six-day trips departing on Saturdays from Puerto Montt. This is THE luxury line. An open bar and excellent food are as much a draw as the scenery. Everything is first class on this trip including the scotch you drink with ice from the glacier. Many visitors come to Chile exclusively for this excursion.

CATAMARAN PATAGONIA EXPRESS, *Patagonia Connection, Oteiza 1951 office 1006, Santiago. Tel. 2/2235567, Fax 2/2748111. 54 people. $800 per person. Credit cards accepted.*

This four-day trip includes two nights at the **Termas de Puyuhuapi Hotel and Spa** (see the write-up in the Puyuhuapi section.) The ship has zodiacs, which allow you to get really close to icebergs. For $250, only the San Rafael portion is included.

PATAGONIA CHARTER, *Turismo Rucaray, Merino 848, Puerto Aisén. Tel. 67/332862, Fax 67/332725. 12 people. $6000.*

If you have a group you should consider this option. Not only is it more intimate, but you have some control over your itinerary.

EL COLÓNO, *Transmarchilay, 21 de Mayo 447, Coyhaique. Tel. 231971. 230 people. $227 per person.* **EVANGELISTA**, *Navimag, Ibañez 347, Coyhaique. Tel. 67/233306, Fax 67/233386. 300 people. $210 per person. Credit cards accepted.*

Both of these are excellent options for the mid-range traveler.

TEHUELCHE, *Green Line, Prat 286 office 6, Coyhaique. Tel. 67/238947, Fax 67/235001. 20 people. $140 per person if you use a tent and $185 for a shared cabin.*

This is the budget option. It's not fancy but it will get you there and back.

Seeing the Park By Plane

If you go by plane it's a one and a half hour flight. When you get to the park, most of the pilots give you just one hour to look around. Obviously, your views while flying depend on the weather. There is an additional park entrance fee of $6 once you get there. If you don't have much time or can't imagine being stuck on a ship for two days, this is a viable option. Even if you don't have enough people for a charter, you can leave your name with the airlines and they will get in touch with you when space comes available.

AEROHEIN, *Baquedano 500. Tel./Fax 67/232772. 5 person single engine. $600 charter.*

TRANSPORTES SAN RAFAEL, *18 de Septiembre 469. Tel. 232048, Fax 67/233408. 5 person single engine. $600 charter.*

TRANSPORTES DON CARLOS, *Cruz 63. Tel./Fax 231981. 5 person twin engine-$700 charter, 8 person twin engine-$850 charter, and 9 person twin engine $1000 charter.*

RIO SIMPSON RESERVE, PUERTO AISÉN & PUERTO CHACABUCO

This trip, 70 km one way, is worth taking simply for the views. The road is blessedly paved, which makes the tour an easy one.

The first stop is the **Marchant Gonzales Lookout** just out of town. From there you get a bird's eye view of the steppe around Coyhaique, the river gorges, and the strange bumpy landscape. On the other side of the inky Farellon tunnel, the **Rio Simpson Reserve** begins. The rough and majestic landscape along the Simpson River leaves you anticipating every bend in the road, wondering what glacier or mountain will pop into view next. Upon passing two waterfalls, the Bride's Veil and the Virgin, you come to the **Reserve Information Center**. The museum is not much, but there is an intriguing stump from a 700-year-old alerce tree with Chile's history mapped out on the rings.

The reserve covers 41,000 hectares, but has poorly maintained infrastructure for hiking and camping. It can also be very wet. The Raleigh International volunteers cleared some paths a few years ago, but they are not well marked and becoming overgrown, which makes for slow going. Talk to the ranger to see if they have cleared any of the trails.

Puerto Aisén was the main commercial center of the area until the 1960s. It remains the second largest city in the region. The verdant, tree-shaded square is perfect for enjoying an afternoon stroll and the cathedral is worth a quick visit. Two simple and colorful ports at the end of O'Higgins Street, **Palos** and **Aguas Muertas** are home to a few well-used boats. You can try to get inexpensive rides to San Rafael on the *goletas* (small boats) by talking directly to the captains who supply basic necessities to the people living along the fjords.

From Aisén you cross the impressive, orange **Puente Ibañez**, supposedly the largest suspension bridge in Latin America. If you have your own vehicle you can detour to **Lago Riesco**, an attractive mountain ringed lake ideal for fishing. Continuing along the route to **Puerto Chacabuco** you are treated to the display of glacial mountains dropping straight into the Aisén channel. The majority of the boating activity has moved to Chacabuco because Aisén's port has filled with silt over time. The boat tours of San Rafael leave from here, though many are booked in Coyhaique.

See Coyhaique *Arrivals and Departures* for bus information. In Aisén you can hail a bus or *colectivo* from Aldea street to get to Chacabuco.

Tour Australis, *Moraleda 589, Tel. 239696* does the round trip in a half day. The $17 outing includes transportation, a guide, and a light lunch.

Renting a car is also an option. With your own wheels you have the freedom to stop by **La Pasarela** for a drink or dinner on the way back.

Where to Stay & Eat: Puerto Aisén
HOTEL GASTRONOMIA CARRERA, *Cochrane 465. Tel. 67/332551. 5 rooms. Double $70. Breakfast included. No credit cards.*

This place is clean, but old fashioned. The restaurant, however, features an extensive seafood selection. This is the nicest, albeit most sedate, place to eat in town. Better to dine than stay here, but there aren't a lot of choices.

HOTEL PLAZA, *O'Higgins 237. Tel. 67/332784. Double $22. No cards* and **HOTEL ROXI**, *Aldea 972, Tel. 67/332704. Double $20. No credit cards,* are two inexpensive options if you need them. Both are generally quiet, but the Roxi has bigger rooms.

RESTAURANTE EL RINCON CHILOTE, *Aldea 353. Tel. 67/332811. Moderate. No credit cards.*

While the only thing especially Chilote on the menu is the *curanto*, the food is quite good and the atmosphere in the wood paneled restaurant is pleasant. Seafood is their specialty, although they offer the complete Chilean menu. Try the *marisco* soup.

CAFÉ DINAS, *Aldea 382. Tel. 67/332911. Inexpensive. No credit cards.*

The Dinas is one of several café eateries along the main avenue. The food and service are solid here as well as at the **Café Irlandes**, *Aldea 1077.*

Where to Stay & Eat: Puerto Chacabuco

HOSTERÍA LOBERIAS DE AISÉN, *Carrera 50. Tel. 67/351115. 25 rooms, 10* cabañas. *Double $63, $93 cabins. Breakfast included. No credit cards.*

This hotel is a surprising find in a small port city. It sits above the water and affords great views of mountains and the Aisén channel. The restaurant, with good seafood, particularly benefits from the hotel's location.

MORALEDA, *On O'Higgins. Tel. 67/351155. Double $16. Breakfast included. No credit cards.*

This run-down looking place is the inexpensive option in town.

LAKE ELIZALDE & SEIS LAGUNAS CIRCUIT

This trip through the Simpson valley offers excellent fishing, beautiful hiking, and terrain that varies from desert plains to hunks of rock sprouting out of the earth. It can take one day or be spread out over as many as you'd like. There are fishing lodges and camping spots on the route. We recommend it for people who are not going to be venturing much farther on the Austral Highway.

The trip starts on the road to Balmaceda where you pass the **Difunta Correa Shrine** before crossing over **El Salto**, a multi-level waterfall alongside the route. The paved road snakes through bizarre rock formations before the turn off to Valle Simpson and Villa Frei. After 14 km the dirt road reaches the finger-like **Lake Elizalde** where you can fish or hike along its *lenga* covered shores. Boats are available for hire at the *Puerto de Yates*. To stay overnight, one of the options is the **Hostería Lago Elizalde**, *Tel. 67/231137, cabins $110*, a Swiss style retreat with boats, horses, hikes, camping and a restaurant. A little further up the road is **Camping La Cascada**, *Tel. 67/237951, $8*, with lovely views of the surrounding area as well as boat rentals and lake excursions.

DIFUNTA CORREA, BETTER THAN CAR INSURANCE

Throughout Chile and Argentina, you will pass roadside shrines dedicated to the **Difunta Correa***. The inspiration for these altars is the legend of Deolinda Correa, a conscript's wife who followed her husband through the desert during the Argentine civil wars of the 1840s. She died of thirst, hunger, and exhaustion, but her infant son was found alive at her breast. She is now thought to have the property of granting safe passage on dangerous roads. Truckers are counted amongst the devout, visiting her shrines to leave bottles of water to quench her thirst, small banknotes, and lighted candles. You may want to drop off some Evian on your way out of town.*

Continuing along the same road you cross winter pastureland and skirt by waterfalls to reach the Paloma Fishing Lodge, a remote shelter in a pristine setting:

PALOMA FISHING LODGE, *Tel./*Fax 67/231257. *$2850 week fishing package includes transportation, lodging, fishing, boats, guides, and meals. Credit cards accepted.*

The Paloma is set up as few places are in Aisén with first class service, excellent meals, and fish galore. The isolated lodge with its comfortable rooms and gathering areas (including a fly tying room), caters to serious fly fishers. Carlos Muñoz takes his clients to gorgeously remote and unexplored areas. Huge browns abound in reed lined channels while condors and parakeets fly overhead. Trips must be arranged before arrival as they are completely full during the season. It's not a place that you just drop in.

Return to Villa Frei and take the left to **Seis Lagunas**, six glimmering lagoons creased in between the hills. Continue along to **Lago Atravesado** and the cabins tucked away at the **Rio Negro Lodge**, *Tel. 67/231558. Five cabins. $175. No credit cards.* The Rio Negro, another lakeside oasis, is geared towards anglers and should be booked in advance.

You can either rent a 4 wheel drive vehicle or take a tour. **Tour Australis**, *Moraleda 589, Tel. 239696*, has a nine hour trip for $40 that includes a barbecue on the banks of Lago Elizalde, a boat ride and an optional hike.

DOS LAGUNAS NATURAL MONUMENT

This 70 km half day trip also starts out on the road to Balmaceda, but heads left to the **El Fraile Ski Center**. Even in summer it is worth a visit for impressive views of the valley and the rocky fortress of Cerro Castillo beyond.

Continuing along the route you pass the tree shaded Frio, Pollux, and Castor lakes, famous for their brown and rainbow trout. Lake Frio, due to its water quality and temperature, is a breeding site for rainbows. On the road to Coyhaique Alto you will come to the **Dos Lagunas Natural Monument**, *8:30am-9pm in the summer. Entry $7.50.* You can see the graceful and endangered black necked swan amongst other water fowl while enjoying a picnic. Continue on a bit towards the Argentine border to get a real sense of the vastness of the pampa before heading back. There is no public transportation.

PRACTICAL INFORMATION

Banks: BCI, *Prat 387*; **Banco Santender**, *Condell 184*; and **Banco de Santiago**, *Condell 139*
Business Hours: 9am-1pm and 3pm-7pm

Currency Exchange: **Turismo Prado**, *21 de Mayo 417*; **Lucia Saldivia**, *Condell 140*; **Emperado**, *Bilbao 222*

E-Mail Service: You can get on the internet at the **Entel** phone center at *Prat 340* from 9am-9pm for $.25/minute or $3.75/hour. If you have a computer you can also access a phone line there in cabaña 16 by unhooking the fax machine.

Fishing Equipment: Patagonia Outdoors, *Horn 47, Tel. 232474*; **Ferreteria La Nueva**, *Condell 150*

Laundry: **Lavanderia QL**, *Bilbao 160*; **Lavamatic**, *Bilbao and 12 de Octubre*

Medical Services: **Hospital**, *Calle Hospital off Carrera*

National Parks: The **Conaf** office is on the second floor at *Bilbao 234*. They have another office in town, but this is the place to get maps and information about parks in the area.

Post Office: **Correos de Chile**, *Cochrane 202*

Supermarkets: **Multimas** and **Vyhmeister** can both be found on *Lautraro between Prat and Cochrane*

Telephone/Fax: The area code is 67. The best call center is the **Entel** phone center at *Prat 340*.

Tourist Offices/Maps: **Sernatur**, *Bulnes 35, 9am-6pm*, has loads of helpful, up to date information and the best maps. The tourist office next to the regional museum at *Baquedano 310* is less useful.

NORTHERN AUSTRAL HIGHWAY

The northern part of the road, generally in better condition that the southern section, envelopes you in green. Dark forests rise out of the mist, lime colored fronds surround mossy thermal pools, and the emerald Futulefú runs its course of class IV and V rapids.

ARRIVALS & DEPARTURES

During the summer buses and vans connect most of the cities along the route. You may have to wait in some places, or be crammed in others, but you can get all the way to Chaiten without a car. See the Coyhaique section for listings of the bus companies and their destinations.

If you have the resources, renting a four wheel drive vehicle is the best way to see this area. The freedom to stop and go when or where ever you want is worth the price. If you rent a vehicle, ideally it will come with an extra spare and extra gas tank. We recommend filling up for gas every time you have the chance, even if you just topped off in the last town, because many times places that say they have gas end up being dry. See the Coyhaique listings for rental companies and driving tips.

The last option is by plane. If you are pushed for time, this can get you to Chaiten. See the Coyhaique section for a list of airplane options.

THE ROAD NORTH: COYHAIQUE TO PUERTO CISNES

From Coyhaique you head east through the Rio Simpson Reserve on the paved road to Puerto Aisén (see *Coyhaique Day Trips*) before catching the Austral Highway. Once you head north, this section of the road, hacked out of the woods, is a densely packed, green corridor with little sign of human activity. It does open up a bit for gorgeous views of the Andes. Blue glaciers nestle in the tops of most of the mountains. Waterfalls stream down the sides of hills, tumbling on moss covered rocks before crossing under the road.

PUERTO CISNES

You actually cross the barely-out-of-the-ocean Andes on the drive into this ocean-side village. Puerto Cisnes has one of the longer histories in the region as a port, if not as a town. Ships used to dock here before and after exploration into the Chilean heart of darkness.

For hotels consider the **Cabañas Manzur**, *Ethel Dunn 75. Tel. 346453, Double $45, No credit cards,* in a quiet spot on the edge of town. The **Residencial El Gaucho**, *Golmberg 140, Tel. 67/346514, Double $12, No credit cards,* and the **Hostal Michay**, *Mistral 112, Tel. 67/346462, Double $25, No credit cards,* are about equidistant from the center of town to the north and south. Both have hot water and friendly service. If you need to go budget, try the **Residencial Ibañez**, *Dixon 31, Tel. 67/423227 for $9.*

When it's time to dine, the **Miramar** on *Prat, Moderate, No credit cards,* has a nice view of the ocean. The **Restaurante Kitypunch** and **Café Los Cuchos**, both inexpensive, are near each other on *Mistral.* Seafood is the specialty of the town. Try the traditional dish called *puyes.*

Puerto Cisnes is just a pleasant little town on the sea that offers all the basic services. **Gas** can be found at *Caro 37.* The **artisan shop** is right around the corner. Their knitted handicrafts are well known, as are the unique works done on fish skin. The **phone center** is on *Cerda* right in front of the plaza.

THE ROAD NORTH: PUERTO CISNES TO LA JUNTA

Continuing north, you enter the world of enchantment of **Quelat National Park**. You half expect a dinosaur to step in front of the car as the road curves through primordial rain forests. Leaves the size of twin beds stand together with hundreds of ferns in every shade of green. Glaciers hang so low that even rain clouds can't obscure the view. Waterfalls crash down on all sides. You have never seen anything like this.

The dense forest makes it extremely difficult to venture into the park in areas with no cut trails. At present, there are just two spots in the park with trails, though they are working on more. The first is a trail to the **Pedro Garcia waterfall**, which takes you into the forest at its drippiest. The second is the **Hanging Glacier**, an unusually low glacier with water cascading off its tail into the stream below.

There is a campground at the glacier, a rangers hut, and the beginning of a museum. It is unusually expensive ($7) for access to the glacier trails because of the infrastructure work, but unless you are on an extremely low budget, it is worth it. The view is not too different from the one you get on the road, but you are a lot closer. There is another more secluded campground further north. It has covered tables to help with the constant rain, but the surrounding forest can be claustrophobic. As you leave the park, the road falls to sea level and borders the ocean.

PUYUHUAPI

About 20 km before reaching Puerto Puyuhuapi there is a sign on the left for the **Termas de Puyuhuapi** dock. The hot springs and hotel are 12 km away on the other side of the canal. Ferries depart at 9:30am, 12:00pm, and 6:30pm in the summer. This Fantasy Island resort offers coddling and luxury in the middle of the rain forest.

TERMAS DE PUYUHUAPI HOTEL AND SPA, *Santiago Tel./Fax 2/ 225-6489. Puyuhuapi Tel. 67/325103. 28 rooms. Double $142. Breakfast included. Restaurant. Bar. Pool. Gym. Sauna. Credit cards accepted.*

If you are up for pampering yourself after bouncing along the Austral Highway, this is the spot to do it. Located in a tranquil cove at the foot of the Melimoyu mountains, the resort includes all the amenities you would expect at a five star establishment, with a few special twists. There are thermal pools, hot seawater Jacuzzis, herbal wraps, seaweed steams, and every kind of massage in the book. The food is far above par for Chile and the service is excellent. During the high season they usually arrange four-day packages, but will accept drive-in (or boat-in) guests on Thursday, Friday, and Monday nights.

The resort has teamed up with the **Patagonia Express** to offer trips to the **San Rafael glacier** as well. If the hotel is out of your budget you can still enjoy a day at the thermal pools for $25. Get out of those muddy, wet clothes and indulge.

Continuing on, the port of **Puyuhuapi** soon comes into view. Four Germans who hacked their way through the jungle founded the town in 1935. All their lands were expropriated in 1971 and their descendents, left with nothing, emigrated. Their Teutonic influence in still seen in the town's architecture. A unique stop is a tour of the carpet factory, 11am-4pm, where you can watch high quality rugs be tied.

Puyuhuapi has all the basic services. **Hostería Alemana** and **Hotel La Casona** on the main strip are the best options for a place to stay or a meal. For a quick bite or a German pastry, we recommend the **Café Rossbach** in front of the gas station.

Further north, on the shores of **Lake Risopatron**, another option for lodging is the **Cabañas El Pangue**, *Tel. 67/325128. Double $100. 6 cabins. Restaurant. Pool. Credit cards accepted.* The cabins are very nicely decorated but small for the price. The fishing here is excellent, however, as is the scenery.

LA JUNTA

This town receives a lot of overnight traffic as it is a good stopping point on the trip to Chaiten. There is nothing special to see or do here other than walk around the dusty streets. It has the basic gas, food, and lodging services, but most of them are overpriced.

Where to Stay & Eat

HOTEL ESPACIO Y TIEMPO, *on the Austral highway, Tel. 67/314141. 45 rooms. Double $75. Restaurant. No credit cards.*

This is the nicest hotel in town and they know it. It's not a particularly good value, but heads and shoulders above the other options. There is a large yard and garden as well as the best restaurant in town. They will even prepare fish you've caught.

There are a handful of small hostels a few blocks off the left side of the highway. Most of them are drab and depressing with the exception of the **Hostel Ricalari**. It is small, and you must share a bath, but at least there is sunlight. The owner has his own artwork decorating the walls.

Boat Trip to Hot Springs & Balmaceda Island

If Puyuhuapi is too blue for your blood you can try the wilderness hot springs experience on this seven hour day trip. The boat floats through virgin rain forest to pull up to shore at natural hot springs. Balmaceda Island is an interesting stop to experience a culture totally dependent on the sea. Contact **Hotel Espacio y Tiempo** to arrange the trip.

ANNUAL RAINFALL IN THE AUSTRAL REGION

For comparison purposes, Seattle's annual rainfall is about 1,000 mm and San Diego's is 250 mm.
- **Chile Chico** - *230 mm*
- **Coyhaique** - *1,350 mm*
- **Puerto Aisén** - *2,960 mm*
- **Puerto Cisnes** - *4,300 mm*

THE ROAD NORTHEAST: LA JUNTA TO FUTULEFÚ

The pace is slow on this next section of that road with more people on horseback than in autos. That's okay though, because the setting continues to overwhelm you with its grandeur. Be sure to keep an eye out for cows. As silly as it sounds, they really do *dash* into the road.

At **Villa Santa Lucia** you have the option of heading east to **Futulefú**, which is both a town and a river. The road winds up and up along the water introducing a new green to the pallet; a deep, full emerald flecked with gold that flies by filling the canyon with its roar.

Thirty six km from Santa Lucia is the take out spot for rafters. Called the **Casa de Empanadas**, it has the best hand-juggling-hot, apple *empanadas* in Chile. You can't help but stop again when you cross the concrete bridge and get your first full sighting of the river. You may even have paddlers swoosh by below.

FUTULEFÚ

Continuing up the river you pass two lakes, the **Lonconao** and the **Espolon**, with cabins as well as camping and fishing. The scenery is spectacular along the entire road. The bases of operations for both of the US rafting companies are found along this stretch. A few minutes later you arrive to Futulefú, population 1,000. Designed by the same landscape deity as Boulder, Colorado, the surrounding hills beckon all outdoor enthusiasts.

There are buses to Futulefú from both La Junta and Chaiten in the summer. The Argentine border crossing, just outside of town, is used by people of the region to go both north and south on smooth, paved roads. It is open from 8am-8pm.

The town is set up in the classic grid with a plaza in the center. Its shady benches are a nice place for a picnic.

Where to Stay & Eat

HOSTERÍA RIO GRANDE, *O'Higgins 397. Tel. 65/258633. 10 rooms. Double $60. Breakfast included. Restaurant. No credit cards.*

This clean, airy, log hotel is a hang out for paddlers. The newly furnished rooms are the most comfortable around, the restaurant the best in town, and the beer cold. They also have a gigantic map of the area on the wall in the lobby. It's a good place to hang out even if you are staying or camping elsewhere.

POSADA LA GRINGA, *Sargento Street, Tel. 65/258633 ext. 260. 8 rooms. Double $40. 8 rooms. Breakfast included. No credit cards.*

A pleasant, well-kept inn, Posada La Gringa draws a mainly foreign crowd.

There's a variety of great sports and recreational activities in the area:

Fishing is excellent in the area lakes. The Municipal building at O'Higgins 596 is the place to get your license. The rivers around Palena, south of Futulefú are a fly-fisher's dream. The **Rio Palena Lodge**, *US Tel. 888/891-3474*, is a beautifully maintained, first class, full-package fishing Shangri-la.

The hills and cattle trails of the area are great for **hiking**. The *Tres Monjas* (Three Nuns) Mountain is especially intriguing. You need ropes to get all the way to the top, but you can make good progress and catch some outstanding views without them.

The **Futulefú River** is a place of special reverence for **rafters** and **kayakers**; people travel from all over the world in the summer to run its emerald waters. It is a technical, fast, big river with class IV and V rapids coming one after the other.

There are two outfitters that run the Fut. Both of them organize ten day trips out of the US. Earth River is the high-end option, with a hot tub and masseuse at their base camp. BioBio is more bare bones in terms of accommodations, but does not scrimp on equipment or food. Both are extremely professional and take all safety precautions. BioBio takes one-day walk-ins for $75 when they are between groups. It is not advisable for amateurs to go down the river with non-commercial groups.

The two outfitters are:
- **BioBio**, *US Tel. 800/260-RAFT, www.bbxrafting.com*, $1,200
- **Earth River**, *US Tel. 800/643-2784, www.earthriver.com*, $2,300

If you want to shoot the Fut you'd better get to Chile soon, as a big hydroelectric project is slated to begin in the next three years.

Another option for the less experienced is to raft the **Espolon River**. The local rafting club, located next to the Hostería Rio Grande, runs two trips a day in the summer.

Practical Information

The **tourist office** is right on the plaza as is the **post office**. There is a **phone center** on the plaza next to the church. The area code is 65. There are no banks. Getting **gas** is an interesting experience as it is sold out of wine jugs at the store on *Lautaro and Carrera.*

THE ROAD NORTH: CHAITEN

As you drive towards Chaiten the green corridor continues. If it is clear, the mountains above make for what some rate as the best scenery of the trip. There is a sign for *Aguas Minerales* where a slippery wooden walkway leads back to some natural springs. The water tastes very minerally, but it's a good way to get into the forest for 15 minutes if you want to stretch your legs.

Lake Yelcho comes into view next. The walls of the lake drop almost straight into the water and here, in the middle of nowhere, is the **Cavi Resort**, *Tel. 65/731337.* Perched right on the lake, it has a beautiful dining area as well as comfortable rooms ($75) and cabins ($200.) The food is a bit expensive but the dining and sitting space are so pleasant on a rainy day it is almost worth it.

Just before arriving to Chaiten there is a turn off for the **Amarillo Hot Springs**. The springs have been diverted into two pools, one large and one small. It's a nice place to go if there are only a few people there, which is usually the case.

Like the rest of the region, Chaiten's history is a recent one. In 1933 there were only three houses in this town that now connects the Austral zone with Puerto Montt.

Arrivals & Departures

Ferryboats make the trip to both Puerto Montt (ten hours) and Chiloé (five hours). The Navimag and Transmarchilay offices are around the corner from each other on *Todesco* and *Corcovado* respectively. Their schedules change every month, so you'll have to check with them for ferry departure times.

Buses from Chaiten can connect the traveler to Coyhaique, Futulefú, and points along the way. The bus station is on the corner of *Independencia and Portales.*

There are daily **plane** connections to Puerto Montt in the summer for $50 on Aerosur, *Tel. 67/731228.* We'd be cautious about taking the planes in bad weather.

Orientation

Chaiten, whose name comes from the Indian word for basket, is bounded by the Bay of Chaiten to the west and the Blanco River to the east. On sunny days you can see the Corcovado Volcano standing in the background.

The town is laid out in that classic grid with the exception of the area along the bay. Much of the commercial activity is concentrated along Corcovado, in front of the ocean, instead of around the plaza, which is two blocks back.

Where to Stay

CABAÑAS TRANQUERAS DEL MONTE, *Avenida Norte no number. Tel. 65/731379. 4 cabins. Double $80. Cable TV. No credit cards.*

The owners put some care into building these cabins, which you can see in the details - sturdy tables and chairs, full sets of kitchen utensils, and lots of hot water. They are on a hill above town so it is nice and quiet as well.

HOTEL MI CASA, *Avenida Norte 206. Tel. 65/731285. 20 rooms. Double $65. Restaurant. American Express only.*

Mi Casa means "my house" and this hotel looks like somebody's home on the hill. There is a nice view of the bay from the front yard and the owners are friendly.

CABAÑAS AND RESTAURANT LAS BRISAS DEL MAR, *Corcovado 278. Tel. 65/731284. 10 cabins. Double $80. Restaurant.*

These cabins are right on the waterfront, which is also the town's main drag. It's great for those who want to be in the middle of things, but can be noisy at times.

RESIDENCIAL ASTORIA, *Corcovado 442. Tel. 65/731263. 12 rooms. Double $20.*

A little further down the waterfront, this utilitarian *residencial* offers decent rooms at an affordable price. There is even a bar downstairs. The **Residencial El Progresso**, *O'Higgins 65, Tel. 65/731235,* is another inexpensive option

An even less expensive option is to stay in someone's home. During the summer families will put a sign in the window saying, "*hospedaje*" – which indicates that they host guests. The stay usually costs less than $10 and includes breakfast.

Where to Eat

CANASTO DEL AGUA, *Portales and Prat. Moderate. Credit cards accepted.*

The nicest restaurant in town in terms of ambiance also has the best food. The menu is typical of Chile with seafood and steaks. Their sandwiches are excellent. It gets crowded almost every night so either go early or be prepared to wait a while.

RESTAURANTE LAS BRISAS DEL MAR, *Corcovado 278. Moderate. Credit cards accepted.*

Las Brisas is another solid option in town. You won't leave raving but you probably won't leave hungry either.

MAHURORI, *O'Higgins 141. Inexpensive. No credit cards.*

In the *hospedaje* of the same name, the Mahurori offers a bit more economical fare. It will fill and warm you up, which is what you usually need in Chaiten.

Excursions & Day Trips

Chaiten is more of a coming and going point than a place to spend any time. There is a dearth of things to do and see, which you will experience first hand if you get caught here between ferries. The best advice for travelers is to hit the road.

If you do get stuck in town, the video store near the plaza has a VCR in a room in the back. You can rent a video and watch it there. Take something soft to sit on, as the benches are plank wood; and a coat, because there's a hole in the wall.

Practical Information

Banks: The bank, open from 9am-2pm is across from the plaza. There is no teller machine and they don't take travelers checks.

Business Hours: Commercial establishments are open from 9am-1pm and again from 3pm-7pm. Restaurants are open from 1pm-3pm and 8pm-11pm.

Laundry: The laundry mat is on *Ercilla and Pardo*. They charge by the pound, not the load, so if you have wet clothes you're in for a big bill.

Phone Center: The area code is 65. There is a phone center underneath the **Hostería Shilling** at *Corcovado 230*.

Tourist Office: The Sernatur office is at the end of Todesco, practically dangling over the sea. They have some leaflets, but don't have that many resources. They suggest that you talk directly to the ferry companies for current schedules.

THE ROAD NORTH: CHAITEN TO PUERTO MONTT

There are two ferry rides on this section. One is five hours long and the other 30 minutes, but they irregular departure schedules. For that very reason most people just take the ferry directly from Chaiten to Puerto Montt. There are some interesting things to see on this stretch of the highway however. Heading north from Chaiten you'll hit **Santa Barbara**, which has a nice beach for camping. From there it is another 56 km to **Caleta Gonzalo**, where you board the ferry to Hornopiren. **Caleta Gonzalo** sits within the boundaries of the Pumalin Park.

PUMALIN PARK

This controversial reserve, owned by American millionaire Douglas Tompkins, is now open to the public. The largest private park in the world, it covers 250,000 hectares and is home to glaciers, rivers, volcanoes, and huge stands of *alerce*, the South American sequoia. There are currently just a few trails cut through the Chilean rain forest. The main one, more than worth the schlep, leads to an ancient grove of trees that predate the birth of Christ.

Where to Stay & Eat

CABAÑAS PUMALIN, *Caleta Gonzalo. Tel. 65/250079, Fax 65/255145. 7 cabins without kitchens. Double $60. Breakfast included. Restaurant. Credit cards accepted.*

Tompkins designed every detail of these simple wooden cabins himself, so you can sleep easy knowing it's environmentally correct down to the last nail. The cabins sleep three to six people and have a full bath, and hot water. The adjacent, nouveau-woodsy **Café Caleta Gonzalo** is an outstanding dining option. They have excellent inexpensive meals and delightful pastries.

CAMPING PUMALIN, *Caleta Gonzalo., Tel. 65/250079, Fax 65/255145. Campsites with common toilet and cold water shower facilities. $1.50 per person. No credit cards.*

With the Renihue Fjord on one side and the dense, kelly, forest on the others, you may not even want to go back country. You can buy firewood at the park information center. It's not called a rain forest because it's dry, so be sure to waterproof those tent seams.

Sports & Recreation

As most of the park does not have roads, **hiking** will only reveal a sliver of the diversity of the reserve. Nosing around the park from the water will give you a much better feel for all its wonders. The most common visitor activities are **fishing** or **boat site-seeing trips** through the fjords. Stop in on the park information center in Caleta Gonzalo for details and directions.

To get on even more intimate levels with the reserve, you can paddle along it's winding shores. Two US outfitters run a few trips a year to the park. Latin America Escapes, *US Tel. 800/510-5999* has an **eight day hiking and kayaking** combo-trip and a **nine day kayaking** trip for $1,015 and $1,475 respectively. Ecole Adventures International, *US Tel. 800/447-1483* has a $725, five day **sailboat-based** trip. From the boat you take kayaking day trips along the shoreline.

DOUGLAS TOMPKINS: ENVIRONMENTAL PHILANTHROPIST OR EVIL SPY?

Imagine the following scenario: A Spanish millionaire moves to Florida and begins buying up pieces of land, forming a complete band across the state. He declares that his intention is to create a park for the benefit of all, but rumors begin to fly. How do you think Americans, especially the military, would react?

*That is basically what has happened to **Douglas Tompkins** with Chile. Tompkins, the deep-pocketed founder of both the North Face and Espirit clothing lines, has bought a thousand square mile slice of land whose boundaries are Argentina on one side and the Pacific Ocean on the other. He has created the world's largest private reserve with the intention of protecting this special eco-system from the encroach of logging and people.*

Many of his supporters, as well as the international press, have criticized the Chilean government as short-sited and mean for its less than enthusiastic response to his purchases. A non-biased look at the situation however, shows not only that Tompkins philanthropy is commendable, but also that the Chilean government's attitude is not completely incomprehensible, especially in light of how other countries might respond in a similar situation.

The ferry, which only runs during the summer, takes you through the **Reñihue fjord**. The boat then hits the open sea to eventually sidle along the Llancahue and Ciervos Islands before landing at **Hornopirén**. There is gas, food, and camping in this town of 1,100. **Hornopirén National Park** lies just to the east. From here it is 55 km to the next ferry boarding spot at **Caleta Puelche**.

Thirty minutes after boarding that ferry you land at **La Arena** on the edge of the **Alerce Andino National Park**, which is covered in the "Puerto Montt" section. It is only another 45 km to **Puerto Montt**.

SOUTHERN AUSTRAL HIGHWAY

The road south from Coyhaique is a bumpy, washboard, poor excuse for a highway but it has outrageous, once-in-a-lifetime views. The beauty literally becomes absurd when you see lakes and rivers whose colors come from pallets designated for bottles of food coloring. Glaciers tucked into mountain crooks are almost commonplace. The microclimate around Chile Chico is something else entirely with painted-desert spires and lunar rock formations. As difficult as access can be on this one-lane dirt road, you are missing something very special if you pass over this section of the region.

ARRIVALS & DEPARTURES

During the summer buses and vans connect most of the cities along the Austral highway. You may have to wait in some places, or be crammed in others, but you can get all the way to Cochrane without a car. See the Coyhaique section for listings of the bus companies and their destinations.

If you have the resources, renting a four wheel drive vehicle is the best way to see this region. The freedom to stop and go when or where ever you want is worth the price. If you rent a vehicle, ideally it will come with an extra spare and extra gas tank. We recommend filling up for gas every time you have the chance, even if you just topped off in the last town, because many times places that say they have gas end up being dry. See the Coyhaique listings for rental companies and driving tips.

The last option is by plane. If you are pushed for time, this can get you to Chile Chico and Cochrane much faster than by car. It's the only way to get to Villa O'Higgins. See the Coyhaique section for a list of airplane options.

THE ROAD SOUTH: COYHAIQUE TO BERTRAND

From Coyhaique you join the southern section of the highway for the first of many kilometers of dirt road.

CERRO CASTILLO NATIONAL RESERVE

The highlight of the reserve is its namesake peak that reigns above the region as a 2320-meter rocky fortress. Other notable sights in the 134,000 hectare park are old growth *lenga* forests, guanacos, pumas, foxes, condors, and even the rarely seen *huemul* deer.

The trail system is a bit confusing as the Conaf campsite and ranger station next to Laguna Chiguay are not at any trailhead. The campsite itself is wonderfully maintained, with bathrooms, firepits, picnic tables, and beautiful wooden signs. You can get a map at the ranger station and be pointed in the direction of the trails. Two of them start within nine km of the station and end further south along the Austral highway; inconvenient if you are driving but nice if all you have is your pack.

If you are interested in climbing Cerro Castillo, the best access point is from the town of **Villa Cerro Castillo**. Cowering at the base of the imposing hill, Villa Cerro Castillo is a dusty, depressing place but it does have food and lodging if you are in a bind.

A few kilometers south of town is the **Hands of Cerro Castillo National Monument**, an excellent example of Tehuelche hand paintings. The self-guided trail offers information about the Indians and their lives.

WHO WERE THESE PAINTERS?

A nomadic tribe whose stomping grounds ranged from southern Patagonia to as far north as Bariloche, the Tehuelches left their marks in numerous caves and rock walls in the region. They roamed the valleys of the cordillera hunting guanacos and ñandues, basically unmolested until the early 20th century. The large land concessions granted to the livestock companies brought their nomadic days to an end. This, coupled with disease introduced by Europeans, essentially wiped out the tribe.

PUERTO IBAÑEZ.

Puerto Ibañez is important because it is the place to catch the ferry to Chile Chico. Ferries depart four days a week (Monday, Wednesday, Friday, and Saturday) for the two and a half hour crossing. The ferry schedule varies by season, but depending on the day, boats leave at 9am or 3pm. The trip costs $4.50 per person. For current schedules call the two companies that handle the route: **Ferry Chelenco** at *Tel. 67/233466* or **RR Pilchero** at *Tel. 67/234240*.

The alternative route to Chile Chico is about ten hours on a rough, albeit stunning section of the Austral highway. Buses leave Puerto Ibañez for Coyhaique soon after the ferries pull in.

If you get stuck in Puerto Ibañez you can try the **Hostería Monica** at *Bertrand Dickson 29, Tel. 67/423226* or the **Residencial Ibañez** next door. Both are rather sparse, but for $10 you can't expect much more.

Puerto Ibañez has a few artisan workshops with ceramic and leather goods. Pieces indigenous to the area are made of fired clay covered with sheep or goats skin.

Twenty-six km from Puerto Ibañez, the **Levican** peninsula sticks out into the lake, almost completing a circle around the port. On the way there you pass waterfalls as well as Tehuelche wall paintings. The real reason for taking the detour is the views of the water; emerald on the port side and deep blue out on the lake.

THE ROAD SOUTH: PUERTO IBAÑEZ TO PUERTO BERTRAND

The road from Cerro Castillo to Puerto Murta is a living (barely) monument to the effects of a strong volcanic explosion. In 1991 the Hudson volcano erupted, spewing ash for hundreds of kilometers. Nature has absorbed the shock in most of the region, but the pass along this section of the road, only 60 km from the volcano, is still covered in ash. You'll see entire forests along the road drowned in swirling ash.

There is not much of note in **Puerto Murta** with the exception of the convenience store/gas station straight out of an Isabel Allende novel. The grandmother sits on the front porch in a running dialog with lost spirits while the strong-willed mother runs her business with efficiency and charm. Her daughter streaks around like a whirling dervish in cowboy boots, eating ice cream and dragging an animal skin stole. This is one of the few places in Aisén to get an ice cold beer.

South of Puerto Murta, **Lake General Carrera** finally comes into view. This gargantuan, bi-national lake is the largest in Chile, covering 978 square kilometers. It is known as Lake Buenos Aires on the Argentine side. The fact that a body of water of this size was not known to exist until 1880 is a testament to the isolation of the region.

The lake dominates the landscape of this part of Chile. The deep azure of its center fades to a brilliant turquoise, which is contrasted with milky blues and greens where glacial rivers spill into its bays. White capped mountains stand as silent sentinels across the lake while glaciers from the ice fields peak through across the road.

The road itself is an engineering marvel wrested and hewn from rocky ledges. As stunning as the scenery is, keep your eyes straight ahead if you are driving or you may find yourself much closer to the lake that you want to be. It's also a good idea to check the road's status if you are driving during a rainy period.

There is gas and food in **Puerto Tranquilo**, which is also the jumping off spot for a visit to the *Capilla de Marmol* or **Marble Chapel**. This lake peninsula has been shaped by wind and water into a stunning series of sculptured caves and formations. From Puerto Tranquilo it is a 30 minute boat ride to the caverns where you then spend time floating through the glowing rock. Trips can be arranged with Juan Carlos Garrido, *Tel. 67/231008* for $60. You can also go down to the docks in Puerto Tranquilo to find him or arrange a ride with somebody else.

The road continues south towards Bertrand with colors and scenery that will proceed to blow your mind. A few kilometers down the road, Lake General Carrera narrows and dumps into **Lake Bertrand** where it again changes colors – this time to a blue like neon, only richer and fuller.

There are a couple of places to stay on this section of the highway, but we recommend **La Pasarela 2**, *Tel. 67/234246, 4 cabins, cabin $200, Credit cards accepted,* a first class lodge set on the edge of the lake that is geared for anglers but comfortable for all.

PUERTO BERTRAND

Bertrand is truly worth the effort it takes to get there. The pace is slow in this tiny town that is home to only 44 families. There is one telephone and no gas station, but there are weeks worth of things to do.

Where to Stay & Eat

RIO BAKER LODGE, *dead end of the Costanera. Tel. 67/411499. 4 rooms. Double $120. Breakfast included. Restaurant. Credit cards accepted.*

The best thing about this blond wood hotel is the sunny, windowed sitting room that juts out over the river. It's a great place to read, play cards or just watch the water shimmy. As is the case with most of the better hotels in the region, it is set up for anglers, with boats leaving from the attached dock. The rooms are also right above the water. The restaurant is the best choice in town.

HOSTERÍA PUERTO BERTRAND, *in front of the dock. Tel. 67/411499.3 rooms with private bath. 6 rooms with shared bath. Double $50. Breakfast included. Restaurant. No credit cards.*

This is the best lower budget option in town and the central meeting point for backpackers.

You can **camp** for free in the park next to the dock. It's hard to find better lake front property anywhere in town. You can also go a little further south on the highway and camp basically anywhere you want.

Sports & Recreation

The neon blue Rio Baker begins its run to the Pacific Ocean right in town. Just witnessing the color of Chile's longest and most voluminous river is justification alone for a visit to this place, but there is much more to keep you interested. World class fly fishing, rafting, and horseback riding are accessible by walking out your front door.

If anybody has heard of Bertrand, it is usually because of the **fishing**. You can arrange guides at the docks or with any of the people who hang out shingles on their front fence.

Horseback riders have an incredible opportunity to take a multi-day ride to the Northern Ice Fields with Anselmo Soto. Anselmo, in his mid-60s, taught us volumes about simplification and generosity. The $150 per person trip includes boat rides to his homestead land; horseback riding through and over valleys, streams and mountains; camping at the base of the stunning Soler glacier; and walking on the ice field. It is well worth the money as it will probably be the most memorable experience of your time in Chile. Arrange trips with his wife at their house directly up the hill from the docks. Ask anyone to point it out. There are other guides in town that arrange multi-day trips, but none to the glacier.

Jonathon Leidith, an American who had been coming to Chile since childhood, moved to Bertrand a few years ago and opened a white water rafting business. The trip is a fun way to experience the impossibly beautiful Rio Baker and see the nature along the river's shores. The best way to arrange a trip is to ask for him in town at the phone center or you can call *Tel. 67/419900* and leave a message.

CHILE'S LAST TERRITORIAL DISPUTE

*Covering 14,000 square km and stretching 320 km, you would think there would be enough ice on the **Southern Ice Field** (Campo de Hielo Sur) to go around. Hundreds of meters thick, the ice has filled in the spaces between mountains leaving all but the tallest peaks frozen in time. The majority of the Campo de Hielo Sur sits on the Chilean side of the border, but some of it reaches over the boundary into Argentina. That's the problem. Chile and Argentina cannot exactly agree on the dividing line.*

There are a number of reasons for the dispute. All of them have nothing to do with the present, but rather look into the future as the glaciers continue to melt away. Argentines don't want "their ice" to run into Chilean lakes and rivers. Chileans don't want the Argentines to have access to the Pacific through the fjords that will be created. The Pope has given stern warnings to both sides to work it out before he has to step in and mediate.

THE ROAD SOUTH: PUERTO BERTRAND TO COCHRANE

If you ever manage to pull yourself away from Bertrand, the road continues south along the Rio Baker towards Cochrane. The glacial tongues of the ever-present Northern Ice Field lick away at the landscape, sculpting the hills before melting into rivers that rush to the Baker. You'll cross several of these on the road south, the most impressive being the waterfall where the Neff and Baker come together.

The Chacabuco river valley, kneaded into strange lumps and humps by the constant wind, is the best sheep grazing land in the region. Stop to sample some fresh goat cheese.

COCHRANE

Cochrane, population 3,000, was founded in 1930. It seems like not much has changed since then as it still has the feel of an old west pioneer town complete with horses roaming the streets.

In the summer Cochrane is connected by bus to Coyhaique and Chile Chico. **Los Nadis** at *Helechos 420* and **Acuario** at *Rio Baker 349* are the two bus companies. Flights to Coyhaique depart once a week. The **Don Carlos** airline, *Tel. 67/231981* makes the trip for about $130.

Where to Stay

HOTEL ULTIMO PARADISO, *Lago Brown 455. Tel. 67/522361. 7 rooms. Double $70. Breakfast included. Visa and Mastercard only.*

This is the best place in town hands down. The lodge-style hotel, made from local cypress and other hardwoods, is a joy for weary travelers. It is simple, but it's comfortable and the service is good.

CABAÑAS ROJERIS, *Teniente Merino 502. Tel. 67/522264. 3 cabins. Double $70. Restaurant. No credit cards.*

If you want more space you can spread out bit in these cabins right in town. The small complex also includes a café/restaurant that is a popular place for meals. The cabins, all fully stocked, come with heaters, which can be a blessing in these climes.

RESIDENCIAL SUR AUSTRAL, *Arturo Prat 334. Tel. 67/522150. 8 rooms without bath. Double $12. Breakfast included. No credit cards.*

This is a good option for the more budget minded as it's clean and has hot water.

Camping: There is camping outside of town in the CONAF administered **Las Correntadas**.

Where to Eat

CAFÉ ROGERI, *502 Teniente Merino. Inexpensive. No credit cards.*

This is a good place to hang out with the rest of town. Most of them lead the life of unhurried public servants. You can also try **Restaurante El Farolito** down the street at *Merino 546*.

Sports & Recreation

Forty-two km southeast of Cochrane, **Cerro San Lorenzo** is a 3700-meter peak ideal for mountaineering. **El Puesto Expediciones**, *Moraleda 229, Tel. 233785* in Coyhaique guides trips to the summit.

The abundant rivers of the area run into magnificent milky lakes, both of which offer grand choices for sport fishers. You can get a license at the Municipal building *at 398 Esmeralda*.

Excursions & Day Trips

Lake Cochrane is worth a visit. A good way to get there is from **The Tamango National Reserve**, only nine km from Cochrane. The reserve is home to a large community of threatened huemul deer. There are cabins, camping and picnic areas as well as trails to the lake. Check with the National Parks office to make sure they are open. For $12 you get a guided tour to see the huemules that includes a boating excursion on the lake.

Estancia Valle Chacabuco is a true working ranch that accepts guests for week-long stays during the spring and summer. Visitors have the chance to work on horseback, go on photo safaris, or just take it easy. You stay in the guest house, eat the same food as the cowhands, and really become part of the crew during your stay. The best time to visit is during the *señalada*, a time of branding and parties. Contact Viviana Candenas at their office in Coyhaique for reservations at *Lillo 311, Casilla 1-D, Tel. 67/236320.*

Practical Information

The bank, post office, National Parks office, supermarket, and tourism office are all on the main plaza. **Gas** is available at O'Higgins and Prat. There is a **travel agency** *at Merino 750* and **cars rental** *at Dr. Steffans 147.*

THE ROAD SOUTH: COCHRANE TO CATELA TORTEL

For eight years Cochrane was the end of the road, but in 1996 the highway was pushed through to Puerto Yungay. The road is gorgeous, with rugged forests standing at attention before majestic mountains literally dripping with glaciers. Once you get to the end, however, there is nothing in Puerto Yungay but a military camp.

More interesting for tourists is **Caleta Tortel**. The entire Tortel community, 21,000 square kilometers for 448 inhabitants, is a series of fjords, canals, and islands wedged between the Northern and Southern Ice Fields. The draw to the area is the Steffens and Jorge Montt Glaciers, three and five hours respectively by boat from Caleta Tortel. Caleta Tortel itself is an interesting place with stilted houses connected by cypress, above-ground walkways. It can be reached by boat along the Baker from the **Rio Vagabundo** docks on the way to Yungay. Ask for Mr. Casanova in Vagabundo.

VILLA O'HIGGINS

This southernmost community of the Austral region has a total population of 337 people. It is completely isolated from the rest of Chile by ground and only accessible by plane from Coyhaique and Cochrane. The Don Carlos airline, *Tel. 67/231981* has flights that depart once a week for about $240. The government keeps boasting that the road from Cochrane will reach it soon, but that is entirely doubtful.

This area is truly one of the last frontiers. It is extraordinarily beautiful and even more remote. Lakes, rivers, and glaciers abound, providing a home for gargantuan trout. Entire sectors of this community are unexplored and there are plants and animals that are yet to be classified. Icebergs calved from the Southern Ice Field float in **Lake O'Higgins**. The wall of the Grande Glacier, at 150 meters, soars twice as high as that of the San Valentin Glacier in Laguna San Rafael. **Mount Fitzroy**, one of the tallest peaks of the area at 3441 meters is a rock climber's dream. There is room available at *98 Rio Pascua* for $5 a night.

THE ROAD SOUTH: BERTRAND TO CHILE CHICO

Another option from Bertrand is to head northeast to Chile Chico. The first town on the route, **Puerto Guadal**, was founded to bring supplies over from Argentina. Guadal, with its beautiful bay, is still a supply point for food, gas, and a phone.

The road from Guadal to Chile Chico mixes that volatile combination of eye-catching scenery with narrow passes and sheer cliffs. The most impressive road work was done on this section of the highway, especially the dangerous and expensive *Paso Las Llaves* (the key hole.)

CHILE CHICO

Chile Chico was founded by a group of Chileans that entered the region via Argentina. It was called Chile Chico to distinguish it from the part of the country north of Puerto Montt, that people from Aisén called Chile Grande.

The next wave of people came in during the years of fruit production. These years are coming to an end. There are still orchards in the area, but as transportation improves, it is slowly being squeezed out by competition from the Central Valley. The new industry keeping the 2,300 person town alive is mining.

Chile Chico, on the banks of Lake General Carrera, has its own microclimate. In a part of Chile that is generally no stranger to rain, Chile Chico, otherwise known as "The City of Sun" lolls in over 300 sunny days a year. This alone is a huge selling point for rain-pounded travelers

THE WAR OF CHILE CHICO

In 1914, a group of pioneers was granted the land that is now Chile Chico. Two years later, Mauricio Braun of Punta Arenas fame (and fortune) was awarded concession of a huge tract of Aisén that included the land along the banks of Lake General Carrera that the pioneers had already settled. He sent word that they had nine months to vacate the premises.

This came as a surprise to the pioneers as they already had title to the land. After fruitlessly petitioning the government, they took matters into their own hands. In a five month struggle they held fast against the army and decimated a unit of carabineros.

Finally, in 1918, the government called off the troops and cancelled the Braun concession, opening the way for many more settlers to the area. Many people in the region still look to the conflict as a symbol of Aisénian gumption over government and big business.

coming up from Magallanes. There is not much happening on the tree-lined streets, but it's a good base for exploring the surrounding area.

Arrivals & Departures

Chile Chico is connected by ferry to Puerto Ibañez. From there travelers can take buses to Coyhaique or points further up the Austral highway. The ferry docks are directly below the town plaza. **Boats** leave at 5:30pm on Tuesday, Wednesday, Friday, and Sunday. You can make reservations by calling *Tel. 67/234240.*

During the summer, Chile Chico is connected by bus to Puerto Guadal. From there other buses go south to Cochrane and north to Coyhaique. The **bus station** is across the street from the hospital on *Portales and Lautaro.*

Many tourists enter Chile Chico by **car** from Argentina, having driven up the excellent Argentine roads from Rio Gallegos to Perito Moreno (the town, not the glacier.) The border is open from 8am-9pm. To cross this particular border from Chile to Argentina, you need a document called a *salvo conducto,* which says you are not wanted by the Chilean police. You can get from the International Police in Coyhaique or, with a 24-hour wait, from the Carabineros in Chile Chico at *O'Higgins and Lautaro.*

The Don Carlos airline, *O'Higgins and Gozales, Tel. 67/231981* has round trip **plane** flights six times a week between Chile Chico and Coyhaique for about $90.

Orientation
Located just 3 km from the Argentine border, the town was dependent on Argentina until 1952 when the road was opened from Puerto Ibañez to Coyhaique. In the winter it still is, as the road is impassible much of the time. The town itself, planned in a grid around the plaza, lies on the banks of the lake.

Where to Stay
HOSTERÍA AUSTRAL, *O'Higgins 501. Tel. 67/411274. 6 rooms with bath. Double $55. Restaurant. Store. Pharmacy. Credit cards accepted.*

The Austral, a comfortable, new hotel, is the nicest place in town. The rooms themselves have light, new bathrooms and extremely comfortable beds. They all share a common sitting area with a TV, so it can be loud if other guests are hooked to the tube, but in general it's a very pleasant place to be. It is also the best place to arrange excursions.

The wood paneled bar and restaurant downstairs is an excellent place for a good beer and the best option in town for lunch or dinner. The fresh salmon is tasty, as are the sandwiches. If you're on a budget you should stick with the daily fixed meal for lots of food at a decent price.

RESIDENCIAL AGUAS AZULES, *Rodriguez 252. Tel. 67/411320. 8 rooms. Double $30. Restaurant. No credit cards.*

One block up from the water and a half a block from the park, the Aguas Azules is the midrange hotel in town. Set up more like small houses, some of them also have shared kitchens.

HOSPIDAJE DON LUIS, *Balmaceda 175, Tel. 67/411384, 9 rooms. Double $12. No credit cards*

This clean, family run hostal has the advantage of being the one place in town where laundry is done. You can kill two birds with one stone by staying here.

Where to Eat
The best restaurant is in the **Hostería Austral**, *moderate*. **Café Holiday**, *Gonzales and O'Higgins, inexpensive*, is a snack joint with decent sandwiches and burgers. There are always lots of people hanging out here. There are really no other good options. Our favorite thing to do is go to the **Bakery On O'Higgins**, *O'Higgins*, and buy a roasted chicken with warm bread to enjoy a picnic overlooking the lake on the green rocks above town.

Sports & Recreation
The area around Chile Chico, as in all the Austral region, is replete with outdoor activities. The great thing here though, is that chances are you will be warm and dry. The **Hostería Austral** is the best place to

arrange trips or line up transportation. They guide river and lake fishing trips, horseback excursions, and camping trips as well as rent jeeps.

Fishing is excellent both in the lake and area rivers. The owner of the Hostería Austral is a popular guide. The cost is roughly $25 per person. Fishing licenses can be obtained at the Municipal Building at 333 O'Higgins.

For **horseback riding**, there are two nice overnight options. **Pico Sur**, the highest point in the area, affords stunning views of the surrounding countryside. The ride there takes you past small lakes as you climb to this special lookout point.

Another alternative, the **Hands Cave**, is a fine example of Tehuelche art. You ride past strange desert pinnacles up to a 1300 meter peak. A group of tourists broke off some of the paintings a few years ago so the entrance to the cave is barred. Make sure your guide has a key. Trips can be arranged at the **Hostería Austral** for $30 per day.

Excursions & Day Trips

One of the most beautiful and least visited national parks in the Chilean system, **Jeinimeni National Park** basks in the sun about 52 km (a three hour drive) from Chile Chico. The trip there takes you through desert canyons with incredible rocky spires and wind shaped formations. Green rock slashes across a red background that free falls into celestial waters. Pink flamingos are known to dot the flats during part of the year as are black necked swans. It's no wonder that the area was considered a spiritual place for the indigenous people.

The park's highlights are two lakes, one blue and the other green, whose hues push the limits of credibility. It's like walking into a colorized movie. We highly recommend camping along the banks of **Lake Jeinimeni** where we have seen Orion reflect off its crystal waters. A climb to the top of **Cerro La Gloria** is a must for an unforgettable 360-degree view of glaciers, mountains, and lakes.

Jeinimeni has excellent fishing and hiking, but be sure to take mosquito repellant or it will be a long, itchy day. The camping fee is $5 per day. The park ranger will sign you in and give you a map of the area.

Getting there requires a four-wheel drive vehicle because there are two substantial river crossings. It is important to cross early as the glacial melt makes it impossible later in the day. If you are without wheels you can try to hitch, but the park receives an average of two people a day during the high season in the summer, so that could be a long endeavor. The best option is to rent a jeep at the Hostería Austral.

Practical Information

There are **no banks** or formal places for changing money but the Hostería Austral is happy to take dollars at a lucrative exchange rate. For **laundry** try the Hospedaje Don Luis. **Mail** is handled in the office on the right after the Port Administration building. There are a number of **phone centers** on O'Higgins. The area code is 67.

17. MAGALLANES –
CHILEAN PATAGONIA

If you ever had a few spare grade school moments to daydream while staring at a map of South America, you must have wondered what was happening on that continental tail dangling precariously near the frozen jaws of Antarctica. Fueling the mental adventures were rumors, which had not been completely dispelled since the age of exploration of the Americas, that Patagonia was a land of giant natives and strange beasts

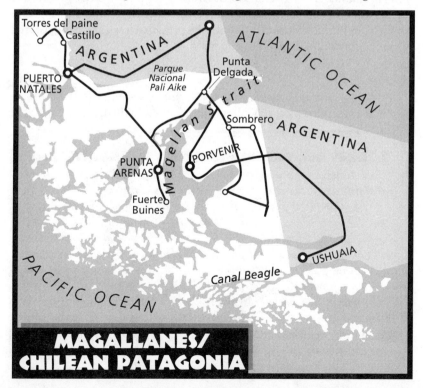

MAGALLANES/
CHILEAN PATAGONIA

inhabiting a wild, contorted landscape. Now you can actually go to that cartographic question mark, chew on a leg of lamb across a cantina from crusty sailors, set foot on the linguistically aerobic Ti-e-rra del Fu-e-go, critique the swagger of a penguin, and reconnoiter the area's wind-sculpted spires. Perhaps rumors get their start from a kernel of truth.

Factually, the **Magallanes** region consists of the end of the **Southern Ice Field**, hundreds of coastal islands, and the Chilean portion of **Patagonia**, located both on the mainland and on **Tierra del Fuego**. The Chilean government's administrative area includes Magallanes measuring about 1.4 million square km and the claimed Antarctic territory of roughly the same size.

Two distinct sections of the Andes chain run along the coastline. The **Patagonian Andes** are submerged at times forming the jigsaw puzzle of archipelagos and channels, while the rugged **Fuegian Andes** extend glacial tongues into the **Beagle Channel**.

To the east of the Andes, the grassy Patagonian pampas, serve as livestock grazing areas and as home to the three primary cities in the region. **Punta Arenas**, a historical port town with its elegant pioneer roots preserved, is the regional capital, transport hub, and commercial center. **Puerto Natales** is an agricultural and mining center as well as the gateway to the magnificent **Torres del Paine National Park**. Across the Magellan Strait from Punta Arenas is **Porvenir**, the principal town and capital of the Chilean portion of Tierra del Fuego.

History

Nomadic hunters first arrived to Magallanes as long as 12,000 years ago as is evidenced by archaeological finds such as the hand paintings in

TORRES DEL PAINE: PLANNING & PRIORITIZING

Travelers almost always underestimate the time it takes to get to **Torres del Paine** *due to the various transportation links involved.*

For example, if you leave Santiago at 9am, get into Punta Arenas by 2pm, then take a bus from downtown Punta Arenas to Puerto Natales, you'll get into town at about 7pm that evening. From Puerto Natales you still have to take a bus to the park the next morning, which is about three hours away. You can see, that you need to include 2-3 days transit time round-trip from Santiago. It seems like a lot, but it's worth it.

Another common error is miscalculating the time necessary to see the main points of interest in the park because they are so spread out. Prioritizing and making realistic objectives before going will contribute to your satisfaction.

Pali Aike National Park. When the Spanish arrived in 1520, they encountered four indigenous groups. The nomadic **Tehuelche** and **Onas** hunted guanaco on the Patagonia pampas. Two seafaring groups, the **Alkalufs** and **Yamanas**, navigated the rainy channels in canoes as they hunted sea lions and collected shellfish.

The **Onas**, also known as **Sélkman**, hunted guanaco on the island of Tierra del Fuego. Tall and robust, the Onas were known to be the most aggressive of the four groups. When the Onas discovered it was easier to hunt sheep than the traditional guanaco, the large landholders hired bounty hunters to capture or kill the Onas, awarding a pair of sheep per capture. More than 1,000 Onas were held in a reserve set up by the Salesian missionary Jose Fagnano in 1888, where they were meant to be protected, but eventually died.

The four tribes traded, fueded, and intermingled until slaughter, alcoholism, venereal and other diseases imported by Europeans all but extinguished them. There remain a few small communities of Alkalufs in the Aysén region around Puerto Eden and of Onas near Puerto Williams.

Portuguese explorer **Ferdinand Magellan** (*Hernando de Magallanes*) discovered the strait later named for him in 1520 while on a Spanish-funded expedition seeking a westerly route to India. He continued on through the ocean he dubbed the "Pacific" ultimately reaching the Philippines, where he was killed in battle with the islanders that same year.

After a few failed efforts by Spain to colonize the area, no one attempted to establish a foothold in Magallanes for another 250 years. Several scientific expeditions passed through the strait including second expedition of the **Beagle** in 1832 with **Robert Fitz Roy** as captain and **Charles Darwin** as naturalist.

To head off other nations from extending their sovereignty over the Magallanes, Chilean President Manuel Bulnes sent a mission with the objective of claiming and colonizing the land for Chile. After initially establishing Fort Bulnes near Puerto Hambre in 1843, the governor chose a more sheltered location farther north, that of the British-named Sandy Point, which was translated first as *Punta Arenosa*, then as Punta Arenas.

In 1876, the regional governor Diego Duble brought in 300 sheep, utilizing Magdalena Island to fence them in. This was the first step for large-scale sheep ranching which, along with a nascent mining industry and maritime revenue, would fuel the region's economic growth. By the turn of the century Punta Arenas was renowned for having attained high levels of economic, social, and cultural growth, and this period became known as its Golden Age.

Since the Golden Age, the region's economy has endured cyclical setbacks and rebirths. When the Panama Canal opened in 1914, ship traffic passing through Magallanes dropped off dramatically. The economic decline was reversed in 1950 with the discovery of petroleum, but by the 1980's profitable reserves began to dry up. Carbon and methanol mining are now the key industrial employers while service industry strategists look toward tourism development as the key to their future.

PUNTA ARENAS

The tidy port city of Punta Arenas was forged by immigrant pioneers whose elegant, turn-of-the-century mansions have been preserved by an economic Rip Van Winkle effect. Alongside the mansions stand humbler dwellings capped with corrugated tin roofs and stone chimneys painted in bold primary colors. When the rooftops meet the intense, windswept blue overhead the result is an engagingly jazzy skyline.

Punta Arenas, with a population of 114,000, is recognized as the world's southernmost city and serves as the capital of the **XII Region of Magallanes and Antarctica**. Located on the Brunswick peninsula, a few hundred kilometers from the southernmost point on the continental mainland, it is hemmed in by numerous islands, the largest of which is **Tierra del Fuego**, visible from Punta Arenas across the Magellan strait.

The city could be the outdoor-wear layering efficiency test center. Although relatively temperate considering its latitude, the four-seasons-in-an-hour weather makes dressing for a stroll a challenge. It is not unusual for raindrops to pelt you while you are perspiring in the summer sunshine, then a few minutes later, for a chilling wind to bolt through making your teeth chatter. The moderate precipitation is spread evenly throughout the year.

Since the Punta Arenas airport is currently the main point of entry to the region, travelers whose primary destination is Torres del Paine National Park must at least go through the town to catch the bus north. This detour frequently results in a serendipitous bonus. A few days in Punta Arenas should be included in your regional travel agenda, to investigate the colorful pioneer town and to amble about near the end of the continent. The number of travelers to Punta Arenas will probably drop once the Puerto Natales airport can accommodate larger planes, but even when this happens, you should consider going through Punta Arenas at least one way, either flying into or out of the region.

The rugged surroundings provide a couple of interesting day trips, including visits to the local rookeries of **Magellanic penguins**, a ferry ride to **Tierra del Fuego**, and a drive south taking the road as far as it runs on the continent. In town, restored **pioneer mansions**, open to the public, and **historical museums** recount the days of a remote settlement booming in the wilderness.

Cemetary

Salesian Regional Museum

Sarmienta de Gamboa

Avenida Sanueza

Señoret

Avenida España

Carrera Pinto

O'Higgins

Jorge Montt

Navarro

Avenida Colón

José Menéndez

Magallan Regional Museum

Waldo Seguel

Catedral

Plaza

Fagnano

Noguiria

21 de Mayo

Errázuriz

Balmaceda

Av. Independencia

PUERTO PORT

MAGELLAN STRAIT

PUNTA ARENAS

ARRIVALS & DEPARTURES

By Boat

Service to/from Tierra del Fuego is handled by **Transbordadores Austral Broom**, *Bulnes 05075, Punta Arenas, Tel. 61-218100.* •**Punta Arenas-Porvenir** The Melinka sails daily carrying up to 20 cars and 200 passengers. The two and a half hour trip costs $8 for passengers and $40 for vehicles. It is advised to reserve vehicle space a few days ahead of time, which you can do by phone. The Austral Broom ticket office and Tres Puentes Terminal are near the Zona Franca on the way to the airport.

• **Punta Delgada-Bahía Azul**: The 20-minute Bahía Azul crossing is normally used by those traveling between Argentina and Tierra del Fuego, but it is an acceptable option for vehicles if the Melinka doesn't work out for you on the day you want to go. There is continuous service from 8am to 11pm; $2 for passengers and $18 for vehicles.

• **Punta Arenas/Puerto Williams**: Sailings take 38 hours and leave twice per month. Tickets cost $50-$75. Consult Transbordadora Austral Broom for dates.

By Bus

The main route served by the bus companies is the three hour, 247 km trip to Puerto Natales. If your destination is Torres del Paine, you must catch the bus from Punta Arenas to Puerto Natales, then buy a ticket there to go to the park which is another 145 km north. There are four bus companies which offer service to Puerto Natales.

The bus offices are all at different, but fairly centralized locations in town. The Sernatur office, *Waldo Seguel 689*, maintains an updated chart of all the bus schedules. If you tell them when you want to leave, they can direct you to the bus company with the most convenient departure time to save you walking for the information. Buses Fernández offers the most frequent departures.

Buses to Puerto Natales
• **Buses Fernández**, *Armando Sanhueza 745. Tel 242313*
• **Bus Sur**, *Corner of Magallanes/Colon. Tel. 244464*
• **Austral Bus**, *Menéndez 565. Tel. 241708*
• **Transfer Austral**, *Menéndez 631. Tel. 220761*

Buses to Ushuaia, Argentina
• **Buses Tecni Austral**, *Lautaro Navarro 971. Tel. 223205*

Buses to Rio Gallegos, Argentina
• **Buses Ghisoni**, *Lautaro Navarro 971. Tel. 223205*

• **Bus El Pingüino**, *Armando Sanhueza 745. Tel. 221812*
• **Bus T.M.T.**, *Colon 900, Punta Arenas. Tel. 242174*

By Car

The main route of entry is via highway 9 to/from Puerto Natales. Both lanes of the highway should be paved by the publishing date of this book. This will cut down drastically on the number of rocks pitched at your windshield that results from having only one lane paved. The highway feeds into Bulnes/Bories streets coming into town, a route which takes you directly to the central plaza. Leaving town, you should take España, a few blocks to the east of Bories. This eventually connects into Bulnes which then turns into the highway. Ferries to/from Tierra del Fuego have car service; see the *By Boat* section below.

Car Rentals

• **Budget**, *O'Higgins 964. Tel. 241696*
• **Emsa**, *Roca 1022. Tel. 222810 or 241182*
• **Hertz**, *O'Higgins 987. Tel. 248742*
• **Lubag**, *Magallanes 970. Tel. 242023 or 214136*
• **Lotus**, *Mejicana 694. Tel. 228244*
• **R.U.S.**, *Colon 614. Tel. 221529* (including 4x4 trucks)

By Plane

Most flights to/from Punta Arenas from Santiago stop in Puerto Montt. You might want to consider using the stopover to initiate travel in Chiloé or the Lakes District. Concepción is another stopover point, but less frequently utilized. The Punta Arenas airport is located about 30 minutes north of town on the highway to Puerto Natales. Transport from the airport to downtown Punta Arenas costs $2.50 by bus and $7 in taxi. You need to go into Punta Arenas to catch buses to other destinations such as to Puerto Natales.

Airlines

• **Avant**. *Tel. 228312 or 228322*
• **Lan Chile**, *Lautaro Navarro 1155. Tel. 247079*
• **Ladeco**, *Lautaro Navarro 1155. Tel. 244544*
• **Aerovias DAP**, *O'Higgins 891. Tel. 223340*
• **Kaiken Linea Aérea**, *Colon 521. Tel. 227061*

ORIENTATION

Punta Arenas is the southernmost city in the world. It is bordered on the east by the **Magellan Strait**, across which lies the island of **Tierra del Fuego**. Punta Arenas is situated to the east of the Andes, in the *precordillera* foothills, as opposed to most of the rest of the country which is west of the Andes. There is a small ski resort in the mountains and small national park to the west of the city.

The city is set up on a regular grid pattern. The Plaza de Armas town square is centered between the port, three blocks to the east, and the **Cerro La Cruz** hill, four blocks to the west. Almost all of the hotels, services, and attraction will be found within a sixteen square block area around the Plaza de Armas.

GETTING AROUND TOWN

This is a town easily and enjoyably walked. The only places to which you might want to take a taxi are the Zona Franca and possibly the cemetery, though the latter might be within walking distance for some.

WHERE TO STAY

Expensive

HOTEL FINIS TERRAE, *Avenida Colon 766. Tel. 61/228200, Fax 61/ 248124. 70 rooms. Double $108 special for foreigners. Breakfast included. Cable TV. View restaurant. Credit cards accepted.*

The Finis Terrae is an excellent value, the best overall upscale hotel in town. The hotel is new, immaculate, and boasts attentive service and quiet rooms. Several rooms have views of the Magellan Strait and Tierra del Fuego. The restaurant on the top floor is a homey, lodge-like set-up with mesmerizing views. The fare is unpretentious Chilean fare, light meals, and sandwiches. The bar, located next to the restaurant, is great place to take a load off your feet and gaze toward the end of the earth.

JOSE NOGUEIRA, *Bories 959. Tel. 61/248840, Fax 61/248832. 25 rooms. Double $180. Breakfast included. Cable TV. Restaurant. Bar. Credit cards accepted.*

The Noguiera offers you the opportunity to lodge in the splendid mansion of the pioneer sheep baroness Sara Braun. The house, built by Braun to overlook the plaza de armas in 1896, is a national monument. The exterior is especially gorgeous at night, with flood lights highlighting lustrous wooden window frames contrasting the shadow-darkened stonework. The elegance of the past is maintained with beautiful wooden trim and leather couches in the lobby. The downside is that the doubles are a bit small and the service lags at times. If you do not stay here, be sure to eat at the Pergola restaurant for a relaxing meal.

ISLA REY JORGE, *21 de Mayo 1243. Tel/Fax 61/248220 and 61/ 222681. 25 rooms. Double $130. Breakfast included. Cable TV. Restaurant/ pub. Credit cards accepted.*

This English-style hotel, finished in a rich interior of hunter's green and dark wood, is the newest entrant into the top end category and an

excellent choice. A homey common area near the entryway accommodates patrons relaxing with newspapers. There might be some traffic
noise from buses on the street side during the day, but it is quiet enough
at night. The brick-walled El Galeón Pub downstairs is a good place for a
beer or a sporting event on TV.

TIERRA DEL FUEGO, *Colon 716. Tel./Fax 61/226200. 30 rooms.
Double $110. Breakfast included. Cable TV. Kitchenette. Credit cards accepted.*

This is a centrally located apart-hotel with kitchenettes in each room
in which to cook meals. The hotel's finest asset is a staff that could not be
more friendly or attentive. Another advantage is the extra space in the
rooms, although they are not as big as most apart-hotels. The breakfast
buffet is heartier than most continental breakfasts, with eggs included
upon request. The popular Pub 1900 is connected to the lobby.

CABO DE HORNOS, *Plaza Munoz Gamero 1025. Tel 61/242134. Fax
61/229473. 25 rooms. Double $154. Suites $220. Breakfast buffet included.
Cable TV. Restaurant. Bar. Credit cards accepted.*

This hotel is an elegant blockish structure with views of the plaza and
the Magellan Strait. The five star rating is too stellar for a hotel without
amenities like a gym or a pool and which has noticeably peeling paint in
the hallways. The dark, woody, downstairs bar is worth bellying up to
though. There is a large breakfast buffet included with the price of the
room.

Moderate

HOSTAL DE LA AVENIDA, *Avenida Colon 534. Tel. 61/247532. 7
rooms. Double $50. Breakfast included. Cable TV. Credit cards accepted.*

The best value in the moderate range is this inn offering cheery
rooms, all with cable TV and baths. The rooms face a garden with vines
creeping in every direction and an antique bathtub-turned-flower-planter.
Chairs are distributed on the patio among the greenery for reading. Lots
of natural light illuminates the small common and dining areas. This is
also the best option in the mid-price range for solo travelers with singles
at $40 per night.

HOTEL PLAZA, *Jose Noguiera 1116, Tel. 61/248613. 17 rooms. Double
$68. Breakfast included. Cable TV. Credit cards accepted.*

The Hotel Plaza is another strong moderately priced option. The
hotel is housed within a turn-of-the-century pioneer building with rooms
overlooking the central square. Black and white photos of the region,
tastefully framed, decorate the walls of the hallways and rooms. Hanging
in the reception area are Rob Hall's Adventure Consultants posters,
signed by the climbing guide before his untimely death in the 1996
Everest tragedy. The disaster was described in the book *Into Thin Air* by
Jon Krakauer, among the most riveting non-fiction books we've read. The

hotel was Halls' favorite in Punta Arenas when en route to summit Vinson Massif, the highest peak in Antarctica. The stairway leading up to the hotel continues up to the Residencial Paris so be careful not to overshoot the entry to the Hotel Plaza.

HOSTEL DE LA PATAGONIA, *Croacia 970. Tel/Fax 61/249970. 13 rooms. Double $44. Breakfast included. Cable TV. Credit cards accepted.*

This hotel is located in an A-frame house in a middle class neighborhood. Rooms have cable TV but not phones. A good place for those who prefer to stay outside of the *centro*.

HOSTAL CARPA MANZANO, *Lautaro Navarro 336 Tel: 61/242296 or 248898. 10 rooms. Double $55. Breakfast included. Cable TV. Credit cards accepted.*

This inn is a one-story American ramble- style suburban house tucked into the same middle class neighborhood as Hostel La Patagonia. It's well-equipped with new furniture. Rooms have cable TV and phones.

LOS NAVEGANTES, *Jose Menéndez 647. Tel. 61/244677, Fax 61/247545. 40 rooms. Double $84. Breakfast included. Cable TV. Restaurant. Bar. Credit cards accepted.*

This was probably the premiere hotel in Punta Arenas at one time, but has now slipped in quality. The management has compensated by making the prices lower than top hotels like Finis Terrae. The hallways have that old slightly too dark feel but with some nice features like a varnished wood handrails. We also give the restaurant mixed reviews. Although the meal we had here was bland and forgettable, several locals insist it is one of the better restaurants in town, so maybe we hit it on an off-day. Seafood is the house specialty.

HOTEL MERCURIO, *Monseñor Fagnano 595. Tel/Fax 61/242300. 13 rooms. Double $62. Breakfast included. Cable TV. Restaurant. Bar. Credit cards accepted.*

The Hotel Mercurio has a good location, only about a block away from the main plaza. The bathrooms have been redone, but the halls are decorated in brown making it somewhat gloomy.

Two mid-priced hotels acceptable in a pinch are the **Hotel Savoy,** *Jose Menéndez 1073, Tel. 61/247979 Double $55,* and **Hotel Monte Carlo,** *Av. Colon 65, Tel. 61/222120. Double $50.*

Inexpensive

HOSTAL RESIDENCIAL PARIS, *Jose Nogueira 1116, 4th floor. Tel. 61/223933. Per person $12. Breakfast included. No credit cards.*

The Residencial Paris offers the best views in the inexpensive category. It is located in the same pioneer era building overlooking the plaza as the Hotel Plaza (and it in the same stairwell, so keep going up). Rooms have high ceilings and could be a bit drafty too far out of summer.

HOSTAL AND TURISMO CALAFATE, *Lautaro Navarro 850. Tel. 61/248415. Per person $25. Breakfast included. Cable TV. No credit cards.*

This is definitely the swankiest place for the solo traveler, but note that for two people the cost is the same as a double room of better quality. Rooms are outfitted with cable TV and telephones. The family runs another nearby hostel of equal quality without these amenities for $12 per person. You can count on superior hospitality from the friendly management.

RESIDENCIAL COIRÓN, *Sanhuesa 730. Tel. 61/226449. Per person $12. Breakfast included. No credit cards.*

This is a nice family-run residencial with bright rooms.

RESIDENCIAL ROCA, *Magallanes 888. Tel. 61/243903. Per person $12. Breakfast included. No credit cards.*

This residencial is grandma's house including all of the knickknacks and a tacky clock. It is a good option and a very sweet lady runs it.

LA NENA, *Boliviana 366. Tel. 61/242411. Per person $12. Breakfast included. No credit cards.*

Although a bit less centrally located, the residencial has a, clean, family feel to it.

Out of Town

HOSTERÍA YAGANES, *7.5 km al norte de Punta Arenas. Tel. 61/ 216600, Fax 61/248052. 25 rooms. Double $80. Restaurant. Credit cards accepted.*

Hostería Yaganes is a waterfront hotel with views of the Magellan Strait. The restaurant here is popular among locals who are looking for a nice dinner out of town. The fare is standard Chilean seafood entrees.

WHERE TO EAT

The consistent high quality and variety of Punta Arenas restaurants is impressive considering its end-of-the-earth location. Lamb is the regional specialty.

PERGOLA, *Hotel Nogueira, Bories 959. Tel. 61/248840. Expensive. Credit cards accepted.*

The Pergola restaurant, housed within what was the atrium in Sara Braun's mansion, is the recommended option for an upscale meal in town. Ivy weaves itself through the interior steel framework. Ample sunlight sneaks through the gaps in the green web to create an ambiance that is both airy and intimate. The restaurant is outfitted in rich hues and offers sumptuous regional cuisine such as beer cream soup (*crema de cerveza*), curried lamb (*cordero con curry*), chicken breast stuffed with scallops (*pollo Cruz de Froward*), and the ambrosial coconut carmel flan

(*flan coco casero*). People frequently stop by simply for coffee and dessert or a drink.

SOTITO'S BAR, *O'Higgins 1138. Tel. 243565. Expensive. Credit cards accepted.*

Sotito's is the hot restaurant for local elite looking to strut their stuff. The simple concrete facade disguises an elegant green interior where a vogue model smoking from a long cigarette holder would fit in. Superior service outshines a simple menu of typical Chilean seafood dishes. The towering king crab cocktail is the house specialty.

ASTURIAS, *Lautaro Navarro 967. Tel. 243763. Expensive Credit cards accepted..*

If you are longing for the glory of the conquistador days, the Asturias' walls are adorned with battle armor of the era. Serving upscale Spanish cuisine, specialties include the conger eel or fish filet *a la Vasca*. The fish *a la Vasca* is prepared in a cream sauce enlivened with garlic, paprika, red bell peppers, and white wine. The entire plate is covered in a mound of delicious potato slices that are cooked to the halfway point between French fries and potato chips.

EL MESON DEL CALVO, *Jorge Montt 687. Tel. 225015. Moderate/ Expensive. Credit cards accepted.*

This restaurant is first on the list in home-style regional cuisine with its specialty being lamb prepared with rosemary sauce (*romero*), mint sauce (*a la menta*), with grilled garlic (*al ajillo*) or stuffed with mushrooms (*relleno de champiñones*). The creamed spinach as a side dish is out of this world. The charming ambience is highlighted by checkered table cloths and fireplaces at either end of the narrow dining area.

EL CORAL, *Jose Menéndez 848. Tel. 241972. Moderate. Credit cards accepted.*

This cozy Spanish restaurant featuring an extensive seafood menu is an excellent value. The mixed seafood plate appetizer, Gran Picada Coral is the biggest plate of seafood we have seen in Chile. Ordered with a side of rice. It can be a meal for two people. While many restaurants closed Sunday night, you can count on El Coral being open.

CLUB DEPORTIVO, *Armando Sanhueza 549. Tel. 241415. Moderate. No credit cards.*

We were tipped off to this odd gem when a government official told us, somewhat embarrassed by the simpleness of the place, that her favorite eatery was the small restaurant of the local sports club. Sure enough, the fixed item daily lunch turned out to be one of the best we've had. Effectively responding to the chilly breezes of Punta Arenas, the lunch usually begins with a hot hearty soup. One day, the main course was a delicious bean stew, (*porortos*, literally translated as "beans") bubbling with white beans, pasta, and spicy sausage in a tomato base. On Fridays, the restaurant offers *curanto*, a specialty from the island of Chiloé, a mixture of scallops, clams, fish, pork, steak, chicken, and tamale-like pastries served in a wooden trough. If you can't make it to Chiloé, you should definitely try the dish here. On Saturdays, *empanadas* are the specialty.

FINIS TERRAE RESTAURANT, *Avenida Colon 766. Tel. 61/228200. Moderate. Credit cards accepted..*

There is a good view restaurant with a comfortable wood-finished, lodge-style bar area on the 6th floor of the Finis Terrae Hotel. The prices are reasonable for a sandwiches and standard Chilean dinners in the connecting restaurant. Although six floors up doesn't seem that high, the locale offers inspiring views of the city and the strait through a large picture windows.

DINO'S, *Bories 557. Tel. 347434. Moderate. Credit cards accepted.*

In our earnest search for the best pizza in Chile, a lamentable journey of mediocrity, (escapable, however with a border crossing into Argentina), Dino's is a bright star and perhaps the winner. With a prodigious glob of cheese per pie, these pizzas are gooey ecstasy. To spice up the fare, we suggest ordering the *Españolisima* pizza with *choricillo* (spicy links) or adding *choricillo* to another pizza. You can probably get by with an individual portion for two people, but we always go overboard and gorge on the *grande*. The sandwiches, such as the *barros luco italiano*, - steak, tomato, advocado, and cheese, are definitely a two person lunch. You can eat one alone with some effort and nap the afternoon away. The decor is modern retro with some nice neon work lining the sleek cut of the ceiling.

LA MAMA, *Armando Sanhueza 720. Tel. 225127. Inexpensive. No credit cards.*

Mama recently expanded her restaurant from two to seven tables, but don't worry, the growth induced by demand has not inhibited the hominess of this place. Mama's speciality is pasta in portions that are serious about filling you up. If you try to order a sandwich here, she will argue that you can get a plate of *canalones* or *ñoquis* for the same price, so why not eat something hot? A tack-board wall of napkins with odes, accolades, and sketches penned by visitors from around the world attest to the satisfaction of her clients.

LA CARIOCA, *Jose Menéndez 600, Tel. 223573. Inexpensive. No credit cards.*

Looking around the room, we noticed that the lunch special of the house seemed to be big ol' beers, so we ordered a couple. In this cantina style bar, a setting usually reserved for men, women can dine comfortably. A fixed lunch menu is offered while sandwiches and pizza round out the fare at about the same price. The owner asks you to sign the guest book which includes long entries of travelers' perceptions of the region, some suggesting that perhaps the visitor had seconds or thirds of the house special.

LOMIT'S, *Jose Menéndez 722, Tel. 243399. Inexpensive. No credit cards.*

Lomit's is a decent last resort sandwich shop. Barro Luco cheese steak sandwiches have average prices. The international fast food yellow and red scheme is fully cranked, but it's a quick meal and usually open.

SEEING THE SIGHTS

In the center of the **Plaza de Armas Muñoz Gamera**, is a statue of the Portuguese Explorer **Ferdinand Magellan** (*Hernando de Magallanes*), who sailed from Spain in 1519 searching for a westerly route to India, arriving to the strait in 1520. At the base of the statue is a Tierra del Fuego native known as Selkman or Ona, whose mythical giant feet are portrayed here in properly exaggerated form (sorry ladies, guanaco skins cover their mid-sections in case you were considering checking out biological consistencies). According to local lore, if you kiss or touch the Ona's toe, you will return to the city. The shiny toe indicates that many are planning on coming back. The other native at the base of the statue is from the Telhueche tribe which inhabited the Patagonian mainland north of the Magellan Strait.

The blue and yellow **Cathedral** is on the southwest corner of the plaza. Along the interior walls are wooden sculptures of the apostles, as well as stained glass, depicting missionaries as they show the natives the path to salvation. Several of the other buildings on the plaza are turn of the century pioneer mansions built during Punta Arena's Golden Age, now converted into public or private office buildings.

The most interesting of these is the restored **Sara Braun Mansion** on the northwest corner. The mansion was built in 1896 by the architect Numa Mayer in French Belle Epoque style. Most of the materials and labor were imported from Europe. The mansion currently is divided into two sections which are utilized as a club and a hotel. The part with the entryway facing the plaza serves as the headquarters for the **Club de la Union**, an exclusive social club for community leaders. Ironically, the club's current member list does not include the famous pioneer names of Menéndez, Braun, Nogueira, or Behety, due to the fact that those families left the area with downfall of the sheep trade or were forced out by the nationalization of their extensive landholdings in 1960's.

The Club de la Union opens its doors to the public for a brief but worthwhile tour ($1) Tuesdays and Thursdays from 4pm to 6pm. The portion of the Sara Braun mansion which opens onto Bories Street houses the **Hotel Jose Nogueira**. It's worthwhile to stop in for a meal at its atrium restaurant or at least take a look around the ground floor.

Walking a block north from the plaza on Magallanes street will take you to the Braun Menéndez Palace:

BRAUN MENÉNDEZ PALACE & MAGALLANES REGIONAL MUSEUM, *Magallanes 949. Summer Hours: October-March, Tuesday-Friday 11am-6pm, Saturday-Sunday 11am-2pm; Winter hours: April-September, Tuesday-Friday 11am-2pm, Saturday-Sunday 11am-2pm. Tel. 244216 or 221387. Entry $2.*

We recommend prioritizing a visit to the Braun Menéndez palace as the top Punta Arenas attraction. The palace was built in 1905 as a residence for Mauricio Braun (Sara's brother) and his wife Josefina Menéndez, a matrimony that united the two largest family fortunes in the region. Mauricio Braun emigrated from Russia with his family in 1873 at the age of 18. He entered into commerce early, ultimately building an empire which included companies in shipping, merchandise importation, sheep and cattle ranching, mining, forestry, and agricultural production. He initially founded several of the businesses with Jose Norgueira, who would marry Mauricio's sister, Sara. She proved to be as astute as her husband in managing the business holdings after his death. The most renowned of the partnerships in which the three were involved was the Sociedad Explotadora de Tierra del Fuego, frequently referred to by the acronym SETF, which accumulated a million hectares of ranching land.

The French architect Antoine Beualier designed the magnificent Braun Menéndez Palace, the interior of which was finished with Italian marble, Belgian wood, French wallpaper and curtains, and British furniture. Of particular interest are the dining room walls covered from floor to ceiling in leather as well as the extensive servants' area and boiler room downstairs. English guides are not available, but there is a translated English text at the reception desk to follow as you walk through.

Continuing up Magallanes north you will encounter the **Municipal Theater** between Menéndez and Colon streets. The theater, built in 1895-1897, was inspired by the Teatro Colon in Buenos Aires and designed by Numa Mayer, the same architect that created the Sara Braun mansion. Two blocks west on the corner of Colon and Magallanes is a colorful mural depicting Gabriela Mistral in a Moses-like pose. The Nobel prize winning poet served as director of the girl's school here in 1918.

Backtracking down O'Higgins toward the plaza, to Pedro Montt street, you will find the **Naval Museum**, *Pedro Montt 981, Tuesday-Saturday 9:30 am-12:30pm/3pm-6pm*, which outlines naval history with vessel replicas and photos. If you don't have seasoned sea legs, you might prefer to skip this one. Continuing on Magallanes past the plaza where the street becomes 21 del Mayo and following that three blocks to Independencia will take you to the **Main Pier**. In front you will find a clock imported from

Germany in 1913 which displays everything from time to weather to phases of the moon.

For a great view of the city, especially just before sunset, take Fagnano street from the Plaza, following it up the hill to the **Mirador** lookout. From here you can gaze out over the ships lounging in the Magellan Strait and across to Tierra del Fuego.

Heading out from the plaza six blocks north on Bories, on the corner of Sarmiento de Gamboa is the massive church **Santuario Maria Auxilidora**, inspired by the Santuario de Fourvier in France. Attached to it, and run by the church, is the oddball museum **Museo Salesiano Mayorino Borgatello**, *Bulnes No. 374, Tuesday-Sunday, 10am-12:30pm/3pm-6pm, entry $2*. As you buy your ticket, the pungent smell of mothballs spears your nostrils. Cruising the first several rooms is like stumbling into a mad taxidermist's lair. The rooms are crowded with badly weathered, stuffed animals from the region which provide the rare opportunity of getting up close to an albatross and condor with the awesome span of their wings spread out. Another area is dedicated to a papier-mâché replica of the milodon cave located near Puerto Natales.

The dwelling was once inhabited by the giant prehistoric sloth whose skin and fur were found intact, preserved by glacial ice. There is also a regional photo exhibit by Alberto d'Agostini, the Italian priest who mapped much of the southern Andes. With his extraordinary eye for black and white photography, Agostini documented the natives and nature of Patagonia when it was still populated by indigenous tribes.

Three blocks farther north on Bories is the **Cemetery**, *Bulnes 949, daily 7:30am-8pm*. Towering cypress shrubs dominate the gardens, while imposing mausoleums of wealthy pioneers such as Braun and Menéndez rival their mansions in town. Of particular interest is the black statue of the Ona Monument at the northeast end of the cemetery, as well as the many simple grave markers with English and Slavic surnames, a testament to the 18th century immigration.

On the northern outskirts of town, is the **Instituto de la Patagonia** which houses the **Museo del Recuerdo**, *Bulnes km 4 Norte, 8:30am-11:30am/2:30pm-6pm, entry $2*. Take a taxi or bus here, since it is a solid fifteen minute drive from the center. The institute, now part of the University of Magallanes, was founded by its current director Dr. Mateo Martinic, the region's foremost historian. The museum is composed of turn-of-the-century horse-drawn carts that litter the institute's huge lawn as well as several small cabins displaying pioneer artifacts. The carts illustrate the specialization of vehicles even before the automobile with examples of dairy delivery carts, luxury coupes, and ambulances. The individual cabins include a garage with a 1908 Peugeot, a provincial worker's home built in 1875, restored with decor of the era, and a well-organized display of rural work tools. Ask at the library for someone to unlock the exhibit buildings and while there, take advantage of the opportunity to check out the fascinating Alberto d'Agostini photos in the antique 3-D view finder.

Near the institute is the **Monument to the Sheep Herder**, a favorite spot for postcard and personal photos. The bronze shepherd is followed by a flock of sheep grazing on the grassy median. The **Zona Franca** duty free mall is also in this area.

NIGHTLIFE & ENTERTAINMENT

The most popular spot on the bar scene is the **Pub 1900**, *corner of Bories and Colon*. The corner location allows for good people watching. There is nothing special about the modern decor and it is not recommended for those averse to cigarette smoke, but the bar is always packed with a mix of locals and travelers. Another favorite is the **Olijoe Pub**, *Errazuriz 970, Tel. 223728*. The upscale watering hole offers sleek decor and drinks that are a bit pricey as a tradeoff for the elegance.

The **Calipso**, *Bories 817*, seems to be going through an identity crisis. Formerly a popular coffee shop, the new owners changed the locale to a tropical music and dance floor renaming it Calipso, but when we queried about salsa, the manager enthusiastically offered karaoke. You say to-mato?

SPORTS & RECREATION

The **Cerro Mirador Ski Center** is located just beyond town to the east in the *precordillera* portion of the Andes. This is a small complex with one chair and one rope tow. The lift ticket costs $20/day. Ski season runs from mid-June to mid-September. Rental equipment is available. The lift operates in the summer elevating tourists for a one of a kind view of the peninsula.

Best bet for a gym is the **Complejo Solarium**, *Croacia 926, Tel. 221148*, which charges $9 per session for weight room/aerobic equipment and the same for aerobics. The space is small but well-organized. There is also a basketball gym for which they charge $25/hour for a group, but you might be able to talk them into letting you shoot around for the regular session price if there is no one using it. If you're sore from a Torres del Paine hike, consider the massage service, $12 for a 45 minute session.

SHOPPING

The **Zona Franca Duty Free Zone**, *Ave. Bulnes km 35 Norte, 10am-8pm*, is located on the road to the airport. The duty free zone is quite mall-like with teenagers and families loitering on the weekends among the shops selling liquor, appliances, clothing, camera supplies, a groceries, and tires. The actual savings on some items are debatable. Check the expiry date on any film you are about to buy because they sometimes sell rolls that are on the verge of passing the indicated date.

EXCURSIONS & DAY TRIPS

There are up to 10 million **Magellanic penguins** inhabiting the east and west coastlines of the southern cone. They nest in open beaches, sand hills, grassy slopes, and woodlands, digging burrows to protect themselves from the elements. Magellanic penguins are average-sized when compared to their peers. A black band under the chin and a black horseshoe outline around the chest distinguishes them from their closest relative, the Galapagos penguin.

The easiest way to hobnob with the area's best-dressed is to visit the **Ottaway Pinguinera**. Two thousand Magellan penguins make up the Ottaway rookery. The nesting area was saved by the local high school, Colegio Alemán, in 1990 when there were only 500 birds, with assistance from World Wide Nature Fund. The half day trips are easily arranged through one of the many travel agencies advertising their services with impossible-to-miss signs on every street in town. The agencies essentially provide the hour and half mini-van transport directly to and from the nesting area. The cost for the excursion is $10 plus an entry fee of $4 at the site. The visiting season runs from October to March, open daily. Dress warmly with a coat and pants capable of blocking the fierce winds shooting through the exposed dune area where the penguins burrow.

SURVIVAL OF THE ROLY-POLIEST

*Whenever you see a **penguin** waddling comically around shore, you have to wonder, how did these guys pass the survival-of-the-fittest challenge? One advantage that contributed to their endurance is that they can actually outmaneuver their predators. A penguin can out waddle a cloddish seal on land. It can usually fend off the few predatory bird species in a duel of beaks, such as a gull intent on snatching eggs from its nest. In water, penguins are incredibly skittish, utilizing their wings-turned-flippers to propel themselves toward land at up to 15 miles per hour if even so much as a shadow comes near. With Orca whales, seals, (a real threat in the water), and sharks on the hunt for a black and white tie dinner, penguins have good reason to be nervous while free diving for their own meals of fish and squid.*

Another penguin viewing option is a boat excursion to the **Los Pinguinos Nature Monument** on Isla Magdalena and Isla Marta. The tour takes six and a half hours which includes a walk on the island of Isla Magdalena, home to over 200,000 penguins. The cost of the excursion is $60-$70 per person with regular service between December and February. Inquire with **Turismo Comapa**, *Independencia 830, 2nd Floor, Tel. 241322 or 241437*, or with **Catamaran Hielo Sur**, *Av. Colon 782, Tel. 244506*. You can also ask at any of the other numerous agencies that broker their excursions for the same price.

PENGUIN PARTY TRICKS

If you grow weary of simply "ah"ing over the penguins' charm, try to identify some of the following typical penguin behavior:

• **Bowing**: *A penguin will bow to its mate when it approaches the nest as a form of appeasement and social bonding.*

• **Bill-to-Armpit Gesture**: *A signal given by males indicating general ownership of an area.*

• **Ecstatic Displays**: *The bird straightens vertically, pumps his chest several times, and emits a harsh braying sound while arching the flippers back as far as possible. This display is given by unpaired males to attract females, or incited by the approach of other penguins or humans, or simply a consequence of mass ecstatic displaying.*

• **Huddling**: *Penguins, especially the young, will huddle to conserve warmth.*

• **Point and Gape**: *An aggressive gesture, in which the penguin points his bill at a threatening entity, possibly followed by charging.*

• **Preening**: *Penguins gather oil from a preening gland located at the rump. This oil is applied to the feathers to prevent water infiltration, thus maximizing their warmth. Pairs may engage in mutual preening.*

• **Venting Heat**: *When overheated, penguins will pant, flap their wings, or take a swim to cool down.*

• **Vertical Sway**: *The penguin bows and raises its head, then sways from side to side. This is a common gesture indicating territorial ownership.*

Reserva Nacional Magallanes is a small state park seven kilometers to the east of town. It is set up mostly for picnicking and camping with tall shrubs for wind blocks and covered picnic areas at each site. There is a short walking circuit from which you can look into a river canyon. Unfortunately you have to drive through an area with a lot of garbage before hitting the park entrance which, combined with the limited trails offered, makes it a less appealing draw. If you are looking for good picnic or camping spots however, the park grounds themselves are well-maintained inside. People usually visit the **Cerro Mirador Ski Area** on the same trip. In summer, you can take the ski lift up to the top of the mountain for a good view of the peninsula.

A great way to spend a day is driving south as far as the road goes on the continental mainland. The road hugs the coastline and is occasional dotted with a house or two which beg the question - what would possibly motivate someone to set up house on this remote wind and rain battered end of the earth? One elderly resident told us he liked it because it got him out of the hustle and bustle of Punta Arenas.

The turnoff to **Puerto Hambre** is 51 km from town. Spain grew more serious about colonizing Magallanes after the English seafarer Francis Drake was found to be sailing nearby on a mission from the English crown. **Pedro Sarmiento de Gamboa** set sail in 1584 with a fleet of ships to colonize the Brunswick peninsula. Severe weather and disease had the reduced fleet to about 100 men when they set shore to found the settlement they named **Rey Felipe**. The colony's food supply ran low, forcing them to contend with nourishing themselves from the harsh landscape. One afternoon Sarmiento's ship was blown out to sea in a tempest while he was aboard, and he was only able to steer the ship to safety on Brazilian shores. He tried but failed to convince the crown to finance the colony further. When the English corsair Thomas Cavendash arrived in 1587, he found one survivor, one cadaver swinging from a tree, and many residents dead in their homes from starvation. Cavendash aptly renamed the place **Port Famine**. There is some rubble left of the original church, which overlooks a pretty horseshoe bay.

Heading back to the main highway you will encounter another branch at the turnoff to take you to the log and rock **Fort Bulnes**. Originally established in 1843, some portions were reconstructed recently to establish it as a historic point of interest. At about km 55, three km before arriving to San Juan and the end of the road, is the hillside cemetery patch with the intriguing grave of **Pringle Stokes**, the original captain of the Beagle. Upon his death "from the effects of the anxieties and hardships incurred" as the marker indicates, the Beagle returned to England. The new captain Fitz Roy would select the young Charles Darwin as the ship's naturalist. He chose Darwin mainly for the companionship someone his own age would provide, hoping he would not suffer the same fate as poor Pringle Stokes, who reportedly was losing his mental rudder at the time of his death.

The cross on the grave site is a replica of the original, which is on display in the Salesiano Mayorino Borgatello Museum in Punta Arenas, but you can read both front and back inscriptions at that grave site. If you are taking a group tour offered by one of the agencies to Fort Bulnes, talk the mini-van driver into making the brief detour to the Pringle Stokes grave if it is not already included.

Other excursions from Punta Arenas include sailing along the spectacular **Darwin Chain** on Tierra del Fuego. An overnight trip to the cross channel town of Porvenir is worthwhile to set foot on the island of **Tierra del Fuego** (see *Tierra del Fuego* section).

The 5,000-hectare **Pali Aike National Park** on the Argentine border is a bit difficult to access, but some tour agencies offer a lengthy day trip excursion, six hours of which would be drive time. Rolling pampas inhabited by grazing guanacos and armor-clad armadillos lead to a crater-pocked, volcanic landscape. Here you can visit **Fell Cave** painted with hand imprints estimated to be 9,000 years old.

Tour & Travel Agencies
• **Arka Patagonia**; *I. Carrera Pinto 946. Tel. 248167*
• **Aventour,** *Jose Nogueira 1255. Tel. 241613*
• **Estrecho de Magallanes**, *Roca 998, Of. 104-105. Tel. 247220 or 248860*
• **La Hermandad,** *L. Navarro 1099. Tel. 248090*
• **Runner,** *L. Navarro 1065. Tel. 247050*
• **Turismo Cabo de Hornos,** *Pza. Munoz Gamero 1039. Tel. 241321*
• **Turismo Comapa,** *Independencia 840. Tel. 241321*
• **Turismo Pehoe,** *Menendez 918. Tel. 241373 or 244506*
• **Viento Sur,** *Fagnano 565. Tel. 225167*

PRACTICAL INFORMATION
Banks: Banks with ATM machines include: **Citibank**, *Magallanes 990, Tel. 248080*; **Banco De Edwards**, *Plaza Munoz Gamero 1055, Tel. 241175;***Banco de Chile**, *Roca 848, Tel. 224885*; **Redbanc ATM** machine on *Bories 930* adjacent to the hardware store (*ferretería*)
Bookstore: Southern Patagonia Souveniers and Books, *Bories 404*
Currency Exchange: Bus Sur, *Corner of Colon/Magallanes, Tel. 244464;* **La Hermandad**, *L. Navarro 1099, Tel. 248090*; **Runner**, *L. Navarro 1065, Tel. 247050;* **Scott Tour**, *Av. Colon/Magallanes corner, Tel. 244464* (the only one open Sunday); **Sur Cambios**, *L. Navarro 1001, Tel. 225656*
E-Mail Service: Canadian Institute of Languages, *O'Higgins 688, Tel. 226333 or 227943*, offers computer use with e-mail service.
Laundry: Lavasol, *O'Higgins 969, Tel. 243607*
Post Office: Correos de Chile, *Bories 91*
Telephone Long Distance/Fax: The area code is 61. Long distance offices: **CTC**, *Nogueira 1116* and **Entel**, *L. Navarro 957*
Tourist Office/Maps: Sernatur, *Waldo Seguel 689, Tel. 225385, daily 8am-6pm*

TIERRA DEL FUEGO

Ferdinand Magellan named the 76,000 square km island "Land of Fire" for the multitude of smoke spires he observed funneling upward from the shoreline. The four thousand Ona Indians who inhabited the island in 1520 depended on fires more than clothing to warm them, even keeping small blazes lit in their canoes.

The island, which currently is more or less split down the middle by the Chilean-Argentine border, stretches from the **Beagle Channel** to the **Magellan Strait**. Its three main topographical elements are the icy, nearly impenetrable **Fuegian Andes** to the south, a central valley in which lies **Lake Fagnano**, and to the north, the grassy steppes of the pampas used as grazing land.

The island's grassy steppes, once dominated by large landholdings, are broken up into hundreds of smaller ranches today. Since the discovery of reserves in 1945, the petroleum industry has been the biggest employer, with extraction facilities positioned on the island and in the strait. **Porvenir**, located on the west side of the island, is the provincial capital with 4,000 inhabitants, and serves as the main point of entry by ferry from Punta Arenas. **Puerto Williams**, is mainly a military city of 1,500 on Hoste Island, south of the Argentine town of Ushuaia.

ARRIVALS & DEPARTURES

Porvenir

By Boat: See Punta Arenas *Arrivals and Departures, By Boat* for information on passenger and vehicle ferry transport to and from the island.

Puerto Williams

By Air: **Aerovias DAP**, *O'Higgins 891, Punta Arenas, Tel. 61-223340* offers service from Punta Arenas to Puerto Williams.

By Boat: From Punta Arenas, there is a cargo boat with spots for 12 passengers, $60 for the 38 hour passage including meals. Contact **Barcaza Patagonia**, *Bulnes 5075, Tel. 61/218100*. The only boat service from Ushuaia across the Beagle Channel to Puerto Williams is via private charter on a catamaran.

ORIENTATION

Most people will go to Tierra Del Fuego by boat from Punta Arenas to Porvenir for a day trip or en route to the Argentine town of Ushuaia. This ferry crossing puts you on the west side of the island. For those going into Porvenir for the day without a vehicle, take the short cab ride into town from the boat dock for $4. Local buses serve other destinations on the island.

WHERE TO STAY & EAT

Porvenir
• **Hotel Central**, *Bernardo Phillipi 298. Tel. 61/580077. Double $40*
• **Hotel Rosas**, *Bernardo Phillipi 296. Tel. 61/580088. Double $50*
• **Hostería Los Flamencos**, *Teniente Merino. Tel. 61/580049. Double $75*
    For a meal try the **Club Croata**, *Senoret 542. Tel. 61/580053* or one of the hotels listed above.

Cerro Sombrero
• **Hostería Tunkelen**, *Cerro Sombrero, Tel. 61/296688*

Puerto Williams
• **Hostería Wala**, *Ruta a Aeropuerto, Puerto Williams, Tel. 61/621114. Double $100.* January-April only
• **Hostería Camlor**, *Via 2 s/n, Puerto Williams, Tel. 61/621033. Double $75.* January-April only
• **Residencial Onashaga**, *Corner of Uspashun & Nueva, Tel. 61/621081. Double $30*

SEEING THE SIGHTS

The main reason to engage in a three hour ferry crossing to Porvenir is to set foot on Tierra del Fuego. If you have an extra day, the romantic images the island conjures up are reason enough to go there. With calm conditions the ferry ride is a pleasant voyage. As we entered Porvenir's hidden bay, a school of dolphins called *toninos* played alongside the boat, undulating dexterously through the water to keep pace with us.

In Porvenir, the main point of interest is the **Provincial Museum**, *Corner of Valdivieso and Schythe, Hours Monday-Friday 9am-1pm/2:30 pm-6pm, open weekends during December-January.* This is a historical and archaeological museum with artifacts and exhibits on the Onas. There are sometimes flamencos and black-necked swans in the bay along the boardwalk.

If you traveling through by car or feel like hiring a taxi, take the drive along **Bahía Inútil** to see the rugged, snow-covered Darwin chain across the bay. **Lago Branco** and **Rio Grande**, 150 kilometers from Porvenir, offer good trout fishing. You can also enjoy bird watching, beach campsites, and perhaps an encounter with the wild horses that run there. To line up an organized fishing excursion contact **Aventour**, *Jose Nogueira 1255, Punta Arenas Tel. 61/220174.* **Cerro Sombrero**, is curious company village built on a unique, amoeba-shaped mesa 120 kilometers north of Porvenir.

PUERTO NATALES

The capital of **Ultima Esperanza** province is a pleasant enough town of 18,000, with folksy dwellings reflected onto the bay, black-necked swans cruising along the shoreline, and views of the **Paine Massif** in the distance. Most travelers that stop here do so for the minimum amount of time possible, as they are focused on pushing their hiking boots along a **Torres del Paine** trail or catching a bus onward to the next destination in their journey. A quick stay in Puerto Natales is OK because you can quickly take in all there is to do here.

ARRIVALS & DEPARTURES

By Boat Puerto Natales-Puerto Montt

A frequently utilized option for transport for one way between Puerto Natales and Puerto Montt is sailing on the *Puerto Eden*. The cargo ship, converted to accommodate passengers and autos, offers a three night, four day voyage between Puerto Montt and Puerto Natales. It navigates through the fog-shrouded, verdant archipelagos and fjords along the southern Chilean coast, inaccessible any other way except by water.

Time allocation should be the main factor in deciding whether to take the voyage or not. If you have a week planned for Magallanes, it is better to fly in, because you will feel shorted on time allotted to Torres del Paine. If you have two or more weeks scheduled for Magallanes, then the time spent on the boat starts becoming worthwhile. However, if it comes down to making a choice between the boat trip and say, spending a few days in the Austral region or Chiloé for example, stay off the boat. The scenery is beautiful, spectacular if you catch clear days with sunshine, but you are captive on a boat with less than stellar food and lounging time that grows a bit tedious by the end of the voyage.

The *Puerto Eden* sails weekly during the summer and three times per month the rest of the year. The high season pricing for room and board passage per person, ranges from $300 for the cheapest class to $1,500 for a single cabin. We booked AA Bunks for $400 per person, which are located in a shared four person cabin, with a bathroom and sufficient storage space. The AA bunks are spacious and comfortable enough with individual reading lights over each bed. We lucked out by rooming with two of the nicest guys on the boat, two Brits, one of whom was an obstreperous snorer and actually relocated to sleep in the common area, (unsolicited), when his snores hit a crescendo. We advise avoiding the cheapest section unless your discomfort tolerance is extremely high.

Rows of triple stacked bunks, separated only by curtains, are located in the belly of the ship next to the engine room, laden with all its noise, odors, and vapors.

A few items to take with you that will make your trip more comfortable include extra fruit and other snacks, picante sauce or other spices for the bland food, and seasickness pills to be taken before crossing the turbulent Golfo de Pena (literally, the *Gulf of Sorrows*). Although you can buy water, soft drinks, beer and wine-in-a-box on the boat, consider packing on bottles of your favorite beverage to save some cash and pamper your taste buds with exactly what they crave.

Navimag Offices
• **Puerto Montt**: *Angelmo 2187. Tel. 65/253754, Fax 65/258540*
• **Puerto Natales**: *Pedro Montt 262B. Tel./Fax 61/411421*
• **Punta Arenas**: *Independencia 830. Tel. 61/244448, Fax 61/225804*
• **Santiago**: *El Bosque Norte 0440. Tel. 2/203-5030. Fax 2/203-5025*

By Bus
Puerto Natales is a natural regional hub for routes to Torres Del Paine and Punta Arenas, as well as to Calafate and Rio Gallegos in Argentina.

There is no central bus station. Most of the offices are located just northeast of the main plaza.

Several buses run to Punta Arenas each day, but it is a good idea to buy your ticket in advance. The trip to Punta Arenas takes three hours. They will drop you off at the airport if you let them know you want to get off there.

Turismos LB and Bus Sur offer the most regular service to Torres del Paine, including service during the off season. The trip to the park takes three to four hours depending on where you get off. During the high season, when there are more bus options, the flexibility of one way tickets more than compensates for the small savings of the round trip ticket.

To Punta Arenas
• **Buses Fernández**, *Eberhard 555. Tel. 411111*
• **Bus Sur**, *Baquedano 534. Tel. 411325*
• **Buses Transfer**, *Baquedano 414. 412216*

To Torres del Paine
• **Andescape**, *P. Montt 308. Tel. 412592*
• **Bus Sur**, *Baquedano 534. Tel. 411325*
• **Patagonia Ice**, *B. Encalada 183. Tel. 411325*
• **Servitur**, *Arturo Prat 353. Tel. 411858*
• **Turismos LB**, *Arturo Prat 258. Tel. 412824*

To Calafate
• **Bus Sur**, *Baquedano 534. Tel. 411325*
• **Turismo Zaahj**, *Arturo Prat 236. Tel. 412260*

By Car
All means of entry and exit to/from Puerto Natales are via Pedro Montt which runs along the waterfront. On the way out, Pedro Montt forks. The left route runs toward Cerro Castillo, Torres Del Paine, and Calafate. The right fork heads south toward Punta Arenas on Highway 9. You should be extra cautious with your speed on rubble rock roads such as that which runs to Torres del Paine. The loose walnut-size rocks tend to slide the car around like a patch of ice. Some auto rental companies show pictures of rolled and mangled vehicles to emphasize the danger.

Be sure to fill up the tank before heading out of Puerto Natales. There is a gas station in Cerro Castillo, and gas from a barrel available near the Administrative Center in Torres del Paine, but it is better not to have to depend on these sources.

Car Rental Agencies
• **Andes Patagonicos**, *Blanco Encalada 266, Puerto Natales, Tel. 61/411594*
• **EMSA**, *Ramírez 278, Puerto Natales, Tel. 61/410775. In the Hotel Martin Guinde*
• **Todoauto**, *Bulnes 20, Puerto Natales, Tel. 61/412837. In the Hotel Costaustralis*

By Plane

None of the commercial airlines have flights into Puerto Natales. Construction is being done at the airport that will allow planes large enough to fly in from Puerto Montt and Santiago. Once it is done you will be able to fly into the region and arrive to the park in the same day.

ORIENTATION

Puerto Natales lies on the eastern side of the weather-protected **Ultima Esperanza Inlet**, 247 km north of Punta Arenas. Beyond the inlet are thousands of islands. The Dorotea mountains rise gently behind the city. On the other side of the mountains is the Argentine border, a mere 16 kilometers away. One hundred and fifty km to the north is **Torres del Paine National Park**, within which is the **Paine Massif** and the beginning of the **Southern Ice Field**.

All commerce and hotels that you will need in Puerto Natales are located in a 16 block triangle contained within the sides of Manuel Bulnes running east to west, Pedro Montt running along the waterfront, and Phillipi on the back side. The Plaza de Armas is four and a half blocks from the waterfront. The banks, grocery stores, and many other retail stores are on Manuel Bulnes between Magallanes and Blanco Encalada.

WHERE TO STAY

Expensive

COSTA AUSTRALIS, *Pedro Montt Esq. Bulnes. Tel. 61/412000, Fax 61/411881. 50 rooms. Double $173 with view. Double $140 without view. Breakfast included. Two restaurants. Bar. Travel agency. Credit cards accepted.*

The premiere upscale hotel of Puerto Natales comes in the form of an mustard-yellow, oversized German style villa. The entryways leading into the rooms are of finely-finished pine providing an elegant nautical feel. All of the view rooms look out over the Ultima Esperanza Inlet. There are two dining rooms open during the high season.

MARTIN GUSINDE, *Lautaro Navarro 1061. Tel/Fax 61/225986. 20 rooms. Double $116. Breakfast included. Cable TV. Restaurant. Bar. Credit cards accepted.*

The Martin Gusinde is tastefully finished in every detail and offers superior service, making it the best option in the expensive category. The interior of the two story hotel is richly decorated in floral- striped wallpaper and cushioned bedspreads. The hotel is located across the street from the casino and a few blocks away from the square. The restaurant serves a fixed menu which includes a pisco sour, appetizer, fish or meat option, desert and coffee. The chef strives to make each daily menu unique.

HOTEL LADRILLERO, *Pedro Montt 161. Tel 61/411652, Fax 412109. 14 rooms. Double $95. Breakfast included. Restaurant. Bar. Credit cards accepted.*

The Ladrillero is a ski lodge-style hotel with the open second floor hallway overlooking the dining room and bar. There are good views of the water from the second floor inlet-facing rooms. The restaurant offers some of the most reasonable prices in town and good food.

CAPITÁN EBERHARD, *Av. Pedro Montt 58. Tel. 61/411208, Fax 61/411209. 25 rooms. Double $100. Breakfast included. Cable TV. Restaurant. Credit cards accepted.*

Although once the premiere hotel of Puerto Natales, there have been some quality debates of late. Granted it needs some refurbishing, but the hotel still rates first in uniqueness. Milodons hold keys for the guests behind the reception desk. The bar is a *huaso* cowboy montage with green shag carpet deep enough to lose change in, while saddles, stirrups, and spurs adorn the walls. A stuffed hawk is strategically perched to nab an armadillo for dinner. A stylish dining room looks out onto the water.

Moderate

HOSTAL LADY FLORENCE DIXIE, *M. Bulnes 659. Tel. 61/411158, Fax 61/411943. Rooms 12. Double $65. Breakfast included. Cable TV. Credit cards accepted.*

Named after the first non-indigenous woman to venture to Torres del Paine and author of the book "Across Patagonia," the hotel is owned, appropriately, by two pioneering sisters. The hotel is centrally located, two story, motel style with open hallways overlooking a grassy parking area and lawn. The rooms are a sufficient distance from the main street for quiet nights. The friendly service makes this the best option in the mid-price range.

HOTEL MILODON, *Manuel Bulnes 358. Tel. 61/411727, Fax 61/411286. Rooms 10. Double $48. Breakfast included. Cable TV. Credit cards accepted.*

This is a strange lovable place with lavender walls, odd geometry, and light invited in through skylights wherever possible. The hotel is as unique as its namesake and homey too.

LOS GLACIARES, *Eberhard 104. Tel. 61-412189, Fax 61-411452. 18 rooms. Double $81. Breakfast included. Cable TV. Restaurant. Credit cards accepted.*

We arrived here twice completely exhausted and found much comfort in the large simple rooms, great showers, and cable TV. The quality is a cut above the rest in the price range. The owner is a bit gruff, but you don't see him much anyway, and the rest of the staff is nice. However, beware of the Don Pepe restaurant attached to the hotel with an entrance around the corner. They served the most inedible piece of meat ever encountered and were reluctant to take it back once they had gotten rid of it.

LUKOVIEK'S, *Ramírez 324. Tel. 61/411120, Fax 61/411120. Rooms 8. Double $57. Breakfast included. Credit cards accepted.*

The common areas are better than average here. There is an immaculate European style living room. The rooftop has been set up with tables to take advantage of clear days when the Paine Massif is visible poking through a gap in the landscape. The family that owns the place puts emphasis on personalized service and works hard to satisfy you. Breakfast features homemade jam and bread.

HOSTAL LOS PINOS, *Phillipi 449, Tel. 61/411735, Tel/Fax 61/411326. Rooms 12. Double $50. Breakfast included. No credit cards.*

This place features a big comfortable living room and dining area. Eooms are farther back without TV's to maintain quiet. The ownership does not recognize the discounting of IVA (sales tax) for foreigners. Usually it is automatic with hotels in this price range. Give it a try though to see what happens. It is still a good deal even with IVA included.

HOSTAL MELISSA, *Blanco Encalada 258. Tel. 61/411944. Rooms 7. Double $48. No credit cards.*

The rooms of this hotel are located over an old fashioned coffee shop. Accommodation is simple but still better than average for the price.

Inexpensive

CASA CECILIA, *Tomas Rogers 60. Tel. 61/411797. Per person $10. Breakfast included. Shared rooms and bathrooms. No credit cards.*

This is the best option in the inexpensive range as evidenced by travelers who leave raving about Cecilia's fresh bread. It was the only full residencial in town during a low season visit which means space goes fast. All rooms and bathrooms are shared. The living room is stylishly comfortable with an ample purple couch to sink into while mellow jazz music massages the soul. The hostel rents camping equipment and bicycles. Someone please tell the host a joke in one of the many languages he speaks to make that pensive man smile! If you fail, it is okay; warm smiles are doled out freely by the hostess.

OASIS RESIDENCIAL, *Senoret 332, Tel. 61/411675.. Mostly shared rooms and bathrooms, a few rooms with private bathrooms. $12 per person. Breakfast included. No credit cards.*

This is a really strong option if the Casa Cecilia is full and it is located just around the corner from it. The family home atmosphere didn't fade when the business started. It feels as if you were a relative invited into the guest room for a visit.

AMERINDIA CONCEPT, *Ladrilleros 105. Tel. 61/410678, Fax 61/410169. $12 per person. Shared rooms and bathrooms. Breakfast included. Restaurant. Bar. No credit cards.*

The Amerindia is the hippest place in town and is distinguished by an active communal backpacker atmosphere. The cafeteria downstairs is a great place to spend an afternoon or evening swapping info with other travelers, reading outdoor adventure magazines, or lounging in the indoor hammock. The menu includes real brewed coffee, brownies, muffins, and cheesecake. The owners are climbers and run an adventure tour service as well.

RESIDENCIAL TEMUCO, *Ramírez 324. Tel. 61/411120, Fax 61/411120. Shared rooms and bathrooms. $10 per person. Breakfast included. No credit cards.*

This residencial is run by the same hard working family that runs the Hotel Luckvieks next door. They offer personalized service assured to satisfy and lots of flowers in the hallways.

Both **La Casona**, *M. Bulnes 280. Tel. 61/412562* and **Laura Residencial**, *Bulnes 222. Tel. 61/412452* are clean and homey enough. Both have shared rooms and bathrooms for $10 per person including breakfast.

Out of Town

HOTEL CISNE DE CUELLO NEGRO, *4 Km from Puerto Natales on the road to T. Paine, Puerto Bories. Tel. 61/411498, Tel/Fax 61/411101. Double $120. Restaurant. Bar. Credit cards accepted.*

This hotel is located among the quaint old estancia buildings in Puerto Bories. The rooms are simple, but most have fabulous views of the strait, the Balmaceda glacier, and the Torres Massif in the distance. The dining room shares the same soothing views. Just beyond the gate, there are pastoral walks along a shoreline adorned with black-necked swans. The service in the hotel and restaurant is outstanding. This is a great option for those who want a rustic experience while maintaing proximity to the Puerto Natales' services.

WHERE TO EAT

CAPITÁN EBERHARD, *Av. Pedro Montt 58. Tel. 61/411208. Expensive. Credit cards accepted.*

The dining room in the Capitán Eberhard Hotel is minimalist elegance with sleek black chairs and pink table cloths. Prices are at the upper end of the scale, but it is the most stylish place in town. Seafood is the house specialty.

LA ULTIMA ESPERANZA, *Eberhard 354. Tel. 411391. Moderate. Credit cards accepted.*

This is the best seafood restaurant in Puerto Natales so it is sought out by both locals and travelers. The decor features white table cloths in an intimate setting. We had the most tender and tasty squid we've eaten in Chile, prepared *al pil-pil*, in oil with garlic and red chile - delicious.

HOTEL LADRILLO RESTAURANT, *Pedro Montt 161. Tel 61/411652. Moderate. Credit cards accepted.*

The restaurant offers some of the most reasonable prices in town. The specialty of the house, not listed on the menu, is the *Salmon Aluza* - salmon with bacon, tomato, onion, and spices, baked in tin foil. Both the restaurant and the adjoining bar feature the ski lodge style of the Ladrillo hotel.

LA TRANQUERA, *Manuel Bulnes 579. Tel. 411039. Moderate. Credit cards accepted.*

Antique phonographs and lamps decorate one wall while antique trumpets dangle from the other. The oversized draft beers are one of the big drawing cards. The specialty of the house is salmon.

LA HERRADURA, *Bulnes 371. Tel. 412538. Moderate. Credit cards accepted.*

This is a pub restaurant with the specialty of house being the seafood chowder *paila marina*. There is live *peña* style music in the January-February high season. Shows are Friday and Saturday nights beginning about 11pm.

EL MARÍTIMO, *Pedro Montt 214. Tel. 410455. Moderate. Credit cards accepted.*

The El Marítimo is a popular seafood restaurant on the waterfront. Among the house favorites are its delicious salmon and scallops. A similar seafood restaurant nearby is **Los Pioneros**, *Pedro Montt 166. Tel. 410783.*

EL CRISTAL, *Manuel Bulnes 439. Puerto Natales, Tel. 411850. Moderate/Inexpensive. No credit cards.*

This is a popular place with the traveler crowd. Garlic lovers should try the Martinez sandwich, consisting of steak, cheese, advocado, tomato, and a heft of garlic. Torres del Paine Park Ranger Carlos recommends the substantial *lomo a lo pobre* (steak, fried eggs, grilled onions, covered in fries) for the ravenous trekker. He doubts one person can eat it all.

LA REPIZZA, *Blanco Encalada 294, Puerto Natales, Tel.410361. Moderate/Inexpensive. No credit cards.*

This rustic pizza parlor makes a darn good pizza. They also offer an extensive list of sandwiches.

AMERINDIA CONCEPT, *Ladrilleros 105. Tel. 410678. Inexpensive. No credit cards.*

Like the hostel above it, the Amerindia cafe is a funky, laid-back place which caters to the backpacker crowd. The menu includes fresh brewed coffee and American style munchies like pizza, cheesecake, and brownies. Some evenings they show videos and slides about regional parks, wildlife, and adventure sports.

CAFE MIDAS, *Tomas Rogers 169. Tel. 411606. Inexpensive. No credit cards.*

This coffee shop has a good atmosphere and looks out onto the main square. There is a book exchange in the corner where travelers are invited to swap books on a take-one-leave-one basis. The shelf also includes non-circulating travel guides. The fundamental menu item that the place lacks is brewed coffee, sadly only instant is available, but there is a good selection of pastries.

EL CENTRAL, *Valdivia 662. Tel. 411415. Inexpensive. No credit cards.*

Although this greasy spoon begs a thorough scrubbing, it merits mentioning for anyone needing an off-hours meal. It is open daily from 9am-2am. The speciality of the house is *cazuela de mariscos* seafood chowder.

SEEING THE SIGHTS

About the only thing to see in town is the newly remodeled, bite-size, regional museum, **Museo Histórico Municipal**, *Bulnes 285, Tel. 411263, daily 9am-12:30pm/3pm-5:30pm*. The museum outlines regional history, focusing on the colonization and sheep ranching at the beginning of the century. The interior of the museum is finished with typical pioneer materials – beech wood and *arpillera*, a coarse fabric that was used to cover pioneer cabin walls.

NIGHTLIFE & ENTERTAINMENT

Best bets for *vida nocturna* include **El Trébol Loco**, *corner of Magallanes and Bories*. For live music and bar atmosphere try **La Herradura**, *Bulnes 371*, with music beginning at 11pm on weekends during the high season. The Mexican style pub **Tío Cacho**, *Phillip 553, Tel. 41021*, occasionally has live music. **Amerindia**, *Ladrilleros 105*, sometimes shows slides or videos on Torres del Paine or other Patagonian subjects in the evening. The local discotec is the **Milodon**, *Blanca Ensenada 854*.

EXCURSIONS & DAY TRIPS

The majority of excursion activities in this area will be found in the **Torres del Paine**. The ones listed here are near Puerto Natales, but outside of the national park.

MILODON CAVE, *24 km north of Puerto Natales. Entry $4.*

Deciding to visit the legendary giant sloth's cave is kind of like trying to decide to spend the time to see the world's largest ball of string or a scale model of the Notre Dame Cathedral made from beer cans. If you have nothing to do or if your curiosity is big enough, you will probably take a look.

Traveling to the Conaf-run exhibit is most easily arranged through one of the agencies advertising the tour for about $10. A nice picnic area is set up in front of the cave where Captain Eberhard discovered bones and fur of a milodon. There is also a statue of the 15 foot tall creature. It will take you about twenty minutes to wring all possible entertainment out of the exhibit.

A MILODON OF MY OWN

"The Milodon was a Giant Ground Sloth, rather bigger than a bull, of a class unique to South America.

The skeleton astonished naturalists of Cuvier's generation. Goethe worked it into an essay which appears to anticipate the Theory of Evolution. The zoologists had to picture the antediluvian mammal, standing fifteen feet high, which was a magnified version of the ordinary insect-eating sloths that hung upside-down from trees. Cuvier gave it the name Megatherium and suggested that Nature had wanted to amuse herself with 'something imperfect and grotesque'.

Darwin found the bones of a milodon among his 'nine great quadrupeds' on the beach at Punta Alta, near Bahía Blanca, and sent them to Dr. Richard Owen at the Royal College of Surgeons. Owens laughed at the idea of giant sloths up giant trees before the Flood. He described Mylodon Darwini as a cumbersome animal that reared up on its haunches, using its legs and tail as a tripod, and, instead of climbing up trees, clawed them down."

– Bruce Chatwin, from his book **In Patagonia**

Boat Cruise to Bernardo O'Higgins National Park

CUTTER 21 DE MAYO, *Ebberhard 554. Tel. 61/411978 or Ladrilleros 171. Tel. 61/411176.*

This excursion sails through the **Ultima Esperanza Inlet** and through the **Eberhard Fjord**, to view the magnificent **Balmaceda and Serrano**

glaciers. Both of these glaciers drop almost all the way into the bay, with the Balmaceda descending from the rugged 2,035 meter mountain of the same name. You have the opportunity to walk alongside the Serrano glacier as well as the possibility of observing sea lions. This trip is a good option for anyone who was thinking about doing the *Puerto Eden* cruise but couldn't fit it into the schedule. It represents a full day, from 8:30am to 6pm, with a cost of $55 during the high season and $40 during the low season. Dress warmly.

Calafate, Argentina & Parque Nacional Los Glaciares

Calafate, 358 km from Puerto Natales, is the service center for the nearby attractions of **Parque Nacional Los Glaciares** within which is located the Perito Moreno Glacier, and the **Fitz Roy Range**, renowned for climbing and trekking. There is bus service from Puerto Natales to Calafate which includes a border crossing so you should expect about a six hour trip. Tour agencies such as Turismo Zaahj offer package excursions, but you can also make arrangements in Calafate upon arrival.

Travel Agencies

• **Andescape**, *Pedro Montt 308. Tel./Fax 61/412592*. Adventure tours.
• **Andes Patagonia Expeditions**, *Blanco Encalada 226. Tel./Fax 61/411594*.
• **Amerindia**, *Ladrilleros 105. Tel. 410678*. Climbing and ice climbing.
• **Cutter 21 de Mayo**, *Ebberhard 554. Tel. 411978* or *Ladrilleros 171. Tel. 61/411176*. Boat tour to Balmaceda Glacier.
• **Onas Aventour**, *Bulnes 463. Tel./Fax 61/412707*. Kayak, ice climbing, adventure tours.
• **Knudsen Tours**, *Blanco Encalada 284. Tel./Fax 61/411976*.
• **Turismo Zaahj**, *Arturo Prat 236, Tel. 61/412260, Fax 61/411355*. Calafate Glacier.

PRACTICAL INFORMATION

Banks: Banco de Santiago, *Bulnes 637* (ATM Machine); **Banco de Chile**, near *corner of Bulnes and Prat* (ATM Machine)
Bookstore: Southern Patagonia, *Bulnes 688*
Business Hours: 9am-1pm and 3pm-6pm
Camping Gear Rentals: Onas Aventour, *Bulnes 463, Tel. 412707*. A good selection of tents, sleeping bags, stoves; **Casa Cecilia**, *Tomas Rogers 60, Tel. 411797*
Camping Gear Sales: Evasion, *Prat No. 353, 2nd Floor, Tel. 411259*; **Supermercado Record**, *Bulnes 710, Tel. 411127*
Currency Exchange: Stop Cambios, *Baquedano 380*
E-Mail Service: CTC, *Baquedano 383*
Laundry: Servitravel, *Bulnes 513*

National Parks: **CONAF**, *Ignacio Carrera Pinto 566. Tel. 411438*
Post Office: **Correos de Chile**, *Eberhard 423*
Supermarkets: **Don Brusco**, *Bulnes 650*
Telephone/Fax: **CTC Office**, *Baquedano 383*
Tourist Office/Maps: **Sernatur**, *Corner of Pedro Montt and Phillipi. Tel. 412125 or 223798*. If you are headed to Torres del Paine, we recommend that you buy the excellent "Torres del Paine Trekking Map" sold in Puerto Natales stores and at almost all of the refugios and kiosks in the park.

TORRES DEL PAINE

As your bus enters the park, a few of the golden-fleeced guanacos might nonchalantly curve their necks away from the grassy steppes, yet the mastication of the protruding weeds, accomplished with a mechanical sideways thrust of the jaw, continues uninterrupted. Behind the herd lies the cobalt blue water of a salt-encrusted lake. Just beyond that, jutting out of the low altitude plain is the burly Paine Massif, from which claw the blackened horns known as Los Cuernos.

The 181,000-hectare Torres del Paine, is a vast, nature lover's playground, the trails of which run 270 km through diverse terrain and climates. Founded in 1959, the park is composed of a series of lakes and glaciers surrounding the **Paine Massif**. The independent mountain mass shoots out of the grassy Patagonian steppes near sea level to a height of 3,248 meters at the peak of **Paine Grande**, a contrast which serves to enhance the massif's grandeur from below.

The park's trio of renowned features includes the namesake **Torres**, three wind-carved, pink granite towers, rising from the eastern edge of the range. The **Cuernos**, two sharp, curved horns, darkened by their broad bands of compressed sedimentary shale, are located to the south of the Torres. The Cuernos are the most frequently seen peaks because they face most of the camping and hiking infrastructure. The third major feature is **Glacier Grey**, which extends along the west side of the massif, originating in the Southern Ice Field and terminating in Grey Lake into which it launches luminescent blue icebergs.

The park's unique weather system can be a vexing factor. In addition to the variability of the clouds, the wind in the park is almost constant. It can literally blow you off of the trail at times. You are guaranteed at least some extreme weather. Packing for rain, wind, and low temperatures is an absolute necessity. Don't let the direness of the downside scare you off. Out of the twenty-five days we've spent in the park, about twenty have been sunny or partly sunny.

Another perplexing factor that people misplan for is time. Almost always travelers underestimate the time required to arrive to the park, how much there is to do, and how far apart the main points of interest are. For example, to hike to the Torres, the Cuernos, and Glacier Grey on the popular **"W" trek**, you will need six full days in the park. If you are departing from Santiago, two more days are needed for transport to the park, resulting in a total of eight days, with zero tolerance for snafus, and requiring you to push along the trails everyday at a wearying clip.

If you are already in the region, wondering if a mere day or night in the park is worth the effort, the answer is definitely "yes". We are sure of this because we've met people who were thrilled with the experience provided by a round-trip bus ride to the administration center combined with a short hike. If blessed with clear or partially clear skies, the ride in alone allows for viewing of guanacos, rheas, waterfowl, the Torres, Cuernos, and eight lakes.

Unless you are a ranger, it seems that no amount of days in the park are enough. As you are leaving, you will inevitably feel separation anxiety and will begin plotting what hikes to do on the next visit. That is exactly the reason to go in the first place.

ARRIVALS & DEPARTURES

Entry into the park is accomplished via one of three gates, most frequently via Laguna Amarga or Lago Sarmiento, and in rare cases via the southern entrance of Laguna Verde. The cost to enter is $15 for foreigners and $6 for Chileans and residents.

By Boat

One adventure tour company is planning to offer a boat trip to its cabins on the edge of Torres del Paine, in the sector Rio Serrano. The boat will leave from Puerto Natales, travel through the Ultima Esperanza Inlet, by the Balmaceda glacier, then up the Rio Serrano river. Contact **Aventour**, *Jose Nogueira 1255, Punta Arenas. Tel. 61/220174 or 241197, Fax 61/243354.* The company owns cabins, *Cabanas del Paine*, seven km south of the Administrative Center.

By Bus

Bus is the most frequently used mode for getting to the park. You should plan on the ride taking at least three to four hours to get there depending on where you get off. The buses make three scheduled stops, but you can ask to be let off or on anywhere along the way. The stops are:

1. Laguna Amarga Park Station Entrance. From here it is a two hour hike to Camping/Hostería Las Torres which is where the Valle Ascencio trail head to the Torres is located. You begin the "W" and the Circuit here, going counter-clockwise.

2. Refugio Pudeto Dock. This is the departure point for the one hour boat ride across Lago Pehoe to Refugio & Camping Pehoe. Refugio & Camping Pehoe is the starting point for hikes to the Cuernos via Valle del Frances and to Glacier Gray, as well as the "W" from that side.

3. Administration Center. From here it is a five hour hike to Refugio & Camping Pehoe, the starting point for hikes to the Cuernos via Valle del Frances and to Glacier Gray. This is also the beginning of the circuit going clockwise.

The order of stops is reversed on the way out. The most convenient way out is to catch the first bus stopping at one of the named points. This allows more flexibility than buying a round-trip ticket originating in

TORRES DEL PAINE NATIONAL PARK

Puerto Natales. The cost of the ticket is about $10 each way. For bus lines and arrivals, see the Puerto Natales *Arrivals & Departures* section.

By Car

From Puerto Natales, follow the signs to Cerro Castillo, 57 km away. As you approach the group of buildings at the "T" in the road, you will pass a *carabinero's* station. It is not necessary to check in here unless an official is out stopping motorists. If you need gas, the gas station is straight through the intersection in the small town of Cerro Castillo, otherwise take the left.

From Cerro Castillo, you will travel an additional 20 km until you hit a fork in the road. Here you will have to decide if you prefer to enter the park via the Lago Sarmiento or the Laguna Amarga entry. The Laguna Amarga entrance is used for Hostería Camping Las Torres, the hike to the Torres, the circuit going counter-clockwise, and to access Laguna Azul. The Lago Sarmiento entrance is used for all other destinations.

By Taxi

If you want to get to the park in the evening due to a time crunch, you can enlist a taxi in Puerto Natales to take you to the Laguna Seca entrance for about $70.

ORIENTATION

The **Paine Massif** is the centerpiece of the Torres del Paine Park, somewhat shaped like a thick "E" tilting to the northeast, with two valleys forming the gaps between the arms. Entrance into the park is from the east side. The majority of time spent by visitors in the park is on the range's southern edge. The access points to the **Torres**, the **Cuernos**, and **Glacier Grey** are located in this southern area, as well as the five largest lakes. The lakes, from east to west, are **Sarmiento**, **Toro**, **Nordenskjold**, **Pehoe**, and **Grey**. There are four smaller lakes on the north side of the range, **Amarga**, **Dickson**, **Azul**, and **Paine**. The Glacier Grey runs along more or less north to south along the west side of the range.

Beyond the park lies the **Southern Ice Field** to the west, the **Toro mountain range** to the south, and the extensive Patagonian pampas to the west.

GETTING AROUND THE PARK

Most of the territory in the park can be covered on foot via well-marked trails. For more remote trails, such as the Lago Pingo, it would be convenient to get a lift to the trail-head. You will probably have good luck hitchhiking to such points in the high season. For transport within the

VANTAGE POINTS: WHERE TO GET THOSE POSTCARD SHOTS

Everyone toting a camera wants to snap great shots of the park's wildlife and unique peaks. Here are some ideal locations to satisfy your Kodachrome desires:

The Torres
　　From a Distance: *Just across the narrow bridge 15 minutes hiking from the Laguna Amarga Park Station toward Refugio Las Torres.*
　　Up Close: *At the base of the Torres; Villa Ascencio hike from Refugio Las Torres.*

The Cuernos
　　From a Distance: *Great shots are possible across Lake Nordenskjold from the lookout at the end of the Mirador Nordenskjold hike. Other good views are from Refugio Camping Pehoe, Hostería Pehoe, and from the Explora hotel.*
　　Up Close: *Along the Valle del Frances trail, especially near the British Camp*

Glacier Grey
　　From a Distance: *From the John Garner Pass between Los Perros Camp and the Upper Camp.*
　　Up Close: *From Refugio Grey and on the tour boat from Hostería Grey*

Paine Massif:
　　From a Distance: *Best shots are from the Lago Pingo Trail on the way to Refugio Zapata*
　　Up Close: *From the John Garner Pass between Los Perros Camp and the Upper Camp.*

Icebergs In Lago Grey
　　Although there are some icebergs floating around near Refugio Grey where they break off from the end of the glacier, the shots with the multiple massive icebergs are taken from the end of Lago Grey. You hike a short distance from the Guardería Lago Grey to a sand spit in front of where the icebergs accumulate.

Guanacos
　　In the western grassy area of the park, especially along the 19 km roadside between either of the park entrances leading up to Refugio Pudeto. Lago Sarmiento provides a brilliant blue lake in the background.

Bird Life
　　The rheas tend to stick to the same area grassy areas as the Guanacos on the west side of the park. There is good bird life on Lago del Toro behind the Administrative Center, especially at daybreak.

area that the buses cover, that is from Laguna Amarga to the Administration Center, you can flag them down and negotiate a ride.

There is frequently confusion about a similarly named lodging and camping sites that serve as geographic reference points, but which are actually a long way apart. These included Refugio Camping Pehoe versus Hostería Pehoe versus Camping Pehoe, as well as Refugio Grey versus Hostería Grey. You might want to take note of these immediately on the map.

By Boat

Refugio Pudeto to/from Refugio Camping Pehoe across Lake Pehoe is a popular boat trip because it takes you to the trail-heads of two of the most popular hikes in the park – the **Grey Trail** to **Glacier Grey** and the **Valle del Frances** trail to the **Cuernos**. You purchase tickets at the Refugio Pudeto dock for $6 each way. The boat sails continuously during the high season, but due to the popularity of the trails at the destination, you sometimes have to wait for a later boat if the earlier ones are full.

If you get stuck at the dock, it's okay, because the **Mirador Nordenskjold** lookout, accessed by a two hour hike round-trip, provides an extraordinary view of the Torres, and is reason enough to delay the boat ride for a few hours.

WHERE TO STAY

Torres del Paine boasts some of the most diverse, well-maintained camping areas in Chile, and at the opposite end of the spectrum, is home to what many argue is the country's most spectacular hotel, the Explora.

In addition to the upscale Explora, there are five full service hotels in the park called **hosterías**, which are at the quality level of moderate hotels, but due to the location and demand, the pricing is the expensive category. Two sets of **cabañas** (family unit cabins) round out the options for those looking for an outfitted bed. In total there are only 220 beds available in the park, so if you are depending on a bed with blankets to be there for you, it is imperative to make reservations in advance.

The park has recently developed a network of privately run, inexpensive cabin type **refugios** that cost about $15 per person per night. This is dormitory style lodging with undressed bunk beds so you need a sleeping bag to stay in these. There are usually about eight people to a room, but occasionally the refugios will have doubles or triples available. In each refugio are shared bathrooms with showers, a lodge-style cafe, a cooking area for guests, a dining room, and a lounge area. The common areas are warm, comfortable, and full of lively, polyglot conversation.

Authorized **camping areas** are divided into free areas without services and pay sites with services. Services offered at the pay sites include water, waste disposal, cooking grills, showers, stores, and since most are located next to the *refugios*, campers can utilize the cafes and common areas there as well. The free sites have no services available, but are usually located next to a water source. Sometimes there is a **refugio rustico** in the free camping areas (not to be confused the dormitory style *refugios*). A *refugio rustico* is a simple shelter, usually a shack. Some are better than others, with roofs that don't leak and wood burning stoves, but none is big enough to hold more than a few people so you shouldn't count on staying inside. The rangers ask that you camp only in authorized camping areas to minimize environmental damage.

Overall the great majority of visitors camp. Our strategy in the park has always been to camp whenever possible, but if the elements are making us miserable, our outdoorsperson pride is tame enough to handle a night or two with a roof over our heads.

Very Expensive
HOTEL EXPLORA, *Sector Salto Chico, Torres del Paine, Reservations Santiago Tel. 2/2066060 Fax 2284655. E-mail: explora@entelchile.net. Website: www.interknowledge.com /Chile/explora. Rooms 30. Paine Massif View Room $1,706 per person, four night package, double occupancy. Price includes transport from Punta Arenas airport, all meals and all tours. Restaurant. Bar. Gym. Pool. Jacuzzi. Gift shop. Library. Video projection room. Day care center during tour hours. Credit cards accepted.*

Staying at this hotel is to choose to experience Torres del Paine in the highly interactive Explora culture. The attentive service begins as a hostess greets you at the Punta Arenas airport while the chauffeur pulls your luggage from the carousel. Built into the rolling hills on the shore of Lake Pehoe, the elongated, minimalist, yellow edifice takes advantage of its position for mesmerizing views of the Cuernos from the front and the Salto Chico waterfall from the rear. The rooms optimize the views, even in the bathrooms which are designed with porthole windows so that you can look at the scenery as you brush your teeth.

The hotel offers 16 different excursions. These include hikes to destinations such as the Torres and Glacier Grey as well as mountain biking and sea kayaking. The excursion groups meet with their bilingual Chilean guides each evening to preview the following day's activities. Slide shows and books in the library provide supplementary information.

The dining looks out over the extraordinary blues of Lake Pehoe. The meals are fixed-menu style with your choice of meat and fish entrees available for lunch and dinner. The hotel also features a lap pool, outdoor jacuzzi, and gym nearly level with the languid Paine River.

Selected as one of our best places to stay – see Chapter 10 for more details.

Expensive

You can't really consider any of these lodgings a good value, except perhaps the Hostería Lago Grey. The prices are high due to the remote location and the strong demand during the high season. A good combination of hotels for a four or five night stay might be splitting up the time between the Hostería Lago Grey and the Hostería Las Torres. The phone service in the park is poor making card verification nearly impossible so none of the locations accept cards without approval in advance.

HOSTERÍA LAGO GREY, *Lago Grey. Tel. 61/229512. 25 rooms. Double $180. Breakfast included. Restaurant. Credit card charges in advance only.*

This is the nicest of the hotels in this price range. Most of rooms and the dining room have extraordinary views of the gigantic icebergs that break off Glacier Grey and loiter at this end of the lake. Although the hotel isn't very centrally located, the boat service to Glacier Grey compensates for this. There are two good day hikes nearby too, one is the Lago Pingo hike and another to Ferrier lookout.

HOSTERÍA LAS TORRES, *Sector Las Torres. Tel./Fax 61/226054. Rooms 20. Double $175. Breakfast included. Restaurant. Horse rentals. Credit card charges in advance only.*

The Hostería Las Torres was converted from a ranch house on the old hacienda. The *hostería* is at the base of the trail-head to the Torres, but unfortunately the rooms do not have a view of them. There is a good restaurant and horse rentals available.

HOSTERÍA PEHOE, *Lago Pehoe. Tel. 61/411442. Rooms 30. Double $130/night. Breakfast included. Restaurant. Credit card charges in advance only.*

The Hostería Pehoe, constructed in 1969, was the first lodging structure built in the park. Although situated in an ideal location on an island in Lago Pehoe, the rooms are set behind a rock so they do not have views. The restaurant has a better design however, and serves up excellent meals to go along with the vista of the Cuernos across the lake. Be prepared for a structure that is showing its age, but that is enhanced by a courteous staff.

POSADA RIO SERRANO, *Administrative Center. Tel. 61/410684. 14 rooms. Double $100. No credit cards. Store. Gasoline. Tire repair.*

Located behind the Administrative Center on Lake Toro, the Posada Rio Serrano offers simple accommodations and dining facilities.

HOSTERÍA ESTANCIA LAZO, *Laguna Verde, Torres del Paine. Tel. 61/223771. Fax 61/411141. 15 rooms. Double $120. No credit cards. Horse rentals.*

Hostería Lazo is a converted hacienda located at the infrequently utilized Laguna Verde entrance to the park. There are two good hikes nearby, one along the Laguna Verde trail and another to the Sierra del Toro lookout.

HOSTERÍA CABAÑAS DEL PAINE, *Sector Rio Serrano, Torres del Paine, Tel. 61/220174. Rooms 15. Double $130. Restaurant. Rafting. Fishing. Tours. Credit cards in advance only.*

The *hostería* is located 9 km south of the Administrative center. A rafting trip is possible on the Rio Serrano to its confluence with the Ultima Esperanza Inlet. The company also has a cabins at the end of the run.

Refugios with Beds

The *refugios* listed beloware comfortable dormitory style cabins with beds, showers, cooking area, and a cafe, but you need a sleeping bag. Cost per night is about $15 per person. If you are going during the high season it is imperative to reserve in advance, especially if you don't have a backup plan (like a tent).

• **Refugio Pehoe** *Lago Pehoe, Torres del Paine. Tel. 61/412592, Santiago Tel. 2/235-5225*
• **Refugio Grey**, *Lago Grey, Torres del Paine. Tel. 61/412592, Santiago Tel. 2/235-5225*
• **Refugio Dickson**, *Lago Dickson, Torres del Paine. Tel. 61/412592, Santiago Tel. 2/235-5225*
• **Refugio at Hostería Las Torres**, *Las Torres Sector. Tel. 61/226054*
• **Refugio Chileno**, *Valle Ascencio*
• **Refugio Lago Toro**, *Administration Center. $5/night.* CONAF run. Unsavory compared to the privately-run hostels.

Pay Camping Areas

Camping areas on this list charge a fee, usually $3 per person per night. They provide water, bathrooms, and other services. In many cases they are next to a *refugios* (dormitory style cabin). The refugios offer additional services such as a stores, cafeterias, lounging areas, and showers (some showers at additional cost) which can be used by campers.

• **Camping Las Torres**, *next to Hostería Las Torres*
• **Camping Refugio Pehoe**, *Lago Pehoe*
• **Camping at Refugio Grey**, *Lago Grey*
• **Camping at Refugio Dickson**, *Lago Dickson*
• **Camping Pehoe**, *Lago Pehoe*
• **Campamiento Serón**, *Sector Lago Paine*
• **Campamiento Los Perros**, *Glacier Los Perros*
• **Camping Los Cuernos**, *Lago Nordenskjold*
• **Campamiento Chileno**, *Valle Ascencio Trail*
• **Camping Laguna Azul**, *Laguna Azul*

WEATHERING THE PARK

More than likely you will get rained on while in the park. Here are a few ideas to help you escape the moisture and chill:

•*Waterproof the seams of your tent before leaving on the trip.*

• *Leave the cotton garments at home. If possible use a layering system of non-absorbing fabrics such as capeline long underwear as your first layer, fleece pants and pullover as your second layer, and as the final layer, rain pants and a rain coat made of Gore-tex or similar impermeable, breathing fabric.*

• *If it is raining elsewhere, head for the dry micro-climate of the Laguna Azul, often at 25-30 degrees in the summer, and spared the rain at times when the rest of the park is wet.*

• *Stay a night in one of the affordable refugios or hang out in the warm cafes.*

• *Pack some red cayenne pepper to mix in with your instant soups.*

The warmest and most popular months to visit the park are January through March. The 710 mm of annual rainfall is spread out fairly evenly. The winter months of July through August are nominally drier with an average of 48 mm per month versus the 60 mm per month average for the year. Although colder in winter, the wind dies down substantially, which combined with views of frosty peaks and bluer skies, makes visiting the park worthwhile year round.

Free Camping & Refugios Rusticos

These camping areas, sometimes located alongside a *refugio rustico* (small shelter). They do not have bathrooms, water, or other services.

• **Refugio Laguna Amarga**, *Laguna Amarga Entrance*
• **Refugio Pudeto**, *Lago Pehoe.*
• **Campamiento Coirón**, *Lago Paine*
• **Refugio Lago Paine**, *Lago Paine.*
• **Campamiento Paso**, *Glacier Grey*
• **Campamiento Los Guardas**, *Glacier Grey*
• **Campamiento Italiano**, *Valle del Frances*
• **Campamiento Británico**, *Valle del Frances*
• **Campamiento Torres**, *Valle Ascencio*
• **Campamiento Japones**, *Valle Ascencio*
• **Campamiento Las Carretas**, *Grey Valley*
• **Refugio Pingo**, *Lago Pingo trail*
• **Refugio Zapata**, *Lago Pingo trail*

WHERE TO EAT

Most people pack in their own food, a camping stove, and cooking gear. It is best to buy all of your provisions, including fuel, before you get to the park because the supplies within are pricey, and usually out of your way. If you do need supplemental supplies, consult the list of stores in the practical information section. The small stores and kiosks usually offer items like pasta, tomato sauce, bread, tuna fish, soap, and other such rations.

Other dining options include sit-down meals at the various *hosterías* listed above or at the cafeterias in the refugios.

GUANACOS AND PUMAS AND RHEAS, OH MY!

The permanent residents of the park have adapted to the presence of admirers, and in fact, the park's creation saved their habitat from development by local ranchers.

__Guanacos__ are usually the first wild creatures that you encounter. Their numbers are great, especially in the eastern side near the park entrance where they migrate in the summer, but it hasn't always been that way. In 1975, the guanaco count was down 100 in the park until a successful recovery program was initiated bringing the population to over 3,000 currently. As with the other lamoids, such as the llama and vicuña, guanacos express disdain by lowering their ears and rasing their tales. Be careful of bothering them too much because their ultimate expression of ire is a snot-projectile fired from flared nostrils.

__Darwin rheas__, (ñandú), frequently associate with guanacos forming mixed herds like those of antelopes and ostriches in Africa. The males bare the brunt of child care in that they build the shallow, grass-lined nest, incubate the eggs for six weeks, and then herd the little tykes around for another six weeks. If caring for up to fifty eggs from one female wasn't enough, the birds are also polygamous which means that one male broods the eggs of several females laid in the same nest.

Up a rung on the food chain is the __puma__, a name given to the cat by the Incas. The feline inhabits mountains, deserts, and jungles from Patagonia to North America, where it is known as the mountain lion and cougar. The puma, weighing in at up to 100 kg, is the second largest of the American felines behind the jaguar. Puma spottings in the park are rare, and attacks on humans moreso.

Other fauna to keep your eyes open for include __gray foxes__, __skunks__, __condors__, __woodpeckers__, and even flocks of bright green __parrots__ squawking above the glaciers.

SEEING THE SIGHTS
HIKING THE PARK

There is such a excellent variety of hikes in the park, you will find yourself wishing for more time to do the ones you can't get to. You will encounter a lot of people on the most popular routes during the high season. However, if you get tired of the company, simply choose one of the many remote routes, such as those connecting to Lago Pingo, Lago Dickson, or Laguna Azul, and you will feel like you have the park to yourself.

All of the trails are marked by orange dots painted on rocks and trees, as well as orange-tipped stakes planted into grassy fields. Only occasionally are the markers spaced out far enough to make you start wondering where the next one is. The rangers ask that you observe low impact trekking – that you pack out your garbage, use designated latrine areas at the campsites without bathrooms, and occupy only authorized trails and campsites.

Our ratings of the exertion levels for the hikes in this section are:
• **Easy**: Anyone including kids can do this hike at an enjoyable pace.
• **Moderate**: A fit person will find this to be respectable exercise.
• **Difficult**: The hike includes obstacles such as numerous fallen trees in the trail, lengthy steep ascents or descents, mountain passes, or bogs. A fit person will discover muscles he hasn't used in a while on these trails. However, the *difficult* rating does not indicate that the trail is too technical for the average weekend hiker.

Torres del Paine seems to be a place where fellow travelers are particularly interested in dislodging any insecurities about having been forced to choose among the many good options, thus asserting that their particular path was the best one. If you aren't careful, their comments can have you pondering, "I wonder if I should've done it that way?" Your peer's adventure probably was superlative to her, and yours to you, so forget it, and focus on enjoying what you've planned instead.

We are listing the hikes in the order of their popularity. People usually prioritize the hike to the Torres above the others because it is the namesake of the park. If you are forced to choose between them, we recommend the hike to Glacier Grey slightly over the one to the Torres, especially for those who have not seen many glaciers. The glacier should also be bumped up on your list if the park is socked in with rain and clouds because the icy blues of the glacier manage to enchant despite the foul weather.

At the end of the list we include two renowned multi-day hikes known among trekkers as **"The W"** and **"The Circuit"**. These challenging routes link up several of the hikes. The greatest debate among trekkers is whether to do the Circuit, the "W", or a series of individual hikes. Rest assured that whatever you choose to do with your time, it will be inspiring and memorable.

Valle Ascencio to the Torres
Three hours (11 km), one way. Moderate

The payoff for your effort on this hike is a mesmerizing view of the three pink granite Torres from across a glacial lagoon. Leaving on a trail from behind Hostería Las Torres, in about 15 minutes you cross the river via a bridge. You must cross this bridge rather than try to shortcut from the campsite, otherwise you will ascend the wrong side of the valley. The first hour and a half of the hike is the most difficult, with a long steep ascent to reach Campamiento Chileno. From there, you hike through smooth, gradually ascending trails in a beech forest.

The last twenty minutes of the hike, after passing the entrance to Campamiento Torres, is spent climbing from boulder to boulder until reaching the a rock filled bowl containing the glacial lagoon at the base of the Torres. Some people avoid the steep ascent on the first portion of the hike by doing the section from Hostería Las Torres to Campamiento Chileno on horses available at the *hostería*.

Glacier Grey
Three hours (12 km), one way. Moderate

This hike ends at the snout of the magnificent 50 km long Glacier Grey. The area has a comfortable *refugio* and a beautiful, but somewhat windy, beach-front campsite where small natural ice sculptures bump against the shore. It is quite an amazing experience to open your tent flap in the morning to see giant icebergs floating about.

Take the trail up from behind the Refugio Pehoe camping area to begin an hour long ascent through a windy canyon. You are still exposed to strong winds while walking on the plateau with a small lake until relief comes with your descent into a beech forest. The trail circumnavigates several ravines that were cut out by the glacier, so you will zig-zag and engage in several ascents and descents during this long, two-hour section. About twenty minutes before reaching Refugio Grey, you will cross a bridge over the Olguin River.

Valle Frances to the Cuernos
Six hours (17 km), ending at the Italian Camp. Difficult

This hike will take you to a spectacular observation point to view the **cuernos** while being sandwiched on the other side by the tallest peak in the range, Paine Grande, (3050 meters). Leaving Refugio Camping Pehoe from the east side of the campsite, enjoy the relatively flat portion of the hike along Lago Skottsberg. About two hours into the hike you will cross a bridge over the Del Frances River and begin the rigorous ascent. In a short while you will reach Campamiento Italiano, a campsite without services. Most who continue up the valley, drop their pack here, taking only a day pack the rest of the way. Another two hours of rigorous ascent will take you to the incredible viewpoint from the British Camp.

Mirador Nordenskjold Lookout
One hour (4 km), one way. Easy
This short walk through parched spiny landscape on shore of Lake Nordenskjold provides a spectacular view of the Cuernos from across the lake. From Refugio Pudeto, ascend the dirt road to the Salto Chico waterfall. From there follow the trail to the lookout point.

Lago Pingo
One hour (3 km), to Refugio Pingo; then four hours (10 km), to Refugio Zapata. Moderate
This is a great hike to escape the crowds while wandering through impressive beech and oak forests with views of the crystal-like Paine Grande. We passed only about four people per day during the high season. The trail begins at the Guardería Lago Grey ranger station. Before you start on the Lake Pingo Trail, we recommend taking the short hike in front of the ranger shack to the sand spit to where the giant blue icebergs from Glacier Grey accumulate.

Walk east from the ranger shack along side the Pingo River crossing small streams until you reach *Refugio Rustico* Pingo shack. From the refugio the trail will follow the river until you cross over a densely forested hill. You cross an open field, then reenter forest to encounter a short turnoff to the churning Cascada Pingo waterfall. From the waterfall, you will hike another hour around a bend in the Pingo River to arrive at the *refugio rustico* shack. This is a superb remote camp spot in a wide open grassy field with a mesmerizing view the Paine Massif. There are day hike possibilities to a lookout point, and to Lake Pingo, depending on the condition of the bridge over Los Hielos River.

Lago Paine
Four hours (15 km), one way. Moderate
The area around the starting point, Laguna Azul, is a microclimate, so you might be able to find clear skies here if nowhere else in the park. Follow the trail west traveling above and past Laguna Azul until the trail intersects with another. Here you will follow it to the right in a northeast-

erly direction passing Laguna Vega and ascending until you reach the *refugio rustico* shack at the northern end of Lago Paine.

Laguna Verde
Four hours (9 km), one way. Moderate/Difficult

The starting point for this hike is about a km north of Webber Bridge which is two kilometers north of the Administrative Center. The hike begins with fairly steep ascent until reaching the plateau where Laguna Los Ciervos is located. The trail continues over uneven terrain around the base of the Toro range during which time you must traverse several streams until reaching Laguna Verde. There is a full service pay campsite here, as well as the Hostería Estancia Lazo, accessible by dirt road from the east. You can ride the trail on horseback by coordinating with Estancia Lazo.

SUGGESTED ITINERARIES IN TORRES DEL PAINE
One Day
Option A: *Mirador Nordenskjold Walk, Administrative Center.*
Option B: *Hike to the Torres with organized tour through a tour agency, (you can fit it all in a long day with vehicle transport to Hostería Las Torres instead of the bus to Laguna Amarga).*

Four Days/Three Nights
Option A:
Day 1: Bus to the Laguna Amarga; Hike to Hostería Camping Las Torres
Day 2: Valle Ascencio Hike to the Torres
Day 3: Hike along the shore of Lakes Nordenskjold and Lake Skottsberg from Hostería Camping Las Torres to Refugio Camping Pehoe
Day 4: Boat to Refugio Pudeto. Bus to Puerto Natales

Option B:
Day 1: Bus to Refugio Pudeto. Boat to Refugio Camping Pehoe
Day 2: Hike to Refugio Glacier Grey
Day 3: Hike to Lago Pudeto
Day 4: Hike to Administration Center
*   To either of these options, time permitting, add the Mirador Nordenskjold Lookout hike from the Refugio Pudeto dock*

Seven Days
Option A: *The "W"*
Option B: *The Circuit*

Lago Dickson
Ten hours over two days (26 km). Moderate
This hike takes you through varied terrain to the idyllic, remote Refugio Lago Dickson.

Pehoe Lookout
One hour (1 km), one way. Moderate
Cross the street from Camping Pehoe following the nature signs describing the flora. A steep ascent leads to the lookout point with a view of the Cuernos and lakes. The view from behind reveals several hidden lakes, including Laguna Negra, to which you can hike if you want to continue.

The "W"
From the Laguna Amarga Ranger Station to the Lago Pudeto Boat Dock, 6-8 days (63 km). Moderate/Difficult
The "W" has become the most popular of the multi-day hikes because you can hike to the big three features of the park – the Torres, the Cuernos, and Glacier Gray. If the park is socked in, you might want to start with the glacier first, and hope it clears before arriving to the Torres. You could possibly do this route in five days if you really hammered it, but with no time for lounging to enjoy what there is to admire.

These are the seven segments:
- **Segment 1**: Laguna Amarga Ranger Station to Hostería Camping Las Torres. *Two hours (7 km). Easy..*
- **Segment 2**: Hostería Las Torres via Valle Ascencio Trail to the Torres and back. *Six hours (22 km) round-trip. Moderate*
- **Segment 3**: Hostería Las Torres to Refugio Camping Los Cuernos. *Five and half hours (12 km). Moderate.*
- **Segment 4**: Refugio Camping Los Cuernos to the Cuernos via Valle del Frances, then to Campamiento Italiano. *Seven hours (12 km). Difficult.*
- **Segment 5**: Campamiento Italiano to Refugio Camping Pehoe. *Two and a half hours (8 km). Easy.*
- **Segment 6:** Refugio Camping Pehoe to Glacier Grey and back. *Six hours (24 km), round-trip. Moderate.*
- **Segment 7**: Refugio Camping Pehoe Boat Ride to Refugio Pudeto Dock. *One hour boat ride or easy five hour hike to the Administrative Center.*

The Circuit
From Laguna Amarga Ranger Station to the Administrative Center. Six to nine days (70 km). Moderate/Difficult
This extraordinary hike presents myriad terrains and microclimates to the trekker. You will traverse grassy fields of wild flowers, slog through

unrelenting muddy bogs, scramble through scree to cross a mountain pass, and glissade through a slippery rainforest above Glacier Grey. Some of the trails are quite rigorous, but in the end you've earned a respectable hiking badge of accomplishment, having just looped the entire Paine Massif.

The rangers prefer that no one hike the circuit alone. If you are traveling solo, try to hook up with someone in Puerto Natales or on the bus on the way out, so you can advise the rangers accordingly when they ask. As opposed to the "W", where you will fairly constantly encounter fellow trekkers on the trails, the Circuit includes long solitary stretches. We've presented the Circuit in a counter-clockwise route, but hikers also do it clockwise beginning from the Refugio Pudeto dock or the Administrative Center.

These are the seven segments:
- **Segment 1**: Laguna Amarga Ranger Station to Campamiento Seron. *Four hours (17 km). Easy.*
- **Segment 2**: Campamiento Seron to Refugio Dickson. *Six hours (9 km). Moderate.*
- **Segment 3**: Refugio Dickson to Campamiento Los Perros. *Six hours (10 km). Difficult.*
- **Segment 4**: Campamiento Los Perros to Campamiento Paso. *Five hours (7 km). Difficult.*
- **Segment 5**: Campamiento Paso to Refugio Grey. *Five hours (8 km). Difficult/Moderate.*
- **Segment 6**: Refugio Grey to Refugio Camping Pehoe. *Three and half hours (12 km). Moderate.*
- **Segment 7**: Refugio Camping Pehoe to the Administrative Center. *Five hours (18 km). Easy.*

SPORTS & RECREATION
Climbing & Ice Climbing
The park offers challenging climbing with Paine Grande renowned as one of the most difficult to climb peaks in the world. Experienced climbers who plan on attempting such climbs should contact a Chilean consulate in the US to obtain the permit known by the acronym "DIFROL."

For climbing or ice climbing guides, contact **Amerindina**, *Tel. 61/411176,* or **Onas Aventour**, *Tel. 61/412707*, both in Puerto Natales.

Fishing
The trout fishing spots inside the park are on Rio Serrano and Lago Toro.

Horseback Riding
• **Hostería Las Torres**, *Sector Las Torres, Tel./Fax 61/226054*
• **Hostería Estancia Lazo**, *Laguna Verde*

Rafting
    Aventour, *Tel. 61/220174*, offers rafting trips down the Rio Serrano. You can also inquire directly at their **Hostería Cabanas del Paine** in the park on Rio Serrano.

PRACTICAL INFORMATION

Banks: There are no banks or ATM's in the park. The closest bank is in Puerto Natales.
Gasoline: Posada Rio Serrano, *behind the Administrative Center*
Laundry: The *hosterías* and hotels offer laundry service.
Medical Service: Administrative Center offers first aid.
Post Office: Administrative Center
Stores: Mini-markets or kiosks with food supplies include the following:
• **Laguna Amarga Kiosk**, *Laguna Amarga entrance*
• **Hostería Las Torres**, *Las Torres Sector*
• **Refugio Camping Pehoe**, *Lago Pehoe*
• **Camping Pehoe Kiosk**, *Lago Pehoe*
• **Rio Posada Serrano**, *Administrative Center*
Telephone/Fax: Administrative Center
Tire Repair: Posada Rio Serrano, *behind the Administrative Center*
Tourist Office/Maps: The Administrative Center serves as the tourist information center. We recommend that you buy the excellent "Torres del Paine Trekking Map" for $5 sold in Puerto Natales stores and at almost all of the refugios and kiosks in the park.

18. OFF THE CONTINENT

Chile's non-continental holdings cover the range from a Polynesian island to a slice of Antarctica. Throw in the islands upon which the story of Robin Crusoe is based and you'll start to wonder if you're not dreaming about these far-flung possessions.

EASTER ISLAND

Easter Island, known as *Isla de Pascua* in Spanish and *Rapa Nui* in its native language, is a small Polynesian island in the middle of the Pacific. Its tropical climes, warm waters, and unique archaeological heritage offer visitors a distinctively non-Chilean Chilean experience.

History

It remains a mystery how the island was originally populated. The most widely accepted theory proposes that the island was inhabited by a group that migrated from the Polynesian Marquees Islands. Another suggests, because of the similarity between Andean and *pascuense* construction, that boatloads of South Americans made their way to the island hundreds of years ago. This theory was given some credence when a Dutchman made the trip from Peru in a raft built by Bolivian craftsmen. The adventure is documented in Heyerdahl's book *Kon-Tiki*.

Regardless of how they got there, the Easter Islanders created an interesting and mysterious society. Separate family groups, each ruled by a king, settled throughout the island. Each clan had its own piece of coastline where it worshipped deified ancestors in the form of the large statues, *moai*, for which Easter Island is so famous. It remains unknown how they could have created and erected the huge stone images. Pressure on island resources due to overpopulation led to wars and the decline of the society, but many of the statues remain.

MOAI

These statues are the single most prominent image of Easter Island throughout the world. Some key facts:
- *Most of the statues range from about three to six meters in height*
- *The largest that once stood on an alter was almost 10 meters tall and was carved from a single block that weighted about 82 tons; its red topknot weighed 11 tons*
- *There is an unfinished moai in the quarries, with its back still attached to the rock, that is 32 meters tall*

Initial contact from the western world was made on Easter Sunday 1722 by Dutchman Jacob Roggeven. In 1888, Chile incorporated the island as part of its territory during its expansionist phase. A large sheep raising corporation was granted use of the land in 1897, and for nearly 60 years it, more than the Chilean government, controlled the island. Following that, control was ceded to the Chilean navy. Only recently have the islands 2700 inhabitants been granted some autonomy.

ARRIVALS & DEPARTURES

By Plane

LanChile, *Policarpo Toro and Pont, Tel. 600/600-4000,* has a few flights a week to Tahiti that stop on Easter Island. The five and a half hour flight costs between $800-$1200 depending on the time of the year.

ORIENTATION

Easter island is 3600 km west of the Chilean coast. South of the Tropic of Capricorn, its latitude is close to that of Copiapó. The island, covering 160 square km, is 20 km at its widest point and 24 km at its longest.

The triangular land mass was created by the eruption and subsequent confluence of lava flows from volcanoes at each of the island's points. *Isla de Pascua* has only one city, **Hanga Roa**, which sits at the western end of the triangle's hypotenuse. At the other end of the hypotenuse lies **Rapa Nui National Park**, with most of the island's archaeological sites.

There are only two beaches on Easter Island. These beaches, **Anakena** and **Ovahe**, are on the side of the triangle opposite town.

GETTING AROUND TOWN

While the town is small enough to cover on foot as long as you are not staying out by the airport, a good way to get around the island is on mountain bike. Horses, motorcycles, and boats are also available to rent in Hanga Roa.

If you are going to try to fit in a lot of sites in a short period of time, jeep rental is the best option. You can rent from a hotel or just find a sign and rent from an islander.

WHERE TO STAY

Prices are generally high on Rapa Nui, but go down quite a bit in the off-season. There are a few nice hotels, many *residenciales*, and some campgrounds. Be aware that only the most expensive hotels accept credit cards.

The **Hotel Iorana**, *Atamu Tekena, Tel. 108/223312, Santiago Fax 2/698-1960*, perched on a cliff away from the downtown, is one of the finest hotels on the island. For $160 a night for a double you can enjoy excellent ocean views. A less expensive, more central hotel option is the **Hotel Ota'i**, *Te Pito Henua, Tel. 108/223250, Double $100*.

Residenciales run between $25 and $50. They are all over as this is how most of the townspeople earn their livings. You can camp at Anakena beach out of town, or some people in Hanga Roa will let you set up in their yards for a small price.

WHERE TO EAT

The **Playa Pea** restaurant, near the town's main docks, offers excellent seafood with a pleasant view. Other good options for seafood around the Hanga Roa docks include **La Taverne du Pecheur** and **Avarei Pua**. **Mama Sabina**, at *Avenues Policarpo Toro and Pont*, is further away, but well worth it. Once you've had all the fish you can stand, head to **Giovani's** *Pizza on Te Pito* for a change of pace.

SEEING THE SIGHTS

A few hours walking will take you through the sights of the entire village. Life in town centers around the **plaza** and the **fishing docks**, *caleta*. Notice the two damaged *moai* looking down on caleta Hanga Roa. Heading west from the main docks along Apina Avenue, you'll find a second, smaller *caleta*, **Hanga Piko**. The **church**, at the end of *Te Pito Avenue* is another worthy sight, as is the **artisan's market** across *Ara Roa Raki*.

The **Sebastian Englert Anthropological Museum**, with its interesting displays on the island's culture, is definitely worth a stop. It is closed on Mondays and during lunchtime.

SPORTS & RECREATION

It seems like getting exercise just comes naturally while you're on the *Isla de Pascua*. The best way to get around the island, and work out at the same time, is by **mountain bike**. You can rent bikes in various places around town. **Horses**, for rent near the Hotel Hotu Matua, are also an option. **Scuba diving** and **snorkeling** are popular island sports. You get rent gear and hire a guide at the main *caleta*. Night dives are also a possibility. There are only two **beaches** on the island, but both Anakena and Ovahe are beautiful choices.

SHOPPING

The main Easter Island souvenirs, which you'll see for sale all over Chile, are small carvings of the famous *moai* sculptures. There are shops sprinkled through Hanga Roa, but you should try the artisan market, near the church, first.

EXCURSIONS & DAY TRIPS

Although the tropical weather is nice, it's the archaeological sites that bring most visitors to *Isla de Pascua*. You can cover the island in a series of excursions from Hanga Roa. On foot, horse, or bike you can visit the ceremonial sites at **Ahu Tahai** in one afternoon and hit the **Rano Kau Volcano** and **Orongo** site in another. With a motorized vehicle it just takes a half day to visit the *moai* at **Aku Akivi**, see where the red top knots were made in **Puna Pau**, and explore the **Dos Ventanas** cave. For a full day excursion, try a trip to the ruined temple at **Vinapu** and the 397 *moai* at **Rano Raraku**, finishing off with a dip in the ocean at either Anakena or Ovahe beach.

PRACTICAL INFORMATION

The **bank, telephone, post office**, and **Sernatur tourist office** are all on the plaza. The **hospital** is behind the church off Ara Roa Rakei. The area code is 108.

ANTARCTICA

Wildlife and spectacular scenery are generally what draw people to the last continent. The world's largest ice sheet has been blown and banged into strange and wonderful forms, creating a dramatic landscape that makes even the biggest of egos feel small.

The clarity of the air and utter lack of pollution make for a visibility on clear days that can almost be dangerous. Glaciers drop into the water and calve outrageously large icebergs. Penguins and whales rule the roost.

ARRIVALS & DEPARTURES

By Boat

Most people arrive in Antarctica via cruise ships. The boats depart from Punta Arenas to the Antarctic Peninsula from November through March each year. Most of the tours are booked from outside of Chile. From Punta Arenas the ships sail to Ushuaia, Argentina, cross the Drake Passage, and then continue on to Antarctica.

The tours generally last from eight to 15 days. Crossing the Drake Passage both ways takes five days. The rest of the time is spent cruising around the continent with the chance to disembark on zodiacs at scientific bases and animal colonies.

The cost of the cruises ranges from $3000 to $6000 per person, depending on the type of accommodations. Most of the ships are re-fitted Russian boats with English-speaking Russian crews. Make sure the company you're traveling with is part of the IAATO, the International Association of Antarctica Tour Operators.

You can make your reservations from outside Chile through numerous tour companies. Try:

- **Mountain Travel/Sobek**, *6420 Fairmont Avenue, El Cerrito, California, 94530. Tel. 510/527-8100. Fax 510/525-7710*
- **Noble Caledonia**, *11 Charles Street, London, W1X 8LE. Tel. 0171/409-0376. Fax 0171/409-0834*
- **Quark Expeditions**, *980 Post Road, Darien, CT, 06820. Tel. 203/656-0499. Fax 203/655-6623*

If you are willing to take a chance, you can try for reduced fairs by booking in Ushuaia, Argentina. You usually have to make your reservation no more than three weeks and no less than ten days out, but you can get fares that are reduced as much as 30%. Ideally you could book your space two weeks out, travel through Chile for two weeks, and then fly from Punta Arenas to Ushuaia to go to Antarctica.

The following agencies all have access to reduced fare tickets:

- **All Patagonia**, *Juana Fadal 26,(9410) Ushuaia, Argentina. Tel. 54-901/30725, 35220, 33622. Fax 54-901/30707*
- **Rumbo Sur**, *San Martín 342, (9401) Ushuaia, Argentina. Tel. 54-901/22441,23085. Fax 54-901/30699*
- **Antartur**, *Maipú 237, (9401) Ushuaia, Argentina. Tel. 54-901/23240. Fax 54-901/24108*
- **Tiempo Libre**, *San Martín 863, (9401) Ushuaia, Argentina. Tel. 54-901/31374,21017. Fax 54-901/21017*

Another option, but not a very good one, is to go to the port in Punta Arenas and try to hitch a cheap ride with one of the Chilean navy boats. Be forewarned – there are many more boats leaving from Ushuaia.

By Plane
ADVENTURE NETWORK INTERNATIONAL, *27 London End. Beaconsfield Bucks. HP9 2HN United Kingdom. Tel. 44/1494 671808. Fax 44-1494/671725. Website: www.adventure-network.com.*

There is one commercial group, Adventure Network International, taking people over from Punta Arenas by plane. ANI started as a logistical and support group for climbers wishing to tackle Vinson Massif, the highest peak on the continent. They now offer a number of types of trips. All of them are first class and all cost into the tens of thousands of dollars. These are once-in-a-lifetime excursions. They offer expeditions to the South Pole, emperor penguin photo safaris, and climbs to the Vinson Massif and Transantartic Mountains amongst other things. Once you see their brochure you'll start playing the lottery.

ORIENTATION

Antarctica sits on the bottom of the world covered with a huge ice sheet. The dimensions of this sheet, twice the size of Australia and up to 4000 meters thick, are difficult to fathom. It is the world's highest, driest, and coldest continent. It is also its most remote and perhaps most fascinating.

The Antarctic Peninsula is an icy arm pointing at the east coast of South America. Most human activity takes place here. There are bases from Chile, Argentina, Brazil, China, Great Britain, Korea, Poland, Spain, the United States, and Russia.

Chile assert rights to a wedge of a half million square miles that overlaps claims by Argentina and England. A twelve-country summit on the territorial dispute tabled the subject indefinitely, neither recognizing nor invalidating claims on the continent. The participants did agreed to guarantee the universal right to engage in peaceful activities.

During the summer, when cruise ships make the trip to the continent, sunlight is standard both day and night. This can be disorienting, but it's actually a really neat experience.

SEEING THE SIGHTS

Most of the programs put special emphasis on the **observation of wildlife**, with on-boat naturalists lecturing about the abundant fauna. Three kinds of penguins; leopard, elephant and fur seals; and minke, killer, and humpback whales are amongst the animals normally sighted.

Most ships have inflatable boats called zodiacs that let you get up close and personal with much of the animal life. These are also your transportation vehicle if you want to go to shore when you call upon one of the bases.

PRACTICAL INFORMATION

You can usually sign for all your extras on the ships, but need cash if you're going to buy anything when you go ashore.

JUAN FERNANDEZ ARCHIPELAGO

Robinson Crusoe Island, the largest of the archipelago, has gained its fame as the site where Alejandro Selkirk was put ashore in 1704 with a Bible, knife, rifle, pound of powder, tobacco, and some clothes. He was rescued almost four and a half years later to become the inspiration for Daniel Defoe's *The Incredible and Amazing Adventures of Robinson Crusoe*.

Today's traveler to the island will worry less about being left ashore than having to leave. With outstanding hikes, isolated beaches, and inexpensive and abundant lobster, getting shipwrecked here is more a dream than nightmare.

ARRIVALS & DEPARTURES

By Boat

The **Motonave Navarino** leaves from Valparaiso to Robinson Crusoe once a month. The trip lasts two days and costs roughly $200 round trip. You can make reservations at *Tel. 32/667730*.

By Plane

There are three airlines than fly 10 seater planes from Santiago to Robinson Crusoe. The round trip flights cost between $420-475. The two and a half hour flights leave from the Aeródromo Tobalaba in La Reina. The airport on the island is an hour and a half boat ride from **San Juan Bautista**, the island's only town.
- **Lassa**, *Avenida Larraín 7941 inside the Aeródromo Tobalaba. Tel./Fax 2/ 224-5691*
- **Servico Aéreo Ejecutivo**, *Apoquindo 7850, torre 3. Tel. 2/224-5691. Fax 2/ 229-3419*
- **Transportes Aéreos Isla Robinson Crusoe**, *Monumento 2570, Maipú. Tel. 2/531-4343. Fax 2/531-3772*

ORIENTATION

The Juan Fernandez Archipelago lies in the Pacific roughly 675 km west of Chile on about the same latitude as San Antonio and Santo Domingo. The mountainous islands are actually the highest peaks of a 400 km submarine mountain range.

The main island, **Robinson Crusoe**, covers 94 square km. The second island, **Santa Clara**, is 500 meters south of Crusoe, while the third, **Alejandro Selkirk Island** lies 187 km to the west.

The shape of Robinson Crusoe looks a smiling elephant in profile. **San Juan Bautista**, the only town on the island, is at the nape of the elephant's neck, while the **airport** lies at the end of its extended trunk. The 560 meter **Selkirk Lookout Point** is the elephant's bulging eyeball.

THE REAL ROBINSON CRUSOE

*The son of a shoemaker, the Scottish sailor **Alejandro Selkirk** ran away to sea in 1695. Shortly after that he joined a group of privateers in the Pacific and by 1703 was sailing master of a ship on a pirate expedition. He quarreled with his captain in September of 1704 and was put ashore at his own request on the uninhabited Más a Tierra Island. He remained there alone for almost five years until February 1709, when he was discovered and taken aboard an English ship.*

GETTING AROUND TOWN

Everybody walks everywhere in San Juan Bautista, but to get anywhere else on the island, including the airport, you have to go by boat. The main street in town is Alcalde Larraín.

WHERE TO STAY & EAT

There are just a handful of hotels and restaurants on the island. Most are more expensive than they would be elsewhere, but you are out in the middle of the Pacific Ocean. For around $80 a night for a double, your choices are the **Hosteria Aldea Daniel Defoe**, *Tel./Fax 32/751075*, **Hosteria Villa Green**, *Tel./Fax 32/751044*, and **Hosteria Martinez-Green**, *Tel/Fax 32/751039*.

Good restaurants include **La Bahia**, *down Alcalde*, and **El Remo**, *on the plaza*. Don't miss the local lobster.

SEEING THE SIGHTS

The highlight of the island is the **Selkirk Lookout**. A roughly three hour hike takes you to views of the entire island and seas beyond when the top in not covered in clouds. The are two plaques recognizing Selkirk at the top.

Another three km trek leads to **Plazoleta del Yunque**, a small lookout at the base of Yunque Hill. This popular spot, where a German castaway lived for 12 years, offers excellent views and picnicking spots.

The trail to the lookout starts behind the municipal building at the **Santa Barbara Fort**. The fort was constructed to ward off French pirates. Another point of interest near the fort, **Patriots Caves**, is the caverns where Chilean liberationists were jailed by the Spanish after a failed coup attempt in Rancagua.

At the northern tip of town by the lighthouse you can walk through the **cemetery** to better understand the island's distinct heritage.

EXCURSIONS & DAY TRIPS

There are a number of boat trips that you can take from San Juan Bautista. Twenty minutes by boat from town you can see the **Robinson Cave** where Selkirk lived during his time on the island. An hour from town you can visit the **French Port**, where French pirates first landed on the island. A lovely two hour trip will take you to the sandy **Arenal Beach** after passing around small islands, steep cliffs, and fur lion colonies. You can camp here if you bring fresh water, or even hike here from the Selkirk Lookout if you have a few days.

You can hire boats at the dock or check with the tourist office for available captains.

PRACTICAL INFORMATION

Alcalde Larraín is the main street in town, and most services can be found where Larraín hits the plaza. The **post office**, **telephone**, and **tourist office** are all here. The area code is 32. There are no banks on the island and nobody accepts credit cards, so bring lots of cash. The **clinic** is on the south side of town at the end of Vicente Gonzales, as is the **Conaf** office.

INDEX

THINGS CHANGE!

Phone numbers, prices, addresses, quality of food, etc, all change. If you come across any new information, we'd appreciate hearing from you. No item is too small! Drop us an e-mail note at: Jopenroad@aol.com, or write us at:

Chile Guide
Open Road Publishing, P.O. Box 284
Cold Spring Harbor, NY 11724

TRAVEL NOTES

TRAVEL NOTES

TRAVEL NOTES

TRAVEL NOTES

TRAVEL NOTES

TRAVEL NOTES